GROWING OLDER
IN AMERICA

GROWING OLDER IN AMERICA

Robert J. Riekse

Grand Rapids Community College
Calvin College-Grand Rapids Community College
Consortium on Aging

Henry Holstege

Calvin College
Calvin College-Grand Rapids Community College
Consortium on Aging

The McGraw-Hill Companies, Inc.

New York   St. Louis   San Francisco   Auckland   Bogotá
Caracas   Lisbon   London   Madrid   Mexico City   Milan   Montreal
New Delhi   San Juan   Singapore   Sydney   Tokyo   Toronto

McGraw-Hill

*A Division of The **McGraw·Hill** Companies*

This book was set in Times Roman by York Graphic Services, Inc.
The editors were Jill S. Gordon and Katherine Blake;
the production supervisor was Richard A. Ausburn.
The cover was designed by Joan Greenfield.
The photo editor was Anne Manning.
Project supervision was done by Tage Publishing Service, Inc.
R. R. Donnelley & Sons Company was printer and binder.

Photo Credits for Chapter Openers:

1: Howard Dratch/Image Works; 2: Jeffrey Muir Hamilton/Stock, Boston; 3: Jonathan Rawie/Stock, Boston; 4: Stock, Boston; 5: Michaels/Image Works; 6: Rhoda Sidney/Stock, Boston; 7: Stock, Boston; 8: Peter Menzel/ Stock, Boston; 9: P. Gentier/Image Works; 10: T. Michaels/ Image Works; 11: Alan Carey/Image Works; 12: Courtesy Dr. Robert Riekse; 13: Addison Geary/Stock, Boston; 14: Elizabeth Crews/Stock, Boston; 15: Peter Menzel/Stock, Boston; 16: Nita Winter/Image Works; 17: Courtesy of Dr. Robert Riekse; 18: Susan Woog Wagner/Photo Researchers; 19: David Stricker/Image Works; 20: Mitch Wojnarowicz/Image Works; 21: W. Marc Bernsau/Image Works; and 22: Elizabeth Crews/Stock, Boston.

Growing Older in America

This book is printed on acid-free paper.

1 2 3 4 5 6 7 8 9 0 DOC DOC 9 0 9 8 7 6 5

ISBN 0-07-052742-3

Library of Congress Catalog Card Number: 95-81850

ABOUT THE AUTHORS

ROBERT J. RIEKSE is Professor of Gerontology/Coordinator of Aging Education at Grand Rapids Community College and the Director of the Calvin College-Grand Rapids Community College Consortium on Aging. He received his Ed.D. from Michigan State University, where he was a Fellow in the Kellogg Community College Leadership Training Program. A pioneer in gerontology education, he has developed a wide range of educational programs for college students, service providers in the aging network, and older persons and family members. He was awarded a fellowship in the American Council on Education's Academic Leadership Program, and he is a recipient of the Everett J. Soop Distinguished Adult Educator Award, presented by the Michigan Society of Gerontology. He has authored and co-authored numerous research grants in aging education and has made many presentations to state and national gerontology associations. He is a past president of the board of directors of Senior Neighbors, Inc., vice chair of the Northwest Michigan Coalition of Older Adult Learners, board member of the Michigan Society of Gerontology, regional representative of the Michigan Coalition of Older Adult Learners, committee member of the Association of Gerontology in Higher Education, and a member of various other organizations promoting aging education. He is the co-author of *The Christian Guide to Parent Care* and, most recently, the recipient of an Administration on Aging grant to develop a demonstration older workers' training program.

HENRY HOLSTEGE is Professor of Sociology/Gerontology at Calvin College in Grand Rapids, Michigan. He received his Ph.D. in Sociology from Michigan State University, where he was elected to Alpha Kappa Delta, the national sociological honorary society. He is Associate Director of the Calvin College-Grand Rapids Community College Consortium on Aging. He is the recipient of the Everett J. Soop Distinguished Adult Educator Award, presented by the Michigan Society of Gerontology. He is the co-author of *The Christian Guide to Parent Care* and the author or co-author of numerous monographs on aging. He has received federal and state grants for research on the aging process and has been a keynote speaker at conferences throughout the nation on various aspects of aging. He is a member of the American Society on Aging, the National Council on Aging, and the Michigan Society on Gerontology.

To Ellen, for patience and support.
To Jon, Amy, and Rob for positive
intergenerational living.
                                    RJR

To Lois, for patience and understanding
for missed vacations and for concerts and
theatrical performances not attended.
                                    HH

CONTENTS

PART 3

The Economics of Aging   155

PREFACE

As we move toward the 21st century, our nation is experiencing a major revolution. Its population is growing older at a rather remarkable rate. For the first time in its history, America is beginning to move away from a youth-based culture. This is not the result of a decision powerful persons or groups have made. In fact, there has been a lack of recognition and even a reluctance to recognize the realities of an aging population on the part of many movers and shakers in the worlds of business, government, entertainment, religion, and advertising. But the realities must be faced. Between 1960 and 1990, while the general population of the United States grew by 39 percent, the number of persons 65 years and older grew by 89 percent, and those 85 years and older (the oldest old) grew by a whopping 232 percent (U.S. Bureau of the Census, 1993). This trend will accelerate in the 21st century.

Some years ago the term "gerontology" was coined to describe the study of aging. Like many terms used to describe a subject area or discipline taught in college, gerontology is the joining of two Greek words; it literally means the scientific study of the old. What an appropriate study this is, given the realities of an aging America as well as an aging world. The study of aging is not only more acceptable and more fashionable than it once was, it is also essential to cope with the real needs of the fastest-growing sector of our population. According to the 1990 U.S. Census, there were 31,241,832 persons over the age of 65, representing 12.6 percent of the population. When those 55 through 64 are added to the 1990 count, the number reaches 52,389,754 persons, or 21 percent of the population. Moreover, projections for the 50-plus age group in America indicate that this sector of our population will grow very rapidly between 1990 and 2000 when the Baby Boomers begin to be counted in this category. When we look to the 21st century, the older population will increase dramatically, with those 65 and older reaching 21.8 percent of the population by 2050. It is interesting to note that all of the persons who will make up this large number of older people in 2050 have already been born.

Although gerontology has rightly and logically focused on the study of the old, it really should be viewed more broadly, since aging is a life-long process. With the Baby Boomers beginning to turn 50 in 1996 and 62 soon after the beginning of the 21st century (2008), the processes, realities, and consequences of aging will be elevated to a level of national attention never experienced before. Already, millions of Baby Boomers are counted as "older workers" and are experiencing the consequences of being thus categorized.

Still, gerontology remains somewhat hard to define, despite the high level of professionalism of both the pioneers in the field and its current academic leaders. This is due in part because, as Professor David Peterson of the University of Southern California has pointed out, gerontology is both an academic discipline and a profession. It has the characteristics and functions of both.

As a profession, "it is a field of practice in which professionals and para-professionals plan, provide, administer, and evaluate a variety of programs and services aimed at meeting the needs of older persons and their families" (Peterson, 1993, p. 1). As Professor Peterson points out, the "real purpose of professionals is to apply knowledge in order to solve problems rather than to create knowledge for its own sake" (p. 2).

There is a range of jobs that utilize the knowledge and skills of professional gerontologists. What typically comes to mind are the jobs in the "aging networks" across the nation in the wide array of agencies and organizations that focus all or part of their activities on meeting the needs of older people—for example, senior centers, Area Agencies on Aging, respite care centers, adult daycare facilities, senior meal programs, and many others. But businesses are now beginning to recognize the explosive growth of the older portions of the population, to appreciate older people as consumers of products and services, and to acknowledge the need to have staff members who are knowledgeable about the field of aging. Opportunities for professional gerontologists should grow rapidly in the years ahead.

As a discipline, gerontology is multifaceted and interdisciplinary. By necessity, it encompasses a broad range of subject areas that address the issues and conditions older people, their families, and persons who work with them experience as a result of growing older in contemporary America. They include, but are not limited to:

- Psychology, because of the psychological changes and challenges older people and those around them experience as a result of the aging process, including personal adjustment to losses, interaction with family members and peers, and adjustment to dependency;

- Sociology, because older people live in social settings that affect their lives and experience social forces such as racism, sexism, and ageism, as well as social stratification and deviancy;
- Humanities, because older people and society can benefit from the reminiscence of lifetime experiences as well as the enrichments derived from religion/spirituality and the arts;
- Political Science, because societal decision making—who makes decisions and how they are made—directly relates to the political power of older people and the development of governmental programs that address their needs;
- Public Policy, because assessing the needs of various groups in society and devising strategies to balance and address these needs—particularly in the face of competing demands for limited resources—require public policy expertise;
- Medicine, because chronic conditions increase dramatically as people grow older and require an inordinate amount of hospital and physician resources;
- Public Health, because nutritional needs/awareness/safeguards and coping with the high degree of disability among the old present challenges to public health policies and strategies;
- Economics, because while some older people are concerned with investment strategies and estate management, million of others are challenged by basic economic survival, and must often choose between paying for food or paying for prescription drugs;
- Biology, because the biological process of aging is integral to the human condition and directly affects the lives of older people;
- Public Safety, because older people are the special target of confidence schemes, scams, and particular forms of abuse;
- Communications, because communication strategies can help older persons in their interpersonal relationships, and communication training will improve the ability of care and service providers to be more productive in diagnosis, advocacy, and the delivery of social services;
- Architecture, because the physical living environments of older people in their homes, apartments, retirement homes, and long-term care facilities greatly affect the quality of their lives;
- Vocational Skills, because home repairs and adapting everyday items to the physical needs of older people are vital to safe and secure living;
- Education, because through educational programs older people can train/retrain for appropriate jobs, acquire coping skills for changing life circumstances, and gain enjoyment through avocational/recreational activities; and
- Law, because millions of older persons face legal issues in trying to qualify for benefit programs, in attempting to comply with tax and governmental regulations, and in coping with estate planning.

Indeed, gerontology encompasses every academic discipline that in some way relates to the lives of older people and their families in contemporary America.

In view of the reality that gerontology is both a profession and a multifaceted academic discipline, what type of book is appropriate for an introductory gerontology course? Having taught gerontology courses for many years in community and four-year college settings, we have felt the need for a text specifically designed for the range of students who typically populate the introductory courses. Although many fine gerontology texts have been developed over the past few years, for a long time we have looked for a text that covers the range of issues that persons interested in aging or persons working with or preparing to work with older people face on a practical level. This book is designed to systemtically address the conditions, issues, and problems people face as they grow older in contemporary America. It is designed to acquaint the reader with the realities of the aging process and with what it means to grow older as the 21st century approaches; to provide some theories about aging; and to explain the social and economic realities of aging in our society, the importance and impact of living environments and specific housing options, the types and limitations of the various support systems for older people at risk, and the public policy issues that affect everyone, young and old alike.

The methodology of the book is direct. Each chapter addresses the issues at hand, utilizing extensive research in a simplifed, applied manner. The application of important and current research to the issues older people face in contemporary America is the primary goal of this text. Current demographic and research data, including those data currently available from the 1990 census, are used wherever possible. Some older research findings are included where more current data are not available and where they are appropriate.

This book is designed for the broad range of students typically found in community colleges, four-year colleges, and state universities, including those who take courses while working in the aging networks. While colleges offering higher degrees are more likely to offer gerontology courses, community colleges are important institutions in disseminating information concerning older people and in promoting community-level discussions on the issues that relate to this information. Community colleges are within commuting distance of 95 percent of the nation's population. With their extensive continuing education programs, they attract a wide range of persons who take courses for personal or job-related reasons. This is true of gerontology courses, as gerontology is a relatively new area of study and many persons need or want a basic course. This type of course requires a text that is appropriate to the interests and objectives of the variety of students it attracts.

A 1991 study by the Association of Gerontology in Higher Education and the Andrus Gerontology Center at the University of Southern California indicated that only 10 percent of the persons who responded to the survey from Area Agencies on Aging and State Units on Aging got into the field as a result of studying aging in college (Peterson, Wendt, and Douglass, 1991). These same respondents "strongly agreed that in the future professionals in the aging network will need more training in aging with 85.1 percent of those in the Area Agencies on Aging and 86 percent in the State Units on Aging recommending that prospective employees obtain aging education while in college" (p. 29).

This book is intended for the students in these classes. It is designed to be academically sound, but it is written to be consistent with the interests, ability levels, and objectives of persons who are likely to enroll in introductory gerontology courses. These include college students and those who are working or interested in working with older people in the aging networks, businesses, community schools, churches, community-based agencies, and family settings.

REFERENCES

Peterson, D.A. 1993. "The Professional Field of Gerontology." Los Angeles: University of Southern California.

Peterson, D.A., Wendt, P.F., and Douglass, E.B. 1991. "Determining the Impact of Gerontology Preparation on Personnel in the Aging Network: A National Survey. Los Angeles and Washington, D.C.: University of Southern California and Association for Gerontology in Higher Education.

U.S. Bureau of the Census, 1993. Current Population Reports, Special Studies, p. 23-178RV, *Sixty-Five Plus in America*. U.S. Government Printing Office, Washington, D.C.

ACKNOWLEDGMENTS

Many people have provided us with their support, assistance, and advice during the development of *Growing Older in America*. At McGraw-Hill, the authors wish to thank Phillip Butcher for having the foresight to publish this particular type of textbook as the field of gerontology evolves in the context of the current social/political climate. We appreciate the excellent work our editor, Kathy Blake, provided in the editorial development process, including coordinating and analyzing the efforts of the reviewers. The supervisory work of sponsoring editor Jill Gordon is also appreciated. Anne Manning did a great job finding appropriate photos, and we thank her. Tony Caruso of Tage Publishing Service did an excellent job coordinating and supervising the copyediting process, which is so vital to the finished project.

The following reviewers provided helpful advice on our behalf: M. Violet Asmuth, Edison Community College; Carla J. Gosney, Retired Senior Volunteer Program/John Wood Community College; David M. Ishizaki, Community College of Philadelphia; James J. Magee, College of New

Rochelle; Dennis Myers, Baylor University-Waco; and Andrew T. Nilsson, Eastern Connecticut State University. Their comments and suggestions enabled us to refine and improve the presentation of complex material in our effort to provide an integrated overview of gerontology.

This book would not be possible without the long-term support of our respective institutions—Grand Rapids Community College and Calvin College—and their commitment to aging education, along with the translation of that support in the Calvin College-Grand Rapids Community College Consortium on Aging, which has been generating creative approaches to aging education since 1974. At Grand Rapids Community College, President Richard Calkins and Vice President Bill Foster implemented this support and commitment. At Calvin College, President Anthony Diekema and department chairs Gordon DeBlaey and Don Wilson were instrumental in facilitating acquisition of the resources we needed. We are very grateful to Ann Annis, Assistant Director of the Social Research Center, for her valuable editorial assistance. Finally, none of this would have been possible without the sterling assistance of Maxine Comer.

On a personal level, we express our appreciation and love to our families, particularly our wives, aging parents, and adult children, all of whom have continually provided us with their moral support, indulgence, and a myriad of illustrations from real life.

Robert J. Riekse

Henry Holstege

GROWING OLDER
IN AMERICA

GROWING OLDER IN AMERICA

CHAPTER 1

We Are
Getting Older

A recent report by the American Psychological Report *said that commercial television poorly serves the people who need it and use it most— children, the elderly, ethnic minorities and women. In another study of 100 randomly se- lected television commercials, the messages were almost always delivered by young actors and actresses, despite the fact the people older than 55 constitute 22 percent of the audience. We asked seniors if television is fair in the way it portrays senior citizens.*

Lee Murray
Free Press Special Writer

We Don't Fit the 'Geezer' Image*

Television shows and commercials, especially, do ignore older people and, what is worse, commer- cials usually portray us as frail, dippy or unat- tractive. I have noticed that grandparents of small children are usually played by actors who are old enough to be great-grandparents. Don't advertisers have parents? Haven't they noticed that older people of today, by and large, are much more active, dress more fashionably, and look younger than previous generations?

Jean Barnard
Rochester Hills

Still Sexy After All These Years*

Watching the tube, you'd think that no one works anymore and they're all under 30. Look around! There's some mighty attractive and sexy seniors around—many over 60. And don't forget the buy- ing power of the over-60 group—it's still sub- stantial.

William J. Carruth
Clawson

And We Like Romance!*

We've come up with the conclusion that all the cruise lines much prefer the younger generation. Never do we see seniors partaking in all the fun—the dancing and romancing in the moon- light. It gives us the definite impression that at

our ages, we don't enjoy those things. Are they wrong!

Mr. and Mrs. Raymond H. Vincent
Detroit

*Reprinted from May 12, 1992 edition of the Detroit Free Press with permission.

AN AMERICAN REVOLUTION

America is going through a revolution. No, we are not being undermined or overthrown by a for- eign power. Communism has not come back in the Russian form or any other form to bring down our democratic way of life. No, we are not referring to the technological revolution that has swept business, industry, and education and that we read and hear about all the time in our news- papers and on our TVs. We are recognizing a rev- olution that very few people ever talk about—the aging of America. Americans are getting older, and there are many more older people among us than ever before in our history.

Upon first hearing this news, it may not sound too exciting or even interesting. We now have the opportunity to see what the aging of America re- ally means to the life of each of us as individuals, as persons in relationships, family members, stu- dents, workers or potential workers, retirees, and citizens, and we can begin to understand how this social revolution is changing America. This revo- lution is not over—it is not even slowing down. In fact, with the impending aging of the 76 mil- lion baby boomers (who begin turning 50 in 1996), this revolution will become more pro- nounced. If the United States is experiencing problems dealing with all the needs of an aging population today, "you ain't seen nothing yet!"

AGE CATEGORIES OF OLDER AMERICANS

The reason for this is simple. Early in the twenty- first century we will have an explosion in the num- ber and percentage of older people. These older people will not just be classified in the general category of persons 65 and older that has been common in the past. We will need to use subcategories of the older-age population to adequately address the characteristics, issues, and needs of each age grouping. For convenience and simplicity, the U.S. Bureau of the Census (1993) provides three subcategories of the elderly population:

1. The young old (65 to 74 years)
2. The aged (75 to 84 years)
3. The oldest old (85 years and older)

In addition to these major subcategories of older people, the term *frail elderly* refers to persons 65 and older with significant physical and mental health problems.

The reason these subcategories are important is because the characteristics, desires, strengths, and needs of people at different stages of life can be very different. As we will see, there can be great differences between the vigor and good health of so many of those classified as young old to the multiple chronic conditions and frailties of so many of the oldest old. This obviously does not mean that all persons who are in the young old category are vigorous and healthy, but there is a greater likelihood of this being the case. Nor does it mean that most of the oldest old persons are frail and living in a nursing home, but there is a greater likelihood of having some form of dependency as a person moves into the oldest years of life.

It is important to know that the fastest growing sector of the American population is made up of persons 85 years and older. This is not the largest sector of our population—far from it. Indeed, in the thirty years from 1960 to 1990, the oldest old sector of the population (85 years and older) grew 232 percent compared to a 39 percent increase for the total population and 89 percent for the population 65 years and older. Why is this important? Persons in this group—the oldest old—consistently need the most assistance with their daily activities and the most support from their families, community agencies, and long-term care facilities to survive (U.S. Bureau of the Census 1993).

WHAT AN AGING AMERICA MEANS TO PEOPLE

To get a better handle on what the aging of America will mean to the average person, the following facts may be startling:

- For the first time in history, the average American has more living parents than children (Beck, 1990).
- The average American woman will spend more years helping her aging parents (18 years average) than raising her own children (17 years average) (U.S. House of Representatives Report, 1988).
- Never in our history have so many middle-aged and young-old persons had living parents (U.S. Bureau of the Census, 1993).
- More people than ever before are providing difficult and demanding care for elderly relatives, mostly parents (U.S. Bureau of the Census, 1993).
- American families, especially adult daughters and daughters-in-law, give 80 percent to 90 percent of the personal care needed by elderly family members (U.S. Bureau of the Census, 1993).

A Changing America

In colonial America, half the population was under the age of 16. Most people never made it to old age. At age 83, Benjamin Franklin was a rarity among the framers of the U.S. Constitution. Two factors kept America a youthful nation in terms of population: high mortality (death) rates and high fertility (birth) rates. In the twentieth century, fertility rates have dropped dramatically, from an average of seven births per woman to two. Death rates also declined (U.S. Bureau of the Census, 1993).

By 1990, fewer than one in four (23 percent) Americans were under the age of 16 and roughly 50 percent were aged 33 and older. By 2010, half the population is expected to be 37 and older. By 2050, at least 50 percent will be 39 and older. According to the Bureau of the Census (1993), by 2050, half the U.S. population will be 50 and older if birth, death, and net migration rates are lower.

Never before in our history have we had so many older people. While the overall population tripled from 1900 to 1990, the number of persons 65 and older increased ten times. In 1900 there were 3.1 million persons age 65 and older; by 1990, there were 31.1 million. This category of persons (65 years and older) is expected to more than double by the middle of the twenty-first century—up to 79 million persons. In 1990, about one in eight Americans was considered to be elderly (65 years and older). By 2030, one in five Americans is likely to be in this category (U.S. Bureau of the Census, 1993).

Not only have the numbers of older persons in the United States continued to increase dramatically throughout the twentieth century, their percentages by age groups of the whole population have also increased markedly as Table 1-1 indicates.

Table 1-1 clearly shows the rapid growth of the older population in America both in numbers and percentages. In 1900, when the elderly population numbered just over 3 million people, they made up just about 4 percent of the total population. By 1950, half way through the twentieth century and at the beginning of the Korean War, there were over three times as many older people as there were in 1900, making up about 8 percent of the population.

By 1960, just ten years later when John F. Kennedy was elected President, older people numbered just over 16.5 million which was 9.2 percent of the population. By the 1990 census, the elderly numbered about 31.2 million, 12.6 percent of the population.

THE DRAMATIC INCREASE OF THE OLDEST OLD

Examining this same table also gives us a better understanding of the dramatic numerical increases that have occurred, and will continue to occur, for the most elderly of the older population—the oldest old. In 1900, there were 122,000 persons 85 and older in the United States. By 1990, that number had increased to over 3 million. By 2020, the number of persons 85 years and older is expected to more than double, to 6,480,000. By the middle of the twenty-first century, the oldest old will reach 17,652,000, a phenomenal increase. As we have already noted, persons in the oldest old category are projected to continue to make up the fastest-growing sector of the older population well into the twenty-first century.

Even persons 100 years and older are expected to increase in numbers rather dramatically. In the ten years between 1980 and 1990, their number more than doubled, to 36,000 persons. The chances of living to be 100 have clearly improved. For persons born in 1879, the odds of living to 100 were 400 to 1. By 1980, the odds were reduced to 87 to 1 (Spencer, Goldstein, and Taeuber 1987).

Not only are we seeing dramatic increases in the older population in America, we are also seeing the "aging of the aged" (U.S. Bureau of the Census 1993). To gain a better understanding of this reality, we can use a method developed by Jacob S. Siegel called the "ratio of two elderly generations" (Siegel and Taeuber 1986). The ratio of the two elderly generations is the number of persons 85 years and older for every 100 persons 65 to 69 years of age. As Table 1-2 indicates, in 1950 there were twelve persons 85 years and older for every 100 persons aged 65 to 69. By 1990, the last general census, there were thirty persons 85 years and older for every 100 persons aged 65 to 69. By 2050, there are expected to be ninety-three persons 85 years and older per 100 persons aged 65 to 69.

The U.S. Bureau of the Census (1993) pointed out that if death rates continue about the same as they are currently, there will be some 9 million Americans aged 90 years and older by the middle of the next century compared to 1 million persons in this age category in 1990. If death rates decline among the oldest old, there will be many more than 9 million persons 90 years of age and older. Likewise with birth rates: If they decrease,

TABLE 1-1

GROWTH OF THE OLDER POPULATION, ACTUAL AND PROJECTED: 1900 TO 2050

(In thousands. "Data for 1900 to 1990 are April 1 census figures. Data for 2000 to 2050 are July 1 projections.)

Year	Total number (all ages)	65 to 74 years		75 to 84 years		85 years and over		65 years and over	
		Number	Percent	Number	Percent	Number	Percent	Number	Percent
1900	75,995	2,187	2.9	772	1.0	122	0.2	3,080	4.1
1910	91,972	2,793	3.0	989	1.1	167	0.2	3,949	4.3
1920	105,711	3,464	3.3	1,259	1.2	210	0.2	4,933	4.7
1930	122,775	4,721	3.8	1,641	1.3	272	0.2	6,634	5.4
1940	131,669	6,376	4.8	2,278	1.7	365	0.3	9,019	6.8
1950	150,697	8,415	5.6	3,277	2.2	577	0.4	12,269	8.1
1960	179,323	10,997	6.1	4,634	2.6	929	0.5	16,560	9.2
1970	203,302	12,447	6.1	6,124	3.0	1,409	0.7	19,980	9.8
1980	226,546	15,581	6.9	7,729	3.4	2,240	1.0	25,550	11.3
1990	248,710	18,045	7.3	10,012	4.0	3,021	1.2	31,079	12.5
MIDDLE SERIES (Middle fertility, mortality, and immigration assumptions)[1]									
2000	274,815	18,258	6.6	12,339	4.5	4,289	1.6	34,886	12.7
2010	298,109	21,235	7.1	12,767	4.3	5,702	1.9	39,705	13.3
2020	322,602	31,680	9.8	15,467	4.8	6,480	2.0	53,627	16.6
2030	344,951	37,865	11.0	23,592	6.8	8,381	2.4	69,839	20.2
2040	364,349	33,678	9.2	28,689	7.9	13,221	3.6	75,588	20.7
2050	382,674	35,217	9.2	26,008	6.8	17,652	4.6	78,876	20.6

[1]For the base years (1992): Lifetime births per 1,000 women, 2.052; Life expectancy at birth, 75.8; Yearly net immigration, 880,000. Assumptions for the year 2050 are respectively: 2.119; 82.1; and 880,000.
[2]For the base years (1992): Lifetime births per 1,000 women, 2.052; Life expectancy at birth, 75.8; Yearly net immigration, 880,000. Assumptions for the year 2050 are respectively: 2.522; 87.6; and 1,370,000.
[3]For the base years (1992): Lifetime births per 1,000 women, 2.052; Life expectancy at birth, 75.8; Yearly net immigration, 880,000. Assumptions for the year 2050 are respectively: 1.833; 75.3: and 350,000.
Figures for 1990 to 1950 exclude Alaska and Hawaii. Figures for 1900 to 1990 are for the Resident population; Projections for 2000 to 2050 include Armed Forces Overseas.
Source: U.S. Bureau of the Census. Current Population Reports, Special Studies, P23-178 RV, *Sixty-Five Plus in America.* U.S. Government Printing Office, Washington, D.C., 1992. Table 2-1, p. 2-2.

TABLE 1-2

TWO-ELDERLY-GENERATION SUPPORT RATIOS: 1950 TO 2050

(Ratio of persons aged 85 years and over to persons aged 65 to 69 years)

Race	1950	1990	2010	2030	2050
Total	12	30	47	42	93
White	12	31	49	44	97
Black	11	26	36	31	77
Other races	14	17	34	46	78
Hispanic origin[1]	(NA)	21	35	32	72

NA Not available.
[1]Hispanic origin may be of any race.
Source: U.S. Bureau of the Census. Current Population Reports, Special Studies, P23-178 RV, *Sixty-five Plus in America.* U.S. Government Printing Office, Washington D.C., 1993, Table 2-3, p. 2–5.

the elderly in America will become an even larger proportion of the population.

THE IMPACT OF THE BABY BOOMERS

So far we have focused on three categories of older people in America as defined by the U.S. Bureau of the Census, the young old (65–74), the aged (75–84), and the oldest old (85 years and older). We have seen how the numbers and percentages of these groups have increased, dramatically changing the nature of the American population to the point of a social revolution. To fully understand the scope of this revolution, however, we need to turn to another group in the American population, the "emerging old." For planning purposes, preparations need to begin now to accommodate the largest group of persons ever born in one period of American history—the baby boomers. The aging of the baby boomers will solidify the social revolution America is experiencing with the aging of its population.

Born between 1946, following World War II when millions of service personnel returned from overseas duty, and 1964, the baby boomers number about 76 million. The huge number of births in this period was 70 percent greater than the number of babies born in the previous two decades (U.S. Bureau of the Census, 1993).

When the baby boomers were babies, there were not enough of the things they needed. For example, when they began to go to school, there were not enough schools. Such has been the way with this generation. Their numbers have always given them visibility and power in American society. It was no accident that the TV program "thirtysomething" aired when it did—many of the boomers were moving through their thirties.

By 1990, the baby boomers were nearly one-third of the U.S. population (U.S. Bureau of the Census, 1993). They were in their economically productive years and raising their families. The children of the baby boomers made up what was called the "baby boomlet" or "baby echo" and followed the "baby bust" generation that followed the baby boomers. While in 1990 the Baby Boomers made up about one-third of the American population, the elderly population (65 years and older), after dramatic gains we already illustrated, made up one-eighth of the population.

By 1996, the Baby Boomers began to enter their fifties, not old yet, but old enough to be looked at as older workers with all the problems that entails.

By 2010, not too many years ahead, the Baby Boomers will be aged 46 to 64. They will become the "grandparent boom." Assuming that women continue to outlive men, this will really be the "grandma boom." Between 2010 and 2030, the baby boomers will be the young old (65 to 74 years) and the aged (75 to 84 years). During these two decades, the number of persons aged 64 to 84 is expected to grow by 81 percent (U.S. Bureau of the Census 1993).

After 2030, the U.S. will experience the final spurt of its aging revolution. This will be called the "great-grandparent boom" when those persons aged 85 years and older will more than double, from 3 million in 1990 to 8 million by 2030. This age group will more than double in size again by 2050, to over 17 million persons, as the baby boom survivors reach the oldest old category (U.S. Bureau of the Census 1993).

LIFE EXPECTANCY

Life expectancy refers to the average number of years a person is expected to live. It can be measured from birth, which is the most common, or from any given year. For example, the Bureau of the Census (1993) defines "life expectancy at birth as the average number of years a person would live given the age-specific death rates of the specified year" (p. 3-1).

For a variety of reasons, not the least of which are biological, women outlive men in America. As Table 1-3 shows, from 1900 to 1992, for example, the life expectancy of men at birth increased from 46 years to 73.2 years. For women, the life expectancy over the same time period increased from 48 years to about 79.8 years (Kochanek and Bettie 1994).

TABLE 1-3

LIFE EXPECTANCY AT BIRTH BY RACE AND SEX: UNITED STATES, 1940, 1950, 1960, AND 1970–92

	All races			White			All other					
							Total			Black		
Year	Both sexes	Male	Female	Both sexes	Male	Female	Both sexes	Male	Female	Both sexes	Male	Female
1992	75.8	72.3	79.1	76.5	73.2	79.8	71.8	67.7	75.7	69.6	65.0	73.9
1991	75.5	72.0	78.9	76.3	72.9	79.6	71.5	67.3	75.5	69.3	64.6	73.8
1990	75.4	71.8	78.8	76.1	72.7	79.4	71.2	67.0	75.2	69.1	64.5	73.6
1989	75.1	71.7	78.5	75.9	72.5	79.2	70.9	66.7	74.9	68.8	64.3	73.3
1888	74.9	71.4	78.3	75.6	72.2	78.9	70.8	66.7	74.8	68.9	64.4	73.2
1987	74.9	71.4	78.3	75.6	72.1	78.9	71.0	66.9	75.0	69.1	64.7	73.4
1986	74.7	71.2	78.2	75.4	71.9	78.8	70.9	66.8	74.9	69.1	64.8	73.4
1985	74.7	71.1	78.2	75.3	71.8	78.7	71.0	67.0	74.8	69.3	65.0	73.4
1984	74.7	71.1	78.2	75.3	71.8	78.7	71.1	67.2	74.9	69.5	65.3	73.6
1983	74.6	71.0	78.1	75.2	71.6	78.7	70.9	67.0	74.7	69.4	65.2	73.5
1982	74.5	70.8	78.1	75.1	71.5	78.7	70.9	66.8	74.9	69.4	65.1	73.6
1981	74.1	70.4	77.8	74.8	71.1	78.4	70.3	66.2	74.4	68.9	64.5	73.2
1980	73.7	70.0	77.4	74.4	70.7	78.1	69.5	65.3	73.6	68.1	63.8	72.5
1979	73.9	70.0	77.8	74.6	70.8	78.4	69.8	65.4	74.1	68.5	64.0	72.9
1978	73.5	69.6	77.3	74.1	70.4	78.0	69.3	65.0	73.5	68.1	63.7	72.4
1977	73.3	69.5	77.2	74.0	70.2	77.9	68.9	64.7	73.2	67.7	63.4	72.0
1976	72.9	69.1	76.8	73.6	69.9	77.5	68.4	64.2	72.7	67.2	62.9	71.6
1975	72.6	68.8	76.6	73.4	69.5	77.3	68.0	63.7	72.4	66.8	62.4	71.3
1974	72.0	68.2	75.9	72.8	69.0	76.7	67.1	62.9	71.3	66.0	61.7	70.3
1973	71.4	67.6	75.3	72.2	68.5	76.1	66.1	62.0	70.3	65.0	60.9	69.3
1972[1]	71.2	67.4	75.1	72.0	68.3	75.9	65.7	61.5	70.1	64.7	60.4	69.1
1971	71.1	67.4	75.0	72.0	68.3	75.8	65.6	61.6	69.8	64.6	60.5	68.9
1970	70.8	67.1	74.7	71.7	68.0	75.6	65.3	61.3	69.4	64.1	60.0	68.3
1960	69.7	66.6	73.1	70.6	67.4	74.1	63.6	61.1	66.3	—	—	—
1950	68.2	65.6	71.1	69.1	66.5	72.2	60.8	59.1	62.9	—	—	—
1940	62.9	60.8	65.2	64.2	62.1	66.6	53.1	51.5	54.9	—	—	—

[1]Deaths based on a 50-percent sample.
Source: National Center for Health Statistics Monthly Vital Statistics Report, Vol. 43, No. 6(S), December 8, 1994, Table 4, p. 19.

With women living about seven years longer than men, the typical young adult woman wishing to live about as long as her husband, statistically at least, would need to select a mate about seven years younger than she. Yet it is still common for American women to marry men who are several years older. From understanding the facts of aging in America, it is easy to understand why there are so many widows in our nation.

The leading causes of death among the elderly are heart disease, cancer, and stroke. Influenza and pneumonia become increasingly important after the age 85 (National Center for Health Sta-

tistics 1991). Smoking has clearly been associated with these three causes of death among older persons. Research has shown that men have been more likely to smoke and to smoke more than women (National Center for Health Statistics 1991), but very important for today's women, men in these studies were relatively more likely to have quit smoking than were women.

OLDER WOMEN AND OLDER MEN

The death (mortality) rate for males is higher than for females at every age (U.S. Bureau of the Census 1993). As a result, for persons aged 65 to 69, women outnumber men five to four. As age progresses, there are even fewer men than women. This is called the sex ratio—the number of men in a given age group for every 100 women in the same age group (see Figure 1-1).

While there are eighty-one men per 100 women at the ages 65 to 69, we can see from the previous figure that by ages 75 to 79, there are only sixty-four men per 100 women, By the ages 85 to 89, only forty-two men survive for each 100 women. By the ages 95 and older, there are only 27 males per 100 females. It is not difficult to see that when we talk about the elderly at any age category, females predominate (U.S. Bureau of the Census 1990). In 1990, among the oldest old in the United States, 841,000 were male and 2.2 million were female.

This female advantage is not new. It has been expanding for decades. The U.S. Bureau of the Census (1993) projects that this trend may ease in the twenty-first century as men 85 years and older are expected to increase their numbers. It

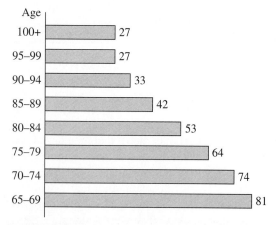

**Number of Men per 100
Women, by Age: 1990**

FIGURE 1-1

Sex ratio (males per 100 females) in the later years. (*Source:* U.S. Bureau of the Census, 1960 Census of Population and Housing, Series CPH-L74, *Modified and Actual Age, Sex, Race, and Hispanic Origin Data.*)

should be noted that even with this projection, there are still expected to be 4.7 million more women than men in the oldest old category by the year 2050.

RACE AND ETHNICITY OF THE OLD

Currently in America the elderly population is mostly white. Of all older people in the United States in 1990, about 28 million were white; 2.5 million were African American; 116,000 were Native Americans including Eskimo and Aleuts (AIEA); 450,000 were Asian and Pacific Islander (API); and 1.1 million were Latino of any race (U.S. Bureau of the Census 1993).

This racial and ethnic composition is expected to change in the twenty-first century. By 2050, the African American elderly population is expected to quadruple, with their percentage of the elderly increasing from 8 to 12 percent. The Latino elderly population is expected to double its numbers by 2010, not many years away. By 2050, the elderly Latino population is expected to be eleven times greater. Older persons of Latino origin are expected to be 15 percent of the elderly population in the United States compared with less than 4 percent in the early 1990s. In this same period, 1990 to 2050, Asians, Pacific Islanders and Native Americans combined would see their percentage of the elderly population increase from less than 2 percent to 9 percent (U.S. Bureau of the Census 1990).

Clearly, in the decades ahead, there will be much more racial and ethnic diversity among the elderly population. This is yet another part of the aging revolution that is occurring in America (see Figure 1-2).

REVOLUTIONARY CHANGES IN AMERICA

If all these numbers indicate that we are indeed experiencing a social revolution in America, it is logical to ask, What will be revolutionized? What will change in how we Americans think, work, play, worship, experience relationships, vote, and

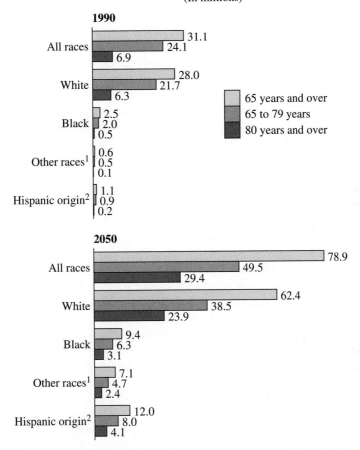

**Persons 65 Years and Over,
by Age, Race, and Hispanic
Origin: 1990 and 2050**
(In millions)

[1]Includes Asians and Pacific Islanders, American Indians, Eskimos, and Aleuts.
[2]Hispanic origin may be of any race.

FIGURE 1-2
The elderly population in 1990 and 2050 by age, race and Hispanic origin.
(*Source:* U.S. Bureau of the Census. Current Population Reports, Special Studies, P23-178RV, *Sixty-Five Plus In America.* U.S. Government Printing Office, Washington, D.C., 1993, Figure 2-11, p. 2-11.)

do all the other things we do today? The changes in how we do all these things will not take place overnight. They will probably be subtle, and they will be profound. Many of these changes are already under way. They are bound to gain momentum as more and more people reach their later years or begin to think about reaching the later stages of life. This trend will only accelerate as the baby boomers move into their fifties and begin to look ahead to their retirement.

What are some of the major changes and challenges our age revolution is having and will continue to have in the years ahead? Here is a sampling of some of the hot topic areas:

Who Takes Care of Older People? Are Women Exploited?

As the Bureau of the Census pointed out in 1993, never before in the history of America have we had so many middle-aged and young-old people with living parents. Never before have we had so many old people, especially in the oldest old category. As people move into their oldest old years, they are more likely to need help with getting by each day. Among persons aged 85 and older, nearly one in four lives in a nursing home. Of those not in long-term care institutions, 45 percent need help with everyday activities.

As medical technology continues to move ahead, the experts tell us that we can expect to see more people living to the oldest old ages but with chronic illness and physical and mental impairments. Caring for these old, impaired people will be increasingly demanding. Who takes care of our oldest old? Contrary to some popular beliefs and some accounts in the newspapers about "granny dumping," families provide 80 percent to 90 percent of all personal care and help with household tasks, transportation, and shopping for dependent older persons (U.S. Bureau of the Census 1993). Of these family caregivers, over 75 percent are women (U.S. Select Committee on Aging 1990). The women who bear the greatest burden of older adult caregiving in the family are the daughters and daughters-in-law (U.S. Bureau of the Census 1993).

The rapid increase in the need for older adult care in families has come at a time when vast numbers of women have returned to the paid labor force, adding to their traditional roles in society. Are they expected to cut their outside-the-home work hours short or give up their employment, as so many have, to care for dependent older family members? Why are our national policies designed to place so much pressure on family caregiving to meet the long-term care needs of the elderly, pressures that in America fall mostly on women? Is this another form of exploitation of women? This issue will be examined later in this book.

What About Advertising and Selling?

As we have already noted, America has been a youth-centered nation. The vigor, freshness, and drive of youth go back to our pioneer roots. When Horace Greeley was quoted as saying "Go west young man," it was not advice to the old. In America, youthful characteristics have always been "in." This has been particularly true in American advertising. How many middle-aged or older women have leaned over the hoods of convertibles to sell cars?

A recent newspaper article pointed out the reality of the typical advertising/marketing of the past. "When a 25-year-old woman makes a fashion statement, she is rarely at a loss for words. Wooed by the effusive language of a hundred glossy magazines, she is plied with five total looks and twenty-five new colors, Lolita lines, and the seductive wardrobe," wrote Jennifer Foote (1994, p. J2). She went on, "and then, roughly 30 years later, she is speechless. There are no new looks, new styles or colors. Every year is devoted to a single garment—the housecoat—and the mood never swings." The article went on to quote Alan J. Greco, professor of marketing at Winthrop University in South Carolina: "Fashion retailers have mistakenly believed for some time that older women are fat and like to wear polyester. They don't want to offer anything for those women because they don't want to be associated with 'Granny Bait' " (Foote 1994, J2). Ms. Foote further stated that most businesses are finally coming to grips with the marketing necessities of the graying of America. Some 50 percent of the nation's discretionary money (money to spend on extras) is in the hands of people aged 50 to 74 (Foote 1994). They make up 40 percent of all consumer demand. As shown in Table 1-4, this group is in the best financial position of any age group—a group marketers cannot ignore for long.

TABLE 1-4

MATURE MARKETPLACE

The Numbers and Purchasing Power of Older Adults in America

The group of Americans age 50 and older is one of the fastest growing markets, with plenty of discretionary income.

The demographic balance reverses in millions, 1970–2020

	1970	1980	1990	2000	2010	2020
Americans under age 18	69.8	63.7	63.6	65.7	62.6	62.9
Americans 50 and over	49.9	59.1	63.5	76.4	96.5	112.0

More Americans and their money

	Per capita after tax income	Percent of households with discretionary income	Per capita discretionary income
All ages	$ 9,087	28.9%	$4,633
50–54	10,513	31.8	4,899
55–59	10,931	35.0	5,759
60–64	11,165	28.8	6,188
65–69	10,472	25.0	6,280
70 and older	9,567	22.8	6,073

Source: Detroit Free Press, June 8, 1993, p. 3C, created by the Los Angeles Daily News.

The actual trend to market to a fast-growing wave of older consumers is developing slowly, but changes are beginning to be seen. For example, McDonald's Corporation is only one of many restaurant chains beginning to seek older customers. The president and chief executive officer, Ed Rensi, has recognized the growth and importance of the older buyers. He said, "Their busy life style makes them an important market segment" (Yu 1993, p. 3c).

General Motors' electric car program is targeting older buyers. They have found a lot of interest in this type of car from people 60 and over. Maybelline, Inc., is also trying to lure older buyers. The company is marketing a new line of makeup called "Age-Denying Makeup," which provides moisturizers to promote elasticity of the skin. Schumacher & Company has sold 150,000 copies of a book entitled *Understanding Living Trusts*, aimed at the mature market (Yu 1993).

Not many people know that the magazine with the largest membership circulation in America is *Modern Maturity*, published by the American As-

sociation of Retired Persons. It sells 22.5 million copies a year (Yu 1993).

More and more companies are starting to target the mature market according to Frank Conaway, president of a marketing and communications firm in California. "A lot of companies haven't realized this market's potential because of stereotypes and perceptions," Conaway said. "The reality is that 80 percent feel healthy and they feel good about themselves. They have time and money to purchase products. They own 77 percent of all financial assets in the country" (Yu 1993, p. 3c).

Although much of today's advertising still ignores the older persons or depicts them as creaky, deaf, befuddled, cranky, or in need of products to catch their leaking urine, a handful of older models, such as Lauren Hutton, have appeared recently in ads (Foote 1994). Banana Republic featured white-haired models in some ads, and some Gap ads included older celebrities and models. The *New York Times Sunday Magazine* even featured twelve glossy pages of expensive, contemporary clothes in a feature called "The Look of the Nineties" which used female and male models in their late eighties and in their nineties (Boyle 1993). These very elderly models posed in evening wear by Calvin Klein, Romeo Gigli, and Ralph Lauren. There was no attempt to hide any wrinkles or gray hair.

A study by the Institute of Gerontology of the University of Michigan in 1993 demonstrated that as the elderly have grown in numbers, they have declined as advertising models (Muha 1993). W. Andrew Achenbaum, co-author of the study, pointed out that not only are fewer older people showing up in ads, but the products they are promoting have changed from prestige items to more ordinary ones. Once portrayed in ads as dapper authority figures, older men were more recently depicted as folksy types selling popcorn or margarine. Older women are most commonly shown promoting hair coloring and anti-wrinkle creams, but given the reality of the sheer numbers of older people and their buying power, change is coming even to the world of advertising. As one analyst pointed out, it is not likely that advertising will ever give up the idea of selling through "fresh, smooth, and sag-free faces and bodies." A growing number of ad campaigns is beginning to portray people in their forties, fifties, and beyond in a different and positive way (Boyle 1993).

Has the Age Revolution Hit Television?

We all know that television is one of the most powerful forces in American life. How do older people do on TV? Not too well, according to a UCLA School of Medicine survey of television insiders (A.I.M. 1992). This UCLA study concluded that TV, considered by many to be the most important medium of this century, is not prepared to cover what will probably be the most important happening of the twenty-first century—the aging of America.

The TV insiders who participated in the study indicated that their industry does a poor job of representing the interests of the elderly. It is also plagued by age discrimination and outdated ideas about older adults (A.I.M. 1992).

As one TV critic put it, even turning 51 years of age meant that he no longer existed by most network TV standards. Doug Nye (1992) of the Knight-Ridder Newspapers pointed out that over the years, the networks have become less and less interested in people who are over 50 years old. ABC has targeted the 18-to-49-year-old audience. Fox has gone after an even younger audience, the 18-to-34-year age bracket. NBC has targeted the 18-to-54-year-old market. Only CBS is going with the aging flow says Mike Duffy (1994), TV writer for the *Detroit Free Press*.

CBS's "Burke's Law" starring Gene Barry, 71, was a surprise Friday night hit in the winter of 1994. James Arnet, 70, also made a CBS comeback in "Gunsmoke, One Man's Justice" in 1994. And 63-year-old Robert Culp teamed with 56-year-old Bill Cosby in a 1994 "I Spy Returns" for CBS. Perhaps the best example of a CBS hit starring an elder is the highly rated and long-running "Murder, She Wrote" with Angela Lansbury. Another example is "Golden Girls," a situation comedy about four older women living together, that ran on NBC from 1985 to 1992. It starred Estelle Getty who was 61 when the series began, 63-year-old Betty White, 59-year-old Bea Arthur, and 49-year-old Rue McClanahan.

CBS Entertainment Vice President Steve Warner said, "We're all getting older. I don't see any problems with programming for an older audience" (Duffy 1994, p. E1). CBS has argued that an aging public means valuable older viewers. Warner points out, "Thirty years ago, if you were 70, you were old. But today, people who are 70 play tennis and lead active lives. They're healthier, they live longer, and they have more money. There are even new studies that indicate that they are also more willing to change their product preferences" (p. E1).

In spite of their primary age targeting previously outlined, some of the other networks are beginning to realize the importance of the older market. The "Colombo" movies with Peter Falk, 66, and "Matlock" with Andy Griffith, 67, brought upbeat ratings to ABC in 1994. NBC revived "Hart to Hart" with Robert Wagner, 64, and Stefanie Powers, 51. Even without Raymond Burr as Perry Mason, the "Mason" mystery series carried on with Hal Holbrook, 69 (Duffy 1994). The indications are clear—people are tuning into the age revolution on TV. This trend will undoubtedly gain momentum as the nation's population continues to grow older.

How Will the Senior Boom Affect Medicine?

In the late 1940s and through the 1950s, when the baby boomers were infants and toddlers, pediatricians were the "in" doctors. It was no accident that Dr. Spock and his book *Infant and Child Care* became not only a best-seller, but one of the better-known books of that time. Babies and toddlers were everywhere.

Today, the situation has changed dramatically. Older Americans are the largest consumers of health care. By the beginning of the next century, the elderly will consume half of all the money spent on health care in the nation, over $1 trillion (U.S. House of Representatives Select Committee on Aging 1992).

Dr. Robert Butler, chair of the department of geriatrics (medical practice focusing on older people) of the Mount Sinai School of Medicine in New York, has pointed out that a student in medical school in the 1990s can expect that half of his or her patients will be in the older age categories (65 years and older) by the time he or she begins practicing medicine. Dr. Butler said he likes to remind medical students that if they do not feel comfortable working with older people, they only have one choice—pediatrics. Those not in pediatrics will deal predominately with older patients (U.S. House of Representatives Select Committee on Aging 1992).

There is a tremendous unmet need for geriatricians, doctors who focus on the health needs of older people. Out of over 550,000 physicians in the United States in 1992, only 4,084 have certificates of competence in geriatrics. This is only 1.32 geriatricians for every 10,000 older Americans. These are mostly internists, family physicians, and psychiatrists. Of the 126 medical schools in the United States, only thirteen had required courses in geriatrics. Only 3.5 percent of medical students took electives in geriatrics in 1992 (U.S. House of Representatives Select Committee on Aging 1992).

Dr. Butler indicated that although 20,000 physicians with expertise in geriatrics were needed in 1992, there were only 4,084. By 2030, there will be a need for 36,000 physicians with these skills.

Training physicians in geriatric medicine is and will continue to be a major problem because of a lack of medical school staff to do the training. In 1992, about 500 physicians had the combination of medical, academic, and scientific training to teach geriatric medicine. At that time, 2,100 were needed to train the number of physicians we need with expertise in geriatrics to serve the greatly enlarged older population.

So there is a revolution in medicine. Who will treat the multiple chronic conditions so many older people experience, especially the oldest old?

Do Relationships and Sexuality Change in Old Age?

Personal relationships are very important to persons of any age. Our lives begin and revolve around relationships—lovers, parents, children, grandparents, siblings, relatives, and special friends. We share and enrich our lives with relationships. Relationships give life closeness and meaning.

Typically, our culture has given us the message that the relationships of older people are limited and narrowly defined. The older married couple, the widow or widower, and the occasional divorced older person were just there—not doing anything exciting, just there. The spice and excitement of their lives, if they ever existed, were things of the past.

In fact, it is difficult, if not uncomfortable, for many college-age young persons to think about their parents being sexually active. As the comedian Sam Levinson quipped, "My parents would never do such a thing: well, my father—maybe. But my mother—NEVER!" (*Mayo Clinic Health Letter* 1993, p. 51).

As a 1993 *Mayo Clinic Health Letter* pointed out, "For many [older] people, sexual intimacy isn't an available or desired form of closeness. A close friendship or a loving grandparent-grandchild relationship, for example, can provide rewarding opportunities for nonsexual intimacy. For some older people, though, sexual intimacy remains important. Despite this importance, sexuality in people after age 60 or 70 is not openly acknowledged" (p. 51).

In America, sex has been considered reserved for only the young. With the revolution of an aging America, this is a perception, whether portrayed by the media, perceived by the young, or depicted by advertisers, that is a myth—a myth that will be exploded and explained in depth in chapter 6.

Indeed, in an age-changed America, we will begin to deal with the reality of the importance of life-long relationships between men and women—married and single—and life-long sexuality. Research has shown that both the quality and quantity of sexual activity among older persons can be defined as "astonishing" (Mayo Clinic Health Letter 1994, p. 51). "The myth is that age makes sexual pleasure fade and idle," wrote researcher Arno Kavhen (1992). "The truth is that middle and later life give us a second chance at sexual pleasure and harmony, often a better one than we had in youth" (p. 52).

CHANGES AND POSSIBILITIES IN AN OLDER AMERICA

These are just some of the issues and changes America needs to address as we collectively realize the extent of the social revolution we are experiencing, and will experience more intensely in the immediate years ahead, with the aging of our population. In their pioneering work, *The Age Wave*, Ken Dychtwald and Joe Flower (1989) pointed out what may be the revolutionary

changes America will experience as the nation continues to grow older. They contended that:

- The concept of marriage will change. As people live longer and longer, some will be married for 75 years. Others will turn to serial monogamy, choosing different spouses for different stages of life.
- The nuclear family centered around children will be replaced by the "matrix" family, an adult-centered family unit spanning generations that is bound together by friendships and circumstances as well as by blood relationships.
- More people will work into their seventies and eighties. They may retire several times to go into something different or to take a year or two off to enjoy themselves.
- Environmental factors will change to accommodate the physical realities of an older population. Traffic lights will change more slowly; steps will be less steep, bathtubs will be less dangerous, and lights will be brighter (p. 8).

Dychtwald and Flower pointed out that the aging of our population will affect more than America's ways of doing things. This aging revolution will touch our innermost thoughts, hopes, and dreams. These authors showed that the revolution brought about by the dramatic aging of our people will force us to rethink and reevaluate the purposes, goals, tempo, and challenges of our lives, at each stage of our lives. This can lead to new and positive perspectives as well as new possibilities in our later years. In these new perspectives and possibilities, the later years of life can be less pressured and more reflective, opening up opportunities for better development of the intellect, memory, imagination, emotional maturity, and spirituality. Persons in this phase of life will be able to give back to society the lessons, resources, and experiences they have gathered over their lifetimes. From this perspective, older people become valuable assets, not social outcasts. In our age-based revolution in America and around the world (the aging of populations is a worldwide phenomenon), we will need to rethink what "old" is, what it means to be old, and how growing older is really a life-long process. When people aged 65 and older outnumber teenagers by more than two to one, as is projected by 2025 in America, our age-based revolution will have reached its peak. Will we be ready? Are we able to cope with today's older people? The rest of this book focuses on the major issues, conditions, and obstacles older people and their families face in their daily lives along with the resources, opportunities, and options available to them today.

SUMMARY

America is experiencing a social revolution based on the aging of its population. This age-based revolution will become more pronounced as the 76 million baby boomers reach their golden years early in the twenty-first century.

For the purposes of this book, older people are classified into three categories: (1) the young old (65 to 74 years); (2) the aged (75 to 84 years); and (3) the oldest old (85 years and older). "Frail elderly" refers to persons 65 years and older with significant physical and mental problems. The fastest growing sector of the population is made up of persons aged 85 and older. From 1960 to 1990, while the overall U.S. population grew by 39 percent, persons aged 65 and older increased by 89 percent. The group made up of persons aged 85 and older increased by 232 percent. Persons in this group—the oldest old—generally need the most assistance with daily living.

For the first time in American history, the average woman will spend more years helping her aging parents (18 years) than in raising her own children (17 years). Never before have so many middle-aged and young-old persons had living parents. More people than ever before are providing demanding care for elderly relatives. American families, especially daughters and daughters-in-law, give 80 percent to 90 percent of all the personal care needed by aging family members. Never before have we had so many older people.

The number and percentages of older people are expected to continue to increase dramatically in the twenty-first century, which begins in just a few years.

Although this book primarily focuses on the three categories of older people identified by the U.S. Bureau of the Census, there is another group of Americans that needs to be included in our discussions—the "emerging old." They are not old yet, but they are moving toward the later years of life. We refer to the 76 million baby boomers, many of whom are already classified as "older" when it applies to the workplace. The baby boomers will have a tremendous impact on the continuing age-based social revolution in America. By 2010, the baby boomers will become the "grandparent boom" according to the Bureau of the Census. By 2030, they will become the "great-grandparent boom."

Older women outnumber men. At ages 56 to 69, women outnumber men five to four. By the ages 85 to 89, there are only 42 men for every 100 women. Women currently live about seven years longer than men.

Life expectancy in the United States has increased from about 47 years for both sexes in 1900 to an average of 75 years by 1989. Throughout this century, women have outlived men. Currently in America, most of the elderly population is white. There will, however, be changes in the ratios of all the minority elderly populations in the years ahead with increased numbers and percentages of minority elderly persons.

As we face a social revolution in America based on an aging population, many major issues and realities will need to be faced. These include caregiving for an exploding elderly population; the personal relationships and sexuality of persons throughout their lives, even among the oldest old; advertising and marketing products; television's inclusion and exclusion of older people; and the changing medical care needs of an aging population.

The changes that an older America will bring about might be startling. Changes in the structure of families, marriage relationships, working patterns, and environments could result from an aging population. The later stages of life can open new opportunities for intellectual development, imagination, emotional maturity, and spiritual identity.

We will need to rethink what old is, what it means to be old, and how growing older is a life-long process. With the number and percentage of older people we have today, and when people 65 and older outnumber teenagers by more than two to one (as projected by 2025), we have no option but to deal with the realities of an aging America.

REFERENCES

A.I.M. (Aging in Michigan). 1992. UCLA Study Finds TV Does Poor Job in Addressing Aging. (May/June) 20(3): 9. Lansing, MI: Michigan Office of Services to the Aging.

Beck, M. 1990. The Geezer Boom. *Newsweek: The 21st century family*, CXIV (27): 62–68.

Boyle, J. 1993. Mature Message: Pitches Are Tailored to Older Buyers. *Detroit Free Press* (September 30): E1, 6.

Duffy, M. 1994. TV's New Golden Age. *Detroit Free Press* (February 14): E1.

Dychtwald, K., and Flower, J. 1989. The Age Wave. From *Utne reader*. (January/February 1990): 82–86. In *Annual Editions: Aging*, 7th ed. 1992. Sluice Dock, Guilford, CT: Dushkin Publishing Group.

Foote, J. 1994. In the Booming 'Gray Market,' Old Rhymes with Sold. Newhouse News Service. In *The Grand Rapids Press*, (January 16).

Kavhen, A. 1992. Appreciating the Sexual You. *Modern Maturity*, (April–May) 35(2): 52–57.

Kochanek, K.D., and Bettie, M.A. 1994. Advance Report of Final Mortality Statistics, 1992. *Monthly Vital Statistics Report* (December). Hyattsville, MD: National Center for Health Statistics.

Muha, L. 1993. Elderly Grow in Numbers, But Decline as Ad Models. *Newsday*. In *The Grand Rapids Press* (November 28): A16.

National Center for Health Statistics. 1992. *Health United States, 1990*. Hyattsville, MD: Public Health Service 1991, (Table 15, 1989). At Birth. (Data from *Monthly Vital Statistics Report*, Vol. 40, No. 8 (S) 2. At 65 years. (Data unpublished; final data from mortality statistics branch.)

Nye, D. 1992. Networks Tune Out the 50-and-Up Crowd. Knight-Ridder Newspapers. In *Detroit Free Press* (August 18): D1.

Mayo Clinic Health Letter. (1993, February). Sexuality and Aging. In *Annual Editions: Aging*. 9th Ed. 1994. Sluice Dock, Guilford, CT: The Dushkin Publishing Group.

Siegel, J.S., and Taeuber, C.M. 1986. Demographic Perspectives on the Long-Lived Society. *Daedalus*, 115(1).

Spencer, G., Goldstein, A., and Taeuber, C. 1987. *America's Centenarians: Data from the 1980 Census*, U.S. Bureau of the Census, Current Population Reports, (Series P-23, No. 153). Washington, DC: U.S. Government Printing Office.

U.S. Bureau of the Census. 1990. Census of Population and Housing, (Series CPH-L-74). Modified and Actual Age, Sex, Race, and Hispanic Origin Data.

U.S. Bureau of the Census. 1993. Current Population Reports, Special Studies: (P23–178RV), *Sixty-Five Plus in America*. Washington, DC: U.S. Government Printing Office.

U.S. House of Representatives Report. 1988. Cited in Beck, M., Kantrowitz, B., Beach, Y.L., Hager, M., Gordon, J., Roberts, E., and Hammill, R. July 16, 1990. Trading Places. *Newsweek*, CXVI(3): 48–54.

U.S. House of Representatives Select Committee on Aging. 1992. *Geriatricians and the Senior Boom: Precarious Present, Uncertain Future*. Washington, DC: U.S. Government Printing Office.

Yu, D. 1993. Cornering the market: Americans 50 and over gain clout with advertisers. *Los Angeles Daily News*. In the *Detroit Free Press*, (June 8): 3C.

CHAPTER 2

Growing Older As a New Century Approaches

Theories of Aging

Robert George Riekse

Different Views of Growing Old

Mr. VanderHoven is 76 but does not want to associate with "old people" because he says that they have lost a zest for life and complain too much. Mr. VanderHoven walks about five miles every day, swims periodically, takes care of his own lawn, travels overseas at least once a year, and devotes a lot of time to his hobby, photography.

Mrs. Tendens is 69 and is proud of her ability to choose clothing that accentuates her figure and her red hair. She enjoys going to movies and then discussing with her friends the plot, acting, directing, cinematography, and symbolism. She also enjoys the local orchestra and rarely misses a performance and, in addition, has a season ticket to the "pops" concerts. She is vibrant, energetic, and opinionated.

Mr. Snowly is 61. He has severe diabetes, is arthritic, has a lack of energy, and looks as if he might be 80 years old. He cannot take care of his own yard. He has been retired for three years. He is very overweight. He smokes a pack of cigarettes a day and drinks a six-pack of beer a day. He complains constantly about his pain, his lack of energy, the "rotten" younger generation, the changes in his church, and corrupt politicians. He is opinionated and is convinced he has the answers, all of which are simple and easy, to the problems of the nation and the world. His wife is as unhappy as he is, as obese as he is, and as complaining and opinionated.

Mrs. Jeffries is 71 and is taking multiple vitamins in massive dosages, because she believes that they will retard the aging process. She is very active in her church. She has a positive, upbeat attitude toward life but is concerned about the excessive wrinkling of her face and talks a great deal about various skin "preservatives." She reads avidly any article she can find on "aging well." Although she is energetic and positive in her outlook on life, she does look her age; in fact, some say she looks older than her age.

Mr. Fortner is, at age 81, beginning to take up weight lifting, as he has read some articles on the benefits of weight training at any age. He has been lifting weights for six months and is convinced it has increased his strength, his feelings of well-being, and his agility. He is trying to convince his 80-year-old wife to begin a weight-training program. He also is trying to convince his four middle-aged children to begin to lift weights. They humor him but talk about his strange new obsession. After six months of weight training, he is proud of his body and is beginning, to the embarrassment of his wife, to do lawn work in his shorts without a shirt.

Mrs. Launder does not take any vitamins and does not exercise because at 79 she believes that aging is purely a genetic factor. Her mother lived to be 91 and she is convinced that she is "programmed" for a long life. She looks 79 and is in fairly good health. She is living independently and does her own shopping and housework. She eats well and likes going out with her friends for lunch or breakfast. She believes that what one eats or does has little impact on how one ages. She frequently says that one either has "good" or "bad" genes for aging, and that she has "good" genes.

PERCEPTIONS OF GROWING OLDER CHANGE

What is it like to grow older in America as the twenty-first century approaches? What is "old" anyway? It is important to keep in mind that there are distinct stages or periods of old age. The young old, persons aged 65 to 74, are very different in many ways from the oldest old, persons 85 years and older. And the aged, people 75 to 84 years, are unique from the other two categories. In addition, persons in their fifties and early sixties are important to recognize because growing older is an ongoing process; people in this age category already experience some of the consequences of being older, especially in employment; and the huge number of people moving into this category in the immediate years ahead requires that we alter our concepts of what it means to be old.

As the nation prepares to move into a new century, we are in a state of transition regarding our view of older people and their place in society. Since America has changed in many ways, and is continuing to change, the status and role of older people have changed and will continue to change.

Current Perceptions of Old Age

As we will see in the following sections of this chapter, over the years there have been many views of older people, of growing older, and of old age. These views change as a result of changing circumstances in any society; America is no exception. We will look at specific factors that affect the role and status of the elderly in a society and how these factors came into play as America became an industrialized nation. We will then examine the changes that will occur as we move into a post-industrial era and that should affect our views of being older and of older people.

First, let us take a snapshot of what Americans think about old age and old people in the mid-1990s. In a scientifically constructed poll, Mark Clements Research, Inc. (1993) surveyed persons across the nation for *Parade Magazine* to determine the views Americans have regarding getting older and older people. Men and women aged 18 to 75 were interviewed, representing various geographic areas by age, household income and household size which were weighted to the latest census data for age, race, and household income. Some of the highlights of this survey follow.

What It Means to Be Old   Two-thirds (66 percent) of all those surveyed thought old age begins at age 70 or older. In this group, 28 percent thought somebody 80 years and older was "old." Of those surveyed who were 65 and older, only 8 percent thought of people under age 65 as "old." However, persons surveyed who were under 25 felt that "old applied to persons anywhere from age 40 to 64.

Old Is Bad?   Only 27 percent of those surveyed, of all ages, thought growing old was "bad." This varied somewhat by age with 35 percent of those between the ages of 18 to 24 having said that growing old is "bad." Among those questioned between the ages of 65 to 75, only 14 percent had a negative view of aging.

Being Afraid of Getting Old   Of all those surveyed, 28 percent indicated that they were afraid of getting old. This fear decreased dramatically with the increased age of the persons questioned. Of the persons aged 65 to 75, 85 percent were not afraid of getting old. As a 56-year-old said, "Aging is quite natural. To me, getting older is good news: it means I didn't die." A 65-year-old, on the same subject, said, "Turning 60 was a plus. Now I'm 65, and I've lived longer than my parents. As you get older, you see more of the beauty of the world. There is a peace that you gain" (p. 4).

Quality of Life of the Elderly   Close to half (45 percent) of all those interviewed thought that life for the elderly had gotten better in the past twenty years. Again, there were some different responses based on the age of those questioned, with 64 percent of persons aged 65 and older feeling that life had gotten better for elderly persons in the United States. As a 65-year-old woman stated, "Society at large has made things easier with senior citizen discounts and other things that help make these years more pleasant. There are more ways for us to keep our bodies and minds as active as we can" (p. 4).

Being Able to Work and Retire   Almost all Americans (93 percent) thought that people should be able to work as long as they want. They also look forward to the opportunity to retire and be free from the demands of a regular full-time job. It is interesting to note that people aged 35 to 49 looked forward to retirement the most, with 65 percent indicating this desire for the future.

Sexuality in the Older Ages   Seventy percent of all those interviewed from all age categories disagreed with the statement that "most people over 65 don't have sex anymore," but this perception differed by the age of those questioned. Of those surveyed between the ages of 18 and 24, 41 percent thought that people cease having sex at age 70 or older. Considerably more men (31 percent) than women (17 percent) were concerned about decreased sexual ability as they grow older.

Physical Appearance in Old Age   A high percentage (84 percent) disagreed with the statement, "When you become old, looks are no longer important." A 65-year-old woman said, "I don't try to look like a 20-year-old, but I think you should take pride in your appearance and look as young and pleasant as you can. It makes you feel good" (p. 5).

The Biggest Worry About Getting Old Among those surveyed of all ages, 35 percent worried the most about illness and failing health in old age. This was closely followed by 31 percent who worried about not being able to care for themselves, which is closely tied to fears about illness and failing health. Among the youngest people questioned, persons 18 to 24 years, 66 percent were fearful of being victims of violent crime when they become old.

What Will Provide Security in Old Age?   The number one response to this question was having enough money in old age, regardless of the age, sex, income, race, or education of those surveyed. In order of importance for security, having money was 40 percent, spouse was 29 percent, children was 12 percent, friends was 5 percent, career/job was 4 percent, and home was 4 percent.

Who Should Care for the Elderly?   A majority of people (57 percent) expressed the desire to go to a retirement home rather than move in with their children or other family members. More

women (44 percent) than men (28 percent) worried that someday they will have to have their children take care of them. This concern decreases somewhat as people grow older. Some 32 percent of persons aged 65 to 75 expressed this concern. When thinking about their parents, almost half (47 percent) of those surveyed thought that they will need to take care of them. More women (52 percent) thought they would become the caregivers for their parents than did men (41 percent). This reflects the reality in American society.

Society's View of Older Persons   Although 82 percent of those surveyed thought that older people had stronger moral values than younger people, and 82 percent disagreed with the notion that most elderly people are, or are becoming, mentally incompetent, only 27 percent believed that older people were respected by younger people. This low degree of perceived respect was in spite of the fact that 75 percent of those questioned said that wisdom comes with age and that 96 percent thought young people can learn from the elderly.

Much of the disparity in these views can be traced to the emphasis American culture has placed on youth. Indeed, 87 percent of the respondents to this survey indicated that Americans place too much emphasis on youth. As one person in his late thirties said, "It's unfortunate, but in our society, when people get to be a certain age, they're pushed off to the side. Yet old people are a lot smarter than young ones—they've been through more things and have learned a lot. The problem is that everything is so fast-paced that no one takes time to listen to them" (p. 5).

FACTORS THAT DETERMINE THE STATUS OF OLDER PEOPLE

What are the forces in any society that influence how people of all ages view what it means to be old? What are the role and status of older people, and what do older people themselves think about their prospects at any given time? The view, role, and status of older people have changed over time. What has brought about these changes? We will look at this issue and then see how these views have changed in American history.

Professor Harold Cox (1994) has pointed out that there are a number of interrelated variables, separate or combined, that directly relate to the place older people are given in a particular society. These include

1. The means of production in a society
2. The form of the family structure
3. Religion
4. The knowledge base of a particular culture
5. The harshness of the environment
6. The speed of social change

As a general observation, long-standing research has indicated that in nonindustrial, settled, agricultural societies older persons have quite a bit of power and are given high status. In industrial societies, the opposite is usually true. Older people generally have relatively little power and are given lower status (Cox 1994).

Regarding the specific factors in any society that determine the power and position of older people, it can be shown how moving from a traditional, rural, agricultural society to one that is fast-changing, urban, and industrialized has dramatically changed the view and role of the elderly.

Means of Production

When property is the primary means of production, older individuals are able to exercise power by controlling ownership of property, particularly agricultural lands (Cox 1994). When modern technology emerges as the primary means of production, social and geographic mobility become goals and individual independence becomes a basic value (Sheehan 1976). In this form of productivity in a society, there is no particular reason for younger people to be under the control of parents or grandparents. The primary means of production are no longer family farms. Older people tend to lose their status, decision-making power,

and the position they had in an agricultural society (Cox 1994).

The Form of the Family Structure

Traditional agricultural societies typically relied on the extended family, which most often consisted of mother, father, sons, and their wives and children (Cox 1994). This family form was most often patriarchical, which meant that authority in the family ran through the males who controlled the land (means of production). Ownership and power were passed to the oldest son when the father died. "Old" meant authority and status.

With the coming of the industrial age, the extended family gave way to the nuclear family—husband, wife, and their children. Means of production changed. New jobs and careers opened up in various places requiring mobility of labor (Cox, 1994). Control of land by the old was much less important. In this arrangement, old people lost power and status.

Religion

Many religions teach that fathers and mothers should be honored and supported. According to Cox (1994), the pressures of a modern, fast-changing, industrial society have resulted in less than total compliance with this teaching. Many older people are looked down upon rather than looked up to in spite of traditional religious teachings.

The Knowledge Base of a Culture

In the traditional agricultural cultures, older people are the sources of information and knowledge for a wide range of situations and problems (Cox 1994). In an industrial society this is no longer true. Research outcomes about current issues and problems are transmitted through print media and the information superhighway. The most recently trained person is often perceived as being more valuable to an enterprise than an experienced older person because of changing technology. This can readily contribute to the loss of status for the old and is particularly troublesome when older workers are not retrained in the new technologies of the contemporary workplace, as is often the case.

Harshness of Environment

When hard physical labor is required to survive in a demanding environment, older people can be at a real disadvantage in any society (Holmberg 1969). This, of course, does not apply to a significant degree in contemporary American culture, but it can be a determinant of the status of older people in any society that depends on physical labor.

Speed of Social Change in a Society

Rapid social change in a society tends to lower the status of older people (Cowgill and Holmes 1972). Rapid change leaves the skills and ideas of the old behind; they become obsolete. There is no longer any need to teach those who are younger. Indeed, the young are usually more knowledgeable about the latest technology. It is easy to see the application of this concept in looking at computers in the contemporary workplace. Other aspects of rapid social change leave many thinking that the ways of older people are either totally out of date or not applicable to the changed, new circumstances younger people face in their daily lives.

Another factor that Cox (1994) indicated as a reason the status of older people has declined in modern societies is the size of their group compared to the rest of the population. When older people made up less than 3 percent of the population, it was easier to set up a special status or role for such a group. However, when older people make up 10 to 15 percent of the population, it is harder to preserve a privileged place for them in society.

The United States experienced many of the historical factors that diminished the role and status of older people in a society as cited by Cox. The great industrial development within the United States throughout the last part of the nineteenth century and most of the twentieth century resulted in profound social changes that directly affected the way older people are perceived and treated.

To gain a better understanding of how America arrived at its current views on aging and the elderly, and to put in context the realities of the emerging postindustrial era, it is helpful to look at some American history as it pertains to changing perceptions of the old.

HISTORICAL PERSPECTIVES ON BEING OLD IN AMERICA

The Colonial Period

An examination of social perceptions of what it means to grow old indicates that perceptions of aging vary over time. In Colonial America, the aged had a place of honor, especially if they owned land or had other sources of wealth, prestige, or power. Fischer (1977) argued that in Colonial times sons had reason to give deference to their fathers because the fathers controlled the farm, owned the land, and had power in the community. Frequently at public gatherings special seating arrangements were made for older people. A study of the use of language of that time indicates that words of honor, prestige, and power were used to describe older persons. There was also a religious emphasis on honoring older persons; religious leaders stressed "Thou shalt honor thy father and mother."

While not rejecting Fischer's contention that honored terms and special places were reserved for some older persons, other studies (Haber 1983) have pointed out that impoverished widows and landless transients were often treated poorly. Impoverished widows often had to beg for food and lodging. Some had to wander from village to village trying to find basic food and shelter. It is from this context that a perception of the old crone, an ugly withered old woman, began to surface in American culture. It is also from this era that a belief in "old witches" began to be part of the folklore of rural life.

In Colonial times there seems to have been a mixed perception and treatment of older persons. Those who owned land were given respect; others, the poor, the widowed, and the landless were not respected at all. At this time, though, the pervasive use of terms disrespectful of the elderly had not developed. None of these authors argued that Colonial times were a golden era for older Americans where they were basking in respect from the family and society. Most people in Colonial times did not live into old age, and it is doubtful that overworked family members were eager to care for a deranged, frail, or incontinent older relative. Neither were there community resources comparable to today to give assistance to families struggling to care for older relatives. Older people of this era were honored more than in the period that followed, however, a period which produced the industrial revolution and a massive migration from the farm to the city.

The Industrial Era

When Americans began to leave the farm to move to the city and work in the factories, older people began to lose honor and respect, because they had neither the knowledge of industry by which they could instruct their children nor the knowledge of city life which would enable them to be tutors to their children and grandchildren. In addition, older people began to be a serious financial burden. Furthermore, they had no power by which they could help their children get positions in the new world of work. Increasingly in the nineteenth century very negative terms began to be used to describe older persons. These included terms such as *old crock, old goat, old fashioned, over-the-hill, fuddy-duddy, geezers, old codger, washed up, out to pasture, hag, gummer* (a person with no teeth), *crone, old duffer, old fogy, old maid, dried up old prune, old galoot,* and even less flattering terms referring to sexual incompetence. There is no comparable list of antonyms. Just try listing the exact opposite of each of these terms, words which have been used in American society to refer to older persons. It cannot be done.

America was beginning to change with a marked shift from a rural to an industrial society. Farming, which had been the focus of employment, began to decrease in importance. American young people began to leave the farms and move to the cities. Increasingly, employment opportunities were being created in the cities, employment opportunities that involved fewer hours of work and higher pay than workers received on the farm. Between 1880 and 1930, the hours worked in the city-based jobs decreased from 60 to fewer than 45 a week. America became increasingly urbanized. Between 1800 and 1890 cities grew by 87-fold while the population increased only 12-fold. During this time, a national youth culture began to develop. Young people created fads that were featured in the national media and that exploded into a national mania in the post-World War II years.

Older Americans were among the last to be affected by these changes. It was mostly the young who moved to the cities. Young people became a more dominant group in the population. Older persons mostly stayed on the farm and continued to work as long as their health permitted; there were no governmental pensions such as Social Security or Supplemental Security Income. Very few farmers had any type of private security in old age other than their children to help them farm, the value of their property, and their savings. Society Security did not begin in the U.S. until 1935. There is no evidence that prior to the twentieth century there was any widespread and significant change in the lifestyle of older Americans.

Achenbaum (1983) stated that there were several changes that had an impact on older Americans. They slowly began to make up a larger percentage of the population. Prior to the Civil War less than 5 percent of Americans were aged 65 or older. Since that time there has been a steady increase in the percentage of the elderly population. At the present time close to 13 percent of all Americans are 65 or older.

The Old As a Problem

Increasingly, Achenbaum (1983) pointed out, Americans began to perceive older people as a problem. More and more articles appeared describing the older person in terms of "pathological deterioration, eccentric behavior, and painful irrelevance" (p. 15). The rapid changes that occurred in American life emphasized the adaptability of youth and the irrelevance of the "wisdom" of the "old farmer," who increasingly was the brunt of jokes about "country hicks."

Social workers, policy makers, politicians, and writers increasingly portrayed the impoverished elderly, and maudlin stories began to appear concerning the tragic plight of America's aged. Out of this type of environment, as well as the changes taking place in Europe in regard to the acceptance of various forms of social welfare, a movement began in the U.S. to help the elderly, which culminated in the Social Security Act of 1935. This movement and emphasis resulted in a political orientation that old age was a legitimate social-welfare category. That emphasis, though, is being challenged by a contemporary view that does not see old age as a legitimate social-welfare category and contends that social-welfare policy should be based on need, not on age. The emphasis by some today is that Social Security in the 1930s fulfilled a widespread social need of older citizens, but that today with private pensions, private savings, and a lifetime of earnings, many older people should not be getting benefits on the basis of their age alone. This changing emphasis is tied to cultural changes that increasingly perceive older people, at least the young old, as affluent, vigorous, and consumer oriented. There is an element of truth in this perception, but it is an overgeneralization that ignores the oldest-old, minorities, and those suffering from chronic and catastrophic illness who are struggling to survive. Achenbaum (1983) stated,

> Because the society in which we live is constantly changing, the normative foundations and socio-cultural political economy that sustain the realm of ideas and social policy are continually shifting. Thus if we truly hope to address people's real needs and help them satisfy their desires, we must forever be sensitive to the tension between tradition and novelty. We must be prepared to alter our conceptions and policies to conform more accurately to current circumstances (p. 176). . . .

Historians, moreover, have been very interested in tracing the value implications of American culture, as it has been transforming from a relatively youthful, industrial base to a demographically older and service-oriented political economy (p. 186).

Clearly a particular society has perspectives on aging related to the history, the demographics, the degree of industrialization and urbanization, and the traditional views of what it means to be old. According to Crews (1993), "Cultural definitions of old age developed during earlier periods were related to the prevailing patterns of declining physical and mental functioning." (p. 30).

Further, Sokolovsky (1993) warned, "It is becoming clear that culturally constructed perceptions of becoming old and fading into a stage of nonfunctioning senescence can have dramatic implications for how a given society metaphorically thinks about its elders." (p. 51).

SOME MYTHS ABOUT OLD AGE

Every society has a conception of what it means to be old. In contemporary, rapidly-changing societies these concepts are also in a process of change, and yet the myths and conceptions of the past persist. Are the modern conceptions of aging and the elderly based on reality, or are they just new myths developed within a specific cultural context? What does old mean? What should it mean? When is one old? How does one determine when a person is old? Is aging affected by cultural definitions or is it primarily a genetically-driven biological process? Are old people wiser than young people? What is wisdom? Do we learn from experience and from wisdom acquired over the decades? Does the media accurately portray aging and the aging process?

Fischer (1977) argued that there are two main periods in American history that relate to social perceptions of the aging person. He referred to the years between 1600 to 1800 as a period of "gerontophilia" when old age was honored and in general, older persons were respected. He did not disagree with those who pointed out that there were older persons during this period who had characteristics which resulted in their being mocked and discriminated against. He pointed out that beginning about 1800 there was an increase in "gerontophobia," in which older persons were increasingly mocked and disparaged and the aging process was feared. He contended that we may now be entering a different era. Fischer may prove to be correct, because there is some indication that the fear and loathing of the aging process is decreasing. Certainly at the present time the aged are not the most impoverished or isolated people in society. It is also true, though, that many Americans still believe many myths about the aged and the aging process.

All Are Poor, Lonely, and Isolated   A Louis Harris poll back in 1981 showed that many Americans believed that older Americans are poor, lonely, isolated, in poor health, and decrepit. The reality is that most Americans 65 and over are not living in poverty, are not lonely, are not in poor health, are not isolated, are certainly not abandoned by their families, and are not in living institutions (U.S. Bureau of the Census 1993; Cispell and Frey 1993).

Most Live in Nursing Facilities   Only a small minority (about 5 percent) of Americans 65 and older are in institutions. The majority (62 percent) of those not in institutions have no limitations that prevent them from independently taking care of themselves in their everyday lives (Cispell and Frey 1994). The need for assistance with everyday activities varies greatly by older age category. Only 9 percent of persons aged 65 to 69 needed assistance. Just 10.9 percent of persons aged 70 to 74 needed help compared to 45.4 percent for persons aged 85 and older (U.S. Bureau of the Census 1990).

Most Are in Poor Health   Poor health is not a common feature of life for the elderly, especially among the young old. Three out of four (73.7 percent) persons aged 65 to 74 not in institutions

consider their health to be good, very good, or excellent. The vast majority (68 percent) of persons aged 75 and older who are not in institutions also consider their health to be good, very good, or excellent (National Center for Health Statistics 1991).

Most Have No Interest in Sex   Certainly many Americans in the past, and many younger persons today, perceive older people as being asexual. Even today many birthday or anniversary cards for the elderly feature jokes about sexual impotence. Some older people internalize these myths and think that there is something wrong with them if they continue to have sexual desires into old, and even oldest, old age. In reality, many older people enjoy active sex lives that they indicate are better than what they experienced in earlier years (Sexuality and Aging, 1993). Later chapters will point out additional studies which indicate that older people think about, desire, and participate in sexual activities.

Aging Means Mental Decline   Some people think that with aging comes an inevitable mental decline, an inability to learn new procedures, and a significant loss of memory. If one tests older persons who are not suffering from some chronic debilitating disease, the differences between old and young begin to disappear. It is true, for whatever the reason, that older persons need a longer time to take tests. Reaction time does seem to decline somewhat with the aging process. However, older persons can learn, be creative, and remember quite well (Kausler 1987). The evidence is clear that older persons should not be seen as incapable of doing their jobs, learning new procedures, being promoted, being in positions of authority and power, or being judged solely on the basis of their chronological age. We are probably moving into an era in which older persons, as well as others in society, will be judged on the basis of their unique abilities and competencies rather than on the basis of their age. We have not yet arrived at that stage of American society, however.

Palmore (1988) stated that two-thirds of persons surveyed believed that older persons have more mental impairments than younger persons. However, community research studies have indicated that older persons have fewer psychiatric problems than younger persons (Myers et al. 1984). If one refers to the oldest old, those 85 years and older, this begins to change in regard to the senile dementias brought about by such conditions as Alzheimer's disease, strokes, and arteriosclerosis (hardening of the arteries). However, research has shown a reduced probability of such illnesses as schizophrenia, manic-depression (bipolar disorder), endogenous depression, and some of the major neuroses.

Families Forget Them   Older Americans are visited regularly by their children and are part of holiday festivities and family celebrations such as birthdays, anniversaries, and graduations. Older people are not being abandoned by their children. For about the last thirty years, the percentage of older persons who live within 25 miles of their adult children has remained at about 75 percent (Cispell and Frey 1993). The U.S. Senate Special Committee on Aging (1988) found that over two-thirds of the elderly live with a family member, either spouse or children (Saluter 1991). Fifty-eight percent of grandparents see their grandchildren quite often (Cispell and Frey 1993).

Most Older People Have About the Same Amount of Money   The stereotype of financial need or financial greed on the part of older people points to complex questions which are discussed in great detail in later chapters. It should be stated, though, that the vast majority of older Americans are not living in poverty. Until the advent of the cost of living adjustment (COLA) to Social Security, there were many more older Americans living in poverty than at the present time. There are categories of older people, primarily single women, minorities, and the oldest old, who have many of their members living in poverty. One's perspective of older Americans'

relative wealth involves questions of values and definitions of terms. To assert that older Americans have greater financial assets than younger Americans, with the hint that this is an indication of their affluence, involves a misunderstanding of financial progression during a person's life span. It seems logical that over a lifetime a person would acquire more assets than a person who just started working. What should the income and assets of older persons be in contrast to younger folks? After a lifetime of employment should older people have more assets than younger persons? Should older people receive special benefits just because of their age? (Palmore 1988).

Older People Are Poor Workers   As long ago as 1977, Palmore found that a third of college students believed that older workers were not as effective as younger workers. Contemporary research evidence has indicated just the opposite. Older persons work as well or better than younger persons. They have less absenteeism, work harder, have fewer acute illness, and have fewer accidents (Krauss 1987). In addition, older workers pay more attention to satisfying customers and are more willing to work overtime (Krauss 1987; The Commonwealth Funds Studies 1991).

A YOUTH-ORIENTED CULTURE

We have had a youth-oriented culture in the United States. The Baby Boom (1946–1964) brought about a tremendous bulge in our population. Because their numbers represented a huge market for sales, the baby boomers got tremendous attention from the media and from retailers. In addition, the media began to emphasize youth as crime began to increase. There was an increase in the number of schools that had to be built to accommodate the baby boomers. Youth began to emphasize their own interests in music, clothing, television, movies, and sexuality. The baby boomers are now well into middle-age and are just beginning to see older age as their next reality. They are going to demand a different concept of the aging process and what it means to be old.

Who Is Old?

Crews (1993) stated that "chronological age alone is a poor proxy for the study of measure of aging and senescence" (p. 30). We are almost surely entering a new period in American society where age by itself will mean less and less in our judgment of others and of ourselves.

In American society, the age 65 has been emphasized simply because of a historical event. Count Otto von Bismarck of Prussia, in the late 1880s, was under pressure from political forces to give assistance to the elderly poor. He instructed his legislators to pass such a law. They agreed to enact the law but were uncertain as to what age recipients should be to collect benefits. After his advisors told the Count that the average Prussian lived to be about 65, benefits were granted to Prussians when they reached 65. France, Britain, and then the U.S. followed in passing Social Security-type legislation. The debate in the U.S. over this legislation was ferocious. Those advocating Social Security were frequently referred to as communists, Marxists, socialists, or leftists. There was, however, little debate over the concept that one was old at 65, and should retire or be retired from employment. The fact is that from birth to death, the age 65 does not take on any physical or psychological significance. We have in American society taken that age, 65, and *reified* it (constructed a reality about it that is not true, but which we believe is true). We therefore treat people who are 65 or older as "old people." That concept is beginning to be questioned. Who is old? How does one determine who is old? Is old primarily a question of chronological age or of functional ability? If determining what is old is based on functional ability, then what significance should age play in political, economic, and educational decisions? Should age by itself give a person certain advantages or disadvantages in governmental programs and policies? What do you think of when you use the word *old*?

CHANGING ROLES FOR THE OLD IN A POSTINDUSTRIAL ERA

Given the reality that we are in transition between the twentieth and twenty-first centuries as well as moving into a postindustrial society, the question needs to be asked, What will be the roles and status of older people in this new era?

A postindustrial era will see a shift away from the ongoing expansion in manufacturing and industry, even though they will still be important. Fewer people will be required to maintain efficient productive enterprises. This change is already under way in many of the major manufacturing plants of the nation, including auto factories. Many believe that the postindustrial age will bring reduced working hours, a four-day work week, and a diminished emphasis on the Protestant work ethic which placed total emphasis on the role of work in a person's life with recreation and leisure being a waste of time or even sinful (Cox 1994).

The postindustrial society will put more emphasis on the expansion of social services, entertainment, athletics, recreation, and leisure activities. All of this should open new nonwork roles for older people, which will give them a higher status in a postindustrial environment than they experienced in an industrial environment. Indeed, older people in this new era should have a range of options to choose from. In a society that puts less emphasis on the importance of productivity and more emphasis on the quality of life, older people can choose roles that are more socially supported than they have been for so much of the twentieth century. They may choose to focus on family roles, recreation and leisure roles, volunteer roles, political roles, or second careers (Cox 1994).

A Normal Phase of Life

In an era of competition for limited governmental resources in the form of assistance programs, and given the realities of contemporary aging as outlined above, we are going to need a perception of aging that fosters individual creativity and productivity regardless of age if we are to avoid worsening the intergenerational tensions that have already surfaced. As Theodore Koff and Richard Park (1993) stated in their book, *Aging Public Policy,* "It appears likely that older people will feel better about themselves when being old is accepted as being of no real consequence" (p. 274). What this will do to age-based assistance programs is discussed in detail in the chapter on public policy and the politics of aging. The thrust of this approach to aging and the support systems that have been put in place to assist the elderly is that they should be intergenerational in nature. One could argue that even a program such as Social Security, typically identified with older people, has provisions to help workers of all ages when they become disabled, as well as their family members of all ages if they lose the support of a covered worker at any age.

Overcoming Ageism

Getting people of all ages to perceive older people in a more favorable light, including older people themselves, is no easy task. Prejudice against the elderly—ageism—is real. It is real in the way much of society, including the elderly themselves, perceive what are believed to be the inevitable declines of aging. A University of Michigan psychologist has contended that our society has "inappropriately focused on decline as a telling characteristic of aging." She stated:

> So much of gerontology has been studying the impairments of aging. I want to understand the pinnacles of human functioning. I expect to find some of the greatest human achievements produced by the elderly (Perlmutter 1990: 8).

Certainly Jessica Tandy, who won the 1990 Academy Award for Best Actress at age 81, Georgia O'Keefe, Benjamin Franklin, Frank Lloyd Wright, and a long list of other creative individuals did some of their best work in their later years. Examples of people excelling in old age have been around for years; still there is a general disregard of the abilities of the elderly, as if these examples were exceptions.

Researchers have found that cognitive (thinking process) decline is not as severe or widespread with advancing old age as has been believed. While younger persons, using measures of mental performance, tend to do better than older persons, some elderly persons do as well as the younger subjects tested. For example,

> In some abilities, older adults may not have the same stamina as the younger person, but they may have other abilities that the younger person does not have. As I have worked with more and more older adults, I have observed tremendous variability and seen many qualities that made these people interesting and vital (Perlmutter 1990: 8).

Indeed, there is good reason to believe that there is no inevitable cognitive decline in old age as previously thought by so much of society. Cognitive gains and losses can occur at all stages of life and are not necessarily tied to being old. Some cognitive abilities may actually blossom in old age, with wisdom being one of the best examples. Wisdom has been said to come from a lifetime of learning and experience, and it shows up in the thinking styles of older adults (Perlmutter 1990).

Liberating the Talents of All

What do these broadened perceptions of old age mean? In a complex society with all of the needs that are evident every day, the nation cannot afford to discard or ignore the ongoing contributions people can make, even in their oldest years, given reasonably good physical and mental health. Recognizing the diversity of the elderly population, within and between the elderly age groups, a reality needs to be developed that avoids stereotypes that have molded society's perception of older people and the perception older people have of themselves, which has too often become a self-fulfilling prophecy. Too often in American society people have acted "old" because they thought this was expected. By acting "old," they began to demonstrate the negative characteristics of what they thought was old. For example, how many older people upon misplacing an item such as car keys say, "I must be getting old," as if younger people never misplace or lose anything.

What does it mean to grow older as the twenty-first century approaches—when society begins to realize the social revolution it is undergoing, when more and more people reach the oldest old years and the ranks of the youngest old are flooded with millions of baby boomers who reach their mid-sixties with more vigor, vitality, and better health than any previous generation? Growing older increasingly will need to be viewed simply as another phase of life without intrinsic negative characteristics. People need to be encouraged to continue to work if they need to or want to. Training and retraining should be open to all regardless of age to secure, retain, or advance in employment. The example of George Burns booking himself to play at London's Palladium and Caesar's Palace when he turns 100 should become the symbolic norm instead of the proverbial rocking chair after age 65 (67 in the future) when full Social Security benefits are available. This does not mean that the social programs for the elderly should be abandoned; they are vital. It does mean that our society needs to stop closing doors to people simply because of advancing years. The technologies of the new age, including the information superhighway, should open opportunities for older people to play a vital role in determining their own destinies and have an impact on their families and their communities as the nation moves into the twenty-first century.

WHY WE GROW OLD—BIOLOGICAL PERSPECTIVES

A discussion of what it means to grow old inevitably leads to some examination of why people grow older in the first place. What brings about biological aging? Why do we grow older? Can anything be done to slow or even stop the biological aging process? What is the maximum life span? Can it be lengthened? These are questions that relate to scientific research. While the focus of this book is not on biological research, it is important for the person studying the aging process and the consequences of growing older in American society to be aware of the major biological themes of aging and some of the current thinking and research that relates to the aging process and the potential length of life. With the explosive growth of the older population, the social, economic, and political consequences of an ever-older population are enormous.

How Long Can We Live?

There is a very important difference between the terms *life expectancy* and *life span*. *Life expectancy* refers to how long the average person in a particular society is expected to live. Therefore, life expectancy varies tremendously from one society to another. Obviously nutrition, medical care, and lifestyle, including smoking and exercise, can all make a tremendous difference in life expectancy.

Life span refers to how long human beings can live under optimal conditions. How long can human beings live given the best nutrition, best medical care, best lifestyle? What is aging? Why do most humans tend to die well before the age of 100? Can the life span be extended? Are there specific genes that control the aging process? Can the life span be extended to 120 or 140 years or beyond? Have there ever been societies where being 120 years was not unusual? Life expectancy in the U.S. is now about 75 years, but it varies significantly between men and women, racial categories, ethnic groupings, and by socioeconomic status. Can genes be changed so that within ten years babies born in the U.S. can be expected to live 140 years? Whether we want to do this is another question.

BIOLOGICAL THEORIES OF AGING

In the past few years, much research has been done in biogerontology, the scientific area that specializes in studying the aging processes (Kotulak and Gorner 1992). For many years researchers have attempted to describe what happens to the body as it ages. Several theories have been formulated in order to explain the aging process. According to Raybash, Roodin, and Santrock (1991), these theories can be understood by dividing them into three basic categories: microbiological, physiological, and cellular.

Microbiological Theory of Aging

According to the microbiological theory, the aging process is controlled by maintaining an internal balance within the body. Contained in this theory is the *homeostatic imbalance theory* which explains that various organs within the body attempt to maintain an internal balance between the heart, lungs, kidney, and liver. When these organs undergo an external threat in early adulthood, they can rapidly combat the threat and restore its internal balance. Young adults have greater reserves in the organs, which translates to a greater capacity for an organ to combat an external threat. This is not generally true of elderly individuals. The organ reserve of persons in early adulthood is four to ten times greater than those in the later years of life. However, even after age thirty, people begin to lose the ability to restore their internal balance. After age thirty, research has indicated that there is a linear decline between aging and the ability to restore balance between the organs. As Raybash, Roodin, and Santrock (1991) stated, "Eventually even the smallest external stress prevents the body from restoring homeostasis" (p. 76). The inability of a person's body to restore homeostasis may lead to death. For example, after the age of thirty, a person's mortality rate doubles every eight years (Upton 1977).

Physiological Theories of Aging

Physiological theories of aging attempt to describe the aging process on a smaller scale than the microbiological theories. The physiological theories propose that aging occurs because there is a breakdown in the functioning of a particular organ system or a particular physiological control mechanism. This breakdown may be caused by either internal or external agents. Two popular theories which describe this breakdown are the *autoimmunity* and the *hormonal* theories.

Autoimmunity Theory One of the most important mechanisms controlling human physiology is the immune system. The immune system protects us from foreign agents such as viruses, bacteria, and mutant cells, which attempt to break down either an organ or a control mechanism in the body. Fortunately, the body produces substances called antibodies which attempt to break down these invading substances by reacting with the proteins of the foreign agents. This response, called the autoimmune response, renders the foreign agents inactive. The immune system may also produce cells that "literally eat up the invading cells" (Raybash, Roodin, and Santrock 1991).

Unfortunately, as people age, the efficiency of the immune system declines. In early adult life, the immune system operates at its highest potential. However, with increasing age, the cells and antibodies produced by the immune system, which should break down the invading substances, begin to break down normal, healthy body cells. According to Crandall (1991), two important changes occur in the body as a person ages. First, since the body begins to lose the ability to distinguish between foreign and nonforeign particles, antibodies and cells begin to attack normal, healthy cells. Second, the body begins to produce more mutations in its DNA structure as a cell divides. According to Crandall, "The consequence is that the body responds to these mutant cells as foreign matter" (p. 126). Even though this theory may describe what happens, it does not attempt to describe why the body suddenly produces mutations or loses the ability to recognize between self and nonself matter.

An organism's immune system declines with age because it is unable to stimulate the reproduction of white blood cells, the cells responsible for the formation of antibodies. This was demonstrated in rats by the fact that the ability of white blood cells to produce a substance called inter-leukin 2 (IL 2) decreases with increasing age. IL 2 plays an important role in the reproduction of white blood cells (Richardson et al. 1985).

Hormonal Theory Another theory that at-tempts to describe biological aging on a physio-logical level is the hormonal theory. This theory explains that aging occurs because the endocrine system begins to "shut down." The endocrine sys-tem produces hormones, molecules formed by one organ that regulate or control other bodily functions via the bloodstream. As the activity of the endocrine system slows down, fewer hor-mones are produced. These hormones may be necessary for maintaining cell functions. Accord-ing to C.E. Finch (1988), aging pacemakers in the pituitary gland and the hypothalamus, regions in the brain that control hormonal production, may inactivate the endocrine system. Research has in-dicated that the amount of various hormones may contribute to the aging process. For example, a significant decrease in sex hormones, which oc-curs in females after menopause, accelerates the aging process (Crandall 1991). As a person ages, the production of estrogen is greatly reduced. The symptoms of menopause can be treated through estrogen supplements. Another example is hy-pothyroidism, a condition in which the thyroid gland diminishes in size and which causes prema-ture aging. Hypothyroidism can be treated by in-jecting additional hormones into the body. As the thyroid gland shrinks, it is unable to produce a significant amount of thyroid hormones. After the injections, the symptoms of hypothyroidism dis-appear. The thyroid gland resumes its normal size and becomes active (Crandall 1991).

Since hypothyroidism and menopause can be controlled through hormonal injections, some scientists believe that the aging process can be regulated by replacing hormones that are de-pleted as a person ages. In fact, some scientists believe that with hormonal injections, a person may be able to live up to 115 years. Research has indicated that hormones are able to control genes responsible for aging. According to Ronald Kotu-lak and Peter Gorner (1992), some of the genes involved in aging are controlled by hormones which act as chemical messengers to the genes; when the hormones are depleted, aging sets in. "Like keys that will fit only specific locks—tar-get receptors on cell surfaces—hormones switch genes on and off, and speed up or slow down cell functions" (p. 3).

In an attempt to control aging, some elderly individuals have consequently begun taking hor-mone injections to retard the aging process. Dr. Daniel Rudman injected men in their sixties and seventies with the human growth hormone, a powerful secretion of the pituitary gland. When people reach about 60 years of age, the hormone naturally markedly decreases. Rudman recruited volunteers and divided them into two groups. One group was given hGH, the growth hormone, the other group was not given the hormone. Those who were given the growth hormone in-jected themselves three times a week for six months. It should be noted that there are side ef-fects if one gets too much hGH: arthritis, hyper-tension, and enlargement of the heart.

The results of the injections were amazing and widely publicized. The men using the growth hor-mone lost 14 percent of body fat, gained 9 percent in their muscle mass, and their skin regained a more youthful firmness. For some there was so much muscle expansion that they complained of pain in their hands, as the expanding muscles compressed the nerves in their hands. The hGH treatment did seem to reverse some of the effects of the aging process. Volunteer Fred McCoullugh, a 66 year-old retired factory worker, stated, "I never felt so strong in my life." His body regained twenty years of lost vigor as his internal organs, which had shrunk with aging, resumed their nor-mal size (Kotulak and Gorner 1992).

Rudman indicated that if genes are implicated in the aging process, there now is evidence that the neuroendocrine system is also involved. Can we find pharmaceuticals that can be taken safely and that will, for most, have the above observed effects? What would the cost be? What would the impact be to those who could not afford the treatment? Might we have 71-year-old crooks?

Other researchers, Dr. Walter Pierpaoli and R. William Ragelson, have treated mice with the hormone melatonin which increased their life span by 30 percent. Dr. Arthur Schwartz has found that by giving laboratory animals DHEA (dehydroepiandosterone), an adrenal hormone, he can reduce their body fat by one-third, enhance their immunological system, reduce the probability of atherosclerosis, and increase life span by about 20 percent.

Hormonal changes controlled by the pituitary and hypothalamus glands are clearly implicated in the aging process (Finch 1988). The hormonal theory of aging states that these glands function as pacemakers in the aging process. Denckla (1974) and Rosenfeld (1976) believed that the hypothalamus stimulates the pituitary gland to produce hormones that travel in blood cells, that these hormones keep the body cells from absorbing an adequate supply of thyroxine, and if thyroxine is not in adequate supply, metabolic imbalances take place. Denckla and Rosenfeld believe that these imbalances produce free radicals, toxins, and autoimmunity.

Cellular Theories of Aging

Some of the most interesting theories that attempt to explain the aging process are cellular theories. Researchers believe that if we are able to control aging through gene therapy and drugs at the cellular level, the average life span for an individual may increase to 200 years! The cellular theories postulate that process within the cell malfunction, which leads to aging. Several theories have been developed in order to describe "cellular aging." These include the *mutation*, *error catastrophe*, *cellular*, *genetic switching*, and *free-radical* theories. All of these theories describe aging on the molecular level.

The Mutation Theory   The mutation theory claims that the process of aging can be directly re-

lated to the production of mutations in cellular DNA of vital organs. A variety of nucleic acids, including purines and pyrimidines, make up the complex structure of DNA, the basic material of life. Through this information, the genetic code is able to be transcribed and translated in order to produce proteins, which are needed for the maintenance and survival of cells. Through the process of transcription, the genetic message is transferred from DNA to RNA, another essential component of all living matter. Finally, through translation, RNA transfers the message to ribosomes to produce the life-sustaining proteins. Unfortunately, the genetic message may not always be transferred error-free. A breakdown in the communication between DNA and RNA may occur. This may lead to the production of mutations in the DNA of cells which constitute vital organs. Other mutations may be caused by genes that specifically introduce mutations and by external factors, such as toxins in air, water, and food (Raybash, Roodin, and Santrock 1991). Unfortunately, these mutations may be passed on to new, daughter strands of DNA in cells. This may alter a cell's identity, function, and rate of reproduction (Crandall 1991). According to Raybash et al., "Eventually, the number of mutated cells in a vital organ would increase to the point that the organ's functioning is significantly reduced" (p. 74). In addition, according to Crandall, "For cells that do not reproduce, the theory holds that over time more and more cells in a certain organ or area are damaged" (p. 127). Crandall further stated that the organ or area would become so damaged over time that it would fail to work properly.

Error Catastrophe Theory   The error catastrophe theory, proposed by Dr. Leslie Orgel in 1963, is very similar to the mutation theory (Smith-Sonneborn 1987). However, this theory explains that aging is caused by damaging RNA, enzymes, and certain proteins, not by damaging DNA. According to this theory, errors in RNA cause a decrease in the production of specific enzymes that are essential for a cell's metabolism. The improperly working enzymes, or lack of them, may cause certain cell functions to be reduced, which may lead to cell death (Raybash et al. 1991).

Fortunately, not all mutated daughter cells remain mutated. In fact, the post-replication repair process corrects most mutations. Enzymes identify the damaged site and repair it. According to John Hampton, Jr., (1991), "If aging is characterized by accumulated DNA damage, efficient repair mechanisms should characterize long-lived species" (p. 43). In other words, since DNA damage may cause aging, organisms that have the highest repair rate should have the longest life span and organisms that have the lowest repair rate should have the shortest life span. This is demonstrated in Figure 2-1. The shrew has the lowest repair rate and the shortest life span. The human, on the other hand, has the highest repair rate and consequently the longest life span. Unfortunately this theory is not totally credible, since the correlation between DNA repair rate and maximum life span is not a phenomenon exhibited among all organisms (Hampton 1991).

Cellular Theory   This states that cells have a finite number of replications. According to this theory, after cells have replicated as many times as possible, termed the *Hayflick limit*, the cells die. Researchers Leonard Hayflick and Paul Moorehead (1961), discoverers of this unique phenomenon, believe that most cells are able to replicate approximately fifty times in vitro (Hayflick and Moorehead 1961). Some cells, such as fibroblasts (cells responsible for forming fibers in connective tissues), only replicate twenty times before they die. In addition, as a person ages, the rate at which a cell is able to divide diminishes. For example, in an experiment conducted by Hayflick and Moorehead, the rate at which human lung cells were able to divide decreased as the cells matured. Hayflick and Moorehead placed these cells in a medium and allowed them to replicate. They discovered that it took ten days for the second replication to occur, whereas the first replication only required seven days. Researchers who promote this theory believe that there is a limited amount of DNA in each cell that is eventually depleted (Hayflick 1970). By decreasing the amount of available DNA, the amount of RNA also decreases, which in turn limits the production of enzymes responsible for properly maintaining a cell (Goldstein and Reiss 1984).

Even though normal cells may have finite lifetimes, abnormal cells, which differ from normal cells in structure and genetic makeup, may divide indefinitely. For example, cancer cells are able to have an unlimited number of divisions. Therefore, cancer cells eventually outnumber the normal cells, which may leave various organs unable to function properly.

Even though normal cells may have limited replications, proteins are still accurately produced in older individuals. The rate of transcription may decrease, but DNA is still transcribed very accurately as a person ages. However, even though a minimal amount of DNA may be mutated, the accumulation of small mutations will eventually render the cell inactive.

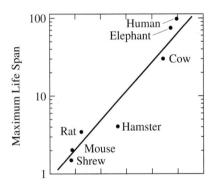

FIGURE 2-1   DNA Repair Rate.
The ability to repair DNA correlates well with the life spans of many species, indicating that this cellular property is important for longevity. In this example, the DNA synthesis measured was not due to cell multiplication but due to DNA damages. (*Source:* Hart, R. and R. B. Sellow, 1974. Proc. Natl. Acad. Sci. U.S.A. 71: 2169–2173. Hart, currently Director, National Center for Toxicological Research, Jefferson, AR 72079.)

Genetic Switching Theory   One of the most interesting theories that attempts to explain the aging process is the genetic switching theory. This theory proposes that certain genes can be switched on and off. When genes that encode DNA become inactive, DNA is no longer produced and the cells "age" (Strehler 1973).

Some researchers have attempted to find the "death gene," a gene that may either turn off, thus stopping the production of DNA, or turn on, generating the aging process. A few researchers have suggested that they have found it. Similar genes have been found in other organisms, such as the roundworm. Biologist Thomas Johnson of the Institute for Behavioral Genetics at the University of Colorado discovered one gene in the roundworm's genome, which comprises approximately 10,000 genes. By manipulating this one gene, called Age-1, Johnson was able to double the life span of the roundworm. As a result, he declared that "aging is under direct genetic control" (Kotulak and Gorner 1992: 13). According to Johnson, this was the first experiment that indicated that one gene may control the life span of organisms. He and many other researchers are now attempting to sift through the human genome in search of a gene that may be able to double the life span of humans to 230 years!

Some molecular biologists have been able to control the life span of specialized cells. For example, molecular biologist Thomas Maciag of the American Red Cross Jerome Holland Laboratory for the Biosciences in Rockville, Maryland has been able to double the life span of skin cells by turning off the interleukin 1 gene. Maciag believes that this gene directs the production of interleukin 1, a protein that causes rapid aging. This "antisense" technique alters the interleukin 1 gene, thus diminishing the aging process. Antisense has already been used extensively in the agricultural industry by preventing premature ripening of fruits and vegetables. For example, through genetic manipulation, the production of ethylene, the chemical responsible for ripening tomatoes, has been able to be blocked. By blocking the production of this chemical, tomatoes are able to be shipped and stored without aging.

When the tomatoes are exposed to ethylene, they once again begin to age and ripen in the supermarket (Kotulak and Gorner 1992).

Researcher Michael West, a molecular biologist at the University of Texas Southwestern Medical Center in Dallas, believes that he has found two genes responsible for aging in mammalian cells. By switching these genes, M-1 and M-2, on and off, he believes that he can increase or reverse the aging process. According to West, when these genes operate, aging occurs. However, when gene M-1 is switched off, the cell's youth can be restored. The cells can actually divide two times as often when the gene is off. If gene M-2 is turned off, the cells divide indefinitely. Therefore, the cells always remain youthful. When either of the genes are turned back on, the aging process continues. According to West, by controlling these genes the human life span may be able to be expanded to 300 to 500 years. West stated, "By switching these genes on and off, we can cause the cells to become younger or grow older at will" (Kotulak and Gorner 1992: 14).

Free Radical Theory   A final cellular theory is the free radical theory. This theory, which has gained significant attention in the past few years, claims that oxygen radicals, or superoxides, are able to destroy cells. Superoxides, highly reactive compounds, are primarily produced during the intermediate biochemical reactions of metabolism. During this process, the body breaks down foods and additives in order to use them for energy. However, as the process takes place, oxygen free radicals are produced as a side product. Superoxides can also be produced from tobacco smoke and the chemical effects of ionizing radiation such as x-rays, gamma rays, beta particles, cosmic radiation, and ultraviolet light (Harman 1987). Since these electrically charged particles contain an unpaired electron, they attempt to abstract an electron from another molecule. This leads to a chain reaction in which the cell's vital structure can be damaged. The cell sustains approximately 10,000 hits by free radicals (Green 1992).

According to Denham Harman who developed the free radical theory in 1954, "Chances are 99 percent [free radicals] are the basis for aging. Aging is the ever-increasing accumulation of changes caused by free radicals" (Kotulak and Gorner 1992: 7). The theory is that this constant pounding by free radicals eventually wears down the system over a period of time, and that it requires antioxidants to be constantly working against the effects of free radicals. It is thought that free radicals damage the protein needed to make cells and that they damage the DNA strands that transmit messages to genes. Antioxidants, or free radical scavengers, are able to stabilize free radicals, rendering them inactive. Antioxidants, including vitamins C, E, and beta-carotene, which can be converted into vitamin A, are believed to neutralize, degrade, and detoxify free radicals. However, antioxidants have not been proven to be antiaging remedies. Attempts to increase the life span of animals by injecting them with antioxidants have not increased their life spans (Green 1992).

Some of the damage caused by free radical attacks can be repaired, but not all. This cumulative cell damage may lead to wrinkled skin and a decline in kidney function. Free radical damage can also be traced to the development of cancers.

The effects of free radicals are believed to contribute to the cause of a range of diseases including atherosclerosis, cancer, essential hypertension, senile dementia of the Alzheimer type, osteoarthritis, senile macular degeneration, acute pancreatitis, senile cataract, adult repiratory distress syndrome, and Parkinson's disease (Harman 1987).

In addition to vitamin supplements, other measures have been attempted in order to inactivate free radicals. For example, many "life-extension pills" have been developed. Coenzyme Q10 (CoQ10), an enzyme produced naturally in the body, serves as an antioxidant in blood lipid particles. In addition, this CoQ10 carries cholesterol in the body helping to prevent atherosclerosis, the build up of plaque on arterial walls. Unfortunately, the ingestion of this enzyme has not increased natural enzyme levels. Likewise, the ingestion of superoxide dismutase (SOD), the enzyme responsible for converting superoxide radicals into harmless hydrogen peroxide, has not been demonstrated to be an aid in increasing the life span. As a protein, SOD is broken down in the digestive tract before it can combat free radicals. Others have believed that ribonucleic acid (RNA) may be able to rejuvenate old cells, improve memory, and prevent wrinkling when it is taken as a supplement. However, it is broken down too much by digestion before reaching cells to be effective. It has further been speculated that the lack of dehydroepinandosterone (DHEA), an adrenal hormone, causes aging because its hormonal levels decrease with age. However, no evidence has been found to support the notion that dietary supplements of this hormone retard the aging process (Green 1992).

Even though antioxidants, enzymes, and hormones may be able to inactivate some free radicals, some still bypass the body's protective systems. In fact, free radicals eventually destroy proteins that make up cells to such a degree that each of the body's billion proteins have to be replaced almost every three days (Kotulak and Gorner 1992).

Free radicals are very detrimental to the systems of the body, but human organisms would not be able to survive without them. Free radicals are actually needed to properly maintain the body. For example, they are able to destroy viruses. If a genetic defect prevented the formation of free radicals by white blood cells, the body would be unable to ward off many diseases (Kotulak and Gorner 1992).

Other Theories on Extending Life

Reducing/Restricting Calories Another theory of biological aging that focuses on extending life does not fit neatly in the three major categories discussed above. It focuses on something our society has highlighted in its emphasis on being thin—reducing and restricting calories.

Rats have had a significant increase in life expectancy when their diet is restricted. That is, by feeding them much less than they usually eat, their life expectancy can be increased by about 30 percent. Would significant diet restrictions in humans have a comparable effect? Would humans consider an additional 25 years worth significant restrictions in their diets? What would the quality of life be like in the last 25 years of life? At the present time there is no evidence that human life expectancy would increase the same as rodent life expectancy by diet restriction.

Scientists at Tufts University have been successful in extending the life expectancy and reducing the rate of disease by restricting the caloric intake of rats and mice. The reduction in caloric intake also reduced the probability of the development of all types of tumors. Dr. Roderick T. Bronson, Tufts University School of Veterinary Medicine, and his colleague Dr. Ruth Lipman, at the United States Department of Agriculture's Human Nutrition Research Center on Aging, found in a sample of 1,100 test animals that there were fewer signs of disease and cancerous tumors in restricted-diet mice when compared with mice who had a normal, nonrestricted diet. At 24 months of age, only 13 percent of calorically restricted mice had tumors, compared to a 51 percent tumor incidence in those without restricted diets. Dr. Bronson also found that animals on restricted diets lived 29 percent longer. Half of all the animals on restricted diets were still alive by the time all the animals on unrestricted diets were dead. Dr. Bronson is cautious about applying these findings to humans. At this time, we simply do not know if there would be any type of comparable effect in humans (Special Report on Aging 1992).

> The closest approximation that we can make to this issue is by looking at the relationship between human weight and life expectancy. Studies using life insurance company data reveal that the shortest life span is found at the two extremes of weight, those underweight and those overweight. There-

fore, we have no evidence that caloric restriction will lengthen human life span. Furthermore, it is possible that caloric restriction of rodents simulates the normal feeding habits of rodents in the wild and that the caged, unexercised, overfed laboratory rodent has premature aging and a shorted life span (Schneider 1992: 7–10).

Sprott and Roth (1992) also stated that there is no direct evidence that caloric restriction will be effective in extending longevity in humans, and that by the very nature of the process of investigation, this type of experiment cannot take place involving humans. They then went on to state that while there are great similarities between the processes of aging in rodents and humans, there are many examples of marked differences.

Lifestyle Realities

In some remarkable recent studies on the effects of genetics on longevity, the importance of genetics has been questioned. Dr. Niels Holm, director of the Danish Twin Registry, and Dr. James Vupel, demographer at Duke University, examined life expectancy of 55 identical and fraternal twins and found that genes do matter a little but do not dictate a maximum life span. From a study of twins, they estimated that only 2 percent to 3 percent of the variance in the ages of death in the population of twins could be explained by genetics. The rest was due to lifestyle, which in the U.S. is often referred to as the "Mormon or Seventh Day Adventist advantage" because both groups reject smoking and alcohol and both groups have longer-than-average life expectancies (Kolata 1992). Vaupel pointed out that if genes are the primary determinant of longevity, then identical twins should live to about the same age. However, their study showed that their life span is similar to that of fraternal twins.

A great amount of research has been done in an attempt to discover why persons age. To this end, funding for research on the aging process has increased dramatically. For example, in 1990, the National Academy of Science Institute concluded that federal funding for research on aging should exceed more than one billion dollars. In addition, great amounts of money have been spent to try to cosmetically or physiologically slow the aging process. In 1990, Americans spent almost four billion dollars on cosmetic surgery and another billion on vitamins in attempts to look or feel younger. In addition, many people have spent thousands of dollars trying to replenish their bodies with lost hormones. For example, treatments for replenishing the body with growth-hormones cost nearly $14,000 a year (Green 1992).

Some gerontologists have predicted that in the next ten years scientific advances will allow individuals to better cope with the changes that occur with aging. Already many postmenopausal women are using estrogen replacement therapy to reduce the risk of thinning bones (osteoporosis) and heart disease. Other supplements may be found that could improve the quality of life as people live longer.

In the meantime, sound advice at maximizing longevity as well as promoting a better quality of life still focuses on the following proven strategies:

> Eat a well-balanced, low-fat, high-carbohydrate diet, exercise regularly, refrain from smoking and alcohol abuse, and avoid obesity. Some of those tactics produce the same effects claimed for life-extension products. Aerobic exercise, for instance, has been shown to build muscle effectively even in elderly people, without the potential side effects of human growth hormone. A diet high in fruits and vegetables will give you plenty of antioxidants (Green 1992: 15).

LONGER LIVES: SOCIAL BENEFIT OR THREAT?

Adding years to life could add problems. It could, for example, increase significantly the number of people with Alzheimer's disease and other dementing diseases. It could also increase the number of people with chronic, debilitating disease such as Parkinson's disease, severe diabetes, stroke, and congestive heart failure. Most per-

sons probably would prefer a healthy 80 years rather than an additional 15 years if it would mean spending most of that time in a nursing facility with limited cognitive abilities. In addition, profound social changes would occur if persons could live to be 200 years or more. For example, people might need to have multiple careers. According to Dr. Robert Butler of Mount Sinai Hospital in New York City, "Increasing the life span may result in having the 'terrible twos' for fifteen years, or the teen-age crisis may go on for twenty years" (Kotulak and Gorner 1992: 12).

If science could significantly slow the aging process, what type of world would that produce? Would it lead to more overcrowding? At what age would a person retire? Could one live financially secure in retirement for 100 years? How long would childbearing continue? At what age would one no longer be considered for military service? Would there be age-segregated communities for persons 120 years of age and older? Would nursing facilities be primarily for persons 140 and older? Would the nurses be still working at age 100? Would those over the age of 100 be truly wise? Is it realistic to believe that life can be significantly increased? Would it be desirable? Older persons are often viewed as a strain on the American economic system. Because older people expend one-third of the nation's health-care costs, many people view them as healthy, wealthy, greedy, and a detriment to society. Former Colorado Governor Richard Lemm even stated that older people "have a duty to die and get out of the way" (Kotulak and Gorner 1992: 14).

The overall goal of the National Research Agenda on Aging of the U.S. Institute of Medicine is to extend the productive, enjoyable years of life, focusing on an overall enhanced quality of life. It is not intended to extend a dependent, frail form of existence. Current and future research efforts on the aging process are focused on helping people retain vigor, strength, and enthusiasm for life as productive members of society. As the introductory section of the Institute of Medicine's research agenda states:

Science offers the best hope to improve the older person's quality of life. Research that is directed and supported properly can provide the means to reduce disability and dependence in old age, and can decrease the burdens on a health care system strained to its limits (Lonergan 1991: 1).

SUMMARY

What it means to grow older changes over time for most societies. This is certainly true for American culture. In considering what "old" is in contemporary society, it is important to distinguish between the age categories of the elderly: the young old (aged 65 to 74), the aged (aged 75 to 84), and the oldest old (aged 85 and older). Each category has some general characteristics that tend to result in unique opportunities and problems.

A current snapshot of what it means to be old in America as revealed by a nationwide survey of persons aged 18 to 75, showed that:

- Two-thirds of those surveyed thought old age begins at age 70.
- Only 27 percent thought growing old was bad.
- Just 28 percent were afraid of getting old.
- Under half of those surveyed thought that the life of the elderly had gotten better in the last twenty years.
- Most Americans think people should work as long as they want.
- A high percentage believe sex is important after age 65.
- Over half do not want to move in with their children.

There are some key factors that determine the place older people have in any society. These include the form of family structure, religion, the knowledge base of a particular culture, the harshness of the environment, the means of production, and the speed of social change.

A look at American history shows that older people were treated differently during various periods. In the Colonial period the aged were given a place of honor, especially if they owned land or had other forms of wealth. However, not all older people were so honored. Some, especially poor widows or landless transients, were often treated quite poorly.

In the industrial era, when work moved to factories in cities, the old lost considerable status and power. Older people increasingly became a financial burden, and derogatory terms such as *old goat*, *over-the-hill*, *old hag*, and others came into use. Older people no longer controlled the means of production.

With the coming of the twentieth century, the old were increasingly seen as a social problem that needed to be addressed. This approach resulted in social legislation which began with the Social Security Act of 1935. With the coming of the postindustrial era, some experts believe that new opportunities will open up to older people, with less emphasis on productivity and more focus on the quality of life. In this approach, it is argued that older people will be able to choose roles that are more supported by society—roles that focus on family, recreation and leisure, volunteerism, politics, or second careers.

As the nation moves into the twenty-first century, it will be important to develop a new and broader concept of the role of older people based on three realities: increased longevity, explosive growth of all elderly groups, and the diversity within and across the older age groups. It is important to emphasize that older people can continue to be major contributors to society, that aging is a normal process of life and being older is just another phase of life, and that prejudice against the elderly (ageism) must be overcome as one of society's last-identified negative "isms."

What is the normal life span? How long can humans live? The biological theories of aging attempt to answer these questions and to explain why people grow older. These theories of aging have been grouped into three categories: the microbiological, the physiological, and the cellular. The microbiological theory of aging focuses on the decreasing ability of the body to maintain an internal balance of the major systems of the body. The physiological theories of aging try to describe the aging process in terms of the breakdown of physiological control mechanisms. This approach includes the hormonal theory. The cellular theories of aging deal with the genes, the basic building blocks of the body. Included is the free radical theory, which contends that cells are destroyed by superoxides or free radicals which result in the aging process. This theory has gained notoriety in the last few years. Some researchers have claimed that antioxidants, including vitamins C, E, and beta-carotene, neutralize free radicals and the damage they do.

Various approaches have been developed to extend life. Nevertheless, the question is raised whether normal life spans of 120 or 140 years would result in social benefits or social hardships. What would a nation populated by millions of 120-year-olds or 140-year-olds be like? When would people retire? How long would people be expected to work? Would longer life translate into better quality of life? The answers to these and related questions are becoming more important with each new scientific breakthrough.

REFERENCES

Achenbaum, W.A. 1983. *Shades of Gray: Old Age, American Values and Federal Policies Since 1920.* Boston: Little, Brown.

Cispell, D., and Frey, W.H. 1993. American Maturity. *American Demographics*, (March): 31–42. In Cox, H. (ed), *Annual Editions, Aging*, 9th Ed., 1994. Sluice Dock Guilford, CT: Dushkin Publishing Group.

Clements, M. 1993. What We Say About Aging. *Parade Magazine*, (December 12): 4–5.

Commonwealth Fund. 1991. *New Finding Show Why Employing Workers over 50 Makes Good Financial Sense for Companies.* New York: Case Studies.

Cowgill, D.D., and Holmes, L.D. 1972. *Aging and Modernization.* New York: Appleton Century Crofts.

Cox, H.G. 1990. Roles for Aged Individuals in Postindustrial Societies. *International Journal of Aging and Human Development*, 30(1): 55–62. In Cox, H. (ed.), *Annual Editions: Aging*, 9th Ed. 1994: 62–66. Sluice Dock, Guilford, CT: Dushkin Publishing Group.

Crandall, R.C. 1991. *Gerontology: A Behavioral Science*, 2d Ed. pp. 124–129. New York: McGraw-Hill.

Crews, D. 1993. Culture Lags in Social Perceptions of the Aged. *Generations*, 17(2): 29–33.

Denckla, W.D. 1974. Role of the Pituitary and the Thyroid Gland in the Decline of Minimal Oxygen Consumption with Age. *Journal of Clinical Investigation*, 53: 572–581.

Finch, C.E. 1988. The Neural and Endocrine Approaches to the Resolution of Time as a Dependent Variable in the Aging Process. *The Gerontologist*, 28: 29–40.

Fischer, D.H. 1977. *Growing Old in America.* New York: Oxford University Press.

Goldstein, S., and Reiss, R.J.S. 1984. Genetic Modifications During Cellular Aging. *Molecular and Cellular Biochemistry*, 64: 15–30.

Green, R. 1992. Can you live longer? What works and what doesn't. *Consumer Reports*, (January) 57(1): 7–15.

Haber, C. 1983. *Beyond Sixty-Five: The Dilemma of Old Age in America's Past.* New York: Cambridge University Press.

Hampton, J.K. 1991. *The Biology of Human Aging.* Dubuque, IA: Wm. C. Brown Publishers.

Harman, D. 1987. The Free-Radical Theory of Aging. In Warner, H.R., Butler, R.N., Sprott, R.L., and Schneider, E.L. (eds.), *Modern Biological Theories of Aging.* New York: Raven Press.

Hayflick, L, and Moorehead, P.S. 1961. The Serial Cultivation of Human Diploid, All Strains. *Experimental Cell Research*, 25: 585–621.

Hayflick, L. 1970. Aging Under Glass. *Experimental Gerontology*, 5: 291–303.

Holmberg, A.R. 1969. *Nomads of the Long Bow.* Garden City, NY: Natural History Press.

Kausler, D. 1987. Memory and Memory Theory. In G. Maddox (ed.), *The Encyclopedia of Aging.* New York: Springer Publisher Company.

Koff, T.H., and Park, R.W. 1993. *Aging Public Policy: Bonding the Generations.* In Jon Hendrics, (ed.), Society and Aging Series, p. 274. Amityville, NY: Baywood Publishing Company.

Kolata, G. 1992. *New York Times*, (December 16): A1, A11.

Kotulak, R., and Gorner, P. 1992. Aging: Is It Reversible? *Knight-Ridder Tribune News Wire*. In *The Bradenton Herald*, (February 26): 1–16.

Krauss, I. 1987. Employment. In G. Maddox (ed.), *The Encyclopedia of Aging*. New York: Spring Publishing Company.

Lonergan, E.T. (ed.). 1991. *Extending Life, Enhancing Life: A National Research Agenda on Aging*. Institute of Medicine. Washington, DC: National Academy Press.

Moody, H. 1990. The Politics of Entitlement and the Politics of Productivity. In S. Bass, E. Kutza, and F. Torres-Gil (eds.), *Diversity in Aging*. Glenview, IL: Scott, Foresman.

Myers, D., Weissman, M., Tischler, G., Hazer, C., and Leat, P. 1984. Six Monthly Prevalence Rates of Psychiatric Disorders in Three Communities. *Archives of General Psychiatry*, 41: 959.

National Center for Health Statistics. 1991. *Health, United States, 1990*. Hyattsville, MD: Public Health Service.

Palmore, E. 1977. The Facts on Aging: A Short Quiz. *The Gerontologist*, 17: 297.

Palmore, E. 1988. *The Facts on Aging Quiz*. New York: Springer Publishing Company.

Perlmutter, M. 1990. Older and Wiser. *Research News*, 41(7–8): 8, 9. Ann Arbor, MI: University of Michigan.

Raybash, J.W., Roodin, P.A., and Santrock, J.W. 1991. *Adult Development and Aging*. Dubuque, IA: Wm. C. Brown Publishers.

Richardson, A., Rutherford, M.S., Birchenall-Sparks, M.C., Roberts, M.S., Wi, W.T., and Cheung, H.T. 1985. Levels of Specific Messenger RNA Species as a Function of Age. In R.S. Sohan, et al. (Eds.), *Molecular Biology of Aging: Gene Stability and Gene Expression*. New York: Raven Press, pp. 237–238.

Rosenfeld, A. 1976. *Prolongevity*. New York: Avon.

Saluter, A.F. 1991. U.S. Bureau of the Census. *Marital Status and Living Arrangements: March 1990, Current Population Reports*. (Series P-20, No. 450). Washington, DC: U.S. Government Printing Office.

Schneider, E.L. 1992. Biological Theories of Aging. *Generations*, (Fall/Winter) 26(4): 7–10.

Sexuality and Aging. 1993. *Mayo Clinic Health Letter*. In Cox, H. (ed.), *Annual Editions, Aging*, (9th Ed.) Sluice Dock, Guilford, CT: The Dushkin Publishing Group.

Sheehan, T. 1976. Senior Esteem as a Factor of Socioeconomic Complexity. *The Gerontologist*, 16(5): 433–444.

Smith-Sonneborn, J. 1987. Error Catastrophe Introduction. In Warner, H.R., R.N. Butler, R.L. Sprott, E.L. Schneider (eds.), *Modern Biological Theories of Aging*. New York: Raven Press.

Special Report on Aging. 1992. Aging Research Promises to Enhance the Quality of Life for All Americans, Both Young and Old. Washington, DC: National Institutes on Health/National Institute on Aging.

Sokolovsky, J. 1993. Images of Aging: Across-Cultural Perspective. *Generations*, 17(2): 51–54.

Sprott, R.L., and Roth, G.S. 1992. Biomarkers of Aging. *Generations*, 26(4): 11–14.

Strehler, B.L. 1973. A New Age of Aging. *Natural History*, 82: 9–19.

Torres-Gil, F.M. 1992. *The New Aging*. New York: Auburn House.

Upton, A.C. 1977. Pathology. In C.E. Finch and L. Hayflick (eds.), *Handbook of the Biology of Aging*, 1st Ed. New York: VanNostrand Reinhold.

U.S. Bureau of the Census. 1993. Current Population Reports, Special Studies. *Sixty-Five Plus in America*, 23–178 RV. Washington, DC: U.S. Government Printing Office.

U.S. Bureau of the Census. 1990. *The Need for Personal Assistance with Everyday Activities: Recipients and Caregivers*. Current Population Reports, (Series P-70, No. 19). Washington, DC: U.S. Government Printing Office.

CHAPTER 3

The Oldest Old and the Young Old

Aging Parents Worry Their Adult Children

Shirley finally collapsed with pneumonia.

By 1983, she was caring for her elderly mother-in-law and dying aunt, all of whom lived in different places, as well as a daughter going through a painful divorce. And three teenage children. And she was working part time.

"I was very stressed, extremely stressed, just pulled in all directions, and felt like I could not possibly be everything I should be—and then I felt guilty. If I was a really good daughter, a really good mother, I should be able to do all this. There was one word I was going to have on my tombstone, and it was 'GUILTY'."

One of the main reasons for Shirley's feelings was her mother, Jean.

Jean had moved from her Detroit home of 35 years in 1973, after she was mugged on her street. She lived in a small apartment a mile from Shirley and her son-in-law. She didn't drive, and Shirley did all her shopping, cooking and cleaning.

It's not just burgeoning numbers of elderly people living on their own who are pressured. Their adult children can spend years worrying, angry and guilty, not sure what to do.

Adult children find themselves sandwiched, painfully squeezed between competing demands from elderly parents and children, often as they are about to embark on what were supposed to be their own golden retirement years.

And contrary to the stereotype, "Americans do care about our elderly, we care very much . . . we just don't always know what to do," says Audrey Wasserman Chase of Adult Well Being Services, a Detroit-based nonprofit organization that runs intensive counseling sessions called "Coping With Aging Parents."

By Janet Wilson, Free Press staff writer,
(*Detroit Free Press*,
April 14, 1992, P. B-1)

Old 'Dogs' Can Learn Lots of New Tricks

LOS ANGELES—Hey, aren't you too old for that?

It's a question that many may be asked as the years go by, but don't ask boxer George Fore-

man, who punched a hole in the age barrier by going the distance at age 42 with 28-year-old Evander Holyfield.

And don't ask Nolan Ryan who complained about feeling old at 44 and then promptly pitched a no-hitter for the Texas Rangers.

The accomplishments of these evidently not-so-over-the-hill athletes are changing society's view of just how old is old, according to Dr. T. Franklin Williams, director of the National Institute on Aging.

"It has called attention to the fact that the human body and mind can be astonishingly healthy and functional at middle age . . . and on up into the 50s, 60s, 70s and 80s," Williams said.

"And it has thrown out the challenge to older people to see themselves as having the capability of maintaining good health, functioning and contributing to society."

Dr. David Peterson, director of the USC School of Gerontology, agreed. As a group, older people are healthier and more vigorous than they were 50 years ago," Peterson said. "We seem to be finding, increasingly, that people continue to learn and, even more exciting, begin to learn at any age. And people continue to exercise and begin to exercise at any age.

Although most people won't be Foremans and Ryans, Peterson said, "There is no age that you can't start to improve."

Ron Hoffman, Catherine Chamlis and Robert Nordskog are taking that advice to heart. "It's never too late to do what you want. It's all a mind-set," said Hoffman, 60, the older brother of actor Dustin Hoffman.

By Brett Pauly, *Los Angeles Daily News*
(*The Grand Rapids Press*, June 9, 1991, p. B-1)

THE OLDEST OLD: A PIONEERING GENERATION IN LONGEVITY

The oldest-old sector of the elderly population—persons 85 years of age and older—has already been defined. Having people in this age category among us is not new in America. Benjamin Franklin was in his eighties when he participated in the Constitutional Convention in 1787, but he was an exception. Most of the men who developed the U.S. Constitution were young. America has been a "young" nation, young in years, young in its people, and young in spirit; but the dramatic aging of its population is bringing about a social revolution.

The Growth of the Oldest-Old Population

Nowhere is the aging of America more evident than among its oldest-old population. Never before have we had so many people in this age category. Because we have always had persons of this age group, but never in any significant numbers, not much attention had been paid to their characteristics and needs. Indeed, it was only recently, in 1984, that the term "oldest old" was coined by the American Association for the Advance of Science (Suzman, Manton, and Willis 1992). In that same year the U.S. Senate Appropriations Committee recognized the importance of the rapidly growing oldest-old sector of the population and set up funds for the National Institutes of Health to carry out research concerning persons in this age group. Since that time, research of and interest in this sector of the population has grown rapidly.

We have already pointed out in the introductory chapter the tremendous growth of the oldest old, in the last thirty years and into the future. Between 1960 and 1990, the oldest old increased by 232 percent, compared to an 89-percent growth rate for persons 65 years and older, and 39 percent for the total population. (U.S. Bureau of the Census 1993). Looking back into our history demonstrates the phenomenal growth of this group. In 1900, there were only 122,000 persons aged 85 and older in the United States. By 1990, there were 3.0 million (Taeuber and Rosenwaike 1992).

The future growth of this sector of the population can be described as substantial, if not spectacular, depending on which projections are used.

The reason the projections of the size of the oldest old population differ is our lack of significant experience with people this old (Suzman, Manton and Willis 1992). This is illustrated in Figure 3-1, which shows various projections made by the Bureau of the Census and other experts in demography (Manton, Stallard, and Singer 1992).

In reality, the oldest old are not a large group even today. With all of their growth in the last thirty years, this sector made up just over one percent of the total population in 1990 and under 10 percent of the total elderly (65 years and older) population. By 2000, they will be 13 percent of the elderly. When the baby boomers begin to reach age 85 by 2031, there will be 8 million persons in this age category. By 2050, their numbers will soar to 15 million, which will be 5 percent of the total population and over

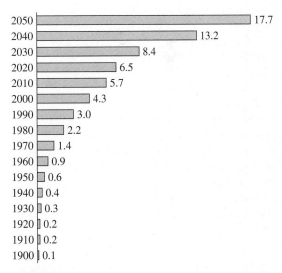

Population 85 Years and Over: 1900 to 2050
(In millions)

Year	Millions
2050	17.7
2040	13.2
2030	8.4
2020	6.5
2010	5.7
2000	4.3
1990	3.0
1980	2.2
1970	1.4
1960	0.9
1950	0.6
1940	0.4
1930	0.3
1920	0.2
1910	0.2
1900	0.1

FIGURE 3-1

Projections of the U.S. population 85 years and older. (*Source:* U.S. Bureau of the Census. Current Population Reports, Special Studies, P23-178 RV, *Sixty-five plus in America*. U.S. Government Printing Office, Washington, DC, 1993, Figure 2-8, p. 2-9.)

one-fifth of the elderly population (Taeuber and Rosenwaike 1992).

While persons 85 years and older make up the fastest growing sector of the U.S. population, persons 100 years and older (centenarians) are also in a rapidly growing group. In 1990, there were about 36,000 100-year-olds in America. This was double the number of just ten years earlier (U.S. Bureau of the Census 1993a).

Characteristics of the Oldest Old

Female Predominance   At all ages, the death rates for men are higher than those for women. As a result, as people grow older, there are fewer and fewer men compared to women. This is called the *sex ratio*. In 1990, there were 42 men for every 100 women aged 85 to 89. For persons aged 95 to 99, there were only 27 men for every 100 women (Taeuber and Rosenwaike 1992). Although the sex ratio of the oldest old is expected to indicate increased numbers of men in the future, it is still projected to show about 50 men per 100 women by 2050, resulting in 5 million more women than men in this age category.

Higher Levels of Disability   As people get progressively older, their chances of having multiple chronic health conditions increase. Similarly, with advancing age, the need for assistance with the basic activities of daily living (ADLs) increases. The ADLs include such functions as bathing, dressing, getting out of bed, going to the bathroom, and feeding oneself. In addition, half of the oldest-old population not in institutions have problems with hearing. More than half have arthritis (U.S. Bureau of the Census 1993).

Less Likely to Be Married   In 1990 about half (48.7 percent) of white men were married at age 85. Only 10.3 percent of the oldest old white women were still married. Four out of five (79.8 percent) women 85 years and older were widowed (U.S. Bureau of the Census, 1993).

More Likely to Live in Nursing Homes   The likelihood of living in a nursing home increases substantially with age. In 1990, less than 2 percent of persons 65 to 75 years old lived in a nursing home. For persons 85 to 89 years, 19 percent resided in a nursing home. For persons 90 to 94, the rate was 33 percent. For persons 95 and older, 47 percent lived in this type of institution. In 1990, 41.8 percent of the nursing home population was 85 years and older compared to 34.2 percent in 1980 (U.S. Department of Commerce 1993).

Predominately White   The oldest old are predominately white. Of the 3 million people aged 85 years and older in 1990, more than 2.8 million were white. In the same census, 273,000 were African American; 9,200 were Native Americans including Eskimos and Aleuts; nearly 30,000 were Asian or Pacific Islander in origin; and 91,000 were of Hispanic origin (Taeuber and Rosenwaike 1992). In the years ahead, the oldest old, like the other two categories of elderly persons, will be more diverse in racial and ethnic origin. The growth rate of the African American and Latino oldest old will outpace that of white persons in this age category.

Poverty Increases with Age   Although persons in the oldest-old population group are more different from each other and economically diverse than previously perceived, in general poverty among the elderly is more widespread as age increases. In 1990, 9.7 percent of all the elderly aged 65 to 74 were in poverty compared to 14.9 percent of persons 75 to 84 years of age. For the oldest old, the poverty rate was 20.2 percent, more than twice the rate for the young old (U.S. Bureau of the Census 1991b). Of widowed men aged 85 and older, 12.6 percent were in poverty, compared to 24.1 percent of the widowed oldest-old women.

Likely to Be Less Educated   Although there are marked differences among the oldest old, as a group they have less formal education than the younger groups of elderly and the rest of the population. This is an important factor as research has shown that persons with more education tend to be healthier, have higher incomes, and demonstrate more self-sufficiency through the life span. As evidenced in the better-educated older persons in the oldest ages, well-being tends to postpone some of the needs for health and social services. The oldest old are less likely to have completed high school or have any college education than are persons 25 to 74 (Preston, 1992; U.S. Bureau of the Census, 1993a). It is important to note that as persons of other age groups move into the oldest-old category, the educational attainment of the oldest old increases because education has become increasingly important throughout the years.

Much Diversity In spite of the previously noted generalizations, this group, perhaps more than most population groups, is made up of very different kinds of people with wide-ranging abilities and social conditions. Even though nearly a quarter of the oldest old live in long-term care institutions and a substantial proportion (45 percent) have various physical or mental limitations, about half are healthy enough and have adequate social and economic supports to live independently in their communities (Taeuber and Rosenwaike 1992; U.S. Bureau of the Census 1993a). Despite this diversity, the general characteristics used to describe this age group overall are very useful because they indicate the likelihood of a person of this age having one or more of these conditions. For example, a person aged 85 or older is more likely to be widowed, especially if the person is female.

Implications of a Booming Oldest-Old Population

The main reason the study of the oldest old has become so important is not simply because there are so many oldest-old people, nor is it because this group makes up the fastest-growing sector of our population—and will continue to do so for years to come. The primary reason these people are so important is because they are having and will continue to have major impacts on themselves, their families, other groups in society, and the government.

Impact of the Oldest Old as Individuals

When the authors surveyed members of the oldest-old group on how they prepared or looked forward to becoming 85, 89, 91, and 94, most laughed and said they had no idea or expectation they would ever live so long. Being so old and knowing there are many like them was not part of their expectations while they were young or middle aged. Oh, to be sure, there were oldest-old people back then, but not so many that reaching oldest age was a common expectation. Hence a large proportion of our current oldest-old people did not prepare for these very elderly years. It could be argued that even if many had expected to live to 85 years and beyond, the social and economic conditions through which they lived offered limited opportunities to plan and prepare for these years. Having been born in the late nineteenth or in the early twentieth century, these people lived through two world wars and the Great Depression plus other foreign and domestic crises.

Compared to today, there was little emphasis on health and wellness in the maturing years of our oldest old. Cigarette smoking was considered a norm, especially for men. Physical fitness and nutrition counseling were almost unknown. Essentially, physicians had no training in nutrition until recent times. And trying to survive through the economic crises of this century has left many of the oldest old incapable of coping with today's prices and expenditures for everyday living.

Women Live Longer—Implications We have already noted that the death rates for men are higher than those for women at all ages. Women simply live longer than men—currently, by about seven years. The longevity advantage of women has great implications on the oldest old. The median age of widowhood for women is about 55 years (Norton and Miller 1990). Women 85 years and older are much less likely to be living in a family setting. Of all persons 85 years and older, only 23 percent lived with a spouse and 47 percent lived alone. As they grow older, there is an increasing likelihood that women (white, African American, and Latina) will live alone. This is primarily due to women's longer life expectancies and their tendency to marry older men. In 1990, 56.8 percent of the oldest-old women lived alone compared to 28.1 percent of men this age (Saluter 1991). This trend has intensified in recent years. In 1980, 39 percent of persons aged 85 and older lived alone; by 1990, the percentage had increased to 47 percent (U.S. Bureau of the Census 1993a).

These factors have significant impacts on the oldest-old women (Figure 3-2):

> The death of a husband often marks the point of economic reversals for the surviving wife. The difference in age at marriage and the gap in life expectancy between men and women are related to

the high proportion of women living alone, the earlier institutionalization of women than men, sharply reduced income and a disproportionately high level of poverty among women, and a need for special support from family members or society (U.S. Bureau of the Census 1993a, 2–9).

Women Predominate the Dependency Years
Longer life expectancies, with women the clear winners, can bring mixed results for the oldest old. The older the person, especially in the oldest-old category, the more likely he or she will suffer from chronic medical conditions that lead to dependency. Poor health and chronic conditions are not inevitable in the oldest-old years, but they are more likely. More and more people, especially women, are living long enough to experience more long-term chronic illness, disability, and dependency. More people are living long enough to suffer from diseases such as senile dementia and Alzheimer's disease. While only 9 percent of all noninstitutionalized persons aged 65 to 69 needed assistance with daily living activities, 45 percent of persons aged 85 and older needed this kind of assistance (U.S. Bureau of the Census 1993a). Needing assistance with one or more activity of daily living (ADL), or *functional dependency*, increases from 20 percent of all persons aged 65 to 74 to 66 percent of the oldest old when nursing home residents were included, according to a major study (Hing and Bloom 1990).

Research has shown that men tend to experience diseases that kill them, while women are more likely to suffer from diseases that lead to chronic, disabling conditions (Hing and Bloom 1990). This has led to the use of the term *active life expectancy* by Sidney Katz and associates (1983). This refers to the expected years of physical, emotional, and intellectual vigor of functional well being—how long a person can be independent in their ADLs. Katz found that while men had shorter life expectancies, the men who survived had a greater percentage of remaining years of independence than did women in all age groups. Women had more years of dependency.

Number of Men per 100 Women, by Age: 1990

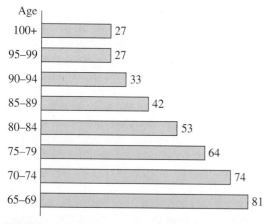

FIGURE 3-2
(*Source:* U.S. Bureau of the Census. Current Population Reports, Special Studies, P23-178RV, *Sixty-five plus in America.* U.S. Government Printing Office, Washington, DC, 1993, Figure 2-9, p. 2-9.)

Of the 1.8 million residents of nursing homes in 1990, 1.3 million (72.3 percent) were women; and in 1990, 41.8 percent of all nursing home residents were aged 85 and older (Figure 3-3), (U.S. Department of Commerce 1993).

Running Out of Money   Reaching the oldest-old years of life can mean running into financial troubles. This may result from a combination of factors, many beyond the control of the aged persons or their families. In looking at the unique characteristics of the oldest-old population and at their implications, it is important to note that many of our oldest-old people experience poverty or near-poverty condition for the first time in their lives. Others continue in poverty in their later years.

All of the current oldest old worked in a time when wages, salaries, and prices were generally much lower than they are today. Even among

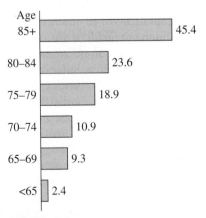

**Precentage of Persons
Needing Assistance
With Everyday Activities,
by Age: 1986**
(Civilian noninstitutional population)

FIGURE 3-3
(*Source:* U.S. Bureau of the Census. Current Population Reports, Special Studies, p. 23-178RV. *Sixty-five plus in America.* U.S. Government Printing Office, Washington, DC, Figure 3-6, p. 3-12.

those who were able to save for their retirements, most were not prepared for today's prices or needs. As we have noted, many had no idea that they would live so long.

For many of the oldest old, saving for their retirement years has been difficult. In 1940, only 12 percent of workers in the private sector labor force were covered by private pension plans. By 1988, the percentage of workers in private industry and business covered by pensions had increased to 41 percent, still less than half of all workers in the private sector (Woods 1989). Even among persons who received a pension in 1990, two-thirds were men (U.S. Bureau of the Census 1993b). Among those receiving pensions, just over half had any cost-of-living adjustments (Short and Nelson 1987). Having a pension definitely decreased the likelihood of older people falling into poverty, both for widows and couples. Only 5 percent of couples with pensions became poor in their elderly years compared to 18 percent of couples without pensions. Among widows, about 15 percent with pensions become poor compared to 28 percent without pensions (U.S. General Accounting Office 1992).

Even though Social Security benefits have had a tremendous impact on the economic lives of the elderly in America, receiving Social Security as the primary or sole income in old age does not protect against poverty. In 1990, Social Security accounted for 71 percent of the total income of the poor elderly households. As a 1992 General Accounting Office report on the economic status of poor elderly Americans stated: "Since nearly all poor elderly households in this category (89 percent) received Social Security benefits in 1990, it is clear that Social Security benefits do not ensure elderly persons—even those with extensive work histories—incomes above the poverty level" (p. 3).

Perhaps the biggest economic threat most of the oldest old face is the possibility of being placed in a nursing home. It is important to note that persons in the oldest-old category have the greatest probability of needing the services of a nursing home. With the yearly costs of these institutions ranging between $35,000 and $50,000, a majority of older Americans are required to "spend down" into poverty to qualify for Medicaid assistance, the only major government assistance program currently available to pay for long-term care.

In fact, a U.S. House of Representatives Select Committee on Aging (1987) study found that this "spend-down" into poverty occurs on average within thirteen weeks after being admitted to a nursing home for 70 percent of single older Americans. After working a lifetime to pay their bills, raise their children, support social institutions, pay their taxes, and try to do all the things required or asked of persons living in our society, a majority of our elders are forced into poverty and need to ask for assistance from a welfare program because they lived too long with chronic, disabling conditions.

The average income of people 85 years and older has been found to be 36 percent less than that of persons aged 65 to 69. The big difference in the average incomes of these two elderly groups is because very few of the oldest old are still working (labor force participation drops 74 percent between persons aged 65 to 69 and those 85 years and older) and lower Social Security benefits of the oldest old (Torrey 1992). For persons 85 years and older, only 7 percent were still in the labor force in 1980, the last date this type of information was available (U.S. Bureau of the Census 1993a).

As with any major population group, the income and economic status of the oldest old varies greatly. The factors that directly affect the income and economic status of the oldest old in addition to their oldest age category are sex, race, ethnicity, marital status, living arrangements, educational attainment, former occupational status, and work history (U.S. Bureau of the Census 1993). Any combination of these factors greatly affects an oldest old person's chances of poverty. For example, poverty rates for women aged 85 and older varied from 8.1 percent for white

women living in families to 72.6 percent for African American women living alone in 1980 (U.S. Bureau of the Census, 1980a).

The Special Vulnerability of Oldest-Old Women

Throughout the discussion of the characteristics of the oldest old, we have frequently pointed out the plight of older women. Their particular vulnerability can be seen by the principal ways so many become unprotected in their oldest-old years. In their examination of the very old, Mary Grace Kovar and Robyn Stone (1992) pointed out that in the United States, there are only two major sources of support as a person moves into their later years. One is the support of family; the other is earnings from work. Our current oldest-old women, born in the late nineteenth century or early twentieth century, are particularly vulnerable because they are at risk of lacking support from either of these sources—family and work.

Our current oldest-old women had fewer children than the cohorts (groups of the population) before them or after them (Heiser 1976). They had few children because of the Great Depression and World War II; birth rates were down significantly during these periods. In addition, infant mortality rates were still quite high when these women had their babies. As a result, many of our oldest-old women may not have many children to provide support for them (Kovar and Stone 1992).

In general, when we focus on vulnerable older people among all the elderly categories, oldest-old women predominate today as they will in the years ahead.

Impact of the Oldest Old on Families

Never before in history has America had so many oldest-old people. This has great implications for American families. We have already seen that as people reach their oldest-old years, they are much more likely to develop a variety of chronic and disabling conditions that limit their ability to perform the range of activities necessary for daily living. The likelihood of needing assistance increases with advancing age. Families, particularly adult daughters and daughters-in-law, provide 80 percent to 90 percent of all the personal care and assistance with household tasks older people need (Brody 1990).

A good way to look at the roles families play in the lives of the oldest old is to be aware that families provide most of the support the people in this age category need, and to consider number of oldest old people relative to the number of people aged 50 to 64 years of age, the likely family-member caregivers. This is called the *family* or *parent support ratio*. The parent support ratio tripled between 1950 and 1990, indicating the explosive growth of the oldest-old population. This same ratio is expected to triple again by the middle of the twenty-first century. Again, these rates are important because the oldest old are the most likely to have daily needs for economic and physical assistance. The pressing needs of the oldest old who require the assistance of their families, especially their adult children, are most likely to come at the very time when their adult children are planning for or have reached their own retirement years. Some of these caregiving adult children of the frailest oldest old have health problems of their own or are caring for a spouse with such problems. Thirty and forty years ago relatively few families needed to worry about caring for their frail elderly relatives (U.S. Bureau of the Census 1993a).

As medical technology opens additional ways to save and extend lives, it is likely that there will be more older people living longer with chronic illnesses. As a result, the need for family assistance for the frail old will increase. With more of the care for the frail elderly coming from daughters and daughters-in-law, the impact on middle-aged and young-old women has been and will continue to be tremendous. This caregiving role of so many female family members has put enormous strain on their physical, emotional, social, and economic well-being. Many have been forced to reduce or give up paid employment when they were trying to save for their own re-

tirement or assisting their own children in some way. Many of those caring for elderly parents are still in some way assisting their own children, even when their children are young adults. The people assisting relatives on both ends—the old and the young—are termed *the sandwich generation*. Some of their children are still in school or college. Some are young adults who need financial or emotional support. Some of these children have been divorced or left a live-in friend and returned to their parents' home. Some have lost jobs and cannot afford to keep their own home. Whatever the case, dual demands are put on this sandwich generation.

As the oldest-old sector of the population increases, more and more people in their fifties and sixties will have surviving parents, aunts, and uncles. The four-generation family will become more common in America. Increasingly, more and more children will know their grandparents as well as their great-grandparents (U.S. Bureau of the Census 1993a). Increasingly, more families will face the concern and financial consequences of caring for their oldest-old, frail relatives. As a result, long-term care policies will be a primary concern of the families of the oldest old. American people do really care about the well-being of their aging relatives. Policies that assist with the real needs of the elderly also help family members of all ages.

Impact of the Oldest Old on Society and Government

The rapid growth of the oldest old has major implications on governmental policy makers, decision makers, and taxpayers. As we have seen, the oldest old are more likely than people in other elderly age categories to have health and disability limitations as well as lower incomes and economic resources. They are likely to need more assistance from their families, from governmental programs, and from community agencies.

One area that directly applies to governmental programs is health care. Medicare, the federal program that insures persons 65 years and older, is available to nearly all of the nation's elderly. Health care costs for the youngest sector of the young old (65 to 69 years) averaged $3,700 per year in 1987 compared to those of the oldest old (85 years and older), which averaged $9,200 (U.S. Bureau of the Census 1993a). Public funds paid for about three-fifth of the costs for both age groups.

Persons in the oldest-old category use hospital days at a rate 123 percent higher than persons in the 65-to-74-years age group and 83 percent higher than persons aged 75 to 84 (National Center for Health Statistics 1987). It is projected that Medicare costs for the oldest old may increase by a factor of six by 2040, using inflation-adjusted dollars (Schneider and Guralnik 1990).

In 1983, Alan Greenspan, chair of the Federal Reserve Board, indicated that 30 percent of Medicare is annually spent on 5 to 6 percent of Medicare-eligible people who die within a year. He wondered if these expenditures were worth it (Schulte 1983).

Another study found that even though federal spending for health and long-term care was 129 percent higher for the oldest old than it was for the young old, this difference was substantially offset by the reduced benefits the oldest old received in Social Security benefits. When the estimated per-person benefits from Medicare, Social Security, and long-term care were added together by age group, the total per-person benefit for the oldest old was only 16 percent higher than was received by the newly retired (Torrey 1992).

Clearly the rapid growth of the oldest-old category in America has real implications for society and the government. There is much discussion in the political arena about "generational equity"—equitable distribution of resources, especially governmental resources, between and among the generations. Cover stories, articles, and letters to the editor in publications such as the *New Republic* and the *New York Times* have portrayed older people as "greedy geezers" who are elderly, affluent, and selfish (Fairlie 1989; Longman 1989). Where in the 1960s and 1970s

elderly people in general were stereotyped as poor, frail, socially dependent, and deserving of assistance, those promoting the greedy geezer stereotype portray them as independent, well, affluent, and greedy, trying to get more and more government assistance. With rising poverty rates among the young, some of the promoters of generational equity are calling for cutbacks in Social Security, Medicare, and other programs that benefit older persons, such as those funded by the Older Americans Act.

Of course, as we have seen, the elderly are a diverse population. Age, sex, race, ethnicity, marital status, health, living arrangements (particularly living alone), educational attainment, work history, and the availability of a pension greatly affect an older person's relative independence and status in life. Further, the oldest old are much more likely to experience the characteristics that make them vulnerable, frail, and dependent.

With the known probability of the needs of the oldest-old sector of our population, and with the predicted steady but manageable growth of the elderly population until 2011 when the baby boomers begin to reach age 65, America (its policy planners, governmental decision makers, and citizens at large) has a window of opportunity to plan for the tremendous needs that will accompany our age revolution (U.S. Bureau of the Census 1993a).

THE YOUNG OLD

In contrast to the oldest-old sector of the population that is more likely to have characteristics that make them vulnerable and dependent, today's young old (65 to 75 years) are more likely to be entering their later years with relatively good health, higher educational attainment, more vigor and vitality, more mobility, and financial security. Of course, this is a generalization. The people in this young-old group are more likely to have these characteristics, just as we have seen the members of the oldest-old category are more likely to have other characteristics. Obviously, all cohorts (age group categories) of the population—youth, young adults, middle-aged, young old, oldest old—are heterogeneous. They are all made up of different people with a wide range of needs and resources. Nonetheless, the young old can be described as a pioneering generation in health, affluence, and vitality.

Who Are the Young Old?

The young old are the youngest category of the population generally referred to as elderly. They are persons aged 65 through 74, by far the largest segment of the elderly population. Of the 31.1 million older persons in the United States in 1990, the last general census, well over half (18.9 million) were in the young-old category compared to 10 million aged 75 to 84, and 3 million 85 years and older (U.S. Bureau of the Census, 1993a). Among the young old, the number of men compared to women is much closer than in the two other elderly categories. In the young-old category, women only outnumber men by five to four. In the oldest-old category, women outnumber men by five to two.

The chances of reaching age 65 are much greater now than in the early part of the twentieth century. In 1900, 41 percent of newborns reached age 65. By 1990, 80 percent of newborns were expected to reach 65 (U.S. Bureau of the Census, 1993a). At age 65, a person has a life expectancy of 16.9 years, many years beyond the average working life of most Americans. It should be noted that calculation of life expectancy does not stop at age 65. For each year thereafter, there are life expectancy figures that clearly show older people continuing to live longer.

Health and Vigor of the Young Old

When some people think about the elderly as a whole, they picture frail, weak, dependent persons, some in nursing homes and many confined to their homes. This is certainly not a picture of the young old. Only slightly over one-quarter (26.3 percent) of the young old consider their health to be fair or poor (National Center for Health Statistics 1991). The rest consider their health to be good, very good, or excellent.

These personal assessments of the health of the young old are borne out by the facts. Less than 2 percent of the young old are confined to a nursing home (U.S. Department of Commerce News 1993). Ninety percent of people aged 65 to 74 who are not in nursing homes do not need personal assistance with everyday activities.

The death rates for the young old have decreased, especially among white and African-American women and white men. Since 1960, there has been about a 30 percent decrease in the death rates for these women and men. African-American men among the young old experienced a 20 percent decrease in deaths (National Center for Health Statistics 1991).

Causes of death among the young old in 1990 are primarily heart disease and cancer. Each major killer caused about one-third of all deaths in this age category. But there have been real decreases in the death rates from heart disease among the young old since 1960 (National Center for Health Statistics 1991). The elimination of heart disease would add the most years to life expectancy for the elderly, especially the young old (National Center for Health Statistics 1985). Eliminating heart disease would add more years to the life expectancy of the young old than eliminating cancer.

Smoking is directly related to heart disease and cancer. Only 25 percent of young-old men had never smoked, compared to 60 percent of women. Since 1965, the likelihood of smoking in their older years has decreased among elderly men but increased among elderly women.

Although Medicare is available to nearly all persons in each of the three elderly categories, supplemental private health insurance is held by more of the young old than by persons in the aged and oldest-old groups (National Center for Health Statistics 1991). Three-fourths of the young old have supplemental private health insurance. This is significant, because research has shown that persons without private supplemental health insurance were more likely to suffer from limitations in carrying out personal care tasks and home management tasks than those with private insurance (McNeil and Lamas 1986).

Helping Their Parents

Even though the health and vitality of the young-old person is likely to be good, it is this group and the middle-aged sector of the population that bears most of the responsibility for caring for aging parents and other elderly relatives. Family members provide 80 to 90 percent of the care needed by the dependent old (Brody 1990). Never before have we had so many middle-aged and young-old caregivers providing so much care to so many oldest-old dependent relatives. A 1993 report pointed out that the present experiences and problems of the young old in caring for the oldest old will become more common as more and more people reach the oldest years of life. This same report indicated that the physical condition of the young old may become a more serious problem as they help their frail relatives with the necessities of daily living (U.S. Bureau of the Census 1993a).

Financial Status of the Young Old

As might be expected, the young old tend to be better off financially than persons in the aged and oldest-old categories. The young old are likely to have higher incomes. In 1990, seven in 10 (69.5 percent) married-couple households in the young-old age category had incomes greater than $20,000 compared with half (51.5 percent) of married-couple households of persons aged 75 and older (DeNavas and Welniak 1991).

In looking at poverty rates among the elderly, in 1990 persons aged 75 and older were almost twice as likely to be poor or near poor as persons in the young-old age category (U.S. Bureau of the Census 1991a). In looking at income and poverty rates for the young old compared to the aged and the oldest old, it is easy to understand why the young old are better off. Even though there has been a trend toward early retirement, many more

of the young olds are working compared to persons in the other elderly categories. In 1990, 26 percent of men aged 65 to 69 were in the paid labor force compared to only 7 percent of men aged 75 years and older. Seventeen percent of women aged 65 to 69 years were in the paid labor force compared to only 3 percent of women aged 75 years and older (United States Bureau of Labor Statistics 1991). Money from paid employment is a major source of income for the elderly.

The young old have greater financial resources for other reasons. The first generation to spend their whole working lives covered by Social Security retired in the 1980s. This same group of workers also gained from the increased availability of pension plans in the 1950s and 1960s (Atkins 1992). The younger retirees have also benefitted by the boom in real wages and disposable income that marked the economy in the years following World War II. The young old have simply earned higher wages in an expanding economy compared to the oldest old. Higher incomes affect the amount of Social Security benefits retirees receive, the amount of pensions if available, and their general level of savings and assets.

Mobility and Location

It is the young old who are likely to move, especially to put some fun in their lives. As research has indicated, it is the healthier, financially secure, and younger old who migrate to better climates or more ideal living environments after retirement. The frail old, particularly the oldest old, are less likely to move unless they need to be placed in a nursing home or return to the geographic location they originally came from to be cared for by relatives, usually their adult children. The migration of the young old, according to research, peaks when people are in their mid-sixties. The oldest old are more likely to move within the same county, which leads to speculation that many of these moves were to a nursing home because of health problems (Rosenwaike 1985).

Elderly people in the United States in 1990 were almost three times more likely to live in metropolitan areas than in nonmetropolitan settings. The young old were slightly more likely to live in metropolitan areas than the oldest old (U.S. Bureau of the Census 1990a). This clearly reflects urban and suburban trends that have come to dominate life in contemporary America.

Widowhood and Living Alone

Widowhood is a common status for elderly American women. In 1990, half of all elderly women were widowed. There is a higher percentage of widows in the population as age increases. Little more than one in three (36.1 percent) young-old women are widowed, compared to four out of five for the oldest-old women. As with any elderly age category, the young-old women are more likely to be widowed than men of the same age. Only 9.2 percent of men aged 65 to 74 are widowed (Saluter 1991).

Closely related to widowhood is the probability of living alone. As women grow older, the likelihood increases that they will live alone, regardless of their ethnicity. This is because of the shorter life expectancies of men and the tendency of men to marry younger women. About one-third of young-old women (aged 65 to 74) lived alone in 1990 (Saluter 1991); but living alone for young-old women does not necessarily mean they are isolated or experiencing a poor quality of life. If their health and economic status are reasonably good, research has shown that women living alone can live satisfying lives (Chappell and Badget 1989; Riley 1983). Women are better at developing and maintaining social contacts. They typically have more and better friends. Many enjoy not being dependent on others: "Today's young-old women are more likely to be in relatively good health and able to afford to live alone than was true in the past" (U.S. Bureau of the Census 1993a: 6-5).

Educational Level

Today's young-old population is better educated than in earlier times. The high-school-completion rate for persons aged 65 to 69 in 1989 was 63 percent compared to 46 percent for persons 75 years and older, a significant difference. Only two in ten persons aged 65 to 69 had an eighth-grade education or less compared to four in ten persons aged 75 and older (Kominski 1991). The educational achievement level of older people will continue to improve in the future because the younger sectors of the population are more likely to have completed high school and gone to college. As the Census Bureau (1993a) pointed out, these improvements in educational attainment will probably make real differences in the interests of the future elderly, their needs, and their abilities to cope with changing life conditions.

Implications of a Vigorous Young-Old Population

The emergence of a pioneering generation in health, affluence, and vitality is having, and will increasingly have, significant impacts on people in this age category, on business, on government, and on the whole of society.

Impact on the Young Old as Individuals   The characteristics of the young old paint a picture of elderly people as quite different from those in the oldest-old category. Indeed, the young old as described today and as they will be defined in the early part of the twenty-first century give new meaning to being elderly in America. As the elderly years grow longer, the stages or categories of being elderly become more distinct. To be young old raises profound questions about work. Is a person ready to retire at 62, 65, or 68? The trend until the late 1980s toward early retirement has been clear. As companies and industries have continued to restructure themselves and downsize, early retirements—some forced, some voluntary—have continued. What is the cost to individuals and to employers?

Can most people find happiness and fulfillment in 25 to 35 years of leisure? Can people afford to be retired over such a long period of time? Will they, like so many of today's oldest old, run out of money with incomes and assets based on today's wages and prices, remembering that there has been a steady and sometimes steep rise in inflation over the past thirty years?

There are conflicting predictions on the economic well-being of the future young old. The Census Bureau (1993b) pointed out that with more women in the paid labor force, and because men are more likely to live somewhat longer than previously, there will probably be more married couples with two private pensions in addition to the Social Security benefits. Even here there are distinct differences in who receives pensions based on racial and ethnic characteristics, with whites receiving considerably more benefits than African Americans or Latinos.

Looking to the future, some experts believe that the current time is the "golden age" of pensions (Woods 1989). With more of the burden for future economic security falling on the individual with the shift from the traditional pension plans that were paid for by the employer to retirement plans that rely on the investments of the employee, many retirees may not have very good pensions in the future. The amount of a person's pension will depend on the amount and soundness of the individual retirement plan and whether the employee has drawn money out of his or her retirement account. Many workers do not choose to be covered in the plans offered by their employers.

In addition, the size of companies greatly determined who had pension coverage in 1991. Projecting to when these workers become part of the young old, in companies with fewer than twenty-five workers, only 23 percent of employees had pension coverage compared to 90 percent in firms with more than 1,000 workers (U.S. Bureau of the Census 1993b).

The young old need to be aware of the likelihood of needing long-term care as they anticipate longevity into the oldest-old years: "A 65-year-old woman, for example, would be wise to make plans to finance her life through at least the mid-eighties and include funding for long-term care" (U.S. Bureau of the Census 1993b: 4-17).

Although less than 2 percent of the 65-to-74-year-old population lived in a nursing home in 1990, the odds of ever being placed in a nursing home in a lifetime are quite high. Of all the people who turned 65 in 1990, 43 percent will enter a nursing home before they die (Kemper 1991). With no universal long-term care program in place in the United States, nursing home placements represent one of the major economic threats to older Americans and their families.

Impact of the Young Old on Business The emergence of a relatively vital, healthy, and more affluent young-old population represents major possibilities for American businesses. First, this segment of the population represents major marketing opportunities for businesses. Marketing experts determined that in 1993, 50 percent of the nation's discretionary income (money that is available to purchase things people want) was in the hands of people aged 50 to 74. This put them in the best financial position of any age group to make purchases (Foote 1994). Some companies are realizing the purchasing power of the middle- and young-old-age groups and are targeting advertising and promotions toward them. This will increase in the future.

Second, the young old present tremendous opportunities for dependable, loyal, and highly trainable workers. As people move into their young-old years healthier and with a better realization of the likelihood that they will live for many additional years, the question of remaining in the workforce or returning to it becomes increasingly important for a number of reasons: supplemental income, being around other people, feeling productive and needed, and having a place to go each day.

Impact of the Young Old on Government and Society The growing number of the young old in the United States has great implications for the government and society at large. There is extensive debate concerning the role of government in the lives of older people. Many now question whether all older people need or deserve programs like the Social Security Act of 1935 and resources provided through the legislation of the 1960s and 1970s.

Some of the old, particularly many of the young old, are seen as better off than some other groups in the population, particularly children. Some public policy leaders and some in the media are asking why these healthy, vigorous, and relatively well-off persons get the benefits of special governmental programs just because they turned 60, 62, or 65 years of age (depending on the program). These types of issues become more heated in times of economic recession and high federal deficit and debt when politicians look for programs to cut or eliminate. Herein lies real potential for conflict between the generations.

Public policy experts such as Assistant Secretary of Health and Human Services for Aging Fernando Torres-Gil (1992) have contended that we need to formulate a new view of aging, a view that takes into account generational claims, diversity, and longevity. In this approach, which Torres-Gil calls "New Aging," there is a need to integrate benefits of the young, middle-aged, and old in the 1990s and in the approaching twenty-first century. An example of this is long-term care, which is a major financial threat to most older people and their families. Torres-Gil advocated, and President Clinton's initial proposal for universal health coverage included, some provision for long-term care for persons of all ages. Social Security, contrary to what many people believe, already provides benefits to persons of all ages through its provisions for disabled workers and their families as well as survivors of deceased workers including their spouses and children.

Harry Moody (1990), another public policy expert, has suggested that the government needs to practice the "politics of productivity," where the elderly are looked at as a pool of skilled, talented, and productive workers. This view moves older people out of the frail, dependent stereotype into self-sufficient produc-

ers. In this approach to aging, older people are offered retraining to upgrade their skills for good jobs in the workplace along with flexible work opportunities. Moody has contended that people in their sixties, seventies, and eighties can be important in overcoming projected labor shortages and in keeping their own lives vital and productive.

Robert Binstock (1990), another public policy expert, has noted that "many older persons remain highly vulnerable with respect to income, health, functional status, and other dimensions of fundamental well-being." This is in spite of the federal programs that have been enacted to help older people.

A New View of Aging

As we close out the twentieth century and embark on new journeys in the twenty-first century, we do so with a rapidly changing population in terms of age structure. From a nation absorbed with the culture of youth from its beginning, we move to a society that is made up of people who are generally older and who continue to grow older. While the total population in the United States tripled in the twentieth century, the number of persons aged 65 and older increased ten times. In 1900, there were 3.1 million people 65 years and older compared to 31.1 million in 1990. By the middle of the twenty-first century, the number of elderly persons in the United States is expected to more than double, to almost 79 million (Day 1992). In 1990, one in eight Americans was elderly. In a relatively short time, about 20 percent of the population will be elderly.

These figures, as startling as they are, do not tell the whole story. As we have seen, the fastest-growing sector of the population is made up of those persons aged 85 and older. As we have noted, these are the people who are most likely to need various forms of support from their families, their communities, and governmental programs. It is clear from looking at the general characteristics of the oldest old and the young old, with the aged a transitional stage between the two groups, that to use one term or one view of the "elderly" is no longer adequate. Just as there are stages in the earlier years of life, there are definite stages for most people in the later years of life. This becomes clearer as life expectancies continue to increase.

All of this calls for a new view of aging—a view that does not automatically classify persons as "over the hill" once they reach age 62, or 65, or 70; a view that takes into account the diversity of persons in each age sector. Some people are "burned out" at 50 or 55. Others are in their prime at age 68 or 70. Some are vulnerable due to chronic health conditions at age 50 to 55, unable to work any longer. Others at age 65, 68, or 72 find work the most important part of their lives. Some have experienced discrimination all their lives because of their sex, race, or ethnic background which has limited their educational opportunities and negatively affected their financial status. Elderly women were nearly twice as likely as elderly men to be poor or near poor in 1990. Elderly African Americans were three times as likely as whites to be poor or near poor in 1990 (U.S. Bureau of the Census 1991a). Adding sex discrimination to racial discrimination only compounds the vulnerable position of so many of the nation's elderly.

With the booming growth of the oldest old, and the newly young old entering their later years as a pioneering generation in health, affluence, and vitality, we need a new and broader view of what growing old in America means. All of us who study aging must realistically understand the aging process; be aware of the major and rapid population changes that are occurring around us; examine what growing older currently means to older people themselves and their families; be aware of the resources and supports that are available to the elderly and the people who care for them; realize the impacts of an aging society on business, government, and the family structure; and participate in the discussions and debates that surround the issues affecting the el-

derly and their families. This book is designed to help the reader in these endeavors.

SUMMARY

Most people are somewhat aware that there are more elderly people in America these days compared to earlier times. However, not many are aware of the explosive growth of the oldest-old population—those persons aged 85 and older. Indeed, this is the fastest growing sector of the population. Between 1960 and 1990, the overall population of the United States grew by 39 percent. The growth of the population aged 65 and older was 89 percent. The sector of the population 85 years and older grew by a booming 232 percent. This fast growth will continue into the twenty-first century, with numbers soaring as the baby boomers reach old age. By 2050, 5 percent of the total population is projected to be 85 years and older.

This age grouping has some unique general characteristics that are important for families as well as the rest of society. With women decisively outliving men, the oldest-old population is, and will continue to be, predominately female. In 1990, there were 42 men aged 85 to 89 for every 100 women of the same age. For persons aged 95 to 99, there were only 27 men for every 100 women. At all ages, the death rates for men are higher than for women. As people grow older, there is a steady decline in the number of men compared to women.

The oldest old are likely to have higher levels of disability than younger-aged people. The oldest old are less likely to be married. They are more likely to live in nursing facilities. Currently, they are predominately white, but this situation is expected to change somewhat with the expected growth in the percentages of the minority oldest old. The oldest old are more likely to live alone. They are generally likely to be less educated, which affects their financial status.

These generalizations obviously do not apply to all oldest-old persons. As with people in any stage of life, there is much diversity among the oldest old. Yet the generalization of these characteristics is important for this group because persons in this age category are the most likely to need assistance in many of their activities of daily living, putting a strain on families and other resources, including government programs, that are in place to help them.

Long life, considered a traditional goal and blessing in literature and religion, can pose real problems for many. With women substantially outliving men, and with men tending to marry younger women, widowhood has become a normal condition for older women in America. This is significant. The Census Bureau points out that the death of a husband often begins the point of economic reversals for a woman. Generally, her income drops. She probably lives alone, which can result in earlier placement in a nursing facility or greater reliance on caregiving from family members. Added to these conditions, older women are more likely to experience multiple chronic health conditions that contribute to their vulnerability. Given the realities that older women generally have shorter paid-work histories than men, worked at jobs with lower wages than men, and received fewer pension opportunities than men, it is not difficult to understand the vulnerable position in which so many older women find themselves.

The booming growth of the oldest-old population has real impacts on families and the larger society. With 80 to 90 percent of all caregiving for the elderly falling on family caregivers, especially daughters and daughters-in-law, the impact of more and more oldest-old people among us is great. The impact on government is significant considering the demands on the social support programs, especially Medicare and Medicaid, with no comprehensive long-term program in place to finance nursing-home placements, which are projected to increase dramatically in the twenty-first century.

The young old (aged 65 to 74) represent a pioneering generation in health, affluence, and vital-ity. People entering their elderly years today are more likely to be healthier, better off financially, more mobile, more vigorous, and better educated than previous generations of the young old. Once again these are generalizations that do not apply to all young-old persons, but they are definite trends. With the baby boomers getting closer to joining this category in the early twenty-first century (beginning in 2011), the ranks of the young old will increase dramatically.

With the coming rapid increase in the numbers of the young old, coupled with their tendency to be healthier, wealthier, and more vigorous, the very nature of being elderly in America needs to be rethought. Is a person at age 65, 68, or 72 really old? Is it reasonable to expect to leave work when a person reaches the age we used to think was old? As longevity has increased and is expected to continue to increase, how can people afford 20, 25, or 30 years of retirement? Will they run out of money?

What is the role of government in a society experiencing an age revolution? Are conflicts between the generations inevitable? Public policy experts such as Fernando Torres-Gil and Harry Moody have pointed out that we need to develop new views of aging, views that take into account generational claims (the needs of people of all ages), the diversity of the older population, and increased longevity.

Harry Moody argued that we need to expand our view of aging where we have focused on the "failure model" of aging to include and practice the "politics of productivity" where people in their sixties, seventies, and even eighties are offered retraining, good jobs, and flexible work opportunities. Of course, this applies to those older people who are physically and mentally able to remain productive. Looking at the characteristics of the young old, and the young old to come, this applies to a lot of people.

Clearly, there are distinct stages in aging and clear differences among the three elderly classifications—the young old (aged 65 to 74), the aged (aged 75 to 84), and the oldest old (85 years and older). As people continue to age, with the oldest old the fastest-growing category, more and more of the young old (and also the middle-aged) find themselves becoming more responsible and directly involved in caring for the oldest old. The care and support of the oldest old by the young old, including financing nursing home placements, is an issue that will increasingly dominate family and political discussions.

REFERENCES

Atkins, G.L. 1992. Making It Last: Economic Resources of the Oldest Old. In Suzman, R.M., Willis, D.P., and Manton, K.G. (eds.), *The Oldest Old*. New York: Oxford University Press.

Binstock, R. 1990. The Politics and Economics of Aging and Diversity. In *Diversity in Aging*, S. Bass, E. Kutza, and F. Torres-Gil (eds.), Glenview, IL: Scott Foresman.

Brody, E.M. 1990. *Women in the Middle: Their Parent-Care Years*. New York: Springer Publishing Company.

Chappell, N.L., and Badger, M. 1989. Social Isolation and Well-Being. *Journal of Gerontology*, 44(5): S169–176.

Day, J. 1992. U.S. Bureau of the Census, *Population Projections of the United States, by Age, Sex, Race, and Hispanic Origin: 1992 to 2050*, Current Population Reports, P. 25–1092. Washington, DC: U.S. Government Printing Office.

DeNavas, C., and Welniak, E. 1991. U.S. Bureau of the Census, *Money Income of Households, Families, and Persons in the United States: 1990*, Current Population Reports. (July) Services P-60 No. 174. Washington, DC: U.S. Government Printing Office.

Elderly Americans: Health, Housing and Nutrition Gaps Between the Poor and Nonpoor. 1992. Gaithersburg, MD: U.S. General Accounting Office.

Fairlie, H. 1989. Talkin' 'bout My Generation. *The New Republic*, 198(13): 19–22.

Foote, J. 1994. In the Booming Grey Market, Old Rhymes with Sold. In *The Grand Rapids Press*, (January 16): J2. Newhouse News Service.

Heuser, R.L. 1976. *Fertility Tables for Birth Cohorts by Color: United States, 1917–73*. DHEW pub. no. (HRA) 76-1152. Hyattsville, MD: National Center for Health Statistics.

Hing, E., and Bloom, B. 1990. National Center for Health Statistics. *Long-Term Care for the Functionally Dependent Elderly*. Vital and Health Statistics, Series 13, No. 104, DHHS Pub. No. (PHS) 90-1765. Hyattsville, MD: Public Health Service.

Katz, S., et al. 1983. Active Life Expectancy. *The New England Journal of Medicine*, (November 17): 1218–1224.

Kemper, P., and Murtaugh, C.M. 1991. Lifetime Use of Nursing Home Care. *New England Journal of Medicine*, 324(9): 595.

Kominski, R. 1991. U.S. Bureau of the Census *Educational Attainment in the United States: March 1989 and 1988*. Current Population Reports, (Series P-20, No. 451; Table 1). Washington, DC: U.S. Government Printing Office.

Kovar, M.G., and Stone, R.I. 1992. The Social Environment of the Very Old. In Suzman, R.M., Willis, D.P., and Manton, K.G. (eds.), *The Oldest Old*. New York: Oxford University Press.

Longman, P. 1989. Elderly, Affluent-and Selfish. *The New York Times*, (October 10): 27.

Manton, K.G., Stallard, E., and Singer, B.H. 1992. Projecting the Future Size and Health Status of the U.S. Elderly Population. *International Journal of Forecasting*. (in review).

McNeil, J.M., and Lamas, E.J. (1986). U.S. Bureau of the Census. Disability, functional limitation, and health insurance coverage: 1984–1985. *Current Population Reports* (Series P-70, No. 8). Washington, DC: U.S. Government Printing Office.

Moody, H.R. 1990. The Politics of Entitlement and the Politics of Productivity. In S. Bass, E. Kutza, and F. Torres-Gill (eds.), *Diversity in Aging*. Glenview, IL: Scott, Foresman.

National Center for Health Statistics. 1985. U.S. Decennial Life Tables for 1979–81 (Vol. 1, No. 1, DHHS Pub. No. (PHS)85-1150-1), Public Health Service. Washington, DC: U.S. Government Printing Office.

National Center for Health Statistics. 1987. Utilization of Short-Stay Hospitals, United States, 1985, Annual Summary. *Vital and Health Statistics*, (series 13, no. 91). Washington, DC: U.S. Department of Health and Human Services.

National Center for Health Statistics. 1991. Data for 1989 Unpublished. In *Sixty-Five Plus in America*. U.S. Bureau of the Census, *Health United States, 1990*. Hyattsville, MD: Public Health Service.

Norton, A.J., and Miller, L.F. 1990. U.S. Bureau of the Census. *Remarriage Among Women in the United States: 1985. Current Population Reports* (Series-P-23, No. 169). Washington, DC: U.S. Government Printing Office.

Nursing Home Population Increases in Every State. 1993. *Census Bureau Reports.* (June 28). Washington, DC: *U.S. Department of Commerce News.*

Preston, S.H. 1992. Cohort Succession and the Future of the Oldest Old. In Suzman, R. M., Willis, D.P., and Manton, K.E. (eds.), *The Oldest Old.* New York: Oxford University Press.

Riley, M.W. 1983. Aging and Society: Notes on the Development of New Understandings. (December 12). Lecture at the University of Michigan.

Rosenwaike, I. 1985. *The Extreme Aged in America.* Westport, CT: Greenwood Press.

Saluter, A.F. 1991. U.S. Bureau of the Census, *Marital Status and Living Arrangements: March 1990, Current Population Reports* (Series P-20, No. 450). Washington, DC: U.S. Government Printing Office.

Schneider, E.L., and J.M. Guralnik. 1990. The Aging of America: Impact on Health Care Costs. *Journal of the American Medical Association,* 263: 2335–46.

Schulte, J. 1983. Terminal Patients Deplete Medicare, Greenspan Says. *Dallas Morning News,* (April 26): 1.

Short, K., and Nelson, C. 1987. U.S. Bureau of the Census. *Pensions: Workers Coverage and Retirement Benefits,* Current Population Reports, (Series P-70, No. 25).

Suzman, R.M., Manton, K.G., and Willis, D.P. 1992. Introducing the Oldest Old. In Suzman, R.M., Willis, D.P., and Manton, K.G. (eds.), *The Oldest Old.* New York: Oxford University Press.

Taeuber, C.M., and Rosenwaike, I. 1992. A Demographic Portrait of America's Oldest Old. In Suzman, R.M., Willis, D.P., and Manton, K.G. (eds.), *The Oldest Old.* New York: Oxford University Press.

The Commonwealth Fund. 1991. *New Findings Show Why Employing Workers Over 50 Makes Good Financial Sense for Companies.* New York: Case Studies.

Torres-Gil, F.M. 1992. *The New Aging: Politics and Change in America.* New York: Auburn House.

Torrey, B.B. 1992. Sharing Increasing Costs on Declining Income: The Visible Dilemma of the Invisible Aged. In Suzman, R.M., Willis, D.P., and Man-ton, K.G. (eds.), *The Oldest Old.* New York: Oxford University Press.

U.S. Bureau of the Census. 1980. Census of Population and Housing, Special Tabulations for National Institute on Aging (Summary Tape File 5A, Table 6). Produced by Age and Sex Statistics Branch, Population Division.

U.S. Bureau of the Census. 1990a. Census of the Population and Housing. Summary Tape File, 1A.

U.S. Bureau of the Census. 1991a. *Poverty in the United States: 1990.* Current Population Reports (Series P-60, No. 175). Washington, DC: U.S. Government Printing Office.

U.S. Bureau of the Census. 1990b. *The Need for Personal Assistance with Everyday Activities: Recipients and Caregivers.* Current Population Reports (Series P-70, No. 19). Washington, DC: U.S. Government Printing Office.

U.S. Bureau of the Census, Current Population Survey. 1991b. Data tabulated by the U.S. Congressional Research Service and published in U.S. Congress, House of Representatives, *Committee on Ways and Means, Overview of Entitlement Programs, 1992 Green Book: Background Material and Data on Programs Within the Jurisdiction of the Committee on Ways and Means,* (102nd Cong., 2nd Session). Washington, DC: U.S. Government Printing Office.

U.S. Bureau of the Census. 1993a. Current Population Reports (Special Studies, P23-178 RV), *Sixty-Five Plus in America.* Washington, DC: U.S. Government Printing Office.

U.S. Bureau of the Census. 1993b. *Preparing for Retirement: Who Had Pension Coverage in 1991?* (Statistical Brief, SB/93-6). Washington, DC: U.S. Department of Commerce.

U.S. Bureau of Labor Statistics. 1991. Data for 1990. *Employment and Earnings,* 38: (1).

U.S. House of Representatives Select Committee on Aging. 1987. Long-Term Care and Personal Impoverishment: Seven in Ten Elderly Alone Are at Risk (Com. Pub. 100-631). Washington, DC: U.S. Government Printing Office.

Woods, J.R. 1989. *Pension Coverage Among Private Wage and Salary Workers: Preliminary Findings from the 1988 Survey of Employee Benefits.* (Social Security Bulletin, Vol. 52, No. 10): 2–19.

THE REALITIES
OF GROWING OLDER

CHAPTER 4

Physical Changes
and the
Aging Process

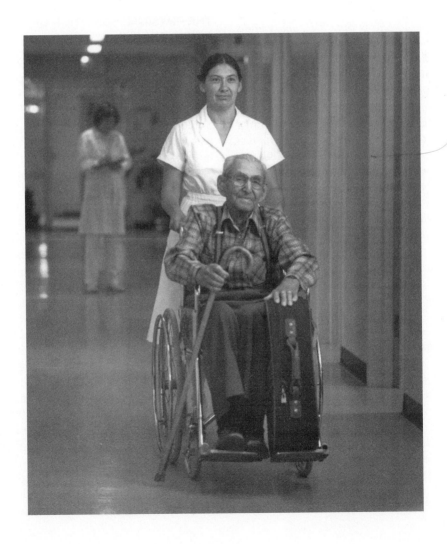

Everybody Is a Little Different—Even the Old

Peter is 86 and is beginning to develop glaucoma. He needs assistance in using the drops that he says he has to put into his eyes several times a day to reduce the pressure on his optic nerve. In addition, he suffers from diabetes, which has resulted in severe pains in his legs because of inadequate circulation. He also has congestive heart failure, and as a result is frequently tired because of a lack of blood being pumped by his failing heart. Through all of these physical difficulties, Mr. Camp remains in his own home because of the assistance of his 79-year-old wife and daily visits by a nurse.

Jennie is petite. She is only 5'1" and weighs only 105 pounds. She is 78 and suffers from osteoporosis. She has a "widow's hump," a curvature of the spine caused by deteriorating vertebrae, which makes her walk with a stoop. Her spine is forcing her upper body to curve outward, bending her head and neck down. She is worried about falling and breaking her hip, as happened last year to her 83-year-old sister. Her doctor has told her she must be very careful because her bones are very brittle.

George is 77. He never sleeps through an entire night without getting up to go to the bathroom. He cannot drive more than two hours because he knows he will by then need a bathroom break. He is beginning to be embarrassed because he is "dribbling" some urine, and he is worried about the odor.

Gilbert is 72 and works out several times a week. He lifts weights at least three times a week and jogs almost every day. He also runs in several marathons a year. He skis, swims, plays softball in a league for people age 70 and older, and is proud of the fact that he can do more pushups than his 19-year-old grandson. He walks with vigor and has a strong firm voice and an even stronger handshake. He says he might reduce his vigorous schedule on his ninetieth birthday, or he might by then decide to take up skydiving.

Jane is 60, but she looks at first glance as if she might be 80. She has very wrinkled skin, em-physema, coughs constantly, and is usually in a depressed state of mind. She is also constantly fatigued. She is obese, at least 40 pounds overweight. She smokes more than a pack of cigarettes a day, never walks anywhere if she can avoid it, and eats compulsively. Her favorite activity is smoking while watching the "soaps" or "interview shows" on television. She is cynical, angry most of the time, and whines constantly. She complains that her children seldom visit her. She is devoted to her cat, who is usually found sleeping on one of the chairs.

THE PHYSICAL CONDITION OF OLDER PEOPLE

According to the most recent available data from the Bureau of the Census (1993), poor health is not as widespread as many people assume among the elderly, especially among the young old. Some three out of four persons aged 65 to 74 who are not in institutions consider their health to be good, very good, or excellent.

The same study found that nine out of ten non-institutionalized persons aged 65 to 74 needed no assistance with everyday activities. However, for persons aged 85 and older, some 45 percent of those not living in institutions did need personal assistance with daily living activities.

Leading researchers such as George Martin, recently retired scientific director of the National Institute on Aging, and George Baker, president of the Nathan W. and Margaret T. Shock Aging Research Foundation, have pointed out that improved nutrition, sanitation, pharmaceuticals (prescription drugs), clinical techniques, and other changes have dramatically increased life expectancy in technologically advanced societies such as the United States (Gunby 1994).

Although most researchers who focus on the aging processes have pointed out that "normal aging can be differentiated from disease, and there is no single timetable for human aging" (Gunby 1994: 1562), there are now more than 600 journal articles based on the Baltimore Longitudinal Study of Aging (BLSA) that have outlined many of the physical changes that occur over the life span. As people grow older, changes tend to occur throughout the physical systems of the body that may be hardly noticeable at first. Over time, however, such changes may result in limited functioning that could interfere with normal activities of daily living (ADLs). As Gunby pointed out, however, all older people do not experience all the documented changes.

These changes are most striking in the physical senses, especially vision and hearing. Although diminished vision and hearing capacity can have devastating effects on a person of any age, the elderly experience the most vision and hearing problems. Decreased ability to smell and taste leaves older people vulnerable to the dangers of spoiled food and gas leaks and denies them enjoyment from enticing aromas and foods.

VISION CHANGES

Changes begin to occur in the eyes for most people after the age of forty. No amount of exercise or nutritional intake will slow certain inevitable changes. Because aging eyes do change and may develop serious eye conditions, it is important for older people to have periodic eye examinations by qualified professionals.

Presbyopia—Farsightedness

Presbyopia, or farsightedness, usually begins to develop when a person is about 40 years of age. Presbyopia is not a disease. It develops earlier for some people, a little later for others. The eye begins to lose accommodation, which means that it cannot adjust for different distances. The condition can be helped by wearing bifocals or trifocals which many people will need by the time they are in their late forties or early fifties. Some people, for what they consider to be aesthetic reasons, delay using bifocals. Others use them periodically but mostly keep them in their purse, on top of their head, or hanging from a chain around their neck. They are only delaying the inevitable.

Eventually most people will need bifocals and will put them on their nose so that they can see better (Stefanson 1990).

Presbyopia also means that as a person grows older, it is more difficult to adjust to darkness, and the adaptation to both light and darkness will require more time. It is much more difficult for a 70-year-old to see adequately at night than a 12-year-old. Any grandparent can test this by going out at night with his or her 12-year-old grandchild and asking what the child sees in the distance. He or she will quickly discover that the 12-year-old is aware of objects that the 70-year-old did not know were out there. This, of course, makes nighttime driving more hazardous for the older person (Kart, Metress, and Metress 1992).

In addition, presbyopia makes it more difficult for the older person to adjust to glare. Adding this difficulty to those mentioned above means that the older eye is at a significant disadvantage driving at night when trying to adjust to oncoming headlights.

Presbyopia also means that it is more difficult for the aging eye to adjust to what are termed "cool colors" such as blue, green and violet in contrast to "warm colors" such as yellow, red, or orange (Kart, Metress, and Metress 1992). Nevertheless, presbyopia should not disrupt the daily lives of most people.

Cataracts

Cataracts are a common and serious vision problem of older people. The evidence seems to be that eventually most persons will develop cataracts if they live long enough. In cataracts the lens become like milk slowly added to water, so there is a clouding of vision; a person with cataracts will suffer blurred or misty vision. As the lens loses its transparency, there is interference with the passage filter. With surgery, the clouded lens can be replaced by a synthetic one. The surgery is becoming routine and its success rate is very high. There is some evidence that connects the formation of cataracts to exposure to the sun (Straatsma, Foos, and Horowitz 1985; Kart, Metress, and Metress 1992).

Macular Degeneration

Unfortunately some people develop macular degeneration as they grow older. This condition is almost always incurable and is the leading cause of legal blindness among older adults in the United States. The region of the eye that is responsible for the most sensitive central vision is the macula. It is a small, oval, yellow area of the retina that is located in the center of the retina in the back of the eye. The macula is the area of the retina that is packed with light receptors. The macula of the eye enables one to see detail, as in reading, sewing, and similar tasks. In macular degeneration, peripheral vision is maintained but central vision is lost (Ferris, Fine, and Hyman 1984).

In some people, after the age of 50 or 60, the macula begins to break down, leading to age-related macular degeneration (AMD). Printed words become blurred, straight lines seem to have a kink in them, and colors tend to become dimmer. The most common form of macular degeneration is the dry, or atrophic (wasting), form of the condition. There is no way to prevent, stop, or reverse this stage of the disease (*Johns Hopkins Medical Letter* 1990).

A more serious form of macular degeneration is exudative, or wet, macular degeneration, which may develop suddenly at any time in patients with AMD. Exudative macular degeneration can cause rapid and severe loss of vision, often in a matter of days or weeks (*Johns Hopkins Medical Letter* 1994c; 1994d). There is some evidence to indicate that AMD is a combination of environmental and genetic factors and not a normal part of the aging of the eye (Kart, Metress, and Metress 1992). Experimentation is progressing in laser-beam therapy, in which an attempt is made to get at the decaying blood vessels of the retina in some persons at the very earliest stage of the disease. A great deal of research is being conducted to determine the causes of AMD and to improve the results of laser treatment (The Johns Hopkins Medical Letter 1994c).

Glaucoma

Another serious eye condition associated with aging is glaucoma. Glaucoma is caused by increased pressure in the eye due to a buildup of aqueous humor, the nutrient fluid that circulates in the anterior chamber of the eye. In glaucoma, fluid is produced faster than it can be eliminated, resulting in an increase in pressure that leads to progressive pressure on the optic nerve. In a normal eye, aqueous humor is produced behind the lens and flows to the front of the eye, bringing with it nourishment and a means to clear the eye of waste products. In the normal eye, the liquid drains as it is produced, maintaining a constant flow. For those who have glaucoma, the drainage becomes blocked. If there is no release of the fluid, it builds up and the pressure damages the optic nerve. This is a serious condition, and all older persons and those who work with them, should be aware of the symptoms of this disease. People with a family history of glaucoma, persons of African ancestry, and all those over the age of 60 are at risk for this disease. Persons who have glaucoma tend to have a gradual loss of peripheral vision. This means that they cannot adequately see objects at the side of the field of vision. It makes driving dangerous because they do not see objects to the side of their car. Persons with developing glaucoma tend to see halos around objects, especially around lights. Any older person who sees halos around objects should have an immediate eye exam. If untreated, glaucoma results in tunnel vision and eventual loss of sight. It can be treated by drugs, usually in the form of eye drops, or surgery; however, it will not be reversed beyond the point at which it was treated (DiGiovanna 1994; Spaeth 1984).

Dry Eyes

Some persons develop dry eyes as they grow older. In some instances this dryness can also cause redness in the eye. One can obtain professional diagnosis and treatment for both dry eyes and redness in the eye. The treatment usually is rather simple, typically consisting of an adequate liquid solution being put into the eye through drops (DiGiovanna 1994; Stefanson 1990).

Retinopathy

The most frequent cause of blindness for persons with diabetes is diabetic retinopathy, damage to the retina, the light-sensing structure in the eye. A common symptom is blurred vision, or for some, complete loss of sight. People with diabetes are 25 times more likely to become blind than persons without diabetes. Nearly all persons with some insulin-dependent diabetes have some form of retina damage by the time that they have had diabetes for 15 years or more. Sixty percent of those who have diabetes, but are not insulin-dependent, usually have retinal damage after 20 years. In both types of diabetes, retinopathy can go undetected for years because vision loss is painless and usually occurs very gradually (*Johns Hopkins Medical Letter* 1994d).

Diabetes damages blood vessels in the eye: Blood vessels in the retina leak, close, or produce new growth, leading to fluid buildup, bleeding, and scarring that can impair or destroy vision.

Adaptations

Somewhat less than 10 percent of persons aged of 65 to 74 are legally blind, although blindness increases to about 16 percent for those aged 75 and older (Stefanson 1990; Hyman 1987).

In addition to surgery and drug therapy, older persons with vision limitations can be helped by the use of large-print books. Most public libraries have these available immediately or by request. For some older persons a magnifying glass can be very helpful. Others with severe vision problems may want to use recorded books. Most libraries have cassettes of books. The Association for the Blind is available to give advice for partially sighted people.

It is important for older persons to have good lighting, because they need more light to see adequately. It would be helpful for older persons if posters, bulletins, etc., used large print with well-spaced letters. In addition, it would help if high-contrast color combinations are used, such as orange on black rather than green on blue.

Some older persons may need to have their appliances color coded because of their difficulty in reading numbers. For example, the temperature numbers on an oven could have an orange dot for 350° and a black dot for 400°.

Changes do occur in the eye with aging. But for the vast majority of older persons, assistance is available in the form of corrective lenses, drug therapy, or surgery. Much progress has been made in effectively treating eye disorders.

HEARING

To illustrate the long-term physical changes that can occur as part of the aging process, research has shown that high-frequency tone hearing can begin to decline in people in their twenties (Gunby 1994). Between the ages of 30 and 80 men lose hearing until the loss is about twice the rate of that in women. Low-frequency hearing usually declines for both sexes in their sixties.

As people grow older, the likelihood of hearing difficulties increases rapidly (U.S. Bureau of the Census 1993). By the time they reach 80 years of age, half of the people have problems with their hearing (Guralink et al. 1989). Estimates vary on the actual number of people with hearing loss in the United States, from 23.5 million to 28 million persons (U. S. Special Committee on Aging 1993). Of the total number of persons in the nation with hearing loss, 60 percent are over the age of 65 (AARP 1993).

To get a better perspective on the number of people with hearing problems, it is significant to note that even though only about 22 percent of the population with a hearing loss wears a hearing aid, these aids are the third most widely used assistive device, after glasses and canes (AARP 1993).

Hearing is an essential component of well-being, especially for people who have enjoyed normal hearing for most of their lives. Losing the

Hearing Aids: Buyer Beware

The reasons for this were highlighted in a hearing of the U.S. Senate Special Committee on Aging hearing in September 1993. Of the 23.5 to 28 million people in the United States who suffer hearing loss, only 3.78 million use hearing aids. Based on these numbers, between 15 to 25 million people could benefit from hearing aids. Not having these aids results in millions of older Americans being cut out of some of the basic aspects of daily living.

Research by the American Association of Retired Persons (AARP) in 1993 found that consumers face serious problems when they shop for a hearing aid (U.S. Senate Special Committee on Aging 1993). The AARP's research took two forms:

- Test shopping in which consumer testers visited 23 different hearing aid sites in Florida with a total of 169 hearing evaluations.
- An analysis of 4,000 letters solicited in an article in the September 1991 *AARP Bulletin* asking members who were users of hearing aids to relate their experiences.

HEARING AID RIP-OFFS

The main finding from the shopping experience research was that while many hearing aid merchandisers met or even went beyond state testing standards, a significant number did not. The quality of the hearing tests that were given, and the recommendations that were made from them, differed a lot. For example, at one hearing aid outlet, 33 percent of the persons the AARP sent to be tested were told they needed a hearing aid. In another outlet, 80 percent of the same people were told they needed an aid. At many sites the consumer testers reported they were tested in noisy rooms. The testers also found the following:

- In many cases, the hearing aid sellers recommended aids to people who did not need them.

- One seller said that it was best for the potential buyer of a hearing aid that she *not* see a physician before buying one.
- One seller said that a hearing aid would exercise the nerve associated with hearing and slow down the loss of hearing.
- One seller said that a 30-day trial period was not needed because his aid used 24K gold circuits.
- One seller said that the patient needed a hearing aid immediately and would not give the price until after the sale was made.

DISSATISFACTION WITH HEARING AIDS

An analysis was made of the first 4,000 letters the AARP received from its members who were users of hearing aids. Most of the respondents were over 70 years of age. They were also people who were long-time users, and 67 percent wore their hearing aids all day long. The main finding of the analysis of these letters was that the users indicated a relatively low level of satisfaction with their hearing aids. Only 43 percent made any positive comments about their use of their hearing aids, and 34 percent made negative remarks (U.S. Senate Special Committee on Aging 1993).

PROFESSIONAL TESTING NEEDED

In a statement before the 1993 hearing of the U.S. Senate Special Committee on Aging, David Kessler, Commissioner of the Food and Drug Administration (FDA), pointed out why so many older Americans are dissatisfied with their hearing aids and end up leaving them in their dresser drawers after spending hundreds or even thousands of dollars on them. One of the major problems is lack of proper diagnostic evaluation prior to buying a hearing aid. About 40 percent of the people who buy a hearing aid only consulted a hearing aid dealer before purchase. Back in 1977, the FDA issued a regulation which restricted the sale of hearing aids to people

ability to hear adequately in the routine activities of daily life can be very detrimental. As Senator David Pryor stated at a Congressional hearing in September 1993,

> As difficult as impaired hearing may be for any person, it is compounded for elderly persons. . . . The loss of hearing affects their independence and

quality of life. For many older people, hearing impairment prevents complete participation in everyday life. Simply trying to understand what is being said around them can be a frustrating experience. Beyond the inconvenience created by hearing loss, hearing impairment can lead to paranoia and depression (U. S. Senate Special Committee on Aging 1993: 3).

Hearing Aids: Buyer Beware (continued)

who had undergone a hearing test by a physician in the previous six months. However, this same regulation allowed fully informed adult patients to waive medical exams. This waiver was intended to be used as an exception, but a 1991 study of hearing aid sellers in Vermont found that 55 percent waived the medical examination, and in 20 percent of the cases, there were no waivers or statements of physicians in the patient files (U.S. Senate Special Committee on Aging 1993).

Dr. Kessler has stressed that it is crucial for a potential buyer of a hearing aid to get a comprehensive hearing exam before purchasing such a device. He pointed out that the hearing aid industry has become "an increasingly aggressive, competitive business. And the current system makes it too easy for salespeople eager to close the deal on the spot to encourage consumers to sign the waiver and bypass the evaluation: in some cases . . . to provide inadequate tests in place of the comprehensive evaluation consumers need" (U.S. Senate Special Committee on Aging 1993).

The AARP, in its statement to the U.S. Senate Special Committee on Aging (1993) recommended the following steps for potential buyers of hearing aids:

1. Be an educated consumer. Go to the library and learn about hearing aids and hearing evaluations prior to making a purchase. There are a number of excellent resources available for first-time buyers. Learn about service providers and the range of services and products they offer. Check your telephone directory's Yellow Pages for practitioners in your area.

2. If you're a first-time buyer, be sure to visit a physician, preferably a specialist in treating hearing impairments, for a medical examination before buying an aid.

3. Try to have your hearing evaluated by a certified audiologist. Audiologists generally are the most knowl-edgeable of the practitioners that evaluate and fit hearing aids. They also conduct the most thorough evaluations.

4. Be on your guard. There are practitioners in all occupations who are more interested in a sale than your welfare.

5. Secure a written quotation for the hearing test, hearing aid, and all other associated costs. Costs do vary but shouldn't be the only consideration in buying an aid.

6. Secure a copy of your audiogram in addition to any other hearing test results. If you don't understand test results, ask more questions.

7. Be skeptical about any claims made for the product and any high-pressure tactics.

8. Demand a 30- to 60-day trial period to test the aid in your hearing environment. The cost to you if you return the aid, should be minimal. Be sure to ask how the trial period works.

9. Practice with the aid during your trial period and attend all scheduled follow-up sessions.

10. Accept the fact that even the best aid, fitted by the most competent individual, may need to be remade or adjusted. It is also the consumer's responsibility to work with the seller.

11. If you're not satisfied, return the aid within the trial period.

12. If necessary, file a complaint with the state licensing board, your attorney general, and the Federal Trade Commission or the Food and Drug Administration.

Consumers can get a free copy of AARP's guide to hearing aids by writing: Product Report: Hearing Aids (D13766), AARP (EE0458), PO Box 22796, Long Beach, California 90801-5796.

Physical Causes of Hearing Problems

As people grow older, a condition known as presbycusis occurs. This refers to a loss in hearing brought about by various, not well understood, changes due to aging. Most people lose the ability to hear higher sound frequencies first. Impaired hearing as a result of aging may be due to a loss of hair cells in the ear known as the organ of the Corti, or interrupted conduction of sound waves due to arthritis of the delicate bones in the inner ear, or it could be due to a wax build up in the ear, which would interfere with the proper conduction of sound. Hearing loss can also be brought about by environmental noises, such as loud rock concerts, walkmans turned up high and industrial noises (Darbyshire, 1984; Surjan, Devald, and Palfalvia, 1973). There is some evidence that in other cultures with less noise pollution there is less loss of hearing with aging (Rosen, Bergman, and Plester, 1962).

Adaptations

In communicating with people who have hearing problems it is helpful to talk slowly and enunciate clearly. Shouting should be avoided. It is beneficial to speak face to face so the person can see lip movements. Since much communication is nonverbal, one can attempt to communicate emotions, moods, and acceptance by body language and facial expressions. It is always helpful to eliminate background noise created by fans, air conditioners, and other appliances. The acoustics in an auditorium should be very good for a presentation to older persons. In addition, it is wise to use good sound equipment, because most persons experience some hearing loss as they grow older.

An important factor in hearing loss is the increasing isolation of the person with impaired hearing. For many persons, hearing loss is gradual. At the beginning of the loss of hearing, it is not unusual for people to be irritable, to seem to be distracted from conversation, and to be unsociable. Often a person may be unaware of the hearing loss and frequently give inappropriate answers to questions that he or she did not hear adequately. As a result, the relationship of others to such a person may become strained as others believe him or her to be a bit confused. As this process continues, this person may begin to feel rejection in the nonverbal communication of others, and there is a real danger that depression may set in, leading to a cyclical process in which he or she becomes even more isolated and more depressed (Voeks et al. 1990).

Older persons who believe they are suffering hearing loss can benefit from having a hearing checkup with an ear, nose, and throat specialist, or with an audiologist. If the hearing loss is due to a buildup of wax in the ear canal, this can be treated rather easily, and the person can be taught how to adequately clean his or her ears of excess wax (Voeks et al. 1990).

If there is a significant organic reason for hearing loss, many aids are available today that can help. Modern hearing aids are marvels of technological advancement. They have been miniaturized so that they are comfortable to wear and are cosmetically acceptable. Hearing aids do not restore the entire ranges of lost frequencies. At first the hearing aid may seem unnatural and strange because it amplifies sounds other than speech. It usually takes some time to adjust to a hearing aid, and families and friends, as well as the user of the aid, will need patience during the adjustment process (Kart, Metress, and Metress 1992). The majority of people who need some type of hearing aid do not have them (Humphrey, Herbst, and Faurgui, 1981). Since hearing aids are expensive and are not covered by Medicare, some people feel that they cannot afford them. It is important for a person to be diagnosed by a certified specialist and not by a person selling hearing aids.

A Quick Test for Hearing

The American Academy of Otolaryngology—Head and Neck Surgery has developed a five-minute hearing test for people to use to initially screen the need for visiting an ear physician.

SMELL

The evidence seems to indicate that about 25 percent of persons aged 65 to 80 lose some ability to smell. After the age of 80 this increases to 50 percent. Usually people do not begin to lose the sense of smell until their fifties. What apparently happens is that the sense receptors for odor in the upper nose begin to lose their ability to function because of disease or to injury. This creates some potentially serious problems: Some older persons have difficulty smelling gas leaks, spoiled foods and beverages, and smoke. At the same time they

5 MINUTE HEARING TEST	Almost always	Half the time	Occasionally	Never
1. I have a problem hearing over the telephone.				
2. I have trouble following the conversation when two or more people are talking at the same time.				
3. People complain that I turn the TV volume too high.				
4. I have to strain to understand conversations.				
5. I miss hearing some common sounds like the phone or doorbell ringing.				
6. I have trouble hearing conversations in a noisy background such as a party.				
7. I get confused about where sounds come from.				
8. I misunderstand some words in a sentence and need to ask people to repeat themselves.				
9. I especially have trouble understanding the speech of women and children.				
10. I have worked in noisy environments (assembly lines, jackhammers, jet engines, etc.)				
11. Many people I talk to seem to mumble (or don't speak clearly).				
12. People get annoyed because I misunderstand what they say.				
13. I misunderstand what others are saying and make inappropriate responses.				
14. I avoid social activities because I cannot hear well and fear I'll reply improperly.				
To be answered by a family member or friend:				
15. Do you think this person has a hearing loss?				

SCORING

To calculate your score, give yourself 3 points for every time you checked the "Almost always" column, 2 for every "Half the time," 1 for every "Occasionally," and 0 for every "Never." If you have a blood relative who has a hearing loss, add another 3 points. Then total your points.

The American Academy of Otolaryngology—Head and Neck Surgery recommends the following:

- 0 to 5—Your hearing is fine. No action is required.
- 6 to 9—Suggest you see an ear-nose-and-throat (ENT) specialist.
- 10 and above—Strongly recommend you see an ear physician.

Source: American Academy of Otolaryngology—Head and Neck Surgery, Inc. Alexandria, VA.

lose the pleasure of smelling flowers, perfumes, and well-cooked and seasoned foods (DiGiovanna 1994; Bittles and Collins 1986).

TASTE

Early research seemed to indicate that with the aging process there was a significant loss in the ability to taste and that by age 70, persons had a greater than 50 percent loss in their taste buds (Arey, Tremaine, and Monzingo 1935). However, more current research has indicated that there is no such dramatic decrease in taste buds associated with the aging process. Bradley (1988) asserted that the number of taste buds varies by persons, but that there is no significant decline with age. Cowart (1989), in reviewing the literature, agreed that there is only a slight decrease of taste buds with aging.

Weiffenback, Cowart, and Baum (1986) stated that the loss of taste, if any does occur, usually affects a person's ability to taste salt more than sugar. DiGiovanna (1994) agreed that aging seems to cause only slight decreases in the ability to detect salty and bitter substances, and that the changes are highly variable among individuals. The loss of the ability to taste that occurs with aging seems to be slight and can be compensated for by adding salt (if high blood pressure is not a problem) or spices to food. The diminished ability to taste can result in an older person's inability to detect spoiled food as well as decreased enjoyment in eating.

SKIN

As people grow older there is an increased probability that their skin will begin to wrinkle. For most that process begins in their twenties. The process is made worse by smoking and frequent exposure to the sun. In addition, the wrinkling process relates to a person's genetic heritage. Blond, fair-skinned persons tend to wrinkle sooner than persons who have darker skin (Kart,

Metress, and Metress 1992; Fenske and Conrad 1988; Gilchrist 1982).

In addition, as a person ages the skin becomes drier and more susceptible to cracking. That process is accelerated by dry air and exposure to the sun (Balin 1990; Sweet 1989).

Also as one ages, the sweat glands cease to function as well as they once did. As a result, an older person does not perspire as much as he or she did in earlier years. This also means that one becomes more likely to experience heat exhaustion (Kart, Metress, and Metress 1992). Because of this, older people should take special precautions in exposure to high temperatures and the sun. In a press release, the U.S. Department of Agriculture contended that there is no such thing as a healthy tan. In a strongly worded statement it pointed out that persons should avoid prolonged direct exposure to the sun as much as possible. It increases the probability of skin cancer as well as the wrinkling of the skin. The report recommended totally covering the skin when in sunlight. If older persons are going to expose their skin to the sun, it is beneficial to have a sunscreen lotion with a rating of at least 15, based on protection from ultraviolet B solar radiation. The Food and Drug Administration (FDA) also recommended that people should avoid tanning parlors (Sweet 1989).

Because of a reduction of blood flow to the toenails as a result of the aging process, they tend to thicken. Because of this it is especially important that older persons inspect their toenails and keep them cut. This problem of thickened toenails is one of the reasons podiatrists (foot specialists) become increasingly important to older people (DiGiovanna 1994).

Because of a loss of subcutaneous fat, and a diminished flow of blood to the skin and extremities, there is an increased danger of hypothermia for older persons. Hypothermia is a reduction of body temperature, with a danger that the body temperature will get so low that a person's life may become endangered. Recent research seems to indicate that the danger of hypothermia among older persons is much greater than previously believed. It is difficult for pathologists to determine whether death was caused by hypothermia, because if they are not particularly looking for the signs of hypothermia, they are easily missed. Studies have shown that many pathologists have missed hypothermia as a contributing factor in the death of older persons. It is important to know the symptoms of hypothermia. They include a bloated face, pale and waxy skin, trembling on one side of the body or in one arm or leg, an irregular and slowed heartbeat, slurred speech, shallow slow breath, low blood pressure, and drowsiness. Whenever an older person has any of these symptoms, immediate medical attention should be sought (Arking 1991; Kart, Metress, and Metress 1992).

Adaptations

It is important for all older persons, but especially those over 75, to keep their room temperature at least 68 degrees Fahrenheit. This may mean that a room temperature that is comfortable for older people probably will seem too hot for those who are younger. This is a special problem in nursing facilities where comfortable room temperature for the residents is usually too warm for the younger, active, working staff. (*Aging in Michigan* 1992).

It is also beneficial for the rooms of older persons to be kept moist so that their dry skin will not crack. If they cannot afford a humidifier, pans of water placed on a heat register can be used to put moisture into the air (Berliner 1986a, 1986b).

As stated earlier, older persons should take special care in the sun. It is advisable to use sunscreen to prevent sunburn. In addition, older persons can make liberal use of creams and ointments to soften their dry skin to prevent cracking. They also need adequate clothing in cold temperatures. Special precautions should be taken in cold weather to make sure that their heads are covered to prevent the loss of heat from their bodies. Most heat loss is through the top of the head (Balin 1990; Sweet 1989).

HAIR

The hair of most persons will eventually turn gray white. No one knows why specific hairs turn gray or white and others do not. It is known that within each hair follicle (tubelike organs in the skin) are cells that add color to the hair shaft. Each specific hair grows for about three years, then it rests for several months before it starts growing again. As one ages, the color-producing cells cease functioning and the hair comes out gray or white. At the present time there is no known process to prevent those cells from discontinuing their color-producing process. It is known that there is a genetic component to the action of these cells, and as a result, persons whose ancestors turned gray early in life have a higher probability of developing gray hair (DiGiovanna 1994).

THE URINARY TRACT

By the time most persons reach 70 years of age, they will have lost 50 percent of their kidney and bladder capacity. This is not a symptom of disease, but simply a result of the aging process. Most elderly persons suffer from *nocturia*, the need to get up in the night to empty their bladder. Older persons should know that having to arise in the night to go to the bathroom is not in itself an indication of any serious disease (Kart, Metress, and Metress 1992). If they have to arise more frequently than once or twice a night, however, they ought to see their physician.

A process called the *micturition reflex* changes when one ages. Micturition is the signal a person receives when he or she has to urinate. For a young person, that signal is usually sent when the bladder is about half full. As a result, young persons have some time left before they must absolutely go to the bathroom. Not so for the elderly. The signal to urinate is given when the bladder is nearly full. Obviously that means when they receive the signal, there is not much time for delay. The reduced capacity of the bladder, coupled with a delayed signal to urinate, can lead to problems of frequent urination and the need to urinate immediately (Kart, Metress, and Metress 1992; Brookbank 1990).

Some older persons also have a problem with dribbling urine or incontinence. This can be viewed as both physiologically and psychologically damaging. There is a higher probability that women will have incontinence than men, probably the result of childbirth and weakening of the bladder outlet and pelvic musculofascial attachments.

The most common type of incontinence is stress incontinence, which is brought about by a laugh, a cough, a sneeze, or lifting. In addition to stress incontinence, some older persons suffer from urge incontinence, the sudden urge to go to the bathroom without time to get there. Others suffer from overflow incontinence, a condition where the bladder becomes too full and urine leaks out (Eastman 1994).

It has been estimated that loss of bladder control affects about 10 million Americans, with the vast majority, 8 million, over the age of 60. It is also estimated that only half of those suffering from incontinence are getting any help for their problem (Eastman 1994).

Katherine Jeter, executive director of Help for Incontinent People (HIP), stated that persons should seek help if they leak small amounts of urine without feeling the need to urinate, have frequent urges to urinate, dribble urine when they cough or sneeze, or urinate during sleep. She pointed out that the causes of these problems may be major or minor, but that most people can obtain some relief (Eastman 1994).

There is an increased chance of bladder infection as a person grows older. Bladder infection is usually accompanied by a low-grade fever, fatigue, and a burning sensation during urination. When these symptoms are present, a person

should see a physician. Bladder infections can be treated rather easily (DiGiovanna 1994).

Adaptations

All types of incontinence can be helped. Current medical procedures can lessen the problems. There are at least three different types of therapies. One is the use of muscle exercises and biofeedback. Persons are taught to use their pelvic muscles that support the bladder, the muscles that can exert a closing force on the urethra, the body's urine-carrying tube. Another type of therapy is for women to monitor on a video screen the strength of their pelvic muscle contractions, while a nurse measures these contractions using a vaginal probe (Eastman 1994).

Others suffering incontinence use behavioral procedures which include being taught to urinate frequently at set times, and then slowly extending the time between urinations, thereby gaining control over feelings of urgency (Eastman 1994).

In 1993 the Federal Drug Administration (FDA) approved injections of collagen, a natural fibrous protein in animal and human bone and cartilage, as a way to treat leaking urine. This can be administered with a local anesthesia in a urologist's office. The procedure adds bulk to the urethra as a way to reduce leaking. The use of absorbent products is another method that enables some elderly persons to function normally without embarrassment. Some need surgery to correct their conditions. Other older persons can be helped by regulating fluid intake or by the use of certain prescription drugs (Kart, Metress, and Metress 1992).

It is usually wise for older persons to have little or no liquid before long-distance trips or before going to bed. Anyone planning tours, for example, for older people should plan frequent rest stops.

Older persons with a problem of dribbling (urinary incontinence) are wise to drink cranberry juice, which reduces the odor associated with this condition. Those with a continuing low-grade fever should also seek medical attention, because this is often a symptom of urinary infection, usually treatable with antibiotics.

The age-related changes associated with the urinary tract, and many of the problems they create, can usually be treated effectively if older persons are aware of the changes and discuss them with their physicians.

BONES AND MUSCLES

As people grow older, they have a tendency to get somewhat shorter. Vertebrae tend to lose mass, and muscles tend to shrink (DiGiovanni 1994). When one sees a 6-foot-3-inch 80-year-old, one can be assured that this person was indeed a tall person in his younger years. Older people also tend to lose some fine and gross muscle coordination. Reflexes tend to be lower. There are not going to be 80-year-olds competing in the 100-yard dash with 18-year-olds. Neither are we going to have 70-year-olds competing with 18-year-olds in the high jump or in the pole vault. However, they can compete with people who are in their same age bracket (DiGiovanna 1994).

Osteoporosis

As people age they become more susceptible to osteoporosis (brittle bones). One of the major reasons for this is loss of calcium, which causes bones to lose density and become brittle. This is especially true of postmenopausal women. Most of the over 20 million cases of osteoporosis in the United States occur in women. Women are more susceptible because they have smaller bones, and changes after menopause—the loss of estrogen, for example—reduce bone mass. After menopause, women have a significant reduction in the production of estrogen. Estrogen assists in the processing of calcium into the bones. With this loss of estrogen the bones tend to lose their density (Kart, Metress, and Metress 1992).

In addition, many persons do not get enough calcium in their diet. Grandchildren should probably ask their grandmothers if they have had their milk today. It is very important that older persons,

if they do not drink milk, obtain calcium in some other way. Using a calcium supplement, though, is probably inferior to the use of estrogen in decreasing the probability of developing osteoporosis among postmenopausal women. The calcium is most needed by women during their teens and twenties (*Johns Hopkins Medical Letter* 1994a; 1994b) when the bones are in a formative stage. In addition, older women do not absorb calcium very well from supplements. It is important for postmenopausal women to have an adequate amount of vitamin D, since vitamin D aids in the absorption of calcium. However, too much vitamin D can be toxic (Hausman 1985; Resnick and Greenspan 1989). Bones retain their density better if people exercise (Sinaki 1989). Physical exercise increases the forces that pull the muscles on the bone. Many older persons stop exercising, and as a result, their bones tend to lose density.

Some older women develop a "widow's hump," a curvature in their spine that makes them round shouldered. This occurs because their vertebrae lose density because of osteoporosis, and in that process, the spine begins to bend, giving the obvious stooping of their shoulders and spine. Women who consume enough calcium and get regular exercise during adolescence have greater bone strength than those who do not, thereby reducing the probability of "widow's hump" developing (Hampton 1991; DiGiovanna 1994).

In addition, older persons become much more susceptible to broken bones. In people with osteoporosis, the slightest fall can bring about a broken hip or arm. A hip fracture is not a minor problem; it is estimated that about 25 percent of persons with a hip fracture end up in long-term care facilities. Over 10 percent of elderly persons with a hip fracture die (Cummings and Black 1986; Magaziner et al. 1989; Owen et al. 1980). Given the rapid growth of the oldest-old population in contemporary America, the problems associated with hip fractures will increase greatly. There is now evidence that indicates that some older people fall because their hips break, not that their hips break because they fall. This also means that bedridden elderly persons have to be handled very carefully, or bones may be broken just by moving them from one position to another (Magaziner et al. 1989).

Adaptations

Older persons need to have adequate calcium intake. If they do not get enough calcium through their diet, they can take calcium supplements. For reasons discussed above, it might be just as important for a grandmother as for her granddaughter to have a glass of milk each day (Kart, Metress, and Metress 1992).

Postmenopausal women can take estrogen placement therapy. It is recommended that older women discuss the advisability of taking estrogen with their physicians. Some have argued that estrogen therapy increases the risk of cancer. However, that risk seems to be exaggerated. Besides, at the present time, estrogen therapy is available in dosages much smaller than it was in the past. In addition, some have argued that the risk of a broken hip is a greater danger than the risk of developing cancer from estrogen replacement therapy. Osteoporosis is a very serious problem, especially among older women. It must be combatted by a variety of means, and estrogen replacement therapy is one approach (DiGiovanna 1994).

The value of an exercise program focusing on weight training with proper medical supervision has become recognized as an effective means to increase bone density.

Arthritis

As people grow older, there is an increased probability that they will develop some form of arthritis. As a result, older persons tend to have more joint and muscle pain. Arthritis is a disease that has been found in ancient skeletons, including Neanderthals from 40,000 years ago. There are over a hundred types of arthritis, but the two major types of arthritis are osteoarthritis and rheumatoid arthritis (Kart, Metress, and Metress 1992).

Osteoarthritis Osteoarthritis is a common type of arthritis which is found in many older persons. It is also referred to as degenerative joint disease. Osteoarthritis (OSA) affects about 24 million Americans, becoming more common in people over the age of 45. It results in the breakdown of joint tissue, producing pain and stiffness in the joints. It can affect any joint, but is most frequently found in the knees, hips, feet, and spine. Symptoms usually develop slowly over time and may be the result of injury, obesity, joint overuse, or other conditions. Heredity is also often a factor in osteoarthritis (DiGiovanna 1992). As cartilage is lost in the joint, the rough underlying bone surface can produce stiffness and pain in the joints. Eventually the joints may become thick, painful, and difficult to move. Osteoarthritis can come from repetitive motions or from injuries from work or athletics. The tendency toward osteoarthritis is inherited. Osteoarthritis can occur in the finger joints, but for most persons, it is found in the larger joints such as the spine, knees, hips, and neck. In the beginning, joint movement may be stiff and painful. As the disease progresses there may even be pain when the joint is not being used. (Altman 1990; Altman and Gray 1985; Kart, Metress, and Metress 1992).

Rheumatoid Arthritis The other major type of arthritis is rheumatoid arthritis (RA). Rheumatoid arthritis is a more serious form of arthritis that is found in almost 2 million Americans. In RA the immune system turns against its own body parts, especially the joints. There usually is swelling, stiffness, tenderness, and pain in the joints. In addition, the person often suffers from fatigue (Hampton 1991). Rheumatoid arthritis is not confined to the joints, but is systemic, meaning that other symptoms such as fatigue, fever, and weight loss frequently are part of the disease. Usually there are swollen, inflamed, painful joints, which unpredictably may involve the hands, knees, elbows, shoulders, and hips (Kart, Metress, and Metress 1992).

There is no consensus as to the cause of rheumatoid arthritis, although it is generally recognized to be some type of problem with the immune system. As a result, many experts see it as an autoimmune disease in which antibodies attack a person's own tissue.

Adaptations

More and more physicians specializing in arthritic conditions are available for people who suffer from the various forms of this disease.

Treatment programs for both forms of arthritis usually involve some combination of exercise, rest, and medication. Aspirin is frequently used as a pain reliever and as an anti-inflammatory, especially in cases of RA. Hot and cold treatments are often used to relax muscles and to relieve joint pain. Exercise is used to maintain strength and coordination and to prevent deformities. A balance between rest and a programmed exercise plan is usually prescribed (Csuka and Goodwin 1990). In the most severe cases, surgery is used to replace hips, fingers, knees, elbows, and other joints (Kart, Metress, and Metress 1992).

The following steps can be helpful to an arthritis sufferer:

1. Ask the doctor about proper regular exercises to strengthen muscles and provide support for the joints.
2. Inquire about proper support devices for the joints.
3. Take rest as needed.
4. Use devices to make it easier to open jars, use zippers, and manipulate buttons.
5. Sleep on an adequately firm mattress.
6. Lose weight, if overweight, to reduce the stress on joints.
7. Obtain proper pain-reducing medications from a physician.

THE HEART

Most older people have some degree of deterioration of the heart as they grow older. As fatty plaques develop in the main arteries, they decrease the flow of blood (*Johns Hopkins Medical Letter* 1994a). As this increases, *angina pectoris* may occur. This pain in the area of the breastbone is caused by inadequate oxygen to the heart. Pain may also occur in the neck, shoulders, left arm, and even on the sides of the face. Because it is caused by inadequate blood supply to the heart, angina can be triggered by physical exertion or emotional stress which requires more blood to the heart. Some persons do not exercise enough to be aware of developing anginal problems. Because they do not exercise, they have no pain and no warning of a heart problem until a significant attack occurs (Gerstenblith and Lakatta 1990). If the supply of blood to the heart is reduced, a *myocardial infarction* (heart attack) may take place. The extent and seriousness of a myocardial infarction depends on the amount of heart tissue involved (Kart, Metress and Metress, 1992). If a coronary artery is suddenly blocked by a blood clot, a *coronary thrombosis* (a heart attack caused by a lack of blood and oxygen going to the heart because of a blockage of the artery) takes place. As a person ages, the indications of myocardial infarction decrease because chest pain is less likely to be present with advancing age (MacDonald 1984; Morley and Reese 1989). Heart disease is the fourth leading chronic disease in persons between the ages of 45 and 64, the second leading chronic disease in persons aged 65 and older, and the major cause of change in lifestyle and of disability in persons 65 and older. It is also the leading cause of death for persons 65 and older. Because of knowledge developed in the last several decades, the death rate due to heart disease is decreasing.

Major Causes of Heart Disease

There are numerous factors that increase the probability of heart disease (DiGiovanna 1994). They include the following:

Smoking Nicotine increases blood pressure and seems to increase substances in the blood that increase the probability that plaques will develop in the arteries. These conditions are significantly increased for women who are taking birth control pills. The combination of smoking and the use of birth control pills increases the probability of heart attacks 18-fold (DiGiovanna 1994).

The American Heart Association (1990) estimated that heavy smokers have an increased risk (two to four times) of a sudden death (within an hour of a heart attack) over nonsmokers. The majority of women who died suddenly from coronary disease were heavy smokers, using twenty or more cigarettes a day (Kart, Metress, and Metress 1992). Cigarette smoke causes injury to the arterial tissue, increasing the atherosclerotic process (Bierman 1990).

High Blood Pressure   High blood pressure seems to increase the probability that repeated minor injuries will occur to the arteries. As the arteries attempt to repair the damage, they form plaques and scar tissue. High blood pressure also makes the heart pump harder, increasing the amount of oxygen it needs, which eventually weakens the heart. Blood pressure tends to increase with age, along with its negative impact on the arteries (DiGiovanna 1994). Research based on the Baltimore Longitudinal Study of Aging (BLSA) has shown that systolic blood pressure can increase up to 25 percent in persons from their twenties to their mid seventies (Gunby 1994).

High Blood LDLs   Blood contains a variety of lipoprotein molecules. Lipoproteins containing mostly cholesterol are called low-density lipoproteins (LDLs). When these are in high concentrations, the cholesterol can accumulate in the walls of the arteries, which contributes to the formation of plaques. This can be reduced if the "good" lipoproteins (HDLs) increase. However, as some persons age, they experience an increase in LDLs and a decrease in HDLs. (DiGiovanna 1994).

Diet seems to play an important role in this process. Foods high in increasing the risk of

forming LDLs are red meats (especially beef), egg yolks, full-fat dairy products, solid shortening, and tropical oils such as palm and coconut oil.

Physical Inactivity   People who have little physical activity require less blood flow, so the heart gets less exercise. Because the heart is a muscle, lack of exercise results in less strength. The heart that is in a weakened condition because of a lack of exercise is not prepared for a sudden jolt of strenuous activity.

Obesity   Being overweight weakens the heart both because the heart is being overworked, and it tends to be invaded by fat. Furthermore, obesity increases the risk of high blood pressure, diabetes, and high levels of blood cholesterol (LDLs) (DiGiovanna 1994).

Stress   Stress in some persons increases periods of significantly elevated blood pressure, which increases the probability that injury will occur to the arteries. In addition, the heart must pump harder (DiGiovanna, 1994).

Menopause   Estrogen is protective of the heart, and as women go through menopause and have a marked reduction in the production of estrogen, protection for the heart is decreased (DiGiovanna 1994).

Personality   There is a continuing debate about the effects of personality on physical functioning. There is some evidence indicating that angry and competitive people, as well as those who are perfectionists, have an increased probability of getting heart attacks. This "Type A" personality also tends to be impatient, tries to do several things at the same time, shows hostility toward others, and usually feels that there is insufficient time to accomplish everything that needs to be done (Rybash, Roodin, and Santrock 1991). Booth-Kewley and Friedman, however, pointed out that the traditional view of Type A personalities does not adequately address the reasons why people get heart attacks:

> The picture of the coronary-prone personality emerging from this review does not appear to be that of the workaholic, hurried, impatient individual, which is probably the image most frequently associated with coronary proneness. Rather, the true picture seems to be one of a person with one or more negative emotions: perhaps someone who is depressed, aggressively competitive, easily frustrated, anxious, (or) angry . . . (Booth-Kewley and Friedman 1987: 358).

Diabetes   Diabetes affects glucose levels and the maintenance and repair of arterial walls. In this process the disease increases the probability of the formation of plaques. The probability of developing diabetes increases as people grow older. It is important to be aware of the symptoms of diabetes: unusual weight gain or loss, slower healing of cuts, excessive formation and elimination of urine, and frequently excessive thirst (DiGiovanna 1994).

Family History   Persons who come from families with histories of atherosclerosis have probably inherited unidentified genes that increase the risk of developing atherosclerosis. Atherosclerosis is a disease which produces weak scarlike material in the walls of the arteries. These genes then interact with the factors mentioned above. To explain this further, DiGiovanna:

> Having two or more risk factors drastically boosts one's chances of developing coronary atherosclerosis because the detrimental effects of each risk factor are multiplied by the effects of the other. For example, smoking almost doubles the risk. Having high blood pressure multiples the risk four times. A person who smokes and has high blood pressure has an eight fold greater risk. Adding high blood lipoproteins, which increases the risk threefold, increases the total risk to 24-fold. Therefore, reducing or eliminating even one risk factor can cause a manyfold decrease in the risk of developing coronary artery disease (DiGiovanna 1994: 58).

Aging by itself also increases the probability of heart disease, because there is arterial hardening as a result of the aging process. In addition, there is an increase in the heart's demand for oxygen because the heart becomes less efficient. Furthermore, aging increases the probability of diabetes and higher LDLs. The aging process also increases the additive effects of all of the factors listed above (Fleg 1986).

Adaptations

Regular physical activity strengthens the heart, decreases blood pressure, helps bring a better ratio of LDLs to HDLs and decreases body weight. A lack of physical activity increases the probability of higher blood pressure and promotes a less desirable ratio of LDS to HDLs. High alcohol consumption may also increase LDLs. Recent evidence seems to indicate that low consumption of alcohol may reduce LDLs, while increasing HDLs (DiGiovanna 1994).

Because postmenopausal women lose the protection of estrogen for their hearts, some take estrogen replacement. However, this should be done only with the continuing direction and supervision of a physician (DiGiovanna 1994).

Since diabetes increases the probability of developing heart disease, it is important to be aware of the symptoms of diabetes: unusual weight gain or loss, slower healing of cuts, excessive formation and elimination of urine, and at times, excessive thirst (DiGiovanna 1994).

Diet and other lifestyle components are major factors in preventing as well as recovering from heart diseases and other diseases.

THE RESPIRATORY SYSTEM

The respiratory system brings oxygen from the air into the blood flowing through the lungs. The circulatory system then takes the oxygen throughout the body. Body cells need oxygen to obtain energy from nutrients. The carbon dioxide in the body, a waste product, is also transported by the circulatory system into the lungs and then expelled (DiGiovanna 1994).

The respiratory system of an older person typically provides adequate service in all but the most physically-demanding situations (DiGiovanna 1994). With aging, however, changes occur that reduce to some extent the capacity of the respiratory system. Respiratory muscles also become weaker. This is especially true if physical exercise is decreased as a person grows older. As a person ages and muscles lose their elasticity and strength, the maximum pressure that the muscles can produce decreases resulting in a decreased rate of airflow (Kart, Metress, and Metress 1992).

Age also changes the bones, cartilage, and joints of the chest, reducing a person's ability to produce large pressure changes in the chest cavity. The cartilage attaching the ribs to the sternum becomes more calcified and stiff, and the ribs become less elastic. In addition, aging affects the positions of the bones of the chest. With aging, the chest becomes deeper from front to back, making deep inhalation more difficult. This, along with other changes, decreases the rate of airflow into the system, making ventilation more difficult and resulting in more difficult breathing. All of this can lead to a decreased amount of oxygen and an increased amount of carbon dioxide in the blood. Aging also affects the volume of air that can be moved, and reduces the maximum respiratory rate (breaths per minute) (DiGiovanna 1994).

As these changes take place, the maximum level at which a person can perform physical activities declines. An older person who starts very vigorous activity may become exhausted more quickly. Usually these age-related changes do not affect daily living. Unless there is some injury or disease, respiratory functioning into old age should be adequate for normal activities.

The changes in the respiratory system that have been described are the result of normal aging processes. If an older person is a smoker, serious life-inhibiting and life-threatening diseases can develop such as emphysema and lung cancer along with a wide range of other illnesses that have been linked to smoking.

Adaptations

There is no doubt that smoking and prolonged physical inactivity can deteriorate the respiratory process. The evidence indicates, though, that respiratory functioning can be regained by stopping smoking and physical activity. For both heart and respiratory functioning, consistent exercise is very beneficial (Porterfield and St. Pierre, 1992).

SLEEP

Differences in the sleep process tend to occur as part of the aging process. People often need more time to fall asleep as they grow older. They tend to sleep more lightly and awaken more quickly in response to noises than do younger persons. Once awake, older persons often find it harder to get back to sleep. There are many reasons for this: There is an increased probability of a need to urinate during the night as a person ages. Older persons also tend to have more circulatory problems and rhythmic leg movements during sleep. They may suffer more pain due to arthritic or other medical problems. All of these factors tend to inhibit sleep and make people more aware of external sounds. Men seem to suffer more from awakenings than do women (DiGiovanna 1994).

Sleep Disorders

Stone (1993), in her investigation of sleep disorders and the aging process, concluded that the three most common sleep disorders for older people are insomnia, sleep apnea, and leg movement. Insomnia, she wrote, is the most common sleep problem and probably affects up to 60 percent of the older population. It occurs when a person has trouble falling asleep, or maintaining sleep. Insomnia's prevalence in the older population has a physiological basis: the flattening of the body temperature curve. She pointed out that normal body temperatures decrease from a high at around 6:00 P.M. to a low between midnight and 6:00 A.M., then gradually rise throughout the day. Older people tend to have body temperatures that remain somewhat level. Without highs and lows, the body does not recognize when it is time to sleep.

Sleep apnea—struggling to breathe, shortness of breath, gasping, snorting, and snoring—tends to restrict adequate oxygen intake. Apnea is more common among the elderly than among younger persons, although it can be found in persons of any age. A lack of oxygen can lead to stress on the heart and brain as well as hypertension. It is considered a risk factor for stroke. Some persons require surgery to reduce the problem, while others can benefit from weight loss or sleeping on their sides rather than on their backs.

Movement disorders, typically periodic leg movements during sleep, can involve 800 movements a night and cause fragmented sleep. Stone (1993) estimated that up to 40 percent of older people suffer from some type of periodic leg movement problems.

Older persons spend more time in light sleep, the least restful of the various stages of sleep. There is a decrease in the amount of time they spend in rapid eye movement (REM) sleep, the most restful stage of sleep (DiGiovanna 1994).

Adaptations

It is not clear how many of the changes in sleep result from the normal aging process or from other factors such as a lack of exercise, napping during the daytime, medications, or disease. It is not a part of normal aging for older persons to be sleepy and feel the need to sleep during the day (Porterfield and St. Pierre 1992). It is important for older people to maintain daytime activities with some exposure to fresh air if possible. In addition, good sleep patterns include keeping a regular schedule of going to bed and rising.

MENOPAUSE

On the average, ovulation and the menstrual cycle cease at about age 50. The normal age at which this occurs ranges from 45 to 55 years.

There is a measurable reduction in estrogen over the two to five years following the last menstrual cycle (Hampton 1991; DiGiovanna 1994; Kart, Metress, and Metress 1992).

Possible Physical Effects of Menopause

The reduction of estrogen increases the probability of osteoporosis, strokes, hypertension, and coronary disease. In addition, breasts begin to lose support, vaginal walls become thinner, and vaginal dryness begins to occur (Hampton 1991; DiGiovanna 1994; Kart, Metress, and Metress 1992).

During menopause some women may experience acute symptoms such as flushes (hot flashes). With flushes come sensation of heat, and for some considerable sweating. Up to three-fourths of women experience flushes and have them for at least a year. A small percentage, 5 percent, have them for five years or more. The duration of flushes varies from woman to woman, but an average of four minutes has been reported. Some women report a sense of pressure in the head that increases until the flush has occurred. Some women have symptoms of vertigo (dizziness) and fatigue. Many will fan themselves during flushes, seek fresh air, remove blankets if in bed, or remove outer clothing. Heart rhythm and blood pressure tend to be unchanged during flushes, but heart rate may increase up to 20 percent above the resting rate (Hampton 1992; DiGiovanna 1994; Kart, Metress, and Metress 1992).

Some other secondary effects of menopause are an increase in facial hair, and a decrease in axillary and pubic hair (DiGiovanna 1994).

Menopause: A Normal Passage

The five-year study by the University of Pittsburgh and the Massachusetts Women's Health Study tracked 2,500 women for six years and found that most take menopause in stride, without any significant psychological problems. The evidence was that they either felt neutral or relieved to have finished menstruating. They did not have negative mental health consequences. Only about 10 percent experienced depression, but most of that was caused not by physiological changes, but by external stresses such as financial, job, or family pressures (Crowley 1994).

There have always been significant cultural differences in how women react to the physiological changes that bring an end to child-bearing. Germaine Greer (1993), in her book *The Change: Women, Aging, and Menopause*, viewed menopause as a significant event and preferred to use the term *climacteric*, from the Greek word meaning critical period. She believed that women going through the climacteric should really go through a ritual indicating that another phase in their life is beginning, a phase which can produce a more profound sense of the meaning of life.

Gail Sheehy (1992), in her book *The Silent Passage: Menopause*, attempted to "demystify" menopause and wrote about "the passage" which brings about a new phase of energy and maturity for many women. This book attempted to answer the many questions that women have about menopause. Most studies find the overwhelming majority of American women pass through menopause without any major problems.

The list of books on menopause, scientific and popular, is almost endless, but as Crowley (1994) indicated, the National Institutes of Health (NIH) is still attempting to determine the physiological implications of menopause, such as whether middle-aged spread, memory lapses, and joint pain are the result of menopause, aging, or other factors.

Estrogen Replacement Therapy

Many post-menopausal changes can be slowed, stopped, or reversed by estrogen replacement therapy (ERT). ERT can reduce or eliminate hot flashes and restore LDL and HDL levels (thereby lowering the risk of atherosclerosis), reduce the probability of osteoporosis, and increase vaginal lubrication (DiGiovanna 1994; Hampton 1991).

However, there are risks with ERT, depending primarily on the woman's genetic heritage. It can increase the probability of breast cancer, gall-

bladder disease, endometrial cancer, and blood clots. Because of this, it is not recommended for women with risk factors of reproductive system cancers, high blood pressure, blood clots, thrombosis formation, or endometriosis. Women who are heavy smokers should not use ERT. These risks can be reduced by using small dosages of estrogen and administering low levels of progestins (DiGiovanna 1994).

ERT can relieve serious consequences of low levels of estrogen in postmenopausal women. Although it does increase certain risks, it reduces others. ERT should be used under close medical supervision. Although much more research needs to be done, ERT does seem to protect women from coronary heart disease (Stampfer et al. 1991).

Most women do not use ERT. Jane Brody (1993) pointed out that only one in seven postmenopausal women decide to take ERT. She cited research that indicated that some find ERT sets off a cycle of irregular bleeding. Others fear the increased risk of developing breast or uterine cancer, while still others find that ERT with progestin has side effects that include bloating, depression, and irritability. However, heart disease is a far more common killer of postmenopausal women than is breast or uterine cancer, and ERT does cut the risk of a fatal heart attack by half.

LIFESTYLE AND PHYSICAL CHANGES

Personal choices are directly related to a person's physical and psychological well-being. These choices not only increase or decrease one's life expectancy, but they also relate to a person's quality of life. Rosenfield, after reviewing the literature about the aging process, stated:

> exercise can hold off many of the functional failings of aging [such as] the loss of bone strength and muscle mass, for example. Overall energy, stamina, agility, aerobic and cardiac capacity remain higher in exercisers than in the sedentary; the same advantage seems to hold for health levels of blood pressure, sugar, and cholesterol, not to mention mental outlook. Just about every study . . . shows

that hardy oldsters . . . remain physically active all their lives . . . (Rosenfield 1986: 68).

Porterfield and St. Pierre stated that in regard to a zest for life and a feeling of planning for the future,

> many experts believe that if you feel good about yourself, especially about your health, you are likely to live longer than someone who is pessimistic. A recent study of 100-year-olds by the National Institute of Aging found that every one of them shared positive attitudes toward life. (Porterfield and St. Pierre 1992: 115).

The following lifestyle choices appear to be key components in maintaining or restoring good health in the later years:

Exercise   As much as possible, older persons need to have a consistent program of exercise because it:

- Improves the cardiovascular system
- Reduces blood pressure
- Reduces the risk of heart attack
- Helps one sleep longer and better
- Reduces stress and nervous tension
- Improves the respiratory system
- Increases blood volume
- Reduces body fat
- Promotes feelings of well-being
- Improves posture
- Promotes joint mobility

Many apparent symptoms of aging are not caused by aging but by a lack of exercise. Persons at all ages, including those in their nineties, can benefit from consistent exercise. Data collected by Tufts University and other research centers have indicated that persons, regardless of age, can increase the size of their muscles, increase stamina, and increase joint mobility by a systematic program of physical training. The deterioration that is seen in some older persons is really not the result of aging but of lifestyle. Almost everyone knows of two 75-year-olds where one is deteriorated, and acts very old, while the other is vibrant

and physically vigorous. Lifestyle is often a major contributing factor to these differences. A major part of a healthy lifestyle is exercise. The American Association for the Advancement of Science has claimed that exercise seems to reduce the probability of breast and uterine cancer for women as well as the probability of diabetes. Physically active women produce a less potent form of estrogen, and as a result, tumors that depend on that hormone do not develop as well. Because physically-active women have less body fat, they reduce the probability of diabetes caused by excess weight (Rosenfeld 1986; Porterfield and St. Pierre 1992). A consistent program of exercise becomes an issue of self-discipline and motivation. It is an individual, conscious choice.

Smoking   Smoking is one of the most destructive habits a person can have. It increases the probability of heart attack, lung cancer, and emphysema among other dangerous health conditions. It has been argued that the use of nicotine is a slow form of suicide. Some have suggested that the tax on all forms of nicotine should be increased with the revenue used for medical insurance. Persons who use nicotine will generally have markedly higher medical costs. It has been contended that a tripling of the tax for the recreational use of nicotine is not unreasonable (Porterfield and St. Pierre 1992).

Alcohol Use   The excessive use of alcohol also increases the cost of medical care. Excessive use of alcohol increases the probability of cirrhosis of the liver, cardiovascular disease, accidents, senile dementia, and cancer. Again, some have argued that those who make choices that increase the probability that they will develop pathological conditions ought to be forced to pay for those choices by an increased tax on the substances that cause these diseases.

Overeating   Overeating is physically destructive. It increases the probability of high blood pressure, cardiovascular problems, respiratory difficulties, and leads to a negative image. It increases the probability of losing mobility, reduces a person's energy level, and saps one's ability to perform tasks. Appropriate nutrition is not only essential for physical well-being, but it is also essential for one's psychological well-being (Porterfield and St. Pierre 1992).

The relationship between psychological factors and physiological functioning is complex and there is a need for much more research. However, the evidence is clear that one's decisions regarding exercise, smoking, eating habits, and alcohol use clearly relate to one's physiological functioning and longevity.

PHYSICAL CHANGES AND FEELINGS OF WELL-BEING

Physical well-being, one's self-image, and feelings of contentment and happiness become a complex mixture of one's actual physical condition and one's attitude toward those physical feelings. Some persons have a body preoccupation in which they exaggerate every ache and pain. They tend to describe every signal of physical change in great detail. They become incapacitated very quickly and seem to "groove" on their symptoms. Others can rise above their troubles and, although in great pain and suffering some real inconveniences, tend to ignore their pain, do not discuss their suffering, and continue on their merry way through life. By tending to have an interest in others, in life around them, and in the daily excitement of another day of life, they continue to function with much better attitudes than those who are preoccupied with their bodies. Keeping active increases opportunities for maintaining personal independence (Cavanaugh 1993).

SUMMARY

Most people experience some age-related changes in the eye. The most universal change is presbyopia. Presbyopia is the inability of the eye to adapt to different distances. After the age of 40 most people will need some assistance with their vision, particularly close vision. Presbyopia also makes it difficult for the aging eye to adjust to changes in light and glare. As a person grows older, there is also an increased probability of developing diseases of the eye such as cataracts, a clouding of the lens of the eye. Some older persons develop glaucoma, the result of increased pressure in the eye. This causes the loss of peripheral vision, eventually resulting in tunnel vision or complete loss of sight. Macular degeneration is another eye disorder that affects some older people. It is a breakdown of the macula, the central part of the retina. As the macula deteriorates, central vision is lost. Nearly all persons with diabetes have a form of retina damage if they have been insulin-dependent for 15 years or more. Although there are a number of eye diseases older people can contract, most see well enough to carry out their normal daily activities.

As people grow older, a condition known as presbycusis can occur which affects their hearing. Presbycusis refers to hearing loss in which the higher sound frequencies usually are lost first. Hearing loss can be brought about by environmental noise, such as loud rock concerts, walkmans turned too high, industrial noises, or the pounding of construction jackhammers. The loss may be directly traceable to nerve-cell damage in the inner ear, arthritic bones in the inner ear, or to a buildup of wax in the ear canal. Most older persons with hearing loss can be helped either by surgery or by the use of hearing aids.

The skin has a tendency to wrinkle with age. Smoking and exposure to the sun increase the probability of wrinkled skin. As one ages, the skin tends to become drier, increasing the probability of cracks in the skin which can lead to infection. Aging also increases the probability of hypothermia, a lowering of body temperature, because of the increased loss of heat through the aging skin.

There are typically significant urinary changes with aging. By about the age of 70, close to 50 percent of kidney and bladder function is lost. It is not unusual for older persons to have to get up to urinate during the night. Incontinence also becomes a problem for many older persons. It is estimated that about 8 million older persons may suffer from some type of incontinence, but significant assistance is available for persons with this condition.

Osteoporosis, or brittle bones, increases as people grow older. Small boned, postmenopausal women are especially vulnerable to osteoporosis. Some older women develop a "widow's hump," a curvature of the spine that makes them round-shouldered. Osteoporosis is a real danger to older persons because it can result in broken bones, in particular hip fractures.

Cardiovascular problems can increase with aging. Heart attacks may be the result of athero-sclerosis, plaques building up in the arterial channels, or coronary thrombosis, caused by a blood clot. Smoking, hypertension, high blood LDLs, physical inactivity, obesity, stress, and a family history of heart disease are all heart disease risk factors.

As one ages, the respiratory muscles, and thus the whole respiratory system, become weaker. In addition, the bones, cartilage, and joints of the chest all have a tendency to become calcified and stiff with the aging process.

As a person grows older, there is a tendency to sleep lightly. When awakened, it is usually more difficult getting back to sleep.

On the average, the ovulation and menstrual cycles for women cease at about age 50. There is a measurable reduction in a woman's production of estrogen with menopause. There can be some negative reactions to decreased estrogen. Estrogen replacement therapy (ERT) can slow or reverse some of these reactions, but it may cause problems. It is important that women use ERT only with the advice and monitoring of a physician.

The physical changes of the aging process are significantly impacted by a person's lifestyle choices. Smoking, excessive use of alcohol, high intake of fatty foods, lack of exercise, and over-exposure to the sun are all physically debilitating.

If a person eats moderately, avoids smoking and the excessive use of alcohol, exercises, and tries to keep a positive mental attitude, he or she measurably increases the likelihood of growing older with good health and vigor.

REFERENCES

Aging in Michigan. 1992. Prevent Hypothermia, Stay Warm. (January/February) 20(1): 1–2.

American Association of Retired Persons. 1993. *Report on Hearing Aids: User Perspectives and Concerns.* Washington, DC: AARP.

Altman, R. 1990. Osteoarthritis. *Postgraduate Medicine,* 87: 66–78.

Altman, R., and Gray, R. 1985. Inflammation in Osteoarthritis. *Clinics in Rheumatic Diseases,* 11: 353–365.

American Heart Association. 1990. *Heart Facts— 1990.* Dallas: National Center.

Arey, L., Tremaine, M., and Monzingo, F. 1935. The Numerical and Topographical Relations of Taste Buds to Human Circumvallate Papillae Throughout the Life Span. *Anatomical Record,* 64: 9–251.

Arking, R. 1991. *Biology of Aging: Observations and Principles.* Englewood Cliffs, NJ: Prentice Hall.

Balin, A. 1990. Aging of Human Skin. In W. Hazzard, R. Andres, E. Bierman, and J. Blass (eds.), *Principles of Geriatric Medicine and Gerontology.* New York: McGraw-Hill.

Bender, B., and Caranasos, G. 1989. *Geriatric Medicine.* Philadelphia: W. B. Saunders.

Berliner, H. 1986a. Aging Skin. *American Journal of Nursing,* (October): 1138–1142.

Berliner, H. 1986b. Aging Skin, Part Two. *American Journal of Nursing,* (November): 1259–1261.

Bierman, E. 1990. Aging and Atherosclerosis. In W. Hazzard, R. Andres, E. Bierman, and J. Blass (eds.), *Principles of Geriatric Medicine and Gerontology.* New York: McGraw-Hill.

Bittles, A.H., and Collins, K.J. (eds.), 1986. *The Biology of Human Aging.* Cambridge, MA: Cambridge University.

Bradley, R.M. 1988. Effects of Aging on the Anatomy and Neurophysiology of Taste, *Gerodontics,* 4: 244–248.

Brookbank, J.W. 1990. *The Biology of Aging.* New York: Harper & Row.

Booth-Kewley, S., and Friedman, H. 1987. Psychological Predictors of Heart Disease: A Quantitative Review. *Psychological Bulletin*, 101: 343–362.

Brody, J. 1993. Personal Health. *The New York Times*, (December 8): B9.

Cavanaugh, S.L. 1993. *Adult Development and Aging*. Pacific Grove, CA: Brooks/Cole.

Charness, N. 1985. *Aging and Human Performance*. New York: Wiley.

Cowart, B.J. 1989. Relationships Between Taste and Smell Across the Life Span. In C. Murphy, W.S. Cain, and D.M. Hegsted (eds.), Nutrition and the Chemical Senses in Aging: Recent Advances and Current Research Needs. *Annals of the New York Academy of Sciences*, 561: 39–55.

Crowley, S.L. 1994. Much Ado About Menopause. *NRTA Bulletin*, (May). 35(5): 2, 7.

Csuka, M., and Goodwin, J. 1990. Rheumatoid Arthritis. In W. Hazzard, R. Andres, E. Bierman, and J. Blass (eds.), *Principles of Geriatric Medicine and Gerontology*. New York: McGraw-Hill.

Cummings, S., Black, D., and Rubin, S. 1985. Epidemiology of Osteoporosis and Osteoporotic Fractures. *Epidemiology Review*, 7: 178–208.

Darbyshire, J. 1984. The Hearing Loss Epidemic: A Challenge to Gerontology. *Research on Aging*, 6: 384–394.

DiGiovanna, A.G. 1994. *Human Aging: Biological Perspectives*. New York: McGraw Hill.

Eastman, P. 1994. A Problem No One Wants to Talk About. *NRTA Bulletin*, (July/August) 35(7): 16–17.

Ferris, F. III, Fine, S., and Hyman, L. 1984. Age-Related Macular Degeneration and Blindness Due to Neovascular Maculopathy. *Archives of Ophthalmology*, 102: 1640–1642.

Fenske, N.A., and Conrad, C.B. 1988. Aging Skin. *American Family Physician*, 37(2): 219–230.

Finch, C.E., and Schneider, E.L. (eds.), 1985. *Handbook of the Biology of Aging*. New York: Van Nostrand Reinhold.

Fleg, J. 1986. The Aging Heart. In Wenger, N.K., Furberg, C.D., and Pitt, E. (eds.), *Coronary Heart Disease in the Elderly*. New York: Elsevier, pp. 253–273.

Gerstenblith, G., and Lakatta, E. 1990. Disorders of the Heart. In W. Hazzard, R. Andres, E. Bierman, and J. Blass (eds.), *Principles of Geriatric Medicine and Gerontology*. New York: McGraw-Hill.

Gilchrist, B. 1982. Skin. In J. Rowe and R. Besdine (eds.), *Health and Disease in Old Age*. Boston: Little, Brown.

Greer, G. 1993. *The Change: Women, Aging and the Menopause*. New York: Alfred A. Knopf.

Gunby, P. 1994. Graying of America Stimulates More Research on Aging-Associated Factors. *Journal of the American Medical Association*, (November) 272(20): 1561–1566.

Guralink, J.M., LaCroix, A.Z., Everett, D.F., and Kovar, G. 1989. *Aging in the Eighties: The Prevalence of Comorbidity and Its Association with Disability, Advance Data*, Number 170 (May 26). National Center for Health Statistics.

Hampton, J.K., Jr. 1991. *The Biology of Human Aging*. Dubuque, IA: W. C. Brown Publisher.

Hausman, P. 1985. *The Calcium Bible*. New York: Warner Books.

Humphrey, C., Herbst, K., and Faurqui, S. 1981. Some Characteristics of the Hearing-Impaired Elderly Who Do Not Present Themselves for Rehabilitation. *British Journal of Audiology*, 15: 25–30.

Hyman, L. 1987. Epidemiology of Eye Disease in the Elderly. *Eye*, 1: 330–341.

Johns Hopkins Medical Letter. 1990. Macular Degeneration: Early Detection May Save Your Sight, (April) 29(3): 2–3.

Johns Hopkins Medical Letter. 1994a. Health after 50. Calcium: Maximizing Its Benefits, (February) 5(12): 4–5.

Johns Hopkins Medical Letter. 1994b. Should You Take Estrogen to Prevent Osteoporosis? (August) 6(6): 4–5.

Johns Hopkins Medical Letter. 1994c. Improving the Outlook for Those With Macular Degeneration, (March) 6(1): 2.

Johns Hopkins Medical Letter. 1994d. Preventing Blindness in Those at Risk, (July) 6(5): 6–7.

Kart, C.S., and Metress, S.P. 1984. *Nutrition, the Aged, and Society*. Englewood Cliffs, NJ: Prentice-Hall.

Kart, C.S., Metress, E.K., and Metress, S.P. 1992. *Human Aging and Chronic Disease*. Boston: Jones & Bartlett Publisher.

MacDonald, J. 1984. Presentation of Acute Myocardial Infarction in the Elderly: A Review. *Age and Aging*, 13: 196.

Magaziner, J., Smonsick, E., Kashner, M., Hebel, J.R., and Kensera, J.E. 1989. Survival Experience of

Aged Hip Fracture Patients. *American Journal of Public Health*, 79: 274–278.

Morley, J., and Reese, S. 1989. Clinical Implications of the Aging Heart. *American Journal of Medicine*, 86: 77–86.

Owen, R., Melton, L., Gallagher, J., and Riggs, B.L. 1980. The National Cost of Acute Care of Hip Fractures Associated With Osteoporosis. *Clinical Orthopedics Related Research*, 150: 172.

Porterfield, J.D., and R. St. Pierre. 1992. *Healthful Aging*. Guilford, CT: Dushkin Publishing.

Resnick, N., and Greenspan, S. 1989. Senile Osteoporosis Reconsidered. *Journal of the American Medical Association*, 261: 1025–1029.

Rosen, S., Bergman, M., and Plester, D. 1962. Presbycusis Study of a Relatively Noise-Free Population in the Sudan. *Annals of Otolaryngology, Rhinology, and Laryngology*, 71: 727.

Rosenfield, I. 1986. *Modern Prevention: The New Medicine*. New York: Simon & Schuster.

Rybash, J.W., Roodin, P.A., and Santrock, J.W. 1991. *Adult Development and Aging*, 2d Ed. Dubuque, IA: William C. Brown.

Sheehy, G. 1992. *The Silent Passage: Menopause*. New York: Random House.

Sinaki, M. 1989. Exercise and Osteoporosis. *Archives of Physical Medicine and Rehabilitation*, 70: 220–229.

Spaeth, G. 1984. From Eye Pressure to Nerve Damage. *Science News*, 127: 351.

Stampfer, M., Colditz, G., Willett, W., Manson, J., Rosner, B., Spizer, F., and Hennekens, C. 1991. Postmenopausal Estrogen Therapy and Cardiovas-cular Disease. *New England Journal of Medicine*, 325: 756–762.

Stefanson, E. 1990. The Eye. In W. Hazzard, R. Andres, E. Bierman, and J. Blass (eds.), *Principles of Geriatric Medicine and Gerontology*. New York: McGraw-Hill.

Stone, A. 1993. Sleep and Aging. *Dialogue: The Emory Clinic Magazine*, 63: 5–8.

Straatsma, B., Foos, R., and Horowitz, J. 1985. Aging-Related Cataract-Laboratory Investigations and Clinical Management. *Annals of Internal Medicine*, 102: 82–92.

Surjan, L., Devald, J., and Palfalvia, J. 1973. Epidemiology of Hearing Loss. *Audiology*, 12: 396–410.

Sweet, C. 1989. Healthy Tan—A Fast-Fading Myth. *FDA Consumer*, 23: 11–13.

U.S. Bureau of the Census. 1993. Current Population Reports, (Special Studies, P23-178 RV). *Sixty-Five Plus in America*. Washington, DC: U.S. Government Printing Office.

U.S. Special Committee on Aging. 1993. Statement of David Pryor. The Hearing Aid Marketplace: Is the Consumer Adequately Protected? (September 15). Washington, DC: United States Senate; Listen Up for Simple Hearing Tests. *Modern Maturity*, (February–March 1994) Vol. 37, No. 1: 76.

Voeks, S., Gallagher, C., Langer, E., and Drinka, P. 1990. Hearing Loss in the Nursing Home: An Institutional Issue. *Journal of the American Geriatrics Society*, 38: 141–145.

Weiffenbach, J.M., Cowart, B.J., and Baum, B.J. 1986. Taste Intensity Perception in Aging. *Journal of Gerontology*, 41: 460–468.

CHAPTER 5

Mental Abilities
and
Mental Health

Different Strokes for Different Folks

Ralph is 85 and is no longer capable of dressing himself, preparing meals, or carrying on any meaningful conversation. When people speak to him he smiles and nods, but clearly he does not understand what is being said. After much family agony, he has finally been placed in a nursing home and is very confused about where he is and how he is supposed to respond to those around him. His eyes show a lack of recognition of what is happening around him, and he seems very sad.

Alice is 77 and is extremely active in her church. She chairs a committee on education and she never misses a church function. She drives not only in town but several hundred miles to visit her children. She reads several magazines a week, is always reading in a new book, is articulate in speech, and has a good memory. She lives independently and does her own cooking, shopping, and house cleaning. She is sought after by her friends and family for advice.

Harold is 68 and has been severely depressed since his wife died two years ago. He has isolated himself. He looks unkempt. He seems to have little interest in the affairs of the world or in anything else. He has insomnia, does not care to eat, has been losing weight, and cannot concentrate long enough to enjoy a book or even read the local newspaper.

Mary is 81 and is taking classes at the local community college. She is enjoying her classes and has a 3.0 average. She is articulate and speaks up in class. She relates well to the younger students and has a keen sense of humor. She complains that she is too old to remember all the material in the books and in the class notes, and then does as well or better than the younger students on her tests. She has learned to use computers and is extremely proud of her computer ability.

Will is 59 and recently retired. He has a great deal of anxiety about his future. He is cynical, angry, and unpleasant to be with, because he constantly complains. He has high blood pressure and is sedentary. He is a hypochondriac and always concerned about his health. He goes to several doctors and is taking many different medications. He is very lethargic, does not exercise, reads very little, and spends most of his time watching television and complaining to his friends. He dislikes politicians, intellectuals, news commentators, and almost everybody else.

MENTAL ABILITIES OF OLDER PEOPLE

Good News About Intellectual Ability and Mental Stability in the Later Years

The mental health and intellectual ability of older people are key components in studying the aging process. They can be affected by many factors, including various diseases. The good news about growing older regarding intellectual ability and mental stability is that they are not necessarily affected negatively by the advancing years. For example, research from the Baltimore Longitudinal Study of Aging (BLSA) showed that more than 25 percent of the volunteers in this study who were older than 70 years of age experienced no decline in their memory (Gunby 1994).

Paul Costa, the National Institute on Aging's director of its Laboratory of Personality and Cognition, and his colleagues have found that a person's personality tends to remain stable over much of the adult life span (Gunby 1994). Their studies have supported the concept that growing older does not change a person's life-long personality, even when physical problems are present. However, various dementias (brain disorders) can cause personality changes.

The first section of this chapter focuses on the mental abilities of people as they grow older. The second deals with personality stability across the life span and the diseases that can impair mental health, diseases that tend to be more prevalent among the old.

The Myth of Inevitable Decline

In the past, it was just assumed that when one became old, the brain would deteriorate and one would go into a "second childhood." Some textbooks in the 1940s stated that this was normal. In the last several decades, much research has been conducted that shows such statements to be myth. To contend that there is no change, however, on average, in the aging brain is not documented by research:

> We have done such a good job of debunking the myth of senility as the symbol of old age that we have created the myth of intellectual stability throughout late life. Unfortunately it is a myth, although there are some people who do hold their own. . . .
>
> The normal brain, free of disease, may well function as effectively and efficiently as the normal younger adult brain, except for speed . . . I believe that significant cognitive impairment is due to disease and not to normal aging. As we get older, we face an increased frequency of disease . . . (Jarvik 1988: 740–741).

There is, therefore, an important "if." If the person does not suffer from a disease, there may not be a significant decrease in the functioning of the brain due to aging. However, by age 85, about 50 percent of persons have some type of dementia (*Harvard Mental Health Newsletter* 1992). Nevertheless, Belsky (1990), along with Schaie and Willis (1986), believed that exercising and training the brain can improve even fluid intelligence if there is no debilitating disease present.

Intelligence in Older People

Early in the debate about intelligence and aging, Botwinick (1977) pointed out some of the problems involved in determining intelligence. These included deciding which tests are to be used, how intelligence is defined, what sampling techniques are used, and the problems associated with specific research methods. In addition, the question of health status as a mediating factor, especially vascular disease problems, needs to be considered in determining intelligence.

Types of Intelligence

Over the years a pattern in research has developed indicating that *crystallized intelligence* (learned patterns of culture and linguistic ability) may remain the same or increase as people grow older. Another type of intelligence, *fluid intelligence*, refers to analytical or instant reasoning ability. Fluid intelligence is a person's innate intellectual analytical ability independent of education and experience. Crystallized intelligence refers to intellectual abilities and knowledge acquired from experience and education. Although there is a disagreement about this, fluid intelligence seems to decline with the aging process. However, Dr. K. W. Schaie and others are not convinced that there is an inevitable decline of IQ with the aging process. Schaie argued that older persons are at a disadvantage in this type of test because they have had less formal education than younger persons, are not as used to taking tests, and have less motivation to take tests and do well in the testing process. Furthermore, evidence has shown that older persons have more anxiety than younger persons in taking tests (Schaie and Hertzog 1986).

Longitudinal and Cross-Sectional Studies A major problem with many studies of intelligence is that they use cross-sectional rather than longitudinal research methods. In longitudinal studies, the same person is tested over a period of time (weeks, months, or years). In cross-sectional studies, two or more groups defined by age are tested at a given period in time. These groups, consisting of people in different age categories, may have had very different experiences, so that the comparisons would not be as accurate as comparing the same persons over an extended period of time as they grow older. Longitudinal studies tend to be more accurate in comparing personality or intellectual changes over time, but they are also more difficult to conduct. The most famous longitudinal study of intellectual abilities and aging is the Seattle Longitudinal Study, which began in 1956. The major work on this study was done by K. W. Schaie. His findings have indicated that after age 60, fluid intelligence, as indicated by tests on space and numbers, shows some decline, but that verbal meaning and reasoning tests, which relate to crystallized intelligence, show no decline until people are in their mid-seventies. However, it is important to be aware of the fact that fewer than half of the participants experienced declines by age 80, and even fewer showed declines in all of the areas being tested. The evidence seems to be that changes in intellectual ability, according to Schaie and his interpretation of the Seattle Longitudinal Study data, are gradual, if they exist at all, and demonstrate long plateaus of intellectual ability (Schaie 1986). After age 70, the range of intellectual ability in the oldest-old population is enormous.

Do Mental Abilities Decline?   Schaie (1994) in his summary of his lifetime's work on aging and cognitive abilities, concluded that decreases in intelligence are modest until persons reach their eighties. Even at the age of 80, fewer than one-half of all observed individuals showed reliable decreases over the preceding seven years. He pointed out that as compared with age 25, at age 88, there is virtually no decline in verbal ability; however, inductive reasoning and verbal memory do decline, as do spatial orientation and numeric ability. Much of the late-life decline can be attributed to the slowing of processing ability and response speed. Schaie argued that there are key variables that increase the likelihood that mental abilities will be maintained in old age. They are: absence of chronic debilitating diseases, such as cardiovascular disease; higher socio-economic status; higher than average educational background; occupational status that requires high complexity in employment; above-average income; substantial involvement in activities typically available in complex and stimulating environments, such as extensive reading habits, continuing education, participation in professional associations, and a flexible personality at mid-life; and being married to a spouse with high cognitive competencies. In addition, persons who rate themselves as being satisfied with life's accomplishment in middle age, or early old age, seem to perform better in late life.

Importance of Educational Programs   Schaie (1994) also argued that intellectual decline can be reversed by educational exercises and programs, a position that is also supported by Willis and Nesselroade (1990). Both researchers concluded that there is considerable elasticity in cognitive functioning even into the oldest-old age, and that older adults, even into their late seventies, can show significant cognitive improvements by remedial educational programs. Lower levels of cognitive performance in older adults may be associated with limited mental stimulation in their everyday lives and not exercising their minds. Ability performance can be enhanced through educational exercises. However, they concluded that the gains from training would be expected to be lost if, after training, the trainees returned to nonstimulating environments or failed to exercise the skills they had learned in the training. Training efforts are effective in sustaining higher levels of cognitive performance even into the oldest-old years. Schaie (1994) stated that persons remain, on average, at a significant advantage even seven years after training.

There are others, though, who believe that there is a real decline in fluid intelligence with the aging process, for example Horn and Donaldson (1976). Schaie (1994) would probably agree that for many persons IQ (fluid intelligence) begins to decline at age 60; however, the situation is complicated by the fact that one has to remove from the decline in fluid intelligence the effect that debilitating illnesses can have on test taking. In addition, it is known that older persons need more time to take tests. To what extent this is due to losses in the central nervous system or is due to a reduction in brain cells has been argued at great length (Botwinick 1978). The evidence does seem to indicate little decline, if any, in the crystallized intelligence of healthy active older persons.

Most of the research seems to indicate that decreases in ability because of age are not as noticeable in everyday testing as in laboratory tests (West 1986). Older persons seem to be more motivated when tested on material that is useful and familiar with everyday life (Perlmutter and Monty 1989).

Salthouse (1991a, 1991b), in a review of the research, argued that there are some age-related declines in certain cognitive abilities. Fluid intelligence does decline with age, whereas crystallized intelligence seems to remain stable across the adult years. He wrote:

> These two patterns have been interpreted as reflecting a reduction with increased age in the ability to acquire or manipulate information, sometimes referred to as fluid intelligence, but with little or no influence of advancing age on access to the products of prior processing, sometimes referred to as crystallized intelligence (Salthouse 1991a: 36).

Salthouse also argued that the few longitudinal studies we have on cognitive testing suffer from losing certain types of participants, because more low-performing than high-performing people fail to return for subsequent testing, and from different test-taking practices, because increased age is related to more prior experience with the tests. In some longitudinal studies the measure of cognition reflects crystallized intelligence, not fluid intelligence. Salthouse did indicate that changes with aging and intelligence are not great, and that the average adult in his or her seventies is well within the normal range of functioning for adults in their twenties and thirties. Indeed, many people in their seventies perform at a higher level than the average 25-year-old. However, declines with increased age and intelligence are well documented. In general, though, performance on many cognitive tests can be improved through practice and training. For most older persons there seems to be relatively few cognitive limits on what can be accomplished in the later years of life (Salthouse 1991a, 1991b, 1991c).

Mental Decline Not Inevitable

Dennis Selkoe (1992), in summarizing the literature on aging and intelligence, asked whether the deterioration of the brain, and thereby the mind, is inevitable with aging. He stated the answer is no; as one ages certain molecules and cells in the brain become increasingly impaired or disappear. However, studies of human behavior suggest that mind-eroding damage is by no means automatic with longevity.

Selkoe (1992) did agree with other researchers that there is a reduction in the speed of some aspects of cognitive processing. He pointed out, however, that given enough time and an environment that keeps anxiety low, most healthy elderly persons score as well as young or middle-aged adults on tests of memory performance.

A message of guarded optimism emerges. If one is free of disease, one may not learn as rapidly during healthy late life, but may learn and remember nearly as well. In addition, Selkoe (1992) cited research indicating that older persons who regularly engage in aerobic exercise perform better on cognitive tests than do sedentary individuals of the same age with low aerobic fitness.

Memory and the Aging Process

There are many questions about how the research studies on memory were carried out, just as there are with IQ studies. Older persons perform best when the testing is relevant to their lives. They do worse on abstract studies that ask a person to remember factors that have no bearing on his or her daily life. There are studies that have indicated older persons did better than younger persons when the words on the tests were relevant to their age (Poon 1985a, 1985b). There is considerable lack of agreement at the present time as to the exact process of encoding, the storage and retrieval of learned material (Salthouse 1985, 1990a, 1990b, 1991a, 1991b, 1991c). There have been problems in the validity of testing memory as to how anxiety, motivation, and practice in testing may influence the results of persons in different age categories. The evidence has seemed to indicate that older persons are not as motivated as younger persons to remember nonsense syllables, pairs of completely unrelated words, or irrelevant numbers.

In a study using the subjects in the Baltimore Longitudinal Study of Aging, Sinnot and Gutman (1986) asked people in different age categories to recall events that took place during the three days they were being tested at the Gerontological Research Laboratory. The young volunteers outperformed the older volunteers on matters that were rather irrelevant to daily living. On matters that were important to daily living, the older volunteers performed as well or better than the younger volunteers.

Variables such as dementia, depression, and physical health account for much of the differences in memory among older respondents; the term *old* should not lead to generalizations. The variables among older people are significant and probably greater than in any group of age-related persons. There is no doubt that some older persons worry more about "losing" their memory, although for many their worry is not related to their ability. They assume they are getting older and therefore they must be losing their memory, when in fact they are not (Kahn, Zarit, Hilbert, and Niederehe 1975). There is no doubt that persons with dementia will have memory loss, and although age increases the probability of having dementia, the majority of older persons do not have dementia. Finally, many researchers seem to agree that there is some memory loss with aging, but they do not agree on the reasons for, or the extent of, loss.

Creativity and Aging

Many years ago Lehman (1953) claimed, after extensive research, that creativity declined with the aging process. Young adulthood was the time of maximum creativity. He found this to be true throughout all the academic disciplines. This conclusion produced a tremendous furor in academia. His methodology was immediately attacked. It was pointed out that he did not adequately take into account the longevity factor, in that many "geniuses" die before they live into older age. He should, it was argued, have restricted his study to "geniuses" who lived into old age, or statistically taken longevity into account.

He also should have taken into account that some high achievers might have become administrators and therefore no longer productive, not because of any age inherent factor, but because they no longer participated in the creative process. Research has seemed to indicate that a person's inherent characteristics are much more important than age in creativity (Cole 1979; Dennis 1956a, 1956b, 1958, 1966). This does not deny that there might be a decrease in creativity with the aging process; but, much more research needs to be done into specific areas of creativity such as mathematics, physics, poetry, and music, as they relate to people in different age categories.

It should be noted that the typical age curve of creativity is just a statistical average of hundreds of separate age curves of individuals. A person is not forced by a statistical curve to give up and say that he or she is "too old." There are always exceptions to the rules of probability.

Simonton (1975, 1977, 1984, 1985, 1988, 1989a, 1989b, 1990a, 1990b, 1991a, 1991b) in numerous studies questioned the magnitude of the supposed creative decline and challenged the trajectory of the decline itself. From his extensive research he argued that creative people in their sixties and seventies often generate new ideas faster than they did in their twenties. He also contended that the expected age decline in creativity in some disciplines is so small that it can hardly be viewed as a decline at all. He did admit though, that in certain areas, such as pure mathematics, the performance peak may be relatively early in life.

Simonton also argued that research suggested creative productivity can undergo a substantial renaissance in the later years of life. For example, some time after the late sixties, there is often a resurgence in output. He concluded by stating,

> . . . these empirical findings should enable us to appreciate that the final phase of life can be, and often is, a period of phenomenal creativity. At the very least we should understand how it can come to pass that certain creators manage to leave posterity with monumental creations that would have been

sorely missed had their late-life endeavors been summarily dismissed (Simonton 1991a: 16).

THE MENTAL HEALTH OF OLDER PEOPLE

Personalities of Older People

The first large-scale empirical studies of personality began in the 1950s with the University of Chicago's Kansas City Studies, which included more than 700 people. The persons in these studies were given a variety of personality tests, including the psychoanalytically oriented Thematic Apperception Test (TAT), which is used to diagnose emotional problems. The research found that as people get older, interiority occurs; that is, persons tend to lose interest in the outside world and become more preoccupied with themselves. By the time people are 50 years old, they start to withdraw emotionally from the world around them and become more concerned with their inner selves. The researchers did not label this as a negative process. They saw it as an adaptive process by which persons accept role losses and limitations that occur with aging. The research also indicated that as they grow older, women tend to become more assertive and men tend to become more passive and mellow. In other words, there is a reversal of gender differences in the aging process with women becoming more aggressive and men more nurturing. Not all researchers have been able to duplicate the Kansas City Studies results (Costa, McCrae, and Arenberg 1980; Costa and McCrea 1980). Gutman (1977), however, essentially agreed that the Kansas City Studies did find relevant gender changes in personality with the aging process.

Stability of Personality Over the Years The Baltimore Longitudinal Study of Aging (BLSA) found that personality over time tends to be stable (Costa and McCrae 1984). In addition to the BLSA, Costa examined the results from the National Health and Nutrition Examination Survey (NHNES), involving 15,000 respondents, and gave them a shortened version of the same personality test that was used with the BLSA subjects. He came up with similar findings, that personality tended to be stable over time.

These findings do not mean that persons cannot have personality changes over the years or that they cannot consciously attempt to bring about changes. It does seem to indicate, though, that most people tend to have stable personalities as they grow older. More research should be done, because the samples, research instruments, and theoretical assumptions of the earlier studies are open to criticism. Nevertheless, the evidence thus far seems to support the idea that no dramatic personality changes occur as a result of the aging process unless a person develops a chronic disease such as one of the dementias or a mental illness (Atchley 1994).

Mental illness occurs less frequently in older adults than in younger persons, and psychiatric symptoms in older people are somewhat different than they are in younger adults. The probability of developing a dementia is low for the young old, but increases rather dramatically for the oldest old.

Senile Dementia and Alzheimer's Disease

The term senile dementia has been used for many years to describe brain disorders related to the aging process. Dementia is used to describe more than seventy disorders. *Senile* refers to old age, and *dementia* means loss of brain function resulting from persistent physical neurological damage. The emphasis is on brain damage caused by diseases are related to the aging process (Billing 1987). Sometimes the condition is referred to as *organic brain syndrome* or *chronic brain syndrome* (Binstock 1993).

A major cause of organic brain syndrome is Alzheimer's disease. This disease was first described by a German physician, Alois Alzheimer, in 1906. At the present time it is the third leading cause of death among adult Americans after heart disease and cancer. It is a progressive, degenerative, irreversible brain disease. Although research is developing various theories, the exact cause of Alzheimer's disease is unknown. It results in changes in the nerve cells of the cerebral cortex and hippocampus of the brain. Apparently, the changes in the hippocampus, the brain's center of thought, language, and memory, result in the devastating symptoms of senile dementia.

Diagnosing Alzheimer's Disease   The diagnosis of Alzheimer's disease in the early stages is very difficult. The most common method to diagnose the disease has been to eliminate other diseases such as strokes, tumors, other neurological diseases, or arteriosclerosis (hardening of the arteries). There are testing procedures that psychologists can use to try to assess brain deterioration, but the tests by themselves cannot distinguish Alzheimer's disease from other physical and emotional problems.

In November 1994, the first simple and possibly accurate test to positively determine the presence of the disease was announced. A team of researchers headed by Leonard Scinto and Huntington Potter of Harvard Medical School gave nineteen patients with known or suspected Alzheimer's disease eye drops containing a very diluted solution of tropicamide, the same drug eye doctors use to dilate the pupil of the eye for routine exams. In nearly all of the Alzheimer's patients (eighteen of nineteen), their pupils dilated by 13 percent. In a control group of persons without Alzheimer's, the pupils enlarged by only 4 percent, less than one-third the degree of dilation of those with the disease (Seligmann and Springer 1994).

Another study released in August 1994 by David Musur, associate clinical professor of neurology at the Albert Einstein College of Medicine and Montefiore Medical Center reported on the use of a combination of four psychological tests to possibly "identify in older people the most and least likely to develop dementia" including Alzheimer's disease (Rubin 1994: 91). The use of

these tests, it was found, could predict the risk of dementia within four years. These tests are more accurate in predicting who will not be stricken. It is emphasized that this is not a do-it-yourself kind of test, but is nonetheless a valuable research tool for professionals.

The most accurate test for Alzheimer's disease has been a microscopic examination of the brain cells after the patient is dead, as there are very definite changes in the brain. Beta-amyloid plaques, waxy protein substances, are deposited in the nerve cells, destroying their function. In addition, neurofibrillary tangles occur. These are twisted filaments of nerve cell endings. Acetylcholine, which is important for neurotransmitter functioning, is leached out of the brain. New research, new findings, and new hypotheses are headlined periodically in the media, but the underlying cause of Alzheimer's disease is still unknown (Aronson 1988).

The Probability of Getting Alzheimer's Disease   There is a disagreement as to how many people have Alzheimer's disease in the general population. Most of the studies put the rate very low for people under age 65. However, after age 65, there seems to be a continual increase in the prevalence of Alzheimer's disease. One study of 467 older persons living in East Boston found very high rates of the disease for persons 85 and older. Using neuropsychological, neurological, and laboratory tests, the researchers estimated that over 47 percent of those over the age of 85 had some form of dementia. They found that in the older age categories, the increase was very dramatic, as they estimated that the rate for persons aged 65 to 74 was only about 3 percent (Evans, Buckwaiter, and Fulmer 1989). Early studies (Smith and Kilosh 1981; Rocca, Amaducci, and Schoenberg 1986) found about a 20-percent prevalence rate for persons aged 80 and older.

Another study cited by the *Harvard Mental Health Newsletter* (1992) put the chances of getting some form of dementia at 50 percent for all persons aged 85 or older, with Alzheimer's disease being the primary cause of dementia. More women than men have Alzheimer's disease, although one reason for that is they live longer than men.

Researchers have found that in the earliest stage of Alzheimer's disease there is a genetic connection. A gene in chromosome 21 is associated with early-onset (before age 60) familial Alzheimer's disease. However, many researchers agree that most cases of Alzheimer's disease do not develop in the younger years but later in life. It is known that an identical twin has a higher probability of developing the disease if the other twin has the disease. However, not all identical twins develop the disease, even if a twin has it. There seems to be a genetic component to the disease, but other factors are involved.

Progression of Alzheimer's Disease   Daniel Andreae (1992) contended that the disease develops in three different stages. The first stage is characterized by slow, subtle changes in ability to learn, memory loss of recent events, confusion about dates or what they are supposed to do, and problems with making coping decisions relating to the activities of daily living.

In the second stage, memory continues to disintegrate. Patients develop noticeable problems in finding the correct words. They become aware that they cannot remember names anymore. They find it more difficult to make daily living decisions and increasingly need supervision.

In the third and final stage, patients need constant care and supervision because they cannot feed, dress, or toilet themselves. Eventually the ability to speak is lost, and the words they use seem to be a meaningless jumble. The loss of bowel and bladder control as well as the ability to walk is part of the progression. Patients may develop delusions and some become paranoid.

Kociol and Schiff (1989) outlined a more elaborate breakdown of the progression of the disease:

Stage 1: No cognitive decline	No functional problem
Stage 2: Very mild cognitive decline	Forgets name and location of objects
Stage 3: Mild cognitive decline	Has difficulty traveling to new locations
	Has difficulty in demanding employment settings
Stage 4: Moderate cognitive decline	Has difficulty with complex tasks (finances, marketing, planning dinner for guests)
Stage 5: Moderately severe cognitive decline	Needs help choosing clothing
	Needs coaxing to bathe properly
Stage 6: Severe cognitive decline	Needs help dressing
	Needs help bathing; may have fear of bathing
	Has decreased ability to handle toileting
	Is incontinent
Stage 7: Very severe cognitive decline	Has vocabulary of six words
	Has a single-word vocabulary
	Loss of ambulatory ability
	Loss of ability to sit
	Loss of ability to smile
	Stupor and coma

Alzheimer's sufferers progress through these stages at their own rates; each is unique.

Each Alzheimer's patient progresses through a series of stages of deteriorations; however, the duration and intensity of each of the stages is idiosyncratic to the patient. Some individuals decline rapidly in the initial phases, but then reach a plateau for a while, and even show occasional glimmers of improvement, before they lapse into further deterioration. Others may decline more slowly in the early stages, but then degenerate more quickly toward the end. Every individual does not suffer the same symptoms during the course of the disease or suffer them at the same time or to a similar degree. There is no way to predict the rate at which a patient will move through the stages that make Alzheimer's disease so frustrating, unpredictable, and frightening for patients, families, and lay and professional caregivers (Andreae 1992: 61).

Causes of Alzheimer's Disease   Many avenues of research have been followed to determine the cause of Alzheimer's disease. Some researchers have found a genetic link to ApoE (apolipoprotein E), a protein that carries cholesterol through the blood. Scientists have been studying a German family with twenty-one members affected by Alzheimer's disease and have traced the disease through six generations (Progress Report on Alzheimer's Disease 1992). This might relate to ApoE because people who inherit a particular type of ApoE-4, are seven times as likely as others to develop Alzheimer's disease.

Beardsley (1993) pointed out that ApoE-4 can be detected with a test that is already widely used for diagnosing a serious cholesterol transport disorder. It seems that people who inherit the gene for a particular variant of the cholesterol-carrying protein apolipoprotein E are much more likely to develop the disease than people who do not inherit that variant:

> Rather than assuming that ApoE-4 causes Alzheimer's, they propose that the other two ApoE variants—ApoE-2 and ApoE-3—help to protect against the disease and that people who inherit the ApoE-4 gene lose all or part of their protection (Marx 1993b: 1210).

Other researchers are investigating whether a virus might be the cause of the disease. A slow-acting virus has been found to be a factor in other brain diseases that cause dementia. If it is a slow-acting virus, at the present time there is no evidence that others, such as spouses, are infected. There are certain viral diseases of the brain that

are somewhat comparable to Alzheimer's disease. However, at the present time there is no evidence that a virus is implied in Alzheimer's disease (Wurtman 1985).

Scientists do not agree on whether something called beta-amyloid plaques are a cause of the disease or an effect. Dr. Selkoe (1992) believes that it is a cause. Others, such as Dr. Allen Roses, have indicated that amyloid plaques do not cause Alzheimer's disease, but are the by-products of the ApoE-4 process. The Alzheimer's research community has been divided for some time into pro- and anti-amyloid factions (Marx 1993a).

Another recent hypothesis (Holloway 1992) relates to the impact of estrogen on the brain. Recent research has indicated that when estrogen levels drop markedly after menopause, the complexity of connections in the brain can slowly diminish, making neurons more likely to degenerate and die. The reason for this is that estrogen operates in brain cells throughout life, producing enzymes that result in the densest possible mesh of fibers connecting one nerve cell to the next. This produces the type of synoptic complexity typical of a robust brain.

This is also important in men because their circulating testosterone is converted to estrogen in the brain. This could explain why more women than men get Alzheimer's disease. Men's testosterone level does not dip sharply at any point, and often remains high even into their eighties, in contrast to the sharp decline in estrogen for women after menopause (Holloway 1992).

Dr. Victor Henderson of the University of Southern California found that women on hormone replacement therapy were 40 percent less likely to develop Alzheimer's disease than women who were not on the hormone. In support of this hypothesis there is evidence that removal of female rodent's ovaries negatively affects the brain (Holloway 1992).

Estrogen also increases the production of an enzyme that allows messages to leap from one neuron to the next in the regions of the brain such as the hippocampus, an area of the brain related to memory and thought processes. This post-menopausal drop in estrogen does not effect all women equally. The body continues pumping out small amounts of sex hormones, even after the ovaries have retired, and some women generate more estrogen than others (Holloway 1992).

It is also known that Alzheimer's patients have an unusually large amount of aluminum in their brains. Dr. Daniel Perl has been attempting for many years to prove that the high concentrations of aluminum are a cause of Alzheimer's disease. Aluminum is found virtually everywhere in the world: in the air, in the water, and in food. It is also found in certain substances, such as many antacids and deodorants. At present, however, there is no scientific evidence that the high concentrations of aluminum in the brains of Alzheimer's patients caused their disease. It is not even well understood why high concentrations of aluminum are present (Perl and Brody 1980; Berg, Karlunsky, and Lowy 1991; Jorm 1990).

Scientists working with twins have found a relationship between anti-inflammatory drugs and Alzheimer's disease. Alzheimer's disease is seen by some researchers as an autoimmune disease, similar to rheumatoid arthritis. A study of 7,490 patients with rheumatoid arthritis found only 0.39 percent of those had Alzheimer's disease, while among people in the same age group without rheumatoid arthritis, 2.7 percent had Alzheimer's disease. Some have contended that anti-inflammatory drugs taken by arthritic sufferers may account for the difference. This study needs to be replicated, and at the present time none of these hypotheses has been proven.

No Effective Cure At this time there is no treatment that will either slow or stop the progression of Alzheimer's disease. There are some treatments that in some instances seem to reduce anxiety and aggression in patients, but they do not cure the disease (Aronson 1988). Antipsychotic medications such as haloperidol (Haldol) seem to reduce some of the symptoms and can also induce sleep. The danger is that it can also be overused because it is a sedative that makes these patients more manageable (Katzman and Jackson 1991).

Experimentation with various drugs to reduce the impact of Alzheimer's disease continues with limited success. Tacrine is a drug that recent research seems to indicate might improve memory and increase word usage. In addition, in some patients it increases the ability to do simple tasks. It certainly is not a cure and does not change the course of the underlying disease. It has probable side effects including nausea and liver damage. Because of this, the drug must be used under medical supervision (Katzman and Jackson 1991).

Impact on Families Whatever the progression of the disease, Alzheimer's has a devastating impact on the families of patients. It is often referred to as a family disease, because all members of the family are affected by it emotionally, financially, and socially. As the disease progresses, families are forced to give more and more time to care for their patients because patients cannot be left alone. If they wander away, they will not be able to find their way back. In addition, patients will eventually need constant care for feeding and toileting. They often sleep strange hours and disrupt the sleep pattern of their caregivers. Many develop a "sundowner's emphasis," meaning that they become very agitated near sundown. They often develop a virtual social death and have no awareness of who their caregivers or other people are. They may explode with harsh words at caregivers or even physically strike out at them (Mace and Rabins 1991).

A person can live 20 years or longer with the disease, with continuing deterioration in cognitive and emotional states. Unless considerable assistance can be given to the family caregiver, placement in a nursing facility usually becomes a necessity.

The value of support groups for the family members of Alzheimer's disease sufferers is discussed in chapter 15. The following statement summarizes the role of support groups:

With no cure or discovery yet of a drug or medical treatment to slow its progress, Alzheimer's disease is a terrible tragedy for any family to face. But when the emotional strain of dealing with the disease and feelings of physical exhaustion are shared with a support group, caregivers seem to find more strength to cope. Not only do they gain emotional and even spiritual support, they gain practical help as well by learning from the support group about community services (Henderson 1992: 24).

Communicating with Alzheimer's Patients

Following are several recommended strategies for communicating with Alzheimer's disease victims:

1. It is important not to assume that the patient does not know what you are talking about. The patient retains the capacity to understand language well after he or she can no longer speak intelligently.
2. As you would not speak about any person to another in the person's presence, do not do so with the patient.
3. Do not hold conversations with another person in close proximity to the patient as if he or she were not there.
4. Sentences and questions should be kept short and simple.
5. The use of pronouns should be avoided, and proper names that the patient can recognize and is familiar with should be used.
6. Conversation should revolve around observable, actual occurrences, not abstract or philosophical ideas that may be difficult to understand or communicate.
7. When talking to the patient, position yourself at the patient's eye level, so the patient does not think that the conversation may be terminated.
8. The patient should be allowed time to listen, comprehend, think, formulate, and express a response to what you have said.
9. Background noise and other stimuli that compete for the patient's attention and make it difficult to pay attention to your message should be reduced.
10. Messages should be stated directly. The patient should not be expected to draw inference from what is said.
11. Metaphor and analogy should be avoided.
12. The patient thinks literally. Such statements as "Why don't you jump into the shower" may elicit a response like "I'm afraid to; I may fall."
13. If your message is not understood, it should be restated and paraphrased.
14. Talk in a low-pitched, audible tone of voice and use appropriate animation and intonational cues.
15. The nonverbal components of communication should be remembered and used to enhance the patient's readiness to listen or to understand your message.
16. You should ascertain whether the patient can hear you by watching the patient's face for signs of comprehension.
17. Avoid becoming overexcited, using wild gestures, or being overly demonstrative; doing so can cause the patient to become alarmed and anxious.
18. Provide cues and help the patient to find the "lost" word while he or she is talking.
19. Alzheimer's patients can read words even after they have lost some of the meaning of a word or phrase. Ambiguous sentences may cause particular difficulty. For example, the sign "Exit" may be interpreted as a command rather than simply as a label for a means of egress.
20. Pay attention to the words and emotional message that are being conveyed. If the patient sounds upset while he or she is talking or begins to cry, it is important to react to the affective response.
21. Ask only one question or give one direction at a time and use short sentences (five to ten words in sequence), rather than make paragraph-length utterances.
22. If the patient loses the thread of a story or is unable to complete a sentence, repeat the last phrase he or she said to prompt the memory.

23. Ask yes-or-no questions when appropriate, but do not restrict all communication to this category.
24. Observe the patient for signs of restlessness or withdrawal, such as agitation (foot movements and hand wringing), restless eye movements or continuous scanning of the room, becoming loud or argumentative, and frowning.
25. Help the patient become tolerant of his or her communication difficulties by supporting the patient's remaining skills and encouraging their use. Reassure the patient that you will take the time to listen.
26. Observe Alzheimer's patients to monitor how they communicate with each other and with their caregivers. Get to know the patient's vocabulary, sentence structure, and normal conversational patterns, so a context can be developed for greater understanding (Andreae 1992: 72–75).

Need for More Research   Some experts have estimated that four million people currently have Alzheimer's disease. Since the fastest growing part of the American population are persons age 85 and older, it is obvious that this disease is going to contribute to a growing crisis in medical care delivery as Alzheimer patients could soon swamp nursing homes (Berg, Karlinsky, and Lowy 1991; Evans, Buckwaiter, and Fulmer 1989). It is estimated that by 2050 there will be seven to nine million Alzheimer's disease victims with an annual health-care cost of $200 billion, if a cure is not found (Butler, Lewis, and Sunderland 1991).

Strokes

The second most common risk factor for dementia is multi-infarct dementia (MID), causing between 15 and 20 percent of all dementia. MIDs are minor strokes that damage the brain by reducing blood flow to the brain. Other strokes are hemorrhagic, caused by a ruptured blood vessel in the brain (*Johns Hopkins Medical Letter: Health*

After 50, 1994). MIDs in the beginning produce few outward symptoms other than a slight memory loss and a slight loss in cognitive abilities. As these strokes increase, there is a decrease in mental abilities because more brain cells die. The functional decline is often referred to as a stepwise deterioration. In contrast to Alzheimer's disease, MIDs do not cause steady deterioration; decline occurs only when the strokes occur (Kart, Metress, and Metress 1992).

About half a million Americans suffer a stroke each year. An improved diagnostic and treatment process has resulted in a 32-percent decrease in stroke-related deaths over the past decade. Even with that improvement in medical treatment, about 150,000 deaths from stroke occur every year, making it the fourth leading cause of death in the United States. In addition, about the same number of stroke survivors are disabled. Part of the reason for this is that some stroke survivors arrive at the hospital too late to receive treatment. Only recently has stroke been recognized as an emergency with the same degree of urgency as a heart attack. Similar to heart attacks, rapid treatment can minimize damage (*Johns Hopkins Medical Letter: Health After 50*, 1994).

Strokes occur when the brain is deprived of oxygen and nutrients, which results in the destruction of brain cells and the loss of their associated functions. Eighty percent of strokes are *thromboembolic*, brought about by a blood clot that lodges in a blood vessel of the brain.

A stroke can affect speech, vision, movement, and other vital bodily functions. In some strokes it takes a number of hours for brain cells to be damaged, and it is during that time that therapies to restore blood flow, or treatment to minimize bleeding, can be effective. Both computer tomographic (CT) scans and magnetic resonance imaging (MRI) are very effective means to diagnose the causes of strokes which is very useful for treatments. In a number of treatable stroke "subtypes," brain damage can be arrested or reversed. Promising treatments for certain categories of thromboembolic strokes include:

thrombolitics, clot-busters like those used in heart attack patients; anticoagulants, which may prevent further strokes; and long-term blood thinners, which provide protection for patients with certain heart-rhythm abnormalities. However patients with strokes brought about by hemorrhaging should not receive these medications, because they can make bleeding worse. In both types of stroke, surgery can sometimes relieve pressure on the brain or remove blood to lessen the damage.

When a stroke occurs, damage is done to the brain that can result in changed behavior. Sometimes there is a weakening or paralysis of one side of the body. Strokes can also cause aphasia. There are different aspects to aphasia. Some persons have *expressive aphasia*, in which they cannot form words. Others have *receptive aphasia*, in which they have a difficult time understanding words spoken to them. Others have *mixed aphasia*, in which they have both difficulty speaking and understanding words. Some persons with a stroke develop *agnosia* which means that they cannot recognize common objects, such as keys, pencils, and combs. Still others might develop *apraxia*, inability to control motor tasks such as writing, feeding, or dressing. There is a danger that friends, and relatives may interpret a person's inability to respond as an inability to completely understand what is occurring. However, the patient may be very aware of what is occurring but unable to form the words to communicate their awareness. Factors such as obesity, high blood pressure, smoking, and diabetes increase the probability of cardiovascular accident (CVA) such as a stroke (Kart, Metress, and Metress 1992).

Depression

Depression is a major mental health problem related to aging. There are several types of depression. In *endogenous depression* there is a biochemical imbalance that leads to a depressed condition. In *reactive depression*, events in the life of the person bring about depression. In addition, some people suffer from seasonal affective disorder (SAD); as winter approaches and the days grow shorter, they begin to feel chronically depressed. Although there is continuing debate as to the exact symptoms and cause of SAD, it seems that a light-sensitive hormone called melatonin may be reduced when a person has decreased exposure to light. With decreasing daylight, these people begin to feel depressed, irritable, and anxious. Increasingly therapists are finding that some persons are reacting well to light therapy, in which light with a composition similar to outdoor daylight is effective in reducing feelings of depression. Ordinary home lighting does not provide this type of lighting. Persons who believe that they suffer from SAD should see a qualified therapist.

In another type of depression, *bipolar depression*, a biochemical imbalance brings about emotional mood swings. The person may change from mania, a hyperactive state, to depression (Phifer and Murrell 1986).

The symptoms of depression include feelings of despair, a denial of self-worth, angry outbursts, and psychosomatic symptoms such as a loss of appetite, sleeping difficulties, constipation, and fatigue. There is considerable hope for persons with depression who get professional help. Again the emphasis has to be on accurate diagnosis and professional help (DSM-III-R 1987).

Loss and Depression As they grow older, people are likely to suffer significant losses in their lives. Eventually most older persons leave their jobs, have a decrease in their incomes, and lose their spouses, as well as many friends. In addition, they may lose one or more of their children; their health may deteriorate; they may lose their homes as they move to congregate living facilities or nursing homes; and they may lose their hope that conditions will improve. Some who have several of these losses amazingly still retain emotional stability and feelings of well-being. Others, however, become overwhelmed by their losses and need professional help. Depression among the elderly is usually not the result of guilt or childhood trauma, but the result of significant loss. Given such loss, the reasons for depression are clear. These people need supportive environments, loving friends, and possibly therapy (Krause 1991).

Lifestyle and Depression Some older persons become mentally depressed because of their personal habits. They might lack exercise and become too sedentary and lethargic. This situation can quickly become cyclical, in that the more they sit, the more tired and fatigued they become, and therefore the more they sit. In the process they become irritable, isolated, and depressed.

Some older persons suffer emotionally and appear to lose some reasoning abilities because of their social isolation. This can become a special problem for some widows who were so dependent on their deceased husbands. Others become isolated because most of their friends are dead. Some become isolated because, in addition to many of their friends being deceased, their children live hundreds or thousands of miles away. Still others may lack the energy to go out and socialize or are too ill to become involved with other people. Whatever the cause, isolation can result in depression and a loss of lucidity. There are some people who have been isolated most of their lives, prefer it, and do not have adverse personality changes as a result. Most people, however, need regular and consistent interaction with others. In their isolation, some persons become alcoholic and increasingly more isolated from others, which increases their drinking. Others cannot sleep adequately and claim they suffer from insomnia. For some, their lack of sleep may be caused by overeating, too many naps during the day, or a lack of exercise. Some get into a vicious cycle of self-centeredness in which they enjoy talking about all their problems and in the process drive others away. Even their children get tired of hearing about all their pains and anxieties. These people probably need professional

help. Their lifestyles often can be changed with professional assistance (Billing 1987).

Anxiety and Depression As they grow older, some persons develop anxiety over their future. They might become anxious thinking about placement in a nursing home that would totally drain all the money they had accumulated over a life time of work and saving. Anxiety might arise over major surgery that will not be covered adequately by insurance or over home repairs they are not able to afford. They might worry about burial expenses that will cause their children financial burdens. It is helpful if these concerns are made known and discussed by family members. If these fears are always the focus of conversations and there seems to be an unrealistic amount of anxiety, however, these persons may need professional assistance (Moritz, Kasl, and Berkman 1989).

Anxiety may be the most frequent psychiatric condition among older people (Myers and Manton 1985). Anxiety is usually defined as having physical symptoms such as sweating, diarrhea, palpitations, headaches, dizziness, and for some, hyperventilation. It is an aspect of the "flight-or-fight" syndrome. In addition, a person with high anxiety has problems with memory, trouble concentrating, and a poor attention span (Benson 1975; Gurian and Miner 1991). Some older persons become argumentative and cranky as they lose self-esteem. Others have anxiety attacks, in which they feel they are losing the power and respect they had in the past. They may try to regain control by controlling others, by threatening others, and by being overbearing and demanding. As a result, people may turn away from them, increasing their isolation and anxiety. This situation may produce anxiety with psychosomatic conditions, resulting in complaints about aching joints, constipation, chest pains, and other symptoms (Quam 1986).

Some older persons become depressed and begin to deteriorate emotionally because they feel that they are disposable. They believe that because they are retired, they are worthless. They feel "over-the-hill," finished, done with, worthless. At times this is made worse by professionals and others who are paternalistic and condescending toward older persons. People who in the past were respected because of their jobs, energy, and wisdom, often find themselves disregarded in their later years. Research has shown that some of the elderly have the same negative view of old age as do younger persons. Some older persons develop gerontological phobia, a fear and distaste of aging. They can benefit from being taught to become assertive, to speak up, to reject a negative view of aging, and to remain involved in activities in their communities (Gatz and Smyer 1992).

Treatment of Depression   Prevention is best where isolation, inadequate nutrition, reactive depression, inadequate medical care, and destructive lifestyles are the major problems. Better funding of senior centers so that older persons could have a place to socialize, to interact with others, to get a hot meal, to obtain referrals to other agencies, to develop a sense of community, and to be observed and evaluated by the professional staff constitutes a preventive approach. To the extent that supportive preventive programs are not available, some elderly persons will be at risk of developing emotional problems.

Early therapeutic treatment is a goal which prevents problems from developing into more serious conditions. Although the aged make up about 12 percent of the population, they constitute only about 3 percent of outpatients in mental health clinics. Too many older people still have very negative attitudes toward the mental health profession and are reluctant to seek help. They think that these types of services are for "crazy" people and that they are not "crazy" (Gatz and Smyer 1992).

Electroconvulsive Therapy   For some older depressive persons, the treatment of choice is electroconvulsive therapy (ECT) or "electro shock" therapy. The movie *One Flew Over the Cuckoo's Nest* probably did more to confuse people about

ECT than anything else. Modern ECT treatment can be very effective with many older patients. The typical candidate for ECT is a middle-aged or older woman who has not responded well to other therapies. Some researchers claim that ECT causes memory loss. However, for patients who do not respond to other types of treatment, it often is effective in treating severe depression. In describing ECT, Korshun (1993) wrote, "Once feared by patients and disparaged by practitioners, electroconvulsive therapy is now considered a safe, first-line treatment for severe depression, particularly in the elderly."

The American Psychiatric Association has endorsed ECT as a safe, effective, first-line therapy for severe depression, especially in older patients. ECT treatment consists of a very slight electrical impulse sent through the frontal part of the brain. A unilateral electrode placement on the right side of the head, rather than a bilateral placement, helps eliminate confusion. A very low amount of current, comparable to that used in a 20-watt bulb, is used for one second. This seems to affect neurotransmitters in the brain, including dopamine, serotonin, and norepinephrine, which are all involved in mood changes. The majority of people respond positively to ECT, with fewer than 5 percent having no positive impact. One full course of ECT treatment usually includes five to eight or more treatments, usually administered two or three times a week. Some patients require outpatient maintenance treatments which may be given once a month. Most of the side effects of ECT have been eliminated by modern procedures. The side effects that were bothersome in the past, including uncontrolled muscle contractions and severe discomfort, are mostly eliminated with the use of anesthesia and muscle relaxants. Confusion and cardiac complications, also present in the past, can now be controlled with improved techniques (Korshun 1993).

Medications   Prescription drugs are part of the treatment process for many depressed persons. It is very important that older patients know the importance of taking their medications exactly as prescribed. Currently many drugs, if adequately prescribed and used, can bring about virtual miracles in helping people through difficult psychiatric conditions. Unfortunately, they can also be misused or abused. That is why it is important to understand that they must be taken as prescribed. More of something is not necessarily better (National Institutes of Health 1991).

Depression: A Major Health Problem Depression in older adults is a major public health problem that is underdiagnosed and undertreated. Neither the victim nor the healthcare provider may recognize its symptoms because many older people have multiple physical problems.

To address this issue the National Institutes of Health (1991) convened a Consensus Development Conference on the Diagnosis and Treatment of Depression in Late Life. Scientists, health professionals and representatives of the public were brought together for two days of scientific presentations by experts and participation by the audience. Among their findings, the panel concluded that:

1. Depression in late life occurs in the context of numerous social and physical problems that often obscure or complicate diagnosis and impede management of the illness.
2. Because there is no specific physical diagnosis test for depression, an attentive and focused clinical assessment is essential for diagnosis.
3. Depressed elderly people should be treated vigorously with sufficient doses of antidepressants and for a sufficient length of time to maximize the likelihood of recovery.
4. Electroconvulsive therapy and psychosocial treatments also can be effective in the treatment of elderly depressed patients.
5. Estimates of the prevalence of depression vary widely, but the highest rates are in nursing homes and other residential settings, and staff in many of these facilities are not equipped to recognize or treat depressed patients.

Suicide Among the Elderly

Suicide is higher among the elderly than among persons of any other age category. Seventeen to 25 percent of suicides are among persons over the age of 65, even though this age group comprises only about 12 percent of the population (National Center for Health Statistics 1988; Meehan, Saltzman, and Sattin 1991; Koenig and Blazer 1992). The evidence seems clear that when older persons talk about suicide, they mean it. When they attempt suicide, they usually succeed. Any older person talking about suicide should be taken seriously. In addition to those older people who take explicit means to end their lives, there are many deaths that are never labeled as suicides because the persons used indirect means to end their lives such as neglecting medical attention, not taking medicine as prescribed, refusing to eat, purposeful exposure to the elements, and overexercising to bring about a heart attack.

Mental Confusion

It is very important that persons with mental confusion be diagnosed correctly because treatment is based on the diagnosis of a particular disease. One of the problems in diagnosis is that the symptoms of irreversible diseases such as Alzheimer's disease are similar to other conditions that are reversible. These reversible conditions, acute transitional confusional states, are sometimes referred to as *pseudodementias*, *pseudosenilities*, or *symptomatic confusional states*. All of these terms refer to underlying conditions which can be treated either to reverse the progress of the disease or halt its progression. These symptoms might be the result of infections such as pneumonia or abscesses; medications; poor nutrition; disorders of the thyroid, parathyroid, or adrenal glands; metabolic disorders due to renal or electrolytic imbalances; trauma to the head; tumors; or severe depression (Abrams 1991).

An infection in an aged person can be devastating since his or her defenses are already often reduced, and as a result, mental confusion might occur. The confusion might also be the result of medications such as L-dopa, digitalis, valium, barbiturates, or a host of other drugs. As a person grows older, the kidneys and liver, which break down and excrete drugs, are no longer as efficient as they once were. In addition, medications often remain in the body longer and thereby increase the danger of overdosage. Mental confusion may also be caused by poor nutrition. When an individual lacks basic vitamins and minerals, his or her system no longer functions adequately, and confusion may result. The confusion might also be due to social-psychological factors, conditions which, with adequate therapy, can be resolved (Shimp and Ascione 1988).

Reality Therapy and Fantasy Therapy

If a person suffers from a pseudodementia, it is important to stress reality therapy, in which one emphasizes the correct time of day, the correct day of the week, one's name and relationship, and where one is living. If, however, the person is suffering significant organic dementia, fantasy therapy is often used, in which one relates to the reality of where the person's memory still exists. It is not unusual for an 87-year-old person to have no significant memory of what happened to him or her 10 minutes ago, but to have excellent memory of what occurred when he or she was ten years old. Such a person can, with directed interaction, "smell the roses" behind his or her house when he or she was a little child. It is not unusual for an aged person, with significant memory loss, to remember vividly songs and poems of childhood (Mace and Rabins 1981).

Schizophrenia

Dilip Jeste (1994) indicated that although schizophrenia usually makes its first appearance in adolescence or young adulthood, there is a second peak in the forties and a third peak in the mid-sixties, especially among women. He believed that schizophrenia is a syndrome rather than a single disease, and that it is not known if late-onset and early-onset schizophrenia are distinct forms of this syndrome or different manifestations of the same disease. He stated that his research showed that late-onset schizophrenics tend to have more paranoid symptoms—bizarre delusions and compelling hallucinations. On the other hand, he indicated that there is evidence that listlessness, apathy, and emotional shallowness are less severe in late-onset patients. Older schizophrenics often have more physical problems than younger patients, use more medications, and tend to have more severe side effects from the use of drugs. Chronic and sometimes irreversible and uncontrollable body movements resulting from drug therapy are more common in older patients than in younger patients. With proper treatment, many late-onset schizophrenics improve, but it is not known how often they fully recover. There are some categories of the elderly that have higher percentages of persons with mental deterioration. About 50 percent of persons admitted to nursing facilities have some type of cognitive or emotional impairment (Gatz and Smyer 1992). That should be kept in perspective, though, as psychiatric conditions represent a major reason for nursing home placements. Confusion, severe depression, high anxiety, and paranoia are often characteristics of older persons placed in nursing facilities.

Other Factors Related to Mental Health and Aging

Physical Health   Physical health is an important factor in the mental health of older people. There are certain chronic illnesses that can affect a person's mental health. Congestive heart failure, for example, can cause a loss of oxygen that can lead to abnormal brain functioning. The tremendous fatigue caused by congestive heart failure can lead to depression. Diabetes can lead to impotence in men, resulting in a damaged self image, depression, and irritability. In addition, severe diabetes in either men or women can result in significant mood swings, depending upon their blood sugar levels. Kidney failure can lead to mood swings, depression, and suicidal feelings. Severe rheumatoid arthritis can lead to extreme fatigue, and the constant pain can result in irritability and depression (Blazer, Hughes, and George 1987).

Inadequate Nutrition   Inadequate nutrition can cause personality changes. Persons who eat too much starch and put on excessive weight can become fatigued, lethargic, and depressed. Some persons who drink an excessive amount of coffee may find themselves tense, anxious, irritable, and unable to sleep. Often persons living alone do not cook or eat wholesome meals and live on coffee and rolls, or tea and cookies. As a result, they do not get the vitamins, minerals, or proteins that their bodies need. Persons working with the elderly need to be aware of their eating habits. Inadequate nutrition over a period of time can have a negative impact on personality (Blazer, Hughes, and George 1987).

Misuse of Medications   At times medications can have side effects that cause personality changes and distortions. Elderly persons have a history of drug misuse. Some older persons with vision problems do not read the instructions on their medications accurately. Others do not tell each physician they consult that they are also going to other physicians, and as a result, they are likely to take a dangerous combination of prescription drugs. Still others, because of limited resources, take only a few of their prescribed drugs, trying to save money by taking the saved drugs at another time. Some, who get up in the middle of the night to go to the bathroom, in their half awakened condition take the wrong drugs. Others take medications from friends because it helped them. Some get into difficulty because their doctors did not explain adequately the side effects of the medications, and they did not ask if there might be side effects (Krause 1991; Cooper 1994). One of the authors worked with a neighborhood senior citizens' center director who had a woman attending her center who was lucid, energetic, and a great helper at the center. Over a period of three months, significant personality changes began to take place. Increasingly she became confused and irritable. The director began to think she might need to be placed in a nursing facility. One day the center director, upon visiting her home, found twenty-one different prescriptions from five different physicians on the woman's dining room table. The woman had not told each doctor that she also was going to other physicians. The director found among the prescriptions psychotropic drugs (major mood changers) such as chlorpromazine (Thorazine) and diazepam (Valium) and a host of other drugs for numerous physical ailments. The woman had deteriorated mentally because of the medications to the point where she was not only mixing the drugs in dangerous combinations, but was taking them in quantities which would make most individuals act irrationally. The happy outcome of this story is that the woman was taken off most of the drugs, put under the supervision of one physician, and recovered her mental and emotional health. When one works with older persons and mood or mental changes take place, it is important to inquire about what medications they are taking, and in what quantities. Physicians need to be informed about other physicians who might be involved in treating a person, just as physicians should make clear to their elderly patients what side effects the drugs might have on their moods or mental condition.

In using prescription drugs, it is important for older people to:

1. Be sure to read all the labels. Use a magnifying glass, if necessary.
2. Be sure to note the expiration date on over-the-counter medications.
3. Be sure to tell their doctor which over-the-counter drugs they are taking.
4. If they are seeing more than one doctor, be sure to tell each one what the other doctor has prescribed.

5. Remember that it can be dangerous to mix drugs and alcohol.
6. Keep drugs in airtight containers and store them properly.
7. Call their doctor if they notice any new symptoms or side effects.
8. Do not take more or less than the prescribed amount of any drug.
9. Do not stop taking prescriptions, even if one feels better or thinks it is not helping.
10. Do not take drugs prescribed for someone else, or give yours to someone else.
11. Do not transfer a drug from its original container to another container.

Older people should ask their doctor the following questions before taking prescription or over-the-counter drugs:

1. What is the name of the drug and what is it supposed to do?
2. How and when do I take it, and for how long?
3. What foods, drinks, other medicines, or activities should I avoid while taking this drug?
4. Are there any side effects, and what do I do if they occur?
5. Is there any written information available about the drugs?

Friendship and Reminiscence in Promoting Mental Health   Many older persons do not need professional help as much as they need the friendship and willingness of others to spend time with them. They need someone who is a good listener. They need someone with whom they can recall and relive the past. Reminiscence is not an indication of senility. Most people like to reminisce. Reminiscence is good for older people because it enables them to recall the past with someone who loves them enough to listen. Family members, friends, neighbors, and service providers who take time to listen to older people will learn about the past, demonstrate their love by taking time to be involved, and strengthen the self-esteem of older persons (Butler, Lewis, and Sunderland 1991; Quam 1986).

SUMMARY

Considerable research on cognitive abilities and the aging process seems to indicate that there are decreases in certain types of intelligence, but there is stability in other mental abilities. There is some research indicating that intellectual decline can be reversed by educational programs, assuming no major chronic major illnesses such as Alzheimer's disease exist.

Creativity is not necessarily lost as a result of the aging process. There have been, and there continue to be, highly creative older persons. Whether creativity in areas such as physics and mathematics declines with the aging process is still to be determined by more research. Certainly the evidence indicates that, free of significantly debilitating illnesses, older persons can learn, be creative, and be productive well into the oldest-old years.

Senile dementia is a broad term that is too often used without the specificity needed to determine why certain older people seem to lack certain cognitive skills. People do not develop a dementia just because they are old. Dementia in old age is the result of a specific disease. The major cause of dementia in older persons is Alzheimer's disease, a progressive neurological disorder for which there is no cure at the present time. A person with Alzheimer's disease will eventually need total care, as the disease destroys both the cognitive and emotional processes. A person with Alzheimer's disease loses memory and eventually the ability to take care of himself or herself in everyday living situations. There is no agreement among scientists as to the cause of Alzheimer's disease.

Alzheimer's disease will continue to be in the news as new research findings are reported. Another reason it will be a news item is the large number of persons—perhaps as high as four million—who have the disease and who will spend a large amount of money in long-term medical care facilities. Because Alzheimer's disease becomes totally debilitating, it is known as a "family disease." The victims typically need family caregivers to provide for their needs. The needs of the Alzheimer patient become so demanding that family members usually need relief from the constant care required. Nursing-home placements typically become necessary.

Another major cause of the development of dementia in the older population is stroke. Strokes block the passage of oxygen to the brain, which causes brain cells to die. Strokes can, depending on the part of the brain affected, cause loss of motor ability or loss of cognitive abilities. Speech, vision, movement, and the thinking process can all be affected.

Depression in older adults is a major public health problem, as it is in younger adults. Older adults respond well to treatment for depression, and electroconvulsive therapy is especially successful with older patients. The American Psychiatric Association has endorsed ECT as a safe, effective, first-line therapy for severe depression in older adults.

Some older persons suffer from acute reversible confusional states. They can be caused by the side-effects of prescription drugs, viral infections, inadequate nutrition, isolation, or depression. These acute reversible confusional states are also referred as pseudodementias, pseudosenilities, or symptomatic confusional states.

REFERENCES

Abrams, R. 1991. Anxiety and Personality Disorders. In Sadavoy, Lazarus, and Jarvix (eds.), *Comprehensive Review of Geriatric*. American Psychiatric Press.

Andreae, D.C. 1992. Alzheimer's Disease: The Family Affliction. In F.J. Turner (ed.), *Mental Health and the Elderly*. Toronto, Canada: The Free Press.

Aronson, M.K. (ed.). 1988. *Understanding Alzheimer's Disease*. New York: Charles Scribner & Sons.

Atchley, R.C. 1994. *Social Forces and Aging*, 7th ed. Belmont, CA: Wadsworth Publishing.

Beardsley, T. 1993. Unraveling Alzheimer's. *Scientific American*, (November): 28–30.

Belsky, J.K. 1992. *The Psychology of Aging*. Pacific Grove, CA: Brooks/Cole Publishing.

Benson, H. 1975. *The Relaxation Response*. New York: Avon Books.

Berg, J., Karlinsky, H., and F. Lowy (eds.), 1991. *Alzheimer's Disease Research: Ethical and Legal Issues*. Toronto: Carswell, Thompson Canada Ltd.

Billing, N. 1987. *To Be Old and Sad*. New York: Lexington Books.

Binstock, R.H. 1993. Plaques and Tangles in Approaching Dementia. *Gerontologist*, 33(1): 133–135.

Blazer, D., Hughes, D., and George, L. 1987. The Epidemiology of Depression in an Elderly Community Population. *Gerontologist*, 27(3): 281–87.

Botwinick, J. 1978. *Aging and Behavior*, 2d Ed. New York: Springer.

Botwinick, J. 1977. Intellectual Abilities. In J.E. Bireen and K.W. Schaie (eds.), *Handbook of the Psychology of Aging*. New York: Van Nostrand Reinhold.

Butler, R.N., Lewis, M.I., and Sunderland, T. 1991. *Aging and Mental Health: Positive Psychosocial and Biomedical Approaches*. New York: Macmillan.

Cole, S. 1979. Age and Scientific Performance. *American Journal of Sociology*, 84(4): 958–977.

Cooper, J.W. 1994. Drug-related Problems in the Elderly Patient. *Generations*, 28(2): 19–27.

Costa, P.T., and McCrea, R.R. 1980. Still Stable After All These Years: Personality as a Key to Some Issues of Adulthood and Old Age. In P.B. Bates and B. Brim, Jr. (eds.), *Life Span Development and Behavior*, (Vol. 3), New York: Academic Press.

Costa, P.T., McCrae, R.R., and Arenberg, D. 1980. Enduring Dispositions in Adult Males. *Journal of Personality and Social Psychology*, 38: 793–800.

Costa, P.T., and McCrae, R.R. 1984. Personality as a Lifelong Determination of Well-Being. In Malatesa and Izzard, C. (eds.), *Affective Processes in Adult Development and Aging*. Beverly Hills, CA: Sage Publications.

Dennis, W. 1956a. Age and Achievement: A Critique. *Journal of Gerontology*, 11(4): 331–333.

Dennis, W. 1956b. Age and Productivity Among Scientists. *Science*, 123: 724–725.

Dennis, W. 1958. The Age Decrement in Outstanding Scientific Contributions: Fact or Artifact. *American Psychologist*, 12(5): 457–460.

Dennis, W. 1966. Creative Productivity Between Ages 20 to 80 Years. *Journal of Gerontology*, 21(1): 1–8.

DSM-III-R. 1987. *APA Monitor*.

Evans, L., Buckwaiter, K., and Fulmer, T. 1993. The Mosaic of Needs for Elderly with Mental Health Concerns. *Gerontologist*, 33(2): 280–281.

Evans, D.A., Funkenstein, H.H., Albert, M.S., Scherr, P.A., Crook, N.R., Chown, M.J., Hebert, L.E., Hennakens, C.H., and Taylor, J.D. 1989. Prevalence of Alzheimer's Disease in a Community Population of Older Persons: Higher Than Previously Reported. *Journal of the American Medical Association*, 262: 2551–2556.

Gatz, M., and Smyer, M.A. 1992. The Mental Health System and Older Adults in the 1990s. *American Psychologist*, (June) vol. 47, no. 6: 741–751.

Gunby, P. 1964. Graying of America Stimulates More Research on Aging-Associated Factors. *Journal of the American Medical Association*, 272(20).

Gurian, B.S., and Miner, J.H. 1991. Clinical Presentation of Anxiety in the Elderly. In C. Salzman and B.D. Lebowitz (eds.), *Anxiety in Elderly*. New York: Springer.

Gutman, D.L. 1977. The Cross-Cultural Perspective: Notes Toward a Comparative Psychology of Aging. In J.E. Birren and K.W. Schaie (eds.), *Handbook of the Psychology of Age*, 1st ed. New York: Van Nostrand Reinhold.

Harvard Mental Health Newsletter. 1992. (August): 9(2).

Henderson, J.N. 1992. The Power of Support. *Aging Magazine*, No. 363–36: 24–28.

Holloway, M. 1992. The Estrogen Factor. *Scientific American*, (June): 26.

Horn, J.L., and Donaldson, G. 1976. On the Myth of Intellectual Decline in Adulthood. *American Psychologist*, 31(10): 701–719.

Jarvik, Lissy, G. 1998. Aging of the Brain: How Can We Prevent It? *The Gerontologist*, 28(5): 739–46.

Jeste, D.B. 1994. How Does Late-onset Compare with Early-onset Schizophrenia? *Harvard Mental Health Letter*, (February) vol. 10, no. 8: 8.

Jorm, A.F. 1990. *The Epidemiology of Alzheimer's Disease and Related Disorders*. London, Chapman and Hall.

Kahn, R.L., Zarit, S.H., Hilbert, N.M. and Niederehe, G. (1975). Memory Complaint and Impairment in the Aged: The Effect of Depression and Altered Brain Function. *Archives of General Psychiatry*, 32: 1569–1573.

Johns Hopkins Medical Letter. 1994. Dial 911 for Stroke. *Health After 50*, vol. 6, no. 5 (July): 1–2.

Kart, C.S., Metress, E.K., and Metress, S.P. 1992. *Human Aging and Chronic Disease*. Boston: Jones and Bartlett.

Katzman, R., and Jackson, J.E. 1991. Alzheimer's Disease: Basic and Clinical Advances. *Journal of the American Geriatrics Society*, 31: 516–525.

Kociol, L., and Schiff, M. 1989. *Alzheimer's Disease: A Practical Guide for Those Who Help Others*. New York: Continuum.

Koenig, H.G., and Blazer, D.G. 1992. Mood Disorders and Suicide. In J.E. Birren, R.B. Sloane, G.D. Cohen, N.B. Hooyman, B.D. Lebowitz, M.H. Wykle, and D.E. Deutchman (eds.), *Handbook of Mental Health and Aging*, 2d ed. San Diego, CA: Academic Press.

Korshun, H. 1993. Another Look at Electroconvulsive Therapy. *Dialogue: The Emory Clinic Magazine*, 6(3): 21–23.

Krause, N. 1991. Stress and Isolation from Close Ties in Later Life. *Journal of Gerontology*, 46(4): S183–194.

Lehman, H.C. 1953. *Age and Achievement*. Princeton, NJ: Princeton University Press.

Mace, N.L., and Rabins, P. 1991. *The 36-Hour Day*. Baltimore: Johns Hopkins University Press.

Marx, J. 1992. Familial Alzheimer's Linked to Chromosome-14 Gene. *Science*, (October 2) 258: 550.

Marx, J. 1993a. Alzheimer's Pathology Begins to Yield Its Secrets, *Science*, (January 22) 259: 457–458.

Marx, J. 1993b. New Alzheimer's Theory Stirs Controversy. *Science*, (November 19) 262: 1210–1211.

Meehan, P.J., Saltzman, L.E., and Sattin, R.W. 1991. Suicides Among Older U.S. Residents: Epidemiologic Characteristics and Trends. *American Journal of Public Health* 81: 1198–1200.

Moritiz, D., Kasl, S., and Berkman, L. 1989. The Health Impact of Living With a Cognitively Impaired Spouse: Depressive Symptoms and Social Functioning. *Journal of Gerontology*, 44(1): S17–27.

Myers, G.C., and Manton, K.G. 1985. Morbidity, Disability, and Mortality: The Aging Connection. In C.M. Gaitz, G. Niedrehe, and N.L. Wilson (eds.). *Aging 2000: Our Health Care Destiny* (Vol. II): *Psychosocial and Policy Issues*. New York: Springer.

National Center for Health Statistics. 1988. *Public Health Service, Monthly Vital Statistics Report*, 36: 25–30.

National Institute of Health. 1991. Diagnosis and Treatment of Depression in Late Life: Consensus Statement. Bethesda, MD: U.S. Department of Health and Human Services.

Perl, D.B., and Brody, A.R. 1980. Alzheimer's Disease: X-ray Spectrometric Evidence of Aluminum Accumulation in Neurofibrillary Tangle-Bearing Neurons. *Science*, 208: 297–299.

Perlmutter, L.C., and Monty, R.A. 1989. Motivation and Aging. In L.W. Poon, D.C. Rubin and B. Wilson (eds.), *Everyday Cognition in Adulthood and Late Life*. Cambridge: Cambridge University Press.

Phifer, J.E., and Murrell, S.A. 1986. Etiologic Factors in the Out-set of Depressive Symptoms in Older Adults. *Journal of Abnormal Psychology*, 95: 282–291.

Poon, L.W. 1985a. Differences in Human Memory With Aging: Nature, Causes and Clinical Implications. In J. Birren and K. Schaie (eds.), *Handbook of the Psychology of Aging*, 2d Ed. New York: Van Nostrand Reinhold.

Poon, L.W. 1985b. Learning. In G.L. Maddox (ed.), *The Encyclopedia of Aging*. New York: Springer.

Progress Report on Alzheimer's Disease. 1992. National Institute on Aging NIH Publication, No. 92-3409.

Quam, J.K. 1986. Life Tasks and Developmental Issues of the Chronically Mentally Ill Elderly. In N.S. Abramson, J.K. Quam, and M. Wasow (eds.), *The Elderly and Chronic Mental Illness*. San Francisco: Jossey-Bass.

Rubin, R. 1994, September. A Test to Predict Dementia. *U.S. News and World Report*, (September): 117(10): 91.

Rocca, W.A., Amaducci, L.A., and Schoenberg, B.S. 1986. Epidemiology of Clinically Diagnosed Alzheimer's Disease. *Annals of Neurology*, 19: 415–424.

Salthouse, T.A. 1991a. Cognitive Facets of Aging Well. *Generations*, XV(1) (Winter): 35–38.

Salthouse, T.A. 1991b. Mediation of Adult Age Differences in Cognition by Reductions in Working Memory and Speed of Processing. *Psychological Science*, 2(3): 179–183.

Salthouse, T.A. 1991c. *Theoretical Perspectives on Cognitive Aging*. Hillsdale, NJ: Lawrence Erlbaum Associates.

Salthouse, T.A. 1990a. Cognitive Competence and Expertise in Aging. In J.E. Birren and K.W. Schaie (eds.), *Handbook of the Psychology of Aging*, 3d ed. pp. 311–319. San Diego, CA: Academic Press.

Salthouse, T.A. 1990b. Influence of Experience on Age Differences in Cognitive Functioning. *Human Factors*, 32(5): 551–569.

Schaie, K.W. 1994. The Course of Adult Intellectual Development. *American Psychologist*, 49(4): 304–313.

Schaie, K.W., and Hertzog, C. 1986. Toward a Comprehensive Model of Adult Intellectual Development: Contributions of the Seattle Longitudinal Study. In R.J. Sternberg (ed.), *Advances in Human Intelligence* (Vol 3). Hillsdale, NJ: Erlbaum.

Schaie, K.W., and Willis, S.L. 1986. Can Decline in Adult Intellectual Functioning Be Reversed? *Developmental Psychology*, 22: 223–232.

Seligman, J., and Springen, K. 1994. Progress on Alzheimer's. *Newsweek* CXXIV, (November 21) (21): 80.

Selkoe, D.J. 1991. Amyloid Protein and Alzheimer's Disease. *Scientific American*, (November): 68–78.

Selkoe, D.J. 1992. Aging Brain, Aging Mind. *Scientific American*, (September): 135–142.

Shimp, L.A., and Ascione, F.J. 1988. Causes of Medication Misuse and Error. *Generations*, 12: 17–21.

Simonton, D.K. 1975. Age and Literary Creativity: A Cross-Cultural and Transhistorical Survey. *Journal of Cross-Cultural Psychology*, 6(3): 259–77.

Simonton, D.K. 1977. Creative Productivity, Age, and Stress: A Biographical Time-Series Analysis of 10 Classical Composers. *Journal of Personality and Social Psychology*, 35(3): 791–804.

Simonton, D.K. 1984. Creative Productivity and Age: A Mathematical Model Based on a Two-Step Cognitive Process. *Developmental Review*, 4: 77–111.

Simonton, D.K. 1985. Quality, Quantity, and Age: The Careers of 10 Distinguished Psychologists. *International Journal of Aging and Human Development*, 21(4): 241–54.

Simonton, D.K. 1988. Age and Outstanding Achievement: What Do We Know After a Century of Research? *Psychological Bulletin*, 104(2): 251–67.

Simonton, D.K. 1989a. Age and Creative Productivity: Non-linear Estimation of an Information-Processing Model. *International Journal of Aging and Human Development*, 29: 23–37.

Simonton, D.K. 1989b. The Swan-Song Phenomenon: Last-works Effects for 172 Classical Composers. *Psychology and Aging*, 4: 42–47.

Simonton, D.K. 1990a. Creativity and Wisdom in Aging. In J.E. Birren and K.W. Schaie (eds.), *Handbook of the Psychology of Aging*, 3d ed. New York: Academic Press.

Simonton, D.K. 1990b. Creativity in the Later Years: Optimistic Prospects for Achievement. *Gerontologist*, 30(5): 626–31.

Simonton, D.K. 1991a. Career Landmarks in Science: Individual Differences and Interdisciplinary Contrasts. *Developmental Psychology*, 27(1): 119–27.

Simonton, D.K. 1991b. The Emergence and Realization of Genius: The Lives and Works of 120 Classical Composers. *Journal of Personality and Social Psychology*. (in press)

Sinnot, J.D., and Gutmann, D. 1986. Dialectics of Decision Making in Older Adults. *Human Development*, 21: 190–200.

Smith, J.S., and Kilosh, I.G. 1981. The Investigation of Dementia: Results in 200 Consecutive Admissions. *Lancet*, 1: 824–827.

West, R.L. 1986. Everyday Memory and Aging. In *Developmental Neuropsychology*, 2: 323–344.

Willis, S.L., and Nesselroade, C.S. 1990. Long-Term Effects of Fluid Ability Training in Oldest-Old Age. *Developmental Psychology*, 26(6): 905–910.

Wurtman, R.J. 1985. Alzheimer's Disease. *Scientific American*, 252: 62–74.

Wurtman, R.J., Corkin, S., Growdon, J.H., and Ritter-Walker, E. (eds.) 1989. *Alzheimer's Diseases: Advances in Neurology*, vol. 51, New York: Raven Press.

Wykle, M.L., and Musil, Carol M. 1993. Mental Health of Older Persons: Social and Cultural Factors. *Generations: Journal of the American Society on Aging* (Winter/Spring): 7–12.

CHAPTER 6

Sexuality
and
Aging

Doris and Ben: Bored and Tired

Doris is 73. Ben is 76. They have rarely had sexual intercourse during the last 10 years. Doris went through menopause at the age of 54, rather late for most women, and her physician never talked to her about estrogen replacement therapy. In addition, at the time she was going through menopause the last of her six children left home. She had been a full-time housewife and mother, and most of her self-image revolved around her children. She never had a great deal of communication with her husband, who worked at two jobs to support his large family. After menopause Doris went into a period of depression, which her very religious husband found difficult to understand. He became angry at her lack of sexual responsiveness during her periods of depression. After menopause, sexual intercourse became increasingly painful. In her earlier years she always found sex rather perfunctory. There was a repetitive sameness in their sex life that even Ben began to find less than stimulating. As a result, their sexual activities decreased markedly, a decrease that Doris found acceptable. Ben, always a heavy smoker, had difficulty after age 50 obtaining and maintaining an erection. He fantasized about sex and periodically masturbated; increasingly as he got older he was ready to ignore their sexual life. In their late sixties, they began to sleep in separate bedrooms, and eventually they ceased most sexual activities.

Jane and Carl: Ever Active

Jane and Carl are both 67 and have a vigorous, active sexual life. Throughout their marriage, they have been sexually active. They see sex as not only a period of intimacy, but also as a fun, creative, and fulfilling process. Neither Jane nor Carl smoke, and their drinking was moderate. They both exercised regularly, were in great physical condition, and had a zest for life. Jane went through menopause with not many physiological or psychological problems. Their three children were out of the home by the time Jane completed the menopausal process. Her gynecol-ogist prescribed estrogen replacement for her, and she took her estrogen pills regularly.

Both Jane and Carl masturbate periodically, fanaticize regularly about sex, and are delighted in the freedom they have, with the children gone, to have intercourse in any room in the house at any time. They both are delighted that at this age they still find sex to be an important part of their lives, and they intend to be sexually active into the foreseeable future.

SEXUALITY AND AGING

Sexuality is best viewed in the context of relationships, attitudes, and values. It involves more than reproductive systems and genitalia; it is more than the hormonal system. Sexuality is an attempt to gain intimacy, to have warmth and closeness with others. It is a physical and psychological closeness that is part of human necessity. With that in mind, sexuality is seen as much more than just sexual intercourse. It includes an embrace, mutual stimulation, a touch, a couple holding hands on their daily walk.

Unfortunately, in the past older people were thought to have no interest in sexuality. The elderly were seen as prudish, asexual people. It was almost as if eventually everyone was expected to lose sexual desire and any interest in the erotic, the sensual. Added to this was the emphasis in our youth culture of relating the erotic to the young, to the perfect bodies of the late adolescent or young adult. Neither *Playboy* nor *Penthouse* magazines feature the mature or older person as a sexual object. Sexual desire, it has been thought, might last through middle age, at a significantly reduced level, but it surely would disappear in later life.

Research, however, increasingly indicates that older people are sensual, have real needs for closeness and intimacy, and are involved in continuing sexual activities of various types.

Whether by intercourse, masturbation, mutual masturbation, or other means, the vast majority of older people are still sexually active. Among happily married older people, most still find the sexual side of their relationship important. About two-thirds of unmarried older persons even over the age of 70 are sexually active. Although they may find sex less intense than when they were young, many older people experience more tender and satisfying sexual experiences.

The biggest problem some researchers have found in studying the sexuality of older persons is their subjects' feeling the need to keep sex secret. Although they feel love, passion, and pleasure, many older people are dismayed by the shock and disapproval they get from their children, some of their friends, and even some health professionals. Of course, not all of the problems facing older people and their sexuality are caused by the reactions of their children and friends. As Dr. Robert Butler pointed out, men may have the physical problems with aging and sex, but women have the social problem—a shortage of men. By the age of 65, there are roughly 150 women for every 100 men. By the time people get into their eighties, the ratio is closer to 250 women for every 100 men. Carol Mayer, a medical social worker at the Turner Geriatric Clinic of the University of Michigan, pointed out that a major unrecognized part of a widow's grief is the stopping of sexual activity. She counsels elderly people without sexual partners to masturbate. This clinical social worker pointed out that both men and women can lose muscle tone, making it difficult to resume sexual theory. It is the old theory "use it or lose it." She indicated that loss of this muscle tone can also promote urinary incontinence (Bruini 1993b).

Not all sexual expression among older people, as in any age group, is heterosexual. After having lived much of their lives in a time when society barely acknowledged the existence of homosexuals, many older gays and lesbians are "coming out of the closet" and acknowledging their sexual orientation (Bruini 1993a). Indeed, many older homosexuals are supporting homosexual organizations as well as public demonstrations so that young homosexuals can live more open and comfortable lives. Story after story is told about lives of gays and lesbians in years past, how they had

to live very secret lives in order to get and retain jobs. The consequences were brutal if they were discovered. Of course, the lives of many of today's homosexuals are not without hardships and even dangers. Nevertheless, they are substantially different than in the era when today's older homosexuals were raised.

In addition, there are the accounts of older persons, upon the loss of their spouses, who experience homosexual contacts for the first time. The story of a St. Petersburg, Florida man relates how lonely he was after the death of his wife. He simply was not interested in another woman. He had had a wonderful marriage and could not think of replacing his spouse. He badly needed companionship and began a relationship with another widower. This led to a temporary physical involvement which he characterized as a helpful phase of life, somewhat similar to the sexual exploration many teenagers experience in passing to adulthood (Towery 1993). Other older people, upon the loss of a spouse, permanently turn to homosexual relationships.

With the social revolution occurring in America brought about by the aging of the population, we will need to view sexuality as an integral part of the whole life span—into the oldest ages. This view will be a dramatic change in itself. As Herbert Covey (1994: 81) of the University of Colorado at Boulder pointed out, "On the whole, sexuality of the elderly population has been viewed as immoral, inappropriate, and negative. Western cultural beliefs at least from the Middle Ages onward have held that sexual drive disappears with old age, that sex is perverse in old age, and those elderly who attempt it practice self-deception." These attitudes must change to match reality.

IMPORTANT RESEARCH STUDIES ON SEXUALITY

Kinsey Studies

The first significant scientific study of sexual behavior in the U.S. was the work of Dr. Alfred C. Kinsey. Kinsey was an entomologist who specialized in the sexual behavior of insects. In reviewing the literature on sexuality, he was appalled to find that there was more written on the sexual behavior of insects than of humans. As a result, he sought a grant to study human sexuality. When it was awarded, he and his staff began interviewing thousands of Americans in depth about their sexual experiences. Their first book, *Sexual Behavior in the Human Male*, was published in 1948. *Sexual Behavior in the Human Female* followed in 1953.

Kinsey and his associates did not have a large sample of older persons. Fewer than 200 of the persons he interviewed were over 60 years of age. However, what he did find from the older people who were interviewed was very significant. He found that most had an interest in sex and that most older people remained sexually active if they had a partner.

The Kinsey study was criticized because of its sampling techniques. Kinsey did not have a random sample, where all Americans would have an equal probability of being chosen. He had a self-selected sample; he had asked people to volunteer to be interviewed about their sexuality. This, unfortunately, led to a highly skewed sample. Out of proportion to their percentage in the population, he interviewed white, middle-class, educated Americans. African Americans, Catholics, Jews, and people of various ethnicities were underrepresented. In addition, he relied on people recalling past events. Memory can distort reality. People might be tempted to distort what happened and not tell the truth about their past sexual history.

Even with all of these criticisms, the Kinsey research is very important because it began the large-scale scientific study of human sexuality. In addition, further research, called replication studies, was done for African Americans, Catholics, Jews, and members of various ethnic groups. These replication studies tended to reinforce the accuracy of Kinsey's work.

Duke Longitudinal Studies

The second important scientific studies on human sexuality and aging were the Duke Longitudinal Studies. In 1955, Duke University began studying 271 older persons and followed them until 1976, when 44 remained alive (Busse and Maddox 1985). In 1968, a study of a second group of 502 participants began, also ending in 1976, with 375 remaining participants.

The Duke Longitudinal Studies used a variety of research techniques, such as physiological and psychological testing, techniques not used by Kinsey. As had Kinsey, they also interviewed the participants. The Duke Longitudinal Studies tended to reinforce the earlier Kinsey studies. The researchers found that sexual activity does decline with increasing age. It is important to put that in perspective: They found a decrease in sexual activity, not a cessation of it. They also found that people who were very sexually active when they were young had a higher probability of remaining more sexually active than others as they got older. The Duke study even found a few people whose sexual activity increased as they got older. In addition, they found tremendous differences in older people regarding sexual desire and activity. As did Kinsey, they found that most older people do not lose an interest in sex.

Masters and Johnson Studies

The next important advance in the scientific study of human sexuality was the work of Dr. William Masters and Virginia Johnson. Masters and Johnson wanted a more scientific, quantitative analysis of human sexual behavior than either the Duke Longitudinal Studies or the Kinsey study provided. They wanted to precisely measure sexual behavior as it took place and asked for volunteers to be filmed and recorded in their sexual behavior. They got hundreds of volunteers. They filmed, recorded, and precisely measured sexual response in hundreds of people, some of whom were older, including one who was 89. Unfortunately, they defined as older women those who were aged 40 and over, and older men those who were aged 50 or older. The result of this research was a book entitled *Human Sexual Response* (1966). They subsequently wrote numerous other books including *Human Sexual Inadequacy* (1970a) and *The Pleasure Bond* (1970b).

In their research, Masters and Johnson found that in order for older people to maintain their sexual responsiveness, it was important to have continuing regular sexual activities. They found that women can be orgasmic well into their eighties, and that although the strength of the male erection decreases with age, premature ejaculation decreases as the male ages.

Starr-Weiner Report

Bernard D. Starr and Marcella Weiner (1981) wanted to add an important dimension to all of the studies listed above by asking older people what sex meant to them in their later years. They asked people aged 60 and older throughout the U.S. to respond to a questionnaire with fifty open-ended questions. Open-ended questions are questions which enable a person to write at length about their feelings and thoughts. Unfortunately they had a low response rate (14 percent) to the large number of questionnaires that they sent out; 518 women and 282 men responded to the study.

They found the vast majority (80 percent) of the respondents were sexually active. Almost all (97 percent) said that they had a positive view toward sex. They found that most people aged 60 to 69 had sexual intercourse more than once a week, and that even people over age 80 who had a partner regularly engaged in sexual intercourse. Only a small percentage of older people (26 percent) said that sexuality was worse in their later years than when they were younger; 36 percent said that sexuality was better in the later years than when they were younger.

It should be noted that Starr and Weiner did not have a random sample of the American population and that the response rate to their questionnaires was very small. At the same time, their findings are similar to the previous research findings in that they also found older people retained an interest in sex, and if they had a partner, they remained sexually active.

Consumers Union Study

The most recent large-scale study of sexuality and aging was conducted by the Consumers Union (Brecher 1984). The Consumers Union placed an ad asking readers to obtain a questionnaire which asked questions about their sexuality. They received 4,246 completed questionnaires. This response was large, but again, it was not a random sample, a criticism of all of the studies on aging and sexuality. The findings of the Consumer Union study on aging and sexuality are very similar to all of the other studies. They reinforce what other researchers had found.

Summary of the Research Findings

Despite all the bad jokes about older people not wanting sex, not enjoying sex, having forgotten what it's all about, the evidence is that they know what it is about, enjoy it, and want more of it. For some older people, sexuality improves with aging. Certainly for many middle-aged persons, sexual life is more fulfilling than ever. Sexuality, broadly defined as touching, embracing, kissing, and intimacy, is something that can continue until the loss of one's partner. Unfortunately, there are too many elderly people who accept the myth that sexuality belongs to the young. This is not to deny the changes that occur with aging; but in spite of those changes, sexual interests, functions, and desires can remain. However, some people believe that because a person gets older, he or she should no longer have an interest in sexual activity. This is simply not true.

The body changes with age. Because sexual response is partly a physical response, it changes with some of the other changes of the body. Fifty- or sixty-year-olds are not going to have the same sexual response as twenty-year-olds. In the younger male, sexual arousal occurs quickly, and frequently ends very quickly. A man who in the past was quickly aroused by visual stimulation, may now find that he needs physical stimulation. Where previously the mere sight of his lover may have aroused him, he now needs her to use physical stimulation to arouse him. A wife, who in the past had her self-esteem increased by her husband's arousal at the mere sight of her, must not assume she is less attractive now because he is aroused more slowly. It might just be the result of hormonal or blood-flow changes (caused by arteriosclerosis) that are taking place in him. On the other hand, it might be that people who have gained considerable amounts of weight, dress slovenly, and take no pride in their appearance may be contributing to the slow arousal of their partners. An extremely overweight person with nicotine-stained teeth who has not bathed in a few days will have less than a sexually stimulating impact on his or her partner. Exercise and physical vitality play a role in sexual response. An overweight, lethargic, badly out-of-shape person probably will have considerably less energy to sexually respond than a person who exercises, is fairly trim, and feels good about herself or himself.

There are some persons who suffer from inhibited sexual desire. Inhibited sexual desire means a person has no known physiological dysfunctions but has no, or very little, sexual motivation. The loss of sexual desire might be the result of anxiety, depression, boredom, or anger. Some people may be so busy at their careers that they simply have no time or interest for sexual arousal. Some people may substitute other interests such as music, eating out, fishing, or sports for sexual activity.

SEXUAL CHANGES IN THE AGING PROCESS

Age-Related Sexual Changes in Males

Research of sexuality in older persons has resulted in the following probability statements, meaning that they are not true for most but not all males:

- Older males will take longer to have an erection than younger males.
- Older males will not respond as quickly to visual stimuli as younger males.
- Older males will not have as firm an erection as younger males.

- Older males will not ejaculate as much semen as younger males.
- It will take older males longer to have an erection than younger males after ejaculation (the *refractory period*).
- Older males will not ejaculate as quickly as younger males during intercourse.
- Older males have a less forceful ejaculation than younger males (Brecher 1984; Butler and Lewis 1976; Palmore 1981).

Reasons for Changes in Male Sexual Response

These changes reflect a combination of physical changes, cultural factors, and interpersonal tensions (Starr and Weiner 1981; Masters and Johnson 1970; Butler and Lewis 1976). Recent research indicates that more of the male's decrease in the sexual drive is caused by a reduction in the testosterone (male hormone) level than had been previously thought to be the case. Some males see a remarkable increase in virility with testosterone treatments. Others have a decreased sexual ability due to diseases such as diabetes. Severe diabetes can destroy the small blood vessels in the penis, thereby making it difficult, if not impossible, for the diabetic to have an erection. In addition, some older males suffer from enlarged or diseased prostate glands which can interfere with urination and sexual functioning. The side effects of some drugs can also reduce the sexual drive; for example, many of the drug treatments for high blood pressure tend to decrease the sexual drive. It is important for people to ask their physicians what the side effects of drugs might be.

Cultural Reasons Some males have decreased sexual drive due to cultural factors. These men might be totally concerned and preoccupied with their careers and earning money. They might become so preoccupied with power, prestige, or wealth that these factors become the total focus of their lives. In addition, they may reach the middle-age plateau where physical changes reduce their sexual drive to the point they fear failure in adequately completing the sexual act. The greater the fear, the less likely they are to enjoy sexual activities. Increasingly, middle-aged women are becoming more assertive about sex at a time in life when some men are becoming insecure about their sexual abilities. The fear of sexual failure may result in a male ignoring his partner's hints or suggestions for sexual activity.

Sexual Boredom   Some persons become bored with their sexual partners, possibly because they have always had a rather boring sexual life. Twenty or thirty years of boring sex will tend to significantly reduce sexual desire. The research evidence is clear that those couples who have had a creative, happy, zestful sexual life are likely to continue that process into old age. The old adage, "use it or lose it," is as true of sexuality as it is of intelligence and physical stamina. People who get into the habit of just going through the same old sexual routine at 11:30, after the evening news, will probably be quite bored with sexuality by the time they reach middle age. They will probably spend many years towards the end of their lives with little or greatly reduced sexual activity.

Too Much to Eat and Drink   Eating too much food and drinking too much alcohol over the years will also tend to reduce the sexual drive. Being considerably overweight can lead to impotence as it brings about tiredness, loss of energy, diabetes, and possibly high blood pressure. Continued use of too much alcohol tends to lead to impotence or a marked reduction in sexual ability. Abuse of other types of substances, such as diazepam (Valium), cocaine, or heroin can also diminish the sexual drive.

Reduced Blood Flow   Probably the most important reason for impotence, however, is a reduction of adequate blood flow to the penis. An erection depends on a surge of blood into the blood vessels of the penis. When the blood vessels become clogged, deteriorated, or injured, blood no longer surges into the penis and an erection cannot occur.

Smoking can obstruct blood flow. The evidence indicates that many vascular obstructions are the result of smoking. When a male has been smoking for years, there is an increased probability that the blood vessels to his penis will become clogged, making it difficult for him to experience an erection. Other conditions that might obstruct blood flow are high blood pressure, diabetes, or high cholesterol. A woman needs to know that if she marries a man who smokes, there is an increased probability that he will be sexually impotent by age 50 or 60.

Inactivity   Some older men may suffer from something called "widower's syndrome." Because they have not had sexual intercourse for some time, they may find it difficult to have an erection. Usually with a patient and loving partner, this difficulty can be overcome. If not, professional help may be needed.

Urinary Tract Diseases   For many older men, an important change is the enlargement of their prostate gland, which can slow down or stop the urinary process. Males having this problem may urinate more frequently, have their urinary flow interrupted, or have a much weaker urinary flow and more difficulty emptying their bladder. All of these conditions can lead to an increase in urinary tract infection. Prostate infections may result in a fever, back pain, or an urgent need to urinate. They can also lead to impotence.

For many men, surgery may be necessary to remove the prostate gland if it becomes cancerous. In the past, the probability of the surgeon injuring the nerves affecting an erection was significant. Although modern techniques lessen the probability of impotence resulting from surgery, those with cancerous prostates may need to have treatments such as estrogen therapy, which will significantly reduce, if not totally destroy, the sexual drive.

The male sexual drive is best retained into old age by those males who are in good health, who have had a history of satisfying and frequent sexual intercourse, who have not abused substances, and who have a satisfying sexual partner.

Therapies

No one knows exactly how many men are impotent. There are some men who are impotent primarily because of psychological reasons. However, most impotent men are incapable of having an erection because of physical factors (Butler and Lewis 1976; Brecher 1984). Most impotency is caused by a lack of blood flow to the penis or because of hormonal deficiencies such as a lack of testosterone. Men suffering from a testosterone deficiency will benefit from testosterone injections.

Some men choose surgery to repair damaged blood vessels. The surgeon may graft arteries from other parts of the body to the penis to increase blood flow. This type of surgery is referred to as *revascularization*. These surgeries are rather new and are generally quite expensive.

Urologists can also use implants in men who can no longer obtain an erection. An implant is a type of prosthesis, usually made of silicone or rubber rods, which is inserted into the sides of the penis. Different types of rods are available. The rods enable the penis to become rigid enough for sexual intercourse to satisfy both partners.

In addition, a vacuum pump device has been developed that can produce an erection. The penis is enclosed in a tube, and a pump is used to force out air around the penis, drawing blood into the penis until it becomes rigid. The majority of the men who use the pump seem to be satisfied with the results.

Age-Related Sexual Changes in Females

Studies of older people and sexuality have resulted in the following probability statements, meaning that they are true for most but not all females:

- The older female, without the use of estrogen therapy, has less vaginal lubrication during sexual stimulation than younger females.

- Older women do not respond as quickly to sexual stimulation as younger women.
- Vaginal elasticity decreases with the aging process.
- The older the woman, the higher the probability that the clitoris has been reduced in size.
- Older woman are still orgasmic, but orgasm may not last as long and may not be as intense. Orgasms, though, are common in women in their seventies and eighties.
- Research indicates that the clitoris continues to respond to stimulation in the older woman, and nipples continue to respond to stimulation by becoming erect (Brecher 1984; Butler and Lewis 1976; Busse 1985).

Female Sexual Changes

As people grow older, both sexes take longer to respond to sexual stimulation (Butler and Lewis 1976; Weg 1983). It takes longer for the female's vaginal lubrication to occur after menopause, and it is generally less effective. In addition, the vagina has reduced elasticity and expansive qualities. After the age of 60, the clitoris is smaller but is still responsive to stimulation. Orgasms tend to be generally less intense and shorter in duration. In addition, the vaginal walls tend to become thinner. The loss of lubrication, the loss of elasticity, and the thinning of the vaginal walls are all primarily due to reduction of estrogen in the post-menopausal woman. Without estrogen replacement or the use of lubricants, intercourse may be painful for the older female.

The female who is addicted to alcohol, diazepam (Valium) or other substances will generally lose interest in sex. The very overweight female who becomes tired easily and doesn't have much energy probably will not be a responsive sexual partner.

Menopause and Related Therapies

Menopause is defined as the end of menstruation. In menopause the production of estrogen decreases significantly. This reduction is so significant that estrogen production is one-tenth of the premenopausal amount. American women go through menopause near the age of 50, although some experience it earlier, some later. Most women going through menopause have hot flashes, or flushes, a feeling of heat that usually spreads over their upper bodies. Some women also have feelings of dizziness (vertigo) and fatigue. Probably as many as 65 percent of women have no significant physical or psychological problems due to the menopause process. Most women can handle the hot flashes with a combination of humor and disregard, but some may need professional assistance because of physiological or psychological problems.

The long-term effects of menopause are significant (Butler and Lewis 1976; Hampton 1991; Katchadourian 1987). A loss of estrogen relates to the inability of the system to take in calcium and can result in osteoporosis, a thinning of the bones. In addition, loss of estrogen relates to the thinning of the vaginal walls and a reduction in lubrication for sexual intercourse.

The psychological effects of menopause are often the result of a change in a woman's social status rather than the result of physiological changes. Most women do not become depressed because they stop menstruating. Around the time of menopause many women see their last child leave home, and for women who have concentrated on being a parent, there may be a sense of loss which can lead to depression.

Some women go into a premature menopause because of a hysterectomy. In a simple hysterectomy the uterus and cervix are removed. In a total hysterectomy, the ovaries and fallopian tubes are also removed, causing, for some, premature menopause.

Estrogen replacement can be effective for many women. It can aid the body in absorbing calcium, thus decreasing the probability of osteoporosis. In addition, it increases vaginal lubrication, making intercourse more enjoyable. Taking into account her genetic history, a woman's gynecologist can determine the extent to which estrogen therapy should be prescribed, and with what combination of drugs.

According to research, hormone replacement therapy, in the form of estrogen, can be helpful in dealing with orgasmic contractions some older women experience (Burnside 1975; Weg 1983). It can also increase the sex drive in postmenopausal women (Brecher 1984). In addition, research has also indicated taking estrogen can increase levels of sexual functioning in eight out of ten measures, including the enjoyment of sex, the frequency of sex, the likelihood of waking up sexually aroused, the probability of having an orgasm when asleep, and the likelihood of reaching orgasm when masturbating.

These demonstrated results of estrogen therapy, according to other research, need to be weighed against possible negative effects of taking estrogen. Concerns about the safety of estrogen therapy include increased risks of uterus and breast cancer (Bergkvist et al. 1989). Additionally, some women have experienced "nausea, vomiting, abdominal cramps, bloating, headaches, dizziness, water retention, breast enlargement and tenderness, and increase in the size of persisting . . . benign tumors of the uterus" (Brecher, in Crandal 1991: 236–237).

These risks of using estrogen therapy can be minimized by taking lower doses, taking estrogen in combination with progestin, and regular medical exams as directed by a woman's physician (Weg 1983). A 1991 study published in the *New England Journal of Medicine* demonstrated the value of estrogen therapy in preventing heart conditions, a problem that becomes more threatening to women after menopause (Stampfer et al. 1991).

For women who do not take estrogen replacement, water-soluble lubricants, such as vaginal creams or KY Jellies, can be used to reduce discomfort brought about by inadequate lubrication. These can be obtained at any pharmacy without a prescription.

RELATIONSHIPS AND SEXUALITY

Older Couples

As they grow older, couples ideally develop an ability to anticipate each other's sexual needs. With years of experience, they can acquire the ability to fulfill those needs. They may develop a mutuality and reciprocity of sexual response that comes only after years of interaction. Masters and Johnson (1970a; 1970b) have indicated that two persons committed to each other in a loving relationship can learn to give sexual pleasure to the other as they communicate their sexual preferences in an atmosphere of trust and acceptance. With the passing years, many learn how to articulate and listen in an interplay of sexual recreation and desire.

For some postmenopausal women, the realization that they will no longer get pregnant liberates them sexually. No longer do they have to deal with the fear of pregnancy and menstrual periods. In addition, many post-menopausal women become liberated from inhibitions that kept them from a free expression of their sexual desires because of fear of pregnancy.

Robert Atchley (1991) indicated that couplehood for older people has four basic functions: (1) intimacy, (2) sexual intimacy, (3) interdependence, and (4) belonging. In some ways, all of these relate to sexuality in older adults even though not all of them focus directly on sexual activities. They all contribute to feelings of closeness, feelings of being needed, feelings of being close, and feelings of having someone to turn to in all aspects of life. In fact, research done by Wright (1989) indicated that many men have difficulties in developing close relationships with anyone other than their wives. Their spouse are an essential part of their being.

In terms of the sexuality of older couples, Brecher (1984) found that 75 percent of wives and 87 percent of husbands believed that sexuality was important in the marriages of persons over 50 years of age. In this study 67 percent of the wives and 59 percent of the husbands felt that the frequency of sex in their marriage was about right; 41 percent of the husbands and 18 percent of the wives indicated that they did not engage in sexual activities frequently enough with their spouses.

Starr and Weiner (1981) found that of the people between the ages of 60 and 91 they studied, 36 percent thought that the sex they were currently experiencing was better than the sex they experienced when they were younger. Twenty-five percent of the people they interviewed felt that sex for them currently was not as satisfying as when they were younger. Some 80 percent were sexually active, engaging in intercourse at least once a week. Participants in this study listed the things they liked about sex: a sense of contributing to others; feelings of desirability, zest, completion, and relaxation; feeling loved and loving; and the comfort of touching and cuddling (Atchley 1991).

However, research has uncovered strains that can develop in older marriages that can affect

TABLE 6-1						
SEXUAL BEHAVIOR IN OLDER PERSONS (PERCENTAGE)						
Frequency of	39–50		51–64		65+	
sexual intercourse	M	F	M	F	M	F
A few times a week	54	39	63	32	53	41
Weekly	29	63	18	33	16	33
Monthly	9	11	11	8	20	4
Rarely	8	21	8	27	11	22

Source: From *The Janus Report on Sexual Behavior* (p. 25) by S.S. Janus and C.L Janus, 1993, New York: Wiley. Copyright 1993 by S.S. Janus and C.L. Janus. Reprinted by permission.

feelings of closeness, mutual interdependence, intimacy, and sexuality. Gilford and Bengston (1979) found that feelings of marital satisfaction do not always persist throughout the long life of a marriage. Other research has found that spouses aged 55 to 62 and 70 to 90 have lower marital satisfaction than do those in the middle range of 63 to 69 (Gilford 1984). Additional research has indicated that over the years of marriage there can be a decline in the amount of love and commitment spouses express to each other (Swensen, Eskew, and Kohlhepp 1981) and "diminished feelings of marital intimacy and belongingness" (Swensen and Trahang 1985).

Retirement, particularly on the part of the husbands, and the ill health of a spouse are factors that can also contribute to marriage strains (Heyman and Jeffers 1968; Keating and Cole 1980; Crossman, London, and Barry 1981; Johnson 1985).

In an important article, Gilford (1986) pointed out that older spouses do not have very many ways to deflect the tensions that rise in their marriages. In general they usually do not have many, if any, relatives, co-workers, or friends with whom to discuss their personal and marital problems. Most do not discuss intimate problems with their children, and few older spouses ever turn to professional help for their marriage problems. According to Gilford, "Service providers in a range of community settings are in a position to strengthen the ties that find spouses in older marriages." She went on to say, appropriately for those who want to help older people,

> Social programs have appeared to overlook well, older couples as a consumer population, possibly on the common assumption that their marital status protects them from distress. Yet older husbands and wives may need social and professional support as they undertake to redefine the marital relationships and reestablish the bases of mutuality that bind them (Gilford, in Cox 1991: 40).

Psychological Factors in Sexuality A decrease in sexual desire in some aging couples is not always the result of physiological factors

(Brecher 1984; Butler and Lewis 1976; Busse and Maddox 1985; Palmore 1981). People can become bored after decades of the same type of sexual activity. Some couples have never experimented with different sexual techniques or positions. Some couples simply have not been creative or playful in their attitude toward sexuality. After 20 years or more they no longer find each other exciting sexual partners.

Some couples drift into sexual apathy because of unresolved anger. They attempt to "get at" their partner by refusing sexual activity or significantly reducing the amount or type of sexual contact. This can happen to couples at any age. Unfortunately, too many older people believe that their reduced sexual contact is simply the result of growing older. As a result they do not get the type of counseling which would enable them to resolve their feelings of anger and once again become a sexually active partner.

Depression can also be a major factor in the loss of sexual desire. Depression can occur at any age; it is a major factor in sexual dysfunction at all ages. Unfortunately, once again, the older the person, the higher the probability that she or he will assume that sexual dysfunction is the result of physical factors and thus will not seek the help that could rejuvenate his or her sexual life.

In instances where there is no physical basis for the loss of sexual desire, professional counseling can be helpful. A competent counselor can assist in understanding the factors and processes that lead to a loss of sexual desire. An effective counselor can also be helpful in recovering sexual drive.

Sexual response is complex and involves a person's physiology including hormones, blood flow, nerve endings, and drug usage. It also includes one's psychological condition: whether one is depressed, has a positive self-image, and is positive in outlook on life. Furthermore, sexual response includes relationships with one's significant other, one's sexual partner. It also includes the values one has regarding sexuality. Regardless of age, sexuality is usually a valued aspect of life, and most people can function sexually into old age.

Mutual Masturbation/Pleasuring

When we hear someone talk about "having sex," being "sexually active" or "sexually involved," being in a "sexual relationship" or "intimate" with someone, we most often think and assume these phrases refer to sexual intercourse. This has been a part of our culture. According to some experts in sexuality, much of the emphasis on intercourse stems from a historical perspective of sexual relations that is based on old norms that focus on (1) sex equals intercourse only; (2) children and older people are asexual and because they are not reproductive, their sexuality is denied; and (3) sexual thoughts, emotions, and fantasies are equally evil as sexual deeds. The major emphasis on sex in this orientation is on procreation—producing children. In this value approach it is not important for women to be sexually satisfied since the pleasurable aspects of sexuality are thought to be rather deviant. These pleasurable aspects would include prolonged sexual play and mutual masturbation (Hacker 1990). In an article proposing a new and more realistic approach to sexuality, Dr. Sylvia Hacker of the University of Michigan advocated new sexual norms for society that include (1) sexuality is far more than sexual intercourse; (2) children and older people are sexual; and (3) sexual thoughts, feelings, and fantasies occur normally. In this new approach to sexuality, Dr. Hacker pointed out that sex and sexuality are not inherently bad. Human beings are by nature sexual and are subject to a wide range of sexual stimuli. She indicated that sexual intercourse is only one part of a wide range of sexual activities that can bring pleasure and satisfaction to people. She also pointed out that intercourse can be a real health hazard with all the sexually transmitted diseases in evidence today, including AIDS.

Dr. Hacker did not propose to stop all sexual pleasures. She pointed out that sexual pleasure can be achieved outside of sexual intercourse. For example, males get pleasure from ejaculation, which can be achieved by masturbation; but the greatest pleasure is achieved when both sexual partners have orgasms, which in many instances are not achieved by women through intercourse. This is particularly true for older, postmenopausal women who lose vaginal lubrication. Not only do many not achieve orgasm through sexual intercourse because of lack of adequate stimulation, but intercourse can be painful without supplemental lubrication.

Dr. Hacker focused on developing "great lover" techniques, which include slowing down and getting in touch with each person's sensuality. This means achieving very pleasurable orgasms by focusing on bringing pleasure to each partner without mandatory intercourse. It means touching, caressing, massaging, hugging, fondling, and bringing to orgasm each partner by manipulation.

Dr. Hacker pointed out that this approach can be very helpful to older people. With aging there is often slower erection response in males, with longer periods of time to achieve orgasm. As we pointed out, older females can find penetration in intercourse painful at worst, not too satisfying at the least. Concentrating on what gives each person pleasure through manual stimulation can be very pleasurable for older adults (as well as younger persons who want to avoid pregnancy, lower the risk of sexually transmitted diseases, or simply want to wait until marriage or a long-term relationship before having intercourse).

Dr. Hacker pointed out that one of the factors that has limited the use of mutual masturbation to achieve pleasure is a cultural reluctance to ejaculate semen on the outside of the body. Somehow this has been looked at as "dirty," or at least not something in which to take pleasure. But towels or other appropriate means can be used to collect semen. One approach is the use of condoms for mutual masturbation. A partner's preapplication of a condom may signal a willingness or eagerness for sexual play, which can begin with very light caressing far from the genital or erogenous areas of the body. Many partners in the mutual stimulation process enjoy the application of a condom as part of this process. With a condom in place ejaculation can occur at any time and place without "messy" consequences, if that is a hang-up to mutual masturbation.

The focus away from standard intercourse as the primary focus of sexual intimacy can bring new opportunities for sexual pleasure in partners of all ages. For older persons who have socialized in the old cultural norm of sexuality, mutual masturbation/pleasuring can be a liberating experience.

Single Older Adults and Dating

The results of the studies of older singles are tremendously diverse. Some older persons have been single all of their lives and see themselves as happily single. They do not appreciate others who assume that something important is lacking in their lives. Many of them value their independence, have developed a network of friends, and do not see themselves as lonely. They have spent a lifetime adjusting to their single status and their sexual needs (Antoniak, Scott, and Worcester 1979; Napolitane and Pellegrine 1977; Stein 1981).

Changing Dating Patterns   Many divorced singles who have been sexually active are forced to adjust to a world where they do not have a regular partner to satisfy their sexual needs. In their research, Wallerstein and Blakeslee (1989) found that ten years after divorce 30 percent of divorced women are still angry and frustrated over their divorce. Many of these women find men who are available as sexual partners, but some of these men are manipulative and untruthful in their relationships. Hunt (1966) found that the average divorced woman was sexually propositioned by the second date. He also found that many older divorced women were not prepared for the quickness with which sexual intimacy developed between daters in the modern era. Many of these divorced women had done their previous dating at a time when sexual activity was more restrained and intimacy developed at a slower pace.

Many divorced men find that the reality of finding sexual partners after divorce does not match the fantasizing they may have done. Research indicates that singles, both men and women, have less sexual intercourse than married couples. Having gone through two sexual revolutions, in the 1920s and in the 1960s, many men are still trying to experience the results of these revolutions.

Dealing with Widowhood   Widowed persons have some of the same problems as divorced singles and some problems that are distinctly different. Some widowed persons are angry with their deceased partners for dying, for not being available to help them with their current problems. At other times they have a nostalgic view of their relationship with their former spouse which mostly emphasizes the positive aspects in their marriage. As a result, when some widowed persons date, they often discuss only the positive characteristics of their former spouse. Others use the dating process to go through an emotional release in expressing their anger about their former spouse.

More Older People Dating   Very little research has been done on dating and older persons, even though it is an important aspect in the lives of many older people. In an important contribution to the study of dating partners of older people, Bulcroft and O'Conner-Roden (1986) conducted research and published their results indicating why so many more older people were dating these days than in previous times. They include (1) the number of older people in America has increased, (2) people are living longer and staying healthier, (3) older people are less likely to have children living with them, and (4) divorces among older people are increasing.

Common Feelings and Dating Activities   Research indicates that both older and younger people have most of the same feelings when they fall in love—sweaty hands, feelings of awkwardness, inability to concentrate, anxiety when away from their loved one, and heart palpations. "Older men tended to equate romance with sexuality," (Bulcroft and O'Conner-Roden, in Cox 1991: 58).

An interesting question was pursued in this research: "What do older men do on dates?" The answers included the same activities that younger people engaged in except they were often more creative and varied. Often this was because the older couple had more money.

More interesting, the research found that the pace of the relationship was speeded up for the older couples they studied. Some of the participants in the study said that there was "not much time for playing the field" (Cox 1991: 59). They found that sexuality tended to develop more rapidly for the older couples. "While sexuality for these couples included intercourse, the stronger emphasis was on the manner of sexual behavior such as hugging, kissing, and touching." Physical closeness was very important to the older people. For those living alone, their dating partner was often their only source of feeling close to someone physically. This research also indicated that the intimacy of sex enhanced their feelings of self-esteem. One 77-year-old said, "Sex isn't as important when you're older, but in a way you need it more" (Cox: 59).

Sex and Personal Values   Bulcroft and O'Connor-Roden also discussed the fact that even though physical intimacy in sexual relationships are vital to many older people, it is often in direct conflict with the value systems they have lived with all their lives. This can result in very mixed feelings on the part of older people as well as attempts to hide their behavior from friends and family. One 63-year-old man said, "Yeah, my girlfriend (age 64) lives just down the hall from me . . . when she spends the night she usually brings her cordless phone . . . just in case her daughter calls" (Bulcroft and O'Conner-Roden, in Cox 1991: 60). Still, not too many of the couples studied wanted to marry their dating partner. Some were not willing to give up their independence. Others said they did not have the same reasons for

marriage that younger people do, such as starting a new life and beginning a new family. Others were fearful of deteriorating health; they did not want to become caregivers of a sick spouse. Many older couples do not marry because of financial considerations including possible loss of pension or Social Security income, complex estate provisions, and inheritances for children.

Lack of Partners   This research indicated the general importance of dating to old single people. It provided their lives with "something that cannot be supplied by family and friends."

The greatest obstacle for sexual fulfillment for single older people (widowed, divorced, or never married) is an available sexual partner. This is especially true for females, as there are many more older women than men. The most typical sexual activity for sexual release for single older people who lack a sexual partner is masturbation. However, some older persons feel uneasy or actually have feelings of guilt about masturbation. It would relieve feelings of guilt and anxiety among many older persons if they understood that they are not engaging in any deviant activity by masturbating; a great many persons, single or not, masturbate. However, masturbation does not provide the closeness and intimacy of a partner that so many older people need.

Older Homosexuals

There is no agreement as to why some persons are heterosexual while others are homosexual. In addition, until the 1970s, there was very little research on older homosexuals (Bell and Weinberg 1978; Bell, Weinberg, and Hammersmith 1981). The research that has taken place indicates a tremendous variety of lifestyles among homosexuals. Long-term relationships are common, some lasting for a lifetime. Many homosexuals experience problems such as relationships to their extended families, acceptance of their lifestyle by children (about 20 percent of gay men have been married and half of those have children through their marriages), broader friendship patterns in the community, acceptance at work, and possible rejection in their religious communities.

The research by Masters and Johnson was the first to point out the sexual responses of homosexuals and how it was similar to, and different from, heterosexual response. They found that many of the sexual problems that heterosexual males experience as they grow older were also found among older gay men. These include the inability to have an erection, a longer time after reaching organism before being able to have another erection, a more flaccid erection, and loss of sexual desire. They also found that therapeutic techniques and procedures that were successful among heterosexual men were also successful among homosexual men.

Some studies have indicated that older homosexuals in some ways adapt better to their homosexuality than do younger homosexuals. One factor supporting this position is that some older gays have less fear of having their sexual orientation exposed; since most are retired, they no longer have to worry about their employer finding out about their homosexuality (Kelly 1977; Weinberg and Williams 1974; Berger 1982a, 1982b).

Other studies have indicated that the homosexual lifestyle can actually help people adjust to growing older (Kimmel 1978). They point out that many homosexuals are more self-reliant in maintaining themselves in their own homes, and this is an important aspect of survival in old age that many older men have not developed. Other studies have shown that homosexuals are better at dealing with devalued identities because they have had to cope with this reality as gays. They contend that this ability is important in coping with being "old" in our contemporary society (Johnson and Kelly 1979; Berger 1982a, 1982b).

Other studies have indicated some other characteristics of older homosexuals.

- Some older male and female homosexuals tend to have more developed friendship patterns than heterosexuals their ages (Harris 1990).
- Most older male homosexuals are satisfied with their sex lives (Kelly 1977). One study

found that some 75 percent of homosexual men were either somewhat or very satisfied with their sex lives (Berger 1982a, 1982b).
- Homosexuals, both men and women, do not see themselves as growing older any sooner than heterosexuals do. In fact, lesbians do not see themselves as growing older as early as nonlesbian women (Minnigerade 1976; Laner 1978, 1979).
- Older homosexuals of both sexes prefer partners their own age (Laner 1978, 1979; Kelly 1980).
- Homosexual men generally have fewer sexual partners as they grow older. Many have only one (Berger 1982a, 1982b).

Some experts on aging have speculated that homosexuality may become more prevalent as a sexual outlet for older women due to the serious lack of male sexual partners (Crandall 1991). This speculation is probably based on the fact that some 10 percent of the older population is homosexual, a figure that parallels the general population (Teitelman 1987); that 59 percent of men and 67 percent of women approved of homosexuality for consenting adults (Starr and Weiner 1981); and that the sexual revolution of recent years would make it likely that more women would choose less traditional sexual lifestyles in the years ahead (Crandall 1991). Much of this speculation developed before the reality of HIV infection and the spread of AIDS.

HIV/AIDS AND OLDER PEOPLE

Older people are not usually thought of as a high-risk group of people to be exposed to the HIV virus. Little attention has been paid by researchers to understanding the risks middle- and older-aged persons take regarding AIDS (acquired immunodeficiency syndrome) (Stall and Catania 1994).

Of the 339,000 Americans who were infected with AIDS as of September 1993, 34,000 were persons aged 50 and older. This was more than double the number of older people who had AIDS in January 1991 (Baker and Crowley

1994). Middle- and older-aged people continue to make up just over 10 percent of the total number of persons in the United States with AIDS.

"It's the last secret of the AIDS game," said researcher Ron Stall of the University of California and San Francisco. "The AIDS epidemic has been treated exclusively as a problem of young people" (Baker and Crowley 1994: 5).

It should be noted that health experts quickly point out that most people aged 50 and over are not likely to become infected with the HIV virus, the virus that leads to AIDS. But those older people who are at risk tend to do very little to protect themselves against the disease. For example, the recent landmark study of AIDS in middle-aged and elderly people by Stall and Catania (1994) found that very few persons over the age of 50 who had behavioral risks for HIV infection used condoms during sex or had had HIV tests. In fact, this same study found that at-risk persons over the age of 50 were one-sixth as likely to use condoms during sex and one-fifth as likely to have been tested for the HIV virus as a similar group of persons in their twenties who had the same types of risk factors.

"Older people just do not perceive themselves at risk . . . They mistakenly believe that AIDS just does not happen in their generation," stated Ellen Stover, director of the office of AIDS at the National Institute of Mental Health (Baker and Crowley 1994: 5).

"Older people haven't gotten the message about what they can do to protect themselves," said Marcia Ory, chief of social science research at the National Institute on Aging's Behavior and Research Program (Baker and Crowley 1994: 5). Ory went on to say that sexual activity is not really discussed as it applies to older people, but older people are engaging in sexual activities, some of which are risky. Even physicians often neglect to take the sexual histories of older patients or to bring up the subject of AIDS. This can be devastating for some older people who are at risk for the HIV virus.

Who Gets AIDS Among Older Adults?

Similar to any other age group, the majority (63 percent) of AIDS patients aged 50 and older become infected through sexual activities (Baker and Crowley 1994). Unlike other age groups, there is a real difference in the proportion of older AIDS patients who became infected through blood transfusions. Older people have a much higher proportion of cases traced to blood transfusions (Stall and Catania 1994). Even more profound are the differences between the age groups of AIDS patients who became infected through heterosexual transmission—persons who got AIDS through heterosexual activity in comparison to homosexual activity. Stall and Catania pointed out that even though AIDS in older persons through heterosexual activity was unknown before the mid-1980s, by 1990, 10 percent of all cases among persons 50 years of age and older were from heterosexual contacts. This is the largest proportion of AIDS cases through heterosexual activity for any adult age group. This rapid increase in the proportion of AIDS cases among persons 50 years of age and older traced to heterosexual contacts occurred after 1986, some three years after finding an initial burst of AIDS cases related to blood transfusions.

AIDS Risk Factors for Older People

The most important risk factors among older people have been found to be:

- multiple sex partners (of either gender);
- a sex partner with known behavioral risks (who practiced or practices unsafe sex); and
- blood transfusion between 1979 and 1985 (Stall and Catania 1994: 59)

This can be a serious situation for older persons who begin to date following a divorce or the death of a spouse. Stall and Catania (1994) found that in a detailed examination of risk factors for AIDS among older people, men were more likely than women to have at least one risk factor. On the basis of race and ethnicity, African Americans had the highest risk factors followed by whites and Latinos. Persons who were separated, divorced, or never married had risk factors higher than those who were married, widowed, or cohabiting. Gay and bisexual men reported the greatest frequency of having at least one risk factor of all of the groups in the study by Stall and Catania, even though they were more likely to use a condom during sexual activity and were more likely to have been tested for the HIV virus.

Because the risk of acquiring AIDS from blood transfusions is currently very low, and intravenous drug use among persons aged 50 and older is also low, the greatest risk for middle-aged and older Americans is from sexual behavior. It is not "surprising that older at-risk Americans are less likely to have adapted behaviors that can slow the spread of HIV infection, since the emphasis of AIDS prevention messages has been almost exclusively on the young" (Stall and Catania 1994: 62). Prevention campaigns targeted at older heterosexual persons are urged, since past education programs aimed at gay/bisexual men proved that persons do respond to these types of approaches. Studies of prevention education programs, targeted at gay/bisexual men, "show that when Americans past the age of 50 are made aware of their risk for HIV infection and are shown specific ways to avoid infection, they can and will reduce their risks" (p. 62).

In addition, Stall and Catania (1994) have called for health care providers to raise the issue of sex and sexual health with their patients who are aged 50 and older. They went on to point out that sex is enjoyed by many older persons well into their oldest-old years, and some do not practice safe sex, especially after becoming single again.

Where to Get Help

A number of resources are available to help older persons and their families dealing with AIDS. These include:

- Fact sheet on AIDS and older adults from the National Institution on Aging: (800) 222-2225.
- "A Guide to Home Care for the Person with AIDS": Local Chapters of the American Red Cross, booklet no. 3 295 42.
- Pamphlets: "Preventing HIV/AIDS" (D-712), "Caring for someone with AIDS" (D-498),

and Surgeon General's Report on AIDS (D-323) from National AIDS Clearinghouse: (800) 458-5231.
- AIDS hotline of the U.S. Center for Disease Control and Prevention: (800) 342-AIDS; Spanish-language Hotline: (800) 344-7432; TDY hotline for hearing impaired: (800) 344-7432.

SUMMARY

Recent research has shown that older people are very interested in sex and need the intimacy that sexual contact provides. Too many elderly persons still believe the myth that sexual activity is only for the young. With the passage of time, the elderly can become less inhibited sexually and more willing to communicate to their partners what gives them pleasure. It is true that some men after age 50 begin to require more direct stimulation of the genitalia, and that needs to be communicated to their sexual partners. On the other hand, the slowing of sexual response in some older males may be an advantage in that it reduces premature ejaculation.

Present evidence seems to indicate that regular sexual activity, coupled with adequate physical well-being, a healthy up-beat attitude toward sexuality, and a zestful orientation toward the aging process will combine to provide a continuing sexually stimulating climate for older people.

Because many people accept society's negative view of aging and sexuality, it is important for older people, and people who work with them, to know that sex can be an important and vital part of aging. Too many myths are believed by too many elderly people about sexuality. Too many assume that growing older results in sexual dysfunction. Sexual dysfunctions that do occur are not seen as reversible, when in fact they often are. The values of older people concerning sexuality greatly influence their sexual practices as they grow older. There are some elderly people who are happy and content to be essentially uninvolved in sexual experiences: This is their preference; they should not feel that they are strange or abnormal if they are not sexually active. Neither, though, should any elderly person feel abnormal about strong sexual feelings and a need to express them. Adequate information is helpful in understanding sexual feelings and in choosing patterns of behavior that are consistent with personal values and desires. Sometimes it is embarrassing for older people brought up in a time when sexuality was not discussed to deal openly with sexual issues. It is important that they realize sexuality is a normal human need that can be discussed openly and can be satisfied in many different ways.

Older people do not have to duplicate the sexual behavior of youth in order to enjoy their sexual experiences. Partners can decide together what pleases the other, what each is capable of, and what contributes to their continuing satisfying relationship.

As at any age, but especially in old age, sexual activity fulfills the human need for the warmth of physical nearness and intimacy. We hope that the myth that if older people desire sexual activity they are deviant has been put to rest. The fact that older people have an interest in, and an enthusiasm for, sexuality does not make them immoral, "dirty" or disgusting. It means that they are in good health, are psychologically stable, and continue to enjoy one of the more satisfying experiences humans can have.

REFERENCES

Antoniak, H., Scott, N.L., and Worcester, N. 1979. *Alone*. Millbrae, CA: Les Femmes Press.

Atchley, R.C. 1991. *Social Forces and Aging*, 6th Ed. Belmont, CA: Wadsworth Publishing Company.

Baker, B., and Crowley, S.L. 1994. AIDS Crisis Reaches Those 50 Plus. *AARP Bulletin*, 35(2): 5, 8.

Bell, A.P., and Weinberg, M.S. 1978. *A Study of Diversity Among Men and Women*. New York: Simon and Schuster.

Bell, A.P., Weinberg, M.S., and Hammersmith, S. 1981. *Sexual Preference: Its Development in Men and Women*. Bloomington, IN: Indiana University Press.

Berger, R.M. 1982a. *Gay and Gray*. Urbana, IL: University of Illinois Press.

Berger, R.M. 1982b. The Unseen Minority: Older Gays and Lesbians. *Social Work*, 27: 236–241.

Bergkvist, L., Adami, H-O., Person, I., Hoover, R., and Schairer, C. 1989. The Risk of Breast Cancer After Estrogen and Estrogen-Progestin Replacement. *New England Journal of Medicine*, 321(5): 293–297.

Brecher, E.M. 1984. *Love, Sex, and Aging*. Boston: Little, Brown and Company.

Bruini, F. 1993b. Difference With Dignity: Older Guys Have Had a Long Wait for This Moment. *Detroit Free Press* (April 27): 3D.

Bruini, F. 1993b. Lust for Life. *Detroit Free Press*, (September 28): 1–3C.

Burnside, I.M. 1975. Sexuality and the Older Adult: Implications for Nursing. In I.M. Burnside (ed.), *Sexuality and Aging*. Los Angeles: University of California Press.

Busse, E.W., and Maddox, G.L. 1985. *The Duke Longitudinal Studies of Normal Aging, 1955–1980*. New York: Springer.

Butler, R.N., and Lewis, M.I. 1994. *Love and Sex After Sixty*. New York: Ballantine Books.

Bulcroft, K., and O'Conner-Roden, M. 1986. Never Too Late. *Psychology Today*, (June): 66–69.

Covey, H.C. 1994. Perceptions and Attitudes Toward Sexuality of the Elderly During the Middle Ages. *Gerontologist*, Vol. 29, No. 1. In *Annual Editions, Aging*, 9th Ed. Sluice Dock, Guilford, CT: Dushkin Publishing Group.

Cox, H. (ed.). 1991. *Aging: Seventh Edition*. Sluice Dock, Guilford, CT: Dushkin Publishing Group.

Crandall, R.C. 1991. *Gerontology: A Behavioral Science Approach*, 2d Ed. New York: McGraw-Hill.

Crossman, L., London, C., and Barry, C. 1981. Older Women Caring for Disabled Spouses: A Model for Supportive Sources. *Gerontologist*, 21(5): 464–470.

Gilford, R. 1986. Marriages in Later Life. *Generations: Journal of the American Society on Aging*, X 4: 16–20.

Gilford, R. 1984. Contrasts in Marital Satisfaction Throughout Old Age: An Exchange Theory Analysis. *Journal of Gerontology*, 39(3): 325–333.

Gilford, R., and Bengtson, V. 1979. Measuring Marital Satisfaction in Three Generations: Positive and Negative Dimensions. *Journal of Marriage and the Family*, 41(2): 387–398.

Hacker, S.S. 1990. The Transition From the Old Norm to the New: Sexual Values for the 1990s. *SIE CUIU*, (June/July): 18(5): 1–8.

Hampton, J.K., Jr. 1991. *The Biology of Human Aging*. Dubuque, IA: William C. Brown Publishers.

Harris, D.K. 1990. *Sociology of Aging*, 2d ed. New York: Harper and Row Publishers.

Heyman, D., and Jeffers, F. 1968. Wives and Retirement: A Pilot Study. *Journal of Gerontology*, 23(4): 488–496.

Hunt, M. 1966. *The World of the Formerly Married*. New York: McGraw-Hill.

Johnson, C. 1985. The Impact of Illness on Late-Life Marriages. *Journal of Marriage and the Family*, 47(1): 165–172.

Johnson, M.T., and Kelly, J.J. 1979. Deviate Sex Behavior in the Lives of Older Gay People. In O.J. Kaplan (ed.), *Psychopathology of Aging*. New York: Academic Press, pp. 243–258.

Katchadourian, H. 1987. *Fifty: Midlife in Perspective*. New York: W.H. Freeman Company.

Keating, N., and Cole, P. 1980. What Do I Do With Him 24 Hours a Day? Changes in the Housewife Role after Retirement. *Gerontologist*, 20(91): 84–89.

Kelly, J. 1977. The Aging Male Homosexual: Myth and Reality. *Gerontologist*, 17: 328–332.

Kelly, J. 1980. Homosexuality and Aging. In J. Marmor (ed.), *Multiple Roots of Homosexual Behavior*. New York: Basic Books, pp. 176–193.

Kimmel, D.C. 1978. Adult Development and Aging: A Gay Perspective. *Journal of Social Issues*, 34: 113–130.

Kinsey, A.C., Pomeroy, W.B., and Martin, C.E. 1948. *Sexual Behavior in the Human Male*. Philadelphia: W.B. Saunders.

Kinsey, A., Pomeroy, W.B., and Gebhard, P.H. 1953. *Sexual Behavior in the Human Female*. Philadelphia: W. B. Saunders.

Laner, M.R. 1978. Growing Older Male: Heterosexual and Homosexual. *Gerontologist*, 18: 496–501.

Laner, M.R. 1979. Growing Older Female: Heterosexual and Homosexual. *Gerontologist*, 4: 267–275.

Masters, W.H., and Johnson, V.E. 1966. *Human Sexual Response*. Boston: Little, Brown.

Masters, W.H., and Johnson, V.E. 1970a. *Human Sexual Inadequacy*. Boston: Little, Brown.

Masters, W.H., and Johnson, V.E. 1970b. *The Pleasure Bond*. Boston: Little, Brown.

Minnigerade, F.A. 1976. Age-Status Labeling in Homosexual Men. *Journal of Homosexuality*, 1: 273–276.

Napolitane, C., and Pellegrine, B. 1977. *Living and Loving After Divorce*. New York: Signet Books.

Palmore, E.B. 1981. *Social Patterns in Normal Aging: Findings from the Duke Longitudinal Study*. Durham, NC: Duke University Press.

Stall, R., and Catania, J. 1994. AIDS Risk Behaviors Among Late Middle-aged and Elderly Americans. *Archives of Internal Medicine*, 154: 57–63.

Stampfer, M.J., Colditz, G.A., Willett, J.E., Rosher, B., Speizer, F.E., and Hennekens, C.H. 1991. Postmenopausal Estrogen Therapy and Cardiac Vascular Disease: Ten-Year Follow-up From the Nurses' Health Study. *New England Journal of Medicine*, 325(11): 756–762.

Starr, B.D., and Weiner, M.B. 1981. *The Starr–Weiner Report on Sex and Sexuality in the Mature Years*. New York: McGraw-Hill.

Stein, P.J. (ed.). 1981. *Single Life: Unmarried and Married Adults in Social Context*. New York: St. Martin's Press.

Swensen, C., Eskew, R., and Kohlhepp, K. 1981. Stage of Family Life Cycle, Ego Development, and Marriage Relationship. *Journal of Marriage and the Family*, 43(4): 841–853.

Swensen, C., and Trahang, G. 1985. Commitment and the Long-Term Marriage Relationships. *Journal of Marriage and the Family*, 43(4): 841–853.

Teitelman, J.L. 1987. Homosexuality. In G.L. Maddox (ed.), *The Encyclopedia of Aging*. New York: Springer, pp. 329–330.

Towery, T. 1993. Readers Respond to Man's Homosexual Relationship. *The Bradenton Herald*, (December 31) PC-10.

Wallerstein, J.S., and Blakeslee, S. 1989. *Second Chances: Men, Women and Children a Decade After Divorces*. New York: Ticknor and Fields.

Weg, R.B. 1983. *Sexuality in the Later Years: Roles and Behavior*. New York: Academic Press.

Weinberg, M.S., and Williams, C.J. 1974. *Male Homosexuals: Their Problems and Adaptations*. New York: Oxford University Press.

Wright, P. 1989. Gender Differences in Adults Same- and Cross-Gender Friendships. In R.S. Adams and R. Bleiszner (eds.), *Older Friendship*. Newbury Park, CA: Sage Publications, pp. 197–221.

CHAPTER 7

Death
and
Dying

Perplexing Cases

James has been in a nursing home for three years. After three major strokes he cannot talk or take care of any of his bodily needs. In his last attempts at communication, he said he wanted to die. He has pneumonia and the staff wants to send him to an acute care hospital for intensive treatment. Should they?

Grace is being kept alive by a feeding tube. She has no lucidity. If the tube is removed she will die. What should the family do?

Alice is 89. She is lucid but suffering from severe diabetes which has led to the amputation of her legs and to blindness. She refuses to eat. She says that she wants to die. Should the staff "force feed" her?

Two years ago Ralph lost his wife after 62 years of marriage. He is still in deep depression because of her death. He mostly talks about how much he misses her. He does not care to continue living and frequently says that he wishes he would die. He has not responded well to psychiatric treatment. He has a severe heart condition and refuses to take his medications. If he has a heart attack he might die, and yet he has thrown away his latest prescription. What should the family do?

David, after 46 years of marriage, is struggling with what type of funeral he should have for his wife. In his grief and lack of knowledge about funerals, he is totally dependent on the funeral director. His bill for the funeral will be $6,750. Excessive? Moderate?

Martha has been attending Widowed Persons meetings for the last fifteen months. It has helped her through the grieving process. She is now beginning to have interesting conversations with some of the men at the meetings. She is 69 and is beginning to think of "dating." Most of the men are in their seventies. Should her children be worried about the relationships that their mother might be developing?

Peter is 63 and quite rich. He has been a widower for two years. He is retired and in excellent health. If he wanted to, he could spend his time traveling around the world. He is dating a 46-year-old divorcée with two dependent children. Peter's three children are worried that their father is going to spend the rest of his life supporting and being devoted to another family. They think he is being set up. Should his children be concerned?

A NORMAL PART OF HUMAN EXISTENCE

In spite of the marvelous advances that have been made in medical technology, the increased availability of medical services, and a better standard of living for many people in the United States that has resulted in a considerable longer life expectancy in this century (75.8 years in 1992), death is still part of all human existence. Death is not abnormal; it comes to all living creatures. As Jan van Eys pointed out, "Dying must be considered as a normal state in and of itself. The process of dying is not extraordinarily different from the process of healthy normal living, for they coexist in the same world" (Leming and Dickinson 1990: 157).

For the older person, death is expected and becomes a normal event (Leming and Dickinson 1990). The problem of death for older people is not so much death itself, but how and under what circumstances death will take place.

Until recently, Americans tended to be willing to discuss death in the abstract but were uncomfortable discussing their own deaths. Death in American society tends to be hidden in hospitals and nursing homes, and few Americans see their relatives die. They are told that death has occurred. Most people say they want to die at home, but most do not die there.

Because so many people in American society are not comfortable discussing death other than in the abstract, many euphemisms are used to refer to death or dying, such as "the departed," "passed on," "expired," "passed away," "succumbed," "croaked," "crashed in," "checked out," and "six feet under." As a result, many people are ill at ease talking to someone about the death of a close relative or about a patient's imminent demise.

Most Americans never see a dead body except one that has been prepared for viewing by a mortician. Stephenson (1985) has contended that death in the United States is characterized by prolongation, bureaucratization, and secularization. Modern medical practice with its array of medicines, surgeries, and other modalities can keep the dying person alive considerably beyond what would have occurred in past years. As a result, dying, for many, has become a very lengthy process of suffering and pain. Bureaucratization occurs because many seriously ill people are treated impersonally, in a complex organization in which the person often becomes a non-person, known more by the disease than by his or her personhood. Secularization occurs because the spiritual dimension of dying and death is ignored or considered irrelevant. In the process, often without close friends and family members around, the patient loses his or her identity and is stripped of dignity.

At one time in American history, most people died at home. Now approximately 70 percent die in an institutional setting. In keeping with banishing death from the homes of America to the hospitals, funerals (including paying respects and sharing grief with relatives, friends, and neighbors) were moved from the family parlor to the funeral parlor (Leming and Dickinson 1990). Following the Civil War, middle-class Americans began to replace the formal parlor in their homes with "living rooms." Corpses were not laid out in living rooms. This process has extended through the twentieth century (Farrell 1980). All of this has made death more distant to the family setting and more removed from the normal life cycle.

FEAR OF DEATH

Similar to people of all ages, older people have some fears and concerns as they get nearer to death. Research has indicated that older persons think about death more often than younger peo-

ple do, but the elderly seem to be less fearful and have less anxiety about it (Leming and Dickinson 1990). Research is not clear as to why older people seem to fear death less than younger people. Kalish (1987) pointed out that there may be at least three reasons. The old may believe that they have lived their lives to the fullest, and as a result, they have a sense of completion and realize that death is the next natural part of the life cycle. Some are in a painful, prolonged, hopeless illness where they see death as a release from pain and suffering. Others have lost so many friends and relatives that they increasingly feel isolated from others. They have seen their spouses and close friends die and have "less to live for." One of the results of living into the oldest old years is that one loses most of one's friends to death at a time when physical debilities make it hard to make new friends.

Fear of the Dying Process

Older people do have some anxieties as to how and under what circumstances they will die. Balfour Mount (1976) found that there are several concerns people have about the dying process. Many people fear that they may die alone, have considerable pain, become a burden on their loved ones, and become a financial burden on their family. In addition, some have indicated a fear of death itself, of the unknown, of what happens after death.

Niemeyer (1988) discussed the fears of dying that people may have as a result of their religious beliefs about a life after death: concern for punishment for what they have done; fear of being abandoned; fear of pain and indignity; and fear of being nonexistent. He pointed out that women seem to have more fear about death than do men, or they may be more open in expressing their fears. He also indicated that research does not show that education about death reduces the fear of death. In fact, there is some evidence that death education may increase the fear of death.

It should be added that most older persons have had relatives and friends who died rather peacefully. In research involving 1,000 persons over age 65 in Connecticut, McCarthy (1991) found that most died quite peacefully. In fact, 10 percent were in good health the day they died, and more than half were in good health a year before they died.

Russell (1989), in *American Demographics*, pointed out that the average American has a better than 50 percent chance of dying without pain. She stated that 61 percent of those who died were not in pain at the time of their deaths and 53 percent died in their sleep. Fifty-three percent were estimated to be in good health a year before they died, with 24 percent in excellent health a month before they died. Nine out of every ten of those who died saw various members of their families in the last two days of life. These facts should reduce the fears that some people have of dying isolated and in pain. Such fears can take the following form:

> They fear a long, painful, and disfiguring death, or death in a vegetative state hooked to sophisticated machines while hospital bills eat up their insurance and savings. They fear that their families will be overburdened by their prolonged care and the expense it entails. They dread losing control of their lives by consignment to nursing home where they may well be in the hands of callous and untrained caregivers (McCarthy 1991: 505–506).

Russell cited the above data to point out that most elderly Americans die peaceful and relatively painless deaths. Their health did not deteriorate until fairly near the end of their lives.

In a recent book, surgeon Sherrin Nulander (1993) was unsparing in his analysis of the dying process. He portrayed clearly and explicitly the dying process to the very last gasp. Dying, he contended, is a messy business. He argued that modern physicians are so unrelenting in their delivery of medical treatment that sometimes they forget what may be best for the patient. What may be best for a particular patient may, in fact, be death. What makes this more complicated now than in years past is not only modern therapeutic processes, but new perspectives on "informed consent," "autonomy," "advanced directives," "Power of Attorney for Medical Decisions," "proxy consent," and dangers that the physician may be guilty of treating the patient as a child.

WHEN IS A PERSON DEAD?

Before some of the major issues of death and dying are discussed, it is important to ask the question, when is someone dead? To a lay person, the question of whether a person is dead may not seem unclear or complex. In the past, if one asked whether a person were dead, it would have been a question of whether the heart stopped beating or the person stopped breathing, or whether there was any blood pressure. Today, however, with modern technology, a person can be kept "alive" by a vast array of machines. In 1968, a task force created by the Harvard Medical School developed criteria for brain death, centering on the absence of electrical activity in the brain as determined by an electroencephalogram (EEG). This is important, because if a person whose heart has stopped for ten minutes or more is revived, the probability is that the brain, deprived of oxygen that long, is dead. Typically, persons with no oxygen to their brain for that length of time permanently lose consciousness but can be kept physically "alive" with sustained assistance of technology (Weir 1986). The question of death in the modern era, therefore, has become a center of debate among family members, medical staff, and various religious groups in American society. Is someone with a flat EEG test (no electrical activity in the brain) dead? Should the technology that keeps them breathing be removed? Who has the right to make that decision? Should people have a right to make that decision before they get into that type of situation?

SUSTAINING LIFE: A THORNY ISSUE

The President's Commission for the Study of Ethical Problems in Medicine and Biomedical and Behavioral Research (1981) stated that there is little debate over the fact that the human body can be kept alive almost indefinitely with intravenous fluids, tube feedings, and advanced medical technology. This commission also stated that humans can be kept physically alive whether or not there is any brain function.

Once they go to a hospital, people can become "trapped" in a situation of complex technology in which their body continues to survive even if there is no lucidity and no hope of recovery. At that point the hospital staff may prefer to discontinue treatment, but they are caught in a maze of legal requirements and continue the treatment because they fear litigation. On December 1, 1991, a federal law was enacted, the Patient Self-Determination Act, which requires hospices, nursing homes, hospitals, and home healthcare agencies to provide patients with information about their right to determine whether they want "extraordinary" or other means used to keep them alive if they become comatose or hopelessly ill. The law requires that each person entering the institution be given information about their right to refuse treatment.

The American Medical Association (1986) declared that whenever the question to sustain life becomes an issue, the patient's choice should prevail. In that spirit, Barbara Bush, wife of the former U.S. President, acknowledged signing a living will, commenting "I had a dog I loved put down because I didn't want the dog to suffer. I certainly hope that someone would do the same thing for me" (Burnell 1993: 8). Burnell stated the dilemma as follows:

> Part of the confusion over the concept of dying lies in the fact that many people are not aware of the new ways of defining death. Formerly, a person who stopped breathing and had no heartbeat was considered dead. Now, brain function is also considered in the definition of death.
>
> In recent years, we have come to recognize that there is more to a person than just a body. The brain plays a major role in providing each of us with a personality, a set of unique behaviors and traits. These, in essence, are what distinguish us from others and give us what we call our identity (Burnell 1993: 16).

A patient's choice may be determined by a legally chosen proponent through a Durable Power of Attorney for Medical Decisions. Although the AMA has been strongly opposed to a doctor taking an active role in helping people to die, not all doctors agree. A Colorado survey (Kanoti and Orlowski 1991) indicated that 35 percent of doctors, in specified cases, would help a person die. In *Dying with Dignity*, Patrick Sheehy wrote:

> We can also predict what the quality of the remaining time will be for the patient. If death is imminent, and if there are only the throes of physical pain and struggle left, I believe that a doctor should be allowed to give you a drug that will painlessly release you to death. As society matures, I foresee a time when this will be possible (Sheehy 1981: 236).

In some countries that time has arrived. The current evidence seems to indicate that the desire of most people to die with dignity is fast becoming a national dialogue involving a definition of terms such as "death with dignity," "uncontrollable pain," "extraordinary methods to keep people alive," and the meaning of "alternative methods of treatment." In addition, there will be continuing theological and philosophical disputes about the meaning of life as well as arguments about the medical costs of sustaining life in comatose patients who are in a vegetative state.

The Cruzan Case

On January 11, 1983, a 26-year-old woman, Nancy Cruzan, was thrown out of a car and landed face down in a ditch. When she finally arrived at the emergency room, she was unconscious and had a brain injury, along with other injuries. Her lack of oxygen while in the ditch apparently did permanent damage to her brain. She did not regain consciousness. On February 7, her husband permitted the hospital staff to place a feeding tube in her stomach. She was finally transferred to the Missouri Rehabilitation Center, a facility run by the state.

Her parents were ultimately appointed her legal co-guardians. After four years they requested that the tube-feeding be removed. With the support of the staff, they went to court to have their request carried out. The court approved, ruling that there was evidence that Nancy would not have wanted her treatment to continue and that her parents were representing her wishes. However, the Missouri Department of Health appealed that decision to the Missouri Supreme Court. On a four-to-three vote, that court stated that the request really required the medical profession to assist in Nancy's death by allowing her to die of starvation and dehydration. It also ruled that the evidence about her wishes to live or die was unreliable, and therefore her parents did not have adequate authority to make the decision to stop treatment. This decision was upheld by the U.S. Supreme Court, citing the need for clear and convincing evidence that Nancy would have wanted treatment terminated.

On December 14, 1990, upon hearing additional testimony from some of Nancy's co-workers, Jasper County Probate Judge Teel decided that their testimony presented convincing evidence that Nancy would not have wanted the feeding tube continued. Nancy died on December 26, 1990 after the feeding tube had been removed.

LIVING WILLS

Through a Living Will, Americans can make their wishes known regarding whether heroic methods should be used to keep them alive. In a Living Will, prior to an emergency situation, people can indicate to the medical staff and their family, in a written document, their wishes about the type of medical care they wish to have, or not to have, under certain conditions. It essentially spells out a refusal of certain types of treatments, but it usually cannot be used for stopping treatment which has begun. As a result, a person with

a Living Will could be taken from a nursing home in a medical emergency and given treatment which seems reasonable. However, during the treatment the person may suffer a severe stroke. If the staff reacts quickly and gives life-sustaining care, and the person then drifts into permanent subconsciousness, at that point the staff will not usually withdraw treatment that has begun. The reason for this is that they probably fear a lawsuit because if they remove the treatment, they may be charged with killing the person. In addition, family members, because of feelings of guilt, love, or other reasons, may not permit the staff to remove the artificial life-sustaining equipment. It is not uncommon for a Living Will to contain vague terms such as "no extraordinary means," or "no heroic methods" which the family will be asked to define, and they may disagree among themselves as to their meaning.

Durable Power of Attorney

For many people the Living Will is a desirable statement, but in itself it is often inadequate. As a result, many experts also recommend a Durable Power of Attorney for Medical Care. The Durable Power of Attorney for Medical Care designates an individual to make treatment decisions for a person who no longer has the mental capacity to do so. The Living Will, then, tells the person designated by the Durable Power of Attorney for Medical Care the wishes of the person who is no longer mentally competent to make those decisions.

EUTHANASIA

Euthanasia is a word so filled with emotional reactions that it probably should no longer be used. In its original derivation it means well (*eu*) and death (*thanatos*). The emphasis is on a "good," painless death. The term became despised by many because of its use by the Nazis under Hitler's orders to exterminate certain categories of people such as the retarded, the mentally ill,

Jews, political dissidents, homosexuals, gypsies, and others. The word *euthanasia* is inappropriately used in that context, because these persons were murdered. They did not choose "good" deaths. They were eliminated because of the criminal acts of Adolf Hitler.

In some ancient societies euthanasia was socially acceptable. In Athens, for example, judges had a supply of poison available for those who wished to die. The evidence indicates that permission to use the poison was not difficult to obtain (Burnell 1993).

Whatever term is used, one's right, in given circumstances, to choose death is the center of considerable debate and political dialogue. The issue became prominent in the mass media when Janet Adkins, a 54-year-old teacher from Oregon, was told that she had Alzheimer's Disease. Adkins was well aware of what would eventually happen to her. She decided that she did not want to "live" through the slow deterioration of the disease. She heard about a pathologist in Detroit, Dr. Jack Kevorkian, who had invented a "death machine," and made an appointment to meet him. He instructed her on the use of his "death machine," and six minutes after activating the machine, she was dead. Newspapers around the nation printed an account of what happened, and Dr. Kevorkian and euthanasia became the center of a national debate.

As our population ages and advances in medical technology allow more and more tragic cases to stay "alive," both governmental and public agencies will be driven to consider the enormous financial expense involved in keeping people alive in a vegetative state. The Society of Critical Care Medicine stated:

> Treatments that offer no benefits and serve to prolong the dying process should not be employed. In the light of a hopeless prognosis, the indefinite maintenance of patients reliably diagnosed as being in a persistent vegetative state (PVS) raises serious ethical concerns both for the dignity of the patient and for the diversion of limited medical and nursing resources from alternative applications that

could offer medical and nursing benefit to others (Society of Critical Care Medicine 1990: 1437).

Basic to the issue is how a particular culture views death and the dying process. All humans will eventually die, and most will have a process of dying in which decisions about their death will have to be made. It is these decisions that will either hasten or delay their death. Many years ago, Phillippe Aries (1974), in his study of death from the Middle Ages to the modern era, concluded that people in the United States have developed a strong death-denial emphasis. If that is true, then it is going to be difficult for people to talk openly about their deaths, and for family members and friends to feel free to discuss a relative's or a friend's dying process. Americans, according to Aries, have a tendency to deny the dying process, or at least, not discuss it openly with the dying person.

The question of prolonging life increasingly will be a major debate in American society. Should Americans have a right to decide to actively take their own life because of continuing severe pain in a hopeless situation? Is Dr. Jack Kevorkian, who has helped many people die, a saint or a demon? Is he a prophet ahead of his time or an unregulated destroyer of life?

Euthanasia is becoming the center of increased political and religious debate and dialogue in the United States. The term *active euthanasia* is commonly taken to mean purposely and deliberately taking action to end an individual's life. The term *passive euthanasia* refers to deliberately not taking any action to prolong the life of someone who is dying or is existing in a vegetative state. Obviously at some point it is difficult to distinguish one from the other. Is withdrawing of life-sustaining instruments active or passive euthanasia? Is it the moral duty of physicians to suggest that life-sustaining procedures be withdrawn when there is no hope of recovery, or when the person is in constant pain, or when there is no hope that the person will recover lucidity? The results of polls seem to indicate that the majority of Americans believe that individuals ought to have the right to make these types of decisions (Ostheimer and Ritt 1976; Summers 1985).

Euthanasia in The Netherlands

There is much misunderstanding about euthanasia in the Netherlands. It is a topic that has been debated much longer there than in the United States. The Dutch do not require that terminal illness be the only permissible grounds for assisted death. They consider death with dignity to be an important consideration. It must also be understood that the doctor-patient relationship in the Netherlands is based on more trust and personal interaction than is the case in the United States. The typical Dutch patient in assisted death is usually a person in his or her early sixties who has an advanced case of cancer. About 85 percent are cancer patients in their last few weeks of life. The remaining patients typically have AIDS, multiple sclerosis, or other neurological diseases that cause paralysis. Active euthanasia in the Netherlands can take place only by meeting the following conditions:

1. The choice of suicide must be a free-will decision of the person and not made under undue pressure by others.
2. The wish to die must be an enduring one.
3. The person must be experiencing unbearable physical pain, emotional pain, or both, and the improvement of this condition can not reasonably be expected.
4. The person must not be mentally disturbed at the time of the decision to commit suicide.
5. The suicide should be carried out in such a way that no harm is caused to others.
6. The person who assists the suicide should be a qualified health professional, and only a medical doctor is allowed to administer the lethal drug.
7. The helper should never handle such cases entirely on his or her own, but should ask for professional consultation from colleagues (e.g., other medical colleagues or members of the clergy).

8. The assisted suicide should be fully documented, and the documents should be made available to the appropriate legal authorities (Diekestra 1987).

As might be expected, there is no consensus on active euthanasia among physicians in the Netherlands. Dr. Richard Fenigsen, a cardiologist, believes that the Netherlands is not setting a good example for the world. Dr. Fenigsen has toured the United States arguing that the United States ought not to follow the Dutch example. Dr. Theo van Berkestijn, Secretary General of the Dutch Medical Society has asked, "Is it wrong for anyone to say someone must stay alive despite their suffering?" Dr. Pit Bakker, President of the Dutch Society for Voluntary Euthanasia continued: "A doctor who follows his conscience and does something that is societally accepted to the benefits of the patient should not be put in a state of jeopardy" (*Grand Rapids Press* 1991: 7A).

Some Dutch argue that euthanasia occurs in the United States but is kept hidden because it would be prosecuted. "A big difference is that we're coming out in the open with it, and in America they don't," said Dr. Johannas van Delder (Ray 1991).

Furthermore, Dutch doctors view euthanasia as a duty. Dr. Herbert Cohen always asks his patients that he is about to put to death, "Are you sure you want to go through with this?" and he says they inevitably say, "Haven't I made it clear enough already?" He always comes with flowers and compassion, along with a lethal dosage. Within minutes of arrival he is putting a cuff on the patient's arm while talking gently. Cohen gives two quick injections; one a sleeping agent and the second a fatally paralyzing drug, curare, and the patient drifts off into sleep. "Whenever I lecture abroad," Cohen said, "doctors come to me in the hallways and say, "We do the same thing, we just don't talk about it" (Ray 1991).

Support in the United States for Euthanasia

In addition to Dr. Jack Kevorkian and his one-man crusade, the Hemlock Society (a group which contends that people have a right to commit suicide) in 1991 published a book, *Final Exit*, by Dereck Humphrey. It became a best-seller. In this book Humphrey not only argued for the right of people to decide to take their own lives, but pointed out how to carry this out. The evidence seems to indicate that the majority of Americans believe that people should have the right, under specific conditions, to die with the assistance of a physician (KCR Communication Research 1991; Older Women's League 1986).

The following is a partial list of other organizations beside the Hemlock Society that promote the right to die with dignity:

Choice in Dying, Inc. In the past this organization was called the Society for the Right to Die. It attempts to inform people of their rights to refuse treatment. In addition, it distributes living-will declarations, Power of Attorney for Medical Decisions forms, and serves as a clearinghouse for lawyers on right-to-die laws. This group is willing to give counsel to patients and their families in regard to legal ramifications of right-to-die questions. It also works in the political arena to get appropriate laws passed which would help give people more freedom of choice in regard to decisions about the right to die.

Americans Against Human Suffering This is a political-action organization dedicated to developing laws which would allow doctors, in specified circumstances, to help persons die. It drafts model laws and gives assistance to persons in various states who are trying to expand the right to make personal decisions about their death or prolonging their life against their wishes.

World Federation of Right-to-Die Societies This is a worldwide organization, with branches in over fifteen countries. It is dedicated to the proposition that people have a right to a painless dying process. It has urged the United Nations Organization to become involved in this question and to deal with it under the Human Rights Commission. It is urging countries throughout the world to pass laws allowing persons the right to choose to die with dignity.

Medical and Philosophical Issues

At the present time, various states have very different laws about who has the right to withhold life support systems. A lucid individual, at the present time, does have the right to accept or refuse treatment. However, Dr. Jack Kevorkian is taking the debate into new territory by assisting people in ending their own lives. This raises such questions as: Does society have a right to refuse terminally ill people, living with terrible pain, the option to end their lives? Does society have the right to refuse permission to physicians to help terminally ill people have a painless, peaceful death? Does society have a right to make criminals of doctors who help these patients end their lives? Does society have a right to force patients to continue treatments they do not want? For example, does society have a right to "force feed" a totally incapacitated patient who refuses to eat? Does society have the right to charge a husband with murder who puts a wife to death who no longer has any lucidity and is in extreme pain?

A related factor is that most of the money spent in a person's lifetime for medical care is spent in the last year of life. The question is posed: Is it worth it to spend that amount of money on primarily very old people when the treatment may do little to increase either the quality or length of their lives? This is a loaded question that involves medical issues as well as religious and philosophical issues. Some argue that it makes little sense to take a third-stage Alzheimer's patient, who has no lucidity left and no future hope of recovery, to the emergency room of an acute-care hospital to treat pneumonia. Some argue that there is nothing gained except enormous expenses with acute intensive-care intervention with this type of patient. Some argue that money could better be used to intervene in the lives of impoverished children. Others argue that life always is sacred in all situations and maximum efforts should be made to keep people alive regardless of their age or condition. In addition, who knows, others argue, what marvelous treatments might be developed in the near future that could cure them? (Callahan 1986)

The Slippery-Slope Argument

Those who oppose active euthanasia often use the "slipper-slope-to-Auschwitz" argument (Leming and Dickinson 1990). They argue that giving some members of society the right to active euthanasia ultimately leaves nobody protected from being killed. This argument contends that through a progression of steps, society moves toward a disregard for human life which could lead to ending the lives of the unwilling, incompetent, and undesirable. This is the reference to Auschwitz, Hitler's concentration camp where the "unproductive," "defective," and "morally and mentally unfit"—Jews, homosexuals, people with handicaps, and others—were murdered (Leming and Dickinson 1990: 224).

While it may be contended that the progression down the slippery-slope is not inevitable, those who oppose permitting active euthanasia argue that the noble intention of those who favor the practice cannot counteract the potential abuse to which mercy killing can be put by those with less noble motives (Bouma et al. 1989).

A Personal Decision: She Did It Her Way

All of this demonstrates that the topic of euthanasia is a controversial one in the United States and elsewhere in the world. Physician-assisted suicide remains an issue that will be debated and be part of the political process for some time; suicide for terminally ill patients who are suffering, although a popular subject for discussion as indicated by the sale of publications that deal with it, is not by any means a widely accepted practice. As we have indicated, most people fear a long, painful death along with the loss of dignity and any control over their lives. Polls have indicated that a majority of people feel they

should have some input into how they might die free from lingering, debilitating illnesses that could result in their being in a vegetative state.

Dr. David Eddy (1994), a physician from Wyoming, in an article in the *Journal of the American Medical Association*, 272(3), pp. 179–181, told the story of how his 84-year-old mother became very ill and wanted to end her life, and how she finally did it legally.

Virginia Eddy, 84, came from a family of four generations of physicians. She had experienced many health problems over the years, but with the advances in modern medicine, she had overcome many illnesses and infirmities. She noted that if it were not "for implants, hearing aids, hip surgery, and Elavil, she would be blind, deaf, bedridden, and depressed."

Virginia was an active older woman until she developed severe bowel disease which hospitalized her. She was treated, but serious complications developed which left her in a painful and debilitated condition. It was at that point that she first talked about gracefully ending her life. She dreaded the thought of being put in a nursing home, unable to care for herself with her body and mind progressively declining.

> I know they can keep me alive a long time, but what's the point? If the pleasure is gone, and the direction is steadily down, why should I have to draw it out until I'm "rescued" by cancer, a heart attack, or a stroke? That could take years. I understand that some people want to hang on until all the possible treatments have been tried to squeeze out the last drops of life. That's fine for them, but not for me.

Her children (one son a physician who wrote the article) convinced her to try additional rectal surgery—which she did. The outcome was total incontinence. She was incontinent at "both ends" (her words), bedridden, anemic, exhausted, achy, and itchy. In addition, her eyesight had failed further and she could not longer read. Assessing her situation, she told her doctor son:

> Let me put this in terms you should understand, David. My "quality of life"—isn't that what you

call it?—has dropped below zero. I know there is nothing fatally wrong with me and that I could live on for many more years. With a colostomy and some luck I might even be able to recover a bit of my former lifestyle, for a while. But do we have to do that just because it's possible? Is the meaning of life defined by its duration? Or does life have a purpose so large that it doesn't have to be prolonged at any cost to preserve its meaning?

I've lived a wonderful life, but it has to end sometime and this is the right time for me. My decision is not about whether I'm going to die—we all die sooner or later. My decision is about when and how. I don't want to spoil the wonder of my life by dragging it out in years of decay. I want to go now, while the good memories are still fresh. I have always known that eventually the right time would come, and now I know that this is it. Help me find a way (Eddy 1994: *JAMA*, 272(3), 179–181).

David (the son) bought Humphrey's *Final Exit* (1991) and read it with his mother. They explored different ways to end Virginia's life, but they were either too messy (she wanted to die with dignity), too difficult for a frail old person, or illegal. Before any approach was finalized, Virginia developed pneumonia and was readmitted to the hospital.

It was determined that her advanced directives gave her the right to refuse treatment, which she did. She requested that the antibiotics used to treat the pneumonia be stopped, and they were. Against the odds, her pneumonia subsided. This made Virginia very depressed, because she wanted to die. She asked what else she could do. Could she stop eating? David told her she could, but that might take a long time. He told her if she really wanted to die she could stop drinking, which would end her life in a few days. This was legal.

Virginia stopped eating and drinking after the last piece of chocolate cake she ate to celebrate her 85th birthday. During the next four days she greeted visitors with a smile—the first smiles she had in months. She relived the good times she had had in the past and talked freely. On the fifth day it was harder to wake her, but when she opened her eyes she would smile. On the sixth day, they could not wake her. "Her face was relaxed in her natural smile, she was breathing unevenly, but peacefully. We held hands for another two hours, until she died."

In recalling the process, David Eddy wrote:

This death was not a sad death; it was a happy death. It did not come after years of decline, lost vitality, and loneliness; it came at the right time. My mother was not clinging desperately to what no one can have. She knew that death was not a tragedy to be postponed at any cost, but that death is a part of life, to be embraced at the proper time. She had done just what she wanted to do, just the way she wanted to do it. Without hoarding pills, without making me a criminal, without putting a bag over her head and without huddling in a van with carbon monoxide machine, she had found a way to bring her life gracefully to a close. Of course we cried. But although we will miss her greatly, her ability to achieve her death at her "right time" and in her "right way" transformed for us what could have been a desolate and crushing loss into a time for joy. Because she was happy, we were happy.

Write about this, David. Tell others how well this worked for me. I'd like this to be my gift. Whether they are terminally ill, in intractable pain, or, like me, just know that the right time has come for them, more people might want to know that this way exists. And maybe more physicians will help them find it.

Maybe they will. Rest in peace, Mom.

David M. Eddy, MD, PhD
Jackson, Wyoming
(Eddy, D.M. (1994) *JAMA*, 272(3), pp. 179–181.)

THE PROCESS OF DYING

Having looked at some of the current major issues and debates surrounding death and dying, it is important to examine the process of dying as well as some of the approaches that have been developed to begin to understand and cope with this process.

The Stages of Dying: Kübler-Ross

Kübler-Ross (1969, 1975, 1981) found that people tend to go through five stages in the dying process. When they are first diagnosed with a terminal condition, they refuse to accept the situation. They *deny* the reality of their situation and live in a condition of unreality in which they believe that the situation will change, that there is a misdiagnosis, and that new developments will help them. In the second stage, *anger and resentment*, they curse their fate, feel that the situation is unfair, and may project their anger and resentment onto the medical staff or family members. In the third stage, *bargaining*, they may plead with God, promise that they will change their behavior, devote themselves to religious or worthwhile causes, and promise that they will no longer engage in certain types of questionable behaviors if they get a "second" chance at life. In the fourth stage, *depression*, they admit that their condition is terminal, that death is imminent, and that they are not going to be cured. They may then go into a stage of grief and isolation. Relatives and friends may find it difficult to communicate with them, and they may reject visits. In the final stage, *acceptance*, they accept their death. This is not a stage reached by all dying persons. It is a stage in which some feel that their life is going to end soon and that they have done all that they could regarding the situation. It is a stage achieved by those who have been able to relate their feelings to others and who have a sense of completion regarding their life's journey.

Kübler-Ross has also asserted that some dying persons, coming to terms with the inevitability of their death, come to a new appreciation of the meaning and purpose of life. She indicated that many persons working with the dying also gain a new and deeper appreciation of their own lives.

It is important to note that not everyone goes through all of these stages. Nor do the persons who go through all of these stages go through them in the same order (Fox 1981; Kastenbaum 1981, 1985). Medical personnel or family members should not try to force dying persons into any one of these specific stages:

> Over the last two decades, I have talked to over one hundred terminally ill individuals and their families. I am convinced that each person has his or her

own way of dying, just as each had his or her own way of living. The people I talked to reacted to their final life event as they reacted to other major events in their lives. Some did it with grace and others did it with regrets, shame, and resentment. I believe that some of those who did it with grace did so because they had a minimum of suffering and pain and because they were able to recognize and resolve residual conflicts. They ended their lives with a good death or "an appropriate death,"—Those who suffered through pain, sorrow, and emotional turmoil ended up with a bad death. In any case, it is clear that dying is as highly individual as the many other experiences of life (Burnell 1995: 19).

Psychologist Edwin Schneidman (1973: 6) added, "I do not believe that there are necessarily 'stages' of the dying process, and I am not at all convinced that they are lived through in that order, or, for that matter, in any universal order."

In any event, people in contact with the dying should recognize the importance of a person's personality and cultural background. Furthermore, how one dies depends not only on one's personality and cultural background, but also on the cause of death as well as one's basic belief system.

Dying in a Hospital

There is some evidence from past research that some medical personnel have had difficulty relating to dying patients. Glaser and Strauss (1966) indicated that dying patients did not experience caring, personal relationships with hospital staff. Glazer and Strauss found various stages of awareness about death on the part of patients in a hospital setting as well as the medical staff's reaction to them.

In the first stage there was a *closed awareness* in which the patient did not know that he or she had a terminal illness and was about to die. In this stage, medical staff members act as if there is hope, and they do not inform the patient about his or her condition.

In the second stage, *suspicious awareness*, the patient begins to suspect that he or she is terminal and that death is approaching, but suspicions are not confirmed. The patient in this stage attempts to get confirmation, but is not certain what the medical charts show and cannot be sure what the attitudes and actions of the nurses mean.

The third stage is the *ritual drama of mutual pretence*. In this stage, the person knows that death is approaching but does not relate this knowledge to the staff. The staff pretends that the patient does not know, and they are not about to inform the patient.

In the fourth stage, *open awareness*, both staff and patient admit and acknowledge that death is approaching. At this point pretence is gone.

In recent years there have been some attempts to educate medical personnel about death and dying, especially the needs of the dying patient. With a greater emphasis on the practice of holistic medicine by many of the nation's medical schools, a greater awareness of the needs of the dying patient and his or her family and significant others should be expected. Without this awareness and approach, a sort of "social death" occurred when the attending medical staff no longer saw the dying patient as a unique person with specific psychological needs, relationships, and spiritual dimensions. Given the current interest in death and dying it is likely that the treatment of terminally ill patients will improve (DeSpelder and Strickland 1991).

Appropriate Death

The term *appropriate death* is used to refer to a death which relates to the dying person's expectations about death, his or her own personal evaluations of life, and of the time and process of dying (Kalish 1987). Kalish viewed an appropriate death as one in which the dying person has a sense of meaning about life, and that philosophically or religiously, life and death can be put into a meaningful framework.

HOSPICE MOVEMENT: BEGINNINGS AND GOALS

An international trend in the care of the dying is the hospice movement. Dr. Cicely Saunders played a key role in the development of the modern hospice movement when she started St. Christopher's Hospice in 1967 in London, England. The goal at St. Christopher's Hospice is to make an assessment of the spiritual, physical, social, and psychological needs of the dying person and of his or her support network. It is based on a belief that dying can occur best at home or in a specialized institution where there is a concerted attempt to reduce pain and to give the person supportive care that allows him or her to maximize relationships with others during their dying process. It is a program for persons who cannot be cured of their physical illnesses, so the emphasis is not on curing the condition, but on enabling the person to die "in comfort" with a caring, supportive staff and with friends and relatives. To define this approach further, Buckingham wrote:

> Hospice is a medically directed multidisciplinary program providing skilled care of an appropriate nature for terminally ill patients and their families to allow the patient to live as fully as possible until the time of death. Hospice helps relieve symptoms of distress (physical, psychological, spiritual, social, economic) that may occur during the course of the disease, dying, and bereavement (Buckingham 1983: 3).

It is important to note that the goal in the hospice movement is to maximize the quality of life for the dying patient and to make the best use of the time remaining with relatives, friends, and acquaintances. In addition, there is a focus on the comfort of the patient.

Key Aspects of Current Hospice Programs

Even though there are different types of hospice programs, they are all unified by their general philosophy of patient care (Leming and Dickinson 1990). Hospice care is focused on patients with life-threatening illnesses. About 95 percent of the hospice patients in the United States suffer from cancer. The key aspects of contemporary hospice programs include the following:

Pain Management The hospice program is based on the discovery that their patients cannot have any quality of life until their physical pain and other "symptoms such as nausea, vomiting, dizziness, constipation, and shortness of breath are under control" (Leming and Dickinson 1990: 175–176). This is in contrast to traditional medical care which is often based on an approach to pain control where the patient must first hurt and ask for relief before the pain can be relieved. Hospice doctors believe that patients should not have any pain. In this approach, medication is given in advance before there is pain. Every symptom is treated separately for pain control.

Home and Inpatient Care Hospice care is provided in both home and institutional setting. In many instances, hospice care becomes a continuum that involves both types of care when necessary, but the emphasis has been on home care. In-home hospice care is sometimes referred to as "hospice without walls." The at-home patient and his or her family receive support from the hospice team, a broad range of professional and volunteer care providers.

Some hospitals have separate units called palliative-care units (PCUs) run on hospice-based principles. Hospice provides coordinated care to the patient on the ward.

Hospice can be paid for by Medicare Part A if a doctor certifies that the patient is terminally ill and has six months or less to live (Stoddard 1978; Zimmerman 1986; Buckingham 1983).

Patient-Centered Care Whenever possible, the hospice approach helps patients make their own decisions about the key aspects of their lives. This approach is "nonjudgemental, unconditional, and empowering" (Leming and Dickinson 1990: 179). As Leming and Dickinson pointed out in their book, *Understanding Dying, Death, and Bereavement*, this approach can mean letting a dying person remain alone in his or her own home, with appropriate staff checking on the person frequently, and even supplying the person

with liquor and cigarettes if he or she is a heavy smoker and alcohol user.

Hospice Team Care in the hospice approach is provided by an interdisciplinary team whose members work together to provide integrated care to the patient and his or her family. These team members include physicians to direct the medical care; nurses (including registered and practical nurses and nurses' aides) who coordinate the care; social workers who assist the family in communicating with each other in this crisis time, and in dealing with specific social problems the patient and family may have; clergy who assist in spiritual concerns; financial counselors to assist the family in dealing with the financial strains of paying for care by completing complicated financial forms and seeking out programs to pay for services; home health aides and homemakers to help with patient care and household chores; physical and occupational therapists to assist the patient with physical functioning; lawyers to assist in settling personal affairs prior to and after the death of the patient; and volunteers who make up an essential part of the hospice team and provide a range of services to the patient and his or her family. It has been said that no hospice could exist for long without strong volunteer support (Leming and Dickinson 1990).

Family Involvement/Family Care In the hospice approach, family involvement and family care require healthcare team members to "know how to cope with the fears, worries, tears, and turmoil of family members; and when to speak, when not to speak, and what to say. It requires that they take time to listen, to determine how they may be most helpful" (Leming and Dickinson 1990: 192).

Burnell (1993) wrote that it is not unusual for family members to be as upset by a terminal illness as is the patient. The hospice movement attempts to develop a situation in which family members and patients can talk easily and meaningfully about the approaching death. After the death of the patient, the hospice staff continues to attend to the needs of the family members by providing counseling and support during their bereavement. Even though the hospice staff members are not responsible for the physical needs of the patient's family, they have real concern for their social, psychological, and spiritual needs.

The Spread of Hospice in the United States

The first modern hospice program in the United States grew out of Dr. Cicely Saunders' lecture in 1963 at Yale University in New Haven, Connecticut, and her subsequent contacts with personnel from Yale Nursing and Medical Schools. Representatives of various disciplines became involved in the development of Hospice Incorporated in 1971, which was later changed to the Connecticut Hospice (Leming and Dickinson 1990).

There are now over 1,700 hospice programs in the United States. The National Hospice Organization (NHO) was developed in 1978 to help coordinate hospice activities and to assure that any program calling itself a hospice would meet quality standards of care. The NHO also provides educational services, technical assistance, publications, and referral assistance to the general public. In addition to this national organization, every state in the nation has its own hospice organization (National Hospice Organization 1989).

Hospice Approach: The Personal Touch

Most of all, the hospice approach attempts to put terminally ill patients into a supportive environment. Hospice workers are specifically taught to take time to listen to and touch the patient. Birthdays and anniversaries become causes for celebration as the emphasis is on celebrating life. There is also a focus on reminiscence as the staff tries help the patients in a life review process (Levy 1987). The hospice movement attempts to keep patients honestly informed about their condition and their prognosis. A key aspect of the hospice movement is to integrate family members into the treatment and dying process of their relative.

The hospice movement also is concerned with staff burnout. Counseling, support groups, and a supportive working environment are provided for the staff (Stephenson 1985).

Although the evaluation studies are not extensive, the research indicates that dying patients in the hospice movement have less anger, depression, and hostility than other dying patients (Kalish 1985; Mor 1982; Morris 1982).

NEAR-DEATH EXPERIENCES

Kübler-Ross (1969) was one of the first researchers to discuss near-death experiences. Other researchers, such as Moody (1975, 1977, 1988), have written extensively about these experiences. Moody interviewed people who were considered clinically dead but were revived. He believed that there is a consistent pattern of experiences that these people claim to have had. They sense themselves leaving their bodies, going down a tunnel toward a bright light. Many felt or saw the presence of dead relatives or other loved ones as well as an intense feeling of love and acceptance and the presence of "an essence" that revealed to them their life's experiences as they saw their lives pass before them. They became aware of a tremendous amount of knowledge that was available to them. Most of these persons believed that they were told that it was not yet time for them to die and that they must go back. Most also reported that the experience gave them new feelings about life and much less fear of dying. Some wished that they had not come back to life but could have stayed near the source of love and acceptance.

Not all near-death experiences are joyous meetings with "the light." A couple of researchers have claimed that some near-death experiences are frightening, with DeSpelder and Strickland (1991) claiming that this type of episodes is as frequent as happier near-death experiences. Walter (1993) disagreed, and contended that a review of the literature indicates that most researchers see the "bad trip" as a much less frequently reported event.

These data do not prove that there is life after death, though they do call for explanations. There are similarities in these experiences which are puzzling. One of the major attempts at a scientific explanation of these near-death experiences was by Siegal (1980), who believed that the experiences can be explained as natural phenomena. He contended that these events are really hallucinations brought about by chemical changes in the brain and that people have similar experiences when they use hallucinogenic drugs. He argued that near-death experiences are brought about by a lack of oxygen, a sudden burst of neurotransmitters or other changes in the brain resulting from the patient's disease, or an accident which brought about changes in the chemical or electrical functioning of the brain.

At this time an adequate scientifically based explanation is not available. The hope of an afterlife is clearly a belief many people hold. The evidence does seem to show that people who believe that they have experienced a loving, peaceful near-death experience find it helps them with their everyday existence in this life.

VITAL ORGAN DONATION PROGRAM

The death of one human being can mean the gift of some key bodily functions or even life itself to another—in some cases several others, if multiple vital organs are used.

Federal law now requires hospitals to inform patients and family members about organ donations. Burnell (1993) pointed out that there are many misconceptions about organ donations. He pointed out that:

- Donating organs will not interfere with receiving medical treatment in the hospital. Doctors are not more interesting in obtaining organs than in providing their patients with proper treatment.

- Organ donation is considered only after all attempts to save a life have been made.
- Organ donation will not take place until the heart has stopped beating or brain death has been established.
- For viable organs, such as the heart, the lungs, the liver, the pancreas, and the kidneys, to be obtained, brain-dead individuals must be maintained on a respirator. However, the donation of eyes, bone, skin, and other tissues does not require maintenance on a respirator. These tissues can be obtained from 6 hours to 24 hours after breathing and heartbeat have stopped.
- The body will not be disfigured by organ donation. After the removal of the donated organs, the surgical team will leave the body intact for proper funeral or burial arrangements.
- The family does not receive any compensation or fee for the donation. It is illegal to buy or sell organs or tissues.
- There is no charge or fee connected with the removal of organs or tissues.
- All major religions support the concept of organ and tissue donation as well as the concept of brain death.
- Organ donation does not interfere with funeral arrangements. Funeral directors can direct embalmers to prepare the body appropriately.
- The most common organ and tissue transplants are skin, lungs, heart, liver, kidneys, corneas, certain bones, pancreas, and middle ear.
- Time is of the essence in most organ transplants except for skin and corneas, so the removal of most organs is likely to occur in the acute-care hospital.
- Even if you have indicated your wish to donate organs, the medical transplant team may not accept the donation. Many variables must be considered, such as the health of the donor.
- Generally speaking, organs are more suitable if they come from people under 70 years old. Also, the organs of cancer patients (except in some cases of brain cancer) or of patients with infections or other serious diseases are not suitable for donation.

- Transportation and other incurred costs are usually covered by the organizations procuring the organs for transplant. There are many organizations that coordinate organ donation, and there is probably one in your area.
- Whether or not you decide to donate your organs, there is already a federal law in the country to enact laws of "required request" that will require hospitals to inform the families of deceased patients of the option of organ donation.
- Organ donation does not interfere with a living will, which refers to your wishes while you are still alive (Burnell 1993: 299, 301).

FUNERALS

Anthropologists have found that every culture they have studied has some form of funeralization process—a rite or ritual recognizing death and a final disposition of the dead body (Leming and Dickinson 1990).

Funerals and Culture

In every culture there are ritualistic aspects to mourning, some type of public ritual that the family and friends go through. Aspects of the ritual vary from one culture to another. In the United States funerals vary enormously according to social class, race, ethnicity, religious affiliation, and geographic location, but it is the funeral that becomes the focus of ritual. In this regard, Leming and Dickinson wrote:

> During the colonization of America, early evidence exists of the care and burial of the dead. There is, however, no evidence of any attempt at body preservation . . . It was not until the late 1800s and early 1900s that states began to promote the practice of embalming to protect the public's health. With the advent of the practice of embalming, laws were soon passed to regulate both the practice and the practitioner.
>
> The current practitioner of the funeral profession evolved from the artisan or cabinetmaker . . . and the livery owner (who provided the special vehicles needed at the time of the funeral—particu-

larly the hearse and special buggies for the family). As the public came to expect the services associated with the casket and transportation, persons began to specialize in providing these services, and the funeral functionary of today evolved as a provider of these services (Leming and Dickinson 1990: 374).

Social Roles of Funerals

The funeral is a social event that brings the chief mourners and community members to the reality of death. In addition, it allows people to express their sympathy and give support to the relatives and friends of the deceased. It develops a context in which people are expected to come and greet the family. It is an event that one attends even though one does not receive an invitation. Even though a person may find it difficult to express his or her feelings of sympathy and support to the relatives, just being there makes a statement of support (Leming and Dickinson 1990).

Another function of the funeral is to provide a theological or philosophical meaning for one's life. For the religiously oriented person, a cleric usually speaks about the purpose and meaning of life, along with a eulogy about the deceased (Leming and Dickinson 1990).

The funeral enables members of the community to express their regards to the living by sending sympathy cards or flowers or by giving to charities named by the relatives of the deceased.

Making Decisions About Funerals

Funeral directors (undertakers, morticians) at times have at times been accused of taking advantage of people who are in a state of shock and depression at the death of a family member or close friend. The most scathing attack on the funeral industry was made by Jessica Mitford (1963), who accused funeral directors of inflating prices, misleading grieving family members, overselling unneeded services, and generally being dishonest in their dealings. She contended that they could do this because many persons are in unfamiliar surroundings at the mortuary and are too trusting of the funeral director. Since the publication of her book and the intense publicity it received, national legislation has been implemented to regulate the funeral industry more closely. The industry contends that Mitford exaggerated the number of dishonest funeral directors and that it now is better at regulating itself. Others argue that self-regulation of an industry is always suspect because of vested and conflicting interests, cronyism, and a reluctance of members of any industry to publicize its problems.

Unscrupulous funeral directors can quickly "ring up charges" by using expensive limousines, caskets, clothing, musicians, and other components of the funeral. They usually do not mention that a casket is not required if there is cremation. Cremation is only about one-eighth of the cost of a traditional funeral, and the number of cremations doubled in the United States between 1980 and 1990. In Japan, 90 percent of persons who die are cremated (Aiken 1991).

One significant attempt to avoid making decisions for a funeral at a time of crisis is to have a funeral planned before death. A pre-planned funeral can be made in an atmosphere that does not have the deep emotions brought about by the death of a loved one. In that type of situation, a person can take the time necessary to make the decisions that are appropriate to his or her values, religious beliefs, and financial situation. The American Association of Retired Persons (1989) has published an explanation of the process involved in a pre-planning funeral, *Prepaying Your Funeral: Product Report*.

Most Americans still have a traditional funeral in which the body is placed in a casket, with about 75 percent having a viewing of the body.

BEREAVEMENT AND GRIEF

The death of a family member, a loved friend, or acquaintance typically results in bereavement and grieving. Bereavement is the condition a person is in upon having lost a significant other to death. Grief is the emotional response to the loss of the loved person. Averill (1968) pointed out that there are essentially three stages in the grieving process: the shock of the dying process and the death of the person; the despair at the death; and finally, a period of recovery. However, the work of others (Parker 1972; Pincus 1976; Pollack 1961, 1978) indicated a greater variety of reactions by some people. Initially there may be physical reactions such as loss of appetite, extreme fatigue, psychosomatic reactions of loosely defined aches and pains, and also an increase in real and clearly defined illness (Thompson, et al. 1984; Lindemann 1979). In addition, there often are reactions of anger, depression, numbness, disbelief, and insomnia (Kalish 1982; Schulz 1978). As anger and depression fade, feelings of nostalgia about the deceased may surface—feelings that may put the dead loved one in a higher place in their minds than they were when the person was alive. This is a process in which they may think if only their spouse were still alive, things would be much better than they are at the present time. These feelings may be mixed with feelings of anger that the deceased left them. One of the authors, in visiting a family friend in a nursing home, listened to the great anger the person had toward her spouse because he died when she needed him and then, in the most flattering terms, discussed the wonderful merits of her deceased husband.

Most grieving persons eventually begin to adjust to the reality of the death and begin to work their way back into their social world without their deceased spouse, child, sibling, or friend. At that point the person begins to get back into their normal routine, although grieving for some brings about a psychological condition which needs professional counseling (Kalish 1985). Research has indicated that there are processes that grieving people go through, but the length and stages of grieving, and the intensity of the grieving process, vary tremendously depending on the personality, the relationship with the deceased, and the way the death occurred.

WIDOWHOOD

There are more than 12 million widowed persons in the United States, with widows (women) outnumbering widowers (men) by a ratio of five to one. Most older women are widowed, while most older men are married, the result of the reality that women live longer than men and that men tend to marry younger women.

Helen Lopata's (1979) classic study on widowhood, *Widowhood in an American City*, found that widows get the most help in the grieving process from other widows. Most metropolitan areas now have some type of widowed persons service or association which helps widowed persons in adjusting to their new status. She also found that one of the challenges family members often face is in not allowing the widowed person to become too dependent on them, but to assist him or her in becoming independent. In addition, Lopata found that it is probably not very wise for most widowed persons to make important financial or living arrangement decisions too soon after the death of a spouse. The widowed person needs time to go through an adequate time of grieving, whether it is six months or a year, before making crucial, important life-adjustment decisions. Lopata (1987) also found that there are widely different reactions by widowed persons. Some become isolated, while others seek out new friendships and experiences; some may develop new talents or find or rediscover abilities that were repressed; and some may become very passive and struggle over a long adjustment time, while others are able to adjust rather quickly.

The American Association of Retired Persons founded the Widowed Persons Service (WPS) in 1973 to meet the emotional and practical needs of newly widowed persons of both genders. There are over 5,500 WPS volunteers located in 222 sites across the United States, serving over 70,000 newly widowed persons each year by telephone calls, visits, and WPS support group meetings.

Mourning for a deceased spouse usually takes more than just a month or two. For some people the mourning process is never totally over, while for others, mourning may involve two or three years of grieving (Gibala 1993). Becoming a widow or widower usually results in severe stress, typically more stress than is involved in losing a job or having a major illness.

The WPS outreach volunteers function as support persons, as "bridges over troubled waters," and for some, as new friends:

> In addition to one-to-one outreach, WPS sponsors group meetings. Because warmth and caring are primary needs of the widowed, WPS meetings first offer hugs, more hugs than you can count . . . The participants share their stories, discuss their worries, offer coping skills, and receive accolades for meeting personal challenges. A guest speaker may talk about anything from crime prevention to cooking for one to help the widowed adjust to their new lives (Gibala 1993: 7).

SUMMARY

Euthanasia in its original form meant well (*eu*) and death (*thanatos*). The term fell into disrepute when the Nazis in the 1930s and the 1940s put millions of people to death. In many ancient societies, euthanasia was acceptable. Currently a person's right to choose death, to avoid pain and indignity, is at the center of debate.

The topic of assisted death has been debated publicly in the Netherlands for many years. The Dutch allow physician-assisted death within specific circumstances. Some Dutch physicians see eliminating pain and suffering through assisted death as a moral obligation. Other Dutch physicians are opposed to the procedure.

Physician-assisted death and the right of a person to choose death are increasingly part of the public debate in the United States. Books, such as *Final Exit*, by Dereck Humphrey, and putting the issue on the ballot are becoming part of the public discourse. Dr. Jack Kevorkian, who has helped a number of persons to die, has also become part of the public's dialogue on assisted death.

Research consistently indicates that older people have less fear of death than young people, but persons in all age categories have some fear of dying in pain and with a loss of dignity.

Kübler-Ross has contended that persons tend to go through five stages in the dying process. Other researchers have indicated that not all persons go through these five stages.

Kübler-Ross was one of the first to discuss near-death experiences in which a person who is near death has an out-of-body experience. Many who have had these experiences have claimed that they went through a tunnel after which they saw a bright light, and then had an overwhelming feeling of love and acceptance. Other researchers have indicated that some persons have not had an experience of love, but an experience of horror; still other researchers have contended that the near-death experiences can be explained as natural phenomena. At the present time there is no generally accepted explanation of these near-death experiences.

An international trend that has developed to care for the dying is the hospice movement. Dr. Cicely Saunders started the movement in England with the goals of making dying as painless as possible and surrounding the dying person with a supportive personnel network. The treatment emphasis is not a cure, but to make the person as comfortable as possible and to construct a situation where family members and the patient can talk easily and meaningfully about approaching death.

Bereavement and grieving are part of the normal reaction to the death of a family member or close friend. Grieving is a process with its own stages which usually takes an extended period of time for most people.

Information about organ donation is now provided by hospital staff. Organ donation does not interfere with medical treatment, take place until death has occurred, disfigure the body for viewing, involve a charge to the family of the donor, or compensate the family for the donation.

In all cultures there are ritualistic aspects to mourning, with the funeral a part of the ritual for most Americans who lose a significant other. Funerals have various positive and negative social aspects.

There are many more widows (women) than widowers (men) in the United States. The American Association of Retired Persons founded the Widowed Persons Service (WPS) back in 1973, and it has grown to include hundreds of local agencies involving thousands of volunteers across the nation. This, and other similar organizations, are vital in helping newly widowed persons adjust to their new status.

REFERENCES

Aiken, L. 1991. *Dying, Death, and Bereavement*. Boston: Allyn and Bacon.

American Association of Retired Persons. 1989. *Prepaying Your Funeral: Product Report*. 1(2). Washington, DC: AARP.

American Medical Association and Council of Education Attitudinal Affairs. 1986. *Withholding or Withdrawing Life Prolonging Medical Treatment*. Dearborn, MI: AMA.

Aries, P. 1974. *Western Attitudes Toward Death: From the Middle Ages to the Present*. Baltimore: Johns Hopkins Press.

Averill, J.R. 1968. Grief: Its Nature and Significance. *Psychological Bulletin*, 6: 721–748.

Bouma, H., Diekema, D., Langerak, E., Rottman, T., and Verhey, A. 1989. *Christian Faith, Health, and Medical Practice*. Grand Rapids, MI: Eerdmans.

Buckingham, R.W. 1983. *The Complete Hospice Guide*. New York: Harper & Row, pp. 1–30.

Burnell, G.M. 1993. *Final Choices: To Live or to Die in an Age of Medical Technology*. New York: Insight Books.

Callahan, D. 1986. Health Care in the Aging Society: A Moral Dilemma. In A. Pifer and L. Bronte (eds.), *Our Aging Society: Paradox and Promise*. New York: W.W. Norton.

DeSpelder, L.A., and Strickland, D.L. 1991. *The Last Dance*. Mountain View, CA: Mayfield Press.

Diekstra, R.F.W. 1987. Suicide Should Not Always Be Prevented. In Rohr, J. (ed.), *Death and Dying: Opposing Viewpoints*. St. Paul, MN: Greenhaven Press, p. 56.

Eddy, D.M. 1994. A Conversation With My Mother. *Journal of the American Medical Association*, 272(3): 179–181.

Farrell, J. 1980. *Inventing the American Way of Death, 1830–1920*. Philadelphia: Temple University Press.

Fox, R. 1981. The Sting of Death in American Society. *Social Science Review*, 49: 42–59.

Gibala, J. 1993. Widowed Persons Service: 20 Years Serving All Generations. *Highlights AARP*, (May–June): 6–7.

Glaser, B., and Strauss, A. 1966. *Awareness of Dying*. Chicago: Aldine Publishing.

The Grand Rapids Press. 1991. Dutch Might OK Mercy Killing Too. (October 22): 7A.

Humphrey, D. 1991. *Final Exit*. Seattle, WA: Hemlock Society.

Kalish, R. 1982. Death and Survivorship: The Final Transition. *Annals of the American Academy of Political and Social Sciences*, 464: 163–173.

Kalish, R. 1985. The Social Content of Death and Dying. In R. Binstock and E. Shanas (eds.), *Handbook of Aging and the Social Sciences*, 2d ed. New York: VanNostrand Reinhold.

Kalish, R. 1987. Death and Dying. In P. Silverman (ed.), *The Elderly as Modern Pioneers*. Bloomington, IN: Indiana University Press, pp. 320–334.

Kanoti, G.A., and Orlowski, J.P. 1991. Ethical Perspectives on the Physician's Role in Patient Death. *Journal of Physicians Management*, 31: 69–72.

Kastenbaum, R. 1985. Dying and Death: A Life-Span Approach. In J. Birren and K.W. Schaie (eds.), *Handbook of the Psychology of Aging*. New York: VanNostrand Reinhold.

Kastenbaum, R. 1981. *Death, Society, and Human Experience*, 2d ed. Palo Alto, CA: Mayfield.

KCR Communication Research. 1991. *Boston Globe*. (October 18–20).

Kübler-Ross, E. 1969. *On Death and Dying*. New York: Macmillan.

Kübler-Ross, E. 1981. *Living With Dying*. New York: Macmillan.

Kübler-Ross, E. ed. 1975. *Death: The Final Stage of Growth*. Englewood Cliffs, NJ: Prentice-Hall.

Leming, M.R., and Dickinson, G.E. 1990. *Understanding Dying, Death, and Bereavement*, 2d Ed. New York: Holt, Rinehart and Winston.

Levy, J.A. 1987. A Life Course Perspective on Hospice and the Family. In *Marriage and Review*, 29–51.

Lindemann, E. 1979. *Beyond Grief: Studies in Crisis Intervention*. New York: Jason Aronson.

Lopata, H.Z. 1979. *Widowhood in an American City*. Cambridge, MA: Schenkman.

Lopata, H.Z. 1987. Widowhood. In G. Maddow (ed.), *Encyclopedia of Aging*. New York: Springer.

McCarthy, A. 1991. The Country of the Old. *Commonwealth*, 505–506.

Mitford, J.A. 1963. *The American Way of Death*. New York: Simon and Schuster.

Moody, R.A., Jr. 1988. *The Light Beyond*. New York: Bantam.

Moody, R.A., Jr. 1977. *Reflections on Life After Life*. New York: Bantam.

Moody, R.A., Jr. 1975. *Life After Life*. Atlanta: Mackingbird.

Mor, V. 1982. *The National Hospice Study: Progress Report*. Providence, RI: School of Medicine, Brown University.

Morris, J. 1982. *Technical Reports: National Hospice Study*. Boston, MA: Hebrew Home for the Rehabilitation of the Aged: Social Gerontology Research Unit.

Mount, B.M. 1976. Use of the Brompton Mixture in Treating the Chronic Pain of Malignant Disease. *Canadian Medical Association Journal*, 115: 122–124.

National Hospice Organization. 1989. *Hospice Fact Sheet*. Arlington, VA: National Hospice Organization.

Niemeyer, R.A. 1988. Death Anxiety. In Wass, H., Berardo, F.M., and Neimeyer, R.A. (eds.), *Dying: Facing the Facts*. New York: Hemisphere, pp. 97–111.

Nulander, S. 1993. *How We Die*. New York: Knopf.

Older Women's League. 1986. *Death and Dying: Staying in Control to the End of Our Lives*. Washington, DC: Older Women's League.

Ostheimer, J., and Ritt, L. 1976. Life and Death: Current Public Attitudes. In N. Ostheimer and J. Ostheimer (eds.), *Life or Death—Who Controls?* New York: Springer.

Parker, C.M. 1972. *Bereavement: Studies of Grief in Adult Life*. New York: International University Press.

Pincus, L. 1976. *Death and the Family: The Importance of Mourning*. New York: Pantheon Books.

Pollack, G. 1978. Process and Affect: Mourning and Grief. *International Journal of Psychoanalysis*, 59: 255–276.

Pollack, G. 1961. Mourning and Adaptation. *International Journal of Psychoanalysis*, 42: 341–361.

President's Commission for the Study of Ethical Problems in Medicine and Biomedical and Behavioral Research. 1981. *A Report on the Medical, Legal, and Ethical Issues in the Determination of Death.* Washington, DC: U.S. Government Printing Office.

Ray, R. 1991. Dutch Doctors View Euthanasia as a Duty. *Detroit Free Press* (November 18): 7A.

Russell, C. 1989. The Facts of Death. *American Demographics.* (April): 13–14.

Schneidman, E. 1973. *Deaths of Man.* Baltimore: Penguin Books.

Schulz, R. 1978. *The Psychology of Death, Dying, and Bereavement.* Reading, MA: Addison-Wesley.

Sheehy, P. 1981. *Dying With Dignity.* New York: Pinnacle Books.

Siegal, R.K. 1980. The Psychology of Life After Death. *American Psychologist*, 35: 911–931.

Society of Critical Care Medicine. 1990. *Consensus Report*, 1437.

Stephenson, J.S. 1985. *Death, Grief, and Mourning.* New York: Macmillan.

Stoddard, S. 1978. *The Hospice Movement: A Better Way of Caring for the Dying.* New York: Vintage Books.

Summers, T. 1985. On Matters of Life and Death. *Gray Panther Network*, 12.

Thompson, L., Breckenridge, J., Gallagher, D., and Peterson, J. 1984. Effects of bereavement on Self-Perceptions of Physical Health in Elderly Widows and Widowers. *Journal of Gerontology*, 39: 309–314.

Van Eys, J. 1988. In My Opinion . . . Normalization While Dying. *Children's Health Care*, 17: 18–21. In Leming, M.R. and Dickinson, G.E. 1990. *Understanding Dying, Death, and Bereavement*, 2d ed. New York: Holt, Rinehart and Winston.

Walter, T. 1993. Death in the New Age. *Religion*, 23: 127–145.

Weir, R.F. (ed.). 1986. *Ethical Issues in Death and Dying*, 2d ed. New York: Columbia University Press.

Zimmerman, J.M. 1986. *Hospice: Complete Care for the Terminally Ill.* Baltimore: Urban Schwarzenburg.

THE ECONOMICS OF AGING

CHAPTER 8

Economic
Survival

Esther: The Unpaid Worker

Esther was the second of six children born to her parents. Her fondest dream as a youngster was to be a schoolteacher. But her family was a working family and she was expected to contribute to the family income as soon as she was able, which in her case was after completing the tenth grade at age 16. This was how it was for working-class families in America in 1920. Only a privileged few actually went on to college.

Esther got a job in an office and by the age of 21 was the manager of the accounting section. By the age of 23 Esther married. She continued to work until the birth of her first child, when she gave up her job completely. She helped her husband start his own business, a small contracting firm. Esther kept all the records, paid the bills, computed the taxes, and managed the small payroll when the company added employees as time went on.

She continued to do this even after the birth of two more children. The Great Depression of the 1930s sent their business reeling for a few years, with very little work and income. World War II also interrupted the contracting business as Esther's husband entered a war plant for three years and left the business for a time.

After World War II things began to pick up and the business flourished. Once again Esther was key to all the office procedures of the business. In addition, she managed a store that she and her husband started to furnish needed household products to returning servicemen and their new families (the beginning of the Baby Boom).

Because their businesses were small and often struggling, Esther was never a paid employee. No Social Security taxes were ever withheld for her. Because they lived and worked at a time when wages and prices were very low by today's standards, Esther and her husband never were able to save any amount of money that could produce income in their later years—especially extended later years, as she and her husband lived into old age much beyond their imaginations.

During all her busy years, Esther was a homemaker, raised her three children, volunteered in the community and in her church for all kinds of activities and projects, cared for her elderly parents until they died in their early eighties, and worked in the family business. For all of these activities lasting over 45 years she received no salary or credits toward any type of retirement, public or private. Her only reward was to get 50 percent of her husband's Social Security benefits based on his earnings and work record, which ended 30 years ago. Needless to say, she and her husband, both over 90, are running out of money as they continue to grow older, spend increasingly more money on medical expenses in spite of Medicare, and spend more on personal assistance as they can do less and less for themselves. If Esther's husband dies first, which is likely, her income will drop by the amount she was receiving as a benefit of her husband's Social Security income (50 percent of his monthly benefit).

Esther was one of the more fortunate elderly Americans. If she were a member of a minority group, widowed earlier, never married, or divorced, her financial situation would be more desperate. Such is the situation of millions of elderly Americans.

THE ECONOMIC STATUS OF OLDER PEOPLE

The elderly population has experienced significant gains in overall economic status since the inception of the Social Security Act in 1935. Widespread poverty, unemployment, and economic vulnerability in the Great Depression of the 1930s provided the stimulus to develop programs that would give some economic stability to the lives of Americans. Title II of the Social Security Act of 1935, the Old Age and Survivors Insurance (OASI) program, was designed to replace a portion of a person's income when he or she retired or died. When people who had worked in jobs where they put money into the Social Security fund retired, they became eligible for a "pension" from the federal government. Later, Title XVI authorized supplemental Security Income (SSI) as a guaranteed minimum income for eligible old, disabled, and blind persons. With the Dis-

TABLE 8-1

1990 POVERTY RATES

Ages	Percent in poverty
24–44 years	10.4
45–54 years	7.8
55–59 years	9.0
60–64 years	10.3
65 years and above	12.2

Source: Bureau of the Census, Current Population Reports, Series P-60, No. 175, 1991, Table 1, p. 15.

ability Insurance (DI) program—combined together to form OASDI—the overall program was designed to cover workers who retire, die, or become disabled. Prior to Social Security, elderly workers had no minimum income base other than money they were able to save, inherit, or were given. Needless to say, most older people were economically vulnerable once they stopped working. As a result, many people worked as long as they were physically able because they could not afford to retire.

TABLE 8-2

POVERTY STATUS OF PERSONS, BY AGE AND RACE: 1959 TO 1990

Year	Total	Age			Race			
		Under 18	18 to 64	65 and over	Total	White	Black	Hispanic origin
1959	22.4	27.3	17.0	35.2	22.4	18.1	55.1	(NA)
1960	22.2	26.9	22.2	17.8	(NA)	(NA)	(NA)	(NA)
1961	21.9	25.6	21.9	17.4	(NA)	(NA)	(NA)	(NA)
1962	21.0	25.0	21.0	16.4	(NA)	(NA)	(NA)	(NA)
1963	19.5	23.1	19.5	15.3	(NA)	(NA)	(NA)	(NA)
1964	19.0	23.0	19.0	14.9	(NA)	(NA)	(NA)	(NA)
1965	17.3	21.0	17.3	13.3	(NA)	(NA)	(NA)	(NA)
1966	14.7	17.6	10.5	28.5	14.7	11.3	41.8	(NA)
1967	13.2	16.6	10.0	29.5	13.2	11.0	39.3	(NA)
1968	12.8	15.6	9.0	25.0	12.8	10.0	34.7	(NA)
1969	12.1	14.0	8.7	25.3	12.1	9.5	32.2	(NA)
1970	12.6	15.1	9.0	24.6	12.6	9.9	33.5	(NA)
1971	12.5	15.3	9.3	21.6	12.5	9.9	32.5	(NA)
1972	11.9	15.1	8.8	18.6	11.9	9.0	33.3	(NA)
1973	11.1	14.4	8.3	16.3	11.1	8.4	31.4	21.9
1974	11.2	15.4	8.3	14.6	11.2	8.6	30.3	23.0
1975	12.3	17.1	9.2	15.3	12.3	9.7	31.3	26.9
1976	11.8	16.0	9.0	15.0	11.8	9.0	31.1	24.7
1977	11.6	16.2	8.8	14.1	11.6	8.9	31.3	22.4
1978	11.4	15.9	8.7	14.0	11.4	8.7	30.6	21.6
1979	11.7	16.4	8.9	15.2	11.7	9.0	31.0	21.8
1980	13.0	18.3	10.1	15.7	13.0	10.2	32.5	25.7
1981	14.0	20.0	11.1	15.3	14.0	11.1	34.2	26.5
1982	15.0	21.9	12.0	14.6	15.0	12.0	35.6	29.9
1983	15.2	22.3	12.4	13.8	15.2	12.1	35.7	28.0
1984	14.4	21.5	11.7	12.4	14.4	11.5	33.8	28.4
1985	14.0	20.7	11.3	12.6	14.0	11.4	31.3	29.0
1986	13.6	20.5	10.8	12.4	13.6	11.0	31.1	27.3
1987	13.4	20.3	10.6	12.5	13.4	10.4	32.4	28.0
1988	13.0	19.5	10.5	12.0	13.0	10.1	31.3	26.7
1989	12.8	19.6	10.2	11.4	12.8	10.0	30.7	26.2
1990	13.5	20.6	10.7	12.2	13.5	10.7	31.9	28.1

[1]Persons of Hispanic origin may be of any race.
Source: U.S. Bureau of the Census, Current Population Reports, Series P-60, No. 179. *Income, Poverty and Wealth in the United States: A chart book*, U.S. Government Printing Office, Washington, DC, 1992, Table 7, p. B3.

As recently as 1959, 35.2 percent of the elderly were classified as poor with incomes below the poverty line (U.S. Bureau of the Census 1990). Poverty rates for older persons continue to be high. Although somewhat higher, the 1990 poverty rate for older persons was not too much different from those of other adult age groups.

Tremendous gains in the overall economic status of older persons have been evident since the implementation of Social Security and cost of living adjustments that were included in the Social Security Amendments of 1972.

A graph of poverty rates by age categories illustrates the position of older persons relative to people in other age groups and the overall improvement that has occurred in their economic status and security (see Figure 8-1).

INCOME OF OLDER PEOPLE

The median family income for older persons in 1990 taken as a whole was lower than persons in any other age category except those 15 to 24 years of age. Many older persons leave the work force and base their incomes on sources other than wages. The following chart shows median family income (number of families must be multiplied by 1,000).

Even though the median income of older people is lower than any other age group except those aged 15 to 24, their net worth as an overall group is second only to the 55-to-64 year age category as Figure 8-2 illustrates.

In order to get an accurate picture of how older people are situated economically in contemporary America, we need to look further.

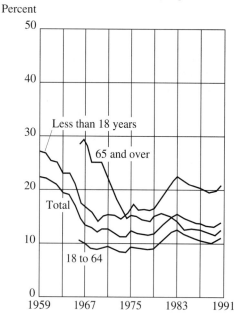

Poverty Rate of Persons, by Age: 1959–90

- Half the Nation's poor in 1990 were either children under 18 years (40.0 percent) or the elderly (10.9 percent).

- The poverty rate for children continues, as it has since 1975, to be higher than that for any other age group. In 1990 the poverty rate for children under 18 years was 19.9 percent.

- The poverty rate for the elderly exceeded that for children until approximately 1973.

- Though the poverty rate for the elderly was lower in 1990 than that for children, a higher proportion of elderly than children were concentrated just over their respective poverty threshold. Consequently, 18.2 percent of the Nation's 11.3 million "near poor" persons were elderly compared with 10.9 percent of persons below the official poverty level.

FIGURE 8-1.
The influence of age on poverty status. (*Source:* U.S. Bureau of the Census, Current Population Reports, Series P-60, No. 179, *Income, poverty and wealth in the United States: A chartbook.* U.S. Government Printing Office, Washington, D.C., 1992, Figure 19, p. 14.)

TABLE 8-3

MEDIAN FAMILY INCOME BY AGE, RACE, AND HISPANIC ORIGIN: 1990

Age	Total			White			Black			Hispanic origin[1]		
	Number	Medium income	Standard error	Number	Medium income	Standard error	Number	Medium income	Standard error	Number	Medium income	Standard error
15 to 24 years	2,726	16,219	453	2,163	18,234	788	476	7,218	707	423	13,009	1,160
24 to 34 years	14,590	31,497	295	12,189	33,457	349	1,943	17,130	706	1,495	20,439	806
35 to 44 years	17,078	41,061	323	14,431	42,632	395	2,023	27,025	1,020	1,323	27,350	1,097
45 to 54 years	11,701	47,164	483	9,990	49,269	595	1,249	30,847	1,445	808	29,908	1,581
55 to 64 years	9,326	39,035	492	8,232	40,416	566	856	25,442	1,674	527	30,839	2,036
65 and over	10,900	25,049	310	9,797	25,864	320	923	16,585	744	405	17,962	1,263

[1]Persons of Hispanic origin may be of any race.
Source: U.S. Bureau of the Census, Current Population Reports, Series P-60, No. 179. *Income, Poverty and Wealth in the United States: A Chartbook.* U.S. Government Printing Office, Washington D.C., 1992, Table 24, p. B-8.

There is considerable debate concerning the economic status of older persons. Much of this discussion is the result of the recent focus on the national debt, the large annual budget deficits, and how America can cope with these realities. One view looks at the elderly as one of the wealthiest groups in the nation continuing to deprive other needy groups of precious federal financial resources. An opposing view sees the elderly as being threatened by economic disaster, noting the rising costs of health care (out-of-pocket costs to older people) and the threat of long-term-care costs, including nursing home costs.

Age is correlated with dollar net worth because increasing age offers an opportunity to accumulate wealth.

- In 1988, median net worth increased significantly from $6,078 for the youngest households (those under 35 years to $80,032 for households in the 55-64 year old category and then declined to $61,491 for the oldest group (75 years and over).

- Although the older group had higher equity in their own homes, the difference in the distribution of net worth and income was not entirely attributable to differences in home equity. Even when home equity was excluded, the oldest group had a much greater net worth than that of the youngest group.

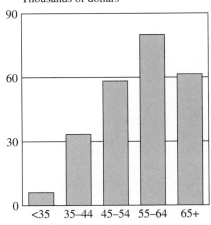

Thousands of dollars

FIGURE 8-2
The median dollar net worth of persons by age: 1988. (*Source:* U.S. Bureau of the Census, Current Population Reports, Series P-60, No. 179, *Income, poverty, and wealth in the United States: A chartbook.* U.S. Government Printing Office, Washington, D.C., 1992, Figure 34, p. 27.)

A true picture of the economic status of older people can be gained by realizing that their overall economic status in America has improved dramatically since the beginning of Social Security and the inclusion of cost of living increases. Nonetheless, numbers of older people are not very well off financially. Indeed, considerable numbers of older people are not able to meet their needs for health care, housing, nutrition, and supportive services (U.S. General Accounting Office 1992).

WHO IS POOR AMONG THE OLD?

The elderly in America are not a heterogeneous group. They are not all the same or even similar in economic circumstances. They differ considerably in many ways. Financial differences among the old are significant. According to the 1991 Current Population Survey, over 5.7 million elderly persons were poor or near poor in 1990. People classified as "poor" are those below the official poverty line established by the federal government. The near-poor are persons at up to 125 percent of the poverty line. This represented 19 percent of the elderly population. It is argued that these figures do not accurately reflect the extent of poverty among the old. There are two reasons for this contention. First, it is argued that these figures do not accurately reflect actual consumption patterns among the elderly because they are based on outdated measures of what older people really purchase with their resources. Second, the poverty figures do not include the older homeless population. (U.S. General Accounting Office 1992).

An extensive review by the General Accounting Office in 1992 of who is poor among the old clearly indicated that elderly women, minorities, and those over the age of 75 were more likely to be poor or near poor than the overall elderly population:

> Elderly women were nearly twice as likely as elderly men to be poor or near poor. Elderly Hispanics were twice as likely—and elderly blacks were three times as likely—as elderly whites to be poor or near poor. Similarly, persons over the age of 75

were almost twice as likely to be poor or near poor as were persons between the ages of 65 and 74. The additive effect of sex, race, and age was dramatic: more than half of all black women over the age of 75 were poor or near poor in 1990 (U.S. General Accounting Office 1992: 16).

It is clear from all the data that older women are much more likely to be poor or near poor than older men. Marital status has a great effect on the poverty status of older women. Indeed, poverty rates for older married men and women were quite similar and relatively low in all the age groups of the elderly in 1990, but being single and old doubled the poverty rate for men and quadrupled it for women (United States Government Accounting Office 1992). This points to the economic vulnerability of older women in American society. Widowed, divorced, separated, or never married older women are among the most economically vulnerable persons in the nation. This is caused by number of factors that directly relate to the traditional roles women have occupied in American society and their economic status in the workplace.

CAUSES OF POVERTY AMONG THE OLD

Older Women

Women, particularly older women in contemporary American society, have traditionally filled roles in society for which they have received no pay and no credits toward retirement income. The roles of wives, homemakers, nurturers of children, caregivers for ill family members (including aged parents), and volunteers in the community, the church, and the school have occupied the lives of countless American women who are currently elderly. As a study by the Women's Initiative of the American Association of Retired Persons stated,

> For women, a lifetime of fewer employment opportunities, lower wages, and more years spent out of the work force raising children or caring for relatives translate into women receiving a much lower retirement income than men. . . . Despite substantial in-

TABLE 8-4

PERCENT OF POOR AND NEAR-POOR ELDERLY PERSONS, BY AGE, SEX, AND RACE/ETHNICITY, 1990

Sex and age	White		Black		Hispanic[a]		Total	
	Poor	Near poor	Poor	Near poor	Poor	Near poor	Poor	Near poor
Both sexes								
65 and over	10.1%	6.3%	33.8%	11.3%	22.5%	11.0%	12.2%	6.8%
65 to 74	7.6	4.9	29.6	11.0	20.6	10.4	9.7	5.4
75 and over	13.8	8.6	40.6	11.9	26.2	12.4	16.0	8.9
Male								
65 and over	5.6	4.6	27.8	10.7	18.6	8.4	7.6	5.2
65 to 74	4.5	4.0	24.6	10.1	18.0	8.0	6.4	4.7
75 and over	7.8	5.4	34.4	12.0	20.1	9.1	9.9	6.0
Female								
65 and over	13.2	7.7	37.9	11.7	25.3	12.9	15.4	8.0
65 to 74	10.2	5.6	33.6	11.7	22.7	12.3	12.3	6.1
75 and over	17.3	10.5	43.9	11.9	30.1	14.4	19.5	10.7

[a]Hispanics may be of any race.
Source: U.S. General Accounting Office, 1992. *Elderly Americans: Health, housing and nutrition gaps between the poor and the nonpoor.* Washington, D.C.: U.S. General Accounting Office, Table 11.1, p. 17.

creases in women's participation in the work place, their access to income security at retirement continues to exist largely through men (AARP 1993: v).

Unless wives who do not work outside the home inherit a large amount of money or win the lottery, their retirement income is totally dependent on their husbands. Upon retirement, a wife who relies on her husband's income for Social Security benefits receives 50 percent of the husband's benefits. In 1990, 63 percent of all women age 62 and older (the minimum age to collect Social Security benefits) received benefits based on their husbands' work records. The average monthly benefit was $316.10 (Social Security Administration 1991).

Of the women who worked outside the home in paying jobs, only 22 percent received a pension compared to 49 percent for men in 1991. Of the women who did receive a pension, their annual benefit was about half the amount men received: $5,186, compared to $9,855 for men (unpublished tabulations from the *March 1992 Supplement to Current Population Survey*, Income Statistics Branch, U.S. Bureau of the Census).

The overall significance of increasing divorce rates among older people, with very few older divorced women remarrying, is the incidence of poverty among these women. A 1993 study by the Policy Center on Aging at Brandeis University showed that after age 62, the poverty rate among divorced older women is higher than among widowed or never married women. This same study revealed that the poverty rate for separated older women was higher than that of any other category of unmarried older women (Crown, Mutchler, and Lowe 1993).

Overall, both women who devoted their lives to being homemakers—wives, mothers, family caregivers—and women who worked outside the home while married or single, are in jeopardy of being economically poor in retirement once they live alone, the way most older women end their lives. Widowed, divorced, separated, or never married older women are at great economic risk in contemporary American society. Most of the elderly poor who live alone are women. Women made up 58 percent of the elderly population overall, but 74 percent of the elderly poor in 1990 (U.S. Bureau of Census 1992). Until there is more equal access to pensions that have equal benefits, women who participate in the American workplace will be more impoverished than men in their later years. In addition, until the contributions women make in all their homemaking and caregiving roles are financially recognized, or these roles more equally divided among the sexes, women will continue to be at a financial disadvantage in old age. Increased rates of divorce will continue to hurt older women financially unless present policies are changed. It is projected that by 2030, more than one in five older women will be divorced, a 400-percent increase over current divorce rates (U.S. House Select Committee 1992). Unless and until more equitable divisions of assets, including pensions, are devised, older women living alone will remain one of the most impoverished groups in America.

Minorities: African Americans

The economic status of older African Americans has declined in recent years. In 1986, 31 percent of all African Americans aged 65 and older were poor. This increased to 33.8 percent by 1990 (U.S. Bureau of the Census 1991). The National Caucus and Center on Black Aged, Inc. attributes this decline in economic status to the struggling national economy and supply-side economics of the Reagan/Bush Years (U.S. House of Representatives 1992). It is pointed out that the poverty rate for elderly African Americans in 1990 was about the same as it was in 1974, indicating virtually no overall economic gain. In fact, the poverty rate for this minority group is considerably higher than for children under 18: 33.8 percent compared to 20.6 percent (U.S. Bureau of the Census 1991). The poverty rate for African-American children under 18 is 44.8 percent. This is similar to the poverty rate for African Americans 75 and older, which is 40.6 percent (U.S. House of Representatives 1992).

Elderly African Americans continue to fall farther behind other older Americans. In 1986, elderly African Americans were almost three times as likely to be in poverty as elderly whites. In 1990, they were more than three times as likely to be poor: 33.8 percent compared to 10.1 percent (U.S. House of Representatives 1992). It is evident that the inclusion of the minority elderly in calculating the overall poverty figures of older Americans raises the overall percentage of the elderly poor in America.

When the economic status of elderly African-American women is examined, the percentages of those in poverty is staggering. In 1986, seven out of eight (87.9 percent) elderly African Americans living alone or with nonrelatives were either poor or economically vulnerable (economically vulnerable defined as having incomes not exceeding twice the poverty rate). By 1990, about nine out of every ten (89.3 percent) were in this category (U.S. House of Representatives, 1992).

Inadequate income in retirement is regarded as the major problem of elderly African Americans. It is regarded as the root cause for almost all of the problems older African Americans face including poor health, deficient diet, dilapidated housing, and other poor living conditions (U.S. House of Representatives 1992).

To improve the poor economic conditions of so many elderly African Americans, advocates recommend raising the Supplemental Security Income (SSI) above the poverty line. They also recommend changes in the way SSI is administered, such as adjusting the way assets are counted, not reducing benefits by one-third when an elderly person lives in the home of a child or another person and receives in-kind support, and aggressive outreach activities to make sure that eligible people are in the program (U.S. House of Representatives 1992).

Increased employment opportunities for older people is another way that is suggested to improve the finances of African Americans. In 1990, only 3.5 percent of all persons 65 and older who were employed were poor compared to 13.8 percent who did not work, about one-fourth as many. Working and older persons is discussed in the next chapter.

In 1990, African Americans made up only 8 percent of the total elderly population, but they accounted for 24 percent of all elderly poor.

Minorities: Latinos

People of Hispanic origin are the fastest growing group in America. This sector of the population is expected to increase to 47 million by the year 2000. In recent years this group increased almost five times faster than the non-Latino population. The number of Latinos age 65 and older tripled in the last two decades. Their numbers will continue to grow at a faster rate than any other ethnic or racial group (U.S. House of Representatives 1992). The 65-and-older group is the fastest-growing segment of the Latino population.

As with other minority groups, poverty rates are high for elderly members. Among Latino elderly persons, 33.5 percent were poor or near poor, compared to 16.4 percent for white elderly persons (U.S. Bureau of the Census 1991).

Reasons for poverty among America's Latino elderly include: (1) lack of access to education, (2) school drop-outs, (3) limited or lack of marketable skills that result in underemployment or unemployment, and (4) discrimination that prevents access to opportunities that could make real changes in the lives of the poor (U.S. House of Representatives 1992).

Because of a history of underemployment, unemployment, or employment in low-paying jobs, Latino elderly are more dependent on Supplemental Security Income than most other groups of older persons (U.S. House of Representatives 1992). One of the biggest problems with the SSI program is the low percentage of the elderly poor who receive it. Among the total elderly poor, only 56 percent get SSI benefits (Committee on Ways and Means 1992). Among Latinos, only 39 percent get SSI benefits. Their participation rate is lower than any other group among the elderly, and lack of participation in the SSI program limits access to food stamps and Medicaid as well as almost every other program designed to improve the lives of the elderly poor (U.S. House of Rep-

resentatives 1992). Reasons for low participation by Latinos in programs for the elderly poor include:

- Fear of the government. One study in Boston found that many poor Latinos were fearful of giving too much personal information to the government due to their experience with repressive governments in their countries of origin (Kassner 1992).
- Language barriers. Limited bilingual printed materials and case workers are available (Kassner 1992).
- Discrimination.
- Inadequate outreach strategies.
- Agency policies, practices, and procedures that discourage application for services (U.S. House of Representatives 1992).

In addition, elderly Latinos are twice as likely to live with someone other than their spouse and therefore more likely to be penalized by household eligibility criteria which lower benefits (Andrews 1989).

Advocates for the Latino elderly recommend improving interpreter services in agencies, assessing bilingual staffing needs and providing resources, developing effective outreach strategies, and emphasizing bilingual skills in recruitment and promotion of agency staffs (U.S. House of Representatives 1992). In addition, education, training, and employment for Latinos are essential to address their long-term income needs in old age.

The Oldest Old

The oldest old (ages 85 and older) make up a group that is overrepresented in poverty classifications for a variety of reasons. In 1990, 20.2 percent of this group were classified as poor compared to 12.2 percent for the overall elderly population. When the "near poor" (125 percent of poverty) were added to those aged 75 and older who were classified as "poor," the percentage increased to 24.9, or one in four of all persons 75 and older. When the economically vulnerable (200 percent of poverty) are included, the percentage increased to 48.6. It is even higher for persons aged 85 and older.

Table 8-5 shows that the poverty rates for elderly Americans increase as the categories of ages increases.

An obvious reason why so many of the oldest old are poor or near poor relates to our previous discussion of poverty being concentrated among older women. Women outnumbered men by more than two to one among the oldest old in 1990. The sex ratio (the number of living males per 100 females) was 42 for persons 85 to 89. For the elderly aged 95 to 99, there were 27 males for every 100 females. This ratio was the same for persons over 100. As a result, the financial problems of the oldest old are primarily the problems of women. As we have already observed, the majority of women will spend their last years widowed or divorced (U.S. Bureau of the Census 1992b).

INFLATION AND LONGEVITY

Long years of retirement result in financial ruin for many of the oldest old. Some simply outlive their money. Even if they do not use up their savings and investments, if they were fortunate enough to have them when they retired, what they have simply does not keep up with the underlying inflation we have experienced in the United States for many years. This is called the *longevity-inflation squeeze*. More and more people are living longer while over time the economy continues to inflate prices. The money older people saved 10, 20, or 30 years ago may no longer pay for their needs today or in the future. The inflation rate does not have to be as high as it was in the late 1970s to feed the effects of the longevity-inflation squeeze. Table 8-6 shows how drastically even a modest inflation rate can decrease savings. On average, consumer prices in the United States have doubled every fifteen years. Living on fixed incomes puts the oldest old at a special financial disadvantage, as they retired at a time when prices and incomes were much lower than 15, 20, or 30 years after they were out of the workplace.

Gil is 90 years old. He retired when he was 61 after working since he was 16. In the depths of the Great Depression of the 1930s he started his own electrical

---

TABLE 8-5

PERCENT OF POOR ELDERLY PERSONS BY AGE, SEX, AND MARITAL STATUS, 1990

Sex and marital status	65 to 74	75 to 84	85 and over	Total
Male				
Married	4.2%	7.2%	11.4%	5.3%
Widowed	13.2	14.3	13.9	13.8
Divorced, separated,				
or never married	16.8	14.7	a	16.1
Total	**6.4**	**9.3**	**12.6**	**7.6**
Female				
Married	4.7	8.1	a	5.7
Widowed	19.5	22.1	24.4	21.4
Divorced, separated,				
or never married	23.4	24.1	a	24.3
Total	**12.3**	**18.3**	**24.1**	**15.4**
Total	**9.7%**	**14.9%**	**20.2%**	**12.2%**

[a]Not available due to unreliability of estimates because of small sample sizes.
Source: U.S. General Accounting Office, 1992. *Elderly Americans: Health, housing and nutrition gaps between the poor and the nonpoor.* Washington, D.C.: U.S. General Accounting Office, Table 11.2, p. 18.

TABLE 8-6

Inflation rate	Value of $1,000 after:			
	5 yrs.	10 yrs.	15 yrs.	20 yrs.
4%	$820	$680	$560	$460
5%	780	610	480	380
6%	750	560	420	310
7%	710	510	360	260

Source: Coopers & Lybrand (*Newsweek*, April 8, 1991, p. 46. All rights reserved. Reprinted by permission).

contracting business which was interrupted by World War II, but flourished in the post-war years. He even added a retail store to his business. The most Gil ever charged for a service call was $5. He only charged that for a couple years. Prior to that the charge was $3. Gil and his wife saved what they could for retirement—what they thought was enough to live on. It was adequate for many years. They purchased a mobile home in Florida where they spent their winters, and they enjoyed a small cottage on a lake up north for the summers. Each residence was purchased for under $20,000. Their expenses were modest. Having been self-employed, Gil had no pension, and his Social Security income was low.

After nearly 30 years of retirement, things have changed drastically. With failing health and vigor, Gil and his wife were forced to move into a retirement home with supportive services. Their monthly bill is over $1,900. It cost them $20,000 for entrance fees. They are living in an entirely different economic world from the one they left as workers. They are using interest and principal from their savings to live. After a short time, their resources will be depleted. What then?

The story of Gil and his wife is not unique. In fact, they are among the fortunate oldest old who started out with some savings and investments. Millions of the oldest old have only modest Social Security benefits on which to rely, and as we will see, those living on Social Security alone are usually the poorest of the old as well as the oldest.

James Schulz (1992), a noted expert on the economics of older people, pointed out five principal ways older people are negative by affected by inflation:

1. Assets such as bonds, checking accounts, saving accounts, and insurance policies often fall in real value with ongoing inflation.
2. Transfer incomes, such as pensions, may lag behind inflation, reducing real income. So far Social Security benefits have increased with inflation, but there is political pressure to cap these increases.
3. Employed older persons may experience earning levels that lag behind inflation.
4. Older taxpayers may experience inflation penalties if tax brackets specified in the laws are defined in money rather than real terms.
5. When inflation is higher in items such as healthcare, which makes up a large portion of so many older persons' budgets, older people suffer.

The benefits of lower inflation have been mixed for older people. With falling interest rates in recent years, a feature the Clinton administration has touted, the incomes of many older people have fallen considerably. At older ages, most people put what savings they have in the most secure investments available. For many this means bank CDs insured by the federal bank insurance programs (FDIC, FSLIC), or government bonds. With $100,000 in CDs or government bonds, a 10 percent rate of return produces $10,000 a year. When rates fall to 3.5 or 4 percent, this translates into income of $3,500 to $4,000 a year. This is a drastic reduction in income for millions of persons living on fixed incomes.

Many retirees are not affected by these rate declines. Many do not have the luxury of interest incomes, especially relatively large ones. But even modest investments provide some measure of security for millions of older people. Deprived of that cushion, or with a much smaller cushion, they must worry about joining the ranks of the elderly poor.

The alternative to investing in CDs and government bonds is to move to riskier investments which so many older people resist and of which many are uninformed.

You can get a little more if you are willing to take a risk," said Albert Lorenz, a retired 75-year-old former car salesman who lives at Deerfield Lake (FL). "But at our age, people are cautious and want security. They are afraid to put their money in the stock market, much less the riskier things like junk bonds (*Grand Rapids Press*, January 1, 1992: A6).

Summing up the feelings of many retired older people as they look at their financial future with underlying inflation and low interest rates, a retired data processor said, "We are working people who worked very hard and saved very hard, and now we find out that we are going to have less than we thought we would have (*Grand Rapids Press*, January 1, 1992: A6)."

ECONOMIC SUPPORT SYSTEMS

As with most conditions among the elderly, there are great differences as to sources and amounts of income. We have already looked at personal situations that reflect on the types and levels of income among the elderly. These include age (oldest old compared to the young old), race, ethnicity, marital status, living arrangements, educational attainment, former occupational status, and work history (U.S. Bureau of the Census 1992a). The Census Bureau points out that although rural elderly and older persons in the Southern states had the lowest median incomes in the 1980 census, the characteristics of older age, widowhood, lower educational achievement, and lower occupational status have been more important factors than geography in explaining income differences (Glasgow 1988).

Social Security

A common denominator of income for the elderly in contemporary America is Social Security benefits. This has occurred since 1940, when fewer than one percent of older people received Social Security benefits. It is interesting to note that at that time, 22 percent of the elderly received general welfare assistance. By 1990, 92 percent of America's elderly received Social Se-

curity benefits, with a mean income of $6,163. Only 6 percent received public assistance or Supplemental Security Income (SSI), a means-tested income program based on poverty status (U.S. Bureau of the Census 1992a).

The importance of the Social Security program is demonstrated by data published by the Bureau of the Census in 1992, indicating that Social Security was the major source of income for 61 percent of beneficiaries in 1987, providing at least 50 percent of their total income. It provided nearly all of the income, 90 percent or more, for 25 percent of retirees, and was the only source of income for 14 percent of the beneficiaries (Sherman 1992).

As we indicated earlier, Social Security came out of the Great Depression of the 1930s as one of the most, if not *the* most, important achievements of President Franklin Roosevelt's New Deal. Begun in 1935, the program continues to be one of the most important pieces of social legislation in the history of the United States. This type of program traces its roots to Europe in the 1880s, where Otto von Bismarck of Germany developed a program to require employers and employees to contribute to a fund first for disabled workers and then for retired workers. It should be noted that not many people lived to age 65 at that time. Not too much was paid out in extended benefits.

By 1905, France had enacted a similar program for unemployment. In 1911, England adopted both old-age and unemployment insurance plans. Roosevelt followed the outlines of the European plans:

- government-sponsored
- compulsory
- independently financed

It is an error to view Social Security only as a program for older people. From the beginning it had intergenerational aspects. By providing a base of financial income for retired workers and their spouses, younger family members were relieved from supporting their elderly parents. Younger workers also gained financial security by having in place income for their families in the event of their death at any age. In 1956, Disability Insurance was added to Social Security to replace a portion of a worker's income when he or she became disabled and unable to work. Title II of the Social Security Act of 1935, the Old Age and Survivors Insurance (OASI) and the Disability Insurance program (DI) together formed the OASDI program. The combined program is intended to replace a portion of a worker's income upon retirement, disability, or death. Generally referred to as "Social Security," monthly benefits are based on a person's work record (years of covered employment) and earnings. In August, 1992, as a snapshot of how the program actually works and pays, $23 billion were paid in benefits, with retired workers averaging $630 monthly and disabled workers, $608 (U.S. Senate Special Committee on Aging 1993).

In 1992, 41 million Americans received Social Security benefits. Of these, 26 million (62 percent) were retirees, almost 5 million (12 percent) disabled workers and dependent family members, and 7 million (17 percent) surviving family members of deceased workers. At the same time about 135 million workers were in jobs covered by Social Security, approximately 95 percent of the total work force in the United States (U.S. Senate Special Committee on Aging 1993). Although the Disability Insurance program of Social Security is an important component, covering about 5 million disabled workers and their family members, the overall program is viewed as a compact between younger and older generations as well as a contract with the federal government.

Debates over Social Security

In recent years, serious questions have emerged regarding the viability, fairness, and desirability of the Social Security program. These questions involve the following issues:

1. The huge national debt and annual multibillion-dollar national deficits.

2. The large number of people living longer and longer.

3. The prospect of the baby boomers overwhelming the retirement systems, including Social Security, as they begin to retire early in the twenty-first century.

Viability   Many workers, particularly younger ones, are concerned that Social Security will be bankrupt when they retire. A 1993 study by Yankelovich Partners indicated that among persons aged 30 to 35, 80 percent had doubts that Social Security would be there for them when they retired. Among those aged 36 to 40, the percentage was 76 percent; among those aged 41 to 50, the percentage of doubters was 66 percent. Going back five years from 1993, confidence in Social Security decreased among 64 percent of those surveyed, with only 30 percent maintaining the same confidence as five years earlier. Some 69 percent of all the respondents expected Social Security to pay less than it did during their parents' generation.

Despite major financing changes in the 1983 amendments designed to restore solvency to the system, it is clear that a majority of younger and middle-aged people in America fear that Social Security will run out of money when their time comes to collect benefits. It should be noted that because of higher payroll taxes and higher limits on which Social Security contributions are paid ($57,600 in 1993), the system is running at a surplus in its trust funds. Also contributing to the growth of the trust funds is the leveling off of people retiring in the 1990s, the Great Depression babies of the 1930s when birthrates were low. In fact, it is projected that reserves will continue to grow. By the year 2020, the surplus is expected to grow to 2.3 trillion dollars in 1991 dollars (Schulz 1992). With the trust funds dwindling as Baby Boomers retire, the OASI fund is projected to be depleted by 2042, ample time to make adjustments to continue it further into the future. The DI trust fund is projected to be depleted by 1997, a smaller fund for which adjustments can be made more easily (U.S. Senate Special Committee on Aging 1993). A former director of the Actuarial Division of the Internal Revenue Service says that with relatively minor tax increases, the Social Security system is expected to pay full benefits for the next 75 years (Brubbs 1992).

The threat to the viability of the Social Security System is the disposition of the surplus funds. By law, the trust funds can only be invested in U.S. Treasury securities. In other words, the federal government owes itself for the investments of the funds; but because the federal government has operated in deep deficit financing for so many years, the surplus trust funds have been used to finance the daily governmental operations. In fact, for many years the surplus of the Social Security Trust Funds have made the yearly federal deficits appear less than they actually were by some 50 or more billion dollars a year.

In 1990, as part of the Omnibus Budget Reconciliation Act, Social Security was finally removed from the budget process in determining deficit reduction guidelines (the Gramm-Rudman-Hollings deficit reduction budget-cutting process). This legislation made it difficult to diminish Social Security reserves. They are known as the "fire wall" provisions, erecting a fire wall between the reserves and the Congress. However, as federal deficits pile up and the trust funds increase at a dramatic rate (a surplus of over one billion dollars per week in 1993), the long-term viability of the trust funds is questioned as they are subject to the political process. "Indeed, political and economic pressures in coming years to use the trust funds to reduce the Federal deficit may overshadow the attention paid to maintaining Social Security's solvency" (U.S. Senate 1993: 11).

Fairness The increased payroll taxes, or "contributions," to fund the Social Security System at its present income level have prompted some workers, particularly younger and lower-income workers, to question the fairness of the system. Why should low-income workers pay the same

rates as high-income workers? Why should younger workers pay into a system that supports older people, many of whom are better off economically than they are?

As to the first question, why everyone pays the same rate, the answer is recognizing "that the benefit structure of Social Security is heavily weighted in favor of low earners" (Schulz 1992). The system was designed so that the ratio of contributions to payouts is higher for low-paid workers than for higher-paid workers. "The formula recognizes that lower workers need to have more of their earnings replaced because they spend a higher proportion of their earnings for basic needs," said Louis Enoff, acting commissioner of Social Security (Dixon, *The Grand Rapids Press*, March 14, 1993: E4). Lower-income workers are generally not as likely to have supplemental income from investments and other sources in retirement as are higher-income persons. As such, Social Security is designed to replace a greater percentage of a lower-income worker's earnings.

An equally probing question for some younger workers relates to the fairness issue. A 1993 analysis of Social Security found that the average worker who retired in 1960 got back all he or she paid into the system in 10 months. Av-

---

TABLE 8-7

TARGET REPLACEMENT RATE GOALS AND REPLACEMENT FROM SOCIAL SECURITY, SINGLE PERSON, IN 1988

Gross preretirement earnings	(1) Replacement goal[a]	(2) Social Security replacement[b]	(1)–(2) Gap
$15,000	72%	44%	28%
20,000	68	41	27
25,000	68	38	30
30,000	69	33	36
45,000	72	23	49

[a] The goal is to provide sufficient retirement income in order to maintain prior living standards upon retirement.
[b] Assumes retirement at age 65.
Source: Schulz, J.H. 1992. *The Economics of Aging*, 5th ed. New York: Auburn House, an imprint of Greenwood Publishing Group, Inc., p. 129.

erage workers retiring in 1992 recovered their contributions after 68 months. The payback period for workers retiring in 2027 is projected to be 103 months. As a result of the changes in the system by the 1983 amendments, workers born in 1960 and later will not get full benefits until they are 67, not 65 (Dixon 1993). Even with these facts in mind, Schulz (1992) has pointed out studies that show Social Security is a good long-term buy for workers overall. Without such a universal system, the U.S. would probably return to an era of widespread poverty among the elderly, given the current savings and investment rate among younger workers. The 1993 Yankelovich Partners' study of views of Social Security among younger workers also indicated that most people have insufficient savings and investment practices for future retirement needs. Among workers aged 30 to 50 earning $30,000 or more per year, only 32 percent had an estate plan. More than half (53 percent) felt they could invest more toward retirement than they were. Between current living expenses, mortgages, car financing, saving for vacations, saving for their children's education (with ever-increasing college tuition), and emergencies, even relatively well-off workers find it difficult to save for retirement. Most lower-income workers find it nearly impossible. In this context, Social Security becomes a good buy for even younger workers who pay more and work longer to receive their benefits.

Desirability   The question of the desirability of having a Social Security system in place as part of a universal governmental program continues to be raised. This question goes to the heart of the role of government in American society. What things ought to be left to the individual? What programs deserve governmental intervention and support? Persons with different political philosophies support differing views. In the United States, public policies, particularly as they relate to specific programs, usually come out of crisis or near-crisis situations. This was the case with Social Security. In the Great Depression of the

1930s, two major needs were addressed by the Social Security Act of 1935. The first was the establishment of a financial income base for older people because so many were in poverty. The second was an incentive for older people to retire to make jobs available for younger unemployed workers (Schulz 1992). Over a quarter of the work force was unemployed at that time.

In signing the 1935 legislation, Franklin Roosevelt asked, "Now, this is a pension program—it isn't welfare, is it?" (Martz and Thomas 1990: 54). In a memorandum to the U.S. Senate, J.D. Brown stated,

> Overall, the advantages of uniform proportionate contributions toward one's social insurance protection are of great psychological, social, and political importance. They clearly differentiate benefits as a matter of right from those available only on individual proof of need. They reflect a natural desire for self-reliance (Brown 1973: 220–221).

It is one thing for those in society rich enough, disciplined enough, and with adequate foresight to systematically put money away for retirement throughout their working lives. However, not many people are able to do this. Even if they were able to put money away every week they worked, in most cases these funds would not be matched by employer contributions.

Social Security, as it is constituted, is a matter of right for all workers—rich, middle-class, and poor. There is no test to determine if one needs benefits upon retirement. Everyone who works and contributes into the system (which is now mandatory for most U.S. workers) earns benefits. So the third of each month is "payday" for Social Security recipients. It is not welfare day. Politicians from time to time (including some prominent current ones) think they have a ready answer to the national debt and the annual budget deficit by controlling and limiting Social Security benefits through capping annual increases tied to inflation (Social Security cost of living adjustments—COLAs) or by means testing, making benefits available only to the needy poor. But means testing would destroy one of the most successful programs of the U.S. Government. Social Security is a contract workers have with their government as well as a contract between generations. As has been pointed out, the program also protects younger workers, not just old retirees, and relieves younger persons from much of the financial responsibility of caring for aging family members. With proper management, it will be a major component of younger workers' financial future.

Supplemental Security Income

The Supplemental Security Income (SSI) program was authorized as Title XVI of the Social Security Act of 1972. It went into effect two years later. It is a cash-assistance program designed to provide nationally uniform guaranteed minimum income for eligible old, disabled, and blind persons. SSI replaced federal assistance to old state-administered poverty programs for the old, the blind, and the permanently and totally disabled. Three congressionally mandated goals were part of SSI:

1. Construct a coherent, unified income assistance system.
2. Eliminate large differences between the various states in eligibility and benefits.
3. Reduce the stigma of being on welfare by having the program administered by the Social Security Administration rather than state-sponsored welfare offices.

Before the enactment of SSI, there were great differences between benefits the state gave out. Michigan, for example, in 1972, had a monthly old-age benefit of $224. Maryland paid out $96 in monthly benefits, and Mississippi $75 (U.S. Department of Health, Education, and Welfare 1972).

Means Tested The SSI program is means tested (only available to persons who meet income and asset tests). Eligibility in categories has not changed since 1974. Individuals must be aged 65 or older. Blindness refers to persons with 20/200 vision or less with the use of a corrective lens in a

person's better eye or those with tunnel vision of 20 degrees or less (as some in glaucoma sufferers). Disabled are those persons unable to engage in any substantial gainful activity due to a physical or mental impairment that is expected to result in death or has lasted, or is expected to last, for a 12-month continuous period (U.S. Senate 1993).

Eligibility To be eligible, monthly income had to be below $434 for an individual and $652 for a couple in 1992. Assets include real estate (except a person's home), personal belongings, savings and checking accounts, cash, and stocks. In 1992, the asset limit was $2,000 for an individual and $3,000 for a married couple. Also excluded are cars ($4,500 current market value), $1,500 cash value of life insurance policies combined with the value of burial funds and burial plots (U.S. Senate 1993).

This is truly a poverty program intended only for the proven poor. It is totally unlike the old-age benefits of the Social Security program. The SSI program also includes a person's living arrangements when it is calculated. If an older person is living in the household of another person, which many do, and getting some support, the value of that support is regarded as being equal to one-third of the SSI benefit. As a result, the SSI benefit is reduced by one-third.

It is important to note that in most states if persons qualify for SSI, they automatically qualify for Medicaid (medical coverage for the poor in the U.S.) and food stamp benefits (U.S. Senate 1992).

In 1992, 5.5 million people received benefits under SSI—$422 for an individual, $633 for a couple. About 1.5 million recipients were elderly poor. The federal SSI benefits for 1992 were estimated to be only 75 percent of the poverty line for individuals and 89 percent for couples (Committee on Ways and Means 1992).

SSI Problems Three problems have been identified as major issues facing SSI. One is the inadequacy of benefits to lift the truly poor elderly out of poverty (U.S. Senate 1993). The second revolves around the strict financial criteria cited previously. The third is the lack of participation in the program by eligible persons. SSI benefits were provided to only 56 percent of the elderly poor in 1990 (Committee on Ways and Means 1992). A Louis Harris and Associates (1988) survey of persons aged 65 and older who live below or near the poverty line found that more than one-third of those potentially eligible for SSI benefits had never heard about the program. Coordinated outreach for this and other programs designed to aid the elderly are greatly needed. Some have been initiated with good results.

In 1940, fewer than one percent of the elderly received Social Security benefits, with 22 percent receiving general welfare assistance. By 1990, 92 percent of older people in the United States were receiving Social Security benefits and 6 percent received public assistance or SSI (U.S. Bureau of the Census, 1992a).

Pensions

Pensions are another major source of income for many elderly Americans, but the coverage is quite uneven. Five categories of pension plans cover a range of American workers and retirees:

1. Private pensions (private industry and business)
2. State and local public employee pensions
3. Federal civilian employee pensions
4. Military retirement pensions
5. The Railroad Retirement System.

By far the largest of these pension categories is private pensions, with some 50 million workers and retirees covered by employer-sponsored plans. Employees of larger firms are much more likely to be in an employer-sponsored pension program than employees of small firms (U.S. Senate 1993).

Pension Coverage   In 1990, pension income was received by 34 percent of elderly whites, 22 percent of older African Americans, and 19 percent of older Latinos (U.S. Bureau of the Census 1992a). Of all retirees receiving pensions in 1987,

68 percent were men. While the mean monthly pension for men was about $744, women's pension income averaged $417 per month (U.S. Senate 1992). As was pointed out earlier, women are at a distinct disadvantage in pension coverage and in pension levels of income.

It is interesting to note that although the coverage of different racial and ethnic groups varies, for those who are covered by pensions, the overall mean pension incomes of white, African American, and Latino retirees were not significantly different. About one in five retirees with pensions had four or more years of college, with mean pension incomes nearly twice as high as high-school graduates and almost three times the amount non-high-school graduates received (U.S. Bureau of the Census 1992a).

A 1993 survey by the Gallup organization found that only 27 percent of respondents knew what percentage of preretirement income is necessary to keep in retirement the same standard of living enjoyed while working. The same study indicated that about one in five persons surveyed overestimated the amount that most people can expect to get from Social Security and pension plans (Matas 1993).

Changes in Pensions   What makes this so crucial is the fact that private pensions are undergoing significant changes. Not even introduced in the United States until the end of the nineteenth century, pensions covered very few workers until the 1940s and 1950s, when the post-World War II industrial boom occurred. The typical pension plan was the *defined-benefit* plan where the worker is guaranteed specific retirement benefits by the employer. The real change in pension coverage is a retreat from the defined-benefit approach, to *defined-contribution* plans. Defined contribution pension plans are those that allow employees to set aside part of their wages in tax-sheltered accounts for their retirement. Employers may contribute to these plans, but they are not required to do so. The level of a worker's pension under these plans depends on the amount he or she is able to set aside during working years and the performance of the investment funds. Often these plans are referred to as *401K plans*, named after the section of the Internal Revenue Code that authorizes them (Lewis 1992).

The defined-contribution plans will affect retirees in the future, as they are rapidly outpacing the older defined-benefit plans. In fact in 1993, 401K plans covered some 10 million more workers than were covered by the traditional defined-benefit plans (Wise 1993).

Efforts to Include More Women in Pensions

Legislation to address the pension inequities of women was included in the Retirement Equity Act of 1984 and the Tax Reform Act of 1986. These legislative acts were designed to address a 1982 survey which showed that only 27 percent of older women were receiving pensions, 24 percent from their own employment, and 3 percent from survivor benefits (Woods 1988). The 1984 act lowered minimum age for participation in pension plans to age 21, so many more female workers could benefit, because the 20-to-24-year-old age group had the highest female labor force rate (Schulz 1992); provided survivor benefits to spouses of vested workers; and clarified the division of benefits in a divorce (U.S. Senate 1992). The 1986 legislation included more rapid vesting—the right to receive benefits from a pension plan. Vesting has been reduced to five years where there is no partial vesting prior to five years. If there is partial vesting, then full vesting takes place after seven years. This provision significantly helps women workers who move in and out of the workforce for a variety of reasons.

Pensions are an important source of income for retirees fortunate enough to get them. Only about one-third of the retirees in 1990 were receiving pension benefits, and the great majority of these were men who had worked in large corporations for long periods of times. Still, the percentage of elderly households receiving pensions is three times the number it was thirty years ago (Lewis 1992). In 1993, half of all workers were

covered by private or public pensions, including about two-thirds of men and half of women in their forties and fifties. Nevertheless, the persistent inequities of pension coverage for women, both as workers and surviving spouses, the shift to defined-contribution plans, and the lack of pension coverage for employees of many small businesses pose key issues for future retirees. Only 16 percent of companies with fewer than twenty-five employees, which is where much of the job growth occurred in the 1980s and early 1990s, offered pensions in 1992 (Lewis 1992).

Savings and Investments

Income from dividends, interest, rents, estates, and trusts were received by 71 percent of the elderly population in 1990 (U.S. Bureau of the Census 1992). The mean income from these sources was relatively low, however, $5,245 per year.

Income from assets continues to be a key source of cash for many older Americans. For families with heads of household 65 years of age and older, it was the third most important source of income in 1990. For unrelated persons 65 and older, those persons living alone or with persons who are not relatives, income from assets (interest, dividends, rents, etc.) was the second most important. It is important to note that in each case, families with heads of household 65 and older and unrelated individuals 65 and older, Social Security continues to be the most important source of income. Looking at the older persons who fall below the poverty line, there is, as expected, a dramatic reduction in the importance of asset income with an accompanying steep increase in the percentage of income derived from Social Security. Families with heads of household 65 and older whose income was below the poverty line received only 3.8 percent of income from personal assets, compared to 21.2 percent for those above the poverty line. For unrelated older persons the percentage of total income from assets was 26.1 percent. For those below the poverty line, income from interest and dividends was 4.1 percent (U.S. Bureau of the Census, Current Population Reports 1991).

Income from savings and investments has increased gradually as more affluent persons retire. In 1962, 54 percent of the elderly had some income from assets. By 1984, this had increased to 67 percent (U.S. Senate 1992).

There are significant differences among various subgroups of the elderly: The oldest old receive less income from savings and investment than do younger elderly persons; elderly men receive more asset income than do elderly women; older white Americans have substantially more income from savings and investments than do elderly African Americans or Latinos (U.S. Senate 1992). Obviously most of the differences in income from savings and investments are directly related to levels of income during working years. People who earn lower incomes find it difficult to save money for their retirement. Many have a tough time making ends meet, and, as indicated previously, it is particularly difficult for economically disadvantaged groups including minorities and women.

Beyond this, Americans have had difficulties saving money. Except for the period during World War II when workers saved some 25 percent of their incomes because there was a scarcity of consumer goods, the personal savings rate in America has been rather low. In 1990, it was 4 percent; in 1991 it was 4.3 percent. This is only about one-half to one-third of the savings rates in European countries (U.S. Senate 1992).

America is a consumptive society. Many fiscal experts have pointed out that contemporary Americans tend to spend what they earn beyond the essentials of life (discretionary income) on instant pleasures, instant gratifications shortchanging their future economic security.

The increasing importance of savings as a portion of retirement income points out the problems low interest rates pose for older adults. Low interest rates mean a drastic reduction in income. What is not often considered is the realization that on the whole, low interest rates generally benefit the young at the expense of the old. Young people, families and singles, buying homes, cars, boats, furniture, TVs, stereos, and anything else that they may purchase with credit making payments over time, benefit from low interest rates. Low interest rates for home mortgages can literally save buyers hundreds of dollars a month.

Work

Income from work provided the highest mean income for older people, but only 16 percent of the elderly had this form of income in 1990. The income from earnings differed greatly among the races, with the mean income for whites $14,498, for African Americans $9,400, and for Latinos $10,331 (DeNavas and Welniak 1991).

One of the most significant trends in the United States has been the trend toward early retirement. Men are retiring early, before the age at which they get full retirement benefits (U.S. Bureau of the Census 1992). Older men today are much less likely to be in the labor force than in earlier times. In 1950, 68.6 percent of men aged 55 and older, and 45.8 percent of men aged 65 and older were in the labor force. By 1990, 39.3 percent of men aged 55 and older, and only 16.4 percent of men aged 65 and older were counted in the labor force. It is projected that labor force participation rates for men aged 55 to 59 and 60 to 64 will continue to fall through the year 2005. But men aged 65 to 69 and 70 to 74 will participate at a slightly increased rate through 2005 (U.S. Bureau of Labor Statistics 1991).

Older women participate in the labor force less than younger women and older men. In 1990, the rates of older women in the work force also dipped dramatically with advancing age. For women aged 55 to 59 the participation rate in the labor force was 55 percent. For women aged 65 to 69 the rate was 17 percent. Over age 75 the rate was 3 percent (U.S. Bureau of the Census 1992). The growth in the participation of women in their fifties in the work force is notable. In 1950, only 27 percent of women aged 55 to 64 were employed compared to 45 percent in 1990. The real growth for women in the work force was in the 55 to 59 age category (U.S. Bureau of the Census 1992).

For women aged 65 and older, participation in the labor force has remained low. In 1950, 9.7 percent were employed. In 1967, the rate was 9.6 percent, and by 1990, it was 8.7 percent, not much change. As they grow older, women tend to reduce the length of their work week as well as the number of weeks they work per year (U.S. Bureau of Labor Statistics 1991).

There is conflicting evidence as to the future trends for older people in the work force. In a 1992 report citing Bureau of Labor Statistics, the Bureau of the Census indicated that a lower percentage of older persons may choose to be in the labor force as a result of broader pension coverage. This same report pointed out that despite better pension coverage in terms of the percentages and types of workers covered, it would be difficult to predict whether such a large percentage of older workers would be able to retire in their early sixties as has been the case. This report stated:

> In 1983, 4 in 5 pension plans had no minimum retirement age or provided full benefits at age 62; over 1 in 3 permitted retirement as early as age 55 with 30 years of service. Since then there have been definite signs that pension plans will be less generous. Increasingly workers are supporting a larger portion of the cost of retirement plans than has been generally true in the recent past (U.S. Bureau of the Census 1992: 4–5).

With people living longer and longer, with costs continuing to rise to maintain even a minimum standard of living, and with the contributions and the management of pensions falling increasingly on individual workers, the pressure on older people to keep working longer or to return to work seems to be building.

SUMMARY

The economic status of older people in general has improved dramatically since the enactment of the Social Security Act of 1935. Remarkable advances in reducing poverty among the elderly have been made since 1959, when 35.2 percent of older Americans were classified as poor. In 1990, 12.2 percent of the elderly were classified as poor.

It is important to note that the gains in economic status are not shared by all groups of the elderly. Older women, particularly widowed, divorced, and never married older women, are generally disadvantaged financially. The reasons older women are so often economically distressed include lack of pension coverage, lack of or insufficient survival benefits when husbands die (women generally live longer than men), job discrimination, income discrimination within jobs, gaps in work records due to years spent as homemakers and caregivers which diminish retirement benefits, and unjust divorce settlements.

The economic status of older minorities clearly shows their economic disadvantage. This is particularly true for older African Americans and older women of Hispanic origin. Ways to improve the economic status of older minorities include changing the administration and coverage of Supplemental Security Income (SSI). Also recommended is increased employment opportunities for older persons. Recommendations also include better education and outreach for targeted benefit programs on the local, state, and federal levels.

The oldest old make up another category of older persons who tend to be poor. Many simply outlive their money. So many elderly people never thought they would live so long. Inflation, even at modest yearly rates, over time catches many older people in the longevity-inflation squeeze. Prices continue to rise and people living on fixed, or relatively fixed incomes are caught in the resulting squeeze. Even though Social Security benefits have been indexed to the cost of living increases since the 1970s, the other sources of income for many elderly persons have not. In fact, the low interest rates of the early 1990s, so beneficial for younger people who are buying homes, cars, and other consumer items, have hurt the incomes of older people who relied on supplemental income from savings.

Being female, a member of a minority group, and among the oldest old can be a cumulative disadvantage—a triple whammy. It is having three strikes in the financial ball game of life. These people too often find themselves among the poorest people in America.

The economic support systems of the elderly in America include Social Security, Supplemental Security Income (SSI), pensions, savings/investments, and work. The viability, fairness, and desirability of Social Security is often questioned. Although a major focus, Social Security is not just for retirement income. Protection for disabled workers, widows, and dependent children are key parts of the system. Social Security, with the huge surplus reserves in its trust funds, has been projected to be sound for some 40 to 50 years.

Pensions are a major component of retirement income for some older people. Although increasing in breadth of coverage, pensions are rapidly changing form from defined-benefit plans to defined-contribution plans. This shift puts more responsibility to save for retirement on the worker as well as more responsibility to manage his or her own investments of the plan. This is significant because it appears that more and more workers will be covered by pensions, but the question needs to be asked, What will these pensions be like? Will they be there when a person retires? Today about one-third of older people in America receive pension benefits, with men the clear winners as to numbers covered and amounts received.

Savings and investments are important components of retirement income. Obviously the level of savings and investments depends on income amounts during working years and the discipline to save. Work is the highest source of income for older people, but only 16 percent remain in or reenter the work force.

REFERENCES

Andrews, J. 1989. *Poverty and Poor Health Among Elderly Hispanic Americans.* Commonwealth Fund Commission on Elderly People Living Alone. (September). Baltimore, MD.

Brown, J.D. 1973. Memorandum. In U.S. Senate Special Committee on Aging. *Future Directions in Social Security.* Part 3. Washington, DC: U.S. Government Printing Office.

Committee on Ways and Means. 1992. *Overview of Entitlement Programs: 1992 Green Book.* Washington, DC: U.S. Government Printing Office.

Crown, Mutschler, J., Schulz, J., and Lowe, R. 1993. *The Economic Status of Divorced Older Women.* Waltham, MA: Policy Center on Aging, Heller School, Brandeis University.

DeNavas, C., and Welniak, E. 1991. U.S. Bureau of the Census. *Money, Income of Households, Families and Persons in the United States*: 1990 Current Population Reports, (Series P-60, No. 174). Washington, DC: U.S. Government Printing Office.

Dixon, J. 1993. Social Security Won't Be Boon It Is Now to Retirees in the Next Century. In *The Grand Rapids Press.* (March 14): E4. Associated Press.

Glasgow, N. 1988. Department of Agriculture, Economic Research Service. *The Nonmetro Elderly: Economic and Demographic Status.* Rural Development Research Report, (No. 70). Washington, DC: U.S. Government Printing Office.

Grubbs, D.S., Jr. 1992. Social Security: Too Little to Live on For Many. *NRTA Bulletin,* 33(1). Washington, DC: AARP.

Kassner, E. 1992. *Falling Through the Safety Net: Missed Opportunities for America's Elderly Poor.* Washington, DC: AARP.

Lewis, R. 1992. Pensions: A Mixed Bag. *NRTA Bulletin,* 33(7): 1.

Louis Harris and Associates. 1988. Follow-up Study of Poor Elderly People, Strategies to Increase Participation in the Supplemental Security Income Program. Study No. 874012, (February).

Marshall, R. 1991. *The State of Families.* Milwaukee, WI: Family Service America.

Martz, L., and R. Thomas. 1990. Fixing Social Security. *Newsweek,* (May) CXV, No. 19: 54.

Matas, A. 1993. Retirement Is Top on Agenda. Knight-Rider Newspaper, *Detroit Free Press,* (April 23): 12F.

Mayer, M. 1993. Pensions: The Naked Truth. *Modern Maturity,* (February/March): 40–44.

Schulz, J. 1992. *The Economics of Aging.* New York: Auburn House.

Sherman, S.R. 1989. *Fast Facts and Figures About Social Security.* Social Security Administration, Office of Research and Statistics.

Social Security Administration. 1991. *Social Security Bulletin, Annual Statistical Supplement*. U.S. Department of Health and Human Services.

U.S. Bureau of the Census, Current Population Reports. 1991. *Poverty in the United States: 1990* (Series P-60, No. 175). Washington, DC: U.S. Government Printing Office.

U.S. Bureau of the Census, Current Population Reports. 1992a. *Sixty-Five Plus in America* (Special Studies, P23-178). Washington, DC: U.S. Government Printing Office.

U.S. Bureau of the Census. 1992b. *Profiles of America's Elderly: Growth of America's Oldest-Old Population*. Washington, DC: U.S. Government Printing Office.

U.S. Bureau of Labor Statistics. 1991. Data for 1990, Employment and Earnings. 38(1) Table 3; data for 1950. Unpublished tabulations from 1950 Current Population Survey.

U.S. Department of Health, Education, and Welfare. 1972. *Public Assistance Programs: Standards or Basic Needs*. Washington, DC: U.S. Department of Health, Education, and Welfare.

U.S. General Accounting Office. 1992. *Elderly Americans: Health, Housing, and Nutrition Gaps Between the Poor and Nonpoor*. Washington, DC.

U.S. Senate Special Committee on Aging. 1993. *Developments in Aging*: 1992, Vol. 1. Washington, DC: U.S. Government Printing Office.

Wise, D.A. 1993. Demise of Pensions Leaves Many Lacking Enough Retirement Funds. *Grand Rapids Press*, (May 16): A10.

Wilson, V. 1991. An Inflation Fright . . . Again. *Newsweek*, (April 18): 46.

Women, Pensions, and Divorce. 1993. Women's Initiative. Washington, DC: American Association of Retired Persons.

Woods, J.R. 1988. Retirement-Age Women and Pensions: Findings From the New Beneficiary Survey. *Social Security Bulletin*, 51: 5–16.

Yankelovich Partners. 1993. *Generations at Risk: 30 to 50 Year Olds Not Financially Prepared for Retirement*. Unpublished Report for Phoenix Home Life: Hartford, CT.

CHAPTER 9

Work and
Older Persons

Bias On, Then Off, the Job

Gray hair is either a mark of distinction or a sign to the world that you've joined the old-age bunch.

Wrinkles are either a badge of earned wisdom or a notice to everyone that you're over the hill. No matter how young and vigorous we may feel, the way we look to others can determine their attitude toward us. In spite of laws against discrimination, the real world is often cruel and unfair. We asked some people if they have ever been victims of age discrimination on the job.

Lee Murray
Free Press Special Writer
Detroit Free Press, March 3, 1992, p. 3C

Gray Won't Wash

At about this time last year, I applied for a hotel job. On the phone, they sounded enthusiastic. When I arrived for the interview, they took one look at my gray hair, and the interview lasted less than one minute. I mentioned the job to a younger friend who had half the credentials I did. He applied and was interviewed for half an hour.

Fritz Spademan, 62
Birmingham

Forced to Quit

The boss and I didn't hit it off. He kept piling more and more work on me, far more than anyone could handle. I could have, and did, handle a normal day's work, but he had someone younger in mind for the job. They don't want to fire you, they want you to quit, and I finally had to.

—Jesse Austin, 61
Detroit

No Promotions

In 6½ years I received four promotions, but in the past six years I have not received any. Isn't it strange? I got dumber with age and experience. One would think 12 years of experience and merit would be more valuable. But all anyone has to do is say, "No, I didn't discriminate," and case closed. I have to prove it and they are going

to deny it. But after age 47, I never received another promotion.

—M.M., 53
Warren

Sue'em

Is there age discrimination? That's a laugh. I can think of at least 10 incidents where a prospective employer passed me over in favor of a younger person who was less qualified. In fact, some of those hired were not even born when I started in my profession. There is nothing like being introduced by someone who is young enough to be your kid. There are many unscrupulous employers out there. How some of these idiots get into management never ceases to amaze me. Don't be afraid to retaliate. Hire an attorney. I just settled my last suit in November.

—W. K., 62
Farmington Hill
Detroit Free Press, "Bias on, then off, the job,"
March 3, 1992, p. 3C.

Under 55 Got a Push

At the utility where I once worked, the pension plan for management was discounted for younger people. At age 55, you could get your full pension, but anyone younger had a substantial reduction. In some cases, pressure was put on those under 55 to leave even though that wasn't official company policy. It was hard on the younger personnel who often had children to care for but were pushed out anyway.

—J. Z., 65
Birmingham

Boss' Forecast Goofed

When I was doing the weather show at Channel 2 back in 1983, they told me, "98 percent of the viewers recognize you, but most of them are over the age of 48 and their buying habits are firmly established. We're buying out your contract." Later on, my boss admitted that it was the biggest mistake he ever made. At that time, I was almost pleased. Actually, it created more furor than the Ernie Harwell affair.

—Sonny Eliot, 60-plus
Southfield

Kept Waiting

I worked as a waitress at an entertainment complex, and although our union contract states that I was in line for the job of hostess and I was qualified for it, the boss said, "You're too old." Later he denied saying it, but there isn't much you can do about it. I was pretty bitter for about a year, but these days I'm just glad I'm still working at all, even though lifting those heavy trays is hard work and I'd like the better job at better pay.

—A. E., 67
Warren

Source: Detroit Free Press "Bias on, then off, the job," March 3, 1992, p. 3C.

WORKING AND OLDER PERSONS

Work provides the greatest amount of money among all sources of income for those older people who are working. However, only 16 percent of all persons aged 65 and older were actively working in 1990. The mean income for elderly people who were working was $14,146 in 1990 compared to $7,825 from pensions, and $6,163 from Social Security (U.S. Bureau of the Census 1991).

The reason for this is that society values productivity—people who produce things or provide services. So barring large inheritances, winning the lottery, or lucky investments, those people who work are generally paid more than those who do not, even those with relatively good pensions who worked for 30 years or more.

Although most of this book focuses on the elderly or older persons in America (those in their sixties and older, usually those 65 and older), this chapter will include persons in their fifties and older as they are approaching retirement and have been the focus of early retirement pressures. Much

of the industrial base in the United States has been downsizing, merging, or retrenching in one way or another in recent years. This is also true of certain sectors of education, government, and other economic components of the American labor force.

TRENDS TOWARD EARLY RETIREMENT

In addition to job losses, changes, and restructuring which have hit middle- and older-aged workers hard, there has been a dramatic movement in the United States since World War II toward early retirement. In 1950, some two-thirds (68.6 percent) of men age 55 and older, and almost half (45.8 percent) of men 65 and older were in the labor force. By 1990, about two in five (39.3 percent) men age 55 and older, and only one in six (16.4 percent) men 65 and older were still working (U.S. Bureau of the Census 1992). Although older women have participated in the labor force less than younger women and older men, their rates in the work force also decrease rapidly with age. Women in their fifties, however, have increased their participation in the work force. In 1967, 48 percent of women aged 55 to 59 were in the paid labor market. By 1990, 55 percent were in this category. However, for women aged 60 to 64, there was no real increase in those working (Bureau of Labor Statistics 1991). Well-paid part-time jobs for any age group are difficult to find, and fringe benefits are usually not part of this type of work.

TRENDS TO CONTINUE TO WORK

Pressure is building (1) to continue to work longer, reversing a trend from the end of World War II to the Mid 1980s toward early retirement; and (2) for retirees and older persons to return to work. The sources of these pressures to continue to work or return to work are varied, ranging from personal psychological reasons to overall labor force trends. As noted economist James Schulz pointed out, "Some people are concerned about the rising trend toward 'no work' " (Schulz 1992: 67). As long ago as the late 1970s, some physicians claimed that some people die earlier, partly as a result of changing from an active to sedentary lifestyle (Bradford 1979). A retired labor leader with whom one of the authors worked on numerous community boards often remarked about the number of his auto-worker friends and co-workers who, upon retirement, saw the television set as their main activity and were "carried feet first" out of their homes in not too many years. Needless to say the retired labor leader who told this story lived until his early nineties, totally involved in all kinds of activities which kept him mentally and physically active.

Also important is the need for income or supplemental income (Schulz 1992; Torres-Gil 1992). Schulz (1992) pointed out that many economists are concerned about the problems associated with financially supporting a growing number of retirees. Social policy analysts such as Fernando Torres-Gill (1992) have pointed out the need for older persons to continue to work longer or to return to work, if they have retired, in order to provide financial support for themselves as part of a rapidly growing elderly population as well as diminishing the intergenerational conflicts that show clear signs of developing as competition for financial resources increase. Other analysts, in spite of the economic slowdowns of the early 1990s and widespread unemployment in numerous sectors of the economy, are worried about future shortages of workers. Indeed, the percentage of people aged 20 to 29 will drop from 18 percent to 13 percent of U.S. population by the year 2000. It is estimated that by that time, more than 21 million new jobs will be created. Many experts think the resulting labor shortage will encourage businesses, organized labor, and workers themselves to reconsider the need for older workers and make a number of changes to include many more in the labor force (Maloney 1990).

In addition, some have argued that greater life satisfaction would be brought about if leisure time were not focused at the end of life (Schulz 1992). According to Bill Stanley of King, Chapman, Bronssard, & Gallagher, a New York consulting firm, more and more people are saying, "What am I going to do for the next 30 years and how am I going to pay for it?" (Beck, Denworth, and Christian 1992).

TO WORK OR NOT TO WORK

In examining work and older persons, there are really two issues to be addressed: (1) whether to continue to work into one's late fifties, early sixties, and beyond the age of 65; and (2) the circumstances of returning to the work force after retiring or being squeezed out of a job as a result of age discrimination, corporate mergers, company downsizing and cutbacks, or the demise of business.

Whether to continue to work past a certain age depends on a number of factors, not the least of which has been the attraction of early retirements; some jobs provide pensions targeted at relatively early ages, for example, reaching age 55 with 30 years of service or some other combination of age and number of years worked—it depends on how eager the employer is to get rid of workers. As we have seen, this has been a trend in the United States since World War II until at least the mid-1980s, a trend that some experts now see being reversed.

Other factors had an impact on the continuation of work in the later years of life. Some 4.3 million jobs were eliminated from 1980 to 1993 by the *Fortune* 500 companies, and another 1.4 million defense-industry jobs were to be eliminated in the early to mid-1990s. Older workers, making up the more experienced and senior-level personnel of the work force, were the hardest hit. "The situation is bad," said Martin Sicker, director of AARP's Work Force Programs. "From October 1991 to October 1992, the increase in the rate of unemployment for people 55 and older was seven times that of people 16 through 54" (Stern 1993: 25). The Bureau of Labor Statistics confirms this finding. During the 1991 to 1992 period, the unemployment rate for workers 16 through 54 rose from 6.8 to 7.1 percent, an increase of 4.4 percent. The rate for workers 55 and older rose from 3.5 percent to 4.6 percent, an increase of 31.4 percent (Stern 1993). Sicker thought that the unemployment situation for older workers in this period was worse than the statistics indicated. The figures do not include the "hidden casualties" of unemployment: older workers who take hourly jobs, part-time jobs, or temporary jobs; people who start their own businesses which are often very marginal; and people who give up trying to work and simply retire earlier than planned. Once again, figures from early 1992 by the Bureau of Labor Statistics showed 994,000 workers aged 55 and over who were either working part-time because they could not find full-time jobs or who stopped looking because they were so discouraged about finding jobs (Stern 1993). A Commonwealth Fund study pointed out that persons aged 55 to 64 have the longest time of unemployment for any group of workers (Bass and Barth 1991). Discouraged workers who are not counted in regular unemployment statistics would double the unemployment rate for older workers if they were counted.

LONGER UNEMPLOYMENT FOR OLDER WORKERS

Once out of work, older workers take longer to find jobs, if they are fortunate enough to find them at all. In 1992, according to the Bureau of Labor Statistics, the median job-search time for all workers was 8.8 weeks. For persons 55 and older seeking employment, those lucky enough to find a job took 16.7 weeks.

Not only have individual companies reduced employment opportunities for older workers, but whole industries in the United States have experienced contractions leading to job losses for mature workers. This has included the textile, agricultural, steel, shoe, and automobile industries (Schulz 1992). The results of the restructuring of many American industries because of the sluggish economy of the early 1990s and increased global competition have not ceased. In the authors' home state of Michigan, some additional

54,000 General Motors employees are to be laid off by 1998. When the effect on suppliers and others in communities who depend on auto workers as customers are counted, these additional 54,000 G.M. jobs translate into 200,000 jobs lost in Michigan alone (Schall 1993).

TOUGH PROBLEMS FACING OLDER JOB SEEKERS

Once they become unemployed, either by retiring early or by losing their jobs, mature workers face a number of serious problems trying to re-enter the work force. As expected, one of the biggest problems they encounter is financial. Jayne Bryant Quinn (1992a), in one of her columns, pointed out that the loss of a job in a person's later middle years can easily result in a permanent reduction in one's standard of living. Of the one million middle-aged people who were looking for work in 1992, most will never regain what they had before losing their jobs, especially the professionals and middle managers who were hit so hard by the economic disruptions of the early 1990s. First, she pointed out, they will use up their savings that otherwise would have compounded in earnings until they normally retired. Second, corporate employees' pensions will be smaller than they expected because the value of pensions usually gains the most between the ages of 50 and 65. As an example, Quinn cited a person with an income of $80,000 leaving work at age 50 rather than at age 65. If that person had worked until age 65, pension benefits would have totaled some $28,000 a year, but at age 50, that person's pension at age 65 will be only about $8,000. Even if the laid-off or early-retired worker were to get another job at the $80,000 rate—something almost impossible to do in today's economic climate—that person would still suffer economic hardship in retirement. That is because the $8,000 pension from Company A, where he worked until age 50, combined with the new pension from Company B (where he worked from age 50 to age 65) would be $8,000 less than if the person continued with Company A until retirement at age 65. And if there is a period of unemployment, which is generally longer for older workers than younger workers, there would be a greater loss of retirement income in the form of a pension.

In addition to pressures to retire early, rapidly increasing rates of unemployment among workers in their middle and later years, longer periods of unemployment among older workers, and financial dislocations as the result of early retirement of job loss, persons in their later years face significant problems as they try to continue to work or reenter the work force. Schulz (1992) pointed out that these include:

1. Age discrimination
2. Job obsolescence
3. Changing job-performance capabilities
4. Adverse institutional structures, including management policies that discriminate against older workers and pressure to retire

Age Discrimination in Employment

Of all the barriers to the employment of older workers, age discrimination is one of the most pernicious and pervasive—it is one of the worst, to put it simply. A U.S. Senate report in 1993 indicated that age discrimination exists for millions of older Americans and that most Americans see age discrimination as a serious problem (U.S. Senate 1993). It cited two nationwide surveys by Louis Harris & Associates conducted in the 1970s and the 1980s indicating that eight out of ten Americans believe that most employers discriminate against older people and make it difficult for them to find work. The Senate report also cited another nationwide study in the 1980s of employers conducted by William M. Mercer, Inc. indicating that 61 percent of employers thought that older workers are discriminated against on the basis of age. This same study found that 22 percent of these employers surveyed did not think that age discrimination in employment would change without negative legal consequences—penalties; 20 percent admitted that older workers, other than senior management people, had less opportunity for promotions or training; and 12 percent admitted that older worker's pay raises were not as large as younger workers in the same category.

Recent studies have continued to point out age discrimination by employers. Research conducted by the AARP Work Force Programs Department revealed negative attitudes toward older workers. Employers tended to view older workers as inflexible and unwilling to accept new ideas and worried that older workers would cost them more money both in salary and healthcare benefits (Lewis 1993a). With the release of a 1990 study of older workers by Louis Harris & Associates for the Commonwealth Fund of New York, Thomas W. Maloney (1990), senior vice president, pointed out the continued discrimination of older workers on the basis of age.

Age Discrimination Legislation

Age discrimination in employment first came to national attention in 1965. At that time a report issued by the U.S. Department of Labor documented that more than 50 percent of all available job openings were not open to persons aged 55 and older due to employers' policies. The report went on to point out that 25 percent of job openings were closed to persons over the age of 54 (Schulz 1992). In 1967, Congress enacted the Age Discrimination in Employment Act (ADEA) "to promote employment of older persons based on their ability rather than age; to prohibit arbitrary age discrimination in employment; and to help employers and workers find ways of meeting problems arising from the impact of age on employment" (U.S. Senate Special Committee on Aging, 1993: 84). This act followed a 1964 Executive order issued by President Johnson declaring a public policy against age discrimination in employment. Three years later the President called for the congressional legislation that became ADEA. A major issue in the debate leading to the legislation was the need to balance the rights of older workers to be free of age discrimination in employment with the right of employers to manage their own business. The law balanced these competing rights by prohibiting decisions as to whether a person may or may not work based on age alone with employment decisions regarding older persons based on individual assessments of each older worker's potential and ability. This approach, which may seem technical and somewhat complicated, is very important because research done at the National Institute on Aging and at Pennsylvania State University many years later clearly indicates the reliability and potential of older workers both physically and mentally (U.S. House of Representatives Select Committee on Aging 1991; Schaie 1989).

In its original form, ADEA prohibited employment discrimination against persons aged 40 to 65. Along the way a number of amendments were made. In 1974, age protection was extended to federal, state, and local government employees. The range of employees covered was also increased, limiting exemptions for employers with fewer than 20 employees. In 1978, ADEA increased the age covered to 70 (the first step to eliminating an upper age limit), and removed the upper age limit for federal government employees.

In 1982, ADEA was amended by the Tax Equity and Fiscal Responsibility Act (TEFRA), which included the "working aged." This legislation required employers to retain their over-65 workers on the company health plan rather than automatically shifting them to Medicare. In 1984, ADEA was extended to U.S. companies in foreign countries. The 1986 legislation removed all age limits in protecting older workers, with the exception of college professors and state and local public safety officers. The age limit on college professors was lifted in 1994.

In 1990, Congress again amended the ADEA with the Older Workers Benefit Protection Act. This came about because the Supreme Court in 1989 had held that the ADEA did not protect older workers' benefits. Another provision of the 1990 legislation was to prevent abuses by some employers who asked (required) employees to sign waivers of their ADEA rights.

Originally ADEA was put under the jurisdiction of the Department of Labor, but switched in 1979 to the U.S. Equal Employment Opportunity Commission (EEOC) which also administers (1) Title VII of the Civil Rights Act of 1964; (2) the ADEA of 1967; (3) the Equal Pay Act of 1963; (4) Sections 501 and 505 of the Rehabilitation Act of 1973; and (5) the Americans with Disabilities Act of 1990. If older workers think they have been discriminated against in hiring, discharge, compensation, and other terms of employment, they can contact a field office of EEOC, or write to: EEOC, 1801 L Street, N.W., Washington, D.C. 20507.

Age Discrimination Following Legislative Action

The enactment of the Age Discrimination in Employment Act of 1967 and all the subsequent amendments and accompanying legislation would appear to be enough to solve the problem of age discrimination in employment in the American workplace. Such has not been the case. Although the more obvious and overt forms of age discrimination, such as age limits in newspaper ads and openly forced retirements at specified ages, have almost disappeared, more subtle and cleverly disguised forms of age discrimination against older workers is evident in the 1990s. Age discrimination in employment is often difficult to substantiate statistically, and as a result, there is not much comprehensive data on this issue (Schulz 1992). Nevertheless, hearings in Congress on age discrimination in the workplace clearly point out the continuing nature of the problem into the 1990s (U.S. House of Representatives Select Committee on Aging 1992). In a 1992 hearing on the issue, Rep. William Hughes, a Democrat of New Jersey, stated:

> While we have made some strides in reducing age discrimination in the workplace, insidious and incorrect myths about the physical and mental capabilities of older workers still persist throughout the job market today. During periods of recession, in particular, it seems that many employers can often

find an excuse which justifies a discriminating practice when it comes to hiring and retraining older workers (U.S. House of Representatives Select Committee on Aging 1992: 11).

In the same hearing Rep. Matthew Rinaldo, Republican of New Jersey, said:

Unfortunately older workers are too often forced out of their jobs to make room for younger employees. This is patently illegal and the Equal Employment Opportunity Commission (EEOC) is the agency in charge of enforcing the law. As we will hear today, too many times older workers are driven into early retirement, left without severance pay, and saddled with a reduction in their pension benefits. All too frequently older workers are pushed out of their jobs because an employer wishes to avoid paying higher benefits (U.S. House of Representatives Select Committee on Aging 1992: 20).

There is no indication that age discrimination in the workplace is diminishing. The EEOC's own data on the percentage of age discrimination cases filed over recent years compared to other types of discrimination is revealing. In 1980, the first full year EEOC had responsibility for administering the ADEA, age discrimination cases made up 11.8 percent of all discrimination cases filed. By 1990, age discrimination cases made up 20.9 percent of all the cases filed (U.S. House of Representatives 1993). The number of age discrimination claims continued to increase in 1991, with a record number filed in 1992. At the same time, the number of complaints against the EEOC because they failed to file suits as a follow-up to the complaints also rose (U.S. Senate 1993).

Although the mechanisms were in place to root out age discrimination in employment, between 1984 and 1988 more than 8,000 ADEA charges may have exceeded the two-year statute of limitations due to EEOC's neglect. At a 1990 Senate Judiciary Committee hearing to confirm the nomination of EEOC Chairman, Clarence Thomas, to the U.S. Circuit Court of Appeals, it was revealed that the EEOC had allowed an additional 1,500 ADEA charges to lapse since 1988.

In fiscal year 1989, EEOC received 14,789 complaints and filed only 133 suits on behalf of older workers (U.S. Senate 1993).

Older Women and Minorities

The plight of older women and older minority persons in regards to age discrimination in employment is not good. The Older Women's League (OWL), in testimony to the Congress in 1991, stated that older women bear a double, and often a triple burden of age, sex, and race discrimination. Its spokesperson pointed out that this discrimination is both overt and subtle (U.S. House of Representatives 1992). This is a serious and important consideration. It is even more serious when it is realized that by the year 2000 about one in three women in the work force will be midlife and older (Older Women's League 1991). Women continue to earn less than men in all older age categories. They continue to be segregated into jobs at the lower end of the pay scale, and few older women work as managers or professionals. In 1991, white men held 95 percent of all top management positions. The role of caregiver, so important in our society, penalizes employment opportunities for women. The same OWL Testimony to the Select Committee on Aging stated that some employers wrongly believe that older women workers are not cost effective as employees and that they cost more to hire and train because they do not return as much on the employer's investment as younger workers (U.S. House of Representatives 1992). A study of 1,500 subscribers to the *Harvard Business Review* indicated that employers responded less favorably to situations involving older workers, including older women, than to situations involving younger workers (Older Women's League 1991).

Older African-American women suffer exceptionally pronounced discrimination, according to the Older Women's League. African-American women over the age of 55 are three times more likely to work in service occupations than white women, occupations that traditionally pay low wages. Nearly one-third of African-

American women over the age of 65 work as private household workers (U.S. House of Representatives 1992).

Other Forms of Age Discrimination

Additional studies conducted in the 1990s indicated persistent types of age discrimination in employment. Experienced teachers find it difficult to get teaching jobs once they leave the field. "Hiring policies which favor the inexperienced applicant, which one analyst calls 'public education's well-hidden secret,' make it difficult for older, experienced teachers to land classroom jobs when they move to a new community" wrote Robert Lewis (1992: 10). Other anecdotal evidence from an array of individuals who have been discriminated against in employment on the basis of age abounds: the National Football League (NFL) referee who detailed his experiences of being pressured to retire when he became 60 years old, including his contacts with NFL Commissioner Rozelle; the airline pilot for United Airlines who was forced to resign at age 60, just after he successfully landed a 747 in Honolulu that had 336 passengers, a full load of jet fuel, 18 crew members, with number three and four engines out—both on the same side; the stockbroker who was fired at age 62 even though he was so successful that he earned more in bonus income than from his salary (U.S. House of Representatives Select Committee on Aging 1992); and the displaced personnel manager this author interviewed in a job-training program for older workers at Grand Rapids Community College who easily recognized all the age discrimination ploys that were pulled on him when he tried to get work in a number of companies. Indeed, age discrimination in employment is pervasive in the contemporary American workplace.

Are Older Workers Able to Produce?

Much of the thinking that results in age discrimination in employment revolves around the out-of-date beliefs that older people "are out of it," "can't hack it any longer," "are over-the-hill," "are not with it," or some such.

Research does not bear this out. Dr. T. Franklin Williams, Professor of Medicine and of Community and Prevention Medicine at the University of Rochester School of Medicine and Dentistry, and for eight years until August, 1991, Director of the National Institute on Aging cited some vital medical research to clearly support the potential effectiveness of older workers. He stated:

> Contrary to earlier views that aging is associated with inevitable declines in physical and mental functioning, we now know with great confidence that there are few if any inevitable declines, and that most people can, and many people do, continue to function into their seventies and eighties and even longer at much the same levels as they have functioned in earlier years (U.S. House of Representatives Select Committee on Aging 1992: p. 41).

The evidence to support this statement has come from some important research. For example, in measuring maximum cardiac out—how well the heart can function at maximum output—research by Rodeheffer and others (1984) found that persons in their seventies and eighties who do not have heart disease (50 to 60 percent of the persons studied were free of heart disease) have the same range of heart output as persons in their twenties and thirties.

Research by the National Institute on Aging showed no real changes related to perseverance, distraction, forgetting, or seeking help from others (U.S. House of Representatives Select Committee on Aging 1992). Professor Warner Schaie (1989) of Pennsylvania State University conducted longitudinal studies showing that most of the people he studied remained unchanged in performing tests of perceptual speed in measuring mental functioning. Other research has shown that people can improve mental and physical performance at even very old ages if they work at it.

What is important to note is that there are real individual differences. Not all older workers are "over-the-hill." Not all young workers are fit and able. Lifestyle and the presence or absence of chronic disease is the key, not age (Albert and Moss 1988).

All of this research clearly points out that many persons are able to keep excellent physical and mental function well beyond the traditional retirement years of 60, 62, or 65. The question then needs to be asked, Can reliable tests be given to measure the physical and mental condition of a particular individual to determine whether that person is fit for a given job? The answer, according to the experts, is clearly yes. This principle, according to the scientists, applies at any age to any job. It even can apply to public safety personnel and airline pilots. As Dr. Williams pointed out, "a pilot in his or her forties who has high blood pressure and smokes is at several-fold greater risk of having a sudden heart attack as a pilot in his or her sixties who does not have these risk factors" (Williams 1992: 43). The next time you fly, don't be worried if your pilot looks pretty old. Be a lot more concerned if that young pilot checking in is smoking before he or she gets in the airplane.

HOW OLDER PEOPLE VIEW THEIR HEALTH

Even though research clearly indicates that older people can perform well in a variety of situations, how do they view their own abilities to carry out the duties of a job? A Louis Harris and Associates survey conducted in 1992 for the Commonwealth Fund revealed a very positive picture of adults 55 and over:

- Of those interviewed, 63 percent rated their health as good or excellent.
- Among those who are working, 82 percent stated that they were in good or excellent health.
- Among those who were willing and able to work, 70 percent reported they were in good or excellent health (Taylor, Bass, and Barnett 1992).

Another study by the National Center for Health Statistics (1988) found that the majority of people aged 55 to 75 who were retired indicated that their health was good to excellent and stated that they were not limited in their activities.

DO OLDER PEOPLE WANT TO WORK?

With early retirement a goal of so many people in the American work force, at least from the end of World War II until the late 1980s, the question needs to be asked, do many older people really want to work? Surveys over the last two decades have indicated the willingness, and indeed the eagerness, of large numbers of older persons to either stay in the work force or return to work if they have left. Back in 1974, a Louis Harris & Associates poll found that nearly a third of the nation's retirees over the age of 65 said they would still be working if they could. A 1979 Louis Harris and Associates poll found that almost half (48 percent) of workers aged 50 to 64 said that they wanted to continue to work and not retire at the usual time (Johnson and Higgins, Inc. 1979). A 1989 study by the Daniel Yankelovich Group conducted for the AARP examined the thinking of older workers. It also found that most older employees wanted to continue to work, even until age 70 and beyond. Many of those surveyed were fearful that they would not be allowed to continue to work into older ages. Many believed they were vulnerable, even disposable (Stephens 1989).

The results of two recent national surveys conducted by Louis Harris and Associates for the Commonwealth Fund in 1989 and 1991 indicated that significant numbers of older Americans were willing to return to work or to continue to work past the time at which they think they will be forced to retire.

- An estimated 5.4 million people aged 55 and older who were not working reported that they were willing and able to go back to work.

- Of those aged 50 to 64 who were retired, 3.8 million would have wished to continue to work for their last employer if they could have negotiated to work for fewer hours with less responsibility.
- Among people aged 50 to 64 who were working, 5.3 million would have been willing to extend their careers if their employees had offered to retrain them, give them jobs with reduced hours and responsibilities, or continue to contribute to their pension plans past age 65.
- More than one million workers aged 50 to 64 believed that they will be forced to retire before they wanted to; 80 percent of those workers would have liked to work at least three years longer than they thought their employers would have allowed (McNaught, Barth, and Henderson 1989; Quinn and Burkhauser 1989; Taylor and Leitman 1989; and Taylor, Bass, and Bennett 1992).

In spite of the fact that the goal of many in the work force is to retire as early as possible or economically feasible, the evidence is clear from studies over many years that there are substantial numbers of older people who want the opportunity to continue to work into their later years or return to work either on a part-time or full-time basis.

REASONS WHY OLDER PEOPLE WANT TO WORK

Two reasons why older workers will be increasingly important to the American economy have already been cited: (1) the potential impending labor shortage around the year 2000, and (2) the need for continued productivity by older people as they become a larger proportion of the population. In addition to these forces promoting a greater use of older workers, the desire for employment or continued employment (either on a part-time or full-time basis) is based on the value and meaning of work to mature people which include:

- Income to maintain an adequate standard of living
- Meaningful activity to occupy one's time
- Self-esteem/self-worth
- Peer/societal recognition
- Friendship and collegial relationships with co-workers
- Outlets for creativity
- Service to others/society

For many in the American culture, work has been and continues to be a central life interest which gives them purpose as well as identity. This applies to persons of any age (Riekse 1991).

THE CHANGING AMERICAN WORKPLACE

In their study of older workers, Bass and Barth described the U.S. economy as being a fluid and dynamic entity. They stated,

> It is influenced by global competition and technological innovations. Industries evolve, change, and dissolve. Workers need to be able not only to change and upgrade their skills in existing fields and jobs, but also may even change fields altogether. As the workplace becomes more technologically sophisticated, workers at all levels need more sophisticated skills (Bass and Barth 1991: 3).

This same study pointed out the projected changes in skill requirements in the U.S. economy from 1988 to the year 2000. The largest growth sectors are:

- Technicians and related support services
- Professional specialty areas
- Service sectors
- Executive, administrative, and managerial

They pointed to a growing shift from industries that emphasize physical labor to those that depend on advanced technical skills, as illustrated in Table 9-1.

Bass and Barth further stated,

> Corporations, out of necessity, have been forced to be more productive and competitive with fewer

TABLE 9-1

SKILL REQUIREMENTS OF U.S. ECONOMY

Occupation	Percent of labor force—2000	Percent change 1988–2000
Executive, Administrative, and Managerial	10.8	22.0
Professional Specialty	13.3	24.0
Technicians and Related Support	3.7	31.6
Marketing and Sales	11.7	19.6
Administrative Support Including Clerical	17.3	11.8
Service	16.6	22.6
Agriculture, Forestry, Fishing and Related	2.4	−4.8
Precision Production, Craft, and Repair	11.4	9.9
Operators, Fabricators, and Laborers	12.6	1.3

(Bass and Barth 1991:5).

resources. On-demand production techniques requiring computerized networking have proliferated, cutting inventory costs. New methods of manufacturing require workers to be knowledgeable of all facets of their niche in production so that downtime, as a result of specialization, is virtually eliminated. These new management techniques require workers to be skilled in many different aspects of the job including technology and human relations. The workers employed in the increasingly "smarter" more technologically advanced industries need to be better educated and trained to meet current demands and, more important, to have the educational preparation to learn new tasks and skills as industries mature and change (Bass and Barth 1991: 7).

STRATEGIES TO MOBILIZE AND UTILIZE OLDER WORKERS

Various strategies have been put forth to increase the opportunities for older persons either to continue to work or to return to work. These include:

- Modifying work environments for older workers
- Modifying Social Security earnings limits
- Retraining employees as consultants
- Providing on-the-job training for older workers
- Providing classroom training for new jobs
- Creating job-sharing opportunities

- Creating possibilities for in-home work
- Individualizing work hours
- Offering "gliding out" retirement plans
- Redesigning jobs to accommodate physical limitations
- Recruiting older workers

RETRAINING OLDER PERSONS FOR THE CONTEMPORARY WORKPLACE

As needed and valuable as these approaches are to increase the participation of older persons in the work force, most do not address the major barriers to the continued employment or re-employment of older workers. This is particularly true for those with limited marketable skills for today's world of work, those who have been out of the workplace for an extended period of time or who have interrupted work histories, and those with little or negative self-esteem. The Daniel Yankelovich Group study (Stephens 1989) concerning the desire on the part of many older persons to continue to work or return to work also identified the major obstacles which appear to slow or block a fuller utilization of older persons in the American work force. These included the lingering question about the ability of workers ages 50 and older to adapt to new technology and the rising cost of healthcare coverage. Joan Kelly of the AARP's Worker Equity Department, the agency that commissioned the Yankelovich Group study, stated in connection with these findings, "It's up to older Americans to adjust to the labor market, to improve and increase their job skills. You have to go that extra mile that makes certain that the skills you have are what the job market needs, or you'll become a dinosaur. You have to be competitive" (Stephens 1989: 1). This, of course, applies to those older persons who are still working as well as those who wish to re-enter the job market.

Trends Promoting Retraining

According to one study (Caro and Morris 1993), several major trends make retraining older workers increasingly important:

- Older people are the fastest growing segment of the U.S. population. The baby boom generation will vastly swell the size of the older population. Already, many of those in the baby boom cohort are classified as "older workers."
- Because of accelerating technological changes in the workplace, upgrading worker skills is increasingly important.
- Because of uneven economic growth and contraction, and the increased willingness of large corporations to lay off long-term employees in midlife, more and more people must anticipate changing fields during their working lives. Success in midlife entry into new occupational fields will depend on acquiring new skills.
- Older people will show greater interest in extending their work lives because of improved health and longevity.
- The capacity of healthy older people to acquire new skills has been well established.
- More older people will seek to extend their work lives because of anticipated deterioration of private income security protection.
- Because the pool of young people entering the work force is shrinking, some labor economists project that when economic growth resumes, demand for older workers will substantially increase.

- Older people will increasingly engage in organized efforts to seek improved employment access. Two major national organizations, the American Association of Retired Persons and the National Council on Aging, have already made employment a major priority.

In addition, a 1992 Louis Harris and Associates survey found significant interest in additional career-related training among persons 55 and older:

- Forty-four percent of those surveyed who had at least a high school diploma would have been willing to take classes to improve their employment opportunities.
- Forty-four percent of those who were employed would have been willing to take classes for retraining.
- Fifty-five percent of those who were willing and able to work would have been willing to take classes to improve or upgrade their job skills (Taylor, Bass, and Barnett 1992).

Small Business and Training/Retraining

While some major industries operate significant training programs of their own, studies have indicated that most working adults have to look somewhere else for retraining (Caro and Morris 1993; Eurich 1990). Some 48 percent of the work force is employed in companies with fewer than 500 employees, companies which generally lack the resources needed to provide their own training. Small companies are vital to the economy as they are expected to be the major source of job growth in the years ahead (Caro and Morris 1993). Community colleges can play a major role in providing these training needs.

Vulnerable Older Persons and Training/Retraining

According to Morris and Caro,

> Rapid change in technology and the growing importance of global economic forces have made older workers in the United States and in Western

Europe vulnerable to job loss and to prolonged unemployment in their later years. Even workers in their forties are at risk of discovering that their work skills are obsolete. The massive personnel cuts in electronic and high technology industries since 1985 provide evidence of the severity of the problem since middle-management, middle-aged workers bear the brunt of the cuts (Morris and Caro 1991: 1).

Benefits of Training/Retraining/Hiring Older Workers

There have been many misconceptions over the years concerning the productivity, trainability, and dependability of older workers. Many of these are tied to pervasive negative stereotypes concerning older people. But recent studies have clearly demonstrated the benefits of training, retraining, and hiring older workers. The Commonwealth Fund Case Studies (1991) of older workers in firms demonstrated the benefits associated with employing older workers. These include:

- Turnover is dramatically lower: 87 percent of older workers stay on the job one year or more versus 30 percent for younger workers.
- Older workers can be trained as quickly as younger workers.
- Absence rates are much lower: 1.4 percent for older workers versus 3.7 percent for younger workers.
- Recruiting and training costs of older workers are almost three times lower than younger workers because they stay on the job longer.
- In the firms studied, older workers have been found to be better salespeople.
- Older workers can effectively operate demanding software at computer work stations.
- Using retirees as workers avoids additional fringe benefits costs because they are usually covered by some medical plan.
- Older workers are more frequently requested by supervisors.
- Older workers are often more familiar with the culture of work and demonstrate a better work ethic.

- Older workers have been found to be good for the morale of the entire work force.
- Older workers have been found to be more careful on the job and have fewer work-related injuries.
- Older workers pay more attention to satisfying customers.
- Leakage (theft, damage, goods never received) was found to be less where older workers predominate.
- Older workers are more willing to work overtime.

Evidence exists that productivity actually increases as workers grow older (Bass and Barth 1991). A number of studies have indicated that older workers have better attendance records, higher job satisfaction, fewer accidents and illness, and demonstrate less job turnover than younger workers.

Other studies have corroborated these findings. For example, the Yankelovich Group study found that many personnel managers appreciated the "work ethic" of older workers, including commitment to quality, company loyalty, coolness in crisis, and practical knowledge (Stephens 1989). Research done by the AARP Work Force Programs Department into how human resource managers view older members found that many were looking for seasoned job applicants (Lewis 1993a). This same study found that older workers were praised for their values, work ethic, and low absenteeism. In particular, they were cited for being "experienced, skilled, dependable, loyal, and having respect for authority and the company."

Job Training/Retraining Programs

As important as training/retraining is to older people who want to continue to work or re-enter a changing world of work, the evidence is not good concerning older people being the beneficiaries of specific training programs. Schulz (1992) pointed out that while older workers have made up a large percentage of the long-term unemployed, they have never been an important part of various job training programs supported or operated by the federal or state governments. He stated, "Despite contrary evidences, most government officials and employers do not consider it worthwhile or cost-effective to train older persons (compared to younger persons) because of the expectation of shorter work tenures, lower levels of education, and a belief that learning abilities decline with age" (p. 75). As an example, he cited the Comprehensive Employment and Training Act (CETA). In 1980, only one percent of the almost seven million persons aged 45 and older who were eligible for the CETA program actually participated.

Job Training Partnership Act   In 1982, the federal government established the Job Training Partnership Act (JTPA). This was designed to be a nationwide system of job training programs administered jointly by local governments and private sector planning agencies. JTPA has two major training programs. Title II is for economically disadvantaged youth and adults, with no upper age limits. Title III is for dislocated workers, including long-term unemployed older workers. Title IIA has funds for on-the-job training, classroom training, and remedial education. Through June 30, 1989, only 5 percent of the participants in this title of JTPA were persons aged 55 and older (U.S. Senate Special Committee on Aging 1992). Another section of JTPA (124-a-d) is targeted at economically disadvantaged workers age 55 and older.

Governors are required to set aside a percentage (originally 3 percent) of Title IIA funds for persons 55 and older for various forms of job training and job-seeking assistance. There was concern that the JTPA 3 percent set-side funds were underspent and that not enough older persons were being served by this program. By 1990, though, this condition had improved with no new unspent funds (Schulz 1992). Nevertheless, the restrictions of these programs (eligible-income guidelines, lack of outreach to eligible older persons, bureaucratic maze in administra-

tion) often limit their effectiveness with an older age group not familiar or comfortable with government assistance programs.

Senior Community Service Employment Program   The Senior Community Service Employment Program (SCSEP) was first given life in 1973 and was made part of the Older Americans Act as Title V in 1978. The purpose of this program is "to promote useful part-time opportunities in community service activities for unemployed low-income persons" (U.S. Senate 1992: p. 101). Persons 55 and older are eligible for this program with priority given to persons 60 and older who are unemployed and have incomes not exceeding 125 percent of the poverty level guidelines (U.S. Senate 1992). The idea of the program is to provide part-time employment, serve as an assist to find permanent unsubsidized employment, and be a source of labor for a number of community service agencies. About 80 percent of the participants in this program, administered by the U.S. Department of Labor, fall below the poverty line. The actual operation of the program is carried out by the AARP, Green Thumb, Inc., National Association of Hispanic Elderly, National Center of Black Aged, National Council on the Aging, National Council of Senior Citizens, National Urban League, and the U.S. Department of Agriculture and Forest Service.

Private-Sector Programs   In addition to federal programs to train older workers and help them retain or get jobs, some private organizations have taken a keen interest in the plight of mature persons and the changing world of work. The AARP has sponsored AARP WORKS, a series of eight workshops on employment planning for older adults, in about 80 locations in 30 states as of 1993. Forty Plus is a self-help organization for professional and managerial employees aged 40 and older, with chapters in more than fifteen cities. Other specific programs are in place in various communities across the nation such as Operation Able in Chicago and the Five o'Clock Club in New York City. Needless to say, job training/retraining for older adults will be a growth industry as the workplace continues to change and with an ever-increasing number of older persons seeking to stay employed or gain employment.

Key Components of a Successful Job Training Program for Older Workers

- Commitment to serve the educational needs of nontraditional students including mature adults (by federal and state governments, schools, colleges, businesses).
- Coordinated/leadership resources to initiate, develop, and administer a mature-worker training program.
- Resources capable of developing job training/retraining programs that relate to job opportunities in the community.
- Focus on employment skills for mature workers ranging from those required for entry-level positions to those required by managers, technical workers, and paraprofessionals who need to keep pace with developments in their fields.
- Strong ties to regional employers linking training/retraining to specific personnel opportunities.
- Clear achievement expectations for curriculum development and student assessment.
- Sensitivity to mature students, recognizing that older people have different learning styles and experiences that need to be addressed through curricular approaches and evaluation methods.
- Emphasis on short-term training/retraining programs with open-entry/open-exit options.
- Competency approach to student assessment based on performance of assigned tasks.
- Teachers who are sensitive and committed to the needs and circumstances of mature learners.
- In-service training for staff who serve older learners/job seekers.
- Appropriate learning environments to maximize learning opportunities for mature students.
- Adequate support services for older learners, including counseling and orientation to the changing world of work.

- Effective outreach to identify and mobilize mature persons to participate in the training/retraining opportunities.
- Effective job placement services (Riekse 1991). Reclaiming a national treasure: Retraining economically vulnerable older persons for the contemporary workplace. Grand Rapids, MI: Grand Rapids Community College.

OLDER WORKERS IN THE FUTURE

Two studies by the U.S. Department of Labor (DOL) analyzed the status of older persons in the American work force and made some interesting projections for the future, at least to the year 2000. One DOL study, "Older Worker Task Force: Key Policy Issues for the Future" indicated that there is growing concern about the consequences of early retirement (U.S. Senate Special Committee on Aging 1993). Too many persons may simply fall short economically—run out of money. The other report, "Labor Market Problems of Older Workers" (Rones and Herz 1989) recognized that while the trend toward retirement had been at earlier and earlier ages, the trend has stabilized or slightly reversed in recent years. This may even result in a decision by business and industry that it is in their best interests to develop and promote policies and practices to make it possible for the widespread employment of older workers.

SUMMARY

Working provides the most money of all sources of income for older people. However, only 16 percent of older people work. The trend toward early retirement was a feature of the American labor force until the late 1980s. There are now pressures in America leading to employees remaining at work longer before retirement, and retirees returning to work. The factors contributing to these trends range from personal psychological reasons to overall labor force trends. A potential shortage of workers by the year 2000 as the result of fewer people in the 20- to 29-years age group could bring pressure to turn to older workers. The financial requirements of being retired for so many years as people live longer and longer may force retirees and those contemplating retirement to question whether they will run out of money in the face of long-term inflation, even at modest rates.

The question of working or not working and the factors that are involved with this issue are important to late-middle-aged and older persons. Unemployment is a major factor for older workers. Even though the unemployment rate is lower for older workers, once unemployed they stay out of work longer.

Age discrimination is a major problem facing older workers, in spite of legislation enacted to combat it. The Age Discrimination in Employment Act (ADEA) of 1967 was the first major legislation to deal with age discrimination. This legislation has been amended numerous times to include additional workers and to raise, and then eliminate, the mandatory retirement age for most workers.

It is important to note the plight of older women and older minority persons in the workplace. Prejudice against both categories of persons has taken its toll in employment situations. This is compounded when an older woman is also a member of a minority group.

Important recent studies can be used to demonstrate the productivity of older workers. Surveys conducted in the 1970s, 1980s, and 1990s showed large numbers of older persons who either want to continue to work or who wish to return to work. Reasons why they want to work include added income, meaningful activity, self-esteem, peer recognition, friendships, outlets for creativity, and service to others.

Strategies to mobilize older workers include modifying work environments, raising or eliminating Social Security earnings limits, using retirees as consultants, job training, and job sharing. Retraining older workers is a major way to keep them employable in the contemporary workplace. A variety of approaches can be used to retrain them. Retraining older workers has a range of benefits. Older workers will be an increasingly important component of the future American workplace.

REFERENCES

A glimpse of the 90s. 1990. *AARP Bulletin*, (February) 31(2): 10.

Albert, M.S., and Moss, B. (eds.). 1988. *Geriatric Neuropsychology*. New York: Guilford Press.

Bass, J., and Barth, M. 1991. *The Next Educational Opportunity: Career Training for Mature Workers*. Draft: 8-1-91. Background Papers Series. Americans Over 55 at Work Programs. New York: The Commonwealth Fund.

Beck, M., Denworth, L., and Christian, N. 1992. Finding Work After 50. *Newsweek*, CXIX (11) (March 16): 58.

Bradford, K. 1979. Can You Survive Your Retirement?" *Harvard Business Review*, (November/December).

Caro, F., and Morris, R. 1992. Retraining Older Workers. *Community College Journal*, (December/January) 63(3): 22–26.

Deets, H. 1993a. Public Retiree Pensions Need to Be Protected. *NRTA Bulletin*, 34(6): 3.

Eurich, W. 1990. *The Learning Industry: Education for Adult Workers*. Princeton, NJ: Carnegie Foundation for the Advancement of Teaching.

Johnson and Higgins, Inc. 1979. *1979 Study of American Authors Toward Pensions and Retirement*. New York: Johnson and Higgins.

Lewis, R. 1992a. Costly Experiences. *NRTA Bulletin*, 33(5): 1, 10.

Lewis, R. 1992b. Early Out—All at Once, the Party's Over. *NRTA Bulletin*, 33(6): 2, 13.

Lewis, R. 1993a. Networking, New Tactics Lift Older Job Seekers. *NRTA Bulletin*, 34(2): 2, 14–15.

Lewis, R. 1993b. Public Retirees Under Siege. *NRTA Bulletin*, 34(6): 1, 13.

Maloney, T.W. 1990. Millions of Older Workers Ready, Willing and Able. *NRTA Bulletin*, 31(3): 6.

Mayer, M.P. 1993. Pensions: The Naked Truth. *Modern Maturity* (February/March): 40–44.

McNaught, W., Barth, M.C., and Henderson, P. 1989. The Human Resource Potential of Americans Over Fifty. *Human Resource Management*, 28: 455–473.

Morris, R.W. and Carol, F.G. 1991. *Older Worker Retraining: An Important New Direction for Higher Education*. Boston: Gerontology Institute, University of Massachusetts at Boston.

National Center for Health Statistics. 1988. Current Estimates From the National Health Statistics, 1988. Current Estimates from the Interview Survey, United States, 1987. *Vital Health Statistics*, (Series 10, No. 166).

Older Women's League. 1991. *Paying for Prejudice: A Report on Midlife and Older Women in America's Labor Force*, Washington, DC: Older Women's League.

Quinn, J.B. 1992a. Job Loss Nightmare Lingers. *Detroit Free Press* (January 13): 10F.

Quinn, J.B. 1992b. What You'll Need to Retire Early. *Detroit Free Press*. Business Monday (January 13): 13.

Quinn, J., and Burkhauser, R.V. 1989. *Retirement Preferences and Plans of Older American Workers*. Background Paper No. 5. New York: Commonwealth Fund.

Retirees' Lament: Broken Vows. 1993. *U.S. News & World Report* (March 15): 14.

Rieske, R. 1991. Reclaiming a National Treasure: Retraining Economically Vulnerable Older Persons for the Contemporary Workplace. Grand Rapids, MI: Grand Rapids Community College.

Rodeheffer, R.J., et al. 1984. Exercise Cardiac Output Is Maintained With Advancing Age in Healthy Human Subjects: Cardiac Dilation and Increased Stroke Volume Compensate for Diminished Heart Rate. *Circulation*, 69: 203–213.

Rones, P.L., and D.E. Herz. 1989. *Labor Market Problems of Older Workers*. Bureau of Labor Statistics. Washington, DC: U.S. Government Printing Office.

Schaie, K.W. 1989. Perceptual Speed in Adulthood: Cross-Sectional and Longitudinal Studies. *Psychology and Aging*, 4: 443–453.

Schall, J.A. 1993. Training to Cope With a Changing World. *The Detroit News* (June 19).

Schulz, J.H. 1992. *The Economics of Aging*. 5th Ed. New York: Auburn House.

Stephens, R. 1989. New Hurdles at Work. *NRTA Bulletin*, (December) 30(11): 1, 4–5.

Stern, L. 1993. How to Find a Job. *Modern Maturity* (June–July): 25–34.

Taylor, H., Bass, R., and Barnett, S. 1992. *Productive Aging*. New York: Louis Harris and Associates.

Taylor, H., and Leitman, R. 1989. *Older Americans: The Untapped Labor Source*. Program Sponsored Survey. New York: Commonwealth Fund.

The Commonwealth Fund. 1991. *New Findings Show Why Employing Workers over 50 Makes Good Financial Sense for Companies*. New York: Case Studies.

Torres-Gil, F.M. 1992. *The New Aging: Politics and Change in America*. New York: Auburn House.

U.S. Bureau of the Census. 1991. *Money Income of Households, Families, and Persons in the United States: 1990*. Current Population Reports, (Series P-60, No. 174), Washington, DC: U.S. Government Printing Office.

U.S. Bureau of the Census. 1992. *Sixty-Five Plus in America*. Current Population Reports, Special Studies. Washington, DC: U.S. Government Printing Office.

U.S. Bureau of the Census. 1993. *Preparing for Retirement: Who Had Pension Coverage in 1991*. Statistical Brief. Washington, DC: U.S. Department of Commerce.

U.S. Bureau of Labor Statistics. 1991. *Employment and Earnings*, (January) Vol. 38, No. 1, Table 3.

U.S. House of Representatives Select Committee on Aging. 1992. *Age Discrimination in the Workplace: A Continuing Problem for Older Workers*. (September 24, 1991) Washington, DC: U.S. Government Printing Office.

U.S. Senate Special Committee on Aging. 1993. *Developments in Aging*: 1992 Volume 1. Washington, DC: U.S. Government Printing Office.

Weatherington, R. 1990. A Promise Not Kept. *Modern Maturity* (June/July): 30–38.

Williams, T. F. 1992. Testimony at U.S. House of Representatives Select Committee on Aging, September 24, 1991. *Age Discrimination in the Workplace: A Continuing Problem for Older Workers*. Washington, DC: U.S. Government Printing Office.

CHAPTER 10

Retirement

Retiring Together

It isn't always easy for working couples to arrange

NEW YORK—John Synal, a Westchester County school superintendent, was 56, burned out and bored when he told his wife he was going to retire. But Jean Synal, at 49, was just reaching her professional peak.

"He was adamant he was going to retire," said Jean, who reared three children before becoming a teacher and then a principal. "I wasn't too thrilled, because I wondered what he would do with himself. But I never had any doubt that I was going to go on working, because I was in my prime."

So Jean worked full-time for six years after her husband retired—and even after she joined him in retirement, she did part-time consulting for several years.

The Synals, like others of their generation, took it for granted women would stay home to care for babies and wives would move to follow their husband's jobs.

But with the advent of the women's movement, economic necessity and the opening of job opportunities, many wives joined the labor force. And the decision about who should retire, and when, has become complicated.

If the issue of the 1980s was how two-career couples would handle child-rearing, the issue of the 1990s may be how two-career couples will handle retirement.

Half of all men are out of the labor force at age 62, reports the Bureau of Labor Statistics. Women's retirement patterns are less clear, because only recently have large numbers of women been in the work force.

Source: Tamar Lewin, *New York Times,*
November 8, 1993.

Fixing a Faulty Pension

Your payout may be thousands short. Here's what you can do

Walter Kinsey worked 30 years for the same Manhattan restaurant company, secure in the knowledge that he was covered by a pension plan. But after he turned 65 in 1991, he was shocked to find that his union had a record of only six of his years of service—and denied him any pension at all. It took intervention by a lawyer and voluminous correspondence before he received in March even part of what he was due: a retroactive payment of about $3,000 and monthly checks of $82.

In a way, Kinsey was lucky that the foul-up was so monumental: He couldn't help but notice. Pension experts say many people collecting retirement benefits—perhaps 1 in 5—are in fact being shortchanged and don't know it. Errors have become common as pension law has grown more complex, explains Chester Salkind, executive director of the American Society of Pension Actuaries. Meanwhile, the ongoing wave of layoffs and early-retirement nudge-outs has added greatly to pension administrators' workload.

Source: U.S. News and World Report,
June 13, 1994, p. 99

RETIREMENT: AN AMERICAN INSTITUTION

Retirement is a major life event. It touches the lives of most older Americans since almost all workers contribute to the Social Security funds that provide retirement benefits. The overwhelming majority of American workers will reach the age at which they can benefit from Social Security and other benefits and resources they may have for their retirement years.

As Abraham Monk pointed out, retirement has many meanings.

It refers to the termination of and formal withdrawal from a regular job under the provisions of a statutory pension system, a demographic category, an economic condition, a social status, a developmental phase in the human life span, the transition to old age, and a lifestyle dominated by leisure pursuits or, at least, by economically nonproductive activity (Monk 1994: 3).

This time-honored definition of retirement is undergoing change as it becomes more common for people to retire from one job or occupation and reenter the workplace in some way.

Today, most Americans take for granted that they will spend a good portion of their lives in retirement. Indeed, retirement has now become an established institution in America. In fact, people are spending more time in all three of life's major activities: education, work, and retirement.

HISTORICAL PERSPECTIVE OF RETIREMENT

Retirement is not something that has always been part of the American scene. In 1900, when the life expectancy for men was 46.3 years, the average man spent only 1.2 years in retirement or in activities out of the labor force. This was only 3 percent of a man's life. By contrast, in 1900, women spent an average of 29 years working at home and in retirement out of an average life expectancy of 48.3 years, and averaged only 6.3 years in the labor force (U.S. Senate Special Committee on Aging 1992). Societal roles typically mandated that a woman's work be confined to the home setting.

As indicated in Table 10-1, these numbers have changed dramatically over the years. By 1992, life expectancy was 73.2 years for men and 79.8 years for women (Kochanek and Hudson 1994). Life expectancy in the year 2000 is projected to be 73.5 years for men and 80.4 years for women (Monk 1994). With dramatically longer lives, the advent of the Social Security Act of 1935, and additional coverage of pensions in the private and public sectors, retirement became a possibility for millions of Americans following World War II. Early retirement entered the picture as a goal of many workers. By 1990, only 16 percent of men over the age of 65 and 9 percent of women over age 65 were in the labor force. Decreased participation rates in the labor force apply to younger categories of workers as well, especially those aged 55 and older. Indeed, only about two in five (39.3 percent) men aged 55 and older were paid workers in 1990. On the other hand, women in their late fifties were more likely

to work in 1990 than in previous decades, but their participation rate in the labor force drops dramatically in the later years (U.S. Bureau of the Census 1992).

Another indicator of the trend toward early retirement is the proportion of different age groups receiving Social Security benefits. The majority of people over the age of 62 now get Social Security checks (U.S. Bureau of the Census 1992). However, although early retirement has been aided by the advent of broader and better pension coverage, there is evidence that the trend toward early retirement is changing.

For many Americans, retirement is no longer a brief interlude between work and death. In the current context of work and retirement, it is becoming common for people to spend a quarter or even as much as one third of their entire lives as retired persons (Monk 1994).

WHEN AND WHY DO PEOPLE RETIRE?

When to retire in contemporary America is not determined solely by reaching a certain birthday in life's journey. The decision to retire involves a complex set of conditions and circumstances in each individual's life. Experts in the retirement field have said that the timing of a person's retirement is one of the most important decisions he or she will make during a lifetime (Clark 1994). Making this decision involves goal setting, strategic planning, and realistically assessing and determining the various trade-offs of continuing to work as opposed to retiring (Dennis 1994).

Some of the experts in the area of retirement have looked at the key factors a person needs to consider in trying to decide whether and when to retire.

Financial Security and Health Status

Among all the factors that are important in deciding whether and when to retire, the most important are a person's financial status and the

TABLE 10-1

LIFECYCLE DISTRIBUTION OF EDUCATION, LABOR FORCE PARTICIPATION, RETIREMENT, AND WORK IN THE HOME: 1900–1980

Subject	Year					
	1900	**1940**	**1950**	**1960**	**1970**	**1980**
	Number of years spent in activity					
Men						
Average life expectancy	46.3	60.8	65.6	66.6	67.1	70.0
Retirement/work at home	1.2	9.1	10.1	10.2	12.1	13.6
Labor force participation	32.1	38.1	41.5	41.1	37.8	38.8
Education	8.0	8.6	9.0	10.3	12.2	12.6
Pre-school	5.0	5.0	5.0	5.0	5.0	5.0
Women						
Average life expectancy	48.3	65.2	71.1	73.1	74.7	77.4
Retirement/work at home	29	39.4	41.4	37.1	35.3	30.6
Labor force participation	6.3	12.1	15.1	20.1	22.3	29.4
Education	8.0	8.7	9.6	10.9	12.1	12.4
Pre-school	5.0	5.0	5.0	5.0	5.0	5.0
	Percent distribution by activity type					
Men						
Average life expectancy	100	100	100	100	100	100
Retirement/work at home	3	15	15	15	18	19
Labor force participation	69	63	63	62	56	55
Education	17	14	14	15	18	18
Pre-school	11	8	8	8	7	8
Women						
Average life expectancy	100	100	100	100	100	100
Retirement/work at home	60	60	58	51	47	40
Labor force participation	13	19	21	27	30	38
Education	17	13	14	15	16	16
Pre-school	10	8	7	7	7	6

Source: U.S. Senate Special Committee on Aging, the American Association of Retired Persons, the Federal Council on Aging, and the U.S. Administration on Aging, 1991. *Aging America: Trend and projections.* Washington, D.C.: U.S. Department of Health and Human Services, Table 3-1, p. 87.

condition of his or her health (Clark 1994; Kelly 1994).

Financial Security In regards to financial security, Robert Clark has stated that "the optimal retirement age is the age at which an older worker decides that he or she has sufficient income from pensions, Social Security, and personal assets to provide the desired level of compensation in retirement" (Clark 1994: 38). Other researchers have found that people who are thinking about retiring have identified financial security as their greatest concern (Dennis 1994).

Sara Rix (1994), another retirement specialist, has said that uppermost in the mind of everyone who approaches old age is the matter of financial security. Rix pointed out that this applies to women and men, with financial security in later life generally more elusive for women.

Retirement, as an American institution, would not be possible without some level of replacement income when a person stops working. W. Andrew Achenbaum (1994), a noted historian of aging in America, pointed out that as late as the 1940s and early 1950s, most of the people who retired did so because they were in poor health or had been laid off. When Social Security benefits became more liberalized in the 1950s, retirement became a more realistic option for American workers.

Because some degree of economic security in the later years of life is the key to being able to retire, a major part of this chapter will be devoted to a discussion financing retirement and the financial pitfalls some persons experience as they live through their retirement years.

Health Status The health condition of people trying to decide whether and when to retire influences their decisions in various ways (Clark 1994). Poor health may limit a worker's ability to carry out certain tasks. It may become difficult for a worker in declining health to keep up with the work load of a given work situation.

In addition, a person's poor health may make work in general more difficult, resulting in a marked reduction in wanting to work. Going through the effort of getting to work and being there all day simply becomes too difficult. Most all studies of retirement have shown that a person's health is a very important consideration in making a retirement decision (Anderson and Burkhauser 1985; Sammartino 1987).

The health condition of a worker's spouse also has a bearing on his or her decision to continue to work or to retire. Poor health of a worker's spouse could result in two options. If the spouse who is experiencing poor health was in the paid labor force, the worker contemplating retirement may be forced to continue to work to maintain the family's income. The worker may increase hours at work to replace some of the income lost by the ill spouse. If, however, the spouse with failing health needs extensive caregiving, the worker may feel the need to reduce hours at work or totally give up her or his job. In American society, it is usually a "she" who gives up a job for family caregiving. Which way the decision goes depends on the cost and availability of home health care, the family's income, and the earning power of the healthy spouse (Clark, Johnson, and Mc-Dermed 1980).

Other Key Factors in Deciding to Retire

In addition to the key determinants of financial security and health status, other considerations are important in this major life-course decision. They include attitudes toward retirement, family commitments and relationships, and the meaning of work.

Attitudes Toward Retirement For some people, retirement is a negative concept. To them being retired means being at the end of the line, on the shelf, over the hill, or put out to pasture (McCluskey 1989).

Some people fear being treated as old persons who are essentially worthless. Not too long before his death, Norman Cousins, the former editor of the *Saturday Review* and professor of medicine at UCLA, wrote, "The worst thing about being 75 years old is being treated as a 75-year-old" (Dennis 1994: 47). Society may well view retired people as no longer serving a useful purpose.

Others fear losses that come with retirement including friends and co-workers, the essence of their work, being part of an organization, the opportunity to learn and travel, new challenges, the contributions they make, and the loss of status. Losses, however, are part of any major change or transition in life. Helen Dennis (1994) pointed out that those planning for retirement can enhance their attitudes toward retirement by compensating for various aspects of their jobs that they value and do not want to lose. She suggested that retirees can seek some of the satisfactions they get from their jobs by participating in volunteer opportunities, through new employment opportunities which may involve some retraining, through training in dependent business ventures, or by becoming involved in activities that are personally rewarding as home repairs or additions.

A positive attitude toward retirement is based on people's perception that retirement is socially acceptable. The American work ethic, which puts high worth on being industrious and self-reliant, is not really part of the retirement most people experience. Because of this, Ekerdt (1986) has suggested that American society has embraced the "busy ethic" to try to justify being retired in a way that is consistent with the American work ethic. This busy ethic puts value on leisure in retirement if it means the retiree is busy with activities and involved in various endeavors.

Even though work is of high value in American life, research has shown that most people view retirement as a positive situation—something they want (Cockerham 1991). Most people look forward to their retirement as a time of freedom from routine work and an opportunity to create a lifestyle of their own choice.

Family Relationships Family commitments and the interactions between family members have a bearing on retirement decisions.

1. *Impacts on women.* Women workers in particular are affected by family relationships when it comes to retirement decisions. Married women tend to retire when their husbands retire. The amount of a husband's pension and his becoming eligible for it have real impact on when a married woman retirees (Atchley 1991; Vinick and Ekerdt 1989). Further a woman's decision to retire, whether she is married or single, is influenced by the health needs of family members (Matthews and Brown 1987). This applies to caring for older parents and spouses.

2. *Impacts on men.* Not too much has been written on the influences of family considerations or the decisions of men to retire (Dennis 1994).

Some men become primary caregivers for disabled spouses. The evidence is that men's decisions to retire are not influenced very much by the decisions of working wives to retire. It is not even clear if the opinions and feeling of wives are determinant factors on the decisions of men to retire (Matthews and Brown 1987).

3. *Impacts on couples.* Working couples often find the decision to retire quite complex (Dennis 1994). As one writer put it, many women are just beginning to "make their mark (in the workplace), while men are leaving their mark" (Karp 1989: 755). As a result, husbands and wives may have difficulty trying to find the right time to retire together. Ongoing communication between a husband and wife who are working is essential for a "good" retirement decision for both spouses (Dennis 1994). Dependent aging family members can adversely affect a couple's decision to retire. One study indicated that retired couples felt their retirement to be "spoiled" when they became the caregivers for an elderly parent who lived with them (Vinick and Ekerdt 1989).

The Meaning of Work The meaning of work to people has an impact on retirement decisions. Various groups of workers have different views of work, which affect their decisions concerning retirement.

1. *Blue-collar workers.* Blue-collar workers tend to retire earlier in life than white-collar workers (Mitchell, Levine, and Dozzebon 1988; Burtless 1987). This is particularly true for workers in mining, manufacturing, construction, and transportation. For men aged 55 and older, more blue-collar workers than white-collar workers retire as the result of health problems (Mitchel et al. 1988).

2. *Professional workers.* A study of working professional men and women aged 50 to 60 found that those least likely to look forward to retirement had unfinished agendas, saw retirement as financially unfeasible, and were healthy and

very satisfied with their jobs (Karp 1989). But another study found that job satisfaction alone does not mean that professionals do not look forward to retirement (Atchley 1991). Rather, it found that many persons can enjoy their jobs and still want to retire.

Planning for Retirement

One of the most important things people of all ages can do to have positive experiences in retirement is to prepare for it by planning ahead. Not until the years following World War II was there any organized effort to help people plan for their retirements. In 1948, Clark Tibbitts and Wilma Donahue of the University of Michigan and Ernest Burgess of the University of Chicago began developing preretirement educational programs (Cooper 1994). In 1956, Woodrow Hunter of the University of Michigan offered the first preretirement education program that was sponsored by a union (Hunter 1968). Since that time, planning for retirement has become an integral part of a successful transition to another part of the life cycle.

Planning for retirement often includes

- Lifestyle planning and attitudes toward retirement and retirement goals
- Legal issues such as wills, powers of attorney, and disposition of property
- Financial planning including income, savings, and investments
- Health and wellness: as nutrition, exercise, and stress management
- Roles and relationships, including aging parents, roles of spouses, and widowhood
- Housing arrangements, including housing options, geographic locations, and continuing care facilities
- The use of time, including part-time work, volunteering, and leisure activities (Cooper 1994).

FINANCIAL TRAPS IN EARLY RETIREMENT

"When General Motors announced recently it was launching a new early-retirement campaign,

52 year-old Carl Lukaszewski got interested," wrote Stephen Advokat in a 1993 *Detroit Free Press* story on early retirement (Advokat 1993: 3F). "I've raised my family, and now I'd like to get into some field that I've always wanted to get into," said Lukaszewski who had worked for GM 29 years. But he decided to stay put. He realized he could not afford to retire. "I think a lot of people really don't know what it takes to retire," said Lukaszewski.

Advokat pointed out that many retirement specialists warn that taking early retirement is a decision that should not be made hastily. He pointed out that retiring as early as age 50 requires a lot of money, as much as $1 million or more. Even retiring at age 55 means one may have to support one's self for another 25 to 35 years. Advokat cites Russ Jalbert, a retirement planning expert, who pointed out that many people will live as long in retirement as they did in their working years. In fact, very few people he deals with who took retirement at 53 were able to maintain their lifestyle without working. Table 10-2 illustrates how money shrinks over the retirement years.

A senior consultant from the Wyatt Company, a Chicago consulting firm, Joanne Daubner pointed out that even those persons who choose early retirement bonuses find that money does not go as far as they thought it would, especially if they are still years away from collecting Social Security benefits. Falling interest rates have eroded the income from lump-sum payments, and declining real estate prices in many parts of the nation have made it harder to realize assets from the family home (Beck, Denworth, and Christian 1992).

She also pointed out that many people in the early-retirement age categories still have mortgage payments. Nearly one third of people in the early stages of retirement have responsibilities for aging parents. This can cast a cloud over their financial futures when possible inheritances and possible commitments to the financial shortfalls of aging parents are considered. In addition, it is not un-

TABLE 10-2

THE VALUE OF RETIREMENT INVESTMENTS SHRINK OVER TIME AS A RESULT OF INFLATION

Many retirees underestimate how far their savings will go. Often, retirement investments grow in the beginning. But after only a few years, inflation outpaces the investments' growth and retirees start draining their principal. Look at what can happen to a nest egg of $120,000.

	Year	Living expenses	Nest egg	Balance (12/31)
• This person intends to	1	$20,900	$120,000	$126,300
live on his $20,000-a-year	2	21,841	126,300	132,038
pension. His $120,000 nest	3	22,823	132,038	137,136
egg is earning 6 percent	4	23,850	137,136	141,514
interest after taxes	5	24,924	141,514	145,081
• Because inflation makes	6	26,045	145,081	147,741
everything more expensive,	7	27,217	147,741	149,388
he'll need $20,900 to live on.	8	28,442	149,388	149,910
In the second year (assuming	9	29,722	149,910	149,182
inflation at 4.5 percent). No	10	31,059	149,182	147,074
problem; his nest egg has	11	32,457	147,074	143,441
earned $7,200 in interest.	12	33,918	143,441	138,130
• The nest egg continues	13	35,444	138,130	130,974
to grow for eight years.	14	37,039	130,974	121,794
But so does the cost of	15	38,706	121,794	110,396
living. By the ninth year,	16	40,447	110,396	96,572
inflation forces this person to	17	42,268	96,572	80,099
tap his principal to maintain	18	44,140	80,099	60,735
his life-style.	19	46,157	60,735	38,222
• At the end of 21 years,	20	48,234	38,222	12,281
the nest egg is gone.	21	50,405	12,281	0

Assumptions: 4.5 percent inflation, 6 percent rate of earnings on nest egg.
Source: Buck Consultants in *Detroit Free Press*, March 18, 1993 p. F3.

common for grown, unemployed, or recently divorced children to return to their parents' old family homes (Beck, Denworth, and Christian 1992).

In addition to the distinct possibility of running out of money, early retirees need to be very careful about health insurance, keeping in mind that Medicare, the national health insurance for older people in America, does not begin until age 65. Sometimes the employer a person is leaving will pay the health insurance premiums allowing him or her to stay on its plan. If that is not possible, employees are usually entitled to stay with a group plan for up to 18 months after leaving employment (Advokat 1993).

Some pension plans include health insurance coverage either as a benefit or with modest contributions by retirees. "It's critical that a retiree have health care coverage, particularly catastrophic coverage," said Rick Dirksen, a partner in a consulting firm (Advokat 1993: 3F). There are very few things that are a bigger risk to someone's financial security than a long-term illness. Early retirement can mean a drastic change in lifestyle due to reduced income. Couples used to the freedom and mobility of two cars may be forced to cut back to one. Recreation, travel, and entertainment costs may have to be reduced just at a time when a person finally has the time to really enjoy life. But much of this is directly related to adequate early financial planning. Another big help may be earned supplemental income from working at something a person always wanted to try, or from part-time employment in an area that is comfortable for the retiree. It should be noted that employment in the later years is not always an easy accomplishment.

WOMEN AND EARLY RETIREMENT

As in many financial areas of life, women are at a particular disadvantage regarding early retirement. According to a study by the University of Miami's Center on Adult Development and Aging, under our economic system, men typically are able to retire earlier and with fewer cares than women are. According to one of the authors of the study, "Working women don't retire, or plan to retire, as early as men do unless they are married and their husbands have a good income or a lot of money stashed away" (Taft 1991: 3E). The study goes on to point out that the difference between the number of men and women seeking early retirement exists partly because women usually enter the labor force later than men and, as a result, have fewer credits in Social Security or private pension plans.

According to the same study, divorced and separated women are at a further disadvantage regarding early retirement. Divorced women need to plan to spend three more years being employed than married women. Separated women can plan to spend two more years in the labor force. Divorce and separation have no negative effect on men's decision for early retirement. This study reinforces others that clearly indicate that a woman usually comes out of a divorce financially worse off than men do.

WHAT DOES IT TAKE TO RETIRE EARLY?

In a column on early retirement, Jane Bryant Quinn wrote a memo to workers who retired early or are planning to:

You probably won't make it financially unless you find a part-time job. At 55 you could easily live another 30 or 40 years. If you're not working, you'll need more savings than most people ever see in a lifetime" (Quinn 1992: 13).

Quinn pointed out that the early retiree's silent enemy is inflation, long-term inflation. If a retiree was living on $30,000 in 1992, by 2002 he or she will need $44,000 to pay for the same things, assuming a 4 percent annual increase in the cost of living. By the year 2017, 25 years after retirement, the retiree will need $80,000 a year. About one-fourth might come from Social Security, which has a cost of living adjustment built into the system. Pensions generally do not increase with inflation. The rest will have to come from savings or work, but it is usually difficult for most people to work 20 to 30 years after retirement.

To estimate how much a person will need in order to retire early and have enough money for the next 35 years assuming a 4 percent inflation rate, Quinn set forth the following formula:

- Add up how much money is needed in the year a person retires. Reduce that by the income derived from a pension and Social Security. The remaining money has to come from savings.
- For every $10,000 generated from savings, a retiree needs $198,000 in savings yielding an average 8 percent a year. At 6 percent interest, a retiree needs $258,000 for every $10,000 he or she derives from savings.

If a person has not saved that kind of money, he or she cannot afford to retire early, according to Quinn.

IS THE EARLY RETIREMENT PARTY OVER?

"Early retirement became a kind of status symbol," according to Harold Sheppard, gerontology professor at the University of South Florida (Lewis 1992: 2). He went on to say that early retirement was an outward sign of success, indicating that a person did not have to work if he or she did not choose to. However, analysts now say that the trend toward early retirement is definitely changing. The change began in the late 1980s. According to the Bureau of Labor Statistics (unpublished figures), beginning in middle years and going through age 65, the percentage of men in the labor force has increased. The trend toward early retirement appeared to peak in 1988, when 68.8 percent of men were in the labor force. In 1989, the percentage rose to 70.7 percent and stayed in that range (Lewis 1992).

"We have reached a turning point," said Martin Sicker, director of the AARP Work Force Programs Department. "The trend to retire at earlier and earlier ages has ended, and we can now expect gradual increases in the working lives of Americans" (Lewis 1992).

Although not all experts agree that the trend toward early retirement has been reversed permanently, Lewis showed clear indications that would lead to such a conclusion. They include:

- Married couples are putting off starting families, leaving them with children to pay for in the early retirement years.
- Generous early retirement incentives, popular in the 1980s as a way to cut payrolls, are reported to be declining. A 1990 survey by A. Foster Higgins & Co., a benefits consulting firm, found that fewer employers (33 percent down from 41 percent) were offering their workers early retirement options.
- More and more employers are shifting the cost of retiree health insurance, motivating middle-aged workers to keep on working.
- Greater longevity of Americans increases the likelihood that people will have to work longer to accumulate enough resources to sustain them in their extended years of life.
- Large "bonus credits" are offered by Social Security for those who keep working past the age of 65 (beginning in 1990, Social Security started raising the 3-percent credit workers get for deferring benefits by one-half percent every two years until the credit reaches 8 percent).

- The age for full Social Security benefits phased in after the year 2000 increases to age 67.
- More and more people want to work in the middle and later years as indicated by surveys already cited.

Martin Sicker of the AARP said, "Rare will be those who can retire at age 55 and maintain their preretirement standard of living" (Lewis 1992: 13). Dan Lacey, editor of *Workplace Trends* newsletter said, "The whole idea of retirement should be put to rest. I don't think anybody wants to spend their sixties and seventies watching Phil Donahue" (Lewis 1992: 13).

THREATS TO RETIREMENT FINANCIAL SECURITY

In addition to long-term inflation, which can literally use up the value of a retiree's nest egg, there are other factors in the American economy that pose threats to financial security in retirement.

Underfunded Pensions

One immediate threat to current retirees is the unsoundness of the pension plans under which they retired. To protect pensions and the retirees who depend on them, the Employee Retirement Income Security Act (ERISA) became law in 1974. ERISA was designed to expand the supervision and regulation of private pension plans by the federal government and create tax-exempt individual retirement accounts for persons not covered by a qualified pension plan. Also established under ERISA was the Pension Benefit Guaranty Corporation (PBGC) as part of the Department of Labor. This agency is designed to guarantee payment of pension checks to retired workers and future payments to vested workers (workers who have worked long enough to collect under a pension plan) when a pension plan is terminated or runs out of money, which occurred frequently in the turbulent economic times of the late 1980s and early 1990s. In 1992, PBGC estimated that some five million workers and retirees were in underfunded pension plans. By 1992, Eastern Airlines, Pan Am, and some large steel companies had gone under. Some 400,000 American workers were directly dependent on PBGC for pensions that their employers had not funded sufficiently.

Underfunded PBGC

In 1992, the executive director of the PBGC estimated that by 1997 that agency might have as much as a $19 billion shortfall, with more red ink to come (Mayer 1993). This warning was not intended to scare retired workers. It was intended to motivate Congress to prepare for the responsibility it faces in funding the PBGC adequately in the face of pension plans that are projected to go broke. It is also a warning to the taxpayers who have already been saddled with bailing out the savings and loan industry in America for at least a half a trillion dollars as of 1993. Underlying all of this is a warning of the number of underfunded or potentially underfunded pensions in the American economy, even though the vast majority of them are well funded and safe (Mayer 1993). Public pension plans—federal and state workers, teachers, other public employees—also face underfunding. The Government Accounting Office (GAO) in 1993 estimated that one in three state and local pension funds was underfunded. At that time, it was estimated that the federal pension programs were underfunded by $1.6 trillion, which in effect adds that amount to the federal debt (Lewis 1993). Although these are not in danger of insolvency because they have the governmental units (especially the federal government) behind them, this situation could have political implications as taxpayers feel less inclined to pay for retiree benefits. This could result in cutbacks in cost of living adjustments, cuts in specific benefits such as vision or dental care (if contained in specific plans), or even scaling back in levels of income. Unlike private pensions, public pensions are not covered by ERISA. Most states have some laws protecting public pensions, but they need standardizing federal legislation to better safeguard the integrity of all public pension plans (Deets 1993).

Diminishing Healthcare Benefits

Tens of thousands of retirees are facing the prospect of losing healthcare coverage that was promised to them when they retired. This is the result of a number of factors according to Richard Weatherington, a specialist in small business, tax, and human services:

- Employees have been retiring earlier, before age 65. Not being eligible for Medicare, early retirees cost companies a lot of money to insure for health care before they become eligible for Medicare.
- Retirees are living longer. The companies have to pay healthcare costs for longer periods of time.
- The government has increased the amount of healthcare costs not covered by Medicare. Higher deductibles and greater co-payments force company health plans to pick up more of the costs of health care.
- Most medical cost controls are ineffective. Since 1966, medical-care costs have increased three times the increase of the rest of the cost of living (Consumer Price Index).
- There are more retirees today. In 1980, there were about fifteen employees working who helped support one retiree's benefits. By 1990 that ratio had fallen to three to one (Weatherington 1990). As a result, according to a 1993 survey of employers by the consulting firm of A. Foster Higgins and Co., about a dozen big corporations are cutting employees' health benefits over the next few years, an additional seventy are reducing benefits for future retirees, and about 800 are revising their health plans, usually by asking their retirees to pay more (*U.S. News and World Report* 1993). Large companies cutting back on these benefits include General Motors, McDonnell Douglas, Unisys, and Primerica (*U.S. News and World Report* 1993; Weatherington 1990).

Where to Turn for Help   These nonprofit organizations provide free advice on pension problems by mail or phone, and they may be able to provide references to pension experts in a specific geographic area: (*U.S. News and World Report*, March 15, 1993, p. 14.)

- Technical Assistance and Inquiries Division
  Pension and Welfare Benefits Administration
  Department of Labor
  200 Constitution Avenue, N.W.
  Washington, D.C. 20210
  (202) 219-8776

The division also has branches at 15 Labor Department offices around the country.

- The American Association of Retired Persons
  Pension Equity Project
  601 E Street, N.W.
  Washington, D.C. 20049
  (202) 434-2070

- Pension Rights Center
  918 16th Street, N.W.
  Washington, D.C. 20016
  (202) 296-3776

DEMISE OR SHIFT OF PENSIONS

The biggest threats to financial security in retirement are the drastic decline in company-supported pension plans and the rapid shift in pension plans from defined-benefit plans to defined-contribution plans. Both trends will result in millions of American workers not having the money needed to support themselves as they grow older, according to many experts and several recent studies (Vise 1993). Both of these trends are the latest example of American business transferring financial risks and costs to their employees.

> For decades, thousands of American companies provided employees with pensions. But in the last several years, large firms have embraced savings plans that rely heavily on voluntary employee contributions. In addition, most small and mid-size companies—which have created most of the new jobs in recent years—have abandoned pension plans, opting instead for savings plans or no retirement benefits at all (Vise 1993).

Writing in *Modern Maturity*, Linda Stern (1993) called the shift from defined-benefit to defined-contribution plans perhaps the biggest change in the area of retirement in recent years. In a defined-benefit pension plan, the employer saves and invests for the workers, guaranteeing a certain level of benefits in retirement. In a defined-contribution plan, such as a 401(K) plan, the employer offers a choice of investments for pre-tax dollars, and may or may not match a portion of the employee's contributions to maximize growth. Defined-contribution plans in 1993 made up some 80 percent of the qualified private-sector plans according to the Employee Benefit Research Institute.

The major problem with the defined-contribution plans is that many workers do not choose to participate in them, leaving themselves very vulnerable financially in their later years. "This trend away from pensions is going to dramatically increase the number of older Americans who cannot make ends meet in retirement," said Karen Ferguson, director of the Pension Rights Center in Washington, D.C. (Vise 1993: 16). A Securities and Exchange Commission member has noted that many employees, when choosing between saving for retirement or buying a new car, paying doctor bills, or vacation expense, ignore their contributions to their pension plans. This will result in major problems as the baby boomers begin to reach retirement age (Vise 1993).

The new approach to pensions, the 401(K) approach, is not necessarily bad if employees systematically invest part of their income in retirement accounts and do not withdraw from them. This approach, in fact, has some beneficial aspects such as higher-paying investments and portability (being able to shift monies for retirement when an employee changes jobs). But at Apple Computer, Inc., for example, where more than 90 percent of the employees participated in a 401(K) plan, many withdrew money to pay for homes and other items during their working years (Vise 1993). Taking funds out of the retirement account of a worker can be very damaging. If, for example, a worker withdraws $5,000 from their defined-contribution account and has some 20 years to work until retirement, the worker loses $23,305 in compounded earnings at 8-percent interest for those 20 years (Stern 1993).

A major problem associated with the defined-contribution plans is where to invest the funds. Even if Americans learn how to save, it is another matter to know where and how to invest. As a Securities and Exchange Commission member said, "Taking assets out of the hands of professional money managers and putting them into the hands of individuals almost ensures people are not going to have enough money to retire on" (Vise 1993: A10).

IMPACT OF PENSION CHANGES ON FUTURE RETIREES

Some experts believe that right now America is experiencing the "golden age of the golden years" in pensions (Weinstein 1988: 7; U.S. Bureau of the Census 1992: 4–11). They believe that the baby boomers in retirement will be less well off than many of today's retirees. It is contended that the retirees of the future will have less personal savings and fewer benefits, and that more of the burden for financial security will fall on each individual retiree (U.S. Bureau of the Census 1992). A 1993 Bureau of the Census report indicated that 68 percent of workers were covered by employer-provided pension plans in 1991, which was an increase from 66 percent in 1987, not much different from 1984. It is important to note that not every covered worker participated in the pension plans offered by their employers. In 1991, 51 percent of workers participated in pension plans, the same percentage as 1987, but lower than the 55 percent in 1984 (U.S. Bureau of the Census 1993), a reverse of a trend to pension coverage that began in the 1940s. Not all workers choose to join pension plans offered by employers, especially the 401(K) plans which require employee contributions.

This same study also showed how pension coverage of current workers, the retirees of the future, differed by industries as Table 10-3 indicates.

The 1993 Census Bureau study of pensions also indicated that the size of an employee's company had a tremendous impact on whether a worker was covered by a pension. In 1991, firms with more than 1,000 employees had 90-percent pension coverage compared to 23-percent coverage for firms with fewer than twenty-five employees. The level of earnings also had an impact. Employees earning $2,000 or more a month had an 82-percent coverage rate. Workers earning less than $500 a month had a 43-percent coverage rate. In terms of race and ethnic origin, whites and African Americans had the same 68-percent coverage rate, but only 52 percent of workers of Hispanic origin were covered.

TABLE 10-3

PENSION COVERAGE RATES VARY BY INDUSTRY

Percent of wage and salary workers age 25 years and over covered by employer-provided pension plans, by industry: 1991

Industry	Coverage rate
Armed Forces	100%
Public Administration	92%
Professional and Related Services	76%
Mining	75%
Transportation, Communications, and Public Utilities	75%
Manufacturing	74%
Finance, Insurance, and Real Estate	70%
Wholesale Trade	60%
Entertainment and Recreational Services	53%
Construction	50%
Retail Trade	49%
Business and Repair Services	47%
Personal Services	37%
Agriculture, Forestry, and Fisheries	34%

Source: U.S. Bureau of the Census. 1993. Statistical *Preparing for retirement: Who had pension coverage in 1991?*, 2.

The reason why many workers did not participate in a pension plan available to them were also outlined by the Bureau of the Census as illustrated in Figure 10-1.

It is significant that 23 percent of those who did not participate in a pension plan simply chose not to. These Census Bureau data certainly support the comments and projections made by many experts that many future retirees will have major problems making ends meet once they retire. Indeed, the lack of adequate income may force them to work longer or find new employment once they leave the jobs they had. In fact, the definition of the word "retirement" may change. One financial columnist stated, "It used to be a proxy for 'the end of productivity.' Now it's more likely to mean 'the day on which you take your first pension and move on to something new' " (Stern 1993: 52).

PSYCHOLOGICAL IMPACTS OF RETIREMENT

The major focus of this chapter has been on the financial implications of retirement. After all, financial security, or at least a perception of financial security, is what has made retirement possible. However, as it was noted in the earlier part of this chapter, retirement is more than a financial consideration. It is a major life event, especially for people whose identities are tied to their life's work. This has been particularly true for men in the past whose lives have been mostly identified by the jobs they held, the professions they have had, or the work they did. Increasingly, this type

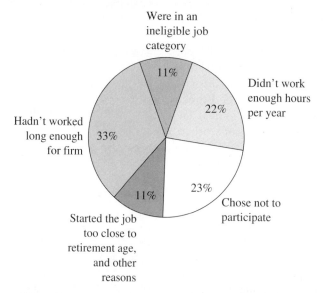

Reasons workers age 25 and older do not participate in employer-sponsored pensions: 1991

Were in an ineligible job category — 11%

Didn't work enough hours per year — 22%

Chose not to participate — 23%

Started the job too close to retirement age, and other reasons — 11%

Hadn't worked long enough for firm — 33%

FIGURE 10-1

Reasons why workers do not participate in pension plans: 1991. (*Source:* U.S. Bureau of the Census Statistical Brief. 1993, April *Preparing for retirement: Who had pension coverage in 1991?* Washington, D.C.: U.S. Department of Commerce, p. 1.)

of personal job identity will be true for women as more and more enter the paid labor force for longer periods of their lives.

Some experts think that the hardest adjustments to retirement may be psychological. "If your whole identity is being chief chemist or factory manager for a major company, you're stripped of that when you retire" said Henry Wallfesh, formerly of Retirement Advisors, Inc. (Beck, Denworth, and Christian 1992: 58). In the middle of a corporate shake-up, Wallfesh himself parted ways from his company at age 54. He found being out of the workplace a cultural shock.

Another couple retired to a quiet California town after leaving work in San Francisco. They thought it would be an ideal retirement. Soon, however, they got bored with nothing really to keep them occupied. They missed being with people, interacting with people. So they both became involved with community activities, he in the politics of the water control board, she in specific community projects (Glaser 1992). This story reflects what is happening across America with the average person retiring at about 62 years of age and many in their fifties. The point here is that although many people enjoy getting away from the demands of a job and a 40-hour work week, complete leisure can be too much of a good thing. Retirees who appear to be the happiest are those who spend two or three days a week learning something new, working part-time, or helping others (Marsh 1991).

Leisure Opportunities

Options for retirees include returning to school, working part-time or temporarily, consulting, teaching, starting a business at home, becoming involved in the creative arts, and volunteering. It is estimated that 22 percent of persons aged 65 and older participate in volunteer activities (AARP 1988). Some retirees volunteer to keep busy or out of a sense of duty. Most participate in volunteer activities because it gives them a sense of satisfaction.

There is a wide range of volunteer programs open to retired persons, including community clubs, religious organizations, museums and libraries, hospitals, political groups, nursing homes, senior centers, and various charitable organizations. A Volunteer Bank at AARP matches available volunteers with local community groups looking for assistance (MacNeil and Teague 1994).

National Volunteer Programs

ACTION is an independent government agency set up to administer all domestic volunteer programs under a single authorizing law (U.S. Senate Special Committee on Aging 1993). It administers a number of programs aimed at persons in a variety of age groups including older people.

Retired Senior Volunteer Program   The Retired Senior Volunteer Program (RSVP) is a program to offer a variety of volunteer opportunities to persons 60 years of age and older. These volunteers serve in a wide variety of areas including youth counseling, literacy enhancement, long-term care, refugee assistance, drug abuse prevention, consumer education, crime prevention, housing rehabilitation, latchkey children in after school programs, and respite care for the elderly (U.S. Senate Special Committee on Aging 1993). These volunteers get no pay but are reimbursed for expenses that result from their services.

Foster Grandparent Program   The Foster Grandparent program (FGP) provides part-time volunteer opportunities for low-income persons 60 years of age and older to help them provide supportive services to children with physical, mental, emotional, or social disabilities. These volunteers are placed with nonprofit agencies such as schools, hospitals, daycare centers, and institutions for people with mental or physical handicaps. These volunteers get paid by the hour, but to qualify they need to be below 125 percent of the federal poverty line (U.S. Senate Special Committee on Aging 1993). In 1986, opportunities to serve in this program were expanded to non-low-income persons who are reimbursed for expenses they have as a result of their volunteer efforts.

Senior Companion Program   The Senior Companion Program (SCP) is designed to provide volunteer opportunities to low-income persons 60 years of age and older to help provide supportive services to "vulnerable, frail older persons" (U.S. Senate Special Committee on Aging 1993: 350). These volunteers help homebound disabled older persons as well as those in institutions and those enrolled in community health programs. As with the Foster Grandparent Program, volunteers are paid if they meet low-income guidelines. Non-low-income persons can participate as well without pay, receiving out-of-pocket expenses associated with their volunteer efforts.

Volunteers in Service to America   Volunteers in Service to America (VISTA) was developed as a "domestic Peace Corps" for volunteers to work full-time in projects that are intended to reduce poverty (U.S. Senate Special Committee on Aging 1993). Principal activities have focused on helping the handicapped, the homeless, the jobless, the hungry, and the illiterate. Other activities have addressed problems associated with substance abuse, promoting economic development, remedial education, and employment counseling. Volunteers commit at least one year of their lives at a subsistence allowance plus some benefits. At least 20 percent of the volunteers are intended to be aged 55 and older.

Benefits of Volunteering

By selecting activities that are interesting, Marsh (1991) claimed that retirement can be the happiest time of life. Staying active provides self-worth; it gives meaning to life. The literature is filled with stories about older people involved with all kinds of activities that keep them involved with life, involved with making a contribution to their communities, their families, their religious institutions, and the lives of others. Although the retirees that are written about are often among the rich and famous, such as captains of industry or TV personalities, a person does not have to be among the elite to be involved and happy in retirement. Tess Canja is a good example. She is 64 and retired. A former journalist, Canja is chair of Florida's Task Force on the Department of Elderly Affairs, State Director of Florida's AARP, and active on the state's Long-Term Care Ombudsman Council. She is one of more than 400,000 members active in AARP-sponsored volunteer programs. The AARP maintains a Volunteer Talent Bank which matches members with positions in AARP programs as well as twelve national and international organizations (Glascheen 1991).

The possibilities for volunteering on the part of older people are endless. Matching talents and interests to needs is the key. Needs exist everywhere in society just waiting to be addressed by people with the time, interest, and ability.

MARRIAGE AND RETIREMENT

Marriage and retirement can be a tricky combination. Of course, this depends on the couple. Studies have indicated that about one in five first marriages lasts for 50 years (Springer 1992). People who achieve 50 years of marriage are double survivors, according to Tim Brubaker, director of Miami (Ohio) University's family and children's studies. "They've lived long and stayed married long" (Springer 1992: 2). Although retirement can be a crisis point for marriages because there is a big adjustment to the two spouses spending so much time together, Brubaker's research indicated that the retirement years can be among the most rewarding years of a marriage, right up there with the newlywed years. The most stressful years are generally regarded to be the child-rearing years.

ARE RETIRED PEOPLE HAPPY?

The question needs to be asked, Are retired people happy? Do they find meaning in life away from their life's work? A number of studies have indicated that a high percentage of older people were relatively satisfied with their lives after they retired. These studies covered the past two decades and also indicate that those retired persons who are not happy with their lives often perceive themselves to be in poor health and or lacking in income. Each condition can easily lead to dissatisfaction with life circumstances. Combining them—poor health and inadequate income—can obviously lead to major unhappiness, but these persons are a small minority of retired people. A Louis Harris and Associates poll done for the National Council on Aging indicated that 90 percent of retired persons felt they made the right decision to retire when they did. Six percent felt they retired too early, 1 percent thought they retired too late, and 3 percent were not sure (Schulz 1992). Another report pointed out that the reason so many older workers are happy in retirement is that they are able to leave jobs that are not too desirable. Even though this report was made in 1983, it is applicable to today's world of work.

> Many if not most newly retired persons welcome the opportunity to slow down. . . . It is well to remember that many jobs are not intrinsically satisfying, they do not enhance feelings of self-worth, encourage autonomy, or permit the exercise of independent judgement. Many jobs—in factories, mines, and some types of institutions—are actually harmful. . . . Retirement can be a rewarding experience for what it does *not* entail (Foner and Schwab 1983, in Schulz 1992: 91).

As these studies on retirement satisfaction indicate, the essential ingredient is financial—the ability to retire with some financial security—which has been a major emphasis of this chapter and a major worry for future retirees.

SUMMARY

Retirement as an institution is a phenomenon of the twentieth century. Following World War II and the advent of Social Security and pensions,

retirement and even early retirement became a goal and a reality for millions of U.S. workers. There can be financial traps in early retirement, including running out of money as people continue to live longer and longer with ongoing inflation. Also, many people in the early retirement ages still have financial obligations such as home mortgages, support for young adult children, and support for aging parents.

Many experts believe that the trend toward early retirement is passing. Some indicate that this trend peaked in 1988 and that the trend is now to continue to work. Martin Sicker of the American Association of Retired Persons has predicted that the 55-year-old retiree who can maintain his or her preretirement standard of living will be rare indeed. Threats to retirement financial security include underfunded pensions, inadequately funded Pensions Benefit Guarantee Corporation, and diminishing healthcare benefits.

One of the major changes that has occurred in regards to pensions is the shift from defined-benefit plans to defined-contribution plans. In the defined-benefit plans, the employer puts aside funds for an employee's retirement income, specific amounts usually depending on length of service and level of income while working. In the defined-contribution plans, the employee can invest a portion of his or her income, tax free, in an investment program to be used for retirement income. Often referred to as 401(K) plans, these plans require active participation by employees. Many choose not to participate, jeopardizing their financial security in retirement and indeed, jeopardizing the ability to retire.

The psychological impacts of retirement include the loss of roles and the loss of identity for many persons. However, once retired, people can achieve great life satisfaction through the variety of activities available to them. Research on this issue indicates that the vast majority of people are happy in retirement, but financial security, or at least a perception of financial security, is a key element of successful retirement.

REFERENCES

Achenbaum, W.A. 1994. U.S. Retirement in Historical Context. In Monk, A. (ed.), *The Columbia Retirement Handbook*. New York: Columbia University Press, p. 22.

Advokat, S. 1993. Get the Facts on Early Retirement Before It's Too Late. *Detroit Free Press* (March 18): 3F.

American Association of Retired Persons. 1988. *Attitudes of Americans Over 45 Years of Age on Volunteerism*. Washington, DC: AARP.

Anderson, K.H., and Burkhauser, R.V. 1985. The Retirement-Health Nexus: A New Measure of an Old Puzzle. *Journal of Human Resources*, 20(3): 315–330.

Atchley, R.C. 1991. *Social Theories in Aging*. Belmont, CA: Wadsworth Publishing.

Beck, M., Denworth, L., and Christian, N. 1992. Finding Work after 50. *Newsweek* (March 16): 58.

Burtless, G. 1987. Occupational Effect on the Health and Work Capacity of Older Men. In Burtless, G. (ed.), *Work Health and Income Among the Elderly*. Washington, DC: Brookings Institution.

Clark, R.L. 1994. The Decision to Retire: Economic Factors and Population Trends. In Monk, A. (ed.), *The Columbia Retirement Handbook*. New York: Columbia University Press.

Clark, R.L., Johnson, T., and McDermed, A.A. 1980. Approaching Retirement. *Social Security Bulletin*, 43(4): 3–16.

Cockerham, W.C. 1991. *This Aging Society*. Englewood Cliffs, NJ: Prentice Hall.

Cooper, J.W. 1994. Getting Ready to Retire: Preretirement Planning Programs. In Monk, A. (ed.), *The Columbia Retirement Handbook*. New York: Columbia University Press.

Dennis, H. 1994. The Decision to Retire: Individual Considerations and Determinations. In Monk, A. (ed.), *The Columbia Retirement Handbook*. New York: Columbia University Press.

Deets, H. 1993. Public Retiree Pensions Need to Be Protected. *NRTA Bulletin*, 34(6): 3.

Ekerdt, D.J. 1986. The Busy Ethic: Moral Continuity Between Work and Retirement. *Gerontologist*, 26(3): 239–244.

Foner, A., and Schwab, K. 1983. Retirement in a Changing Society. In Mitilda White Wiley, Beth B. Hess, and K. Bonds (eds.), *Aging in Society: Selected Reviews of Recent Research*. Hillsdale, NJ: Lawrence Erlbaum Associates.

Glasheen, L. 1991. It Makes Me Feel 9 Feet Tall. *NRTA Bulletin*, 32(6): 8–9.

Glaser, V. 1992. Meaningful Activities Can Help Make Retirement More Rewarding. In *Detroit Free Press* (January 14): 36. *Maturity News Service*.

Hunter, W.W. 1968. *Preparation for Retirement*. Ann Arbor, MI: Institute of Gerontology, The University of Michigan—Wayne State University.

Karp, D.A. 1989. The Social Construction of Retirement Among Professionals 50–60 Years Old. *Gerontologist*, 29(6): 750–760.

Kelly, J.R. 1994. Retirement and Leisure. In Monk, A. (ed.), *The Columbia Retirement Handbook*. New York: Columbia University Press.

Kochanek, M.A., and Hudson, B. L. 1994. Advance Report of Final Mortality Statistics, 1992. *Monthly Vital Statistics Report*, (December 8) 43(6): Supplement. Hyattsville, MD: National Center for Health Statistics, 1–76.

Lewis, R. 1992. Early Out: All at Once the Party's Over. *NRTA Bulletin*, 33(6): 2, 13. Washington, DC: AARP.

Lewis, R. 1993. Public Retirees Under Siege. *NRTA Bulletin*, 34(6): 1, 13.

MacNeil, R.D., and Teague, M.L. 1994. Leisure Opportunities, Leisure Resources. In Monk, A. (ed.), *The Columbia Retirement Handbook*. New York: Columbia University Press.

Marsh, D.L. 1991. Retirement Careers: Combining the Best of Work and Leisure. Charlotte, VT: Williamson.

Matthews, A.M., and Brown, D. 1987. Retirement as a Crucial Life Event: The Differential Experiences of Women and Men. *Research in Aging*, 9(4): 548–551.

Mayer, M.P. 1993. Pensions: The Naked Truth. *Modern Maturity* (February/March): 40–44.

McCluskey, N.G. 1989. Retirement and the Contemporary Family. *Journal of Psychotherapy and the Family*. 5(1–2): 211–224.

Mitchel, D.S., Levine, P. B., and Dozzebon, S. 1988. Retirement Differences by Industry and Occupation. *Gerontologist*, 28(4): 545–551.

Monk, A. 1994. Retirement and Aging: An Introduction to the Columbia Retirement Handbook. In Monk, A. (ed.), *The Columbia Retirement Handbook*. New York: Columbia University Press.

NRTA Bulletin. 1990. A Glimpse of the 90s. 31(2): 10.

Quinn, J.B. 1992. What You'll Need to Retire Early. *Detroit Free Press*, (June 25): 10F.

Rix, S.E. 1994. Retirement and the American Woman. In Monk, A., (ed.), *The Columbia Retirement Handbook*. New York: Columbia University Press, p. 433.

Sammartino, F.J. 1987. The Effect of Health on Retirement. *Social Security Bulletin*, (February): 50: 31–47.

Schulz, J.H. 1992. *The Economics of Aging*, (5th Ed.). New York: Auburn House.

Springer, I. 1992. Staying in Step . . . Over Time: A Combination of Magic and Old-Fashioned Hard Work. *NRTA Bulletin*, 33: 2, 9.

Stern, L. 1993. Nothing Ventured. *Modern Maturity*. (January): 52–54, 82–83.

Taft, A. 1991. Thinking of Retiring? Women Find They Have to Think Again. *Detroit Free Press* (September 3): 3E.

U.S. Bureau of the Census. *Sixty-Five Plus in America*. Current Population Reports Special Studies. 1992. Washington, DC: U.S. Government Printing Office.

U.S. Bureau of the Census. 1993. *Preparing for Retirement: Who Had Pension Coverage in 1991*. Statistical Brief. Washington DC: U.S. Department of Commerce.

U.S. News and World Report. 1993. Retiree's Lament: Broken Vows. (March 15): 14.

U.S. Senate Special Committee on Aging. 1992. *Developments in Aging: 1991. Age Discrimination in the Workplace: A Continuing Problem for Older Workers*. Washington, DC: U.S. Government Printing Office.

U.S. Senate Special Committee on Aging. 1993. *Developments in Aging: 1992*. Washington, DC: U.S. Government Printing Office.

Vinick, B.H., and Ekerdt, K.J. 1989. Retirement and the Family. *Generations*. (Spring): 53–56.

Vise, D.K. 1993. Demise of Pensions Leaves Many Lacking Enough Retirement Funds. In *The Grand Rapids Press*, (May 16): 16. *The Washington Post*.

Weatherington, D. 1990. A Promise Not Kept. *Modern Maturity*, (June/July): 30–38.

Weinstein, M.H. 1988. The Changing Picture in Retiree Economics. *Statistical Bulletin, Metropolitan Life Insurance*, (July–September), 69(3): 7.

THE LIVING ARRANGEMENTS OF OLDER PEOPLE

CHAPTER 11

Living Environments
of Older People

Jane and Pete: Ending Up Isolated?

Jane and Pete moved to the suburbs of their medium-sized eastern city in 1954, when Pete got a promotion to sales manager and their three children were two, four, and seven years old. The American dream of their own home in a new area with space for the kids and new schools was a goal they realized along with millions of other Americans in the 1950s and 1960s. Life, it turned out, was not paradise in the suburbs, but compared to many other settings, it was pretty good. But as they got older and the children moved away, Jane and Pete thought it might be good to try a new way of life after Pete retired. They had enough money from the sale of their house to buy a mobile home in Florida and a small cottage on a lake in the northern, rural part of their state.

This was great living as some of their friends moved to the same area of Florida for the winter months. In the spring they moved up north to their cottage. This went well until they were in their early eighties. All of their friends had died or were too ill to go back to Florida. Pete could no longer drive very well to get to the bank or store. They gave up trying to go to church. It was too hard to get to and besides, they didn't know many people anymore. Up north at their cottage, things got pretty tough, too.

Pete had a heart attack one summer, and he was 35 miles from the nearest hospital. The adult children were busy with their own lives and lived in different cities; the closest lived 40 miles away. After his hospitalization, Pete needed a range of services, some of which were not available in their rural area. When their neighbor was gone, there was no one to get their groceries. Jane felt isolated and helpless. Like so many of her generation, she had let Pete do all the driving. Their kids, helpful and caring, also felt helpless so far away.

Ellen: Where Will She Go?

Ellen had never married. She had a fine education and devoted herself to her profession of social work. She began working in the 1930s and cial work. She began working in the 1930s and

for a time was paid in scrip (IOUs from her employer) because of a budget crunch. Her salary was never large; she worked at a time of relatively low wages in an area of the country that was not too prosperous. Ellen lived frugally and helped her brother send his three children through college.

In 1968, Ellen retired at the age of 65. She had lived in apartments ever since graduation from college, and had moved only twice in all those years. Now her apartment building was being torn down as part of a new shopping center development. Where can Ellen move? What kind of living facility can she afford? The savings she accumulated are now quite modest, given the ongoing inflation since her retirement. The income she earns on this money has decreased dramatically with falling interest rates. In addition, Ellen's income from her pension and Social Security is very small because both are based on her prior wages which were always rather meager, particularly by today's standards. Does Ellen have to move to substandard housing in a deteriorating neighborhood?

WHERE DO OLDER PEOPLE LIVE?

This chapter begins a unit on the living environments of older people. Where do older people live? What is the importance of living environments to older people? What are the factors that directly influence the satisfaction or happiness of older people in their living environments? What conditions make them unhappy or unable to function adequately in particular living arrangements? Where can older people live? What are their options? Finally, we will look at the progression of dependent living environments from retirement communities to nursing homes.

This chapter begins by examining the importance of living environments to older people. Then an overview of where older people live in America, using the 1990 census data, is presented. What does it mean for older people to live in urban or rural America? What are some of the implications of living in the suburbs as a person continues to grow older? These types of questions have important implications for older persons as well as for people who work with them in social agencies, health services, religious organizations, and businesses. They also have real implications for planners and policy makers on all levels in the public and private sectors.

This chapter concludes by examining some of the major factors of the living arrangements that directly affect how older people are able to function. These factors affect the satisfaction and happiness of older people as well as their ability to carry on independent lives. What are the things about living environments that affect the ability of older people to survive with dignity and independence? What can be done to improve these conditions? What can people who work with older persons do to assist them in coping with some of these important factors? These factors will be looked at and some of the current research and programs that address them will be cited.

IMPORTANCE OF LIVING ENVIRONMENTS TO OLDER PEOPLE

Where a person lives has a great impact on the quality of his or her life. The type and condition of a person's living unit and the general characteristics of the neighborhood make up a person's living environment. Until relatively recent times, a person's environment was not a very important consideration in the study of the social sciences (Howell 1980; Lawton 1983, 1985). More recent research has shown the vital importance an older person's living condition has on his or her overall well-being, including physical and psychological health. It also relates to an older person's ability to interact and relate to other people. In fact, according to the 1971 White House Conference on Aging, except for an older person's spouse, his or her living arrangement is probably the single most important aspect of daily life.

According to a recent publication of the American Association for Retired Persons focus-

ing on the needs and preferences of older people in housing arrangements, appropriate housing for America's exploding older population has become a critical issue. This publication stated:

> Unfortunately, the connection between the growth in numbers of older Americans and their special housing needs has been woefully ignored. How older Americans are housed now and in the future will impact upon the long-term care policies, health and housing industries, neighborhood and community practices, and family relationship" (American Association of Retired Persons 1990: 4).

Aging in Place

It is generally agreed that living environments are vitally important to life satisfaction. This is particularly true for older people, because they spend so much of their time in and around their homes. Most no longer go off to work any more, at least on a regular basis. Many are limited in their ability to get in their cars and go away for trips. As people continue to age, many are even limited in their ability to get to the grocery store, the regional mall, their place of worship, or the doctor. As people continue to "age in place"—to get older in the places they have been living—they find themselves more and more confined to their immediate living environments.

Availability of Services

The living environments of older persons include not only the housing units in which they live, but other aspects, such as the availability of shopping facilities, medical services, transportation, and access to relatives and friends. Good transportation and access to relatives and friends can be more important than the quality of the living unit itself. For an older person who does not drive, a home, apartment, or other type of living unit may become a virtual prison if transportation is not readily available. Accessibility to relatives and friends includes the availability of transportation. In America's mobile society with its fragmented family units, many older persons find themselves hundreds or even thousands of miles from children, grandchildren, and friends. All of these factors have a great influence on the quality of life for older persons in our society.

This chapter focuses on where and under what conditions older people live. Because where older people live is so important to their happiness, their sense of well-being, their ability to feel secure, their ability to feel that they are still somehow in charge of their own lives, and their ability to relate to others, especially "significant others" in their lives, it is important to look at some of the major factors that contribute to their overall happiness in their living environments.

METROPOLITAN AREAS, CENTRAL CITIES, SUBURBS, RURAL AREAS

According to the 1990 census, most older persons in America (74 percent) live in metropolitan areas consisting of central cities and suburban areas around the central cities. (U.S. Bureau of the Census 1991). The others live in small towns and rural areas. Of those in the metropolitan areas, 60 percent live in the suburbs. This continues a trend that began in 1980 when, for the first time, older persons in the suburbs outnumbered those in the central cities (10.1 million to 8.1 million) (U.S. Senate 1991a). The 1990 census shows suburban older people outnumbering those in the central cities 13.14 million to 9.07 million (U.S. Bureau of the Census 1991). The suburbanization of America became a major phenomenon in the 1950s. At that time younger families moved to the suburbs for a variety of reasons: to live and raise their children in "ideal" conditions, thus "escaping" crime, pollution, congested traffic, and deteriorating housing. Left behind were lower-income persons, including many minorities, ethnics in ethnically oriented neighborhoods, and older persons who had purchased their homes before the suburbanization movement. These older persons tended to stay put in the houses in which they had raised their families, felt comfortable, and had memories and community ties. Prior to 1980, we saw the suburbs exploding with younger families,

with most older urban people remaining in the old family homestead in the central cities. Currently this original suburban population is aging in place, in areas of the suburbs that are getting older, and experiencing most of the problems once thought confined to the inner city. Those types of suburban areas typically have more rental housing, lower average-income levels, and higher population densities (U.S. Senate 1991a). Looking at where our older residents live, we see many of our oldest old (85 years and older) persons remaining in central areas of our metropolitan areas. Many of these persons move only when they are forced to by failing health and strength, and then usually to some form of congregate living situation such as a retirement or nursing home. Often these folks have few if any alternatives to improving their living situations. As observed in chapter 8, the oldest old among us are very vulnerable to poverty brought on by an expanding economy with continuing inflation. After living on fixed incomes that were based on earnings and wages of 20 or more years ago, many of the oldest old are economically vulnerable.

Older Suburban Areas

In the older suburban areas, where the younger old persons (65 to 75 years of age) now form the majority of older persons in America, the problems of aging in place are just emerging. These problems will become the focus of aging in America as they apply to housing in the near future.

The American suburb was built around the automobile—its widespread ownership and use. The automobile revolutionized how Americans live, work, and play. Workplaces, shopping centers, recreational facilities, and many houses of worship are all built around the use of the automobile. As people grow older, physical changes occur that affect their ability to perform certain tasks, including driving an automobile. For most people these changes are very gradual and hardly noticed at first. However, they are real and in time will affect people who are dependent on the use of automobiles.

What makes this situation worse is that public mass transportation is minimal or nonexistent in most American suburbs. Much of what is available is geared toward moving suburbanites to central city business and financial districts. As the majority of older people now live in suburban settings in America, advocates for the elderly are calling for ways to help them get to stores, doctors' offices, houses of worship, and other services when driving becomes difficult, particularly in the hours of darkness and on congested freeways and crowded streets.

The problems associated with getting around the suburban areas are not as evident now as they will be in the future, because many older people in the suburbs are in the young-old category (aged 65 to 75) and have not yet experienced the range of limitations of older-aged persons (75 years and older). However, it is important to become aware of these problems now and plan for them before so many of the older suburban population becomes "trapped" and isolated in their living units, unable to get to needed services. This was recognized in 1991 by the U.S. Senate Special Committee on Aging:

> The dispersion of older persons over a suburban landscape poses a challenge for community planners who have specialized in providing services to younger, more mobile dwellers. Transportation to and from service providers is a critical need. Institutions that serve the needs of elderly persons such as hospitals, senior centers, and convenience stores, must be designed with supportive transportation services in mind. In addition, service providers must provide transportation services for their elderly clients. Primary transportation systems or mass transit must ensure accessibility from all perimeters of the suburban community to adequately serve the dispersed elderly population. (U.S. Senate Special Committee on Aging 1991b: 393.)

The problem of older people living in the suburbs will become even more important in the future as the suburban elderly population is expected to continue to increase at an even faster pace in the future as a result of the large number of the "pre-elderly" (ages 50 to 64) currently living in the suburbs (U.S. Senate Special Committee on Aging 1991b).

Aging in Place: Kay and Jim

Like the suburban couple featured in the beginning of this chapter, Kay and Jim moved to the suburbs to buy a home away from the congestion of the central city but still close to Jim's work in the city. The commute to work was not too bad, 20 to 30 minutes, depending on the traffic. Like so many people in the late 1950s, Kay and Jim wanted to get away from all the problems of the central city, have more space for the kids, have access to newer schools, and live the American dream as it was developing after World War II. But like so many others, they continued to live in the same home even after the children grew up and left home. Forty years later Jim is now retired and wondering what will happen to Kay and him as newer suburbs continue to be built farther and farther from the central city. Most of the problems of the city have spread to Kay's and Jim's suburb, which now has more rental units compared to owner-occupied units and streets and freeways that have become more and more crowded. What will happen to Kay and Jim as they continue to "age in place" in their older suburban area? Will they stay in their old house or will they move? If they were inclined to move, where would they move? These are the realities facing millions of older people who occupy the older suburban areas of America. There are no easy answers to these questions, because finances have such a major impact on the lives of older people, particularly in their housing decisions.

Small-Town Living

According to the 1990 census, only about 5 percent of older persons live in small communities (less than 2,500 residents), reflecting the long-term trend toward urbanization (including suburbanization) in America. Research has found that older persons in small towns have fewer services, lower income, and poorer health than older persons who live in metropolitan areas (Lawton 1980). However, older persons in small towns tend to interact more with friends and neighbors—with younger people, and with persons their same age—than do their counterparts in metropolitan areas. For many older persons, small towns are a much easier place in which to live. Generally, things move slower, including traffic. Points of interest as well as other services (the store, the house of worship, the bank, the post office) are closer. Change is usually less pronounced, and relatives, friends, and neighbors are not likely to move often. Knowing more people around town gives older people a sense of security. If they are ill, a neighbor, friend, or even a store owner or manager, will deliver food. Knowing where everything is in a small town and being able to get around are great comforts. However, services to deal with crises or prolonged-illness situations are limited. With the closing or threatened closing of many rural hospitals, this is particularly true of emergency medical care, a real crisis for many people in rural and small-town America.

It is important for people who deal with older persons in small towns and rural areas to make sure they are able to meet their needs such as shopping and doctor's appointments. Ways can be devised to meet these needs while maintaining the dignity and self-worth of older persons. For example, organized assistance programs can be developed that enlist the youth of a club or religious institution to do chores for older persons, allowing them to pay for services (modest payments) so they do not feel they are charity cases. Exchanging services can be a creative way to provide direct in-home services and allow older persons to stay in charge of their own lives. Instead of direct payment for the services, older people may provide other services such as arts and craft products, tutoring, or child care. The idea here is to provide needed services in helping older people both maintain their own homes and retain their independence and dignity.

TRANSPORTATION AND OLDER PEOPLE

Transportation is a major problem facing older people who live in the suburbs, small towns, and rural areas. In 1984, transportation was cited as one of the major problems facing rural older persons by the Senate Special Committee on Aging. According to their report:

> An estimated 7 million to 9 million rural elderly lack adequate transportation, and as a result, are severely limited in their ability to reach needed services. Lack of transportation for the rural elderly stems from several factors. First the dispersion of rural populations over relatively large areas complicated the design of a cost effective, efficient public transit system. In addition, the incomes of the rural elderly generally are insufficient to afford the high fares necessary to support a rural transit system (U.S. Senate Special Committee on Aging 1991: 391).

The report went on to state that the lack of access to transportation in rural areas is a major factor that leads to the underutilization of specific programs designed for older persons such as congregate meal programs, adult education, and health promotion activities.

A hearing by the U.S. Select Committee on Aging of the House of Representatives in January, (1991), revealed that almost one-half of the rural communities in the United States do not have a public transit system and that nearly 60 percent of the older persons who live in rural areas are not licensed to drive. The report went on to point out that the trend in many areas of the nation is toward a decrease in public transportation. The same report pointed out that Title III of the Older Americans Act is a major source of funding for transportation for the elderly in the United States. In fact, transportation is the third largest expenditure of Area Agencies on Aging (AAAs) of Title III funds, just behind congregate and home-delivered meals. In addition, AAAs are eligible for funds to transport the elderly under Section 16(b)(2) and Section 18 of the Urban Mass Transportation Act of 1964 (UMTA). The same report stated, "While AAAs are the single largest recipients under this program, the funds received only begin to address the transportation needs of the elderly" (U.S. House of Representatives 1991: 58).

In spite of the problems that are identified with living in small towns and rural areas, and in spite of the numbers and percentages of older people who actually live in these areas compared to those who live in metropolitan areas, the 1990 AARP housing survey, which reported on older people sampled in 1986 and in 1989, indicated quite different results in preferences. It can be speculated that these preferences may have some nostalgic overtones, looking back to an earlier time when America was more rural/small-town oriented—an orientation that has persisted in values and ideals (see Figure 11-1).

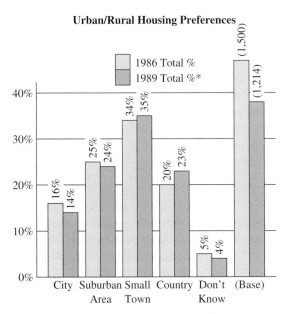

FIGURE 11-1

Asked to choose their preferred type of community if they were to move. *Source: Understanding senior housing for the 1990s.* AARP. 1990, Table 5, p. 15.)

AGE-SEGREGATED OR AGE-INTEGRATED HOUSING

One of the factors that has been debated by gerontologists for decades is the importance of age-segregated versus age-integrated living situations for older persons. Age-segregated means older persons living among persons about their own age. Age-integrated means older persons living among people of all ages, young, middle-aged, and older. This issue is not very important for people living in their own homes in typical neighborhoods across America. Generally, there is a natural mixture of ages in most American neighborhoods. Where the question of age becomes more important is in the development of apartment buildings, mobile home parks, public housing complexes, condominiums, or planned unit developments (PUDs) involving a defined tract of land. The question is, are older people happier in housing that is designed and maintained specifically for people of the same approximate age? Are older people happier living among people who are at least 50, 55, or 60 years of age? Hundreds of studies have been done since the mid-1960s to try to answer this question; this is an important issue for older people, those who work with them, the relatives of older people, city planners, and private developers who are in the business of developing housing alternatives for the rapidly expanding number of aging persons in America.

Mixed Answers from Studies

The results of the studies are mixed. Some studies have indicated greater life satisfaction of people living among residents their own age. Back in the 1960s a study found that people in age-segregated housing environments seemed happier than those who were living in age-integrated housing (Messer 1967). This study also found that those in age-segregated housing had more contact with other people than did those in age-integrated housing. However, another study (Sherman et al. 1968) found that there were some negative aspects to living among only people who were elderly. This study found that only 38 percent of the residents of age-segregated housing reported that they liked living in a place where there were few young people; 34 percent said they did not come in contact with young people often enough. Later research (Winiecke 1973; Fishbein 1975) found that the older people they studied liked age-segregated housing because companionship, a sense of having "buddies," safety, convenience, social activities, and contacts improved living conditions.

Different Choices for Different People

A more recent study indicated that there were no differences in life satisfaction among age-segregated or age-integrated residents, but those in age-segregated housing had longer and more supportive social networks (Poulin 1984). Back in the 1950s Wilma Donahue of the University of Michigan, one of the pioneers in social gerontology, probably put it best when she pointed out that one formula could not be developed for older people as to their "best" living environment because they are a varied group representing people of all tastes, interests, and needs (Donahue 1954). Some people go to bed early and do not want to be kept awake by loud music or parties. Others do not want to be around any situation that might seem threatening to them. They want to live in a controlled environment without disturbing noises or surprises. Still other older people benefit from being around children playing, or babies taking their first steps, or young people strolling hand-in-hand down the street. It is a matter of personal taste and preference.

It is important to understand that where living conditions are close, where there is little space between housing units, and where the residents share common grounds and facilities, preferences for age-segregated housing facilities can become more marked. For example, according to the latest comprehensive housing survey conducted by the American Association for Retired Persons (1990), older people who are willing to move, especially those who are limited by their

health, are more receptive to age-segregated housing than in a survey done three years earlier. Forty percent of the older persons surveyed preferred an age-segregated building compared to 32 percent in the earlier survey. This same survey indicated that 76 percent of the older people surveyed preferred to live in neighborhoods that accommodate people of all ages while only 12 percent preferred to live in an age-segregated neighborhood, with 12 percent undecided (AARP 1990) (see Figure 11-2).

The issue of age-segregated or age-integrated housing is clearly a matter of personal choice. Still in close living arrangements, such as apartment buildings, mobile home parks, and public housing developments, the results of different lifestyles of the young and the old can become annoying to persons as they continue to grow older.

FINANCIAL STATUS AND HOUSING

One of the major factors that affects where and how older people live is their finances, including income and resources. The financial status of older people is discussed in the chapter on economic survival, looking at who is poor or near poor among the old. This section briefly examines what an older person's financial status means to his or her living arrangement.

As with other segments of the population, an older person's financial status has a direct relationship to his or her ability to live in a housing unit that adequately meets the needs of daily living. For some, this may mean upgrading and remodeling existing single-family homes to adapt them to the changing needs of older people, including such things as bathroom and washing facilities on the ground floor, new insulation for warmth in the winter or cooling in the summer, and adequate lighting to accommodate vision limitations. For others, it may mean the ability to move to a new neighborhood when essential services leave the old neighborhood or when the neighborhood becomes less safe. For still others, financial resources may mean the ability to leave their old

Neighborhood Preference

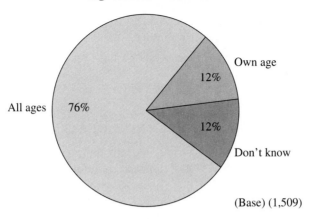

Apartment Building Preference

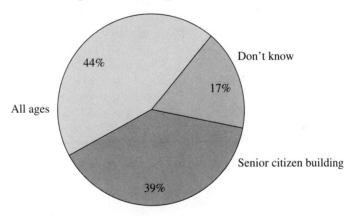

FIGURE 11-2
Preference of age-segregated or age-integrated neighborhoods and apartment buildings. (*Source: Understanding senior housing for the 1990s.* AARP. Table 9, p. 31.)

home location to move to a retirement area in another section of their state or the nation. Included in these are the "snowbirds" who migrate to warmer climates upon retirement. For others, as they continue to age, it may mean moving to some form of congregate living arrangement when they need additional support services on a daily basis.

For many older people, finances are a matter of survival in housing. Keeping a roof over their

heads becomes a major struggle. Some do not win that struggle; they join the ranks of the homeless. Of the 93.3 million households in the United States in 1990, 20.2 million (22 percent) were headed by people age 65 and older (U.S. Senate Special Committee on Aging 1991a). According to this report, older people form a higher percentage of householders than the rest of the population because their average household is smaller. The same report went on to say that although housing may appear to be an asset for most older people because so many live in their own homes, it can actually represent a serious burden for others. Obviously, for many older people who own their own homes and do not have to pay monthly mortgage or rental payments, their homes can represent an asset. In addition, some older people can sell their homes at a handsome profit and use the money to finance other forms of living arrangements. However, for many others, the cost of utilities, real estate taxes, insurance, repair, and maintenance can be burdensome (U.S. Senate Special Committee on Aging 1991a). Older renters can quickly be priced out of the housing market. According to a recent General Accounting Office report:

> Despite the fact that so many poor elderly households own their own homes, they nevertheless incur substantial housing-related costs relative to their incomes. In fact, according to the Annual Housing Survey, half of all poor elderly homeowners spent at least 46 percent of their income on housing in 1989. Housing costs as a percentage of income are generally high for poor homeowners— even those who no longer pay a mortgage—apparently because real estate taxes, the cost of utilities, and insurance are a burden on their low incomes (U.S. General Accounting Office 1992: 29).

The GAO report went on to state that in addition to these normal costs of maintaining a home, poorer elderly homeowners can look forward to difficulties in trying to rehabilitate their older homes to make them functional for their needs as well as acquire needed supportive devices such as handrails in bathrooms. Few federal programs exist to help these older people adapt their homes to their changing needs. What programs do exist are mostly geared toward the rural population and are relatively modest.

Unfortunately, poor elderly renters also spend a large percentage of their low incomes on housing. Although some live in public housing or receive rental assistance, half of all poor elderly renters spent about 46 percent of their income on housing in 1989 (U.S. GAO 1992). To make matters worse for the poor and near-poor elderly in America, appropriations for federally subsidized elderly housing that is designed to remedy the housing plight of low-income older people peaked some 20 years ago, despite the continued demand for such assistance (U.S. GAO 1992).

HOMELESSNESS AND THE ELDERLY

High rents compared to incomes, deteriorating housing conditions, and an increasing shortage of housing options are problems which are affecting a substantial number of older people according to a 1991 book which addressed the problem of homelessness among the elderly (Keigher 1991). According to Sharon Keigher and Faith Pratt (1991), "the 1980s saw a startling erosion of America's commitment to the provision of housing for low-income people as a national goal." The authors further stated that the nation's basic housing resources are eroding at a time when the number of older people will continue to grow into the twenty-first century.

Homelessness has grown dramatically in the 1980s and is expected to continue to do so in the future. "Homelessness appears to be increasing at least as fast among the elderly as among younger population groups, and the elderly appear to have unique vulnerabilities to it" (Keigher and Pratt, 1991). According to these authors, the elderly homeless are "poor, alone, and aging in place." They went on to point out that little is really known about new elderly homeless, but homelessness seems to be the result of a decade of:

- The gentrification of housing units in older neighborhoods, which is the revitalization of houses and apartment buildings to original or better condition
- The demolition of low-income housing units
- Federal program cutbacks in constructing low-income housing and in rent subsidy programs
- Changing tax benefits for entrepreneurs to build low-income housing units

• Prepayments and buyouts of federal mortgages on rent-subsidized buildings so that rent-subsidized units are available in decreasing numbers for a population of older people that continues to increase

With little new construction of low-income housing under way or planned, this problem is expected to get worse in the years ahead. This trend is seen in the drastic drop in the amount of money in the assisted-housing category of the Department of Housing and Urban Development (HUD) budget, which went from 25 billion dollars in fiscal year 1981 to 8.9 billion dollars in fiscal year 1990. In real dollars this was an 80 percent reduction (Keigher and Pratt 1991).

LIVING ALONE

One of the most important factors in determining the quality of the living environments of older people is whether they live alone. Obviously some people prefer to live alone at any adult age. Some choose to live alone because of a variety of circumstances at various stages in life. Some people are single by choice and enjoy their freedom and independence as well as their own company. Some people lose a spouse and make the adjustments necessary to live alone. After years of marriage, some people find new independence in their own lives after the death of a spouse or a divorce. However, for many others, living alone is not a preferred choice but the result of circumstances they find difficult to change.

According to recent studies, nearly one-third (30.5 percent) of all older people live alone. Almost half (47 percent) of all people live alone (U.S. Senate 1991a). That trend is expected to continue into the next century. Living alone is a very important consideration in examining the living environments of older people who make up one of the most vulnerable and impoverished segments of the American population. On the average they have lower incomes than older couples, especially if they are women, members of minor-

ity groups, or 85 years of age and older. As people continue to advance in age, their likelihood of living alone increases, especially among women.

> Many elderly people who live alone have chronic health problems that make it difficult for them to remain independent. While family and friends provide a great deal of assistance with daily activities, many frail, older individuals who live alone have no one to help them. Such people either receive no services, or must rely entirely on paid assistance or formal social service programs. The provisions of adequate services and care to the elderly who live alone represents an enormous challenge to our nation's long-term care systems (U.S. Senate 1991a: 208).

Figures 11-3, 11-4, 11-5, 11-6, 11-7, and 11-8 (U.S. Senate 1991a) illustrate the realities and consequences of older people living alone.

Living alone has an impact on the health recovery rates of people who survive heart attacks. As with all studies or general characteristics, all persons do not fall into all projections or generalities. Obviously all older people who live alone are not poor, lonely, in poor health, or have all of the other characteristics that were illustrated by the charts. But it is important for people who work with older persons in any kind of setting to be aware of the conditions to which older people who live alone are prone.

RESIDENTIAL SETTING

Another vital factor in examining the living environments of older people is their surroundings—the setting of their living unit—whether it is in an apartment building, a retirement home, a mobile home park, a nursing home, or any other type of dwelling. The immediate surroundings of individuals in living units have a great impact on the quality of their lives.

An older person's living environment includes not only the living unit he or she occupies, but the surrounding area including access to vital services such as shopping and medical care, and to friends and relatives. This is particularly important for older people who still live independently

Projected Increases in Number of People 65+ Living Alone: 1990–2020

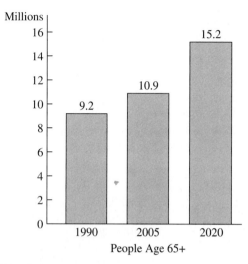

FIGURE 11-3

Projected increase in number of people 65+ living alone: 1990–2020. (*Source:* U.S. Senate Special Committee on Aging. The American Association of Retired Persons, the Federal Council on Aging. 1991. *Aging America: Trends and projections.* Washington, DC: U.S. Department of Health and Human Services, Chart 7-3, p. 212.)

Proportion of Older Peolple Living Alone Increases with Age: 1989

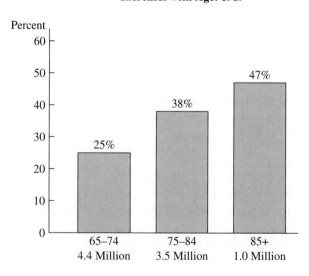

FIGURE 11-4

Proportion of older people living alone increases with age: 1989. (*Source:* U.S. Senate Special Committee on Aging. The American Association of Retired Persons, the Federal Council on Aging, and the U.S. Administration on Aging. 1991. *Aging America: Trends and projections.* Washington, DC: U.S. Department of Health and Human Services, Chart 7-5, p. 214.)

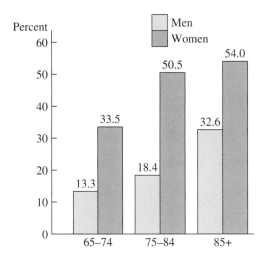

Older People Living Alone, by Age and Sex: 1989

FIGURE 11-5

Older people living alone, by age and sex: 1989. (*Source:* U.S. Senate Special Committee on Aging, the American Association of Retired Persons, the Federal Council on Aging, and the U.S. Administration on Aging, 1991. *Aging America: Trends and projections.* Washington, DC: U.S. Department of Health and Human Services, Chart 7-5, p. 214.)

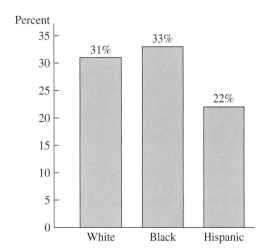

Percent of Elderly People Living Alone, by Race and Hispanic Origin: 1989

FIGURE 11-6

Percent of elderly people living alone, by race and Hispanic origin: 1989. (*Source:* U.S. Senate Special Committee on Aging, the American Association of Retired Persons, the Federal Council on Aging, and the U.S. Administration on Aging. 1991. *Aging America: Trends and projections.* Washington, DC: U.S. Department of Health and Human Services, Chart 7-10, p. 219.

in their own homes, apartments, condominiums, or mobile homes. However, the quality of an older person's surroundings goes beyond the importance of access to services, friends and relatives. It directly relates to the ability of older people to function effectively with some degree of confidence and some degree of security in their environment. This is true with any type of dwelling, from single family homes with total independent living to confinement in nursing facilities.

Many older people do not want to leave their old neighborhoods because they may have friends or family there. They may feel secure in old memories in the area they lived for so many years. Many do not move to a different location because they cannot afford a living unit that better meets their changing needs. Others move because health conditions force them to seek as-

sisted living situations. From changing neighborhoods to changing housing units as the result of moves, many older people feel overwhelmed by not being able to cope with their surroundings, whether they are neighborhoods, retirement homes, or nursing facilities.

SOLVING LIVING ARRANGEMENT PROBLEMS THROUGH MEDIATION

A relatively new movement is developing across much of America that is already offering, and has great potential to offer, services for older people in helping them cope with their surroundings (neighborhoods/environments). It is identified by various labels including "community mediation," "alternative dispute resolution," "reconciliation center," "neighborhood justice center," or just "mediation."

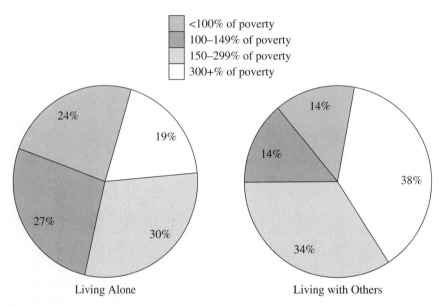

Economic Status of People 65+ Living Alone or with Others: 1990

<100% of poverty
100–149% of poverty
150–299% of poverty
300+% of poverty

Living Alone

Living with Others

FIGURE 11-7

Economic status of people 65+ living alone or with others: 1990. (*Source:* U.S. Senate Special Committee on Aging, the American Association of Retired Persons, the Federal Council on Aging, and the U.S. Administration on Aging, 1991. *Aging America: Trends and Projections.* Washington, DC: U.S. Department of Health and Human Services, Chart 7-8, p. 217.)

The goal is to resolve disputes without going through the formal legal system by coming to a resolution of problems so that all parties to the dispute can live together in peace. Having one party "win" and the other "lose" is not the objective. Reaching a negotiated agreement that reflects the best interests of both parties is always the overriding objective (Hoffman and Wood 1991–92). A "win-win" result to disputes is the goal. Community mediation is being used by older people in some model projects in a wide array of living environments, from neighborhoods with single- and multiple-family homes to nursing facilities.

Mediation in Neighborhoods

In neighborhoods, alternative dispute resolution centers are handling a range of cases that involve older people. Disputes between neighbors over property use, driveways, trash, barking dogs, loud music, noisy parties, lot lines, unruly children, and a number of other issues are being mediated by some 450 mediation centers in communities across the nation. In addition, the American Association of Retired Persons' Standing Committee on Dispute Resolution looks for ways to include mediation in disputes that involve some types of criminal activity. This is particularly useful with neighborhood youth who engage in activities that affect the homes and lives of older people. Community mediation is particularly effective in landlord/tenant disputes. This can involve the older person either as a landlord or as a tenant.

Mediation in Congregate Living Facilities

Mediation can be very beneficial as older people leave traditional neighborhoods and move to

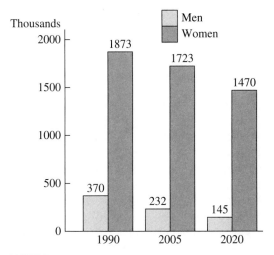

Number of Elderly People Living Alone Below Poverty, by Sex: 1990–2020

FIGURE 11-8

Number of elderly people living alone below poverty, by sex: 1990–2020 (*Source:* U.S. Senate Special Committee on Aging, the American Association of Retired Persons, the Federal Council on Aging, and the U.S. Administration on Aging. 1991. *Aging America: Trends and projections.* Washington, DC: U.S. Department of Health and Human Services, Chart 7-6, p. 215.)

other types of living arrangements. For example, the Dispute Resolution Center in St. Paul, Minnesota, has developed an exciting pilot project to educate residents of senior housing about the benefits of mediation, provide mediation services to the people in these complexes, and recruit and train older persons to become mediators. People moving into senior high-rises or complexes usually have to make many adjustments to high-density living which can lead to conflicts with neighbors, tablemates in dining rooms, or persons using the same facilities in a common setting. These situations often have a profoundly negative effect on residents because this is their neighborhood, their surroundings. Personal conflicts often loom larger to older people who are home most of the day because they no longer work outside the home. When Jennie is assigned to a dining table in a senior housing facility that provides meals with someone who constantly irritates her, this becomes a big issue in her life. When the landlord of Jim's mobile home park continues to raise the rent for lots and imposes restrictions on washing one's car or prohibiting one's grandchildren from staying overnight, to whom can he turn? He knows that he cannot move his mobile home because it is not really mobile any more, and other parks will not take older mobile homes.

Mediation in Assisted Living Facilities

Mediation is also used to resolve disputes that arise in dependent living situations. The National Institute for Dispute Resolution, beginning in 1989, sponsored a program to provide mediation and negotiation training for long-term care ombudsmen, nursing home administrators, and staff (Hoffman and Wood 1991–92). The goal is to help improve the quality of life for nursing-home residents by introducing negotiation and mediation skills to resolve day-to-day recurring problems that affect them, their families, and caregivers. The problems they handle range from unwanted transfers and financial matters to intrafamily disputes. The Nursing Facility Mediation Project, a pilot project in Cincinnati, Ohio, deals with vital nursing-home problems, including unanswered calls for help, cleanliness, food, lost and stolen belongings, visiting hours, and roommate and family disputes.

Other mediation programs focus on problems associated with the home care of elderly people. "My aide frequently shows up late without calling to warn me," and "My client is expecting me to work past the number of hours agreed," are examples of problems that home-care mediation can address effectively. Future efforts in housing/neighborhood mediation will address the issues and problems that arise from the Americans with Disabilities Act (ADA) of 1990, which involves some 43 million Americans, and the Fair Housing Amendments Act. These acts require a range of public and private individuals and organizations to make "reasonable accommodations" to very diverse needs. However, the question is, what is reasonable? How far, for example, does a landlord have to go to meet the needs of a prospective or current tenant with various disabilities? Regulations sometimes add confusion to disputes over individual situations. Mediation can provide a creative way to facilitate the implementation of these specific acts as they apply to housing situations.

Having a mechanism to effectively deal with differences of opinion and conflicts in their living environments gives older people more secure feelings about maintaining a sense of control over their own lives. Having some control in matters pertaining to one's own life is a vital ingredient to self satisfaction and happiness. This is true whether a person lives in a single-family home in a neighborhood, or in any other living situation, from high-rise senior centers to nursing facilities.

CRIME AND FEAR OF CRIME IN LIVING ENVIRONMENTS

Older people react in various ways to the reality and fear of crime in all types of environments. The types of crimes that threaten and harm older people in their homes and surroundings include breaking and entering, armed robbery, purse snatching, destruction of property, and assault.

There has been a common perception that the elderly are victimized by violent crime at a higher rate than the rest of the population (Harris 1975, 1981; Hooyman and Kiyak 1991). Studies have shown that this is not true. A 1988 report indicated that criminal victimization rates for the elderly between 1973 and 1984 had a greater decline than for the rest of the population (Covey and Menard 1988). Even older studies reported that crime against the elderly is lower except for personal larceny with contact (such as purse snatching), which is either equal to or slightly higher for elderly persons (Antunes et al. 1977; Alston 1981). Fear of crime among the elderly is a problem that affects older people more than actual crime victimization (Braungart et al. 1980).

This can lead to a fearful and negative existence. Some people become afraid to leave their homes, and when at home, they can perceive normal sights and sounds as potentially threatening. Another study showed who among the elderly were the most and least likely to be fearful of crime (AARP 1990: Understanding Senior Housing for the 1990s. Washington, DC: 50):

- People with annual incomes of $36,000 a year or more are more likely to feel "very secure" from crime.
- Those who are divorced, separated or never married are somewhat less likely than widowed and married to feel "very secure" from crime.
- Minorities are over three times as likely as whites to feel "not secure at all" from crime.
- Those in retirement communities and buildings for older adults are more likely than those in naturally occurring retirement communities to feel "very secure" from crime.
- People living in rural areas are more likely than those living in non-rural areas to feel "very secure" from crime.
- People who are limited a great deal by their health are over twice as likely as those with no health limitations to feel "not secure at all" from crime.

MOVING AND OLDER PERSONS

One of the most important considerations in examining living environments and older people is the issue of moving—from one type of housing to another, from one geographic area to another, from one living arrangement to another.

For many older people, moving their residence is one of the most traumatic things they can do. Older studies had indicated that when some older persons move against their will, the move not only impaired their health but contributed to their death. This phenomenon was described as "transplantation shock," "transfer trauma," and "relocation stress" (Liberman 1961; Aldrich and Mendkoff 1963; Jashau 1967).

More recent research has indicated that the early studies were flawed and that age, health status, radical as opposed to moderate living arrangement change, as well as personal involvement in the move had not been taken into consideration in the earlier studies (Liberman 1974; Wittels and Botwinick 1974; Schulz and Brenner 1977). When these factors are considered, and when the move promotes independence of living, positive results from the move can occur (Marlowe 1974).

Why Some Older Persons Resist Moving

At this point, the question can be asked, "Why are some older persons opposed to moving when a move could greatly improve their living accommodations?" One reason is money, or the lack of it, as was discussed before. To move from deteriorating housing into a better housing unit costs money, both in the form of higher housing costs and moving expenses. Insufficient funds, real or perceived, is often the cause of older people not wanting to move. Second, some people, young or old, simply resist change, especially a change that affects so much of their lives. Fear of the unknown is a limiting factor for people of all ages, but particularly for the old who no longer have the physical or emotional resources to cope with unknown changing life conditions. Third, relocation is a traumatic event, especially when a person's life centers on his or her place of residence. Relocation means leaving behind the old neighborhood, familiar surroundings, old friends and acquaintances, and neighborhood ties built over the years. Familiar surroundings in old neighborhoods give older persons a sense of stability and security. These losses are mourned by many elderly people both physically and psychologically.

Until relatively recent times, living in older residential areas offered a convenience for many older persons because these areas were close to facilities such as stores, physicians, and dentists. As services of all types continue to move toward the suburbs, many older people are left without them, unless they have access to reliable, cheap transportation.

In evaluating their existing housing situations, most older people refer to distances from medical and shopping facilities as a key factor, followed by distance from relatives, the climate, and assistance with housekeeping and meal preparation. When these factors become more remote and inaccessible, older persons are bound to feel the negative results of isolation in their lives.

Helping Older People Move

Relocating older people involves much more than providing better housing units. It is important to recognize that moving has the potential to threaten the entire world of an older person. Children, spouses, clergy, and agency workers need to be particularly sensitive to the needs of the older person if a move is planned. Hooyman and Kiyak (1991) pointed out that the negative effects of relocation can be reduced by working hard to prepare the older person for a move. This can involve making several visits to the new housing unit or facility, looking at rooms, meeting staff in institutional or congregate living situations, and generally looking around the facility over a period of time. Personal involvement in the move by the older person is the best strategy if time and circumstances permit. Having older persons themselves decide to move, where to move, and when to move is the best approach. Unfortunately, this is not always possible or feasible.

Types of Moves

Moves may be required because of the inadequacy of an older person's present living arrangement, the closing of a retirement home or some type of supportive facility, or the physical or emotional deterioration of the elderly person. In addition, some older people move after they retire to enjoy recreational areas or beneficial climates. Some move to be near their adult children who can interact with them socially and look after them if and when they need assistance.

Those who move upon retirement typically are married couples who want to enjoy the recreation and climate new locations offer (Szinovocz, Ekerdt, and Vinick 1992). The move and the activities surrounding the establishment of a new home in a new location typically become the focus of a couple's life (Cuba 1992). A move to a new location is described by one man who recalled:

> When we came down here for retirement there was no agenda for us, we were for the first time sort of starting over. We wondered why the phone didn't ring . . . and nobody was screaming at us to go to meetings. We were very thankful that we had a house and yard to occupy our energy and our time (Cuba 1992: 216).

The other moves, to be closer to adult children, are often called kin-oriented moves (Gober and Zonn 1983). Some of these moves are made by older people who have become ill or frail. Others are by older people who simply want to be near their adult children to have a role in their lives (Barsby and Cox 1975; Rowles 1983; Litwak and Longino 1987; Speare and Meyer 1988).

Most Older People Do Not Move

Most older people do not move at all. Only 5 percent of older people moved compared to 35 percent of 20- to 24-year-olds and 18 percent of the total population. Indeed, 84 percent of older people indicated on an AARP (1990) survey that they wanted to stay in their own homes and never move. There is evidence that people who migrated to other states upon retirement came back home when they wanted to be closer to family members. This often occurs when they lose friends in the new locations because of death or disability, when their own physical or mental status forces them to lose independence, or when their financial situations make it difficult for them to maintain their living arrangement (AARP 1990).

SUMMARY

Where and under what conditions people live is vital to their overall life satisfaction. This is particularly true for older people. Most of their lives are spent in their dwelling units in the context of their overall living environments. The geographic settings of older people as well as their housing arrangements directly affect the quality of their lives. Metropolitan areas, central cities, suburbs, and rural areas have different effects on the lives of older people.

Different older people have different preferences for age-segregated and age-integrated living environments. The importance of finances on the living environments of older people cannot be minimized. Homelessness among America's elderly has become a major problem.

The reality of living alone influences health, financial status, and the overall quality of life for many older persons, often negatively. The environments (neighborhoods/surroundings) of housing units affect the lives of older people. Conflict resolution as a mechanism to deal with conflicts that arise over housing issues can contribute to a sense of control over one's life. This is particularly important for older people.

An overview of violent crime against the elderly showed that there was less victimization of the elderly than the general population, but that the fear of crime plays an important role in the lives of many older people.

The mobility of older people presents important issues: who is likely to move, what are the reasons to move, and how to make moves better for older people. Most older people want to stay in their own homes and never move. The next chapter will systematically look at the kinds of housing units older people occupy as well as the types of housing options available to them.

REFERENCES

Aldrich, C.K., and Mendkoff, E. 1983. Relocation of the Aged and Disabled: A Mortality Study. *Journal of the American Geriatrics Society*, 11: 185–194.

Alston, L.T. 1986. *Crime and Older Americans*. Springfield, IL: Charles C. Thomas.

American Association of Retired Persons. 1990. *Understanding Senior Housing for the 1990s*. Washington, DC: AARP.

Antunes, G.E., Cook, F., Cook, T., and Skogan, W. 1977. Patterns of Personal Crime Against the Elderly. *Gerontologist*, 17: 321–327.

Barsby, S.L., and Cox, D.R. 1965. *Interstate Migration of the Elderly*. Lexington, MA: D.C. Heath.

Braungart, M.M., Braungart, R.G., and Houer, W.J. 1980. Age, Sex, and Social Factors in Fear of Crime. *Sociological Focus*, 13: 55–66.

Covey, H.C., and Menard, S. 1988. Trends in Elderly Criminal Victimization From 1973 to 1984. *Research on Aging*, 10: 329–341.

Cuba, L. 1992. Family and Retirement in the Context of Elderly Migration. In Szinovacz, M., Ekerdt, D.J., and Vinick, B.H. (eds.), *Families and Retirement*. Newbury Park, CA: Sage Publications.

Donahue, W. 1954. Where and How Older People Wish to Live. In W. Donahue (ed.), *Housing the Aged*. Ann Arbor: University of Michigan Press, pp. 21–24.

Fishbein, G. 1975. Congregate Housing With a Difference. *Geriatrics*, 30(9): 124–128.

Gober, P., and Zonn, L.E. 1983. Kin and Elderly Amenity Migration. *Gerontologist*, 23: 288–294.

Harris, L. 1975. *The Myth and Reality of Aging*. Washington, DC: National Council on Aging.

Harris, L. *Aging in the Eighties: America in Transition*. 1981. Washington, DC: National Council on Aging.

Hoffman, R., and Wood, E.F. 1991. *Mediation: New Path to Problem Solving for Older Americans*. Washington, DC: American Association of Retired Persons.

Hooyman, N.R., and Kiyak, H.A. 1991. *Social Gerontology: A Multidisciplinary Perspective*. 2d Ed. Boston: Allyn and Bacon.

Howell, S.C. 1980. Environments and Aging. In C. Eisdorfer (ed.), *Annual Review of Gerontology and Geriatrics*. New York: Springer, pp. 237–260.

Jashau, K.F. 1967. Individualized Versus Mass Transfer of Nonpsychiatric Geriatric Patients from Mental Hospitals to Nursing Homes With Special Reference to the Death Rate. *Journal of the American Geriatrics Society*, 15: 280–284.

Keigher, S.M., and Pratt F. 1991. Growing Housing Hardship Among the Elderly. In Kieger, S.M. *Housing Risks and Homelessness Among the Urban Elderly*. New York: Haworth Press.

Kieger, S.M. 1991. *Housing Risks and Homelessness Among the Urban Elderly*. New York: Haworth Press.

Lawton, M. 1980. *Environment and Aging*. Monterey, CA: Brooks/Cole.

Lawton, M. 1983. Environment and Other Determinants of Well-Being in Older Persons. *Gerontologist*, 23(4): 349–357.

Lawton, M.P. 1985. Housing and Living Environments of Older People. In R.H. Binstock and E. Shanas (eds.), *Handbook of Aging and Social Sciences*. New York: Van Nostrand Reinhold, pp. 450–478.

Liberman, M. 1961. Relationships of Mortality Rates to Entrance to a Home for the Aged. *Geriatrics*, 16: 515–519.

Lieberman, M. 1974. Relocation Research and Social Policy. *Gerontologist*, 14: 494–501.

Litwak, E., and Longino, C.F., Jr. 1987. The Migratory Patterns of the Elderly: A Developmental Perspective. *The Gerontologist*, 25: 266–272.

Marlowe, R.E. 1974. When They Close the Doors at Modesto. Paper presented at NIMH Conference on Closure of State Hospitals (February). Scottsdale, Arizona.

Messer, M. 1967. The Possibility of an Age-Concentrated Environment Becoming a Normative System. *Gerontologist*, 7: 247–251.

Poulin, J.E. 1984. Age Segregation and the Interpersonal Involvement and Morale of the Age. *Gerontologist*, 24: 266–269.

Rowles, G.D. 1983. Between Worlds: A Relocation Dilemma for the Appalachian Elderly. *International Journal of Aging and Human Development*, 17: 301–314.

Schulz, R., and Brenner, G.F. 1977. Relocation of the Aged: A Review and Theoretical Analysis. *Journal of Gerontology*, 32: 323–333.

Sherman, S.R., Mangum, W.P., Dodds, S., and Wilmer, D.M. 1968. Psychological Effects of Retirement Housing. *Gerontologist*, 8(2): 170–175.

Speare, A., and Meyer, J.W. 1988. Types of Elderly Residential Mobility and Their Determinants. *Journal of Gerontology*, 43: 74–81.

Szinovacz, M., Ekerdt, D.J., and Vinick, B.H., (eds.). 1992. *Families and Retirement*. Newbury Park, CA: Sage Publications.

U.S. Bureau of the Census. 1991. *Poverty in the United States: 1990*. Current Population Reports (Series P-60, No. 175). Washington, DC: U.S. Government Printing Office.

U.S. General Accounting Office. 1992. *American Housing Survey, 1989*. Gaithersburg, MD.

U.S. House of Representatives Select Committee on Aging. 1991. *Transportation in the Nineties: Keeping America's Elderly Moving*. Washington, DC: U.S. Government Printing Office.

U.S. Senate Special Committee on Aging. 1991a. *Aging America: Trends and projections, 1991*. Edition prepared by the Senate Special Committee on Aging, American Association of Retired Persons, the Federal Council on Aging, and the Administration on Aging. HHS Publication, No. (FCOA) 91-28001.

U.S. Senate Special Committee on Aging. 1991b. *Developments on Aging: 1990*, 1. Washington, DC: U.S. Government Printing Office.

Winiecke, L. 1973. The Appeal of Age-Segregated Housing to the Elderly Poor. *Aging and Human Development*, 4(3): 293–306.

Wittels, I., and Botwinick, J. 1974. Survival in Relocation. *Journal of Gerontology*, 36: 440–443.

CHAPTER 12

Housing Options for Older People

John and May: Staying Put

John and May were married in 1927. John was a painting contractor with a business that began to flourish by 1928. Until the birth first their first child, May was in charge of an office for a large band instrument company. Her salary was good for the times. The goal of both John and May was to build a home across from a new park in a new section of the city in which they lived. The Roaring Twenties gave them that opportunity, with their new house complete just before the stock market crash of 1929. With lots of hard work, sacrifice, and worry, they were able to hang onto their house through the Depression. They raised their three children there. Within six blocks were their church, grocery stores, and other stores and services including dentists and a physician. The park across the street had baseball diamonds, a swimming pool, and acres of grass for everyone to enjoy in the summer. In the winter there was a nice skating rink that attracted a lot of young people.

Sixty years later a lot of things have changed. John died in 1981. The children are all grown and two of them have children of their own. May continues to live alone in the house she loves so much, a house filled with her possessions and memories. Her church moved to the suburbs in 1979. Most of the stores six blocks away have changed: The old movie theater only shows triple-X movies. The clothing store is now a massage parlor. Two liquor stores now occupy the old drug store and the old ice cream parlor. The dentist and the physician have moved to newer professional buildings. The park, once the center of outdoor recreation for the whole family, has attracted a large number of drug dealers and users. Police are regularly called to break up fights. May is reluctant to move, even though her children strongly encourage her to do so.

Bill and Mary: Planning Ahead

Bill and Mary were married in 1935. The Great Depression was in full swing, but part-time work and help from their parents saw them through the worst times. Although never rich, Bill and Mary had a good living and were able to buy a house they really liked after Bill got out of the navy in 1946. Bill developed lung cancer in 1975 and died in 1979. By this time both of their children had grown and left home, one a few miles away in the same city, the other 800 miles away on the coast. Following Bill's death, the family got together to discuss Mary's housing options. She didn't like living in her house all alone, especially in the winter. Although she was not old, only 64, she wanted to explore the options open to her if she sold the house. The house was still in good condition for a house of its age, but heating bills began to go up with the price of energy and the house was simply too big for Mary to live in alone. She asked her adult children for their input before making the final decision. Mary decided she would sell the house, invest the proceeds of the sale (the house was all paid for) in a variety of investments including government bonds, and move to a garden apartment in a pleasant area, not too far from her daughter who lived in the same city. The plan was that as she got into her seventies, she and her children would investigate a continuum-of-care facility to which her church contributed. She didn't want to give up her complete independence in her sixties, but she wanted to plan ahead so she would not burden her children as she got older—and she wanted to be free to spend three or four months of the year in Florida where some of her friends spent their winters.

HOUSING OPTIONS FOR OLDER PEOPLE

This chapter deals with the types of housing available to older people. Although they are called "options," in some important aspects they are not really options at all because (1) the vast majority of older persons (84 percent) want to continue to stay in the housing unit they are living in and never move; (2) many older people are not willing to consider other types of living arrangements, even if another type of unit may be more suitable to their needs; and (3) many older people simply cannot afford to move to a different or more appropriate living arrangement. The overwhelming trend in America is to age in place, to continue to grow older in the place one is already are living, regardless of the condition of the dwelling unit, the changing nature of the neighborhood, and the special needs many older people have with the tasks of daily living. The result of this trend is the large number of older people in America trying to cope with daily living while remaining in their single-family home in which they have lived for many years. It is the home in which they raised their families, the homestead that holds the memories of a lifetime, the place that represents "home" and all that means (see Figure 12-1).

HOME OWNERSHIP

Almost 95 percent of all older people in America live in some form of independent household. A majority of older people in independent households live in single-family homes. According to the most recent information, of the 19.5 million households headed by older persons, 75 percent were owners and 25 percent were renters. Of the 75 percent who were homeowners, 86 percent had no mortgages. They were fully paid off. It is important to note that 83 percent of older male householders were homeowners, whereas only 65 percent of older females were (AARP 1990). This is particularly significant, as women dramatically outnumber men in the later decades of life.

Studies over many years have indicated that the single-family homes older people live in are generally older and less adequate than those of the rest of the population. Their size (too big for the older couple or surviving spouse), condition, functional obsolescence, high cost of mainte-

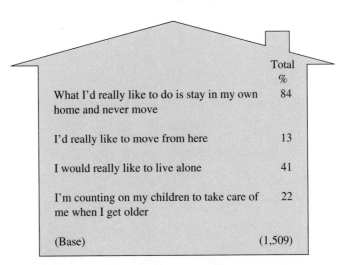

Opinions About Living Situation
(Percent Agreeing)

	Total %
What I'd really like to do is stay in my own home and never move	84
I'd really like to move from here	13
I would really like to live alone	41
I'm counting on my children to take care of me when I get older	22
(Base)	(1,509)

FIGURE 12-1
The vast majority of older persons in America are aging in place. For a variety of reasons, they prefer to stay in their own home and never move. (*Source:* American Association of Retired Persons. 1990. *Understanding senior housing for the 1990s.* Washington, DC: American Association of Retired Persons, Table 15, p. 57.)

nance and utilities, lack of adequate insulation for efficient heating and cooling, deteriorating neighborhoods, and relatively high local property taxes can make an older home a burden for an elderly person. This was clearly indicated in a 1980 Annual Housing Survey, which reported that 40 percent of older homeowners lived in houses built before 1940 compared to 22 percent for the rest of the population (Harris 1981). An American Association of Retired Persons-Administration on Aging (1990) publication indicated that 43 percent of the homes owned in 1987 by older people were built before 1950 compared to 25 percent for the rest of the population, just about the same ratio as indicated in the earlier study. Many older persons live in homes that are too big for their needs, do not measure up to the heating requirements of older persons, are too costly to repair because of their age, and simply do not meet the changing physical needs of people as they continue to age. A person's physical limitations tend to increase with advancing age. For example, a two-story house with steep steps can become difficult and even dangerous for older people. It is common for older homes to have the only bathroom upstairs, which can create a difficult or impossible situation for aging homeowners.

Older homes generally have lower resale values than newer homes. Some studies have indicated that almost a third of all older people in America live in substandard, deteriorating, or dilapidated homes in order to stay close to old friends, house of worship, familiar stores and restaurants, and other facilities they do not want to give up. In addition, it is often cheaper and easier to stay in the old home than to move to a new and more appropriate living arrangement.

Home ownership is part of the American dream, the American way of life. This is particularly true for many older citizens who were able, through hard work and various loan programs such as the Federal Housing Administration (FHA) and the Veterans Administration (VA), to purchase homes at reasonable prices and low in-

terest rates (4 to 6 percent). Home ownership also gives an older person a continued sense of control over his or her own life. If old age is viewed as a series of losses and limitations, as it has been by some experts, it is not difficult to see why so many older people are reluctant to give up the home they have lived in for a long time, the home they own and call their own. For many older persons, home ownership becomes one of the last symbols of control over their own lives. They do not want to give this up. The result is that many older persons are simply "overhoused." They have too much house for their present needs.

All of these concerns with older single-family homes have been substantiated by studies over many years. The most recent study of the preferences and concerns of older Americans in housing is no exception (AARP 1990). Although 70 percent of the older persons who responded to the survey indicated they were able to do their own outdoor maintenance, 65 percent thought they would need help in the future if they continued to live in their own home. The same was true for heavy housework, with 66 percent doing the work now, but 60 percent thinking that they would need help in the future. Similarly, 38 percent thought that they were paying "too much" for both utilities and property taxes. Sixty-four percent of these same people were concerned about future utility costs for their homes. Of this same group, 65 percent were concerned about future property taxes, 59 percent about insurance costs, and 50 percent about maintenance costs.

With all these problems and concerns, what can older people do with their old homesteads? As we pointed out earlier, many older persons cannot move because they do not have enough money to move to a more suitable dwelling. Others simply do not want to move from the home in which they have lived for so long and in which they raised their families. Older people who are financially incapable of moving or who simply do not want to move, can benefit from the types of assistance that are currently available to help them stay in their own homes.

Tax Relief Programs for Homeowners

All of the states (except Hawaii) plus the District of Columbia have some form of property tax relief program for older persons. They may be called "circuit-breaker" programs or "homestead exemptions." Circuit-breaker programs provide tax cuts or refunds to older homeowners when property taxes go above a certain percentage of their household income. Homestead exemptions are usually fixed-percentage reductions in the assessed valuation of an older person's primary residence. For example, when property taxes are raised by a special mileage election for schools, many older homeowners pay very little extra in taxes if these programs are in place and used. It is important that older persons fill out the forms for these types of programs to limit or reduce their property taxes. In some areas, community agencies have set up programs to help them complete the forms so they can get the benefits of the circuit-breaker or homestead exemption programs. (See Figures 12-2 and 12-3.)

Reverse Mortgages for Homeowners

A *home equity conversion mortgage*, or reverse mortgage, turns the equity value in an older person's house into a source of monthly income without the need to sell or move out of the home. In a reverse mortgage, the lending institution makes an older person a loan against the equity value of the house. The equity value is the market value of the property less whatever the person owes on the home. The homeowner gets the loan in the form of monthly checks, which add to his or her monthly income. The amount of the monthly check depends on how much equity a

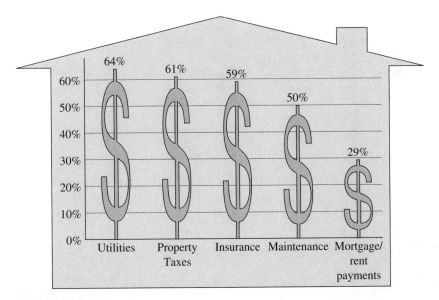

Concern about Future Housing-Related Expenses
(Percent Somewhat or very Concerned)

FIGURE 12-2

The results of an AARP survey indicating the percentages of older people who think they will need help with household chores if they continue to live in their own homes. (*Source:* American Association of Retired Persons. 1990. *Understanding senior housing for the 1990s.* Washington, DC: American Association of Retired Persons, Figure 12, p. 19.)

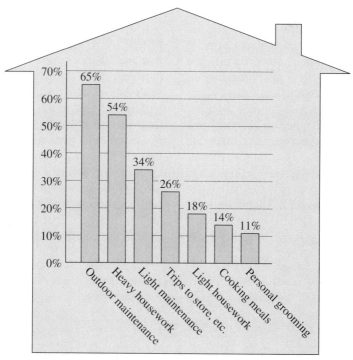

Future Help with Household Activities
(Percent Who Anticipate Needing Help)

FIGURE 12-3
Concerns older people have about future housing—related expenses.
(*Source:* American Association of Retired Persons. 1990. *Understanding senior housing for the 1990s.* Washington, DC: American Association of Retired Persons, Figure 10, p. 45.)

person has in the home and the age of the older couple or person who takes out the loan. The older a person or couple is, the higher the monthly payments. Persons who participate in this federally sponsored program never have to leave their homes, they can stay where they live. When the home is finally sold as a result of the older people moving or dying, the loan, its initial costs and added interest are paid from the sale of the house.

Although the idea has been around for some time, it was not until 1989 that Congress granted the authority to insure 2,500 reverse mortgages.

In January 1991, the program was opened up to all 10,000 lending institutions that make loans insured by the FHA. Reverse mortgages can be a very good source of monthly income for older people, because so many own their houses and their homes are their largest single financial asset. The homes of older people are generally older and less valuable than the homes of the rest of the population; the median value of these homes was $58,900 in the late 1980s (AARP-AOA 1990). The AARP has published a free booklet, *Home-Made Money: Consumer's Guide to Home Equity Conversion*, that describes in detail the various types and specifications of reverse mortgages (Scholen 1990).

Community Resources Services to Assist People in Their Own Homes

Broad-based community resources in most areas are designed to assist older people with transportation, home chores, and other services so they can remain in their own homes. Information about these services can usually be found by calling a community information and referral service such as United Way, First Call for Help, religious organizations, or the local (or regional) Area Agency on Aging.

Adapting Private Homes for Older Persons

Most older homes can be adapted to the changing physical needs of people as they grow older. These physical needs include the limitations in movement by older people, declining strength, loss of physical dexterity, and a range of limitations in eyesight and hearing. Some adaptations to an older person's home to accommodate physical limitations are relatively easy and inexpensive. Removing all throw rugs, installing non-skid adhesive strips in bathtubs, putting in brighter light bulbs, and installing grab bars in key locations in the bathroom as well as other areas of the home are all illustrations of relatively easy adaptations to the changing physical needs of older people. Many of these measures are designed to prevent one of the most serious threats to older persons—falling. According to research conducted at the Center for Locomotion Studies at Pennsylvania State University,

> Falling among the elderly is widely recognized as a major life-and-death threatening problem. Over 11,000 deaths occur annually as the result of falling, and one in three people over the age of sixty falls each year. Research conducted at Pennsylvania State shows that changes to our environment and increased attention to our own movements can increase safety and decrease the risk of falling (Pennsylvania State University 1990: 1).

Clearly, older people and those who assist them need to review their environment and eliminate and correct those things that can result in falls. Other adaptations that require moving or widening doorways, raising or lowering countertops, building a bathroom on the first floor, or making a home barrier-free for persons confined to a wheelchair can be very costly. A publication, *The Do-Able Renewable Home: Making Your Home Fit Your Needs*, available free of charge from the AARP, systematically covers the types of adaptations needed in private homes to meet the physical needs of older persons (Salmen 1988). This publication also lists the sources of financial assistance that are available in the United States to help older people overcome the barrier of inadequate financial resources to make these home adaptations.

The Single-Family Home as an Investment

In recent decades, the single-family home has increased in value at a rather remarkable rate. Although this trend has slowed in the last few years in some areas of the country, the average increased value of homes owned by older persons is significant due to their average length of ownership. The single-family home has been one of the best investments the average American has made. Offsetting this is the fact that many older persons own homes that are old, in deteriorating neighborhoods, and not always maintained adequately. Nevertheless, the true financial value of home ownership must be measured by the equity an older person has in a home. If older people were to sell their homes and invest the equity in secure investments, they might realize enough monthly return to pay for other forms of housing that are more suitable to their needs. The current tax laws permit a once-in-a lifetime sale of person's home after the age of 55 on which they do not need to pay any federal tax on a capital gain up to $125,000. The older person selling his or her home and investing the equity from the same has the benefits of a monthly (or quarterly or yearly) income and the security of having the money available.

APARTMENTS

One of the most workable options for older people who decide to move from their old homestead is to move to an apartment. All styles of apartments are available in a variety of price ranges. It is a matter of personal choice and the ability to pay the rent for the apartment that a person chooses. The apartment market, as all housing markets, varies from one community to another. Before a person decides to choose apartment living, it is important to become familiar with the types and price ranges of apartments that are available in an area, as well as the tightness of the market. This can be difficult for some older people. They may need help in surveying the apartment marketplace, but this is often available from a family member, persons they may know who are still active in the business community, or some real estate agents who include leasing in their services.

For the older person, apartment living can be attractive because it transfers the responsibilities of property ownership to someone else. A person's commitment is usually for a fixed period, typically a year at a time. This can be an advantage or a disadvantage, depending on the circumstances of the older person. During that year housing costs are fixed, so the person can budget housing costs with no surprises such as the need for a new roof or furnace or escalating taxes or utility costs. However, at the end of the year's lease, the price of the apartment may go up. This has been true in certain areas of the nation where particular types of apartments are in short supply. If apartments have been overbuilt in an area, rents tend to be much more stable, so it is important to be familiar with the apartment market. It may be possible for an older person to get a longer-term commitment for the amount of the rent of an apartment, or if not a locked-in price, at least a cap on the yearly increase. Since most older people live on some form of fixed incomes, price stability in their housing is a key factor in their ability to survive financially. On the other hand, if for some reason they become dissatisfied with their apartment, yearly leases give them the flexibility to move to a living unit that suits them better.

Apartment living has the potential of offering older persons the feeling of physical security and the opportunity to meet and interact with other people. However, many elderly people feel they lose privacy in an apartment setting. Others feel loss of ownership or control as a major barrier to living in an apartment. Still others cannot come to grips with a drawer full of rent receipts. They believe this money "down the drain." However, for many older persons, apartment living can be an economical way to gain tax-free, realized invested equity from the sale of the old homestead, as well as to get out from under the escalating cost of taxes, insurance, utilities, and maintenance associated with keeping their own home.

CONDOMINIUMS

Condominiums, or "condos," are a form of real estate ownership. They can take almost any form of housing unit from detached single units on the ground level to "cubes" or apartments in high-rise buildings. They are housing units that are individually owned but part of a multifamily housing setting on a common grounds area that typically have support facilities and possibly recreational facilities. Condominium owners are real estate owners. They own (or are buying) the housing unit they live in plus a fractional share of the common grounds area and facilities. Owning a condominium is just like owning one's own house except the condo owner generally does not do the maintenance and repairs, but as partial owners of the common areas, the condo owner pays a fee that covers the cost of ongoing maintenance and repairs. As property owners, condominium dwellers can get a mortgage on their property, deduct the interest they pay on their mortgage from their tax returns, pay real estate taxes, and sell their property if they decide to move.

For many older persons, condominium living combines the benefits of living in an apartment-type setting with no responsibility for grass cutting, snow removal, and other chores (except for monthly and yearly fees) associated with home ownership. There are no rent receipts. The living unit is owned by the resident, which means it can appreciate in value, as can any property. However, it can also depreciate if the real estate market gets "soft," or if a particular condominium complex becomes less desirable for some reason. Condominium ownership ties up a person's capital as home ownership does, but it does not involve all the personal responsibilities to maintain the property beyond the condominium financial obligations. As with all living arrangements, it is important to weigh all the pluses and minuses of this particular housing situation before deciding whether this is a comfortable option.

An important consideration in weighing the decision to buy a condominium is the *master deed* or *declaration*, as well as the board of directors that is usually elected to run the complex. The board of directors represents the association of the condominium owners. It is important to examine both of these carefully. It is most helpful to have an attorney who is familiar with condominiums and condominium laws review the master deed and the powers and duties of the condominium association's board of directors. In regard to the master deed, it is important to know if there are clear definitions of the rights of the individual owners in resale, reviewing financial records, defining the use of the buildings, and a range of other issues. In reviewing the operation of the board of directors, it is important to know how the association functions, how and to what extent it can make rules governing the operation of the complex, how much can it raise monthly fees, and what happens if an individual owner defaults on his or her fees.

MOBILE HOMES AND MANUFACTURED HOUSING

Mobile or manufactured homes are very appealing to many older people. They are an affordable housing option that gives them the feeling of a secure living environment, if they are in a mobile home park that they enjoy, while at the same time allowing them the independence and privacy of a single-family home. In 1987, the average sale price of a mobile home was $23,700 (Gillespie and Sloan 1990). However, this figure did not include any of the costs associated with getting the mobile home ready for occupancy. Additional costs include closing costs, moving costs (sometimes included in the price of the unit), setup costs, some furnishings and appliances, outbuildings or attached structures such as utility rooms and porches, and attachments such as steps, awnings, and landscaping if the mobile home resides on land owned by the resident. These added costs are reflected in the average price of the completed mobile home ready for occupancy: $30,000 to $75,000, depending on the size and quality of the mobile home and the quality of the mobile home park in which it is located.

Mobile homes are really not mobile. About 98 percent of all mobile homes are never moved from their original sites (Gillespie and Sloan 1990). A major problem in mobile home parks where the spaces are rented by the residents is the spiraling costs of monthly rentals. This is particularly true for prime recreational areas of the South and Southwest. As these rentals tend to increase constantly, often at the whim of the park owner trying to get whatever the traffic will bear, many older persons have been forced to sell out because they could no longer afford the rising monthly rental rates on the property where their mobile home resides.

Most parks will not accept older mobile homes. Even if they were to find a park that would accept their older mobile home, many older persons on modest, fixed incomes cannot afford the expenses involved in moving a mobile home. This points out the importance of the nature of the park and the quality of its management. As 50 percent of all manufactured homes are on rental property, the rental fees and the quality of the management are of great concern to many older people who reside in mobile homes (Foley 1982).

Another economic consideration in mobile home living is the principle that the value of any property will be determined by its highest and best use. This means that at some point a piece of land may become more valuable for another use. Thus, if the property on which the mobile home park is situated becomes more valuable for a shopping center, gas station, or office building, the owner may sell, forcing the residents to move out. This can be devastating for older people.

Another major consideration for mobile home dwellers is restrictions. Most parks have some restrictions, and some are so restrictive that residents are not permitted to wash their cars or have visitors overnight.

A different style of mobile home park is one in which the residents own the lots on which their mobile homes rest. These parks are generally cooperatively managed and have cooperatively owned recreational buildings and services. Some even have their own fire departments and emergency paramedical units, such as Trailer Estates in Manatee County, Florida. There, the elderly residents participate directly in the decision-making processes of operating the park. Cooperatively owned mobile home parks usually keep monthly fees relatively low. Most importantly, there is no "rent" to pay each month beyond the minimal service charges. These parks will not be sold unless there is a cooperative decision by the park's resident owners. In short, resident owners of a cooperatively owned mobile home park are in a much better position to control their living environments. including costs. Older persons who live in these types of parks have much greater control over their lives.

In the past, mobile homes often depreciated faster than many people could pay them off. This has not changed. Depending on the nature and the location of the park, many mobile homes have actually increased in value, especially if the lot a mobile home sits on is owned by the resident.

Living in a well-managed mobile home park can be an excellent housing arrangement for some older persons. The homogeneity of an adult-oriented mobile home park often provides older persons with a sense of community in which they find companionship and security with persons of similar age, interests, and lifestyle.

SHARED HOUSING

Shared housing, or homesharing, is a living arrangement in which two or more unrelated people live in the same home and share the home. It is a concept that is developing rapidly in some sections of the nation. It is economical because it significantly cuts the homeowner's housing cost. It is not easy for many older (or younger) people to have one or more persons move into their home. For some, it is a way to keep their home and have companionship at the same time. The most important part of homesharing is matching appropriate persons. It is important to try to determine whether the persons who are considering sharing a home are compatible. Persons considering this option should explore similarities and differences in tastes and lifestyles. Although there will always be some differences between people, it is advisable to avoid matching persons when basic differences in tastes and lifestyles are too great. It is often advisable to agree upon a trial period which could last a weekend, a week, or one to two months. Even for people who are generally compatible, inevitable differences and tensions may arise. Some agreed-upon way to resolve differences is recommended, whether it is periodic airing of tensions and grievances in a peaceful, orderly manner or using a third party such as a homesharing counseling program or a community reconciliation center.

Information on homesharing can usually be obtained from a local Area Agency on Aging, or from the National Shared Housing Resource Center at 6344 Green Street, Philadelphia, Pennsylvania 19144. The AARP has a free publication entitled *A Consumers Guide to Home Sharing* (1987a) which describes the details of the process as well as things to be aware of in homesharing.

ACCESSORY APARTMENTS

Accessory apartments are private living quarters, including a sitting and sleeping area, a kitchen, a bathroom, and sometimes a separate entrance, in an existing single-family home. It is an independent apartment within a single-family home. These are sometimes referred to as "mother-in-law apartments." Some of the antebellum plantation homes of the South had mother-in-law apartments separate from the rest of the family. The object of this type of apartment is to provide secure living arrangements for older persons close to the family so that family members can help care for the older person while still maintaining the privacy and independence of a person's own living space.

These apartments can be occupied by someone other than an older family member. An accessory apartment can be created in the single-family home of an older person to be occupied by a family member or service provider who comes to live with the older person to assist in daily living. An accessory apartment can be rented out to a tenant for additional monthly income for the older homeowner.

Residential zoning can be a problem in developing an accessory apartment in a single-family zoned neighborhood, but it is possible to deal with zoning restrictions in some communities through revised zoning ordinances, zoning variances, licensing, or special-use permits. Each community deals with this issue in its own way. Zoning ordinances concerning accessory apartments are usually more lenient in rural areas. Several studies have indicated that accessory apartments have no noticeable negative affects on their neighborhoods, and that they generally go unnoticed (Gillespie and Sloan 1990).

Accessory apartments can provide all of the advantages of being near to someone who can provide for the needs of dependent older persons with the advantages of privacy and independence. The American Association of Retired Persons (1987b) has a free publication that describes accessory apartments in some detail.

ECHO: ELDER COTTAGE HOUSING OPPORTUNITY

Elder Cottage Housing Opportunity Housing (ECHO) refers to small, free-standing, removable housing units placed on the side or backyard of a single-family home to provide private, independent housing for elderly parents close to the home of an adult child. This enables the adult child to care for the daily needs of dependent elderly parents without leaving his or her own property. It has the advantage of maintaining the privacy and independence of each family unit. Grandma and Grandpa have their own "space," their own home, their own lifestyle. They do not have to listen to their grandchild's stereo, be in the way when their adult children entertain, and all the other inconveniences of two families living together in the same home. They can go to bed as early or late as they wish. The traumas and adjustments necessary when the old folks move into the home of an adult child are avoided. The adult children, and their children, can help with the daily living needs of the elderly folks, with each maintaining their own space.

As might be expected, one of the major problems of this type of living arrangement is zoning. Putting an additional living unit on the land of a single family home usually requires enabling legislation and procedures to process zoning applications. The AARP has three publications that deal with ECHO housing: *A Model Ordinance for ECHO Housing* (D13791); *ECHO Housing—A Review of Zoning Issues and Other Considerations* (D1023); and *ECHO Housing—Recommended Construction and Installation Standards* (D12212).

The concept of this type of housing is not new. It has been used widely in rural and southern areas of the United States where mobile homes are set up for elderly parents near the home of one of their adult children. In Australia, where this housing formally began, they are called "granny flats." As the need for support services for the elderly increases, this type of housing may become quite common if zoning laws can be dealt with through specific use variances to accommodate older residents.

PUBLIC HOUSING

The concept of public housing came about with the passage of the Housing Act of 1937, two years after the Social Security Act. It was not until 1956 that the Housing Act was amended to provide public housing specifically for the elderly. Through its various sections, public housing for the elderly has been cooperatively provided through federal governmental loan programs to municipalities, religious organizations, private investors, and various social agencies.

Forms of Public Housing for the Elderly

Public housing has been developed primarily through two provisions. One is Section 202 of the Housing Act of 1959. Through this section, long-term loans are made to nonprofit organizations to develop multifamily housing complexes for elderly and handicapped persons. The program was suspended in 1969 after much opposition, but it was revived in 1974 as part of the Housing and Community Development Act. Since 1978, Section 202 housing has developed some demonstration housing projects designed to link housing with vital services needed by the frail elderly, who because of physical limitations need special help in their daily living. Although limited, these projects have proven quite successful (Nachison 1985). This program is called the Congregate Housing Services Program.

Section 8, created by the Housing and Community Development Act of 1974, is a program designed to provide subsidized rent to low-income households, including elderly people. In this program, money is paid through the Department of Housing and Urban Development (HUD) to persons who can show financial need to make up the difference between 30 percent of a person's income and what is considered fair-market rent. In this program the tenants can choose their own rental units (within price ranges) in a wide variety of rental housing styles, including apartment buildings, duplexes, single-family homes, and others.

The Lack of Public Housing

The major problems with federally assisted housing are the lack of it and its limited approach to meet the housing needs of a broad range of needy elderly persons. Since 1981, a period of time that has seen a dramatic increase in the number of older people in America, direct supplements for low-income housing developments and rental assistance programs have been cut by over 80 percent (AARP-Pacific Presbyterian Medical Center 1988). Even though some 1.5 million older households receive housing assistance under federal programs, an additional 2 million qualify. Many waiting lists for publicly assisted housing are so long that the people on the lists will die before their names are selected.

In addition, the federal programs are designed mostly for renters. Given the facts cited earlier indicating the large numbers of older people who are trying to stay in their own homes and the problems they have trying to do this, the lack of federally sponsored programs designed to meet the needs of elderly homeowners is a serious flaw in the nation's approach to housing frail, needy older people. No federal program exists to help older homeowners modify their homes to accommodate their changing physical needs as they continue to age (AARP-Pacific Presbyterian Medical Center 1988). Given the fact that about one in four persons aged 65 and older has at least some degree of disability, with disability increasing as age advances, the lack of assistance to modify existing homes is a serious national problem. This is a matter of public policy that needs to be addressed as the number of older people in the United States continues to increase rather dramatically, especially those persons aged 85 and older.

SINGLE-ROOM OCCUPANCIES

Single-room occupancy (SRO) is a living arrangement that many older persons would not choose. It refers to those single rooms that people of any age occupy in inner-city hotels and rooming houses, usually with a shared or common bath and no kitchen. Research has indicated that older persons occupy a large percentage of SROs (Harris 1990). Researchers have described these older persons as having almost no visibility (Second Conference on the SRO Elderly 1976). The development of urban renewal projects in the 1960s first brought this population to light. Typically, SROs are located in old, decaying hotels in the inner city or in a deteriorating section of town. SROs are generally undesirable housing units for many reasons. They are generally substandard in quality, often have no private bathrooms, no adequate cooking facilities, no common area, and no regular meals service. They generally do not offer any support services and often isolate residents from effective interaction with other persons. Most of these old rooms were designed for transient stays, not for long-term residence.

In spite of all these problems, studies have indicated that some older people actually prefer living in SROs. Some older people feel a sense of personal security in SROs because people are always on the premises, usually a desk clerk and custodian (U.S. Senate 1978). Some older people who prefer these types of arrangements have led mobile, single lives in the past and seem to prefer living alone (Eckert 1980). Although some older women live in SROs, most of the residents are men.

LIVING WITH ADULT CHILDREN

Many people believe that the families of today are radically different from the families of earlier times. Obviously many things have changed, such as much higher divorce rates and fast-paced lifestyles; but contrary to common belief, what has not changed in American family life are intergenerational living arrangements. Many people feel that they have an obligation to automatically take their aging parents into their own homes when one of them becomes widowed or less than fully capable of maintaining his or her own home. Many people feel this is the way it was done in earlier, more stable times. Clark Tibbitts (1968), one of the noted pioneers in gerontology, has noted that the three-generation family, where the old parents moved into the home of a nuclear family, has always been relatively rare. Even in American colonial times, the three-generation family was an exception. The evidence for this comes from examining family wills in Plymouth Colony (Demos 1965). Another study of family life in Massachusetts in the seventeenth century noted the difference between the family of residence, which was mostly nuclear, and the family of interaction or obligation (Greven 1966). This was a kinship group of two or more generations living in a single community, not a single house, who were dependent on each other.

Whether people live in separate homes, apartments, condominiums, mobile homes, or any other type of housing unit, most value some degree of independence with the ability to rely on family members living nearby. This is termed the independent-dependent family, close but not living together (Greenberg and Becker 1988). The reality is that in our culture, for the most part, there has never been an emphasis on older people moving in with a grown child's family unless it was necessary. Arranging for an independent living situation for older parents is not abandoning them. In most instances it is best for both parties, the older people and their adult children.

Key Questions Before Moving a Parent into an Adult Child's Home

Before inviting an elderly parent to move into the home of an adult child, the following questions should be raised:

- Can they tolerate each other's lifestyle? Different generations have different tastes in food, music, TV watching, and a range of other activities.
- Can they relate to each other as mature adults? The aged parent and the middle-aged child have lived apart for many years. The dynamics of early years are very different. The adult child is not the same person who left his or her parents' home years before. In a close living situation, differences can become evident and tensions can surface easily.
- Does the home have enough space? Physical space and adequate privacy are essential if an aging parent is to live successfully with an adult child. An accessory apartment, described earlier in this chapter, could be the answer when an adult child invites a parent to move into his or her home.

RETIREMENT COMMUNITIES

In general, retirement communities are places where people have moved since they retired (Longino 1980). This does not mean that no one in a retirement community works, but rather that the residents have retired from their primary job and have relocated to the retirement community.

Many of these communities are located in the sunbelt. They are usually age-segregated and often focus on leisure activities (Gillespie and Sloan 1990). They usually provide leisure and avocational services and resources in a self-contained setting. Some provide additional services, as in the case of Trailer Estates in Bradenton, Florida, a large complex of mobile homes which has extensive recreational facilities and social organizations in addition to a fire department and paramedical rescue unit staffed by volunteers among the residents.

Types of Retirement Communities

Retirement communities can be mobile home parks, high-rise senior housing complexes, leisure villages, or other forms of resident housing units.

Among the largest and most elaborate retirement communities are Sun City, Arizona, and Leisure World, California. An elaborate range of amenities and services to meet the wishes and needs of retired persons are found in these rather remarkable villages. Housing options, recreational facilities, medical assistance, houses of worship, and a range of educational opportunities seem to have no limit in this type of retirement environment. (Stevey and Associates 1989). Self-governance by elected representatives of the residents is usually a feature of retirement communities. Enhancing the lives of retired persons is the primary goal of these communities.

Costs of Retirement Community Living

Many persons have pointed out that retirement communities are opportunities primarily for the wealthy, or at least the relatively affluent old. In some instances this is truly the case. As of August, 1992, Leisure World in California had two types of ownership of units: cooperatives and condominiums. The lowest priced co-op apartment with one bedroom and one bath was $35,000. Added to that was an underlying loan of $8,000, bringing the price to $43,000. In addition, to be approved by the board of the village, a single person had to verify an annual income of at least $18,000, two persons $21,600. Condos started at $55,000 for one bedroom and one bath. Condo owners needed to verify an income of $25,000 a year regardless of the number of persons in the unit. Condos ranged up to $600,000. The average age in Leisure Village was about 75 years of age, with 55 years being the minimum age of one person in the unit. The other spouse can be 20, 30, or whatever as long as one person is at least 55.

Obviously not all retirement communities are for the wealthy. Some researchers have indicated that some mobile home parks are the working-class equivalent of the wealthier retirement villages (Atchley 1991). Most of these parks also have minimum age restrictions (usually 50 or 55 years). Renters can become part of the park for the price of the mobile home (new or used, but used only if already in place) plus the monthly lot rental fees. The dangers here are possibly restrictive, authoritarian mobile home park owners or managers and no limit on escalating monthly rentals.

Used mobile homes on lots to be purchased could be purchased for $30,000 and up in many mobile home parks on the coast of Florida as of August, 1992. For $40,000 one could purchase a "good" mobile home in a retirement park in Florida with many recreational facilities and social outlets. In addition, low yearly fees including property taxes afford low-cost living for many people. Because of the relatively low cost of living in these types of facilities, many people are able to spend winters in the sunbelt and summers in their northern home region. However, advancing age, health problems, physical limitations, and increasing costs relative to fixed incomes over a period of time often result in the permanent return of these older folks to their native regions to be closer to family and support systems.

Limitations of Retirement Communities

Retirement communities are not generally continuum-of-care facilities. Even at Leisure World, with all of its resources, facilities, and services, when a person needs ongoing supportive care or nursing care, it is necessary to move to a long-term care facility. Buying into a retirement village is not a guarantee of long-term supportive care. It does support retirees in an environment which maximizes their opportunities to pursue their interests, whatever they are, as long as they are mobile, relatively healthy, and financially secure enough to meet the requirements of each particular community.

SUMMARY

Almost 95 percent of older people live in independent households. Older people's housing needs change as they grow older. Physical limitations often make their old homes difficult and sometimes dangerous to live in .

Many older people cannot afford to move to appropriate housing units or to adapt their old homes to their changing physical needs. Home ownership represents the biggest asset that most older people have, yet many are unable or unwilling to convert the equity they have in that home. Many are unaware of the various options older Americans have in the variety of living arrangements available to them.

In addition to home ownership, older people have a range of housing options. Apartments can be one of the most workable options for older people who decide to move from their old homestead. A variety of apartments are available in a range of prices. Apartment living can be attractive to older people because it transfers the responsibilities of property ownership to someone else. However, some older people feel they lose privacy in an apartment setting. Others feel loss of ownership or control as they become renters. Apartment living can be a good way to gain tax-free, realized invested equity from the sale of the old homestead, as well as get out from under the escalating cost of taxes, insurances, utilities, and maintenance associated with keeping one's own home.

Condominiums are housing units that are individually owned but part of a multifamily housing setting on a common grounds area with facilities. Owning a condominium is like owning one's house except the condo owner generally does not do maintenance or repairs. For many older persons, condominium living combines the benefits of living in an apartment-type setting with home ownership. The living unit is owned by the resident, which means it can increase in value as any property. The resident is freed from upkeep and has the security of living in a controlled environment. It is possible that the property can decrease in value and that the resident may not like living with the rules and fees set by the governing board of the condominium complex.

Mobile or manufactured homes can be very appealing to older people. They are an affordable housing option that gives them a feeling of secure living, if they are in a mobile home park, while allowing them the independence and privacy of a single-family home. A major caution is the land upon which the mobile home rests. If the space is rented by a park owner, the rental fees may escalate dramatically over a few years, depending on location. A better option is to live in a mobile home park where the residents own the individual parcels of land upon which their mobile homes are placed. This usually involves a cooperative approach to managing the park.

Shared housing, or homesharing, is a living arrangement in which two or more unrelated people live in the same home and share the home and its expenses. It is a concept that is developing rather rapidly for older people in some sections of the nation. It is economical because it cuts the residents' housing expenses. It also provides companionship. The most important aspect of shared housing is matching appropriate persons to share a home.

Accessory apartments are private living quarters in existing single-family homes. It is an independent apartment within a home that can provide security as well as privacy for an older person. Elder Cottage Housing Opportunity (ECHO) refers to small, free-standing, removable housing units placed on the side or backyard of a single-family home to provide private, independent housing for elderly persons close to the home of a relative, usually an adult child. The major barrier to these two types of housing is community zoning.

Moving in with an adult child is another option for some older people. Most older people do not wish to do this, and it can be disruptive to the lives of their adult children. Other options that promote independent living are more viable in contemporary America.

Public housing, in its various forms, has been very successful for older persons. The major problem has been lack of federal funding to meet the demand for this assisted type of living.

Too many older persons have few or no options in alternative living arrangements due to cutbacks in existing programs, or no programs or

assistance to help them in their present circumstances. As *Aging in America: Dignity or Despair?* concludes:

> Currently, the housing options for most older Americans needing supportive services are relatively limited. Many individuals remain at home, with or without varying degrees of support provided to them there, until disabling conditions require their entry into a nursing home. Intermediate options that would provide additional support in a semi-independent setting . . . are still nonexistent or unaffordable for the vast majority of older persons. The development of a range of housing options to meet the changing health and social needs of aging America is critically needed, especially as the population requiring such options expands (AARP 1988: 25).

There are a range of housing options available to many older Americans. It is important that they become aware of these options and what they can mean to the quality of their lives. However, many older Americans simply cannot afford the benefits these housing arrangements offer. They are "aging in place" in environments that do not meet their changing physical needs.

REFERENCES

American Association of Retired Persons and the Administration on Aging. 1990. *A Profile of Older Americans*. Washington, DC: AARP and AOA.

American Association of Retired Persons. 1990. *Understanding Senior Housing for the 1990s*. Washington, DC: AARP.

American Association of Retired Persons and Pacific Presbyterian Medical Center. 1988. *Aging in America: Dignity or Despair?* Washington, DC: AARP and Pacific Presbyterian Medical Center.

American Association of Retired Persons. 1987a. *A Consumer's Guide to Home Sharing*. Washington, DC: AARP.

American Association of Retired Persons. 1987b. *A Consumer's Guide to Accessory Apartments*. Washington, DC: AARP.

American Association of Retired Persons. 1985. *Your Home: Your Choice*. Washington, DC: AARP.

Angel, S. 1991. Stumbling Into a Hidden Parent Trap. *Los Angeles Times* (February 20): E3.

Atchley, R.C. 1991. *Social Forces and Aging*, 6th Ed. Belmont, CA: Wadsworth Publishing.

Demos, J. 1965. Notes on Life in Plymouth Colony. *William and Mary Quarterly*, 22. (3rd series): 264–286.

Eckert, J.K. 1980. *The Unseen Elderly: A Study of Marginally Subsistent Hotel Dwellers*. San Diego: Campanile Press.

Foley, N. 1982. The Norman Foley Lectures. Grand Rapids, MI: Grand Rapids Community College.

Gillespie, A.E., and Sloan, K.S. 1990. *Housing Options and Services for Older People*. Santa Barbara, CA: ABC-CLIO.

Greenberg, J.S., and Becker, M. 1988. Aging Parents and Family Resources. *Gerontologist*, 28: 786–791.

Greven, P. 1966. Family Structure in Seventeenth Century Andover, Mass. *William and Mary Quarterly*, 23, (3rd series): 234–356.

Harris, L. 1990. *Sociology of Aging* (2d Ed.). New York: Harper and Row.

Harris, L. 1981. *Aging in the Eighties: America in Transition*. Washington, DC: National Council on the Aging.

Longino, C. 1980. The Retirement Community. In F. Berghorn and D. Schafer (eds.), *Dimensions of Aging*. Boulder, CO: Westview Press.

Michigan Department of Management and Budget. 1991. *Population news*. (Winter). Lansing, MI: Michigan Department of Management and Budget.

Nachison, J.S. 1985. Congregate Housing for the Low and Moderate Income Elderly: A Needed Federal-State Partnership. *Journal of Housing for the Elderly*, 3(3/4): 65–80.

Pennsylvania State University. 1990. *Increasing Your Safety: What We Have Learned About Falls in the Elderly*. University Park, PA: Pennsylvania State University.

Quinn, J.B. 1991. Reverse Mortgage Reality. *Detroit Free Press*, (March 11): 13F.

Salmen, J.P.S. 1988. *The Do-able Renewable Home: Making Your Home Fit Your Needs*. Washington, DC: AARP.

Scholen, K. 1990. *Home-Made Money: Consumer's Guide to Home Equity Conversion*. Washington, DC: AARP.

Second Conference on the SRO Elderly. 1976. St. Louis, Missouri. (May 15–16).

Stevey, T.E. and Associates. 1989. *Fulfilling Retirement Dreams*. Laguna Hills, CA: Leisure World Historical Society.

Tibbitts, C. 1968. Some Social Aspects of Gerontology. *Gerontologist*, 8(2): 131–133.

U.S. Bureau of the Census. 1991. *Information From Summary Tape File 1A*. Washington, DC: U.S. Government Printing Office.

U.S. Bureau of the Census. 1991. *1990 census profile*, No. 1. (March) Washington, DC: U.S. Government Printing Office.

U.S. Bureau of the Census. 1990. *Selected Population and Housing Characteristics*. Washington, DC: U.S. Government Printing Office.

U.S. Senate Special Committee on Aging. 1978. *Single Room Occupancy: A Need for National Concern*. Washington, DC: U.S. Government Printing Office.

CHAPTER 13

Congregate/Assisted Living

Henry and Joan—Not Much Choice

Henry and Joan worked all their lives with the goal of someday moving to a retirement community in Florida. They both loved warm weather and sunshine. Working in northern New York, Henry as a plumber and Joan a receptionist, made them eager for a more carefree life with good recreational facilities. Their three children were all grown and on their own. As retirement was near for both, now was their chance. They bought a mobile home in a pretty good park with people their own age and older. All the activities were geared toward "mature" people aged 55 and older. Everything went great until Joan developed macular degeneration in her eyes which made it impossible to do normal household tasks such as cooking. Henry thought he could learn to cook, even though this had always been Joan's job. But Henry suffered a heart attack which required hospitalization and then rehabilitation at home. What can Henry and Joan do? They are in Florida in a retirement community that is not set up for major assistance with daily living. Their children are back in New York and not able to come down to help. Even if they were nearby, who would provide all the care required? Who would cook the meals?

Henry and Joan turned to a resource they had always known about but never really thought they would need: a life-care facility operated by their church—an "old people's home" in their view. At first they weren't too happy at the prospect of living there, but they felt they had little choice.

Some Promises Are Best Not Kept

Dear Ann Landers: My father is 84 and doesn't want to go into a nursing home. My husband and I have hired a woman to stay with him during the week, day and night. I am his only child. I stay with him weekends.

He continues to live in his own home even though he is forgetful and frequently doesn't know where he is. Sometimes he thinks strangers have captured him and taken him to a hotel.

Ann, people don't understand when I tell them my father is "forgetful." I mean he still asks for my mother, who has been dead for several years.

He forgets to take his clothes off before showering. He forgets he has eaten and attempts to eat every hour. He forgets to go to the bathroom. You can imagine what the rugs look like.

I have a part-time job helping my husband in his small business. Besides cleaning and cooking for my own family, I help take care of my grandchildren. In addition to spending weekends with my father, I also do all his grocery shopping, pay his bills, cut his grass and run errands.

There is no time or energy left to enjoy my own life. I know I will be unable to go on like this for much longer.

I can't understand why parents make their children promise not to place them in a nursing home. It's really a very cruel and selfish thing to do. I've told my children that if I should become unable to care for myself, they should put me in a good home and come visit. I don't want them to give up their lives for me.

—*Wrung out*

Dear Wrung: Some promises are best not kept. Circumstances sometimes change. From what you have written, your father needs around-the-clock care. I implore you to find a first-rate facility for him, and soon, or you may end up in a hospital from exhaustion.

Creators Syndicate Inc.
(*The Grand Rapids Press*: July 26, 1992, p. B5)
(Permission granted by Ann Landers and Creators Syndicate.)

MOVING FROM INDEPENDENT LIVING

All of the housing options discussed in the previous chapter, even those that involve sharing a home with others, are essentially independent living environments. This chapter looks at the types of living arrangements that involve various degrees of supportive services. Some of these facilities are chosen primarily for the benefits of interaction with people of similar ages and interests. Others are chosen as planned moves with continuum-of-care services built in as part of the environment, where levels of supportive care are provided as needed. Still others are chosen out of necessity when a person needs immediate assistance with daily living activities. Regardless of the reason for the move, all of the choices in this category of living environments involve a move to an environment that is age-segregated. The most obvious exception is moving into the home of an adult child or relative in order to be cared for by the adult child or relative. The other exception is a nursing home that cares for patients of all ages, which for younger ages usually means developmentally disabled persons or victims of catastrophic accidents. For most, moving from some form of independent living arrangement means moving to an environment designed for older persons and their needs.

CONGREGATE LIVING

Congregate living has many definitions and takes many forms. It continues to take additional forms as the market expands because of the tremendous increase in the number of older persons in America. These living arrangements have been called "homes for the aged," "retirement homes," "old people's homes," and "sheltered housing," and others. The common factors in all of these homes are housing units that have a common dining room in which meals are served on a regular basis along with access to social and recreational services (Gillespie and Sloan 1990).

The goal of congregate living is to provide services in a residential setting for persons who need some form of assistance with daily living but do not require continuing medical or nursing care. They also do not generally require full-time personal assistance.

In the past, many of these homes for the aged were developed and operated by religious institutions, and fraternal or social organizations. Most of these were, and continue to be, nonprofit. They provide rooms of varying sizes and quality depending on the price and the quality of the home, some basic supportive services, and regularly-served meals (also of varying quality). In a sense, it is a

dormitory for the old. One of the authors of this book regularly drives to work down a road which has a college and its dormitories on one side, and a home for the aged on the other. The appearance of both from the outside is remarkably similar. In addition, both have rooms, both have basic services, both have common rooms and space, and both serve meals on a regular basis. However, on the inside, one is much cleaner, quieter, and more orderly. It is obvious which one this is.

A Dormitory for the Elderly

Not everyone likes "dorm life" at any age. There are inevitable rules and set procedures, whether the dorm is for college kids or older persons. It goes without saying that for the college student, the dorm is transitory. With their mobile, active lifestyle and the demands of classes, labs, and studying, college students often spend relatively little time in their dorm rooms.

For older persons, the "dorm room" of the home for the aged is where they spend much of their time. It is difficult for many older persons, after being active and "in charge" of their lives, to give up some of their independence and move to congregate living situations. This is particularly true for older persons who have a perception of homes for the aged from past experiences where the settings were often old, dismal, and generally oppressive. That is one of the reasons new approaches to congregate living situations are being developed, often by entrepreneurs, that cater to the more affluent older persons. They provide a sparkling physical environment with a range of entertainment and recreational options along with upscale services. They are designed to attract persons who are physically mobile, persons who want the security of a controlled, supportive environment along with operational rules and procedures that are designed to promote as much independence as possible for the older residents.

A Way to Bridge the Gap

Congregate living is seen by many experts as a way to bridge the gap between independent and dependent living for persons who need some assistance with daily living but do not need continuous care. According to Gillespie and Sloan (1990), residents tend to be 75 years of age and older in these types of facilities. Typically, congregate living arrangements have social directors for group activities and personal assistance; linen service and housekeeping arranged, sometimes at an additional fee; and some medical assistance, with a nurse who monitors medications, consults with residents on medical problems as they arise, and provides blood pressure screening.

Support for Congregate Living

As was indicated previously, many of the congregate housing facilities were, and continue to be, sponsored by nonprofit organizations. This was particularly true of those developed in the nineteenth century. But these did not house many people. Late in the nineteenth century most old people had to look out for themselves with only the help of their families. For those who had no help, or no families to move in with, the alternative was the "poor farms" of America. These were common across the nation's landscape. With the beginning of Social Security in 1935, America began to look toward a different approach to providing for the needs of the elderly. But Social Security was only a beginning. It was not until a 1963 address to the Congress that President Kennedy proposed a basic concept which later became part of national program for congregate housing. President Kennedy stated:

> For the great majority of the nation's older people, the years of retirement should be years of activity and self-reliance. A substantial minority, however, while still relatively independent, require modest assistance in one or more aspects of their daily living. Many have become frail physically and may need help in preparing meals, caring for living quarters, and sometimes limited nursing.
>
> This group does not require care in restorative nursing homes or in terminal custodial facilities. They can generally walk without assistance, eat in a dining room, and come and go in the community

with considerable independence. They want to have privacy but also community life and activity within the limits of their capacity. They do not wish to be shunted to an institution, but often they have used up their resources; and family and friends are not available for support. What they do need most is a facility with housekeeping assistance, central food service, and minor nursing from time to time. The provision of such facilities would defer for many years the much more expensive type of nursing home or hospital care which would otherwise be required. (U.S. House of Representatives 1963).

President Kennedy went on to recommend the enactment of housing programs that would include a variety of services. In 1970, Congress finally acted to provide funds for the construction of congregate housing. In 1974, Congress authorized funds to include space for central kitchens and dining rooms.

Government Assistance

In 1978, the Congregate Housing Services Program (CHSP) became part of the Housing and Community Development Act. The goal at that time was to demonstrate the cost-effectiveness of this type of living arrangement to prevent premature and unnecessary institutionalization of old and disabled persons (Gillespie and Sloan 1990). In 1987, the Housing Community Development Act authorized the CHSP as a permanent governmental program, but the fluctuating federal funding for congregate housing has been a problem. According to the Special Committee on Aging of the U.S. Senate, Congress kept the program alive throughout the Reagan presidency by appropriating funds to maintain the existing CHSP facilities. In 1989, the fiscal year appropriation was $5.4 million; for 1990 it was $5.8 million; for 1991 it was $9.5 million, and for 1992 it was $17.7 million. Although this seems like a big increase, it was still less than half of the amount authorized by Congress (U.S. Senate Special Committee on Aging 1992). The report went on to say: "While there is no way of precisely estimating the number of elderly persons who need or prefer to live in congregate facilities, groups such as the Gerontological Society of America and the AARP have estimated that a large number of people over the age of 65 and not living in nursing homes would choose to relocate to congregate housing if possible" (p. 281). The same Senate report stated that some states have set up their own housing programs which include support for congregate housing. This is because federal funds have been inadequate to meet the need for additional congregate living opportunities these states hope to provide their elderly citizens who need some assistance with daily living without forcing them into nursing homes.

Gillespie and Sloan (1990) pointed out that congregate housing is attractive to a cross-section of older people at a variety of income levels. Diverse ethnic groups participate in congregate housing opportunities. They provide opportunities for companionship as well as some supportive services, particularly regular meals. Adequate nutrition is one of the major problems older people face; they often put little emphasis on meal preparation, especially if they live alone. Some people face age-related problems that make it difficult for them to prepare meals.

Esther's Need for Congregate Living

Esther was the best cook in her family. Nieces and nephews always talked about Aunt Esther's chocolate cakes. Her dinners were also excellent. After she turned 80, she began to develop macular degeneration (the loss of central vision). Gradually she lost more and more vision due to the deterioration of the retinas in her eyes. It became hard to read even the largest print. Her general health was quite good, with her high blood pressure controlled through aggressive medication. Her husband, so typical of their generation, never learned to cook nor did he want to try. His health too was quite good but he could no longer drive for a variety of physical reasons. Esther and her husband had always been very independent. They did not rely on anybody. They helped lots of people in various ways. With Esther's limited vi-

sion, what were they to do? When they had some friends move into a congregate living facility that did not require an entry fee and rented on a month-to-month basis for $1,300 a month including two meals a day, they saw that as an option for them, too. It was a new facility and really quite nice. Each unit had a living room, bedroom, bath, walk-in closet, and small kitchen to prepare meals they might choose to have in their own apartment. They thought they would try it. The biggest adjustment was eating with other people on a regular basis. At first this was difficult for Esther because she was so used to being in charge of the food preparation and the eating arrangements, but she adjusted quite well after a time. Both Esther and her husband made many friends and actually looked forward to meals as a natural time to get together with their new friends.

Congregate living served real needs for this couple. Not only did the regularly served meals solve Esther's problem of not being able to cook and prepare food, but the congregate setting provided them with a secure environment and the opportunity to meet and enjoy new friends. They did not need, nor did they want, any additional supportive care. It would have been an infringement on their freedom and independence as well as a waste of money.

One aspect of congregate living that needs to be noted (and that finally prompted Esther and her husband to move away from their happy surroundings) is the lack of provision for supportive or nursing care. Over a period of time Esther and her husband saw some of the couples they had become friendly with separated as one of the spouses required supportive or nursing care. Their congregate living facility was set up to serve the needs of older people who could get to meals regularly and who could care for themselves on a daily basis. When problems arose that required ongoing assisted care, the person had to find accommodations in a supportive or nursing care facility. This eventually prompted Esther and her husband to seek entrance into a continuum-of-care, or life-care, facility.

For older people who are able to get around by themselves and are able to care for themselves on a daily basis, who want the security and services of a controlled, supportive environment with operational rules and procedures that are designed to promote as much independence as possible, congregate living facilities may be the answer. Costs generally range from $700 to $2,000 a month, with much lower fees for residents of federally sponsored facilities (Gillespie and Sloan 1990). In fact, residents of federally sponsored programs only pay a percentage of their incomes so they are able to maintain themselves. The problem with these programs is that the limitations and cutbacks in federal funding have caused a shortage relative to the demand.

When looking for a congregate living unit, the following are some of the factors that need to be considered before any decisions are made:

1. Who owns the facility? Is it for-profit or not-for-profit? What is its business reputation?
2. Who manages the home? Is the management competent? Does the facility have a record of sound management? If it is a new facility, who can recommend the management?
3. Is there a support base to carry the facility financially? If it is a nonprofit operation, how much money is behind the facility to ensure its long-term financial health? If it is a for-profit operation, is there enough money behind it for long-term stability without large increases in monthly rates?
4. What happens to an entry fee (if there is an entry fee) if a person changes his or her mind before actually moving in? What happens to this money if a person moves in and decides he or she does not want to stay?
5. What is included in the monthly fees? What costs are extra? Do the fees cover such household maintenance as clean linens changed regularly, room/apartment cleaning, cable TV, and food service to the room when the resident is ill?

6. What are the other residents like? Will a prospective resident feel comfortable living there?
7. What are the rules and regulations of the facility? How free are the residents to decorate or furnish their own rooms or apartments?
8. Is there a choice in the food that is served? Can special diets be accommodated? How good is the food?
9. Do the residents feel happy or content living in this facility? Do they have more than the usual complaints?
10. How are emergency medical situations handled at the facility? (*The Christian Guide to Parent Care*, Riekse and Holstege 1992: 183–184)

CONTINUING CARE RETIREMENT COMMUNITIES

For those who want the assurance of being in an environment that will meet all of their needs as they continue to move through their later years regardless of the status of their mobility and health, there are continuing care retirement communities (CCRCs). They are also called life-care or continuum-of-care communities. They usually provide housing, personal care, supportive care, nursing care, congregate meals, and a range of social and recreational services. The key feature is that incoming residents enter into contractual agreements to pay an entrance fee and monthly fees that will provide for the care of the resident for the rest of his or her life. According to the U.S. Senate Special Committee on Aging (1992), the definition of these facilities is confusing and inconsistent due to the wide range of services offered, differing types of dwelling units, and the wide range of contractual agreements.

The American Association of Homes for the Aging (AAHA) pointed out that "continuing care retirement communities are distinguished from other housing and care options for older people by their offering of a long-term contract that provides for housing, services, and nursing care usually all in one location" (U.S. Senate Special Committee on Aging 1992: 307). As of 1992, there were between 700 and 800 CCRCs, with some 230,000 residents, about 1 percent of the elderly population. Most (up to 95 percent) of these facilities are sponsored by nonprofit organizations (Gillespie and Sloan 1990).

Costs of Continuing Care Facilities

According to the 1992 Senate report, there has been increasing interest by corporations in developing continuing care facilities. Also according to this same report, in 1990 the median entrance fee ranged from about $32,800 for a studio, $47,500 for a one-bedroom, and $68,250 for a two-bedroom apartment. The median monthly fee ranged from $695 for a studio, $830 for a one-bedroom, to $980 for a two-bedroom unit. Other sources have indicated that entry fees can range from $15,000 to more than $20,000, with monthly fees ranging from $200 to more than $1,300 (Harvey 1991).

Types of Life-Care Contracts

Life-care contracts for continuing care retirement communities are designed to take the worry about being provided for in the future away, regardless of the type of care that is needed. It is a form of housing insurance. Like any insurance, the residents who need fewer expensive services, such as supportive and nursing care, help subsidize those who need more of the intensive services. Many of these facilities base their entrance fees on actuarial and economic assumptions similar to those used by the insurance industry.

All life-care contracts are not the same. In fact they can usually be grouped into three categories: (1) extensive, (2) modified, and (3) fee-for-service. Each of these types includes shelter, residential services, and amenities. The major difference is in the amount of long-term nursing care provided. In the extensive category, unlimited nursing care is provided at no increase in fees. The modified contract has some specific length of nursing care provided; it may be 15, 30, or 60

days. After that time the resident pays either a discounted rate or full rate for nursing care services. The fee-for-service contract guarantees the resident access to a nursing facility, as needed, but he or she is charged the full nursing home rate (U.S. Senate Special Committee on Aging 1992; Gillespie and Sloan 1990).

It is important to note that when a prospective resident pays an entrance fee, this does not represent the purchase of a housing unit in the retirement complex. Even though the fee may be large, it does not buy any real estate that can be resold. The entrance fee purchases assurance that a person will be taken care of regardless of his or her needs. The different levels of contracts purchase different levels of long-term security for the older person. Even the lower levels, which provide guaranteed access to a nursing facility and then charge the going rate for nursing services, generally provide security for the resident. Those types of facilities usually accept Medicaid for residents who "spend down" to poverty levels and thus continue to serve their needs.

Many of the newer CCRCs have private apartments in duplex or townhouse arrangements, individual apartments in larger buildings, rooms in a "manor" type of building, supportive care rooms, and nursing facilities all on the same campus. As an older person's needs change, the resident can move within the same retirement community to the next level of assisted-living housing unit, on into nursing-home care. All of this is covered by the life-care agreement.

CCRCs can be nearly ideal situations for older people who can afford the entrance fee and the monthly assessments and who can adapt to living in an environment that is at least somewhat institutional and controlled. This approach can be a solution to guaranteed long-term care. However, because of the relatively large fees involved, this approach does not address the public policy issues of long-term care for the majority of older Americans. For those who have a fairly substantial amount of equity in their homes and can rely on adequate monthly incomes from a combination of Social Security, savings and investments, and possibly pensions, it is worth investigating. Because many of these facilities are nonprofit, operated by religious institutions and other philanthropic organizations, once a person is a resident, even if money for the monthly fees runs out, he or she is taken care of through donations or Medicaid. A large CCRC in Grand Rapids, Michigan, supported by two church denominations, has about half of its nursing-home residents on Medicaid. Many other residents in the independent living facilities cannot meet the monthly fees and are continued as if they were paying their fees in full. No one is put out or discriminated against because of their financial status. This facility is 100 years old and growing.

Pitfalls in Purchasing CCRC Contracts

As ideal as this type of arrangement might be or appear to be, there are potential pitfalls that need to be considered if a person is contemplating buying into a CCRC. Anne Harvey (1991) has pointed out many of these, including the following:

Fraud   Some life-care facilities have been operated fraudulently. Some people put all or most of their money into what they thought was a secure investment that would take care of them for the rest of their lives. Many have been cheated out of their money. It is important to investigate each operation thoroughly before an investment is made.

Mismanagement   Some CCRCs have been mismanaged. The intentions of some the operators have been good, but they ran out of funds to meet the life-long contracts they had with their residents. It is important to examine the record of each facility being considered. If it is a new one, it might be possible to examine another branch of the same operation if it is part of a chain.

Lack of Capital   Some facilities have insufficient funds to support them. They have been undercapitalized to begin with; they may not have projected long-term expenses and income realistically.

Lack of Institutional Support   Some CCRCs, even some associated with churches, do not have adequate support. It is important to learn whether the facility really has the support it claims it has from its sponsors to make up for financial shortfalls. Some facilities that are sponsored by religious organizations have long-standing support mechanisms. Some are in the budgets of the religious institution they are affiliated with. Other facilities do not have this built-in and ongoing support.

Underoccupied   Some CCRCs depend on high occupancy rates which they never achieve. It is important to know occupancy rates to help determine projected financial health.

Rising Medical Costs   Some CCRCs do not adequately provide for rising medical costs that the residents will need. This can lead to financial collapse. It is important to determine how these costs will be covered.

Unclear Contracts   Some CCRC contracts are unclear. All items need to be spelled out in clear language before a prospective resident signs a CCRC contract and invests in this type of facility.

Long Waiting Lists   Long waiting lists, which stretch to two or more years for the good facilities, may prevent a person from entering a CCRC. Many CCRCs have some physical mobility and mental fitness requirements that make it difficult for frail older people to gain admission if they wait too long. Some CCRCs have age limitations for entry. Planning ahead while the older person is still fit enough becomes vitally important. Often these facilities will put a prospective resident's name on a waiting list. When a name comes up the person may be given the option to enter the facility or continue to wait until he or she is ready. Usually there is an application fee, somewhere between $50 and $300. Many people wait too long to begin the entry process, thinking they have to enter the facility as soon as their name comes up.

Things to Look for in Choosing a CCRC

In addition to these factors, persons contemplating a CCRC should think about all the other considerations that were outlined above in the guidelines for selecting congregate care facilities. Much of the decision comes down to whether a prospective resident feels "at home" after a period of adjustment. The place chosen will become "home" and all that means to the life of an older person. Although it may appear that these living arrangements (CCRCs) are primarily for the well-to-do elderly, some contracts can be purchased for reasonable amounts considering the number of older people who own their homes free and clear of mortgages.

Regulation of CCRCs

One of the missing ingredients of the CCRC picture is regulation. Until recently, CCRCs have been the domain of the nonprofit sector. Even here, there have been some problems in financial stability, and in some cases, financial honesty. The CCRC industry is growing and expected to grow rather rapidly during the 1990s and into the twenty-first century (Netting and Wilson 1987). As of 1988, sixteen states had passed legislation to help prospective purchasers of CCRC contracts determine their reliability. In addition, there is no industry-wide or governmental clearinghouse to monitor CCRCs to see if they are living up to their agreements or to see if they are financially healthy (Harvey 1991). It is important to look at the track record of any CCRC facility that is being considered by an older person.

BOARD-AND-CARE HOMES

Board and care homes are also known as assisted living homes, adult foster care homes, personal care homes, sheltered care facilities, residential care facilities, or dormitory care facilities. Essentially these types of homes provide a room, three meals a day, help with daily living activities, transportation, laundry services, housecleaning, and protective supervision. They are designed for persons who cannot live alone because of physical or mental impairments, but who do not need institutional care. With supervision, supportive services, and assistance, these persons can live in family-type arrangements in communities (Gillespie and Sloan 1990; AARP 1989).

It is difficult to determine exactly how many older persons live in board-and-care homes, as many of these facilities are not licensed and their definitions differ among states. A 1987 study by the National Association of Residential Care Facilities identified some 41,000 facilities with some 563,000 residents in the United States. It has been estimated that the need for this type of facility will increase dramatically due to the projected large increase of older persons with functional limitations (doubling from 1990 to 2020). In addition, other factors have been cited as contributing to the growth of these facilities including the following:

- Changing family structure
- Fewer children per family, which means fewer potential caregivers for parents
- Increased number of women who work outside the home and are therefore unable to care for elderly relatives or friends
- Decrease in available low-cost housing
- Rising health care costs
- Desire of many people to remain in neighborhood settings (AARP 1989).

The Operators of Board and Care Homes

Although they vary in size, the majority of board-and-care facilities are for-profit "mom and pop" operations. Some of the "moms and pops" are operated by individuals—a "mom" or a "pop." This manager plays an important role in the facility and in the lives of the residents. In fact, this person (or couple) is the key to the overall well-being of the residents. Whether the operators need to have any special training to operate a board-and-care home varies from state to state. Some operators hire outside help to manage the home. In all of this there is a potential for abuse and neglect of the residents. A fairly large number of these facilities are not licensed (5,000 out of 30,000 such facilities according to the U.S. Department of Health and Human Services) in 1982 (Gillespie and Sloan 1990). Being licensed does not necessarily protect the residents' safety or quality of care. It should be noted that not all states require facilities with few residents to be licensed. Some of these may be quite good overall.

Regulations for Board and Care Homes

Regulations for these facilities vary, making them difficult to enforce in many instances. The basic responsibility for ensuring the safety of residents falls on the states, but state regulations vary a great deal. Some states have minimal standards, while others have rather extensive regulations for the safety of residents and their quality of care. Abuse, neglect, mismanagement of the residents' personal finances, and fires are problems that received attention from the media in the early 1970s, which led to increased efforts to regulate them by the federal government and some state agencies. In 1976, an amendment to the Social Security Act stimulated states to regulate and monitor board-and-care facilities though regulations that apply to homes with three or more residents receiving Supplemental Security Income (SSI). In 1981, a provision was added to the Older Americans Act (OAA) that required state nursing home ombudsmen programs to investigate complaints they receive concerning board-and-care facilities (Gillespie and Sloan 1990). Those federal initiatives have not been supported by any additional funds, so the basic responsibilities of enforcement still falls on the states, which have a variety of enforcement practices. As with any congregate living situation, it is important to check the record of the facility as well as try to determine the following:

- What services are included?
- What is the degree of privacy in the living arrangements?

- Are there rules about alcohol and pets?
- Is the facility licensed?
- Can residents bring some of their own furnishings?
- Is a telephone available?
- Are guests are permitted?
- What is the quality of the food?
- Is the facility safe in terms of locks, fire extinguishers, easy and quick emergency exits?
- How is the overall cleanliness of the facility?
- How is the money handled?
- Is the manager and any staff, competent and friendly?
- What is the opinion of the current residents of life in the facility?

The owners of these types of facilities set the fees, which in 1990 varied from $240 to $2,500 a month (Gillespie and Sloan 1990). Many residents in these facilities are on some form of assistance, including Supplemental Security Income (SSI), which often has a bearing on the amount of fees that are charged. These types of facilities, if run properly, can provide adequate long-term care for some older people.

NURSING HOMES/NURSING FACILITIES

One of the most difficult decisions to make is whether to put one's parent or loved one in a nursing facility. Many older people and their families perceive nursing homes as warehouses where old people just wait to die. In this waiting process, there is a widespread perception of nursing homes as places where abuse and neglect are to be expected. The 1960s and early 1970s, a period of rapid growth of nursing homes, was also a time of well-publicized nursing home scandals (Vladeck 1980). More recent reports by the Inspector General's Office of the Department of Health and Human Services indicated continued abuse and neglect in many nursing facilities despite the passage of the nursing-home reform legislation of 1987. These reports showed that "abuse comes from a variety of sources, including families and visitors, but most of the perceived abuse was attributed to overworked and undertrained aides and orderlies" (McLeod 1990: 10). The most prevalent form of abuse was physical and emotional neglect.

The Number of People in Nursing Facilities

As a result, there continues to be extensive public and professional concern over the quality of care found in nursing homes (Institute of Medicine 1986). This is a serious situation given the fact that on any given day, nursing facilities care for more people than all community hospitals combined (Aiken 1990). Research has indicated that even though only about 5 percent of older people reside in nursing facilities at any one time, of the persons who turned 65 in 1990, 43 percent will be admitted to a nursing facility sometime before they die (Kemper and Mutangh 1991). Projecting to the future based on current disability rates, the Pepper Commission (1990) estimated that the number of older persons who will live in nursing facilities will go from 1.5 million in 1990 to 5.3 million by 2030.

Characteristics of Residents

The residents of nursing homes tend to be the oldest-old, female, and white. People 85 and older made up 41.8 percent of the nursing home population in 1990 (U.S. Bureau of the Census 1993). Seventy-five percent of the residents are women, and 93 percent are white (Hing 1987). The rate of nursing home admission for women 85 and older is 248.9 per 1,000 compared to 13.8 per 1,000 for women aged 65 to 74, and 66.5 per 1,000 for women aged 75 to 84. For those 85 and older, 23 percent of white people and 14 percent of black people live in nursing homes (Rivlin and Wiener 1988).

The need for nursing facility care is expected to rise rather sharply in the years ahead due to the projected increase in the number of older persons and particularly to the rapid increase in the number of people 85 and older, the fastest growing sector of our population.

Omnibus Budget Reconciliation Act (OBRA) of 1987

To address the conditions that were documented by investigations and studies by the U.S. Senate Special Committee on Aging (1986), the U.S. Government Accounting Office (1987), and the Institute of Medicine (1986), which found that thousands of frail elderly people were in nursing homes that did not provide the care that met their most basic health and safety needs, Congress passed the Omnibus Budget Reconciliation Act of 1987 (OBRA). The studies that led to the passage of the OBRA of 1987 urgently recommended a stronger role for the federal government as a way to improve the quality of care in nursing homes. The passage of this legislation was the result of the cooperation of Congress, consumer groups, nursing home provider associations, and aging advocacy organizations.

The 1987 OBRA legislation addressed many issues, from the definition of nursing facilities to the details of staffing and operating a nursing facility. As of October 1, 1990, the distinction between a Skilled Nursing Facility (SNF) and an Intermediate Care Facility (ICF) was eliminated; all nursing homes that participate in either Medicare or Medicaid must meet the same standards for services, the rights of the residents, staffing and training of staff, and other administrative considerations. All nursing homes, former SNFs and ICFs, are now called "nursing facilities" and are held to a single standard of care (National Citizens Coalition for Nursing Home Reform 1990).

Provisions of the Omnibus Budget Reconciliation Act (OBRA) of 1987   The 1987 OBRA focused on a range of provisions that affect the quality of care for nursing facility residents including:

- *Quality of life*: Each nursing facility is required to "care for its residents in such a manner and in such an environment as will promote maintenance or enhancement of the quality of life of each new resident."

- *Provision of services and activities*: Each nursing facility is "to provide services and activities to attain or maintain the highest practicable physical, mental, and psychological well-being of each resident in accordance with a written plan."
- *Participation in facility administration*: "Resident and advocate participation" is to be a criteria for assessing the operation of a nursing facility.

In addition to these general provisions, the OBRA of 1987 provided for specific rights of nursing facility residents including the following:

- *Rights to information:*
  —inspection plans
  —advance notice of change in room or roommate
  —complaint procedures and how to contact the state ombudsman
  —available services
  —applying for Medicaid benefits
- *Self-determination:*
  —choosing a physician
  —planning care and treatment
  —individual needs and preferences
  —voicing grievances
  —participating in resident and family groups
- *Personal and privacy rights:*
  —social and religious activities
  —medical treatment and telephone communications
  —personal and clinical records
- *Transfer and discharge rights:*
  —reasons for transfer
  —notice to residents
- *Visiting rights:*
  —immediate access by personal physician
  —immediate access by relatives with resident's consent
  —immediate access by others with resident's consent and "reasonable" restrictions
  —ombudsman access
- *Protection against Medicaid discrimination:*
  —identical policies and practices regardless of source of payment
  —no transfer or discharge because of change of payment to Medicaid
- *Protection of personal funds:*
  —if resident chooses, manage resident's personal funds in accordance with OBRA provisions
  —upon resident's death, turn funds over to resident's trustee
- *Rights against restraints and abuse:*
  —freedom from physical or mental abuse, corporal punishment, or involuntary seclusion
  —freedom from restraints used for discipline or the convenience of staff
  —freedom from restraints without a physician's written order
  —freedom from drugs to control mood, mental status, or behavior without a physician's order in a written plan of care and an annual review by an independent, external expert
- *Rights regarding incompetent residents:*
  —rights of residents who are judged by a court to be incompetent to be exercised by a person appointed under state law to act on behalf of the resident
- *Rights for families or legal representative:*
  —notified with 24 hours of an accident
  —notified of appeal rights
  —notified of change in room or roommate
  —participate in the planning of care
  —participate in a family council
  —make recommendations to the facility which is required to listen and act on grievances and recommendations

In addition to these provisions, the OBRA of 1987 and other federal and state regulations have outlined staffing requirements for administrators, registered nurses, licensed practical nurses, nurses aides, physicians, medical directors, activities directors, social workers, pharmacists, dietary supervisors, occupational therapists, physical therapists, and medical records supervisors.

Because of size differences, not all staff positions are maintained in all nursing facilities. Arrangements can be made with community resources in some instances to provide services such as pharmacy supplies. In addition, the 1987 OBRA mandated training requirements for nurses aides. It also provided for survey teams to make routine and unscheduled audits to make sure the facilities are meeting their requirements.

About 75 percent of the nursing facilities are for-profit operations (proprietary facilities). Some have argued that the nonprofit (nonproprietary) facilities provide higher quality care than the for-profit facilities. A 1987 study could not document this claim (Duffy 1987). This study found no difference in the quality of care between both types of operations. A survey of the nursing-home industry indicated that for-profit facilities charged higher rates than all categories of nonprofit private rooms (Marion Merrel Dow 1992). The same survey indicated that while the overall average room rates increased for 1991, all types of nonprofit nursing facilities actually lowered their rates for many types of rooms, from 34 percent to 5 percent, depending on type of room and level of service.

Even with regulations and standards, placing a loved one in a nursing facility is still a very difficult decision, often involving strong feelings of guilt on the part of the responsible family members or friends. Salamon and Rosenthal (1990) cited numerous studies which document why so many older people and their families hesitate to seriously consider placements in nursing facilities. These include the following:

1. Fear of institutions, which includes fearing something new, something different, something they have heard bad stories about, something where the care of the parent is in the hands of strangers, and something that is viewed by many to be avoided at all costs. This fear, with all its implications, is real and cannot be ignored. It needs to be dealt with by facts and other approaches (Goffman 1983).

2. The familiarity of the home environment is something that is prized by almost everyone. Even though moving into an adult child's home means leaving their own home, most older people are familiar with their children's homes. They are not nearly as threatening as institutions are (Haug 1985).

3. The high cost of nursing facilities concerns almost everyone. Most people cannot afford to pay the costs of institutions for more than a few months (Brody 1984).

4. The whole concept of continuity of life within the family is a widely held concern. This relates to the extended family relying on each other and how this might be lost when a parent moves into a nursing facility (Kingson, Hirshorn, and Cornman 1986).

5. Reciprocity is another factor in trying to keep an ill parent in one's home. Family reciprocity means that adult children think they owe total level of care to their parents because their parents took care of them when they were young and dependent (Brody, Johnson, Fulcomer, and Lang 1983; Horowitz and Shindelman 1983).

6. The older person's resistance to a planned move to a nursing facility is one of the most important reasons why many people do not seriously consider such a move until conditions can no longer be tolerated. Even then, many caregiving relatives are afraid or uncomfortable raising the issue.

7. Feelings of guilt within the adult child are powerful forces propelling her or him to be an around-the-clock caregiver.

Individually or in combination, these are powerful reasons for people to try to take care of their ill and frail older folks in their own homes. Studies consistently indicate that about 80 to 90 percent of the care older people need is provided by family caregivers. Among the most ill and frail elderly, more than twice as many are cared for by relatives than are placed in nursing facilities or other institutions. The stresses on these caregivers are huge. To make matters worse, only about 20 percent of those elderly persons cared for in the home setting use any of the formal community-based services that are available to them (Osterkamp 1988).

Reasons to Turn to a Nursing Home

In spite of all the pressures on people to care for their sick or frail elderly relatives in their homes, conditions can develop that result in finally considering a nursing facility. According to Salamon and Rosenthal (1990), these conditions usually fall into two categories (1) the continued deteriorating condition of the elderly parent, and (2) the ongoing strain and eventual exhaustion of the caregiver.

Deteriorating Health Conditions   In the category of the deteriorating condition of the elderly parent, the following factors usually are evident:

Multiple Health Problems   Study after study has indicated that family support and active involvement in the care of ill and frail elderly relatives in America are great (Brody 1990). In fact, the support and care of these relatives are the most important factors in keeping older people out of nursing facilities. Family-cared-for old folks are found to have about four health problems per person when they finally enter a nursing home (Osterkamp 1988). These multiple conditions become increasingly difficult for the home caregiver to manage.

Intensity of Care   Closely related to this is the level and amount of care required by the elderly patients. The average home caregiver spends four to five hours a day, seven days a week in direct hands-on care to the elderly patient in her home. When the amount of care needed goes beyond these numbers and becomes continuous care seven days a week, the situation usually becomes impossible and other arrangements must be made to prevent the collapse of the caregiver.

Skill Level Required   When professional medical skills that the adult child caregiver does not

have are needed on an ongoing basis, nursing home placement needs to be considered in fairness to the patient and to the caregiver.

Combination of Physical and Mental Problems   Research has indicated that when the elderly patient develops a combination of physical and mental problems, the amount and level of care required often lead to the careful consideration of a nursing home placement for one's loved one (Brody 1990).

Loss of Bladder or Bowel Control   The inability to control bladder or bowel functions (incontinence) is often the last straw in caring for an ill elderly parent. Many caregivers are simply not prepared to assume the level of care that is needed to provide for patients who cannot control their bladder or bowels.

Burnout of the Caregivers   In the category of the burnout or exhaustion of the adult-child caregiver, the following factors are important:

Demands of Their Own Families   These demands often begin to wear down the resources of the primary family caregiver. In a study done by the Travelers Insurance Company, 80 percent of the caregivers said that caring for the elderly had interfered with other family responsibilities and with their social and emotional needs (Eagan 1986).

Family Tensions   Closely related to family responsibilities which can overwhelm the primary caregiver of an ailing parent is the reality of family tensions (Salamon and Rosenthal 1990). It is one thing to be burdened by the usual family responsibilities which go with being a spouse, parent, and housekeeper. It is another thing to experience the tensions that can develop as a result of being a caregiver in an extended family setting. Strains may develop between the wife and husband when she is exhausted and on edge from all the time and effort spent on caregiving. This strain may easily extend to the couple's sexual life. Strains may develop around the financial costs of trying to be a home caregiver. It is not uncommon to spend thousands of dollars a year doing all the things necessary to provide around-the-clock care for an ill relative, considering the costs of medicines, special equipment, and outside specialized help even a few hours a week. Family tensions may also develop over the lack of space and privacy in the home when an ill elderly parent moves in.

Parent-Child Tensions   Another strain that can enter the picture for middle-aged caregivers are tensions between themselves and the elderly parents for whom they are providing care (Salamon and Rosenthal 1990). These tensions may be the result of unresolved issues that were there since the caregivers were children. They may be the result of Mom or Dad's health condition or the physical exhaustion of the caregivers and their elderly patients, not unusual in situations of ongoing illness. Unresolved, these tensions may be the final factor that causes the caregiver to seek a nursing facility placement.

Employment Needs   The need for the caregiver to go back to work to earn money needed to survive is another reason to finally consider placing a loved one in a nursing facility. Over the past few years, the percentage of women working to help support their families has soared. Also, there are many women who through divorce, widowhood, or never having been married, need to work to support themselves and their dependents, including elderly parents, who rely on them.

Source of Admissions to Nursing Facilities

The majority of admissions to nursing facilities come from hospitals. The percentage of patients admitted to nursing facilities for the first time directly from hospitals was 54.4 percent in 1990, 63.8 percent in 1991. The percentage of readmitted patients to nursing facilities directly from hospitals in 1990 was 47.8 percent; in 1991 it was 69 percent. These dramatic increases in a period of one year reflect the increased use of nursing facilities by third-party payers (insurers) and HMOs (Health Maintenance Organizations) as *subacute facilities*, facilities providing a level of care just below acute-care hospitals (Marion Merrel Dow 1992). For-profit and larger (over 200 licensed beds) facilities received more of their patients directly from hospitals than did nonprofit and smaller facilities.

Choosing a Nursing Facility

Some small towns in America have only one or two nursing facilities. In these instances, choices are extremely limited or nonexistent. However, in most areas of the country, there is a variety of nursing-home-type facilities from which to choose. In 1991, there were 15,324 nursing facilities in the United States offering 1,625,936 licensed long-term-care beds. They are divided into four categories of ownership: (1) government, (2) religious-institution-related, (3) secular not-for-profit, and (4) secular for-profit. Seventy percent of all nursing homes contained from 50 to 150 beds, with some facilities having over 200 beds. The thirty largest nursing home chains operated some 21 percent of the nation's nursing facilities. The occupancy rate of all nursing facilities was 94.8 percent (Marion Merrel Dow 1992). How can a decision be made as to which nursing facility to chose?

First, nursing facilities can be assessed on the basis of the patient's needs and wants, both of which should be taken into consideration as much as possible. Needs refer to the medical, physical, and mental requirements of the patient. Wants refer to the particular personality and lifestyle of the patient. Some places are more comfortable to certain people than others.

Second, active participation in the selection process can ease the guilt adult children typically have over placing their loved one in a nursing home. Most relatives have some difficulties in making this decision. They can take some comfort in knowing they have weighed the important factors in selecting a nursing home, and from all they can see, they have helped choose the best one for their relative.

A variety of pamphlets, books, and experts have offered advice as to what to look for in selecting a nursing facility. Some go into great depth. Others simply list some basic things to ask and look for. One of the best outlines for selecting a nursing facility is in Salamon and Rosenthal's book, *Home or Nursing Home: Making the Right Choices*, (1990). Another is a booklet entitled "How to Choose a Nursing Home" prepared by the Michigan Citizens for Better Care (CBC) and the Institute of Gerontology of the University of Michigan (1989). Other organizations and agencies that serve older people have developed booklets, pamphlets, and check lists that are good guides in assessing nursing facilities.

Questions to Ask and What to Look For In Choosing a Nursing Facility

- Is the facility licensed?
- Who owns and manages the facility?
  —Is it for-profit or not-for-profit?
  —Is it part of a chain?
  —Does the administrator have more than one facility to manage?
  —Who is in charge when the administrator is away?
  —Is the administrator licensed?
  —Does the administrator seem friendly?
- Is the home eligible for Medicare and Medicaid reimbursement?
- Does the home have Medicaid residents?
  —Is the home restricted to private-pay patients?
  —What happens to private-pay patients when their funds run out?
- What are the basic costs of the facility?
  —What do these costs include?
- Does the home make extra charges for special diets or feeding a patient?
- Are there special charges for walkers, crutches or canes?
- Are bills itemized?

- What about physician services?
  —What physician services are included? What are extra?
  —Are there charges to hold a bed while the resident is in the hospital?
- What are the visiting policies?
  —What are the limitations?
- What are the living arrangements?
  —Do all residents share a room?
  —Are private rooms available?
  —How much privacy is there for a patient?
  —Is the facility clean?
  —How does it smell?
- What is the food like?
  —Is there any choice?
  —Are special diets accommodated?
  —Do the patients enjoy the food?
- Are private physicians allowed?
- Who provides eye care, dental care, and mental health care?
- Is there a staff social worker and a recreation staff?
- Are rehabilitation services available?
- Are clergy encouraged to visit?
  —Does the facility recognize and support the religious needs of the patient?
  —Is there a chapel or prayer room in the facility?
- What is the ratio of staff to patients?
- What are the rules concerning personal possession, including some personal furniture?
- Is the location convenient?
  —Is it close the family?
  —Is it in an area that is generally pleasing?
- What happens to residents when they become ill?
  —How ill must they become before they are hospitalized?
  —Does the facility work with a local hospital in the case of ill residents?
- Does the staff try to get to know the resident?
  —Do staff members show respect for the patient?
  —How does the staff address patients?
- Does the home encourage the participation of a resident council?
  —What are the rights of the resident council?

- How are suggestions, questions, and complaints handled?
   —Is there a way to effectively address the questions and complaints of residents and relatives?

It is not necessary to ask all these questions for each specific case, but families should have some knowledge about the areas covered.

Overall Impression   What is your overall impression of the facility? Does it look clean? How does it smell? Is the atmosphere cheery and bright, or dull and dingy? Are staff members courteous to the residents, family and visitors?

Ownership   Who owns the facility? Is it a nonprofit or for-profit operation? Who operates it in either case? Is it licensed? Is it supported or affiliated by a religious organization? Is it a stable operation? Does it appear it will be in operation for a long time? All of these questions get to the quality of ownership and management.

Costs   How much does it cost to be in the facility? What do the costs cover? Are there extra costs? If so, what are they and when do they apply? Is this a self-pay facility only? Does it accept Medicaid patients? What happens if and when a patient runs out of money to pay the costs? These are vital questions because of the enormous costs of long-term care and the inability of so many people to pay for any extended stay in a nursing facility.

Treatment of Residents   How well are the residents cared for? What is the training of the various staff who care for patients? How much freedom do residents have? What restrictions are placed on residents? To what extent are they medicated? Do they have any choice of roommates? Are there any private rooms? How are problems and complaints handled? Is there a resident's council? How are patient and family concerns handled?

Resident and Family Councils

As part of the OBRA of 1987, provisions were made to ensure the establishment of resident councils and family councils in long-term-care facilities. Resident councils provide for the ongoing input of the residents in the operation of a nursing facility as well as a means to disseminate information to the residents. This is an important vehicle to improve the lives of residents in such facilities by giving them a voice and outlet for various conditions as they arise.

Family councils are vehicles for the loved ones of residents of nursing facilities to band together to have input into the operation and address issues and conditions that inevitably arise in any congregate living situation. The vulnerability of nursing facility residents makes the resident councils important features in trying to protect and improve the lives of people who live in these types of facilities.

Placing a loved one in a nursing facility is almost always difficult. However, with the enactment of various legislative provisions and the development of various programs, at least this difficult decision can be made with some objectivity, some standards, and some hope and knowledge that one is not abandoning a loved one when a decision is made to seek a nursing facility placement. In fact, research has indicated that too many people wait too long before they turn to these types of facilities. Family caregivers usually exhaust their own resources before they face the reality of a nursing facility (Osterkamp 1988).

Dealing with Feelings of Guilt and Distress

Placing a loved one in a nursing facility produces stressful feelings, including feelings of guilt, for many in our society. These are common reactions. Many experience strong feelings of guilt as they recognize that they cannot provide the care their loved ones need. They may be burned out and unable to continue the maximum efforts they have expended. They may not be capable of providing the level of care required by their patient

(Kahana and Kahana 1985). One study indicated that putting an elderly parent in a nursing home does not reduce the caregiver's burdens (George 1984). This study found that there were no real differences in the mental health of caregivers whose loved ones were in nursing homes and those who lived with them. Another study found that most stress for caregivers of nursing-home patients came from the patients' mental condition and trying to juggle spending time with the institutionalized patient and the demands of one's own life (Townsend, Deimling, and Noelker 1988). Most people do not "dump" their ailing parents or loved ones in nursing facilities. They did it with great reluctance. Many do it after they have spent great energy trying to care for them themselves (Eagan 1991). Some have no choice following a parent's hospitalization. How can adult children deal with these feelings? How can they feel that they are doing their best to continue to help loved ones who are in a nursing home? How can they continue to be caregivers?

Being a Caregiver for Someone in a Nursing Home

Even after a loved one is in a nursing home, an adult child or friend can still continue to be a caregiver. Relatives and friends who are responsible for elderly persons can have important roles and functions in helping in the care of their institutionalized relatives and friends. There are some very positive steps these people can take.

Visiting　One of the most important things caregivers can do is visit. It is not necessary to visit twice a day, and in most instances, not even every day. Maybe once a week is all they can manage because of distance, jobs, or other responsibilities. Meaningful visits are important—visits where there is a real exchange of care and support. One of the best illustrations of this is demonstrated in a film entitled *Peege*. It is a story of a family visiting Grandma in a nursing home. The whole family goes together: Mom, Dad, and their children. Peege, the Grandma, is not very lucid.

She sits in her chair staring at no one. The family comes just before a holiday. They all talk about their busy lives—lives that Peege really does not comprehend: school activities, business trips, and so on. They all make small talk which pretty much goes over Peege's head. After a relatively short time everybody leaves Peege except one of her grandsons, who stops to reminisce with Peege about some good times they had in the past when she was active and he was a young boy. These memories really get through to Peege, and a beautiful smile lights up her face. She remembers a zest for life, the fun she had with her grandson. It is a beautiful time; it is a beautiful visit. The quality of visits to institutionalized persons is at least as important as the number of visits.

Monitor Care　Another important thing a caregiving adult can do for a parent in a nursing facility is to monitor the care received. This is an important and delicate role. It includes knowing whom to talk to first when a situation arises that does not seem right. It is important to talk first to the person who can do something about a situation. This may be an attending staff person, a charge nurse, a supervisor, or an administrator. When one is in doubt about a condition or situation and unclear as to how to handle it, it can be helpful to ask someone in the local Long-Term Care Ombudsman Program how to proceed. Describing the problem and getting advice on whom to address and how to proceed is useful. It is important for the families and advocates of nursing facility residents to become familiar with and, when necessary, use the services of local Long-Term Care Ombudsman Programs.

Participate in Decision-Making　Participating in the decisions that are made concerning the lives of loved ones who are patients in nursing facilities can be an ambiguous role (Brody 1990). Some decisions are made solely by the nursing facility staff, such as moving a person to a different level of care when the resident's condition has changed. However, there are many decisions that involve input by the resident and his or her primary caregiver in the family or a trusted friend. What if she or he cannot make these decisions? What if she or he is intimidated and afraid to voice her or his wishes? These are instances where the outside caregiver, a child, a spouse, or a friend, can make a meaningful difference.

Acquaint the Staff with the Patient   Another way family members or friends can be helpful is to talk to the staff of the facility about their loved ones. It is helpful to acquaint the staff with key facts so they can know about the lives of their residents and to know their patients as "real people." One story is told about an older man who became a patient in a nursing home. The staff had a real problem with him because he slept much of the day and wandered around most of the night. They did not really know what to do with him. Various medications were considered to help him get his nights and days straight. The staff wondered if this condition was the result of some serious medical situation. The whole picture became clear and the situation was resolved when they learned that the man had been a night watchman most of his life. Sleeping days and working nights was his life. No one in the nursing home knew this until they were told. It has been suggested that a simple but comprehensive biography be placed by a resident's bed so all of the staff may become familiar with their patients. It personalizes the patient. It makes her or him a real person with a past they can relate to instead of just another occupant of a bed. Making the nursing facility resident a real person to the staff is something a relative or friend can do to make life better for a loved one.

Nursing Home Rights   A caring relative or friend can obtain copies of the rights of nursing facility residents as guaranteed by the federal government and each state. Copies of these documents can be obtained from local Long-Term Care Ombudsman Programs, Area Agencies on Aging, or a State Office on Aging (whose tele-

phone numbers and addresses can be obtained from telephone directories or directories of state offices). These rights are updated from time to time, so it is important to have the latest versions. As has been noted, these rights directly relate to the quality of care and the quality of life of nursing home residents.

Resident and Family Councils   Another way to assist loved ones in nursing facilities is to become familiar with and participate in family councils. Not all nursing facilities have family councils. They provide means for ongoing input into the life of the nursing home.

All of these are ways family members and friends responsible for older people can continue to be effective caregivers of their loved ones who have been placed in a nursing facility. Being effective caregivers can help persons deal with the stressful feelings they usually experience after placing their mother, father, spouse, or close friend in a nursing home.

LONG-TERM CARE OMBUDSMAN PROGRAM

A vital resource for older people, their families, and people who work with them is the Long-Term Care Ombudsman Program. Begun as a demonstration program in the early 1970s, it became part of the 1978 amendments to the Older Americans Act. As such, it became available in all states. Under the direction of a full-time state ombudsman, the program is set up to:

1. Investigate and resolve complaints made by or on behalf of residents of long-term care facilities.
2. Monitor the development and operation of federal, state, and local laws, regulations, and policies for long-term facilities.
3. Provide information about the problems of residents of long-term care facilities to appropriate public agencies.
4. Provide training to staff and volunteers to participate in the ombudsman program.

5. As of the 1981 amendments to the Older Americans Act (OAA), serve the residents of board and care homes.

The basic role of the long-term care ombudsman is to be a consumer advocate. The 1987 Amendments to the OAA strengthened this long-term care program. Included were provisions to require the states to:

1. Provide access to facilities and records.
2. Offer immunity for the good faith for the ombudsmen.
3. Offer legal representation for ombudsmen if needed.
4. Make it unlawful to interfere with the official duties of an ombudsman.
5. Make it unlawful to retaliate against the residents of a facility or others who make a complaint or cooperate with ombudsmen (U.S. Senate Special Committee on Aging 1992).

Although they have numerous functions as outlined above, the major role of the Long-Term Care Ombudsman Program is to assist residents of long-term care facilities and their advocates in resolving complaints and problems with the facility operators. Ombudsman programs have some enforcement powers in some states. In other states they have semi-regulatory authority. In all states their goal is to resolve complaints. If the residents or their families are not able to resolve an issue or complaint, the ombudsmen can refer the situations to the state agencies that regulate nursing facilities. Where abuse or neglect are present, cases are referred directly to the state regulatory agencies. In cases other than abuse or neglect, ombudsmen make attempts to resolve the issue on the local level.

The Long-Term Ombudsman Programs are important resources in educating patients and their families. They often have a working relationship with the facility they are called upon to deal with concerning a complaint. They also work with families and facilities in obtaining Medicare or Medicaid coverage for patients.

They know how to apply the rights of nursing facility residents, as guaranteed by federal and state laws. They are rich resources for all kinds of information concerning nursing facilities.

In fiscal year 1990, there were 578 ombudsman programs across America. The number of complaints they handled rose from 41,000 in 1982 to 154,000 in 1990, (U.S. Senate Special Committee on Aging 1992). Of all the complaints received in 1989, about 69 percent were fully or partially resolved. As a result of their knowledge of nursing facilities in specific local areas, Long-Term Care Ombudsmen Programs can be valuable resources for selecting nursing resources. They probably will not recommend one over another, but they can provide information that can be helpful in the selection process.

DEALING WITH TRANSFER TRAUMA

Being placed in a nursing facility can be the most difficult change one can make in a lifetime. This has been called *transfer trauma*. It was thought to even cause death. However more recent reviews of the relocation of elderly persons has suggested that this is not as serious a problem as was previously indicated (Salamon and Rosenthal 1990). This is especially true if certain steps are followed with the patient.

Preparing for the Move Studies have indicated that if the patient is prepared for a move to a nursing facility, the anxiety level on the part of the patient is reduced (Bornp 1982). Discussing the move, talking about the good features of the facilities, having staff members show the potential residents around, introducing them to residents, and pointing out that the other residents are managing pretty well in these circumstances are all part of preparation.

Realizing Limitations Helping potential residents realize the limitations of the care they can get in their home settings tends to help them understand the need for the help they can get in a nursing home. Some people simply cannot get the level of care they need in a private home setting (Koff 1982).

Sharing Situations It can be easier for older people to adapt to a nursing facility placement if they realize that they will be among people who are "in the same boat," who have limitations and conditions that are similar to their own. Being in a setting where one is among others with similar problems tends to make one's own limitations seem less severe. As a result, there is less of a threat to self-esteem (Myles 1970). Being the only person with severe limitations among healthy, able people tends to magnify one's problems and difficulties.

Understanding the Reason for the Move Helping older people understand the reasons for placement in a nursing facility can help them adjust to such a drastic move. When they realize that the quality of their lives depends on the kinds of resources nursing facilities can give them, older people can begin to actually feel uneasy in a private home setting (Salamon and Rosenthal 1990). Coming to this understanding on the part of older persons requires repeating the explanation with openness and warmth.

Keeping Prized Possessions Letting older people take some prized possessions to a nursing facility can help them make the transition to institutional life (Salamon and Rosenthal 1990). It gives them continuity with their past lives. It also gives the staff something to talk about that ties in with past experiences.

Becoming Involved with Activities Most all nursing facilities provide a range of activities for their residents. Activity directors have become an essential part of nursing home life. Taking one's attention off one's problems can be very helpful. Activities can occupy the mind as well as the body. Mental and physical stagnation are generally not beneficial. Getting involved with others

in programs and activities helps residents feel accepted as individuals in a social setting, which is important to everyone. It also helps them see that Mary and Joe, in spite of their age and physical limitations, can still enjoy being active around other people. Being involved with others with limitations can help residents see that even though they are not what they used to be, they are better off than others who have more severe problems: "Look at Pete over there. He sure is in worse shape than I am. I'm lucky I'm not that bad off." This realization can put one's own limitations and conditions in a more positive perspective.

THE COST OF NURSING FACILITIES

Almost everyone knows that nursing facilities are expensive. The overall average for all types of rooms in all types of facilities for skilled care in 1991 was $83 a day. For a private room in a for-profit facility the average was $92 a day. A semi-private room in a religious facility cost $74 per day. The average daily room rates increased 5 percent for skilled care from 1990 to 1991. At $83 a day, the yearly rate averages over $30,000. The yearly cost can be over $50,000 a year depending on the location and facility (U.S. Senate Special Committee on Aging 1992). How can the average American afford over $30,000 a year to stay in a nursing facility? Obviously, most cannot. Various studies have indicated that most people are forced to "spend down" to the poverty level to become eligible for Medicaid, the federal program that is supposed to pay the medical-care costs of impoverished Americans. A study released by the U.S. House of Representatives Select Committee on Aging (1987) indicated that 70 percent of single older Americans spend down to poverty within thirteen weeks after admission to a nursing home. As a result, Medicaid was the largest source of revenue for nursing homes in 1991. It accounted for 60.9 percent of nursing-home revenues in 1991, up from 58.8 percent in 1990 and 57.6 percent in 1989. Medicare payments declined as a source of revenue to nursing homes from 8.3 percent in 1989, 8 percent in 1990, to 6.9 percent in 1991 (Marion Merrel Dow 1992). This was the result of cutbacks by the federal government in Medicare reimbursements that affected all types of nursing facilities. Contrary to what many people believe, Medicare payments for nursing facilities care are very restricted. To receive Medicare support for nursing facility care a person must meet six conditions:

1. The patient's condition requires daily skilled nursing or skilled rehabilitation services which can only be provided in a skilled nursing facility.
2. The patient has been in a hospital at least three days before being admitted to a participating skilled nursing facility.
3. The patient is admitted to the skilled nursing facility within a short time after leaving the hospital.
4. The care in the skilled nursing facility is for a condition that was treated in the hospital, or for a condition that developed while the patient was receiving care in a skilled nursing facility for a condition that was treated in the hospital.
5. A medical professional certifies that the patient needs, and receives, skilled nursing or skilled rehabilitation services on a daily basis.
6. The patient's stay in the skilled nursing facility is not disapproved by the medical intermediary.

If a person meets all of these six conditions, Part A of Medicare pays for up to 100 days in a Medicare-participating skilled nursing facility in each benefit period. In 1991, it paid for all covered services for the first 20 days. In the next 80 days it paid for all covered services, except for $78.50 a day, which for 80 days is $6,280 (U.S. Senate Special Committee on Aging 1991). Most people end up needing custodial care in nursing facilities which is not covered by Medicare.

Most older people are not prepared to pay for long-term care in nursing facilities. Most families cannot afford to help pay the nursing home costs of older relatives. How many families in America can afford to pay yearly costs of $30,000 to $50,000? This is truly a major social problem in the United States.

SUMMARY

There are a wide range of living situations older people encounter as they leave independent living environments. Moving from their old homes means different things to older people depending on what types of moves are involved.

Congregate living situations are called, among other names, "homes for the aged," "old people's homes," and "retirement homes." These arrangements provide rooms or apartments with common dining facilities where meals are served on a regular basis and there is access to social and recreational services. Congregate living is seen by many experts as a significant way to bridge the gap between independent and dependent living for persons who need some assistance with daily living but not ongoing continuous care. Some key factors need to be considered in selecting a congregate care facility.

A type of facility that is becoming increasingly popular is the continuing care retirement community. In this type of situation, for an entrance fee, a person can move from an independent living unit in a congregate care setting to a nursing facility placement, usually all on the same campus or complex. There are, however, some major cautions to be aware of in this type of arrangement.

Board-and-care homes are often relatively small facilities with "mom and pop" operators who provide for the care of people needing assistance with daily living. Regulations for these types of facilities are necessary but not always in place, depending on the state.

Nursing facilities constitute a key element of long-term care in America, but many people have dismal views of these facilities based on widely published stories of abuse and neglect. Nevertheless, nursing facilities are vital to a significant percentage of older people; although only about 5 percent of older people are in nursing facilities at any one time, some 43 percent will be admitted before they die. Nursing facility residents are primarily the oldest old, female, and white. The need for nursing facility care is expected to rise sharply in the future as the population continues to age. The provisions of the Omnibus Budget Reconciliation Act of 1987 detailed the rights of nursing facility residents as well as the guidelines for the operation of these facilities.

There are as many reasons for keeping a loved one out of a nursing facility as there are factors that ultimately lead to admission. There are specific items to look for in choosing a nursing facility.

Long-Term Care Ombudsman Programs are in operation around the nation. They can be very helpful in addressing and finding solutions to problems patients and their families may have with specific situations in nursing facilities. They can also be useful in providing information in selecting a nursing home or board-and-care facility.

Resident and Family Councils have become important components in the operation of nursing facilities. They provide opportunities for patients and their families to have input in the ongoing administration of a nursing facility. Most people experience feelings of stress and guilt when they place a loved one in a nursing home. Continuing to be a caregiver even after a nursing facility placement of a loved one can be helpful in relieving these feelings.

Residing in a nursing facility costs between $30,000 to $50,000 a year. Who in America can afford these costs? Medicare pays only a small portion. Out-of-pocket payments by patients and their families along with Medicaid pay most of the costs of nursing facility fees. However, Medicaid eligibility requires patients to spend down to poverty level before they are covered. Is this what is expected of Americans who have worked all their lives to support themselves, raise their children if they were parents, and support the institutions of our society through taxes and contributions?

REFERENCES

American Association of Retired Persons. *The Board and Care System: A Regulatory Jungle*. Washington, DC: AARP.

Aiken, O.H. 1990. Educational Innovation in Gerontology: Teaching Nursing Homes and Gerontological Nurse Practitioners. The Beverly Lecture on Gerontology and Geriatrics Education (No. 5). Washington, DC: AGHE.

Bornp, J.H. 1982. The Effects of Varying Degrees of Interinstitutional Environment Change on Long-Term Care Patients. *Gerontologist*, 22: 409–417.

Brody, E.M., Johnson, P.T., Fulcomer, M.C., and Lang, A.M. 1983. Women's Changing Role and Help to the Elderly: Attitudes of Three Generations of Women. *Journal of Gerontology*, 38: 597–607.

Brody, E.M. 1984. Women in the Middle. *Gerontologist*, 21: 471–480.

Brody, E.M. 1990. *Women in the Middle: Their Parent-Care Years*. New York: Springer.

Citizens for Better Care. 1989. How to Choose a Nursing Home. Ann Arbor, MI: University of Michigan Institute of Gerontology.

Duffy, J.M. 1987. *The Measurement of Service Productivity and Related Contextual Factors in Long-Term Care Facilities*. Unpublished doctoral dissertation. University of Texas. Austin, TX.

Eagan, A.B. 1986. Options for Aging. *New Age Journal*, 54–59. In *Aging*. 1991. Guilford, CT: Dushkin Publishing Group.

George, L. K. 1984. The Burden of Caregiving: How Much? What Kinds? For Whom? In *Advances in Research*, 8. Durham, NC: Duke University Center for Study of Aging and Human Development.

Gillespie, A.E., and Sloan, K.S. 1990. *Housing Options and Services for Older People*. Santa Barbara, CA: ABC-CLIO.

Goffman, E. 1983. *Stigma: Notes on the Management of Spoiled Identity*. Englewood Cliffs, NJ: Prentice-Hall.

Harvey, A. 1991. Life Care Contracts for the Elderly: A Risky Retirement? In *Annual Editions: Aging*, 7th Ed. Guilford, CT: Dushkin Publishing Group.

Haug, M.R. 1985. Home Care for the Ill Elderly: Who Benefits? *American Journal of Public Health*, 75: 127–128.

Hing, E. 1987. National Center for Health Statistics. Use of Nursing Homes by the Elderly: Preliminary

Data from the National Nursing Home survey. *Advance Data From Vital and Health Statistics*, (No. 135, HHS) (May 14). Washington, DC: Public Health Service.

Horowitz, A., and Shindelman, L.W. 1983. Reciprocity and Affection: Past Influences on Current Caregiving. *Journal of Gerontological Social Work*, 3: 6–16.

Institute of Medicine. 1968. *Improving the Quality of Care in Nursing Homes*. Washington DC: National Academy Press.

Kahana, E., and Kahana, B. 1985. Institutionalization—Bane or Blessing. In Hang, A.M., Ford, A.B., and Scheafor, M. (eds.), *The Mental and Physical Health of Aged Women*. New York: Springer.

Kemper, P., and Mutangh, C.M. 1991. Lifetime Use of Nursing Home Care. *New England Journal of Medicine*, 324(9): 595.

Kingson, E.R., Hirshorn, B.A., and Cornman, J.M. 1986. *Ties That Bind*. Washington, DC: Seven Locks Press.

Koff, T.H. 1982. *Long Term Care: An Approach to Serving the Frail Elderly*. Boston: Little, Brown.

Marion Merrel Dow. 1992. *Managed Care Digest, Long-Term Edition*. Kansas City, MO: Marion Merrel Dow.

McLeod, D. 1990. Abuse Abounds. *NRTA Bulletin*, (May). Washington, DC: AARP.

Myles, J.F. 1970. Institutionalization and Sick Role Identification Among the Elderly. *American Sociological Review*, 431: 508–520.

National Association of Residential Care Facilities. 1987. Directory of Residential Care Facilities. Richmond, VA: NARCF.

National Citizens Coalition for Nursing Home Reform. 1990. *Nursing Home Reform Law: The Basics*, (October). Washington, DC: NCCNHR.

Netting, F.E., and Wilson, C.C. 1987. Current Legislation Concerning Life Care and Continuing Care Contracts. *Gerontologist*, 27: 645–51.

Osterkamp, L. 1988. Family Caregiver: America's Primary Long-Term Care Resource. *In Annual Editions, Aging*, 7th Ed. 1991. Sluice Dock, Guilford, CT: Dushkin Publishing, Group, pp. 180–183.

Pepper Commission, U.S. Bipartisan Commission on Comprehensive Health Care. 1990. *A Call for Action*. Washington, DC: U.S. Government Printing Office.

Riekse, R., and Holstege, H. 1992. *The Christian Guide to Parent Care*. Wheaton, IL: Tyndale House Publishers.

Rivlin, A.M., and Wiener, J.M. 1988. *Caring for the Disabled Elderly: Who Will Pay?* Washington, DC: Brookings Institute.

Salamon, M.J., and Rosenthal, G. 1990. *Home or Nursing Home: Making the Right Choices*. New York: Springer.

Townsend, A., Deimling, G., and Noelker, L. 1988. *Transition to Nursing Home Care: Sources of Stress and Family Members' Mental Health*. Presented at 41st Annual meeting of the Gerontological Society of America, San Francisco, CA.

U.S. Bureau of the Census. 1993. *Nursing Home Population Increases in Every State*, (June) CB93-117. Washington, DC: U.S. Department of Commerce.

U.S. Government Accounting Office. 1987. *Medicare and Medicaid: Stronger Enforcement of Nursing Home Requirements Needed*, (May). HRD-87-113. Washington, DC: G.A.O.

U.S. House of Representatives. 1963. President Kennedy's message to aid elderly citizens. (House Document 72, February 21). The House: Washington, DC.

U.S. House of Representatives Select Committee on Aging. 1987. *Long-Term Care and Personal Impoverishment: Seven in Ten Elderly Living Alone Are at Risk* (Comm. Pub. 100–631). Washington, DC: U.S. Government Printing Office.

U.S. Senate Special Committee on Aging. 1986. *Nursing Home Care: The Unfinished Agenda*. (S. Pvt. 99-160). Washington, DC: U.S. Government Printing Office.

U.S. Senate Special Committee on Aging. 1991. *Getting the Most from Federal Programs: Social Security, Supplemental Security Income, Medicare*. Washington, DC: U.S. Government Printing Office.

U.S. Senate Special Committee on Aging. 1992. *Developments in Aging*: 1991, Vol. 1. Washington, DC: U.S. Government Printing Office.

Vladeck, B. 1980. *Unloving Care: The Nursing Home Tragedy*. New York: Basic Books.

SOCIAL SUPPORT SYSTEMS

CHAPTER 14

Primary Support Systems:
The Family

Help from the Family

Mary has had a stroke and needs a lot of supervision and help in everyday living. She has three children, but only one, a daughter, lives in her small town. That daughter, Jane, is 60 years old, is employed full-time, and has a husband who is thinking of retiring in two years to a southern state. Jane is increasingly angry, stressed, and filled with guilt over her feelings. She is also feeling guilty over not having more time for her own children and grandchildren. In addition, her mother is very controlling and does not accept assistance graciously.

Glen who is 74, has been a widower for two years. He has a very close relationship with a 66-year-old widow. He is thinking about marriage but is concerned about what his two children will think. His significant other has four children who believe that Mr. Diamond is too old for their mother. Both sets of children are concerned about who will get the estates if the parents marry.

Mary is taking care of her father who was and continues to be an alcoholic. He abused her when she was small. They have never talked about the abuse, but Mrs. Murphy deeply resents taking care of her father whom she does not like. Out of religious convictions and feelings of guilt she provides care, but is suffering from insomnia and anxiety attacks. Her sisters and brothers—there are five—will not help in taking care of their alcoholic, abusive father. They want to put him into a nursing home, which is an idea he vehemently rejects.

Bill was always a "Mama's Boy" and was very dependent on his mother. There is tension in his marriage because of the time he spends taking care of his mother. He is unwilling to admit that she has Alzheimer's disease, that her condition is hopeless, and that she will continue to worsen. He has taken his mother to three different medical clinics, and they have all come to the same conclusion: She does indeed have Alzheimer's disease. He has just heard rumors of a new treatment in Mexico and plans to take his mother there and spend $5,000 on "experimental" treatment for Alzheimer's disease. His wife is infuriated.

Clara is 55 and has seen her last child leave home. She cried at the wedding of this daughter, but she admits that the tears were as much over feelings of freedom over having her last child married and having the home to herself and her husband, as it was over any feeling of loss over her daughter leaving home. If there is any "empty next" depression, she was not feeling it—and she had no guilt over not feeling it.

IMPORTANCE OF THE FAMILY FOR SUPPORT

There is no doubt that the family is the basic support system for most older Americans. In spite of the changes that have occurred in the American family, and all the negative things that fill the popular press concerning family relationships, the family is still the backbone of support for most older people. For emotional support, social interaction (visiting, spending holidays together, etc.), and various types of assistance in times of health problems or frailty in old age, the American family remains ready to help its older relatives. For married older couples, the family unit is the basic financial support structure.

The type of family support an older person gets depends to a great extent on his or her family situation—whether married, widowed, separated, divorced, never married, has living children, is living alone, living with adult children, or living with friends or other relatives. To some extent, the type of family support older people get depends on whether they are living in the community or in an institutional setting such as a group home, retirement village, or nursing facility.

MARITAL SUPPORT

All of these various family characteristics have a real impact on the kind and amount of family support an older person receives. Probably the best determinant of family support for older people is marital status. Whether a person is married has great impact on that person's support within a family setting—including emotional, financial, and physical support, such as care in times of illness or infirmity.

Marital Status and Poverty

Whether an elderly person lives in a family setting or lives alone has much to do with whether they are poor or not. In 1991, only 5.1 percent of elderly married couples were poor (U.S. Bureau of the Census 1993c). This is in sharp contrast to older persons who live alone. Among the elderly who lived alone, 17.6 percent of the men and 26.6 percent of the women were poor in 1991. As another report pointed out,

> The death of a husband often marks the point of economic reversals for the surviving wife. The difference in age at marriage and the gap in life expectancy between men and women are related to the high proportion of women living alone, the earlier institutionalization of women than men, sharply reduced income and a disproportionately high level of poverty among women, and a need for

---

TABLE 14-1

OLDER WOMEN OUTNUMBER OLDER MEN BALANCE OF MALES AND FEMALES 85 YEARS AND OVER: 1930 TO 2050 (SEX RATIO IS MALES PER 100 FEMALES 85 YEARS OLD AND OVER)

Year	Sex ratio	Excess of female (thousands)
1930	75.4	38
1940	75.0	52
1950	69.7	103
1960	63.9	205
1970	53.3	430
1980	43.7	877
1990	38.6	1,339
2030	52.0	2,647
2050	57.8	4,727

Source: U.S. Bureau of the Census. Current Population Reports, 1993

special support from family members and society (U.S. Bureau of the Census 1993a: 2–9).

In the age category 65 to 69, there were 81 men for every 100 women in 1990. In the age category 85 to 89, there were only 42 men for every 100 women. As Figure 14-1 indicates, this situation will continue at least to the middle of the twenty-first century.

Widowhood and Poverty

As people grow older, not only are there more and more women compared to men in each age category, but fewer and fewer women remain married. In the young-old category, ages 65 to 74, about four-fifths of the men but only half of the women are married. By the time people reach the oldest-old category, ages 85 and older, about half of the men are still married while four-fifths of the women are widowed (U.S. Bureau of the Census 1993b).

Married-couple families are much more likely to have higher incomes than older people living alone. In 1990, for example, the majority (55 percent) of persons aged 75 and older who lived alone had incomes below $10,000. In contrast, 48.5 percent of married-couple families, where the householder was aged 75 or older, had incomes below $20,000 for the same year (U.S. Bureau of the Census 1993a).

According to the Census Bureau, older people who lived alone in 1990 were more likely to have low incomes than those who lived as married couples (U.S. Bureau of the Census 1993a). Of the 2.3 million older persons who were poor and lived alone in 1990, 2 million were older women. In addition, one million older women who lived alone in 1990 were classified as near poor. While women made up 58 percent of the total elderly population in 1990, they accounted for 74 percent of all poor older people. With the median age of widowhood for women being 55, older men were nearly twice as likely as older women to be married and living with their spouse in 1990 (74 percent for men, 40 percent for women). Elderly women (49 percent) were more than three times as likely as older men (14 percent) to be widowed, see Figures 14-1 and 14-2 (U.S. Bureau of the Census 1993a).

Marital Status and Physical Assistance

It is easy to understand why most older men have a spouse to rely on for help when they get sick or need assistance with chronic (long-term) health conditions. As women get older, the majority do not have help from a spouse. Results from the National Long-Term Care Survey showed that some 36 percent of the caregivers who helped older people who were not in institutions were spouses. Two-thirds of the caregiving spouses were wives, indicating that when men needed assistance in a family setting, a majority had wives to call on for help (Stone, Cafferate, and Sangl 1987). Relatively few older women have spouses to help them, especially as they continue to age. That is one reason why the great majority (75 percent) of nursing home residents are women (U.S. Bureau of the Census 1993c). There are relatively few husbands around to help them in their illnesses and infirmities. By age 85 and older, 51 percent of men but only 9 percent of women lived with a spouse in 1990 (U.S. Bureau of the Census 1993b). As people live longer, they are more likely to have long-term chronic illnesses and disabilities. About half of the oldest old (aged 85 and older) who live in their homes need assistance with the activities of everyday living (U.S. Bureau of the Census 1993b).

Emotional Support and Happiness in Marriage

Marriage, of course, is much more than a financial arrangement or organization for caregiving, at least ideally. It might be noted, incidentally, that many young people going into marriage are not aware of its wide-ranging financial implications. The question needs to be raised, how happy

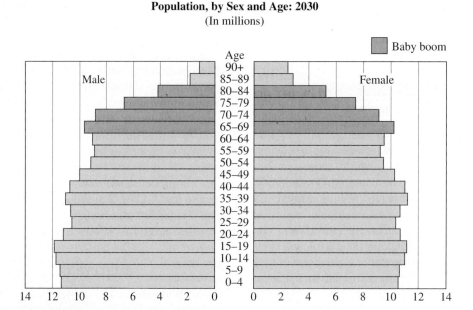

Population, by Sex and Age: 2030
(In millions)

FIGURE 14-1
Older women will continue to outnumber older men into the next century. (*Source:* U.S. Bureau of the Census. Current Population Reports, Special Studies, P23-178RV, *Sixty-five plus in America.* Washington, D.C.: U.S. Government Printing Office, May 1993, Figure 2-6, p 8.)

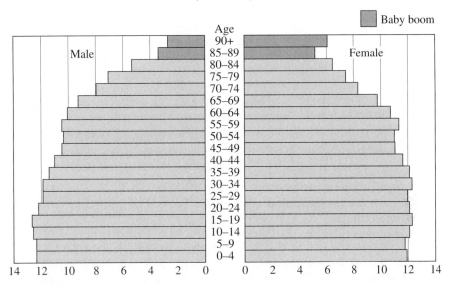

FIGURE 14-2

Older women will continue to outnumber older men into the next century. (*Source:* U.S. Bureau of the Census. Current Population Reports, Special Studies, P23-178RV, *Sixty-five plus in America.* Washington, D.C.: U.S. Government Printing Office, May 1993, Figure 2-8, p. 8.)

are older people who have been married a long time? What do they get out of their marriages?

Generally, most older couples have reported that their marriages actually improved over time (Gilford 1991). However there are gender differences. Men tend to be more satisfied with their marriages and the degree to which their emotional needs are fulfilled than are women (Rhyne 1981; Gilford 1984).

Like marriages in any age group, not everything is perfect with older couples. Older marriages have their strengths and weaknesses. Their strengths revolve around the basic functions of what being a couple is, as outlined by Robert Atchley (1994). These include:

Intimacy   A feeling of closeness to a mate usually involves mutual affection, regard for each other, and trust.

Sexual Intimacy   This is an integral part of any couple's relationship that can continue to be very fulfilling in the later years with the proper attitude and adequate physical approaches to sexual enjoyment.

Interdependence   This includes sharing resources, responsibilities, and activities. As we have already noted, one of the major reasons fewer older couples are poor compared to single older persons is mutual financial support.

Belonging   A sense of belonging is important to most people. Having a close confidant to share values and outlooks on life as well as being part of a couple is important in everyday American life. Having a comfortable partner in life is very satisfying at any age.

Strains in Long-lived Marriages

In spite of these strengths, long-lived marriages can experience particular strains. Gilford (1991) pointed out some of the strains that older people might experience with their marriages. These include:

Feelings of Marital Satisfaction Change Older couples may feel differently about the success of their marriage as time passes. Spouses aged 55 to 62 and 70 to 90 have reported less satisfaction with their marriages than those whose ages are between these two groups.

Loss of Intimacy Over the Years As the years go by, it is possible for spouses to be less involved in each other's activities and to lose feelings of marital intimacy and belonging. This can result in inability to express true feelings and frequent disagreements.

Partners Grow in Different Directions Over the course of the years of a long-lived marriage, it is possible that the partners will grow at different rates and in different directions. This may result from experiences at work, involvement in community activities, or developing personal interests.

Marriage Not the Central Point of Life It is possible that over the years marriage may no longer be the focus of a person's life. Close friendships through associations outside marriage may become more important to some spouses, resulting in strained relationships in older marriages.

Stresses of Caregiving A caregiving spouse is likely to experience a range of stresses that put some strains on marriage. Even though caregiving spouses may report satisfaction with their marriages, there is some evidence of underlying tension (Johnson 1985).

Retirement and Marriage Satisfaction

Most people believe that retirement is a stressful, life-changing event that could pose a real threat to happiness in marriage. Robert Atchley (1992) pointed out that 30 years of research on retirement has shown retirement to be a rather mild change in the lives of most people.

What does retirement do to a marriage relationship? Does the husband, if he is the one retiring, intrude on the wife's domain—the home? Does his being around so much of the time limit the wife's privacy or the way she is used to doing things on her own?

Atchley (1992) pointed to previous research that showed very different results of retirement on marriage: that retirement has negative results on marriage satisfaction; that there is no effect on marriages; that there is a positive aspect to retirement and marriage. Atchley argued that the studies producing these very different results were flawed. In what he contends is more valid research, Atchley found that a large majority (87 percent) of persons reported no change in the quality of marital relationships as the result of the retirement of a spouse. And of those who did report some changes, most were for the better:

> "We have more time together, more pursuing of mutual interests, more loving" (woman, age 64)

> "Retirement definitely improved our relationship. We have considerably more time together, and that is just super" (man, age 69).

> "Retirement improved the quality of our relationship. We have time to do the things we like, go places we desire, and just talk about our interests and concerns. We are more relaxed, less inhibited" (woman, age 67) (Atchley 1992: 153–154).

Of course, not every comment concerning retirement was positive:

> "It is very difficult to get essential things done (around the house) with someone here all the time. I get frustrated and slowed down" (woman, age 66).

"I found it to be more confusing, being with my husband 24 hours a day and giving up much of my privacy and quiet times. There are more meals to cook and more housework" (woman, age 66) (Atchley 1992: 154–155).

An important reason why retirement does not effect marital satisfaction negatively is that it comes at a time in life when most people are experiencing an increased enjoyment in marriage. Research has found that marriage satisfaction tends to follow a U-shaped pattern (Bengston, Rosenthal, and Burton 1990). For couples who marry in young adulthood, have children, and stay married into the older ages, marital satisfaction tends to be high in the early years, fall in the early child-rearing years, and rise steadily thereafter. Once children are launched into adulthood, satisfaction with marriage usually increases for both spouses. It is important to note that for most people, retirement takes place during the period of life when marital satisfaction is rising—the post child-rearing years (Atchley 1992).

Why Some Older Marriages Fail

It usually comes as a shock when couples married for 30 years or more announce they are divorcing. How can this be after so many years? Said one divorcee:

> "A year ago, my husband walked in 10 days after our 30th wedding anniversary and calmly announced that he wanted a divorce", says Kristen. . . . The real shock was that, a few months later, three days after the divorce was final, he remarried" (Broughton 1993: 3D).

There are a variety of reasons why older marriages dissolve, according to Walter Lambinder of Wayne State University (Broughton 1993). As the previous story indicates, infidelity may be one that leads to a new relationship. In addition, Lambinder pointed out, divorce does not have the stigma it used to have. As a result, persons in unhappy marriages are more likely to leave. Some couples stayed together because of the children, but once the children are grown and gone, the

marriage ends. Other couples simply become bored or experience a loss of love.

Elise Snyder, a psychoanalyst at Yale University, pointed out that in some instances divorce after many years of marriage may be the result of traumatic life events such as the death of a child, a parent, or a close friend or other life-changing events. Snyder contended that sometimes divorce after many years can be a sign of growth: "When there are genuine problems in the marriage that simply haven't been worked out, after a long time of trying, it may be healthy to just throw in the towel and move on" (Boughton 1993: 3D).

Divorce

Divorce is a significant event in the life of any person and a major economic threat to women, particularly older women.

Divorce has become a major social reality in the lives of millions of Americans as divorce rates have risen steadily for more than a century. Only about 7 percent of all marriages begun in the 1860s (the Civil War era) ended in divorce. Now, almost half of all marriages are dissolved. Our current divorce rates are double what they were immediately following World War II and three times the rates of the 1920s and 1930s (Marshall 1991).

More than 10 percent of the 41 million Americans who were divorced or separated in 1990 were aged 45 and older (Crown, Mutschler, Schulz, and Loew 1993). About 5 percent of both elderly (aged 65 and older) men and women were divorced and had not remarried in 1990 (Saluter 1991). By comparison, in 1960, fewer than 2 percent of older persons were divorced (U.S. Bureau of the Census 1993a).

Not much was known about the impact of divorce on older people until 1993, when two studies—one by the Women's Initiative of the American Association of Retired Persons (AARP) and the other by the Policy Center on Aging of Brandeis University—focused on the financial plight of older women following divorce. One reason for the lack of information about older divorced people is that government statistics often combine "divorced" women with "never married," "separated", and "widowed" women.

What these studies revealed is that after age 62, the rate of poverty among divorced older women is as high or higher than that of women who were widowed or who never married. The poverty rate for separated older women was higher than for any other category of unmarried older women including divorced women (Crown et al. 1993).

Ironically, one of the major reasons for the financial inequities in divorce, where men generally come out of divorce in much better financial condition than women, is the modern no-fault divorce revolution which began in California in 1970 (Crown et al. 1993). The no-fault approach to divorce was supposed to treat men and women equally. However, this approach ignores the economic realities of the American workplace as well as the typical division of labor in the home where no monetary value is put on women's domestic work. The no-fault standards that no longer routinely award alimony to wives ignores their unequal pay in the labor force. Only 4 percent of older divorcees receive alimony payments (Crown et al. 1993). So with limited income from paid employment and with no credit from domestic work, older divorced women are at a real disadvantage in terms of support.

An area that is under investigation for divorced persons is the growth of pensions as part of compensation for employees. According to Anne Moss (1991) of the Pension Rights Center, today's pension may be one of the most important assets a couple has. Whether a divorced wife gets access to her former husband's pension depends to a great degree on the divorce laws of the state in which she lives. In pure common-law states, separate property stays separate when divorce occurs. Only jointly held property is divided and distributed. In these states, pension benefits are normally classified as separate property and not divided upon divorce. In a community-property state, such as California, a divorced spouse has

access to the other spouse's pension benefits. Common-law states can modify their distribution of property laws by adapting the Uniform Dissolution of Marriage Act, which has the effect of putting community-property rules into operation when a dissolution of marriage action is filed (Crown et al. 1993).

Pension benefits can mean the difference between having enough to live on in retirement and living in poverty according to Moss, author of the 1993 Woman's Initiative Study of the AARP. According to the Census Bureau, of all men and women age 65 and older who received incomes in 1991, less than half as many women (22 percent) as men (49 percent) had income from pensions. For the women who did receive pension benefits, the average amount they got on a yearly basis was about half what men realized (Moss 1993). For many women who get divorced, access to a spouse's pension benefits can be crucial for economic survival.

Looking at pensions as jointly earned and jointly owned property within marriage is relatively new (Moss 1993). This view is based on the concept that pensions are deferred wages. In theory, if there were no pensions, the amounts of money set aside by employers and employees for a future retirement would have been paid to the worker in the form of higher wages or other benefits which the wife would have enjoyed during the marriage. Because each partner is to be a contributor and benefactor from the marriage, deferred wages in the form of a pension should be enjoyed equally after the marriage ends.

The Women's Initiative of the AARP has recommended changing some state and federal laws to ensure a more equal distribution of pensions earned while marriages were intact (Moss 1993).

Possible Negative Outcomes of Divorce

For women, the major threat after divorce is often financial in nature, especially for older women. For men who face divorce late in life, the wounds are often more emotional than financial. It is often very hard for older men to lose the feeling that someone is taking care of their household, that their supper is on the table, and that there is someone at home when they get there. Their care pattern is gone and they are alone. Research has shown, for example, that older men who live alone often have less nutritious diets because so many do not know how to prepare adequate meals (Havlik, Lin, Kovar et al. 1987). Many men find it more difficult to establish friendship networks than women, who are able to develop and maintain them through much of their lives.

So if an older marriage is stalled or has gone into reverse, before any drastic steps are taken it is wise for the couple to seek professional help to jump-start the relationship. As Snyder pointed out, "Divorce is not a solution in itself" (Broughton 1993: 3D).

Divorce of Older People in the Future

The issue of divorce among older people is not going to fade away. The Census Bureau has estimated that between 1990 and 2020, the proportion of divorced older people will increase from 5 percent of elderly men and women in 1990, to 8 percent of elderly men and 14 percent of elderly women in 2020 when the baby boomers are counted among the elderly. The main reason for the expected increase is the higher divorce experience of the age group that will become elderly in the future—the baby boomers. They will carry many of their social patterns into their later years.

Remarriage

Remarriage after divorce for women after the age of 45 is not very common. Peter Uhlenberg and his colleagues showed that only 29 of 10,000 divorced women aged 45 to 64 remarried in 1985 (the last year data were available) compared to 45 per 10,000 in 1960 (Uhlenberg, Cooney, and Boyd 1990). For women 65 and older, the rate was much lower; only 5 of 10,000 remarried in that same year compared to 9 per 10,000 in 1960.

Brubaker (1990) said that the likelihood of remarriage for older persons after widowhood or divorce is small. He estimated that 25 percent of widowers aged 65 or older ever remarry, and less than 5 percent of widows aged 55 or older ever remarry. Only about 3 percent of all people getting married in a given year are persons aged 65 and over (Statistical Abstract of the U.S. 1990).

Second marriages of older persons do seem to be successful. The success of the second marriage depends to a considerable extent on the reaction of the adult children of the elderly couple. Whether the couple likes their children or not, they are bonded to them. Adult children who reject the remarriage of their parents put a tremendous amount of stress on that marriage. Most people spend holidays with their families, and if the children reject their parents' remarriages, there is a tremendous strain on what should be a happy event. Stepparenting is often tough under the best conditions as two different family histories come together and misunderstandings can easily arise. Some adult children are concerned about their parents' estate and how a stepparent may spend, or eventually acquire, what they believe to be rightfully theirs. However, most second marriages of older couples are successful, especially if they have a similar cultural history, approval of their children, and can coordinate without friction their financial resources. The major reason for remarriage in old age is a desire for companionship (Vinick 1978; Brubaker 1985).

Recent studies seem to indicate that those persons who have been widowed after happy marriages have a higher tendency to remarry (Silverstone and Hyman 1992). However, even some survivors of happy marriages are hesitant to marry again, not wanting to risk being widowed a second time or not believing that anyone could take their former spouse's place. The probability is much higher that men will remarry than women. As we have noted earlier, women overall live longer than men so there are many more of them in the older ages—and many more widows than widowers. In fact, elderly women were more than three times as likely than men to be widowed in 1990 (U.S. Bureau of the Census 1993a).

Men have a much larger pool of potential brides to choose from than women have grooms. Not only do men have a potential pool of women about their own age to choose from including never married, widowed, or divorced women, but in American culture it has been more acceptable for men to choose brides younger—sometimes much younger—than they are. The combination of younger men and older women is not unacceptable in our society, it is simply not a norm yet. So the major obstacle to remarriage for older women is the lack of older men. As a result, men have a seven times greater probability of remarriage than do women (Longino, Saldo, and Manton 1990).

Projecting into the next century, Robert Schoen and his colleagues estimated that over their lifetimes, baby boomers will be about twice as likely to experience divorce as did the current elderly population (Schoen, Urton, Woodrow, and Baj 1985). Although the baby-boom generation women are expected to experience widowhood at a later average age (67 years), on average they will still spend about 15 years as widows. This same model projects that fewer than one in ten will remarry. That is why a 1993 Census Bureau report pointed out that it would make sense, in terms of the differences in longevity between women and men and the average years women spend as widows, for women to marry men at least 7 years younger than they are. This, of course is rarely done because it would mean a difficult match for many people who marry in their early or middle twenties.

Homosexual Couples

Many homosexual couples have been estranged from their families and as a result are more dependent on either their partner or the broader homosexual community. The research on older homosexual couples is quite limited. The number of homosexual couples is arguable, as is the number of homosexuals in American society. There is no doubt that homosexual couples have disadvantages regarding the right of their partners to med-

ical insurance, life insurance, and other benefits usually tied to employment. American society is in the process, primarily because of the changes in employment contracts in some localities, of giving homosexuals the same right to be eligible for their partners' benefits as married heterosexual couples.

Research has indicated that a lifetime of sexual discrimination has had an impact on how older homosexual couples perceive life, view life satisfaction, and interact with the heterosexual world (Fried 1990). Older gays are beginning to form organizations such as the National Association of Lesbian and Gay Gerontologists and the Lavender Panthers. American society is slowly moving toward an openness about sexual orientation which will allow for more research funds to be available and for more researchers to study older homosexual couples. Less is known about older gay couples than about the ethnic, religious, racial and socioeconomic status of couples in general. The research so far seems to indicate that lesbian couples are more likely to stay together longer than are gay couples and have sex less frequently, while gay couples tend to have sex less frequently than heterosexual couples. The evidence also indicates that older homosexual couples have problems similar to older heterosexual couples: problems in communication, financial decisions, household tasks, and tension over who has power in relationships (Blumstein and Schwartz 1987).

ADULT CHILDREN PROVIDE SUPPORT

Over the years study after study has shown that most of the help older people get when they need it comes from family members (Brody 1990). Families provide 80 to 90 percent of personal care and help with various tasks around the house to maintain an older person, including transportation and shopping (U.S. Bureau of the Census 1993a).

Recent extensive national studies have confirmed that in spite of all the changes that have occurred in and around the American family in all of its forms, adult children continue to stand ready to help their elderly relatives (parents and others) when they need it. In a large study conducted by the University of Michigan's Institute for Social Research for the National Institute on Aging (NIA), 13,000 people aged 51 through 61 were surveyed across the nation. In a report released in June 1993, the study clearly showed that middle-aged people give substantial help to their frail parents. About two-thirds of the people in this study had living parents or parents-in-law, and about half of those had frail parents who needed personal care or monitoring. In analyzing the data from this study, Beth Soldo, head of the department of demography at Georgetown University said,

> Married people, contrary to what many people believe, help their parents in times of need. In particular, women in their 50s may adjust their work hours to help parents, in-laws, children, or grandchildren (National Institute on Aging 1993: 3).

This same study found that single middle-aged people also were generous with their time and money when parents needed help. About one in ten unmarried men in the study with a dependent older parent gave more than 100 hours of care a year. More than a third of these men had a brother or sister who also gave help. Of unmarried women with a frail parent, one-quarter provided more than a 100 hours of care a year, and nearly one-half of them had a brother or sister who gave help to the parent. The NIA (1993) study found that women were more likely to provide personal-care help and men tended to give financial assistance.

A 1994 study by the Princeton Survey Research Associates conducted for the AARP also surveyed middle-aged people (aged 45 to 59) across the nation. This research also found that about two-thirds (70 percent) of the people surveyed had at least one living parent or in-law.

In this AARP (1994) study, nearly all (92 percent) who had a parent or in-law within an hour's driving distance felt they might be in a position to help a dependent older relative. Even 85 percent of those surveyed who had parents or in-laws living farther away than an hour's drive could put themselves in a helping situation. What was somewhat surprising about this research is that two-thirds (68 percent) of the middle-aged people questioned who had no living parents or in-laws felt some responsibility for the financial well-being of another older relative.

This same AARP (1994) study, not surprisingly, found that in general middle-aged caregivers felt more responsible for helping an older relative deal with illness than with financial difficulties. In other words, adult children felt more compelled to help their parents physically than financially. This is not hard to understand, as many people have limited financial resources which are usually allocated for all the expenses of living. However, when it comes to helping parents or in-laws in times of illness or frailty, most people feel they can make time and spend energy on caregiving.

An interesting feature of the AARP (1994) study is that the degree to which a middle-aged person is likely to help an older relative both financially and physically is related to socioeconomic status. It is not at all surprising that people with more income and assets feel more ready to help older relatives financially. This research also found that more affluent individuals also feel better able to provide personal care to an older relative who is dealing with a serious illness or disability.

Another recent major study by Frank Caro and Scott Bass of the Gerontology Institute, University of Massachusetts at Boston (1993) focused on the productivity of persons age aged 55 and older. This study included a national in-depth survey by Louis Harris and Associates that found a willingness, even an eagerness, by those questioned to help their relatives—parents, children, grandchildren—and even friends and neighbors who were in need of assistance.

For our immediate purposes, this study is important in two ways. First, although the survey included adults over the age of 55, including some persons in the older-age categories, there was a high level of assistance given to parents. Obviously, most people in the older-age categories do not have parents. So the level of care provided to parents by those in the survey—second only to spouses by one percentage point—indicates a broad base of parent care by older adult children.

The second important feature of this report for our discussion is the reasons those surveyed gave for helping, their willingness to do so, and the satisfaction they felt from assisting others. As Table 14-2 indicates, personal relationships in family settings easily top the reasons older persons surveyed in the University of Massachusetts at Boston study gave for why they helped others (Caro and Bass 1993) (See Table 14-2).

Two-thirds (66.3 percent) of those surveyed in this study did not regard giving informal care to their relatives and friends as a burden. In fact, only 7.3 percent regarded their caregiving as a heavy burden.

Equally important, over three quarters (77.6 percent) got a great deal of satisfaction from their informal caregiving as Table 14-3 indicates.

There is no doubt that American families generally stand ready to help their older relatives. This was determined by a range of studies in the

TABLE 14-3

CAREGIVING SATISFACTION

Satisfaction level	Percentage
A great deal	77.6
Some	17.1
A little	3.8
None	1.4

Source: Caro and Bass, *Patterns of productivity among older Americans,* 1993: p. 4–20.

1970s and the 1980s and validated by major national research conducted in the 1990s by institutions including the Gerontology Institute of the University of Massachusetts, Louis Harris and Associates, the Commonwealth Fund, Princeton Survey Research Associates, the American Association for Retired Persons, the Institute for Social Research of the University of Michigan, and the National Institute on Aging, a division of the National Institutes of Health.

Of all family members, daughters and daughters-in-law provide the most care for older adults, even more care than do elderly persons' spouses (Brody 1990; U.S. Department of Labor, Women's Bureau 1986). This does not mean that sons do no caregiving. Pearlin et al. (1990) found that 16 percent of the caregiving adult children were sons. As Brody (1990) pointed out, sons in general love their parents and do not neglect them. However, they tend to do tasks to help their elderly parents that to them reflect more gender-appropriate roles such as home repairs and managing money, rather than direct hands-on care of older people. Sons tend to become the primary caregiver when they have no sisters or none living near the elderly parent who needs help. When they do give aid, they are usually assisted by their wives.

As we have indicated, most of the hands-on care that adult children provide older relatives is given by daughters and daughters-in-law. Most of these women are caught in the middle of competing and conflicting roles and obligations. They have been referred to as "women-in-the-middle" by Elaine Brody (1990: 3). She pointed out that

TABLE 14-2

REASONS FOR HELPING THE SICK AND DISABLED[1]

Reason for helping	Percentage
I love him/her	26.2
It's my family obligation	20.8
That's what old friends are for	12.2
No one else will or can	9.9
He's my husband/she's my wife	8.8
I enjoy it	8.0
It's in my nature	4.6
That's what my religious beliefs tell me to do	1.8
I have better skills and energy than others who are available	0.9

[1]Multiple responses were accepted; some respondents gave no reason.
Source: Caro and Bass 1993, *Patterns of productivity among older Americans:* 4–14.

these caregivers, who provide most of the hands-on assistance for dependent older relatives, are often under much strain because of their many other responsibilities. Women in our culture have had traditional roles of wives, and this role is not a new one. What is new is the vastly increased number of older people who survive to the oldest ages and need assistance. Even though the role of caregiver for elderly relatives is not new to American women in general, it is an added role for millions of women who would not have faced this responsibility if they had lived in an earlier era when many fewer people survived to the oldest ages.

In addition to their role as caregivers for the elderly that contemporary women are assuming, record numbers and percentages of women have entered the paid labor force. The proportion of women who work outside the home has quadrupled since the Great Depression. Brody has given these women-in-the-middle the following characteristics:

- They are most likely to be in their middle-aged years, although they range in age from their twenties to their seventies.
- They are mostly a middle generation in three-or-four-generation families.
- They face the demands of their various competing roles.
- Many are caught between the competing values of: (1) the care of older persons in the family is their responsibility as women, which is a deeply-rooted traditional value; and (2) it is all right—even preferable—for them as women to work outside the home and follow their own interests.
- Some are struggling emotionally with the competing demands placed on them by the elderly relatives they are assisting and the rival attention needed by their husbands and children.

Financial Assistance Between Younger and Older Family Members

As we have already noted, there is a great deal of caregiving assistance for older relatives. Accord-

ing to numerous studies, there is much less financial assistance between the older and younger generations. In the middle 1980s, O'Connel et al. (1988) found that the overall odds of providing financial support to parents was 1 in 208. In their study of Americans aged 55 and older based on a Lou Harris and Associates survey in the early 1990s, Caro and Bass (1993) found that there was no common pattern of income contributions between the generations. In this study, 78.2 percent of those responding to the survey reported essentially no intergenerational transfers. Where there was financial assistance, 19.6 percent was from older persons to children and grandchildren. Only 2.3 percent of the financial assistance went to older people.

An AARP study (1994) conducted by Princeton Survey Research Associates of persons across the nation aged 45 to 59 found that only 18 percent of those surveyed felt well-prepared to give financial support to a parent or older relative. This same study found that 18 percent of those surveyed had already given financial assistance to a parent in the last five years. A major feature of this study showed that "whether they are prepared or not, people age 45 to 59 find a way to help family members who need financial assistance" (AARP 1994: 43).

The NIA study (1993), found that middle-aged people aged (51–61) were much more likely to provide financial assistance to children than parents. Of those surveyed who had both children and living parents, 40 percent provided financial help only to their children. Just 4 percent give financial assistance to parents only. Fewer than 10 percent gave to parents and children.

David Eggebeen (1992), in one of the more extensive surveys of financial assistance among family members (National Survey of Families and Households) found that only 17 percent of adult children received money (at least $200 or over loaned in the past 5 years) from their parents, and only 4 percent gave money. In the month before the interview, about 13 percent of adult children received childcare, 17 percent received household assistance, and 32 percent gave household assistance. Advice and emotional support were the most common forms of exchange, with 27 percent of those surveyed receiving such support and another 25 percent giving such support to their parents (Hogan and Eggebeen 1991b).

The more siblings one has, the less likely it is that one is receiving support from parents. Intergenerational support varies by the marital status of both adult children and aging parents. Married adult children tend to give more assistance to their parents than do their unmarried counterparts (Eggebeen 1992).

Hogan and Eggebeen (1991b) pointed out that the kinds of assistance between generations in families are partly determined by the history of routine exchanges between the individual in need and the provider. It is this history of family dynamics that determines the type and amount of mutual assistance.

Older Parents–Adult Children: Family Dynamics

The family dynamics involving older parents and adult children have been explained extensively by numerous authors (Silverstone and Hyman 1976; Weiner, Teresi, and Streich 1993; Shulman, and Berman, 1988; Smith 1987; Brody 1990; McLean 1987). The following is based on a summary of these works.

For many families, the problem is one of overcoming counterproductive relationships of the past and the present. In all families there are tensions in the parent-child relationship, and some of these tensions continue into old age.

Counterproductive Family Dynamics: Unresolved Tensions Some parents may have been too domineering, some too smothering, some too demanding, and some too immature. Some parents have been abusive or neglectful. In addition, some may have had psychiatric problems that did not allow them to function adequately as parents. The passing of time by itself will not resolve

these types of problems. These children will have to make a real effort to lovingly confront their parents with their feelings, go through an emotional release, and attempt to move the relationship to a more understanding level.

Role Reversal Role reversal means that persons who were independent and took care of others are now dependent and have to be cared for by the very people they raised. True role reversal between children and parents really never occurs.

Rescue Fantasy Some adult children believe that they should rescue their aging parents from illness or other problems. These children may take their sick parent from treatment center to treatment center, trying to find a cure. They may even take their parents to medical quacks in search of quick relief from Parkinson's disease, Alzheimer's disease, cancer, or other serious illnesses.

In the movie *Dad*, starring Ted Danson and Jack Lemmon, the adult son convinced himself that his father was not getting the right treatment in the hospital, so he literally picked him up from the hospital bed and drove him home. The dad was no better at home, and the son was forced to face reality—he could not rescue his dad from his illnesses.

Excessive Demands on Other Caregivers The evidence is clear that children do not tend to "dump" their aged parents into nursing facilities. If anything, they probably bring their parents too reluctantly to these care centers. Because of their guilt, some want to make certain that their parents receive the best possible care, and as a result, they can become too demanding of the professional caregivers.

Generation Gap Some adult children experience considerable tensions in their relationships with their parents because each are members of different generations which have had distinctly different experiences. Each typically has different perceptions and attitudes toward music, entertainment, sex roles, the use of money, and a range of other social issues. These differences can lead to continuing conflict and anger. Each generation needs to recognize the cultural differences and respect each other's feelings.

Facing Generational Conflicts

Dealing with conflicts between members of different generations, particularly aging parents and their adult children, can be very difficult. It is helpful to understand how different aging parents react to conflict. In his book, *You and Your Parents: Strategies for Building an Adult Relationship*, Harold Smith (1987) outlined various ways parents react to conflicts with their children:

- Some parents are *avoiders of conflict*. At the first hint of conflict they back off because they do not want the tension that confrontation brings.
- Some parents are *exploders*. At the first hint of confrontation, conflict, or disagreement, they explode in anger. They try to control their children by always being on the verge of anger, being angry, or threatening to be angry. As a result, basic issues cannot be resolved and children either stay away or try to pacify their parents.
- Some parents are *victors*. These parents will argue because they believe they must win. They cannot tolerate the fact that a child might be brighter, more educated, or more insightful than they are. Their daughter might have a Ph.D. in geology but they will still insist that they know as much about the origins of Earth as their child.
- Other parents are *extinguishers*. These parents deny that there is a conflict. Instead of admitting that a disagreement exists, they will change the subject.

Unresolved tension and conflict between an older parent and his or her adult child can result in one or both hiding behind a wall of silence. This can easily progress to partial or total estrangement—not seeing or calling each other. This kind of suppressed rage usually needs to be dealt with through professionals. It is possible that some parents were ill equipped for the role of parent and were not able to face the realities life brought them. Some older parents dwell on some real or imagined pain in their life and turn away from the very people who could support and help them—their adult children. It is also possible that this type of behavior is the result of undiagnosed depression.

In addressing unresolved tension and conflict between older people and their adult children, Wesley Burr and Clark Christensen (1992) said:

> How many who hear or read these words have some "unfinished" business with their parents? . . . Are there some of us who carry around resentments and grudges about others in our family rather than experience the cleansing that comes from . . . tolerance, acceptance, or mercy? Are there some of us who should try to "give in" a little more so we can try to do things the way others want . . . (Burr and Christensen 1992: 463)

Improving relationships between older parents and their adult children may take considerable effort. Often it requires professional assistance.

GRANDPARENTS GIVE SUPPORT

It is a well-established fact that most older people receive nearly all (80 to 90 percent) of the help they need in times of illness and infirmity from family members—primarily spouses and adult children. In spite of all the changes in the American family, standing ready to help other family members has not changed.

What is changing is the increased role older people are playing in the lives of their grandchildren. To put these changes in perspective, we need to remember that the ranks of the young old are growing rapidly with people who tend to be healthier, wealthier, and more mobile than persons of these ages in previous generations. Added to the young old are many persons in the aged category (aged 75 to 84) who continue to have the health, vigor, and resources to play active grandparenting roles along with the millions of persons who are becoming older (aged 55 to 64), many already retired.

These growing ranks of active, energetic grandparents face requests for intergenerational assistance as a result of many of the changes in the American family. Certainly not all of these changes are "bad." Some are, such as the need to care for grandchildren as a result of the drug culture that has affected much of the nation, leaving many children with no parental support. Other changes are the result of changing lifestyles which lead to changing cultural norms. The rise of single-parent families by choice or as the result of the high national divorce rate has resulted in additional care and attention by grandparents. In addition, the dramatic change in the number and percentage of women working outside of the home has had an impact on the need for direct grandparent help with young children.

Intergenerational family ties remain strong throughout the lives of most persons. The vast majority (85 percent) of all people in the United States aged 55 and older have children, according to a national survey conducted by Louis Harris and Associates as part of a study of people 55 and older by the Gerontology Institute of the University of Massachusetts at Boston (Caro and Bass 1993). Of those who have children, 88.5 percent have grandchildren or great-grandchildren. Putting it another way, 76 percent of all persons aged 55 and older have grandchildren or great-grandchildren. Indeed, grandparenting is a common role for over three-fourths of all people aged 55 and older in contemporary American society.

The Changing Roles of Grandparents

Grandparenting is not a new role. For decades there have been endless stories and anecdotes about grandparents who take pleasure in "spoiling" their grandchildren. Grandparenting has been portrayed as an opportunity to indulge children's children in ways a person never could or would for her or his own.

As some of the popular media have pointed out, times, social roles, and expectations continue to change. With the multigeneration family (including the four-generation family) becoming more and more prevalent, many of today's grandparents are taking on roles that are more complicated and difficult than the stereotypes would have us believe (Larsen, McMorrow, Edlestein, and Cooksey 1990).

Hearings of the U.S. Senate Special Committee on Aging on the changing role of grandparents in contemporary American Society pointed out that "a profile of older Americans reveals that never before in our history have so many persons lived long enough to become grandparents, nor have their activities been so varied and diverse" (U.S. Senate Special Committee on Aging 1992: 55). The following are some of the complicated and difficult roles that grandparents increasingly are undertaking.

Grandparents as Substitute Parents   One of the most significant shifts that has occurred in American society in recent years is the rapid growth in the number of grandparents who have taken on the role of raising their grandchildren. They have become stand-in or surrogate parents for these children.

The 1990 census reveals that 3.2 million grandchildren under 18 years of age in the United States—5 percent of all children—lived in their grandparents' homes (Saluter 1991). This was a 40-percent increase in the decade between 1980 and 1990 (U.S. Senate Special Committee on Aging 1992).

Of the grandchildren living in their grandparents' homes, 15 percent had both of their parents living with them; 50 percent had only their mother living with them; 6 percent had only their father with them; and 30 percent had neither of their parents living with them (Saluter 1991).

Among racial and ethnic groups, African-American children were more likely to be living in their grandparents' homes in 1990 (12 percent) than were white children (4 percent). African-

American children were also more likely to be living with their grandparents alone without any parent (38 percent) than were white children (25 percent). Among Latino children, 6 percent lived in their grandparents' homes. Of the Latino children who lived in their grandparents' homes, 21 percent lived only with their grandparents with no parent present (Saluter 1991).

The reasons for the rapidly increasing number of parents living with grandparents are varied and often directly related to contemporary American life. In many cases the natural parents are unwilling or unable to fulfill their parenting roles as a result of drug or alcohol abuse (U.S. Senate Special Committee on Aging 1992). Some experts contend that drug or alcohol addiction is the main cause for grandparents becoming responsible for raising their grandchildren (Larsen 1991). Other conditions of contemporary life are also contributors to this situation including divorce, abandonment, physical or sexual abuse, death, imprisonment, and even murder. As a U.S. Senate Special Committee on Aging report stated:

> While multigenerational households have long been common in working-class communities and in African-American and Hispanic households of all income levels, this trend cuts across all class and racial lines. These arrangements are most prevalent in the inner cities throughout our country where crack, teenage pregnancy, AIDS, and violent crime have taken their toll, often on several members of a single family. Middle-class suburban and small-town families, however, are also beginning to experience the fallout of the drug epidemic and other social ills. Increasing numbers of white middle-class grandparents are finding themselves caring for their children's children (U.S. Senate Special Committee on Aging 1992: 1).

Problems of Substitute Parenting Grandparents raising their children's children face many problems. Many find the job a second time around very draining physically. They simply do not have the stamina needed to do all the things they did when they were younger and raising their own children. Many have emotional stress—stress over the emotional drain of being stand-in parents, as well as stress over the circumstances that led to their becoming surrogate parents. As one grandparent said, "I resented having to raise a child again and I was angry at my daughter for putting me in this position" (Larsen 1991: 34).

Others feel a sense of guilt. "What did I do to cause this?" asked another grandparent. "Where did we go wrong?" is a cry heard often by grandparents forced into a parenting role as a result of drug or alcohol abuse, child abuse, or abandonment by their own children (Larsen 1991: 34). This is especially difficult when the parents grew up in stable, loving homes.

Another problem many of these surrogate parents face is a financial one. If still working, many are forced to reduce their hours at work or give up their jobs completely to have enough time and energy to be with and care for their grandchildren. If retired, many others are forced to dip into their savings to cover the costs of raising another generation—expenses they had not counted on in planning for their retirement.

Some of these grandparents may qualify for Aid to Families with Dependent Children (AFDC), but this program does not provide the kind of coverage foster-care benefits include. Some states do not allow relatives to be eligible for the foster-care program (Larsen 1991). It is argued that grandparents have enough incentive to provide care for their grandchildren. In addition, there really is no Social Security assistance. This only applies when the natural or adoptive parents die or are disabled, which can lead some grandparents to adopt their grandchildren. However, adoption costs money and can be a complicated process if the natural parents are still alive.

"The burden of raising a child at this stage of life and also coping with the loss of an adult child—for whatever reason—often causes problems between couples who have spent most of their lives together," said Sylvie de Toledo, clinical social worker and founder of Grandparents as

Parents, a support group for grandparents thrust into the role of raising their children's children (Larsen 1991: 32). Their social life changes, previous plans for retirement may disappear, old friends no longer have much in common, and the burdens of parenting a second time around can all put stresses on relationships.

Support groups have played important roles in assisting grandparents who find themselves in these difficult roles. Grandparents Raising Grandchildren, Grandparents as Parents, Grandparents Against Immorality and Neglect, Second Time Around Parents, Grandparents United for Children's Rights, Inc., and From Generation to Generation are examples of these types of support groups: "For sure it helps us—we've all learned to laugh again," said Paula Browne of Grandparents as Parents in California. "But it also helps the kids" (Larsen 1991: 34). Support groups for grandparents raising their children's children are helpful because people come to them in different stages of acceptance and are able to draw emotional support from the participants who have already worked their way through many of the situations that arise in this difficult role.

Grandparents as Babysitters   With the prevalence of the two-spouse working family and the high incidence of the single-parent family (primarily single mothers) in contemporary American life, childcare has become a major issue. Who will take care of the children when both mom and dad (in the two-parent household) or when mom (in the single-parent home) is off to work? This applies to preschool children as well as to school-age children after school, when they are sick and cannot go to school, and during vacation periods.

Unlike most European countries, the United States does not have a coordinated, state-supported system of child daycare. Essentially, each family is responsible for its own childcare. Specific childcare programs are established for specific groups of people or in conjunction with some specific programs. In the main, childcare is the responsibility of each family. It can be very expensive. Child day care can be so expensive for a family that the cost effectiveness of a parent's participation in the paid labor force may come into question depending on how much a parent earns. If, for example, a person earns $200 a week and child care costs $125, is it cost effective for that parent to work? This question especially applies to single mothers on AFDC who, if they return to the work force, are stuck in minimum-wage jobs and lose income and benefits that come with staying on welfare and not going back to work. Why return to work if income and benefits from welfare are lost, and in addition, they must spend a considerable amount of money on child care?

Enter grandparents. In contemporary American society, grandparents provide a sizeable amount of babysitting services for their families. A 1990 report by the Bureau of the Census showed that 750,000 children under the age of 15 were cared for in their own homes by grandparents. In addition to these children who were cared for in their own homes, 1.2 million were cared for in the homes of the grandparents. Of the 1.9 million children in these two categories (cared for in their own homes and the homes of the grandparents), 65 percent were under the age of five (O'Connell and Bachu 1990).

There were some differences among racial groups. Where the mother who was working outside the home was white, 12 percent of the primary child care was provided by grandparents. Where the employed mother was African American, 21 percent of the child care came from grandparents.

As one might expect, and research backs this up, grandparents are especially likely to be the care providers of preschool children when the income of the mother is below or near the poverty line. Where the income of the employed mother is below the poverty line, 21 percent of child care was provided by grandparents. The same level of babysitting services (21 percent) was provided by grandparents when the income of the employed mother was just above the poverty line (100 to 125 percent of poverty). When the mother's income rose to more than 125 percent of poverty, the child care arrangement provided by grandparents fell to 13 percent, a significant drop (O'Connell and Bachu 1990). Clearly, characteristics such as race, ethnicity, and income level affect the level of child-care that is provided grandchildren by their grandparents. With increasing numbers of two-parent families with both spouses employed, and with dramatic increases in single-parent families, the role of childcare provider by grandparents is a significant one in contemporary America. Like many other characteristics or roles of older adults, it is not a new one. What is new is the increasing importance it has assumed.

Grandparents as Bridge-Builders   In an era when life seems to be increasingly more complex and fragmented with multiple family arrangements, with both parents in two-parent families working outside the home becoming the norm, with employees working longer and longer hours, and with increased mobility, the role of the grandparent as bridge-builder or generation-connector has become more significant.

In the fast pace of modern life, grandparents have the opportunity to provide some sense of continuity to their grandchildren. Whether they are down the block or halfway across the country, grandparents can give grandchildren a sense of belonging, a feeling of self-worth, an understanding that they are part of something that reaches beyond their nuclear families, whatever that happens to be. In addition, grandparents can provide for grandchildren a sense of family history which can be tied into cultural history and historical events.

In troubled times, such as the breakup of the child's family through divorce, death, or some other form of parental loss, in addition to providing critical childcare, grandparents can give grandchildren stability and security. These are vital ingredients for most people, particularly for children experiencing family trauma.

Grandparents as the "Club Sandwich Generation"

All of the important activities grandparents carry out have led to a new term to define their position and diverse roles in their families in contemporary America. The term is the *Club Sandwich Generation.*

Based on information collected through an extensive study by professors Frank Caro and Scott Bass of the Gerontology Institute of the University of Massachusetts at Boston, the term *Club Sandwich Generation* has been coined to describe the numerous and important roles many grandparents assume in our complex and multigenerational culture (Davis 1994: 6F).

Where the Sandwich Generation carries heavy responsibilities for aging parents and their own children, the Club Sandwich Generation, using the analogy of the many layers of the club sandwich, has multiple layers or responsibility. Usually in their sixties and seventies, persons in the Club Sandwich Generation are typically trying to deal with their own health and financial problems as they grow older while having responsibility for their parents, their children, and their grandchildren. In addition, it is not unusual for the Club Sandwich Generation members to provide assistance to other relatives and to engage in various forms of community service (Davis 1994). To illustrate what a Club Sandwich Generation member is like, the *Boston Globe* carried a story of a 65-year-old:

> With physical problems that would justify asking others to take care of her and at an age when most people are retired and at leisure, Arlene Russo voluntarily took on a demanding full-time job: parenting. Or more precisely, grandparenting—1990 style.
>
> "There are times when I think the responsibility is more than I can take, but I let the moment pass and I'm fine again," said Russo, a widow who is bringing up a 16-year-old granddaughter by herself.
>
> Russo suffers from a painful rheumatic condition that often leaves her exhausted. Nevertheless,

she serves on a parental advisory committee at her granddaughter's high school, sings in a church choir, does volunteer work with the elderly people and is studying for a degree in gerontology. And she regularly visits an elderly aunt in a nursing home (Davis 1994: 6F).

Arlene Russo is not unique for her generation. Research has shown that Club Sandwich Generation members are generous in giving of their money and time in helping others. According to the University of Massachusetts at Boston study, of the 38 million people aged 55 and older, 70 percent are volunteering for their community, as well as caring for children, spouses, and other relatives (Davis 1994).

One in five (20 percent) older persons provides a sizable part of children's or grandchildren's income. Only 5 percent receive a sizable part of their income from their children or grandchildren. Giving of their time and money in this way does not cause most of these older people worry or anxiety; only 10 percent said it did. Over 75 percent indicated that sharing their resources and their efforts serving and helping others gave them pleasure and satisfaction. The reason, according to an analyst of this study, is that unlike the "Me Generation," most of the Club Sandwich Generation were raised when times were more difficult and families were expected to work together in order to survive (Davis 1994). Helping one's family when needed, as well as serving the needs of the community, comes naturally to most of the members of the Club Sandwich Generation.

There is little doubt that the roles and significance of grandparents will continue to evolve as the revolution of an aging society continues to unfold. By 2010, the baby boomers will be aged 46 to 64. By that time, and in the immediate years that follow, they will become the grandparent boomers—or somewhat more accurately, the grandma boomers, assuming women continue to outlive men in significant numbers (U.S. Bureau of the Census 1993a). By 2030, the baby boomers will move into the great-grandparent boom generation.

SIBLINGS SUPPLY SUPPORT

Most older people live relatively near to at least one brother or sister (McGhee 1985; O'Bryant 1988). After people retire, relationships between siblings tend to become stronger and contacts tend to increase. The reasons for greater sibling interaction are varied. They include:

- Concern with a sibling's health
- Decreased tension over conflicts and hurts as they fade into the past
- More time and freedom with the end of child rearing
- More opportunities to visit and engage in mutual activities as the result of leaving the work force through retirement (Gold 1987).

There is growing evidence that interaction between sisters is more evident in the later years of life than in sister-brother or brother-brother relationships (Scott 1990).

Deborah Gold of Duke University Medical School in her research on sibling rivalry concluded:

> Even if you fought like cats and dogs with your brother or sister in early life, by middle age about 80 percent of siblings have positive relationships of varying intensity while 10 percent have apathetic relationships, and 10 percent are hostile toward each other (Gold 1993: 91).

Gold indicated that there are three conditions that tend to increase closeness between brothers and sisters:

- The death of a parent
- The empty nest—when children leave home
- The retirement of a sibling

She went on to point out that sister-sister and sister-brother bonds tend to be the strongest, while brothers tend to be more distant from each other.

About 20 percent of older people have no children. When they become frail, their care is provided primarily by their spouses. If their spouses are deceased they tend to turn to siblings or nieces and nephews (Beckman and Hauser 1982).

SUMMARY

In spite of all the changes that have occurred in the American family—and all the negative reports that fill the media concerning family relationships—the family is still the backbone of support for most older people.

The marital status of older people has a lot to do with their support system. Whether a person is married has great impact on that person's support within the family unit. In 1991, only 5.1 percent of elderly married couples were poor. In sharp contrast, 17.6 percent of the men and 26.6 percent of the women who lived alone were poor according to the Bureau of the Census. Married older people typically have someone to help them in times of illness or infirmity.

Living alone is a condition many older women experience. Between the ages of 65 through 74, about four-fifths of men are married compared to only half of the women. By ages 85 and older, about half of the men are still married compared to one-fifth of the women.

Older couples with long marriages tend to be happy in their marriages, but there are gender differences. Men tend to be more satisfied with their marriages and the degree to which their emotional needs are met than are women; however long-lived marriages can experience strains. Feelings of marital satisfaction may change; there may be a loss of intimacy over the years; the partners may grow in different directions; and the stresses of caregiving may surface when one partner takes on the role of caregiver for the other over a long period of time. There is no evidence that retirement affects marriage satisfaction negatively. In fact, marriages that begin in young adulthood tend to be happiest in the beginning years, before child rearing, and again in the later years. As retirement usually occurs in the later years, it comes at a time when marriage satisfaction is usually increasing.

Divorce is a major issue in American society. Although the divorce rates for older people are low compared to the rest of the population, some 5 percent of the elderly were divorced and not remarried in 1990. This was more than double the percentage for older people in 1960, 30 years earlier.

Poverty among older divorced women is a particular problem. The rates of poverty among older divorced women is as high or higher than for women who are widowed or never married. The poverty rate for separated older women is higher than for any other category of unmarried women. More attention is being paid to the fair division of pension assets when older couples divorce, as pensions represent a significant marital asset. Looking ahead to the near future, the Bureau of the Census estimates that between 1990 and 2020, the proportion of older people who will be divorced will increase from 5 percent for both men and women in 1990 to 8 percent for men and 14 percent for women. Remarriage is not a likely prospect for most older people.

Assistance from adult children is a major component of the total support system for older people. Recent major national studies have confirmed the high level of support adult children provide their older relatives, particularly in the form of caregiving in all its forms—physically assisting ill and infirm relatives, getting the elderly to doctors appointments and other events, running endless errands, filling out insurance and other forms, advocating on behalf of parents with agencies in the community they need to deal with, and other tasks of daily living.

Research has shown that 80 to 90 percent of all assistance older people get is from their families. Most of this help comes from daughters and daughters-in-law. Never before in history have so many people in the middle years of life been called upon to provide care for so many older people. Often these care providers are still involved in some form of assistance to their own children.

The role of grandparent has taken on new dimensions in contemporary America. More and more people enter their later years healthier, wealthier, and more vigorous. Many more are taking on additional roles as grandparents. The 1990 census showed that 3.2 million grandchildren, which is 5 percent of all children under the age of 18 in the United States, lived in their grandparents' homes. This was a 40 percent increase in the decade between 1980 and 1990. More and more grandparents are taking on the role of babysitter as a result of the rapid increase in the number and percentage of two-spouse working families and the large number of single-parent families where the parent needs to be in the labor force. Daycare can be financially prohibitive for many working parents, who then rely on their parents to fulfill this role.

With so many grandparents being members of four-generation families, and this new generation of grandparents taking on responsibilities for all the generations, the new grandparents have been called the "Club Sandwich Generation" for their multilayered roles. This will not change in the future. The Bureau of the Census has recently pointed out that more and more of us will be members of four- and even five-generation families as we move into the twenty-first century.

REFERENCES

American Association of Retired Persons. 1994. *Concerns of Adults in Their Pre-Retirement Years*. Princeton, NJ: Princeton Survey Research Associates.

Atchley, R.C. 1994. *Social Forces and Aging*. Belmont, CA: Wadsworth Publishing.

Atchley, R.C. 1992. Retirement and Marital Satisfaction. In Szinovacz, M., Ekerdt, D.J., and Vinick, B.H. (eds.), *Families and Retirement*. Newbury Park, CA: Sage Publications.

Beck, M. 1990. The Geezer Boom. *Newsweek, Special Edition: The 21st Century Family* CXIV(27): 63.

Beckman, L.J., and Hauser, B.B. 1982. The Consequences of Childlessness on the Social and Psychological Well-Being of Older Women. *Journal of Gerontology*, 37: 243–250.

Bengston, V.L., Rosenthal, C., and Burton, L. 1990. Families and Aging: Diversity and Heterogeneity. In Binstock, R.H. and George, L.K. (eds.), *Handbook of Aging and the Social Sciences*, 3d Ed. New York: Academic Press.

Blumstein, P., and Schwartz, P. 1987. *American Couples*. New York: Morrow.

Brody, E.M. 1990. *Women in the Middle: Their Parent-Care Years*. New York: Springer.

Broughton, J. 1993. Unexpected Pain. *Detroit Free Press*, (November 9): 3D.

Brubaker, T.H. 1990. Continuity and Change in Later Life Families: Grandparenthood, Couple Relationships and Family Caregiving. *Gerontology Review*, 3: 24–40.

Brubaker, T.H. 1985. *Later Life Families*. Beverly Hills, CA: Sage.

Burr, W.R., and Christensen, C. 1992. Undesirable Effects on Enhancing Self-Esteem. *Family Relations*, 41(4): 460–464.

Caro, F.G., and Bass, S.A. 1993. *Patterns of Productive Activity Among Older Americans*. Boston: Gerontology Institute, University of Massachusetts at Boston.

Crown, W.H., Mutschler, P.H., Schulz, J.H., and Loew, R. 1993. *The Economic Status of Divorced Older Women*. Waltham, MA: Policy Center on Aging, Heller School, Brandeis University.

Davis, W.A. 1994. Grandparents Carry Layers of Responsibility. *Boston Globe*. In *Detroit Free Press* (June 22): 6F.

Eggebeen, D.J. 1992. From Generation Unto Generation: Parent-Child Support in Aging American Families. *Generations*, Vol. XVII, No. 3.

Footlick, J.K. 1990. *Newsweek (Special Edition): The 21st Century Family*, CXIV(27): 14–20.

Gilford, R. 1984. Contracts in Marital Satisfaction Throughout Old Age: An Exchange Theory Analysis. *Journal of Gerontology*, 39(3): 325–33.

Gilford, R. 1991. Marriages in Later Life. In *Annual Editions: Aging*, 7th ed. H. Cox (ed.), Sluice Dock, Gilford, CT: Dushkin Publishing Group.

Gold, D.T. 1987. Siblings in Old Age: Something Special. *The Canadian Journal on Aging*, 6: 211–227.

Gold, D.T. 1993. Sibling Rivalry Eases Over Time. *New Choices* (April): 91.

Havlik, R.J., Lin, B.M., Kovar, M.G., et al. 1987. National Center for Health Statistics, *Health Statistics on Older Persons, United States: 1986*, Vital and Health Statistics (Series 3, No. 25) (June). Public

Health Service. Washington, DC: U.S. Government Printing Office.

Hogan, D.P., and Eggebeen, D.J. 1991a. *Sources of Aid and Assistance in Old Age*. Paper presented at the annual meeting of the American Sociological Association.

Hogan, D.P., and Eggebeen, D.J. 1991b. *American Adults in the Middle: Patterns of Giving and Receiving Between the Generations*. Paper presented at the annual meeting of the Gerontological Society of America.

Johnson, C. 1985. The Impact of Illness on Late-Life Marriages. *Journal of Marriage and the Family*, 47(1): 165–72.

Larsen, D. 1990. Unplanned Parenthood. *Modern Maturity*, (December/January): 32–36.

Larsen, D., McMorrow, T., Edelstein, S., and Cooksey, K. 1990. Grandparent: Redefining the Role. *Modern Maturity*, (December/January): 31–44.

Longino, C., Soldo, B.J., and Manton, K.G. 1990. Demography of Aging in the U.S. In K. Ferraro (ed.), *Gerontology Issues and Perspectives*. New York: Springer.

McGhee, J.L. 1985. The Effects of Siblings on the Life Satisfaction of the Rural Elderly. *Journal of Marriage and the Family*, 47: 85–91.

McLean, H. 1987. *Caring for Your Parents: A Source Book of Opinions and Solutions for Both Generations*. Garden City, NY: Doubleday.

Marshall, R. 1991. *The States of Families, 3*. Milwaukee, WI: Family Service America.

Moss, A.E. 1991. *Your Pension Rights at Divorce*. Washington, DC: Pension Rights Center.

Moss, A.E. 1993. *Women, Pensions, and Divorce*. Washington, DC: Women's Initiative, AARP.

National Institute on Aging. 1993. *Survey Sketches New Portrait of Aging America*, (June 17). Washington, DC: National Institutes of Health.

O'Bryant, S.L. 1988. Neighbors' Support of Older Widows Who Live Alone in Their Own Homes. *Gerontologist*, 25: 305–310.

O'Connell, M., and Bachu, A. 1990. U.S. Bureau of the Census, *Who's Minding the Kids? Child Care Arrangements 1986–1987*. Current Population Reports, (Series P-70, No. 20 U.S.). Washington, DC: Government Printing Office.

O'Connel, M., Jennings, J.T., Lamas, E.J., and Mc Neil, J. 1988. U.S. Bureau of the Census. *Who's Helping Out? Support Networks Among American Families*. Current Population Reports, (Series P-70, No. 13). Washington, DC: U.S. Government Printing Office.

Perlin, L.I., Mullan, J.T., Stemple, S.J., and Skaff, M.M. 1990. Caregiving and the Stress Process: An Overview of Concepts and Their Measures. *Gerontologist*, 30. 383–594.

Rhyne, C. 1981. Bases of Marital Satisfaction Among Men and Women. *Journal of Marriage and Family*, 43(4): 941–55.

Riekse, R., and Holstege, H. 1992. *The Christian Guide to Parent Care*. Wheaton, IL: Tyndale House Publishers.

Saluter, A.F. 1991. U.S. Bureau of the Census. *Marital Status and Living Arrangements: March 1990*. Current Population Reports, (Series P-20, No. 450). Washington, DC: U.S. Government Printing Office.

Schoen, R., Urton, W., Woodrow, K., and Baj, J. 1985. Marriage and Divorce in 20th Century American Cohorts. *Demography*, 101–114.

Scot, J.P. 1990. Sibling Interaction in Later Life. In T.H. Brubaker (ed.), *Family Relationships in Later Life,* 2d Ed. Newbury Park, CA: Sage Publications.

Shulman, G.H., and Berman, R. 1988. *How to Survive Your Aging Parents*. Chicago, IL: Surrey Books.

Silverstone, B., and Human, H. 1992. *Growing Older Together*. New York: Pantheon Books.

Smith, H.I. 1987. *You and Your Parents: Strategies for Building an Adult Relationship*. Minneapolis, MN: Augsburg Press.

Stone, R., Cafferate, G.L., and Sangl, J. 1987. Caregivers of the Frail Elderly: A National Profile. *Gerontologist*, 27(5): 616–626.

Uhlenberg, P., Cooney, T., and Boyd, R., 1990. Divorce for Women after Midlife. *Journal of Gerontology*, 45(1): 55.

U.S. Bureau of the Census. 1993a. Current Population Reports, (Special Studies, P. 23-178 R V), *Sixty-Five Plus in America*, (May). Washington, DC: U.S. Government Printing Office.

U.S. Bureau of the Census. 1993b. *We the American Elderly*, (September). Washington, DC: U.S. Department of Commerce.

U.S. Bureau of the Census. 1993c. *Profiles of America's Elderly: Living Arrangements of the Elderly*, (November). Washington, DC: National Institute on Aging.

U.S. Bureau of the Census. 1990. *Statistical Abstract of the United States: 1990*. Washington, DC: p. 87, Table 128.

U.S. Department of Labor, Women's Bureau. 1986. *Facts on U.S. Working Women. Caring for elderly family members*. (No. 86-4). Washington, DC.

U.S. Senate Special Committee on Aging. 1992. *Grandparents as Parents: Raising a Second Gener-* *ation*. Washington, DC: U.S. Government Printing Office.

Vinick, B. 1978. Remarriage in Old Age. *The Family Coordinator*, 27: 359–365.

Weiner, M.B., Teresi, J., and Streich, C. 1993. *Old People Are a Burden, But Not My Parents*. Englewood Cliffs, NJ: Prentice Hall.

CHAPTER 15

Other
Support Systems

Friends–
Religion/Spirituality–
Support Groups

Hattie's Friends

Hattie has lived most of her adult life in the same house. Her husband built it when they were first married. She raised her three children there. Her church and doctor's office were in a shopping center four blocks away. Hattie is now 89 years old. One of her three children died over ten years ago, and the other two live on opposite sides of the nation. She had a lot of friends over the years, but many of them are either dead, confined to nursing homes, or living with or near their children. With the loss of her husband two years ago, and with her children living great distances away, increasingly Hattie has relied on her friends for mutual support in facing the changes and losses in her life. In the past six months, Hattie's church has announced it is relocating to the suburbs, where most of its members live. Her doctor's office, along with other offices and stores in the neighborhood shopping center, is being demolished for a new urban freeway. Last week her only remaining friend who was still driving in the daylight hours suffered a stroke.

Hattie's children, who have been providing for some home-help services for their mother, are encouraging her to move to a congregate living facility for older people which has a continuing-care option, meaning she can be provided any level of assistance she needs as she grows older.

Feeling all alone in her old house and neighborhood, Hattie is willing to consider moving, but she is afraid because she doesn't know anybody in the facility her children have suggested. How can she survive without her old friends? Will she still be able to see those friends if she moves to the new facility? Will she be able to make new friends at age 89? With her husband dead the past two years and with her children many hours away, friends have been a key component of Hattie's life. She has passed the time with them when they have been able to get together, and she has been able to confide in them in times of happiness and times of stress and loss.

John: Still Coping

John has been an active member of his church most of his life. He grew up learning the stories of his faith and singing the hymns. As a young-married couple, John and his wife focused most of their social life around the church—church suppers, couples groups, being with other people in their age group facing similar experiences including raising children.

At age 62, John developed Alzheimer's disease. At first no one, except his wife, was aware of it. But it didn't take too long for the disease to worsen to the point where John felt nervous and agitated attending church services. To try to cope with those feelings, John's wife suggested that they sit in the back pew so they could leave if John got too disturbed by the service. But soon, this didn't work either.

Even though John was unable to go to church services any longer, and even though he often forgot his own street address, he still derived comfort from hearing some of the old hymns he learned when he was young and hearing some of the old stories he learned as a child. Anything new—new hymns, new liturgy, new approaches to worship even in the home setting—made him very uncomfortable.

A Write-On Support Group

Intrepid authors help each other

Fifteen years ago, after several years working at truck stop kitchens, imprisoned in an oppressive, itinerant life, Sue Rush, at age 57, gave up the world of Merle Haggard cassettes and Caterpillar hats for the imposing calm of the Mississippi River.

Bound for Tiger Lilly, a towboat docked in Memphis, with only a bag of clothes and cooking skills, Rush found humor and order in her life as a river rat. But more important, she says, "I found material for a book."

Rush, now 72 and retired in Ann Arbor, had always loved to write. And like many of the older authors who convene every Friday at the Univer-

sity of Michigan's Turner Geriatric Clinic, she never before had found the time, confidence or motivation to do it.

"I always thought I had the faculties to write but it wasn't until I joined four years ago that I really started to," she says. "It serves as a nice support group."

Founded 16 years ago by social worker Ruth Campbell, the group now has over 25 members. "So many older people have dreams of being a writer," says Campbell, "and once they're in, they're forced to deal with its pitfalls—the intellectual concentration and the block that goes with it."

It is a stimulating process for people who, as they grow older, have less responsibility and activity. Some credit the group with saving them, with giving them discipline.

By Shawn Windsor
Free Press Special Writer
Source: Detroit Free Press,
January 18, 1994, p. 3D

FRIENDS

The primary support network for older people focuses on their families—particularly spouses and adult children, and among adult children, mostly daughters and daughters-in-law. We have also seen that elderly people are not just receivers of assistance within the family unit. As more and more people enter their later years healthier, wealthier, and more vigorous than in previous generations, they are giving increased help to their younger relatives, especially grandchildren.

As important as families are in the support system of older people, most people throughout their lives have an important source of mutual assistance that adds to their quality of life—friends.

Few things are more important than good friends. Friends are important at any age, from toddlers making their first attempts at personal interaction in the sandbox to 99-year-olds recalling past events and reacting to today's news. The only problem for the 99-year-olds is that many of

their old friends are no longer around. So new friends of various types often take on the roles of companions and confidants.

As we look at the subject of friends, it is important to note the roles of companions and confidants. A companion is someone with whom a person can share activities and pastimes—go to the movies together, share a ball game, build and fly model airplanes together. A confidant is someone to confide in and share personal problems with—a person to lean on in times of stress or joy (Barrow 1992).

Roles and Importance of Friends to Older People

Beyond the two major classifications of friends as companions and confidants, friendships have a number of characteristics. These include acceptance, trust, respect, confiding, understanding, spontaneity, mutual assistance, and happiness. These are many of the same characteristics spouses and lovers share, but unlike friendships, relationships with lovers and spouses include strong emotions, such as passionate love and a stronger sense of caring (Davis 1985).

Friends Are Chosen Unlike family relationships that we are either born into or marry into, we choose friends. The interactions we have with family members are not always enjoyable; they can be very trying at times. Friends, on the other hand, are chosen for the joy, fun, support, and pleasure they bring (Larson, Mannell, and Zuzanek 1986).

Friends and Independence Some studies have indicated that friends are very important to older people because they are a means of maintaining independence in their later years (Roberto and Scott 1986). Friends in later life are able to help each other in their goal of maintaining independent living, so important to most older people.

Friends and Feelings of Well-being Feelings of well-being and being satisfied with life are key ingredients of life. Research has shown that having close ties with friends is more important to an older person's well-being than family ties (Crohan and Antonucci 1989). This is true across ethnic lines. For example, research has shown that happiness among African Americans is closely tied to the number of friends they have (Ellison 1990).

Friendships can be critical to an older person's feelings of well-being because growing old successfully depends to a great extent on maintaining a positive self-image (Baltes and Baltes 1988). Friendships tend to help people maintain a positive self-image even in the face of major problems. A positive self-regard is important for happiness and contentment as well as the ability to care for others (Antonucci 1990). Friends supporting each other can build and maintain self-esteem.

Facing Problems with Friends Friends are vitally important to older people as they face the problems of being alone, particularly the large numbers and percentages of older women who become widowed. One study found that both friends and family were equally effective with married and never-married women in dealing with loneliness and isolation (Essex and Nam 1987). Another study reported friends and relatives to be equally important as support systems for older women (Ingersoll-Dayton and Antonucci 1988). An additional study found that many older people feel that both family and friends provide similar functions and that both are equally important (Armstrong and Goldsteen 1990). It is not uncommon for older widows to rely more on friends than family members both as companions and confidants (Atchley 1994).

Friends and Coping with Life Changes In addition to helping older people cope with isolation and loneliness, such as brought about by loss of spouse, friends can help older people with some of the major life changes they face. For example, social support from a group of work

friends has been very helpful for a number of middle-class women at the time of their retirement (Francis 1990). Friends can play a crucial role in older people adjusting to a congregate living situation, such as moving into a retirement community or even a nursing facility (Atchley 1994). Moving into a retirement living environment where a person already has a friend can be a great advantage, but even new friendships can be developed in these kinds of facilities that can make a real contribution to a person's adjustment to new conditions. These friends, although new, can provide a welcome and share mutual life circumstances that led each to giving up their prior lifestyles to move to congregate living. As a former neighbor told this author about how she liked giving up her home and her flower garden when the failing health of her husband persuaded them to move into a life-care community,

> It was really hard at first, but as we got to know our new neighbors and began to share how individually we decided to leave our familiar homes and move here, it became somewhat easier. Getting to know others who were in the same boat, visiting with them and sharing our experiences and feelings helped a lot.

Making New Friends

Old friends, in general, are like old shoes—comfortable; but as we indicated in the beginning of this chapter, the 99-year-old has probably lost most of his or her friends. People in all the older age categories lose friends through death or separation. So developing new friends is vital to the well-being of older adults. One study of friendships over a period of time (longitudinal study) indicated that older women developed more friends than they lost (Adams 1987). Making new friends is not easy for everyone. Certain personality types find it particularly hard to do the give-and-take things that friendships require (Bould, Sanford, and Reif 1989). Very dominant and demanding persons may quickly overload a potential friendship. Changed roles and life circumstances may make it difficult for people to meet others who could become friends. Leaving the workplace reduces for many people the number of contacts that could develop into friends. Continuing to live in neighborhoods where most of the people near the age of an older person have moved away can leave an elderly person with a reduced pool of potential friends. Older people tend to find more friends and neighbors with whom they can interact when they live where the proportion of elderly persons is high, as in retirement communities (Barrow 1992).

Making Friends from People They Meet

Older people, as any other age group, tend to develop new friendships among the people they come into contact with in their daily lives (Atchley 1994). Because of this, some older people have been found to attach friendship characteristics to their service providers (Wolfsen, Barker, and Mitteness 1990). These included physicians, apartment managers, and social workers. Many of the older people in this research shared their feelings with these service providers, confided in them, and counted on them to help them in a variety of situations, many beyond what their normal jobs would require.

Other research (Eustis and Fischer 1991) has found older people giving friendship characteristics to their home-care providers. The clients in this study often confided in their home-care service providers about family problems. The home-care workers frequently used friendship terms when they spoke about their clients. It was not uncommon for the home-care workers to give help beyond the tasks for which they were paid. As one recently widowed 88-year-old told this author when asked about how she was doing with her companion of 60 years gone and trying to live alone in her big, old house,

> It's not too bad as long as Jane keeps coming. I really don't need her too much now that George is gone [Jane was the home-care provider for George in his last years]. I keep paying her to come mornings, but we mostly talk. She tells me all about her family and I tell her about mine. Without her I

would be pretty lonely as my kids live on opposite sides of the country.

The Importance of Making New Friends

The ability to make new friends is important throughout life. This requires some interpersonal skills that need to be nourished across the life span because they may be most needed in the oldest-old years when old friendships are usually depleted through death and disability. It is important for couples to continue to develop friendship skills even though the partners have each other. Some studies of older couples have shown that even though the majority of those surveyed rated their marriages as "very happy," a large number, when asked to name a confidant, named friends rather than spouses (Silverstone and Hyman 1992). In addition, although a married couple tends to do most things together, upon the death of a spouse, the widowed partner—typically the woman—is all alone. Not only is she alone in the home due to death of her spouse, but she is often alone in her social world as couples tend to socialize with other couples. Silverstone and Hyman (1992) have pointed out that married partners are better prepared for the future if each maintains some friends independent from one's spouse. There will be someone there for them beyond the marriage, beyond the world of couples.

Women and Men—Friendship Differences

For more than 20 years, studies have shown that men and women view friendships differently and react differently with friends. Over their adult years, it has been found that women tend to maintain their friendships longer than do men (Riley, Johnson, and Foner 1972; Maas and Kuypers 1974; Essex and Nam 1987). Women, in comparison to men, generally have a variety of relationships in their friendship networks. These differences tend to hold up across various cultures (Antonucci 1990).

It is common for men to develop friendships based on shared activities or interests. Women tend to base their friendships on intimate and emotional sharing (Huyck 1982). Men are likely to go to ball games together or go hunting, where women may go to lunch with their friends and discuss personal issues. Men are much more likely to confide in their wives for personal matters (Atchley 1994).

In the later years, the death of a spouse often narrows the circle of friends for men while expanding it for women. This conclusion was supported in part by an earlier study which indicated that widows in their sixties had fewer contacts with friends than widows in their seventies (Blau 1982). After the age of 70, widowhood for women becomes common. As a result, there are usually many other single women available for friends. Women generally do better than men socially and physically when they end up living alone in their later years. Research has shown that marital status (such as widowhood) and living arrangements (such as living alone) are not necessarily related to an older person's well-being or social isolation (Chappell and Badger 1989). This research indicated that along with health and economic status, the quality and number of companions and confidants are measures of well-being for older people. Some older people live alone because they want to be independent. Others, as is the situation with many widows, have no other choices. Whatever the reason, women who live alone tend to do better because they have better social contacts than men and have more nutritious diets (Riley 1983; Havlik et al. 1987; National Center for Health Statistics 1986).

There is no doubt that friends are very important to an older person's support network. Friendships can bring: enjoyment by spending time with friends; acceptance through valuing friends as they are; mutual respect by knowing that friends have a right to their own opinions; assistance by letting friends help each other; someone to confide personal problems and feelings in; understanding—feeling that friends know each other well enough so they do not have to explain everything; and spontaneity by being able to do and say what one feels like with a friend (Rybash et al. 1991). Friends are important for building and maintaining self-esteem which is so important to life satisfaction. For the older person going through major life changes and losses, friends are a major source of help. Knowing that others have or are experiencing the same circumstances and being able to share thoughts, reactions, fears and joys, can help older people successfully adjust to new situations.

RELIGION/SPIRITUALITY

The focus of this book has been to look realistically at what it means to grow older in America, to look at the changes that occur in a person's life as they move across the life cycle—as well as the losses they face. How do people cope with these changes, losses, and the chronic health conditions that so many of the oldest old experience? This section focuses on the range of support systems that older people use, or could use, in some form or another. Obviously not all support systems are available to all older people. But on the whole, family and friends are vital support mechanisms. The formal support systems described in the next chapter can be vital to the lives of the elderly. Economic supports along with medical and long-term care play key roles in meeting the basic needs of older people. However, some people, because of previous experiences, cultural backgrounds, or personal encounters, tend to rely heavily on religion to help them cope with the changes and challenges of old age.

Optimism and Aging Well

Being optimistic appears to be a significant factor in coping effectively with major life events. There is substantial recent research indicating that optimistic people are better able to overcome defeat and are more likely to be successful, happier, and healthier than people who are not optimistic (Seligman 1991; Myers 1992a, 1992b; Albertson Owens, Berg, and Rhone 1993).

Myers (1992a, 1992b) has indicated that many people believe that happiness is based on being young, successful, rich, and having cultural advantages. What is more important for happiness, he contended from his research, is being content with what one has. He also pointed out that being optimistic is a key factor in happy living. It is assumed that happiness is a factor in a person's concept of well-being.

There is compelling research that indicates that a person's health, as well as feelings of happiness, may be tied to being optimistic (Peterson and Bossio 1991; Guarnera and Williams 1987). Some of this research has indicated that older persons who are optimistic feel more in control of their own lives, which tends to lead to better health. Other research has connected a person's attitudes, especially optimism and positive thinking, with better reactions to disease and even recovery from serious illness (Cousins 1979; Judd 1993; O'Brian 1982; Siegel 1986; Yates et al. 1981). The book, *Learned Optimism*, Seligman (1991) demonstrated how optimism promotes better health.

Faith and Happiness

Myers (1992a, 1992b) has pointed out that there is a close connection between a person's faith and his or her degree of happiness. Citing surveys of people in fourteen nations, Myers (1992a) showed that individuals who had strong religious ties tended to be happier. A number of studies by Koenig (Koenig 1990; Koenig, George, and Siegler 1988; Koenig, Kvale, and Ferrell 1988; Koenig, Moberg, and Kvale 1988; and Guy 1982) have demonstrated that religious attitudes and activities were a source of comfort during stressful times for older adults.

Albertson Owens and McLain (1992), in their research of older adults in southern California, found that the degree to which people in their study were satisfied with life was closely tied to how religious they reported to be. Research by Cox and Hammonds (1988) also showed a link between religion and being satisfied with life among older adults.

Defining Religiosity

What does "being religious" mean? Actually, this is somewhat hard to define. Researchers in the field of religion mostly use the term *religiosity*. Shirley Albertson Owens, of Southern California College, has used this definition: "Religiosity is a complex concept that involves moral belief systems as well as behaviors that may allow the individual to associate with others who share their belief system" (Albertson Owens, Berg, and Rhone 1993: 5). It is important to note that this definition of religiosity has two distinct parts: (1) a belief/reflective aspect that involves personal beliefs, prayer, meditation, and related activities; and (2) an organizational or group activity component that involves being with other people in common activities—from group worship to community service projects to bingo parties. So when the term *religiosity* is used in the rest of this section, it usually refers to both parts of the definition, beliefs and activities.

Religion and Health

In her 1993 research, *Religion, Optimism, and Health in Older Adults* (1993), Albertson Owens and her colleagues cited studies that indicated that religiosity may be a positive contributor to both the physical and mental health of older people. Going back to the middle 1980s, they noted that Stock (1984) reported a link between religiosity, feelings of well-being, and health in the later years of life. Then citing Larson (1992), who is one of the leading researchers studying the relationship of religion and health with the National Institute of Mental Health in Washington, D.C., Albertson Owens and her colleagues showed the link in the 1990s between religiosity and health. Larson, in more than 130 published articles, suggested that levels of religiosity are related to health. As an example, he found that people who attend church have lower blood pressure levels than people who do not attend church. In their own research, Albertson Owens, Ward, and McLeod-Winder (1993) found that older people who were more religious smoked and consumed alcohol at a lower rate than less religious people. Eliminating smoking and reducing alcohol consumption are generally considered good health practices.

Larson (1992) in his research found that faith not only helps people cope with tragedy, but it may even help them recover from physical and mental illness.

Optimism and Religiosity

We have already looked at the relationship between feelings of well-being and optimism. What is optimism? What does it mean to be optimistic? Scheier and Carver (1985) define optimism as expecting that good things, not bad, will happen. Seligman (1991) pointed out that the concept of optimism is more complex. He said optimism includes a person's outlook on events that happen in life, where defeat is not his or her fault, and bad situations are challenges to overcome. In their research, Albertson Owens, Berg, and Rhone (1993) found that "those who rated themselves high on religiosity also rated themselves high on optimism." Those persons who used religion more to cope with life indicated that they were more optimistic than persons who used religion less. People whose faith was more a part of their everyday lives indicated that they were more optimistic than persons who said they were less religious. Although the research of Albertson Owens, Berg, and Rhone (1993) did not show a direct link between religion, optimism, and health in the particular study they conducted in Southern California, a great deal of empirical support for the relation between optimism and health exists. As Albertson Owens and her colleagues cited in the background to their study,

> Optimism may underlie a health style of coping with life events. Seligman (1991) and Myers (1992a, 1992b) have reported substantial empirical evidence that suggests that optimistic people overcome defeat, are more likely to be successful, report themselves to be happier, and enjoy better health than people who are not optimistic (Albertson Owens, Berg, and Rhone 1993: 2).

Are People More Religious As They Grow Older?

If being religious and participating in religious activities are beneficial for older people, which most of the research cited so far has indicated, the question needs to be raised, are older people more religious as they grow older? It seems logical to conclude that in their later years with more free time and getting nearer to the end of life, older people would without question become more religious. Research indicates that this is not really true for most older people. Barbara Payne (1990) found that the assumption that people become more religious as they grow older is incorrect. Evidence indicates that religiosity is related to previous religious activity, the period or time in which they were raised and lived most of their lives, and whether they have chronic health problems.

One of the reasons that many people probably assume older people become more religious as they grow older is the high degree of religiosity of older people compared to younger adults. Koenig (1990) of Duke University reported that, based on Gallup Polls, people age 65 and older have more religious attitudes and behaviors than younger adults. Bearon and Koenig (1990) found that as a group, older adults are highly religious. But Markides, Levin, and Ray (1987) reported that there is little evidence to say that older people become more religious as they grow older and get closer to death. Their research showed that a person's religiosity remained quite even over the years, with a slight decline in religious service attendance which could be linked to declining health and decreased ability to attend services due to loss of mobility. Other research has shown that attendance at religious services could be linked to health, fewer physical symptoms, and lower mortality (Koenig, Moberg, and Kvale, 1988). It should be noted that this also could be because a person in better health can get to religious services more easily.

A decline in attending religious services does not mean that older people are less religious. As we have already noted, many older people attend religious services less frequently because of health conditions which limit their mobility. Other research has indicated that a decline in church attendance may also be a sign of an older person's shift from an outward to a more inward focus of life (Birren 1990b). Religious-service attendance may not be an accurate measure of a person's religiosity. This is probably the case for older people. The inward focus of religion may be more appropriate for personal and emotional expressions of religiosity even as attendance at religious services decreases. This has been found in research dating back to 1976 (Blazer and Palmore 1976) where even though religious activity, such as church attendance, declined for older people as the result of physical limitations, positive religious expressions remained into the later years. This is important to note because religiosity consists of beliefs and religion-related activities ranging from religious services to social events.

Religious TV and Older Adults

There is evidence that older people watch more religious television and read more religious literature than younger people (Hammond 1969; Kivett 1979; Young and Dowling 1987; Moberg 1970, 1972; Briggs 1987). With their continued interest in religion and their generally decreased mobility due to health conditions and infirmities, it is logical to conclude that many older people would turn to religious television programs if they were available and if they fit the religious expressions of individual viewers. Religious television programs in an area that are limited to Roman Catholic or some form of Protestant services certainly are not going to meet the needs of older Jewish people.

Beyond limited physical mobility, it has been found that there are other factors that cause some older people to turn to television and radio as a means of religious expression instead of attending religious services. In their study, *The Relationship between Cognitive Status and Religios-*

ity in Older Adults (1993), Albertson Owens and her colleagues found that some persons with cognitive decline (decreasing mental capacities due to dementia such as Alzheimer's disease) experienced too much stimuli from attending religious services because they do not process information in traditional ways. They cited Davis' book, *My Journey into Alzheimer's Disease* (1989), a personal account of his experiences with this mind-killing disease, where he said it was less distressing for him to tune into religious television or radio programs than to go to church services. When the personally attended church service became too overwhelming to cope with, it was too difficult to leave. It was easier to turn off the religious TV program if it became too frustrating.

The research of Albertson Owens, Ward, and McLeod-Winder (1993) on religious practices and the mental status of older adults confirmed Davis's observations. Those persons who showed poorer scores in tests that measured speed of processing information as well as visual-spatial problem solving tended to watch more religious television and listen to more religious radio programs. Albertson et al. concluded:

> Therefore, when one's speed of processing and/or visual-spacial problem solving ability became progressively impaired, one may prefer to watch religious television or listen to religious radio in the comfort of their own home so he/she may have the option to walk away if the words or picture become too obscure of confusing (Albertson Owens, Ward, and McLeod-Winder 1993: 20).

Religion and Coping Skills

Research indicating that it is not uncommon for older adults to rely on their religion as a source of comfort in stressful times has been noted (Koenig 1990). In 1992 Albertson Owens and McLain reported the results of a study of older adults to determine whether religion could be looked at as a coping mechanism at times when a person has little control over changes and challenges in his or her life. The purpose of this research was to see if it would be helpful for service providers (caregivers) to encourage religious expression on the part of the older people they were caring for as an effective coping mechanism. Their study revealed that increasing age did not result in increased use of religion as a coping mechanism. However, health was a big factor. Declining health often resulted in an increased reliance on the personal aspects of religion as a way to cope with illness. This study indicated that the personal aspects of religion, not whether a person attends religious services, provide a "degree of comfort when the individual has no control over the situation," such as in times of loss and illness (Albertson Owens and McLain 1992: 14).

An interesting, but understandable, aspect to this research was that older adults who were deeply involved with the basics of their religion (personal beliefs) were likely to use religion as an effective coping mechanism for the challenges life brings. However, older persons who were active but more superficial in their religious orientation were no more likely than those who indicated little or no interest in religion to use religion as an effective coping mechanism for the trials of life: "Religiosity/spirituality is conducive to life satisfaction in older adults provided that it is indicative of a more deep-seated involvement with such a belief system" (Albertson Owens and McLain 1992: 15).

Coping skills are particularly important to older adults, Albertson Owens and McLain (1992) pointed out, because their options to change their environment or their circumstances usually are quite limited. Religious attitudes and beliefs can serve as useful mechanisms in helping them cope with the changes, including physical changes, they cannot control. Koenig, George, and Siegler (1988) studied coping strategies among adults aged 55 to 80. The 100 older adults in the study mentioned 556 coping strategies they used in reaction to 289 stressful events. Personal religious responses (such as trust and faith in a deity) were the most cited (30 percent) responses to stressful events which were indicated to be effective in relieving tension and ad-

justing to circumstances. The next most-often cited responses (15 percent) dealt with keeping busy with other things. Religious coping mechanisms to stressful events represent an internal coping mechanism. Older adults typically have more ready access to internal coping mechanisms than to external ones. In most any circumstances older adults can draw upon inner resources that usually include their belief systems.

Coping Skills for Mentally Impaired Older Persons

So far we have seen that older adults can use religious expressions and orientation as effective coping mechanisms in dealing with the changes, problems, and challenges of life. The research that supports these observations involved adults who were lucid and aware. The question arises, What about older adults who suffer mental impairments? What about the millions of people afflicted by dementia, including Alzheimer's disease? Can religion be an effective coping mechanism for these people? Richards (1990) contended that people with dementia can respond to faith rituals and religious symbols. This is because it is easier for people with dementia to remember things from the past than recent events. For many older adults, the religious beliefs they developed in their early years are embedded in their memories which, Richards believes, makes it possible for people who even have late-stage dementia to use religion as a coping mechanism. Koenig, Moberg, and Kvale (1988) found that patients with mild to moderate dementia tended to be more religious than those who had cancer or high blood pressure.

Davis (1989), in his personal story of his own Alzheimer's disease, gave a step-by-step account of his use of religion as a source of support as the disease got worse. Even though his faith was used more simply as his brain deteriorated, it was still a comfort. He did note that new versions of the Bible or forms of worship were of no use. As his Alzheimer's disease got worse, only those religious forms he used in his youth were of value.

This supports the concept that religious beliefs developed in the early years of life which are strongly embedded in the memory can be useful even when a person is suffering from mental decline (Richards 1990).

Because the evidence to support these conclusions was limited, Albertson Owens et al. (1993) undertook additional research to determine whether religion can be a source of comfort to mentally impaired older people. They found that even persons who suffered from mental decline obtained comfort in their religious beliefs. For example, some persons who were not able to remember a telephone number that they had just looked at were able to understand and use their religion or faith as a coping mechanism. Of the people in their study, 91 percent rated God as a source of strength. This same research found that even those who were the most mentally limited rated themselves high on religious measurements. These researchers suggested that these findings can be helpful to the professionals, lay persons, and family members who try to help older people deal with the realities of dementia, including Alzheimer's disease.

Negative Aspects of Religion on Older People

All throughout our discussion on religion and aging, we have focused on the positive effects religiosity in its complete form—beliefs and group interaction—has on older people, even if they fall victim to dementia. But are there any down sides? Are there any negative aspects of religiosity for older people? H.G. Koenig (1990) of Duke University, in his extensive review of research on religion and aging noted, "that in all of the studies that he had reviewed there was not one report of a negative association between religious cognitions and well-being among older adults" (Albertson Owens and McLain 1992: 3). This has been supported by the broad array of studies we have cited. However, Albertson Owens and McLain (1993: 3) cited other studies that "have reported little positive, or else no sta-

tistically significant, relation between religiosity and well-being" (Baugher et al. 1989–90; Levin and Markides 1986; Levin and Vanderpool 1987; Peterson and Greil 1990; Wagner and Lorion 1984).

Ross (1990) found an interesting relationship between the intensity of a person's religious beliefs and well-being. People with strong religious beliefs had lower mental distress in reacting to life's problems than people with weaker religious beliefs. This same research, however, found that people with no religious beliefs also had low levels of distress. In 1970, Moberg pointed out that there may be some negative aspects for older people who participate in religious activities. Some churches create a fear of damnation. Older people may feel that they are unqualified for heaven, that past wrongdoings may be bothering them, and as a result, fear death. They may even believe that their illness is the result of past sins. Larue (1976) stated that in some churches older people are led to believe their illnesses are punishments from God. Hogan (1974) argued that some churches treat their older members like little children rather than as mature functioning adults. Gray and Moberg (1962) argued that some older persons suffer significant spiritual pain as they observe changes in liturgy and beliefs. Today, many religious institutions are reexamining beliefs regarding the role of women, homosexuality, and their role in contemporary society. Without regard to the merits of such changes, many older parishioners see the changes resulting in a church very different from the church of their youth. For many older persons there is a sense of security in the "old ways." In some churches there also is significant change in music and drama, which may create tension, stress and a feeling of loss among older parishioners.

Levin and Markides (1986), in a study of 375 persons aged 65 to 80, found that religious service attendance was not significantly related to how a person rated his or her health; rather, attendance was tied more closely to an older person's physical ability to get to services than the degree to which they are religious. This ties in to another study by Ross (1990) which indicated that people with strong religious beliefs had less distress in coping with life than those who went through the motions of being religious. Although religious service attendance is important to many older people and serves as a vital form of contact with other people, meditation, reflection, prayer, and other inward expressions of faith seem to be key for relying on one's religion in times of change and stress.

One negative aspect of religion is often brought about by religious institutions themselves, according to Robert Atchley, director of the Scripps Gerontology Center at Miami University (Briggs 1992). He pointed out that people adjust to growing older to a great extent by continuing lifelong ways of doing things, and church attendance is part of that for millions of Americans. By not providing easy access to religious services, religious institutions can themselves become a disruptive force in the lives of older people. Even though the population is aging rather rapidly, with the baby boomers next in line to join the ranks of older people, it has been pointed out that most religious organizations still see their future in recruiting younger people for membership.

Monsignor Charles Fahey, a professor of aging studies at the Third Age Center at Fordham University, has referred to the lack of interest by churches and synagogues in older people as "an ageism of neglect. Rather than lead into the culture, churches are generally caught (up) into the broader culture that tends to ignore older persons, at best" (Briggs 1992: B6). At this point, in order to get a better view of religion and older people, it is important to look at the role religious institutions—churches, synagogues, temples, mosques, and all other terms that apply to religious organizations—play in the lives of older people. For simplicity and ease of reading, all of these institutions will be referred to as "churches."

Religious Institutions and Older People

The church is clearly an important and crucial institution for many older Americans, and churches increasingly will have a larger and larger percentage of their members among the elderly. In November 1967, *Christianity Today* reported that 25 percent of Presbyterians, Episcopalians, and Methodists were 65 years of age or older, and that 50 percent were aged 50 or older. Another survey found that more than one-fourth of the parishioners in the average Roman Catholic Church are aged 65 or older (Briggs 1992).

By participating in a religious community, a person can find friends and emotional support. This gives him or her a sense of belonging and acceptance. One of the more important functions of churches is to make sure that their older parishioners are really a part of the church community. Widowed persons frequently find themselves isolated. The church can provide a social network that can enable them to feel a part of a community (Koenig et al. 1988).

Studies have shown that the elderly are more likely to be affiliated with a church than any other organization. The church therefore becomes for most older Americans not only a place of worship, a place for participation in ritualistic processes, and a place to interact with others, but also an anchor for their view of reality and a place to go for direction and assistance in times of need. It is a place of acceptance and, at a deeper level, tells them who they are and who they can be.

The church can be either a positive or negative influence in the lives of older people. It will be a negative force if it ignores them or treats them in a condescending manner. Older people can be very useful to the church if their skills and knowledge are recognized and used.

Increasingly, churches will have older parishioners. Clearly the "graying" of the church will pose major new challenges in American society in general and for religious communities specifically: J. Kirk Gulledge wrote,

Stereotypical attitudes toward aging may result in avoidance of contact with older parishioners, monolithic thinking and characterizations, such as, "Old people are all alike," condescension toward or oversight of elderly in ministry plans, or discrimination against older members in appointments to church leadership when ministry with the elderly may be regarded as an unpleasant necessity by many clergy (Gulledge 1991: 65).

In this context Robb (1991) wrote that many religious institutions are living symbolically in the past. Congregations and their leaders devote too much time, energy and resources to church schools and youth programs. They seem unaware of the tremendous demographic changes that are taking place in American society. They seem unaware that their youth-oriented institutions are shrinking, not so much from lack of good leadership or creative programming, but from enough younger people to maintain former levels of participation. For nearly a quarter century, Americans have not been producing enough children to replace themselves. Many churches have not made the switch to a new reality of membership in which the increases in membership will not come from younger people but from older people. As a result, congregations and their leaders have the dual challenge of ministering to the decreasing numbers of younger people while supporting increasing numbers of older people needing spiritual reality for what they experience in the aging process. For many older persons, Robb argued, the spiritual agenda for youth is inadequate for the reality of the older generation. Older persons need spiritual nurturing just as much as youth do, but whose reality ought to be emphasized? Both of course, but how are spiritual leaders to do that adequately? Increasingly that will be the challenge. To attract attendance by older persons and meet their needs, the church will need to wrestle with questions relating to the purpose in growing old. What is the meaning in a life that is beginning to be seriously debilitated?

Robb (1991) believed that many of the current religious leaders may be committed deeply to equal treatment of women and members of various racial and ethnic minorities, but may still harbor deeply ingrained negative stereotypes about age and the aging process. Robb asserted that in the near future one-half to two-thirds of many congregations will consist of older persons. If denominations see older persons as confused, unattractive, unproductive, uninvolved, and dependent, and younger persons as attractive, intelligent, achieving, and productive, then the church will have internalized a negative societal stereotype of the older person, and the church will not adequately minister to their spiritual needs.

Access to Organized Religion: A Major Problem

Even if the orientation and programming in churches includes the needs, resources, and contributions of older people, it is of little value if they cannot get there. Recent research has clearly suggested that older people do not abandon social activities including participating in church life. A study by researchers from Holy Cross College disputed the disengagement theory of aging that has held that as people grow older they voluntarily withdraw from religious and other social activities. In a random survey of 200 Christians aged 65 and older in Worcester, Massachusetts, 46 percent of those questioned indicated that they would like to attend religious services more often (Briggs 1992). Almost one-third of those questioned cited lack of transportation as the principal reason for not attending church more often frequently. Health problems and poor weather were noted as the reasons 37 percent of those surveyed did not attend services more often. Father Fahey of Fordham University, in response to this survey, indicated that for "those churches and synagogues that do reach out, older people do participate" (Briggs 1992: B6).

One of this study's researchers, Stephen Ainley, said that some churches may unintentionally discourage older persons from attending services by putting so much emphasis on radio broadcasts rather than organizing transportation to bring older people to church. Gerontologist Robert Atchley pointed out that religious institutions endanger their own spiritual health by ignoring older members' needs in transportation to and from church. He said, "If you really want to tell the truth about this, most every church has the resources. It's a lack of commitment" (Briggs 1992: B6).

Attitudes of Religious Leaders Toward the Elderly

Elderly parishioners tend to place a high level of trust in religious leaders (Rowles 1985). When they need personal counseling they tend to go to the clergy before they go to psychiatrists, psychologists, or social workers (Brink, 1977). The pastor is still for most elderly a person of respect, a person in whom they have some confidence, and the person they go to when they are troubled. Is this trust misplaced or is it based on pastoral competence? Is it based on pastors who do really respect and care for elderly persons? Or is this respect of pastors based on clergy who do not understand, nor have sympathy for, the aging process and elderly persons? Gulledge (1991) attempted to determine the attitudes of pastors toward the elderly. He mailed questionnaires to 289 randomly selected pastors from the United Methodist, Southern Baptist, and Evangelical Lutheran churches about their views of aging and the elderly. There were 238 responses, an 82.3 percent response rate. He found that the clergy as a group (at least as represented by these denominations) are generally positive in their attitudes toward older adults. He also found that persons with the most positive attitudes toward aging usually demonstrated the most accurate knowledge of the facts about the aging process. He found that differences in attitudes toward aging are not significantly related to the age, sex, years in the ministry, the size of church, personal position in the church, number of ministers, proportion of older members, or proportion of ministerial time spent with older persons. He did find significant differences in attitudes about the quality of contact between the clergy and older parishioners.

The congregations that are most successful will probably have leaders who have a good awareness of the aging process, an understanding of changing demographics, and programs that are holistic and enabling. A holistic approach emphasizes the whole person: the physical self, the emotional self, the social self, and the spiritual self.

How Churches Can Assist Older People

To be helpful to older parishioners, churches can make a list of regular congregational activities that do exist for older members. Older persons could be used to discuss their "life's journey" and what insights they gained from that process. Churches can set up telephone assurance networks in which someone, at least once a day, calls the older parishioner. They can set up support groups for relatives of older persons suffering from chronic illnesses. Churches can provide transportation services for needed appointments, church services, and to shopping malls or to local entertainment. They can provide respite care for caregivers. Some churches can provide handyman services to help older people maintain their homes. Many churches have become involved with meeting the housing needs of the elderly through supporting and sponsoring congregate living arrangements—homes for the aged, shared housing, board-and-care homes, nursing facilities, and life-care communities.

Churches can provide opportunities for informational speakers, music, or other types of entertainment. They can also provide intergenerational communication opportunities. Some churches provide bus tours to various scenic and entertainment sites. In addition, older people can be used to visit the ill, participate in the educational programs of the church, and encourage the depressed. The enabling functions of churches are also important because of the losses associated with aging. Clearly the church as an institution is going to have to decide what to do with its aging congregation (Dickerson and Myers 1988; Elias 1988; Moberg 1970).

An important role for churches will be the need for staff or volunteers to know about the agencies and organizations in the community that provide assistance to older persons. Medicare, Medicaid, SSI (Supplemental Security Insurance), housing assistance, chore services, and a range of other programs and services are becoming so complex that many older people become confused about their benefits and where to look for help.

Rituals and Older People

All societies have rituals in which members of the society are expected to be involved. At the heart of worship in most religions are traditional rituals, traditions, or rites. These rituals focus on how a person's spirituality is to be focused during the worship process. Robb (1991) stated that many older persons have feelings of dismay when they see the changes taking place in traditional rituals. Rituals frequently point to the spiritual meanings of beliefs. Rituals tend to consist of repetitive behaviors and evoke memories of one's religious heritage. Older persons have a lifetime of remembrances that can be threatened when new forms are used.

Confirmations, bar or bas mitzvahs, and baptisms tend to be rituals celebrating transitions in life. These rites of passage look toward the future. There are often no comparable religious rites involving older persons. As a result, the rites of passage involving youth usually look forward to new possibilities, while the absence of rites of passage for older persons can result in the danger of seeing old age as a slippery slope to oblivion. The absence of religious or social norms for the late years, Robb (1991) argued, leaves people uncertain about the roles they are to play in their old age. The danger, he stated, is that some people may need direction in old age and without it wander spiritually aimlessly. Rites are powerful in their ability to affirm the value and purpose of life, and that the absence of a religious rite tends to label a life transition as lacking in religious importance. He pointed out that this is particularly true for retirement, for which there is no religious ritual. The lack of a religious ritual for retirement tends to affirm society's judgment that the event is of such little importance that it is not worth any type of special event in a religious context.

Spirituality: Searching for Meaning in Life

Abraham Maslow (1970) argued that human needs fall largely into a hierarchy of five levels: physiological, safety, belongingness, love and esteem, and self-actualization. He believed that when one level of need is regularly satisfied it becomes less powerful, causing the next "higher" level need to be more keenly felt. In all of this, the individual's symbolically perceived needs are important, and it is difficult to know how the individual symbolically perceives his or her needs. The basic needs of many older Americans are met. For them, there is a focus on what it all means. It is at this point that spirituality becomes important. Human beings as symbolizing creatures think, question, and look for meaning and purpose in life.

The terms *spiritual* and *religious* are not synonymous. Spirituality reflects one's search for the meaning and purpose in life in general and the attempt to put meaning into the many events of daily living. Religiosity describes individual or group relations with a supernatural power, whether called God, spirit, or vital force. Most older persons are religious, and all have some sort of spiritual orientation. The search for meaning is an expression of the spiritual dimension of human existence and separates humans from the rest of the animal world.

In contemporary society, older persons are breaking out of formerly defined limitations of what it means to be old. Only human beings have the capacity for reflective thinking and the ability to use that reflection for present needs. This perspective is important in viewing religion and spirituality because it relates to the self-identifying process. Life purpose is not assumed to come with biological birth, but rather to have evolved out of relationships with others at a specific time in history, with its unique set of events, values, and norms on which humans can reflect. It is out of this interaction that spiritual orientations develop. Spirituality in old age then comes out of this reflection of past and present experiences and relationships. Payne (1990) stated that spirituality is handled and modified through a reflective process people can use to give meaning to what they encounter in life.

Religious activity and church membership do not necessarily reflect spirituality. A person can be very spiritual and yet not be active in a church or have any church membership at all. On the other hand, people can be very active in a church and not be very spiritual.

David Moberg, in writing on aging and spirituality, used the definition for spirituality of the National Interfaith Coalition on Aging: "Spiritual well-being is the affirmation of life in a relationship with God, self, community, and environment that celebrates wholeness" (Moberg 1990: 6). He then pointed out that the definition and its emphasis have not yet made a significant impact upon the study of aging. Neglecting the spiritual aspects of life ignores the needs of older people because they tend to be very concerned with spiritual perspectives.

Moberg (1990) also stated part of the problem is that research on spirituality is complicated by not being able to measure spirituality empirically. Relationships and the consequences of religious beliefs can be determined, but not spirituality itself. Again, the problem is the lack of an adequate definition. What indicators of behavior can be used to determine spirituality?

In pluralistic American society, people of many different backgrounds tend to agree to disagree about religion. This is understandable and can be helpful in maintaining tolerance and stability in society. But who provides for the spiritual needs of older people, if not the religious institutions? If this is so, then it often leaves practitioners (nurses, doctors, social workers, psychologists, counselors, and others) unable to deal with the totality of the older people they are serving. One does not need to agree with a person's spiritual perspective to use it in working with an older person.

The point here is not a minor one, as again it must be stressed that religion and spirituality are not synonymous. James Birren, who has devoted a lifetime to research on psychological development, wrote:

> I have come to believe that the inner spiritual life of an individual follows a different life course than does religious behavior or participation. I have the impression that mature and elderly adults seek a wholeness, a meaning in life, that is more integrative of actions and emotions, but less analytical in thought. If such a trend is widely found then explorations of the territory of late life spirituality should be undertaken by both empirical psychologists and students of religion (Birren 1990a: 44).

Susan McFadden wrote about spirituality, stating that it is essentially "the quest for ultimate meanings, values and answers to questions like 'For what purpose have I lived?' 'Have my allegiances made a difference to anyone?' 'How can I live knowing the inevitability of death?' " (McFadden 1990: 133).

The Importance of Symbols

Melvin Kimble (1990) pointed out that humans are creatures who use symbols to give meaning and direction to life. Human beings are capable of understanding and creating a world of meaning. Human beings have values which give meaning and direction to life. Without positive symbols that give meaning to growing old, one can quickly come to the conclusion that aging is primarily a biomedical condition. However, for persons with symbols that give direction, meaning, and purpose even in frail old age, happiness and life satisfaction can result. It is within that process of symbolizing, of giving meaning and direction to life, that spirituality begins to be understood. To adequately understand older persons then, as well as younger persons, one must understand the symbols they believe give values and meaning to their lives.

Henry Simmons (1990) wrote that as important as it is to have the research projects tell us about religiosity and aging, we also need research to focus on the spiritual dimension. Much more research needs to be done in this area of religion and spirituality. James Seeber at the end of his book on spiritual maturity wrote:

A true crisis exists in the field of religion and aging. Almost no thorough or intensive research is being done to better understand how spiritual resources and religious life contribute to successful aging nor how it interacts with other variables in later life (Seeber 1990: 195 [sic]).

Religious Cults and Older People

If established religion in the U.S. does not respect or meet the needs of older Americans, there is a danger that cults will. Collins and Frantz wrote:

Respect your elders; cults certainly do. They respect elders' retirement incomes, investment portfolios and paid-for homes. No longer satisfied with recruiting wide-eyed and penniless youths, the cults have shifted their focus to older people—even those who have little more to offer them than their Social Security checks or small pensions (Collins and Frantz 1994: 23).

In their investigation, Collins and Frantz found that as many as a million cult members are over the age of 50. At least five people age 50 and over were among David Koresh's followers. This number would have been higher were it not for the fact that many of the older individuals in the cult left just before the assault by federal agents. Collins and Frantz quoted Kevin Garvey, a Connecticut-based expert on cults, as indicating the evidence shows that about 40 percent of all persons in New Age cult-like groups are over the age of 50. There are in the United States today 2,000 to 5,000 cults with a membership between 3 to 5 million persons.

Collins and Frantz (1994) quoted University of California at Berkeley professor Margaret Singer, who has studied cults for 25 years and has counseled more than 3,000 former members, that 10 to 20 million Americans have had some involvement with cults at one time or another:

That a number of older people are being recruited into cults is no accident, but the result of a sophisticated strategy many of the major groups are carrying out on a nationwide scale. They may contact subjects through nursing homes, hospitals, senior centers, and even go into the homes of sick, lonely, and other extremely vulnerable individuals (Collins and Frantz 1994: 26).

Collins and Frantz (1994) have pointed that cults try to recruit older persons who are looking for answers—those older persons who are attempting to determine why they have lost a spouse or a child, or who are trying to find spiritual answers regarding their own death and questions about life after death. They quoted a former recruiter of older persons who indicated that elders are the perfect targets because they are lonely, have the time to talk, and are usually at home.

In her book *Hawking God*, Ellen Kamentsky (1992) said that she would wander through nursing homes, observe the names of persons above their doors, and then go in and talk to them to recruit them to her cause and to her organization. She would let them first do most of the talking, then she would begin to ask questions, and finally would attempt to bring in her own recruiting agenda. Collins and Frantz add:

It's virtually impossible to anticipate the physical and emotional trauma cult association can unleash. It can also lead to irreparable economic devastation, particularly for older people. . . . The seduction starts out caring and comfortable. Eventually, it becomes cruel and castrating. . . . Worse, the destruction can never be fully undone (Collins and Frantz 1994: 29).

SUPPORT GROUPS

One form of support that has grown rapidly in recent years is support groups. Support groups have developed across the nation to deal with almost any problem people might have or think they have. Older people, and those moving toward the older ages, are included. The previous chapter has already noted a number of support groups to help grandparents deal with the difficult issues and problems they face in their expanding roles.

As some writers have observed, in localities across the nation people are streaming back to churches and synagogues with a fervor that has not been seen since the 1950s. A religious revival? Not really. Instead of sitting in the pews, they are going off to meeting rooms throughout the building sharing their innermost thoughts, darkest fears, deepest secrets, confounding frustrations, and strangest cravings (Leerhsen, Lewis, Pompers, Davenport, and Nelson 1990).

In 1990, it was estimated that there were about 500,000 support groups attended by some 15 million people. In the ten years between 1980 and 1990, the number of these groups has quadrupled (Leerhsen et al. 1990).

Why has this form of support increased so rapidly? Why are these groups so popular? Many people have discovered that sharing feelings, frustrations, and problems through talking and listening to people who are facing the same situations has a soothing and healing effect. They can motivate people to work out solutions through suggestions and encouragement.

Most professionals see these types of groups as effective ways to cope with isolation—a condition that tends to make all other problems worse. "Just the sight of your fellow sufferers tends to make your pain a little more bearable," said one self-help group organizer (Leerhsen 1990: 50).

Defining Support Groups

Self-help groups are known by various names: support groups, mutual aid groups, and mutual aid societies (LaGrand 1992). They are "small group structures for mutual aid and the accomplishment of a specific purpose. They are usually formed by peers who have come together for mu-

tual assistance in satisfying a common need, overcoming a common handicap or life-disrupting problem, and bringing about desired social and/or personal change" (Katz and Bender 1976: 9).

In 1970, psychologist E.T. Gendlin wrote "Soon it will be understood that everyone needs to be in a group" (Gendlin 1970: 23). This came at a time when psychotherapy focused on individual treatment. Gendlin was advocating support groups for persons with or without specific problems. Participating in these groups fills a vacuum brought about by changing family structure, advances in technology, urbanization, and the mobility of the population socially, economically, and physically (LaGrand 1992). These social factors have tended to make people feel more alone in facing the issues and problems of life.

In addition, traumatic life events such as the loss of loved ones through death, life-threatening illnesses, or significantly changed roles in life (such as stepparenting or caregiving) can threaten a person's feelings toward himself or herself as well as one's perception of the world as a stable place (LaGrand 1992). These traumatic events can led to a range of emotions—guilt, anger, and depression—that leaves the person feeling victimized and alone. Enter the self-help support groups.

Support Groups: An American Approach

Although support groups have grown rapidly in recent years and seem to be springing up almost everywhere, the idea behind them is not new. The need for people to come together for mutual assistance and support can be traced back to the Middle Ages, with guilds and brotherhoods, and to even earlier times (LaGrand 1992). There has always been an American tradition of coming together to meet needs as well as provide assistance to those who needed help. In 1976, Hurvitz pointed out that the American values of humanitarianism and pragmatism can be seen in the development of present-day self-help groups. Providing assistance to others in need and doing things in a practical way have been part of the

American way of life. Marcia Colone, director of social services at the University of Chicago's Hospitals, has noted something very American in the self-help support group movement with its emphasis on getting results: "This supports America's values of marshaling resources, taking charge and solving the problem. There is no doubt that these groups help people make real changes in their lives" (Leerhsen 1990: 53).

Types of Support Groups

According to Leerhsen (1990), support groups in contemporary America are generally divided into four major categories:

- Groups focusing on problems of addictive behavior, such as Compulsive Shoppers and Workaholics
- Groups focusing on providing supports for those suffering from physical and mental illness, such as Parkinson's Support Group and Recovery, Inc.
- Groups focusing on those dealing with a major life transition or other crisis, such as Widowed Persons Service and Recently Divorced Catholics
- Groups focusing on the friends and relatives of people with a problem, such as Adult Children of Alcoholics and Children of Aging Parents

Support Groups and Older People

Support groups have proven to be very helpful to older people and the people who help them—particularly their caregiving family members. Previous chapters pointed out the reality of widowhood for older people, particularly older women, and in the chapter on death and dying, the important role of the Widowed Persons Service with support groups was noted. These groups have played a vital role in helping people adjust to a new and frightening phase of life.

There are a number of support groups that provide assistance to patients and their families dealing with illnesses and disabilities that particularly strike older people. Many of these are coordinated on the national level including: United Ostomy Association (for patients and family members of persons who have had an ostomy, an operation to make an artificial opening to empty the large or small bowel or the bladder), American Cancer Society, American Heart Association, Arthritis Foundation, Courage Stroke Network, Huntington's Disease Society of America, Leukemia Society of America, and many others. These support groups deal with a range of issues patients and their families face as they try to cope with their illnesses.

Support Groups for Caregivers

Some of the support groups focus on the people who take care of their elderly relatives and friends. One of the best illustrations of this type of support group is the Alzheimer's Disease and Related Disorders Association. Until it was founded in 1979, there was little organized support for the caregivers of Alzheimer's patients. "The county was just barely becoming aware of Alzheimer's then," recalled Dr. Robert Butler, chairman of the geriatrics department of Mt. Sinai Medical Center in New York City (Barnhill 1994: 15).

In order to survive the strains and stresses of being a caregiver to an Alzheimer's patient, experts say that people need a place to get advice, share their experiences, let off steam, and know that they are not alone in what they're trying to do. Dr. Butler stated that "exhaustion and burnout can make the caregiver a second patient. Support groups provide much-needed relief" (Barnhill 1994: 15). Alzheimer's support groups are springing up all around the nation.

The functions of these types of groups are diverse. On the knowledge side, many of these groups utilize professionals to teach caregivers practical skills and inform them about various services such as transportation, adult daycare, and nursing homes. Doctors, lawyers, and other experts in fields related to the needs of patients are featured in some support group meetings. Information ranges from learning about the disease to how to dress someone larger than the caregiver and how to prevent a wandering patient from leaving the house.

On the emotional release side, these types of support groups offer moral support to devastated participants. Just being with other people facing the same challenges is very helpful.

> "Going to a group meeting and seeing that you're not alone . . . can be very beneficial" said Diane Young, chair of the Patient and Family Services Committee of the Alzheimer's Association. "There's nothing you can say that someone else hasn't said, thought, or felt. And you can say it without being criticized" (Barnhill 1994: 15).

Being able to vent pent-up feelings is a vital aspect of support groups for caregivers. In a support group meeting, the members of a group in St. Louis nodded in sympathy as a woman tearfully told them that she wanted to divorce her husband who has advanced-stage Alzheimer's disease. In another support group, two members expressed their desire to divorce their ill spouses to marry other people. They were able to share these feelings and explore the consequences of these actions with their support groups (Barnhill 1994).

In another group in New York State, sitting around a table with nine other people, one woman said, "Being a caregiver for a person with Alzheimer's is a living hell. It was horrible, like a nightmare" (Barnhill 1994: 15).

The people in the Alzheimer's support groups are the caregivers to some of the 4 million Americans diagnosed with Alzheimer's disease. With the oldest-old population the fastest growing sector of the population, the need for these types of support groups will continue to grow.

Lynn Osterkamp (1992) pointed out the important things a support group can do for caregivers of elderly people:

- Provide comfortable setting in which participants can express their feelings
- Help the members of the group to realize they are not alone in what they are facing and doing

- Help members to set limits to their caregiving responsibilities
- Help members to consider the effects of taking on or continuing their caregiving
- Help members to make difficult decisions—decisions that directly affect the caregivers in their abilities to carry out their roles

Key Resources

The following agencies provide information about support groups around the nation which focus on caregiving of elderly people.

Alzheimer's Association
919 North Michigan Avenue
Chicago, IL 60611
(312) 335-8700

Information Referral Service:
1-800-272-3900 (toll free)
(312) 335-8882 (TDD)

Children of Aging Parents
Suite 302-A
1609 Woodbourne Road
Levittown, PA 19057
(215) 945-6900

National Self-Help Clearinghouse
Room 620
25 West 43rd Street
New York, NY 10036
(212) 642-2944

Supportive Older Women's Network (SOWN)
2805 N. 47th Street
Philadelphia, PA 19131
(215) 477-6000

Support Groups for Fun

Not all support groups focus on serious needs or problems—not even the ones for older people. Some are aimed at helping older people add new dimensions to their lives, new outlets for creativity, new zest for living. The Write-On Support Group of the Turner Geriatric Clinic of the University of Michigan is such a group (Windsor 1994).

Founded in 1978, the group has over twenty-five members. Mildred McGregor, 81, a World War II frontline surgical nurse who for the past 15 years has been working on a memoir of her experience said, "It gave me a deadline. We older people disintegrate without some objective. And though the writing forces me to relive often painful memories, it's still my raison d'être—my reason for being" (Windsor 1994: 3D).

New members are welcomed to the group. The founder of the group, Ruth Campbell, a social worker, stated, "They are very helpful to each other. They take care of each other. The writing and the stories that come out of it create a bond, a commonality" (Windsor 1994: 3D).

Support Groups: A People's Movement

Self-help support groups have been called "a people's movement," a new primary social group or institution. For the most part, the groups provide "resources within strong social systems at times when our emotional guard is down" (LaGrand 1992: 165). The key ingredient of these groups is acceptance—no matter their circumstances or conditions, the participants are looked at primarily as normal people with particular troubles or needs. Self-help support groups are the living example of the benefits that can come from "human interaction focused on mutual interests" (LaGrand 1992: 173).

According to LaGrand (1992), there are still a large number of Americans who are unaware of the availability of self-help support groups that could benefit them at any age, particularly in times of major life changes, losses, or threatening illnesses.

SUMMARY

Friends

Although families are the primary support system for older adults, most older adults have an important source of mutual assistance—friends. Few things are more important than good friends at any age, from toddlers to the oldest old.

There are two major categories of friends: companions and confidants. A companion is someone with whom a person can share activities and pastimes. A confidant is someone a person can confide in, can share problems with—a person you can lean on in times of stress or joy. Friends help older people maintain their independence and cope with life changes. Friends can enhance a person's well-being.

Because people who move into the oldest old ages lose friends through death or incapacity, it is important for them to be able to make new friends in the circumstance in which they find themselves. If, for example, an older person chooses or is forced to move to a congregate living facility, it is important that they make new friends to help them deal with their new surroundings. However, many older people find this hard to do. They are used to their old friends. Some older people, facing this type of situation, have developed friendships, at least the characteristics of friendships, with their service providers—the people who help them with their personal living needs.

Studies over many years have shown that men and women view friendships differently. It is common for men to develop friendships based on shared activities and interests. Women tend to base their friendships on intimate and emotional sharing.

Religion/Spirituality

Being optimistic appears to be an important factor in coping with major life events. There is compelling evidence that a person's health, as well as his or her feelings of happiness, may be tied to being optimistic. Recent research has shown that there is a close connection between a person's faith and levels of happiness. Research has also shown that those persons who rated themselves high on being religious also rated themselves high on optimism. Those persons who used religion more in coping with the changing circumstances indicated that they were more optimistic than persons who used religion less.

People are generally not more religious as they grow older. The evidence seems to indicate that the extent to which a person is religious is related to previous religious activity, the time period in which they were raised and lived much of their lives, and whether they have chronic health problems. Determining a person's level of religion by such measures as attendance at religious services is not an accurate measure. With chronic health conditions and physical limitations, many older people find it difficult to participate in religious activities. Many old people shift from outward religious expressions (such as church attendance) to a more inward focus in life which can be more useful for them. They also tend to watch and listen to more religious television and radio programs.

Religious beliefs and practices have been found useful as coping mechanisms, even when an older person suffers from dementia, including Alzheimer's disease. This is particularly true if the religious beliefs and practices were acquired in the earlier years of life, as it is easier for many of these patients to recall and utilize earlier memories.

All religious institutions, including churches, synagogues, temples, and mosques, can mobilize their resources to assist older people. They can become involved in supporting or developing various housing options for older people. Churches can develop support groups to help the caregivers of the dependent elderly. Churches can sponsor informational and entertainment opportunities for older people. However, access to these events can be a serious problem if adequate transportation is not provided.

Being spiritual and being religious are not the same. Spirituality reflects one's search for meaning and purpose in life in general and an attempt to put meaning into the events of daily living. Religiosity describes individual or group relations with a supernatural power.

Support Groups

In contemporary America, there is a self-help support group for almost everyone for almost any interest or problem. Many people have discovered that sharing feelings, frustrations, and problems through talking and listening to people who are facing the same situations has a soothing and healing effect. This is also true for older people and for those persons who care for them. Many people experiencing losses, facing threatening illnesses, or put in circumstances that drain their resources, such as caring for older people, can be helped by support groups. Researchers contend that support groups represent an American approach to problem solving. Not all support groups focus on losses, problems, and stresses. Some provide support for older people to become more creative and productive.

REFERENCES

Adams, R.G. 1987. Patterns of Network Change: A Longitudinal Study of Friendships of Elderly Women. *Gerontologist*, 27(2): 222–227.

Albertson Owens, S.A., and McLain, S.L. 1992. *The Effects of Religion as a Coping Mechanism on Life Satisfaction of Older Adults*. Paper presented at the 45th Annual Scientific Meeting of the Gerontological Society of America, Washington, DC.

Albertson Owens, S.A., Berg, A.J., and Rhone, R.L. 1993. *Religion, Optimism, and Health in Older Adults*. Paper presented at the annual meeting of the Society for the Scientific Study of Religion, Raleigh, NC.

Albertson Owens, S.A., Ward, C.D.L., and McLeod-Winder, J.S. 1993. *The Relationship Between Cognitive Status and Religiosity in Older Adults*. Paper presented at the annual meeting of the Society for the Scientific Study of Religion, Raleigh, NC.

Antonucci, T.C. 1990. Social Supports and Social Relationships. In R.H. Binstock and K.K. George (eds.), *Handbook of Aging and the Social Sciences*, (3d Ed.). New York: Academic Press.

Armstrong, M.J., and Goldsteen, K.S. 1990. Friendship Support of Older American Women. *Journal of Aging Studies*, 4(4): 391–404.

Atchley, R.C. 1994. *Social Forces and Aging*. Belmont, CA: Wadsworth Publishing.

Baltes, P.B., and Baltes, M.M. 1988. Psychological Perspectives on Successful Aging: A Model of Selective Optimization With Compensation. In P.B.

Baltes and M.M. Baltes (eds.), *Successful Aging: Research and Theory*. New York: Academic Press.

Barnhill, W. 1994. Self-Help Groups Bolster Alzheimer's Families. *NRTA Bulletin*, 35(3): 1, 15–16, 117.

Barrow, G.M. 1992. *Aging, the Individual, and Society*, 5th Ed. St. Paul: West Publishing Company.

Baugher, R.J., Burger, C., Smith, R., and Wallston, K. 1989. A Comparison of Terminally Ill Persons at Various Time Periods to Death. *Omega*, 20(2): 103–115.

Bearon, L.B., and Koenig, H.G. 1990. A Comparison of Terminally Ill Patients at Various Time Periods to Death. *Gerontological Society of America*, 30: 249–253.

Birren, J.E. 1990a. Spiritual Maturity in Psychological Development. In Seeber, J.J. (ed.), *Spiritual Maturity in Later Years*. Birmingham, NY: Hayworth Press, pp. 41–51.

Birren, J.E. 1990b. Spiritual Maturity in Psychological Development. *Journal of Religious Gerontology*, 7: 41–53.

Blau, Z.S. 1982. *Old Age in a Changing Society*. New York: Franklin Watts.

Blazer, D., and Palmore, E. 1976. Religion and Aging in a Longitudinal Panel. *The Gerontologist*, 16(1): 82–86.

Bould, S., Sanford, B., and Reif, L. 1989. *Eighty-Five Plus: The Oldest Old*. Belmont, CA: Wadsworth Publishing Company.

Briggs, D. 1992. Study Says Older Americans Feel Neglected by Churches. *Grand Rapids Press* (September 17): B6.

Briggs, K.A. 1987. Religion in America. *Gallup Report*, 259 (April): 1–76.

Brink, T.L. 1977. Pastoral Care of the Aged: A Practical Guide. *Journal of Pastoral Care*, 31: 262–272.

Chappell, N.L., and Badger, M. 1989. Social Isolation and Well-Being. *Journal of Gerontology*, 44(5): S169–176.

Collins, C., and Frantz, D. 1994. Let us Prey. *Modern Maturity* (June): 22–32.

Cousins, N. 1979. *Anatomy of an Illness as Perceived by the Patient*. New York: Bantam Books.

Cox, H., and Hammonds, A. 1988. Religiosity, Aging, and Life Satisfaction. *Journal of Religion and Aging*, 5: 1–21.

Crohan, S.E., and Antonucci, T.C. 1989. Friends as a Source of Social Support in Old Age. In R. Adams and R. Blieszner (eds.), *Older Adult Friendship:*

Structure and Process. Beverly Hills, CA: Sage Publications.

Davis, K.E. 1985. Near and Dear: Friendship and Love Compared. *Psychology Today*, 19: 22–30.

Davis, R. 1989. *My Journey into Alzheimer's Disease*. Wheaton, IL: Tyndale House Publishers.

Dickerson, B.E., and Myers, E.R. 1988. The Contributions and Changing Roles of Older Adults in the Church and Synagogue. *Educational Gerontology*, 14(4): 303–314.

Elias, J.L. 1988. Religious Education of Older Adults: Historical Perspective. *Educational Gerontology*, 14(4): 269–278.

Ellison, C.G. 1990. Family Ties, Friendships, and Subjective Well-Being Among Black Americans. *Journal of Marriage and Family*, 52: 298–310.

Essex, M.J., and Nam, S. 1987. Marital Status and Loneliness Among Older Women: The Differential Importance of Close Family and Friends. *Journal of Marriage and the Family*, 49: 93–106.

Eustis, N.M., and Fischer, L.R. 1991. Relationships Between Home Care Clients and Their Workers: Implications for Quality Care. *Gerontologist*, 31(4): 447–456.

Francis, D. 1990. The Significance of Work Friends in Late Life. *Journal of Aging Studies*, 4: 405–424.

Gendlin, E. 1970. Forecast and Summary. In J. Hart and T. Tomilson (eds.), *New Directions in Client-Centered Therapy*. Boston: Houghton Mifflin.

Gray, R.M., and Moberg, D.O. 1962. *The Church and the Older Person*. Grand Rapids, MI: William B. Erdmans.

Guarnera, S., and Williams, R.L. 1987. Optimism and Locus of Control for Health and Affiliation Among Elderly Adults. *Journal of Gerontology*, 42: 594–595.

Gulledge, J.K. 1991. Influences on Clergy Attitudes Toward Aging. *Journal of Religious Gerontology*, 8(2): 63–78.

Guy, R.F. 1982. Religion, Physical Disabilities, and Life Satisfaction in Older Age Cohorts. *International Journal of Aging and Human Development*, 15: 225–232.

Hammond, P.E. 1969. Aging and the Ministry. In M.W. Riley, J.W. Riley, and M.E. Johnson (eds.), *Aging and Society* (Vol. 3): *Aging and the Professions*. New York: Russell Sage Foundation, pp. 293–323.

Havlik, R.J., Liu, B.M., Kovar, M.G., et al. June 1987. National Center for Health Statistics, *Health Statis-*

tics on Older People, United States: 1986. Vital Health Statistics, Series 3, No. 25, Public Health Service. U.S. Government Printing Office, Washington, DC: 26–27.

Hogan, W.F. 1974. The Challenge of Aging for Contemporary Religion. In W.C. Bier (ed.), *Aging: Its Challenge to the Individual and to Society*. New York: Fordham University Press, pp. 26–34.

Hurvitz, N. 1976. The Origins of the Peer Self-Help Psychotherapy Group Movement. *Journal of Applied Behavioral Science*, 12(3): 283–294.

Huyck, M.H. 1982. From Gregariousness to Intimacy: Marriage and Friendship Over the Adult Years. In T.M. Field, A. Huston, H.C. Qual, L. Troll, and G.E. Finely (eds.), *Review of Human Development*. New York: Wiley, pp. 471–484.

Ingersoll-Dayton, B., and Antonucci, T.C. 1988. Reciprocal and Nonreciprocal Social Support: Contrasting Sides of Intimate Relationships. *Journal of Gerontology*, 43: S65–S73.

Judd, N. 1993. *Love Can Build a Bridge*. New York: Villard Books.

Kamentsky, E. 1992. *Hawking God: A Young Jewish Woman's Ordeal in Jews for Jesus*. Medford, MA: Sapphire Press.

Katz, A., and Bender, E. 1976. *The Strength in Us: Self-Help Groups in the Modern World*. New York: Franklin-Watts.

Kimble, M.A. 1990. Aging and the Search for Meaning. In J.H. Seeber (ed.), *Spirituality Maturity in the Later Years*. New York: Haworth Press.

Kivett, V.R. 1979. Religious Motivation in Middle Age: Correlates and Implications. *Journal of Gerontology*, 34(1): 106–115.

Koenig, H.G. 1990. Research on Religion and Mental Health in Later Life: A Review and Commentary. *Journal of Geriatric Psychology*, 23: 23–53.

Koenig, H.G., George, L.K., and Siegler, C. 1988. The Use of Religion and Other Emotion Regulating Coping Strategies Among Older Adults. *Gerontologist*, 28: 303–310.

Koenig, H.G., Kvale, J.N., and Ferrel, C. 1988. Religion and Well-Being in Later Life. *Gerontologist*, 28: 18–28.

Koenig, H.G., Moberg, D.O., and Kvale, J.N. 1988. Religious Activities and Attitudes of Older Adults in a Geriatric Assessment Clinic. *Journal of the American Geriatric Society*, 38: 362–374.

LaGrand, L.E. 1992. United We Cope: Support Groups for the Dying and Bereaved. In Cox, H. (ed.), *Aging: Eighth edition*. Sluice Dock, Guilford, CT: Dushkin Publishing Group, pp. 165–174.

Larson, D. 1992. Holy Health! *Christianity Today* (November 23): 18–22.

Larson, R. Mannell, R., and Zuzanek, J. 1986. Daily Well-Being of Older Adults with Friends and Family. *Psychology and Aging*, 117–126.

Larue, G.A. 1976. Religion and the Aged. In I.M. Burnside (ed.), *Nursing and the Aged*. New York: McGraw-Hill, pp. 573–575.

Leerhsen, C., Lewis, S.D., Pompers, S., Davenport, L., and Nelson M. 1990. Unite and Conquer. *Newsweek*, CXV(6): 50–55.

Levin, J.S., and Markides, K.S. 1986. Religious Attendance and Subjective Health. *Journal of the Scientific Study of Religion*, 25(1): 31–40.

Levin, J.S., and Vanderpool, H.Y. 1987. Is Frequent Religious Attendance Really Conducive to Better Health?: Toward an Epidemiology of Religion. *Social Science and Medicine*, 24(7): 589–600.

Maas, H.S., and Kuypers, J.A. 1974. *From Thirty to Seventy*. San Francisco: Jossey-Bass.

Markides, K.S., Levin, J.S., and Ray, L.A. 1987. Religion, Aging, and Life Satisfaction: An Eight-Year, Three-Wave, Longitudinal Study. *Gerontologist*, 27(5): 660–665.

Maslow, A.H. 1970. *Motivation and Personality*, 2d ed. New York: Harper and Row.

McFadden, S.H. 1990. Authentic Humor as an Expression of Spiritual Maturity. In J.J. Seeber (ed.), *Spiritual Maturity in the Later Years*. New York: Haworth Press.

Moberg, D.O. 1970. Religion in the Later Years. In M.A. Hoffman (ed.), *The Daily Needs and Interests of Older Persons*. Springfield, IL: Charles C. Thomas, pp. 175–191.

Moberg, D.O. 1972. Religion and the aging family. *The Family Coordinator*, 21(1): 47–60.

Moberg, D.O. 1990. Spiritual Maturity and Wholeness in the Later Years. In J.J. Seeber (ed.), *Spiritual Maturity in the Later Years*. New York: Haworth Press.

Myers, D.G. 1992a. *In Pursuit of Happiness*. New York: William Morrow and Company.

Myers, D.G. 1992b. Who's Happy? Who's Not? *Christianity Today*, (November 23): 23–26.

National Center for Health Statistics. 1986. *Health Statistics on Older Persons, United States*. Vital and Health Statistics, Series 3, No. 25, Public Health Service: 26–27. Washington, DC: U.S. Government Printing Office.

O'Brian, M.E. 1982. Religious Faith and Adjustments to Long-Term Hemodialysis. *Journal of Religion and Health*, 21: 68–80.

Osterkamp, L. 1992. Family Caregivers: America's Primary Long-Term Care Resource. In Cox, H. (ed.), *Annual Editions: Aging* 8th Ed. Sluice Dock, Guilford, CT: Dushkin Publishing Group, pp. 206–208.

Payne, B. 1990. Spiritual Maturity and Meaning-Filled Relationships: A Sociological Perspective. In J.H. Seeber (ed.), *Spiritual Maturity in the Later Years*. New York: Haworth Press.

Peterson, C., and Bossio, L.M. 1991. *Health and Optimism*. New York: The Free Press.

Peterson, S.A., and Greil, A.L. 1990. Death Experience and Religion. *Omega*, 21(1): 75–82.

Richards, M. 1990. Meeting the Needs of the Cognitively Impaired. *Generations*, (Fall): 63–64.

Riley, M.W. 1983. Aging and Society: Notes on the Development of New Understandings. (December 12). Lecture at the University of Michigan.

Riley, M.W. 1983. Aging and Society: Notes on the Development of New Understandings. Lecture at the University of Michigan, (December 12): 13.

Riley, M.W., Johnson, M.E., and Foner, A. 1972. *Aging and Society* (Vol. 1): *An Inventory of Research Findings*. New York: Russell Sage Foundation.

Robb, T.B. 1991. *Growing Up: Pastoral Nurture for the Later Years*. New York: Haworth Press.

Roberto, K.A., and Scott, J.P. 1986. Equity Considerations in the Friendships of Older Adults. *Journal of Gerontology*, 41: 241–247.

Ross, C.E. 1990. Religion and Psychological Distress. *Journal for the Scientific Study of Religion*, 29: 236–245.

Rowles, G.D. 1985. The Rural Elderly and the Church. In Michael Henderickson (ed.), *The Role of the Church in Aging: Implications for Policy and Action*. New York: Haworth Press.

Rybash, J.W., Roodin, P.A., and Santrock, J.W. 1991. *Adult Development and Aging*, 2d Ed. Dubuque, IA: Wm. C. Brown Publishers.

Scheier, M.F., and Carver, C.S. 1985. Optimism, Coping and Health: Assessment and Implications of Generalized Outcome Expectancies. *Health Psychology*, 4: 219–247.

Seeber, J.J. (ed.). 1990. *Spiritual Maturity in the Later Years*. New York: Haworth Press.

Seligman, M.E.P. 1991. *Learned Optimism*. New York: Alfred A. Knopf.

Siegel, B.S. 1986. *Love, Medicine and Miracles*. New York: Harper and Row.

Silverstone, B., and Hyman, H. 1992. *Growing Older Together*. New York: Pantheon Books.

Simmons, H.C. 1990. Countering Cultural Metaphors of Aging. In J.J. Seeber (ed.), *Spiritual Maturity in Later Years*. Birmingham, NY: Hayworth Press, pp. 153–164.

Stafford, T. 1987. The Grouping of the Church: What Kind of Ministry Awaits the Growing Ranks of Retirees? *Christianity Today*, (November 6): 17–22.

Wagner, K.D., and Lorion, R.P. 1984. Correlates of Death Anxiety in Elderly Persons. *Journal of Clinical Psychology*, 40(5): 1235–1241.

Windsor, J. 1994. A Write-On Support Group. *Detroit Free Press*, (January 18): 30.

Wolfsen, C.R., Barker, J.C., and Mitteness, L.S. 1990. Personalization of Formal Social Relationships by the Elderly. *Research on Aging*, 12(1): 94–112.

Yates, J.W., Chalmer, B.J., St. James, P., Follansbee, M., and McKegney, F.P. 1981. Religion in Patients with Advanced Cancer. *Medical and Pediatric Oncology*, 9: 121–128.

Young, G., and Dowling, W. 1987. Dimensions of Religiosity in Old Age: Accounting for Variation in Types of Participation. *Journal of Gerontology*, 42(4): 376–380.

CHAPTER 16

Formal
Support Systems

Marie: Caught in a Financial Bind

Marie is a 64-year-old widow. Disabled by high blood pressure and diabetes, she was unable to continue working. Because her husband did not work in jobs that were covered by Social Security, he never collected any benefits. At the age of 62, Marie began to collect Social Security from her own employment. Despite her disability, however, she was turned down twice for disability benefits. She was told that with her nursing training she should be able to find employment.

As a result of an SSI outreach program in South Carolina, Marie now supplements her $214 Social Security Check with $228 a month from SSI, bringing her total monthly income to $442. She also now receives Medicaid, which pays for three of the four prescription medications she must take.

While her home is fully paid for, it needs many repairs which she cannot afford. Her daughter and nephew live with her. Because it is difficult for her to get around, her daughter does all the shopping and much of the housework.

Marie would like to receive food stamps, but was told that her income, combined with that of her daughter, is too high to qualify. She had heard that she could apply for food stamps on her own, but she hadn't yet made the 5-mile trip to the food stamp office to apply. (Kassner 1992: 20)

Dorothy: A Hard-Luck Story

Dorothy has not had an easy life. At 77 years old, she can remember when her first husband worked six years for the WPA. Back then, there was a commodities program that provided them with food every week. Although they didn't have much, she never needed to ask for help until her husband became ill and began to use a wheelchair.

Her husband's work history did not qualify him for Social Security benefits, and when Dorothy tried to get assistance, she was told that there was nothing available. When they had no food in the house, she went to social services and was told to go to the grocery store and buy $10 worth

of food, which they would pay for. She was able to do this about three or four times. A worker at the grocery store noticed that she was having a hard time and got permission to give her dented canned goods and wilted produce.

After her husband died, Dorothy supported herself by babysitting for two to three children. After several years she remarried, but her new husband didn't want to live with her mentally retarded daughter and wanted to charge her rent to live with them. As a result, Dorothy separated from her second husband.

She and her daughter, who is now 50 years old, moved into a trailer that her son let them use. They received $20 to $30 a month in food stamps, and she made quilts to pay for the light and phone bills. She hadn't worked enough to qualify for Social Security, and didn't receive Social Security from either of her husbands. After she had a stroke, she was finally able to qualify for SSI.

Now she and daughter each receive an SSI check. They also get $10 a month in food stamps and Medicaid benefits. While her son lets her live in his trailer, she pays the $70 a month rent to park it. She also pays $5 a month for water, $40 a month for life insurance for herself and her daughter, and about $20 a month for the phone.

She owns nothing—no car, no land, no home. A nurse visits periodically to check on her, and occasionally a housekeeper comes to help her wash the clothes and vacuum. (Kassner 1992: 34)

Mr. and Mrs. Smith: A Well-Organized Approach

Mr. and Mrs. Smith live in a semirural area. Everything was fine for them until Mr. Smith had a heart attack at age eighty-five. Mrs. Smith doesn't drive, and she had always depended on Mr. Smith driving her to the store every week to do their shopping.

Mrs. Smith also has severe arthritis and has paid a helper to come in and help with cleaning and cooking. The Smiths' daughter and her family live 50 miles away and usually visit on Sundays, but they are busy the rest of the week.

When Mr. Smith was scheduled to come home from the hospital, his daughter was worried. What should be done? He couldn't drive anymore, so who would do their shopping? Should they be put in a nursing home? What if they had to be separated?

A case management team—a social worker and a nurse—was invited into the Smiths' home. Their help was offered free of charge under provisions of the Older Americans Act. The caseworkers talked to Mr. and Mrs. Smith and found out exactly what kinds of help they needed. Then the caseworkers decided what services could realistically be offered by family, friends, or neighbors and which needs could best be met by private and public agencies whose business is serving older people.

Working together with family and community-based services, the Smiths were able to stay in their own home. The woman who helped with cleaning was retained. A home health nurse was brought in to provide Mr. Smith with nursing services as he recovered from his heart attack. A Red Cross volunteer drove Mr. Smith to his doctor appointments. Someone else was found to take Mrs. Smith shopping. Although this arrangement resulted in some additional costs for the Smiths, staying in their own home with help was much less expensive than going to an institution, and they much preferred to stay together at home. And even though Mrs. Smith had people coming in to help her, she was still in charge in her own home.

Source: The Christian Guide to Parent Care, R. Riekse and H. Holstege © 1992. Used by permission of Tyndale House Publishers, Inc., Wheaton IL 60189. All rights reserved.

FORMAL SUPPORT SYSTEMS

This chapter examines the range of services that are available to older people in the United States. Looking at the services and programs in the 1990s is a bit perplexing; many are underutilized, and there is again pressure to justify their existence.

In the face of increasing needs across our society with limited, and in numerous cases, diminished resources, many people are asking why special programs and services are provided to people just because they have reached a certain age. Much of this type of questioning relates to a more general ongoing debate concerning the basic role of government. Is the role of government limited to basic services to maintain order and provide for the national defense with some emergency relief to the neediest citizens? Does government's role include providing programs, services, and resources to enhance the lives of various categories of people across America? Or does the role of government fall somewhere in between? Obviously, there is no easy or set answer to this ongoing debate. It is rooted in the politics of the nation and dependent on the vitality of the economy. Politics is the art of making choices on a collective basis. In the United States, those choices are made democratically with input, pressure, guidance, and plain old-fashioned clout from a variety of sources. We will look at how this debate translates into formal support for older people in America.

NATURE OF PROGRAMS AND SERVICES FOR THE ELDERLY

Older people in America are the beneficiaries of two types of programs. One is *generic,* meaning that these programs were designed to be of assistance to people of any age (Gelfand 1993). The Food Stamp Program could be characterized as a generic program. Any person can qualify if he or she meets income/asset guidelines. Relatively early in its history, the nation collectively decided that it was not a good thing to have starving people. Emergency aid to the poor usually included some type of starvation prevention, often in the form of excess commodities such as flour, peanut butter, eggs, and powdered milk. Following an eight-county experimental antihunger program established by Executive Order in 1961, the Food Stamp Act was passed in 1964, making it available to all states as an option to giving out food commodities. In 1992, about one in ten Americans was taking part in the Food Stamp Program, including older Americans.

In addition to participating in generic programs, older people have benefitted from *categorical* programs. Categorical programs are designed to benefit all the people who fall into specifically defined groups (Gelfand 1993). The categorical programs this chapter focuses on are designed specifically for older Americans. These programs arose out of collective decisions that it was in the best interests of the nation as well as older people and their families to design and develop programs and services specifically to meet some of the basic needs of older people. From the beginning of the United States under its Constitution in 1789, it took a long time to come to a collective decision to organize a part of government to specifically assist older persons, particularly on the national level. As it has already been noted, it was not until 1935 that the Social Security principle (with Old Age and Survivors Insurance) was enacted into law. Prior to that time, the welfare of older people was the responsibility of families, and to some extent, local governments in cases of abject poverty. Of course, there were not nearly as many older people then as there are today. Nevertheless, older people were part of society. Not until 1965 when the Older Americans Act (OAA) was passed did we see a systematic, organized approach to provide services and programs on a nationwide basis to enhance the lives of older people.

UNDERUTILIZATION OF SERVICES

Although the resources of many programs and services are not adequate to meet the demands on them by the rapidly growing numbers of older adults, according to recent studies many are substantially underutilized.

The programs and services that are currently available to older people have resulted from complex legislation. This has led to problems of frag-

mentation, lack of coordination, and even lack of communication among various service providers. The result is often a maze for older people and their families to try to work through when seeking assistance for problems and conditions they face. Access to these services is often limited by these problems (Gelfand 1993). Current national studies have indicated that millions of older Americans are not getting the benefits of programs and services to which they are entitled because of substantial barriers to accessibility, including:

- Lack of awareness of programs
- Different income and asset levels for eligibility for different programs
- Different age eligibilities for various programs
- Different eligibility criteria within and between states
- Lengthy and complex forms
- No centralized location in which to apply for assistance for various programs
- Lack of outreach efforts to inform people about programs
- Fear of government programs
- Lack of bilingual resources and personnel
- Lack of transportation to access sites

As an example, the Supplemental Security Income (SSI) program reaches only 56 percent of the nation's eligible elderly poor (Committee on Ways and Means 1992). A survey by Louis Harris and Associates (1988) of persons 65 and older indicated that more than one-third of those potentially eligible for Supplemental Security Income had never heard of the program. Among people 65 and older, only 30 percent of the aged poor received Medicaid in 1990 (Committee on Ways and Means 1992). Lack of participation by eligible older persons is also characteristic of other programs, including the Food Stamp Program, the Qualified Medicare Beneficiary Program, the Home Energy Assistance Program, federally assisted housing programs, and the Older Worker JTPA Employment Training Program. Studies have indicated that lack of information was a major reason for low participation rates of eligible older people in these programs (Center on Budget and Policy Priorities 1991a, 1991b, 1991c, 1991d, 1991e). (See Figures 16-1 and 16-2.)

NATIONAL LEGISLATION TO ASSIST OLDER PEOPLE

The Older Americans Act (OAA)

The Older Americans Act (OAA) of 1965 grew out of the deliberations of the 1961 White House Conference on Aging. It has been amended eleven times; the eleventh set of amendments, which was signed into law in 1992, reauthorized the OAA through fiscal year 1995 (U.S. Senate Special Committee on Aging 1993). The OAA laid the foundation for a wide array of community services to older people which has become known as the Aging Network. It is a nationwide system of federal, state, and local agencies designed to provide services to the elderly of the nation (U.S. Senate Special Committee on Aging

1993). Although the Aging Network includes some programs and services that go beyond those supported by the OAA, the 1965 legislation made it possible to develop a variety of programs and services to specifically meet the social and human needs of older people.

It is significant to note that the OAA grew out of societal (political) decisions that the role of government should include meeting the needs of older people beyond the basic income-transfer function of Social Security, which was enacted in the 1930s in the depths of the Great Depression. It should be noted that one of the basic goals of the Social Security Act was to help older people leave the work place to make way for jobs for younger people, jobs that were very scarce in the 1930s. The OAA was one of a number of federal programs that were part of President Johnson's Great Society programs. It was the first major legislation in the history of the United States to organize and deliver community-based services exclusively to older people. It was developed in a framework that was based on the idea that de-

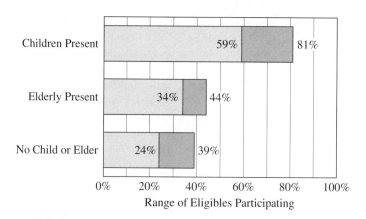

**Percentage of Eligible Households
Receiving Food Stamps**

Children Present — 59% 81%

Elderly Present — 34% 44%

No Child or Elder — 24% 39%

0% 20% 40% 60% 80% 100%

Range of Eligibles Participating

FIGURE 16-1

Many eligible older persons do not utilize food stamps. (*Source:* Kassner, E. 1992. *Falling through the safety net: Missed opportunities for America's elderly poor.* Washington, DC: American Association of Retired Persons, Figure IV, p. 7.)

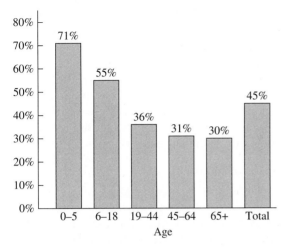

**Medicaid Coverage Among the Poor
Percentage, by Age**

FIGURE 16-2

Only 30 percent of the elderly poor get Medicaid benefits. (*Source:* Kassner, E. 1992. *Falling through the safety net: Missed opportunities for America's elderly poor.* Washington, DC: American Association of Retired Persons, Figure III, p. 6.)

centralization of authority and the use of local control when it came to policy and program decisions would make a more effective and responsive service system for the recipients of the services at the local level (U.S. Senate Special Committee on Aging 1993).

The OAA, as originally enacted, established a series of broad policy objectives intended to meet the needs of older persons. It set up a structure which Congress could use to expand aging services.

Central Mission of the OAA   The central mission of the OAA has remained essentially unchanged since 1965:

To foster maximum independence by providing a wide array of social and community services to those older persons in the greatest economic and social need. The key philosophy of the program has

been to help maintain and support older persons in their homes and communities to avoid unnecessary and costly institutionalization (U.S. Senate Special Committee on Aging 1993: 313).

Objectives of the OAA   The language of the 1965 OAA concerning the objectives for older Americans provides insight into the societal decision that was made which resulted in the legislation. It states:

Sec. 101. The congress hereby finds and declares that, in keeping with the traditional American concept of the inherent dignity of the individual in our democratic society, the older people of our nation are entitled to, and it is the joint and several duty and responsibility of the governments of the United States, the several states and their potential subdivisions, and of Indian tribes to assist our older people to secure opportunity to the full and free enjoyment of the following objectives:

1. An adequate income in retirement in accordance with the American standard of living.
2. The best possible physical and mental health which science can make available and without regard to economic status.
3. Obtaining and maintaining suitable housing, independently selected, designed and located with reference to special needs and functional limitations and available at costs which older citizens can afford.
4. Full restorative service for those who require institutional care, and a comprehensive array of community-based, long-term care services adequate to appropriately sustain older people in their communities and in their homes, *including support to family members and other persons providing voluntary care to older individuals needing long-term care services.*
5. Opportunity for employment with no discriminatory personnel practices because of age.
6. Retirement in health, honor, dignity—after years of contribution to the economy.
7. Participating in and contributing to meaningful activity within the widest range of civic, cultural, education and training and recreational opportunities.

8. Efficient community services, including access to low-cost transportation, which provide a choice in supported living arrangements and social assistance in a coordinated manner and which are readily available when needed, with emphasis on maintaining a continuum of care for the vulnerable elderly.
9. Immediate benefit from proven research knowledge which can sustain and improve health and happiness.
10. Freedom, independence, and the free exercise of individual initiative in planning and managing their own lives, full participation in the planning and operation of community-based services and programs provided for their benefit, and protection against abuse, neglect, and exploitation. (Title I, Sec. 101, Older Americans Act of 1965, Public Law 89-73 including amendments)

Structure to Implement the OAA   To achieve the objectives of the OAA and provide the services that resulted from them, the Aging Network was established. On the federal level, the Aging Network is comprised of the Administration on Aging (AoA) which is located in the Department of Health and Human Services. It administers most of the programs that come under the Older Americans Act and has the responsibility to be the primary federal agency to advocate for older persons (U.S. Senate Special Committee on Aging 1993). The AoA oversees a network of state units on aging (SUAs). The SUAs receive federal funds to implement state plans on aging which have to be approved by the AoA. The SUA can be an independent unit of state government or part of an existing state agency. In some states the office on aging is part of one of the human service departments. In other states it is an independent unit. However constructed, the state office is responsible for developing three-year statewide plans, which are then approved by the AoA, to serve the elderly.

On the state level, regional geographic service areas are established by the state agency, which become Area Agencies on Aging (AAAs). The AAAs develop their own three-year plans to serve the older people of their area. These plans must be approved by the SUA. An AAA agency can be a unit of county, city, or town government. It can even be a private nonprofit agency. In 1990 there were some 680 AAAs in the United States. The SUAs and the AAAs are not permitted to provide services directly to the elderly unless it is absolutely necessary to do so to "assure an adequate supply of such services" (Gelfand 1993: 14). The AAAs are to contract for the services to older people in their areas.

Titles of the OAA

To implement the objectives of the Older Americans Act, various titles were established as part of the act. As noted earlier, the OAA has been amended eleven times, with the 1992 reauthorization in operation through fiscal year 1995. The following titles reflect the basic programs of the OAA as amended through 1995.

Title I: Declaration of Objectives: Definitions
This title outlines the underlying philosophy of the legislation and its sweeping objectives. It also provides for definitions that apply to the act. In 1973, the age of the target population to be served was changed from the original age of 65 to 60. The 1992 amendments expanded objective 4 to include supportive services for the caregivers of elderly people who need assistance (Gelfand 1993). The objectives have been expanded somewhat over the years to achieve an extensive service delivery system for older people on the part of the Administration on Aging (Gelfand and Bechill 1991).

Title II: Administration on Aging   This title established the Administration on Aging with a Commissioner on Aging. In 1993, under the Clinton administration this office was elevated to Assistant Secretary for Aging in the Department of Health and Human Services. The AoA is charged with providing information on the problems on aging, planning, developing statistical reports, developing policies, and coordinating activities at federal and local levels with private and public organizations. The 1992 amendments established the Office of Long-Term Care Ombudsman Programs (to assist people who have problems with long-term care institutions), a Nutrition Officer responsible for all nutrition programs funded through the Older Americans Act, a National Center on Elder Abuse, and a National Information Center (Gelfand 1993).

Title III: Grants for State and Community Programs in Aging   This title defines the types of services that are provided at the local level across the nation. It also provides for the governor in each state to designate an agency to be responsible for aging services—the state units on aging. Title III has been amended since 1965 to include a variety of services and programs. In the amendments of subsequent years, different services were emphasized. In 1975, transportation, in-home services, legal services, and home repair and renovation were emphasized. In 1978, access services were featured, including transportation, outreach, information, and referral. Also emphasized were in-home services (homemakers, home health aides, visiting, and telephone contacts) and legal services. In 1992, case management was classified as an access service (Gelfand 1993).

Title III also includes a range of supportive services including an ombudsman program to investigate and take action on complaints of residents in long-term care facilities. Also included are crime-prevention and victim-assistance programs, job-counseling programs, translation services for non-English-speaking older persons, representation in guardianship cases, insurance counseling, and services for family members who care for older persons needing long-term care (Gelfand 1993).

A major feature of Title III is funding for nutrition programs. Nutrition became part of Title III in 1978. Prior to that, nutrition was Title VII of the OAA. The 1981 amendments provided for flexibility in nutrition, noting that primary consideration be given to meals served at congregate sites but allowing home-delivered meals, an important feature of the current service delivery network.

The 1992 amendments of the OAA also include funding for school-based meals for older persons who volunteer in schools as well as intergenerational social and recreational programs for older volunteers. This is designed to promote intergenerational contacts and understanding.

Title III also currently provides funds for multipurpose senior centers. In fact Title III includes "where feasible, a focal point for comprehensive service delivery" should be created with "special consideration" given to "designing multipurpose senior centers as such focal point" [Sec. 306(a)(3) of the Older Americans Act of 1992]. Senior centers provide a place where seniors can gather for a variety of activities including being the recipients of services that they are entitled to through the OAA.

Title III, as amended over the years, also includes a variety of other services for older people. These include: funds for in-home services for frail older people and their families, funds for transportation to meet the special needs of the elderly, and health-promotion and disease-prevention services. These health services include health assessments and screening, nutritional counseling, physical fitness and dance, and music and art therapy. The 1992 amendments to the OAA included supportive activities for caregivers of frail older people focusing on training, technical assistance, and information.

Title IV: Training, Research, Discretionary Projects and Programs   This section of the OAA has provided research and training in the field of aging. This training and research has ranged from short-term, in-service training for providers and staff of agencies and organizations that serve the elderly to sophisticated college or university research in various aspects of aging.

The lack of training in aging by staff in the Aging Network is a vital concern. Research over the years has indicated a lack of training of staff in the local Area Agencies on Aging as well as the state units on aging. A 1991 study by the University of Southern California and the Association for Gerontology in Higher Education found that only 10 percent of aging staffs had studied aging in college (Peterson, Wendt, and Douglas 1991). In the AAAs, the majority of staff had been employed in their current jobs two years or less. In the SUAs, over one-third of all staff responding to the survey had been in their jobs two years or less. This same study indicated that professional education in the form of professional conferences and continuing education workshops would be valuable help in their work.

Research in recent years has focused on special programs in long-term care, transportation demonstrations that improve mobility of older persons, demonstration programs for older persons with developmental disabilities, ombudsman programs in public housing, and demonstration programs for information and counseling for retirement and pension benefits (Gelfand 1993).

Title V: Community Service Employment

This title authorizes funds to subsidize part-time community-service jobs for unemployed, low-income persons aged 55 and older. These funds are given to ten national organizations as well as state agencies. The ten national organizations get most of the money and include the American Association of Retired Persons (AARP), the Association National Pro Personas Mayores, the National Center on Black Aged, Inc., National Council of Senior Citizens, National Urban League, Inc., Green Thumb, Inc., National Pacific/Asian Resource Center on Aging, National Indian Council on Aging, the U.S. Forest Service, and the National Council on the Aging (U.S. Senate Special Committee on Aging 1993).

Title VI: Grants for Native Americans

This title provides funds for Indian tribes to develop nutritional and social services for older members if they are not provided under Title III. This title also provides for the needs of older Alaskan natives and native Hawaiians (Gelfand 1993).

Title VII: Vulnerable Elder Rights Protection Activities

This is a new Title VII as of 1992. It includes (1) state long-term care ombudsman programs; (2) programs for the prevention of elder abuse, neglect, and exploitation; (3) state elder rights and legal assistance development; and (4) state outreach, counseling and assistance for insurance and public benefits. This new Title VII consolidates some previously sectioned services and represents an effort to make older persons aware of the services to which they are entitled. The last component of this title reflected Congressional concern that too many older people are falling through the safety nets provided for them. This title is directed to "expand state responsibility for the development, coordination, and management of statewide programs and services directed towards ensuring that older individuals have access to, and assistance in securing and maintaining, benefits and rights" (Congressional Record 1992: 8989).

OAA: Coordinated Services for the Elderly

These are the major titles of the Older Americans Act, the primary source of human and social services for older persons in the United States. As originally intended, the OAA was designed to improve the lives of older Americans in such areas as income, health, housing, employment, community services, and gerontological research and education. The intent was to develop a coordinated and comprehensive system of services on the community level. The goal was to provide the support system "necessary to promote independent living and reduce the risk of costly institutionalization" (U.S. Senate Special Committee on Aging 1993: 331). To this end, the OAA has been successful. It has enabled the needs of older persons to be identified as well as the development of a system to meet these needs. The Aging Network has evolved with 57 state units on aging, some 680 area agencies on aging, and about

25,000 local supportive and nutrition service providers (Gelfand 1993). In addition, the OAA has provided for the training of thousands of persons who work with older people as well as research to develop better strategies to meet the needs of the elderly.

A basic premise of the OAA is that it was intended to be the primary way to organize and deliver community-based services to all older Americans regardless of income (U.S. Senate Committee on Aging 1993). The provisions of the OAA are not means-tested. Any person 60 years and older is entitled to OAA programs and services regardless of income and need (Torres-Gil 1992). Congress has resisted any attempts to make the OAA programs and services means-tested, in other words, to have to prove that one's income is low enough or that one has a demonstrated need (U.S. Senate Special Committee on Aging 1993).

The reality is that the actual appropriations of all the titles of the OAA were only somewhat over one billion dollars a year ($1.372 billion in FY 1993, and slightly less than the $1.375 billion in FY 1992). As part of a national budget of some $1.3 trillion for comparable years, it was the proverbial "drop in the bucket" of about one-tenth of one percent. Indeed, Torres-Gil (1992), in his book on public policy on aging, written prior to his becoming Assistant Secretary for Aging in the Department of Health and Human Services, questioned how so few dollars (relatively measured) in the hands of one small agency (AoA) within the mammoth Department of Health and Human Services can meet its goals.

OAA: Stretching Resources

The answer lies in "targeting" services to those with the greatest economic and social needs. This has come to mean primarily low-income persons, minority older persons, residents of rural areas, and the frail elderly. Because the OAA is designed to provide services to all older persons regardless of income and need, Torres-Gil has indicated that targeting services without alienating healthier, active, affluent older persons is a real challenge.

Another approach to make OAA funds go further is cost-sharing—sharing fees or partial fees for services for older persons who can afford them. The current law prohibits mandatory fees, but nutrition and supportive services providers are allowed to ask for voluntary contributions from participants. Older persons cannot be denied any service because they will not or cannot make a contribution for a service. However, cost-sharing may become a feature of the next reauthorization of the OAA in 1995, because of pressures for more services by ever increasing numbers of older people in America as well as fierce competition for funds in view of the national debt and annual deficits. The provisions of the OAA continue to be overextended and underfunded (U.S. Senate Special Committee on Aging 1993).

It is important to note that accessing the services provided by the OAA is accomplished on the local level by contacting the local Area Agency on Aging listed in most telephone books, senior centers, city or county units of governments, or agencies funded by an AAA, Table 16-1.

OTHER LEGISLATIVE SUPPORTS FOR OLDER AMERICANS

Although the Older Americans Act (OAA) is the focal point of services and programs for older persons and has resulted in the formation of Aging Networks across the United States, other legislation not specifically targeted at older adults is of great benefit to them. It is important to be aware of the major pieces of legislation and the programs that can be of direct benefit to older Americans.

Social Services Block Grant

The Social Services Block Grant (SSBG of 1984) is the replacement for the 1974 Title XX

TABLE 16-1

MONEY APPROPRIATED FOR THE OLDER AMERICANS ACT PROGRAMS: 1992–93
OLDER AMERICANS ACT APPROPRIATIONS, FISCAL YEARS 1992–93
(DOLLARS IN THOUSANDS)

	Fiscal year—	
	1992[1]	**1993**
Title II: Administration on Aging		
Federal Council on Aging	$181	$178
ADA program administration	([2])	[2]16,041
Title III: Grants for State and community program on aging	938,644	916,590
Supportive services and centers	299,238	313,708
Disease prevention and health promotion	17,000	([3])
Nutrition services:		
Total	607,162	595,807
Congregate meals	(366,067)	(363,236)
Home-delivered meals	(89,603)	(89,659)
USDA commodities	(151,492)	(142,912)
School-based meals/multigenerational activities	([4])	None
In-home services for the frail elderly	6,898	7,075
Assistance for special needs	None	None
Elder abuse prevention	4,416	([5])
Long-term care ombudsman	3,930	([5])
Outreach for SSI, Medicaid and food stamps	None	([5])
Supportive activities for caretakers	([4])	None
Title IV: Training, research and discretionary projects and programs	25,941	25,973
Training of Service Providers	([4])	None
Title V: Community service employment for older Americans	395,181	390,060
Title VI: Grants for Native Americans	15,086	15,110
Title VII: Vulnerable elder rights protection activities		8,218
Long-term care ombudsman	([5])	[5]3,870
Elder abuse prevention	([5])	[5]4,348
Elder rights and legal assistance	([4])	[4]None
Outreach, counseling and assistance	([5])	[5]None
Native Americans elder rights program	([4])	[4]None
Total	1,375,033	1,372,170
White House Conference on Aging	2,000	None

Source: U.S. Senate Special Committee on Aging. 1993. *Developments in Aging: 1992*, U.S. Government Printing Office, Washington, D.C.

of the Social Security Act. Title XX was added to provide social services designed to help people become self-sufficient, protecting children and adults not able to take care of themselves, and attempting to prevent and reduce placing persons in institutions (Torres-Gil 1992). Title XX was used to fund adult daycare, foster care, homemaker services, services in long-term-care facilities, and community mental health centers (Gelfand 1993).

The block grant approach gives the states more flexibility on how the funds are used. In 1990, the American Association of Retired Persons released a survey indicating how the block grant approach was working for older persons. It found that 44 states used some portion of their funds for services for older people. The most frequently provided services were home-based, adult protective, and case management/access. Other services provided with these funds included family assistance, transportation, nutrition/meals, socialization, and disabled services. Lack of increase in federal support for these block grants has resulted in serving only the very-low-income elderly. A potential problem with these funds, as they are not targeted towards older people alone, is fierce competition for support by persons in different groups (U.S. Senate Special Committee on Aging 1993).

Community Services Block Grant

The community Services Block Grant (CSBG) is the current approach to the previous Community Action Program (CAP), which was the focal point in the War on Poverty of the 1960s. The goal of the CSBG is to "promote self-sufficiency for low-income persons, to provide emergency food and nutrition services, to coordinate public and private social services programs, and to encourage the use of private-sector entities in antipoverty activities" (U.S. Senate Special Committee on Aging 1993: 335). Emergency assistance including clothing, food, shelter, energy assistance, and weatherization for older persons are funded through the CSBG program. These funds are not just for older persons, but they do benefit older people. They are accessed through local antipoverty centers and programs.

ACTION Programs

ACTION is an independent government agency set up to administer all domestic volunteer programs under a single authorizing law (U.S. Senate Special Committee on Aging 1993). It administers a number of programs aimed at persons in a variety of age groups, including older people.

Retired Senior Volunteer Program The Retired Senior Volunteer Program (RSVP) is a program that offers a variety of volunteer opportunities to persons 60 years of age and older. These volunteers serve in many areas including youth counseling, literary enhancement, long-term care, refugee assistance, drug abuse prevention, consumer education, crime prevention, housing rehabilitation, latchkey children in after school programs, and respite care for the elderly (U.S. Senate Special Committee on Aging 1993).

These volunteers get no pay but are reimbursed for expenses that result from their services.

Foster Grandparent Program The Foster Grandparent Program (FGP) provides part-time volunteer opportunities for low-income persons 60 years of age and older to help them provide supportive services to children with physical, mental, emotional, or social disabilities. These volunteers are placed with nonprofit agencies such as schools, hospitals, daycare centers, and institutions for the mentally or physically handicapped.

These volunteers get paid by the hour, but to qualify they need to be below 125 percent of the federal poverty line (U.S. Senate Special Committee on Aging 1993). In 1986, opportunities to serve in this program were expanded to non-low-income persons who are reimbursed for expenses they have as a result of their volunteer efforts.

Senior Companion Program The Senior Companion Program (SCP) is designed to provide volunteer opportunities to low-income persons 60 years of age and older to help provide supportive services to "vulnerable, frail older persons" (U.S. Senate Special Committee on Aging 1993: 350). These volunteers help homebound disabled older persons as well as those in institutions and those enrolled in community health programs.

As with the Foster Grandparent Program, volunteers are paid if they meet low-income guidelines. Non-low-income persons can participate without pay, receiving reimbursement for out-of-pocket expenses associated with their volunteer efforts.

Transportation

Transportation is vital to the well-being of noninstitutionalized older persons. As for any age group, transportation is necessary to meet the basic necessities of life. Two federal departments are involved with assisting older persons with their transportation needs: the Department of Health and Human Services (HHS) and the Department of Transportation (DOT).

The Department of Health and Human Services (HHS) administers a number of programs specifically designed to help the elderly with their transportation needs, including provisions of the Older Americans Act (OAA), the Social Services Block Grant (SSBG), the Community Services Block Grant (CSBG), and Medicaid. Under Medicaid, transportation is provided for the elderly poor to get to medical facilities (U.S. Senate Special Committee on Aging 1993).

The Department of Transportation (DOT) administers programs to develop mass transit in the nation and to assist older Americans with basic transportation services, including 50-percent fare reductions for elderly and handicapped persons. Hearings held by the U.S. Senate Special Committee on Aging have highlighted the unmet transportation needs of older persons, particularly in rural and suburban areas. Transportation is particularly crucial given the Medicare system of DRGs (diagnosis-related groups). DRGs result in Medicare patients being released from hospitals earlier with needs for more follow-up care, which means getting back to the hospital or doctor's office: That requires transportation. A survey conducted by the State of Kentucky cited in the U.S. Senate Special Committee on Aging report (1993) found that 52 percent of those surveyed cited lack of transportation as the reason for not attending social activities. Lack of transportation may set back some of the advances in health care that have been achieved.

Legal Services

Support for legal services for older persons is from two sources. One is the Legal Services Corporation (LSC), which was established in 1974. It is a legal assistance resource for low-income persons with an income no higher than 125 percent of the poverty line. This service is not limited to older persons. In assisting older persons, LSC attorneys do most of their work representing them in government programs such as Social Security and Medicare (U.S. Senate Special Committee on Aging 1993).

The other major source of legal assistance for the elderly focuses on their needs. This is the Older Americans Act (OAA) which with the 1987 amendments mandated that state units on aging designate a "minimum percentage" of Title III social service funds on legal assistance. Another mandate requires state agencies on aging to set up long-term-care ombudsman programs to investigate and handle complaints by residents (or persons acting for them) of long-term-care facilities (U.S. Senate Special Committee on Aging 1993).

In fiscal year 1992, the AoA supported the National Senior Citizens Law Center, Legal Counsel for the Elderly (sponsored by AARP), the American Bar Association's Commission on Legal Problems of the Elderly, the Center for Social Gerontology, the Pension Rights Center, the National Clearinghouse for Legal Services, Inc., the Mental Health Law Project, and the National Bar Association (U.S. Senate Special Committee on Aging 1993).

Older Americans Act funds supported over 600 legal programs for older persons, serving over 323,000 persons in 1991. It is estimated that some nine million persons 60 years of age and older are eligible under income guidelines for Legal Services Corporation programs which are not solely targeted for older people.

An effective approach to legal assistance for the elderly is the use of legal hotlines. Legal advice is given to callers over the telephone by attorneys. Callers can also be referred to a publicly funded legal program or to a social service agency if the advisor decides that the caller's problem is not a legal one (Kolasa and Soto 1990). Legal hotlines overcome the problem many older people have with transportation. However, there have been problems working with older callers who have hearing problems (Porter and Affeldt 1990).

Food Stamps

The food stamp program is set up to alleviate malnutrition and hunger among low-income persons by increasing their food purchasing power. In this program, local welfare agencies issue coupons to purchase food in accordance with guidelines established by the U.S. Department of Agriculture (USDA). This program is not only intended for elderly people, but for persons of any age who qualify. In 1992, some 25.4 million persons participated in the food stamp program, about one-tenth of the entire U.S. population (U.S. Senate Special Committee on Aging 1993).

A U.S. Senate report cited recent studies confirming the correlation between nutritional status and health, especially for the young and the elderly. "Malnutrition may account for substantially more illness among elderly Americans than has been assumed," according to medical experts (U.S. Senate Special Committee on Aging 1993: 23). This same report indicated that concern about malnutrition is rising fast as the elderly population grows, and surveys show that millions of them eat poorly.

Twenty percent of the American households that get food stamps have at least one member aged 60 or older. However, they make up only 11 percent of food stamp recipients and get only 8 percent of all food stamp benefits. Older food stamp recipients generally live on Supplemental Security Income and Social Security benefits (U.S. Senate Special Committee on Aging 1993).

COMMUNITY-BASED PROGRAMS FOR OLDER PEOPLE

The information outlined above describes the kinds of programs that are available to older people across America. The following are specific community-based services that can be found in most communities of the nation.

Multipurpose Senior Centers

The multipurpose senior center has been defined as "a community focal point on aging where older persons as individuals or in groups come together for services and activities which enhance their dignity, support their independence and encourage their involvement in and with the community" (Gelfand 1993: 153).

Although the history of a center for older people goes back to a program developed in New York City in 1943, senior centers were not funded by the federal government until 1975 through the Older Americans Act. By 1990, between five and eight million older persons were involved in 10,000 to 12,000 senior centers across the United States (Krout, Cutler, and Coward 1990).

Depending on the location, support, and resources, multipurpose senior centers can provide a range of resources and services for older people, all in one place. The important thing about them is that they can become a familiar and comfortable place for older people to access a broad range of services and resources. They do not need to venture to a strange place at some distance to participate in a given activity or to access a service.

Center programming is usually of two types: (1) recreation and education, and (2) services (Gelfand 1993).

Recreation and Education   A range of activities falls under recreation and education including the following:

- Arts and crafts
- Nature, science, and outdoor life
- Drama and dance
- Physical activities
- Music and literary activities
- Table games
- Social activities
- Excursions
- Speakers, lectures, movies, and forums

Activities are usually designed to appeal to both men and women.

Services   Services in senior centers can include the following:

- Information, counseling, and referral
- Assistance with living arrangements and employment
- Health programs, including screening clinics, pharmaceutical services, and health education
- Protective services
- Meals
- Legal and income counseling
- Friendly-visit outreach programs
- Homemaker assistance
- Telephone reassurance
- Handyman-fix-up programs
- Transportation assistance

The programs that have generated the most participation are meals, information and referral, and sedentary recreation. The activities that had the most interest were tours and trips (Gelfand 1993). A 1990 study indicated that three-fourths of senior centers are in their own separate facilities (Kront 1990). This gives the centers an independent existence which makes them more attractive to a wide range of participants, unlike being extensions of religious organizations or social agencies.

Funding for senior centers can come from Title III of the Older Americans Act, Block Grants, General Revenue Sharing funds, Social Services Block Grants, the Higher Education Act, and state and local funds. Senior centers can be meaningful resources for older people, and they provide ongoing opportunities for older people to interact with other older people.

Adult Daycare

Adult daycare was defined in the original federal guidelines for demonstration projects as a program that: "provided under health leadership in an ambulatory care setting for adults who do not require 24-hour institutional care and yet, due to physical and/or mental impairment, are not capable of full-time independent living" (U.S. Health Resources Administration 1974: 1).

The National Council on Aging (NCOA) has defined daycare as follows:

Community-based group program designed to meet the needs of functionally impaired adults through an individual plan of care. It is a structured, comprehensive program that provides a variety of health, social, and related support services in a protective setting during any part of a day but less than 24-hour care (Behrens 1986: 5).

First organized in England in the 1940s, adult daycare is a response to the need for family caregivers to have relief from caring for dependent older people on a regular basis. Unlike senior centers, adult daycare programs and centers are usually not "drop-in" situations. They are generally offered on a five-days-a-week basis, with the clients attending a regular number of days each week for eight hours per day. Adult daycare centers offer family caregivers opportunities to continue or return to work outside the home or participate in any activity, free for some hours each day from the responsibilities of caring for a dependent older person.

The range of services provided by adult daycare centers include the following:

- Screening for physical conditions
- Medical care (generally arranged with an outside physician)
- Nursing care
- Occupational, physical, and recreational therapy
- Social work
- Transportation
- Meals
- Personal care
- Educational programs
- Crafts
- Counseling

Funding for these programs can come from Medicaid, Social Services Block Grants, Title III of the Older Americans Act, and fees paid by users and their families. These centers may be located in an independent facility, a senior center, a neighborhood center, a hospital, or a religious organization.

Daycare has become an important component of community services available to older people and their families. It plays a key role in alleviating isolation, preventing or delaying institutionalization, and providing relief in the caretaking responsibilities of families (Gillespie and Sloan 1990).

Respite Care

Another form of community help for a caregiver of a dependent older person is respite care. Closely related to daycare, respite care generally offers more intensive care on a limited-time basis for elderly persons who require ongoing care. This care may be in the caregiver's home, or the dependent older person may be brought to a respite-care facility, which may be a nursing home or other long-term-care facility. The length of the assistance may range from a few hours to a few days.

In a second option for respite care, the elderly patient is brought to a group setting where he or she has the opportunity to socialize with others and participate in program activities. This type of service is increasingly being provided to Alzheimer's patients (Quinn and Crabtree 1987).

This type of service in the community is relatively new and generally underfunded by social-support funding systems. Some are being developed on a fee-for-service basis. Although this is one of the least-available community service programs, a study indicated that it ranked at the top when caregivers were asked what help they needed most (Caserta et al. 1990; Belsky 1990).

Respite care in communities is seen as an effective means of maintaining frail, dependent older people in their own homes for longer periods of time. This service helps the informal support system (family and friends) provide the care that dependent older people need (Quinn and Crabtree 1987).

In-Home Services

Perhaps the most important services that enable older people to remain in their own homes and communities are in-home services. In recent years in-home care has been one of the fastest-growing components of Medicare (Gelfand 1993). Too often admission to nursing homes, chronic-care hospitals, and other long-term facilities are used to meet the needs of impaired older individuals when appropriate assistance at home, or in the home of an adult child or friend, would be a better solution. Not only is staying at home usually much more cost effective, but most older people want to remain in the familiar surroundings of their own house.

A 1992 Census Bureau report reviewed eleven national surveys of the elderly population who required help with activities of daily living (ADLs), including routine functions such as bathing, dressing, getting out of bed, going to the bathroom, and feeding oneself. ADLs are used to measure the need for various types of care and assistance. The study found some differences among the eleven national surveys, but nevertheless, there were similar trends (U.S. Bureau of the Census 1992). There was a strong correlation between age and the need for assistance. Among persons 64 years of age and younger, only 2 percent needed assistance. From ages 65 to 69, some 9 percent needed help. For those persons 85 years and older, the percentage jumped to 45 percent. As the population continues to age, the need for in-home help will continue to increase dramatically.

Categories of In-Home Services In-home services can be grouped into three basic categories based on the level of service needed (U.S. Senate Special Committee on Aging 1972).

- *Intensive* or *skilled services* are ordered by a physician and supervised by a nurse. These types of services are for heart patients, persons with bone fractures, open wounds, diabetes, or terminal illnesses requiring catheters and tube feedings, and others.
- *Personal care* or *intermediate services* are for older persons who are medically stable but who need help with some activities of daily living such as bathing, prescribed exercises, and medications.

- *Homemaker services* are provided to older persons who need help with light housekeeping, preparing food, laundry, and other activities to maintain a household in an orderly manner (Gelfand 1993).

Any of these services can be provided in conjunction with the others. The client who needs intensive or skilled services will usually need services from the other categories to be able to remain in his or her own home. The key person of in-home services, in addition to the professionals who screen, monitor, and treat health conditions, is the homemaker–home health aide. This person can perform a wide range of tasks that enable the dependent older person to remain at home. These tasks include: cleaning, planning meals, shopping for food, preparing meals, doing the laundry, changing bed linens, bathing, giving bed baths, washing hair, helping persons move about, assisting with exercises, giving medications, and providing companionship (Gelfand 1993).

Types of In-Home Service Providers A number of community-based agencies provide in-home services for elderly people including the following:

- *Home-care units of community hospitals*, assist discharged patients.
- *Departments of social services* usually provide intermediate and basic-level in-home services through their adult protective services divisions.
- *Private nonprofit community agencies*, such as Visiting Nurses Associations, Associated Catholic Charities, Jewish Family and Children's Services, and Family and Children's Services, usually provide homemaker–home health aides, nurses, and other in-home service providers.
- *Community health centers* provide in-home services for those clients who are involved with the health center.
- *Proprietary* (for-profit) *agencies*, such as Upjohn, offer in-home services to the homebound for a fee (Gelfand 1993).

Ways to Pay for In-Home Service There are a number of ways in-home services are reimbursed. Unfortunately, there is no comprehensive system to cover these expenses. Indeed, paying for these services has been cited as the major problem in their delivery (Gelfand 1993). In addition, public funding is heavily biased toward institutional care, even though homecare is cheaper and has emotional advantages. Methods of payment include the following:

- Client fees; most in-home service agencies will provide services for fees paid by the users.
- Medicare can be used when health-related services and the clients meet the following Medicare eligibility requirements:
  —Service must be provided by a home health agency whose primary function is skilled nursing service and at least one additional therapeutic service.
  —Reimbursable services focus on acute or short-term illnesses.
  —Actual services are restricted to homebound patients (persons unable to leave their homes without the assistance of a person or a device such as a wheelchair or cane).
  —Homecare must be prescribed by a physician caring for the patient.
  —The patient must require either intermittent skilled nursing care, physical therapy, or speech therapy (Leader 1991).
  Services paid for by Medicare include:
  —Part-time or intermittent nursing care
  —Physical, occupational, and speech therapy
  —Medical supplies
  —Home health aide services
  —Counseling for social or emotional problems
- Medicaid can be used to pay for in-home services when the client and the service meet Medicaid eligibility requirements, which include strict income guidelines. Services provided by Medicaid include:
  —nursing services
  —home health aide services
  —medical supplies and equipment

Medicaid does not require that skilled nursing care or therapy be provided to the patient. Medicaid also pays for personal care and non-medical services that are part of ADLs if the person is Medicaid eligible, although because the states are involved in paying for Medicaid services, few actually allow for personal care and nontechnical services (Gelfand 1993). This, however, is changing with Medicaid waivers promoted by the Clinton administration which will result in more Medicaid funds used for in-home services to avoid more costly institutionalization of infirm elderly people.

- Title III of the Older Americans Act provides funds for in-home services through local AAAs. These funds are intended to avoid putting people in long-term care institutions. They provide for:
    —Preinstitution evaluation and screening
    —Homemakers services
    —Shopping services
    —Escort services
    —Reader services
    —Letter-writing services

To be eligible for these services a person must be 60 years of age or older. Like other OAA services, there are no income restrictions on these services. However, efforts are made to target the low-income elderly because these funds are so limited (Gelfand 1993).

Case Management Services

Case management is a community-based service in which the responsibility for assessing the needs of older people and finding and negotiating for services to meet the identified needs is undertaken by a qualified person or team. This is usually done in conjunction with a community agency (Gillespie and Sloan 1990). This service is becoming increasingly critical as service delivery systems become more complex and the number of older people who need in-home services continues to grow.

Types of Services Case management services include assessing needs, developing a plan of care, locating appropriate services, coordinating services, authorizing and arranging for services, monitoring services, and monitoring and re-assessing needs.

In the case management process, the case managers can help determine eligibility for various services as well as assist with applications for government-sponsored programs.

Case management is available not only to help older people remain in their own homes, but also to help people who have an aged family member or friend living with them. Outside professionals, usually a nurse and a social worker, are invited into the home to help the caregiver determine what type of services the older person needs, who can help with these services, and who can help pay for these services.

Reluctance to Use Services It is difficult for many caregivers to call someone into their home to help with this kind of assessment. Most think they know what needs to be done, and most want to do what needs to be done by themselves. Many think it is their duty and their responsibility, but deep down they also know that they cannot do everything. They cannot continue to give around-the-clock care and continually worry about frail, elderly parents without paying the consequences in terms of personal health, family unity, and emotional well-being.

With case management, there is usually no obligation after the initial assessment. Suggestions may be followed, rejected, or modified. Using one of these services and following some of their suggestions for help does not mean that caregivers are abandoning their responsibilities to parents. It means that they are wise enough to know that they cannot do everything by themselves all the time. Using a case management approach, family caregivers can plug in the types of assistance that are needed so that they can continue to be effective caregivers. It means that they are using their own resources in more effective ways.

In some areas of the nation, case management services are offered on a nonprofit or low-cost basis to help keep elderly people out of long-term care institutions as long as possible. In other instances, the service is on a fee basis, which should be discussed ahead of time.

Helping from a Distance   In many instances, case management services provide adult children living distances from their aging parents the opportunity to assist in the care of their elderly parents without moving near them. Some agencies, such as the Jewish Family and Children's Agencies, have developed an Elder Support Network through which family members are able to arrange for case management and supportive services throughout the nation with fees based on a sliding scale determined by the family member's income (Gelfand 1993). Private care managers are springing up across the United States, which can be accessed through the National Association of Professional Geriatric Care Managers. Columnist Jane Bryant Quinn (1991) warned that this field is unregulated. She advised prospective users to check every claim, to get written plans of action, and to interview at least three clients before signing on to any private case manager. The American Association of Retired Persons has a free booklet, *Miles Away and Still Caring*, that deals with this issue.

Nutrition Services

As was indicated previously, adequate nutrition is an essential component of life. This is particularly true for older people. According to the testimony of Dr. Susan Calvert Finn, president-elect of the American Dietetic Association, at a Congressional hearing in 1992, as many as 50 percent of independent living older Americans have nutrition deficiencies, and that an estimated 6 million people are at risk for poor nutritional status. Older persons are at a greater risk of malnutrition due to psychological, socio-economic and psychological factors. Some 85 percent of older Americans have one of more chronic potentially debilitating diseases that could benefit from cost-effective nutrition intervention and services (U.S. House of Representatives, 1992).

Nutrition services in communities fall into two general categories: (1) congregate nutrition programs, and (2) home-delivered meals.

Congregate Meals   Under provisions of the Older Americans Act, the Administration on Aging is mandated to offer meals programs for the elderly which (1) provide at least one hot or other appropriate meal per day and any additional meals which the recipient of a grant or contract may elect to provide, each of which assures a minimum of one-third of the daily recommended dietary allowances as established by the Food Nutrition Board of the National Academy of Sciences; (2) shall be provided in congregate settings; and (3) may include nutrition services and other appropriate services for older individuals (Title III, Part C of the Older Americans Act of 1992).

The purpose of the congregate meals program in communities across the nation is to provide both meals and opportunities to socialize. People who participate in these nutrition programs often have other needs which can be identified and responded to by linking the meals programs with other community services (Gelfand 1993). While improving the nutritional intake of older people, the congregate meals programs have addressed many other problems older people face including social isolation, loneliness, and limited access to social and health services (Gillespie and Sloan 1990). The congregate meals programs have been among the most popular and successful of all the programs for older adults (Gelfand 1993).

Home-Delivered Meals   Home-delivered meals, or "meals on wheels," are provided to homebound older people to enable them to have nutritional meals on a regular basis (Gelfand 1993). Obtaining these meals enables many elderly persons to remain in their own homes. Although the major purpose of the home-delivered meals program is to prepare and deliver nutritious meals to home-bound older persons, it also includes a check on the status of the older persons, who get the meals as well as a brief conversation.

A feature of the home-delivered meals program that is little known is that persons under 60 years of age are eligible for the service as long as they are homebound. However, some 90 percent of those receiving meals on wheels are 60 and older (Gelfand 1993). In fiscal year 1990, 102 million meals were delivered to older people (Older American Reports 1992).

Information and Assistance

Information about services that are available in communities is the key to their being used by older people and their caregivers. Having an array of resources does little good if the intended recipients do not know about them or know how to access them. As such, information and assistance become a community-based social service in its own right.

The functions of information and assistance for older people are similar to those of the general population except they focus on the particular needs of older people. They include putting together information that links older people with opportunities, services, and resources to help them with their needs, and collecting and reporting information concerning the needs of older people to assist in evaluating, planning, and coordinating resources.

According to research, the problems most often requiring referrals involve income, Social Security, transportation, health problems, home health care, housing, home maintenance and repair, food and nutrition, homemaker services, employment, consumer needs and problems, legal problems, companionship, and nursing-home care (Gelfand 1993).

One of the major problems of information and referral services is their underuse by isolated and unconnected older people, the very people who need these services the most (Gelfand

1993). To overcome this problem, various active outreach programs have been initiated. Some use "hot lines" that are publicized. Some of the state legal assistance programs use this format. In 1993, the National Association of Agencies on Aging, with funding from the Administration on Aging, established a national Eldercare Locater service with a toll-free telephone number from any place in the United States. Any older person, or anyone seeking assistance for an older person, can call 1-800-677-1116 between 9:00 A.M. and 11:00 P.M., Eastern time, Monday through Friday, requesting information about the kind of help needed. The Eldercare Locater taps into an extensive network of organizations that are familiar with state and local community resources. Information is provided about such resources as adult daycare centers, legal assistance, home health services, and transportation resources (NRTA 1993).

Even though attempts are being made to make information and referral services more accessible to older adults, current research indicates that there are many elderly persons who are eligible for services who do not use them.

Beyond these specifically targeted programs, in-depth, coordinated information and education programs focusing on resources, services, and coping strategies to deal with the issues and problems older people face are not readily available in formats that reach the rapidly growing numbers of older people and their family caregivers. A major recent study by the Public Policy Institute of the American Association of Retired Persons (Kassner 1992) recommended coordinated community education programs along with outreach strategies as ways to reach this rapidly growing target population. How to cope with the wide range of pressing situations that occurs as people grow older is of vital concern to millions of Americans in all walks of life. These issues are also important for younger people as they begin to prepare for their own advancing years. One of the most effective approaches for assisting older people and their families, who are trying to help them cope with the range of real life situations they face as they move through the aging process, is to mobilize and coordinate community resources in an integrated approach to increase learning opportunities for older persons, their families, and agency staff who work with them.

SUMMARY

A broad range of services have become available for older people across most of the United States. The Social Security Act in 1935, and the Older Americans Act in 1965 laid the foundation for an array of services and programs for older Americans. The national legislative bases of other services and programs include Social Services Block Grant, Community Services Block Grant, ACTION Programs, Transportation, Legal Services, and Food Stamps. These legislative acts are not targeted specifically at older people, but they can participate in them if they qualify. Eligibility for the services and programs of these legislative acts is generally based on low-income and limited resources.

For those programs funded by the Older Americans Act, there are no income eligibility guidelines. Anyone 60 years of age and older can qualify. However, because of the limited funding of these programs, especially in recent years, these services are targeted at those older people in greatest need, those with low incomes and limited resources. Some of the programs are funded by a combination of funding sources including local community support and participant contributions or fees.

Multipurpose senior centers have become a focal point for services, meals, recreation, and socialization for many older people. Adult day-care programs are vital to dependent elderly persons and their caregiving families. Respite care is emerging as a vital resource in providing caregiving family members with relief so they can continue to keep their dependent elderly relatives in community and family settings.

In-home services provide services to older homebound persons who need a range of services, from skilled nursing to assistance with housekeeping chores, in order to stay out of long-term-care institutions. Case management is emerging as an effective way to assess, coordinate, and manage the services needed by older people who need help with the activities of daily living.

Nutrition services in communities consist of congregate and home-delivered meals. Both are vital to the lives of older Americans across the nation. Malnutrition is an ongoing threat to millions of older people for a variety of reasons. The community-based nutrition programs improve deficient diets and lessen loneliness and isolation among the elderly.

All of the programs for older people are of little use if they are unknown and underutilized, especially by those who need them the most. Information and referral services are vital links in this process. Current research indicates that many eligible potential recipients of programs and services for the elderly are falling through the safety nets designed for them. More needs to be done to reach the isolated, hard-to-reach older people across the nation.

REFERENCES

Behrens, R. 1986. *Adult Day Care in America.* Washington, DC: National Council on Aging.

Belsky, J.K. 1990. *The Psychology of Aging: Theory, Research and Interventions.* 2d Ed. Pacific Grove, CA: Brooks/Cole.

Caserta, M.S., Lund, D.A., Wright, S.D., and Redburn, D.E. 1990. Caregivers to Dementia Patients. *Gerontologist,* 27: 209–214.M.S.

Caserta, M.S. 1987. Caregivers to Dementia Patients: The Utilization of Community Services. *Gerontologist,* 27: 209–21.

Center on Budget and Policy Priorities. 1991a. *SSI, Medicaid, Food Stamps and LIHEAP Programs: A Summary Review of Participation Rates and Outreach Activities.* Washington, DC: AARP.

Center on Budget and Policy Priorities. 1991b. *Food Stamps: A Review of Participation Rates and Outreach Activities*. Washington, DC: AARP.

Center on Budget and Policy Priorities. 1991c. *Supplemental Security (SSI): A Review of the Participation Rates and Outreach Activities*. Washington, DC: AARP.

Center on Budget and Policy Priorities. 1991d. *Medicaid: A Review of Participation Rates and Outreach Activities*. Washington, DC: AARP.

Center on Budget and Policy Priorities. 1991e. *The Low-Income Home Energy Assistance Program: A Review of Participation Rates and Outreach Activities*. Washington, DC: AARP.

Committee on Ways and Means. 1992. *Overview of Entitlement Programs: 1992. Green Book*. Washington, DC: U.S. Government Printing Office, 33.

Congressional Record. 1992. *Older Americans Act* (Part II). Washington, DC: U.S. Government Printing Office.

Gelfand, D., and Bechill, W. 1991. Older Americans Act: A 25 Year Review of Legislative Changes. *Generations*, 15(3): 19–22.

Gelfand, D.E. 1993. *The Aging Network: Programs and Services*, 4th Ed. New York: Springer.

Gillespie, A.E., and Sloan, K.S. 1990. *Housing Options and Services for Older Adults*. Santa Barbara, CA: ABC-CL10.

It's Now Elementary: Eldercare by Phone. 1993. *NRTA Bulletin*, 34(5) (May): 13.

Kassner, E. 1992. *Falling Through the Safety Net: Missed Opportunities for America's Elderly Poor*. Washington, D.C.: Center on Elderly People Living Alone, AARP.

Kolasa, M., and Soto, M. 1990. *Legal Hotlines to Serve Older People*. Third Annual Joint (October). Washington, DC.

Kront, J., Cutler, S., and Coward, R. 1990. Correlates of Senior Center Participation: A National Analysis. *Gerontologist*, 30: 72–79.

Kront, J. 1990. *The Organization, Operation and Programming of Senior Centers in America: A Seven-Year Follow-up*. Fredonia, NY: Final Report to the AARP Andrus Foundation.

Leader, S. 1991. *Medicare's Home Health Benefit: Eligibility, Utilization, and Expenditures*. Washington, DC: Public Policy Institute, AARP.

Louis Harris and Associates. 1988. *Follow-up Study of Poor Elderly People: Strategies to Increase Participation in the Supplemental Security Income Program*, (Study No. 874012, February).

National Council on the Aging. 1978. *Fact Book on Aging*. Washington, DC: NCA.

Older Americans Act of 1965 (Public Law 89-73) as Amended by Older Americans Act Amendments of 1992 (Public Law 102-375).

Older American Reports. 1992. AoA Releases FY '90 Data on Title III State Programs (April 17): 16, 152.

Osterkamp, L. 1988. Family Caregivers: America's Primary Long-Term Care Resource. *Aging*, 358: 2–5.

Peterson, D.A., Wendt, P.F., and Douglas, E.B. 1991. *Determining the Impact of Gerontology Preparation on Personnel in the Aging Network: A National Survey*. The University of Southern California and the Association for Gerontology in Higher Education, Washington, DC.

Porter, D., and Affeldt, D. 1990. Legal Services Delivery Systems: An Overview of the Present and a Look at the Future. In P. Powers and K. Klinger Smith (eds.), *Aging and the Law: Looking Into the Next Century*. Washington, DC: Public Policy Institute, AARP.

Quinn, J.B., and Crabtree, J. 1987. *How to Start a Respite Service for People with Alzheimer's and Their Families*. New York: Brookdale Foundation.

Quinn, J.B. 1991. Old, Sick and Far Away. *Newsweek*, 118(9): 39.

Riekse, R., and Holstege, H. 1992. *The Christian Guide to Parent Care*. Wheaton, IL: Tyndale House Publishers.

Torres-Gil, F. 1992. *The New Aging: Politics and Change in America*. New York: Auburn House.

U.S. Bureau of the Census. 1992. Current Population Reports, Special Studies (P23-178), *Sixty-Five Plus in America*. Washington, DC: U.S. Government Printing Office.

U.S. Health Resources Administration, Division of Long-Term Care. 1974. *Guidelines and Definitions for Day Care Centers Under P.L.92-603*. Washington, DC: U.S. Government Printing Office.

U.S. House of Representatives, Select Committee on Aging. 1992. *Hearing: Adequate Nutrition for the Elderly* (July 30). Washington DC: U.S. Government Printing Office.

U.S. Senate Special Committee on Aging. 1993. *Developments in Aging: 1992* (Vol. 1). Washington, DC: U.S. Government Printing Office.

U.S. Senate Special Committee on Aging. 1972. *Home Health Services in the United States*. Washington, DC: U.S. Government Printing Office.

U.S. Senate Special Committee on Aging. 1991. *Older American Act: Findings and Policy Recommendations of the 1990 Workshops*. Washington DC: U.S. Government Printing Office.

CHAPTER 17

Medical
Care

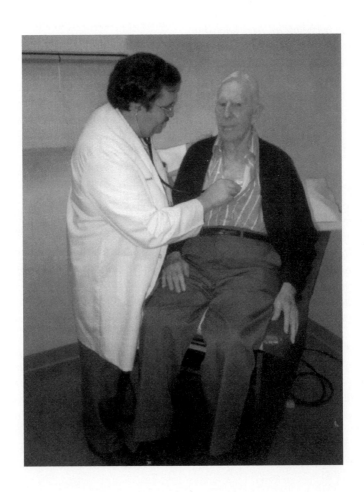

He Was Told He'd Die But He Chose to Fight

In 1990, after doctors told Ira Baldwin of Madison, WI, that his rare form of liver cancer was incurable, he searched for a doctor who would help him find a cure. Paul Carbone, director of the University of Wisconsin Comprehensive Cancer Center, took up the challenge. Says Baldwin, a retired administrator and professor of bacteriology at the university, "I told him, 'if you've got some ideas about things that may work but you're afraid they may do more damage than good, let's try it. I'm 95 and I can't live forever.'" The drug alpha interferon at first kept the cancer in check. But when the tumor started to grow again, Baldwin was switched to a platinum-based drug. "I feel fine," says Baldwin, who grows orchids as a hobby and is teaching Carbone about them as well. "I tell the doctor I'm cured, but he says I have to wait five years before using that word."

Ira Baldwin, 97
Source: U.S. News and World Report,
June 18, 1993, p. 73

She Says She Had a Choice But Found Out Too Late

Margaret Smith of Santa Monica, Calif., was wheeled into surgery in 1984 for a biopsy of a small tumor in her right breast. The surgeon, as she remembers it, had told her that if the tumor proved to be malignant he would remove the breast, and she had agreed. "I was completely in his hands," she says. Sure enough, when she awoke, the lump was gone—and so was her breast. The tumor however, turned out to be minuscule. Breast-saving surgery—an option Smith doesn't recall being offered—would have been an appropriate alternative, says Patricia Ganz, a UCLA cancer specialist who has written extensively about doctors' tendencies to treat old and young people who have cancer differently. Smith who asked that her first doctor not be con-
tacted, is now being treated for an unrelated bone-marrow disorder.

Margaret Smith, 89
Source: U.S. News and World Report,
June 18, 1993, p. 76.

Pressured Into Too Much Care

Because of her Alzheimer's Edna Stanbrough of Fremont, Calif., had moments of great confusion. One day in 1983, at the age of 84, she fell and broke her hip and had to be hospitalized. A neurosurgeon called Stanbrough's kin, Shirley Burris, and explained that her cousin had a blood clot in her brain, Burris recalls. Surgery might clear up her disorientation, he said. Burris, a geriatric nurse, says she rejected the idea, because the clot hadn't appeared until long after dementia had set in. Besides, she insisted, her cousin wouldn't want to undergo brain surgery. But the surgeon persisted. "This man made me feel about as low as I could feel," says Burris. "He wore me down. 'How could I be so uncaring?' he asked, 'that I would not do everything possible to help her?' If that happened to me—someone in the field who knows better—how many others is it happening to?" She approved surgery, Burris says now, that left her cousin unimproved. Stanbrough then became incontinent and unable to walk. She was placed in a nursing home and died there three years later.

Edna Stanbrough, 1899–1986
Source: U.S. News and World Report,
June 18, 1993, p. 79

The Alzheimer's That Was Cured with a Shunt

He started forgetting things in 1989. And as Charles Lavery's memory became increasingly fuzzy, his sense of balance began to erode. Memory tests and brain scans brought no reliable diagnosis, says the Catonsville, MD, resident. One physician intimated that Alzheimer's might be the cause but left it at that with no further explanation. "We didn't know what else to do and be-

sides, we had faith in this doctor," says Lavery's wife, Barbara. His condition continued to deteriorate, and in 1991 Lavery sought the opinion of Thomas Finucane, associate medical director of the Johns Hopkins geriatrics center in Baltimore. Finucane saw in Lavery someone who "didn't fit the Alzheimer's mold." He ordered a full neurologic work-up, which revealed that Lavery's symptoms were due not to Alzheimer's but to pressure on the brain from excess fluid in his skull. Installing a shunt, or drain, relieved the pressure, and within three days of surgery Lavery's symptoms began to diminish. It was a procedure, said the Laverys, that the original doctors had never suggested.

Source: U.S. News and World Report,
June 18, 1993, p. 78.

IMPORTANCE OF MEDICAL CARE AS PEOPLE GROW OLDER

Health care is one of the most pressing issues facing the nation. In studying aging, health care quickly becomes one of the most important issues facing persons as they grow older. This is particularly true for persons in the two groups of the elderly that include the more advanced years—the aged (75 to 84 years) and the oldest old (85 years and older).

As people continue to age, the likelihood of having health conditions that require attention and hinder their ability to perform the daily tasks of living increases. Among the young old (65 to 74 years), only about 9 percent need assistance. Among persons aged 75 to 79, 18.9 percent need assistance; and among the oldest old, 45.4 percent need assistance (U.S. Bureau of the Census 1993).

Even though people are living longer they are more likely to live with multiple illnesses and disabilities. While heart disease, cancer, and stroke are leading causes of death among the elderly (along with influenza and pneumonia for persons 85 years and older), they also contribute to chronic health problems and disabilities (U.S.

Bureau of the Census 1993). Even though doctors are now able to save the lives of many persons who would have died from these conditions, many of the survivors spend years with chronic illnesses and conditions. In addition, many elderly persons suffer from other chronic diseases such as arthritis, diabetes, osteoporosis, and dementias, which increase in frequency after age 85.

Chronic and Acute Health Conditions

Essentially people face two types of illnesses over a lifetime: chronic and acute. A chronic condition is one that is expected to be long-term and possibly permanent, such as heart disease, high blood pressure, hearing loss, vision impairment, diabetes, and arthritis. Chronic illnesses can sometimes be managed by the individual with minimum effect on a person's independence, but some chronic conditions can become disabling.

An acute condition is one that is expected to be of a limited duration. It may be mild or serious. These conditions can range from simple bruises to heart attacks, pneumonia, or broken bones. Acute conditions often require a hospital stay.

Chronic diseases are major threats to the well-being and independence of older people. More than four out of five older people have at least one chronic health condition. Multiple health problems are common among the elderly, particularly older women (U.S. Senate Special Committee on Aging 1993).

The five most common chronic conditions are arthritis, hypertension (high blood pressure), hearing loss, heart disease, and cataracts. Most older people are hospitalized as a result of an acute episode of a chronic disease. The leading causes of hospitalization of the elderly are cancer and diseases of the circulatory, digestive, and respiratory systems. Most visits to the doctor are also for the treatment of chronic conditions (Aging America: Trends and Projections 1991).

USE OF MEDICAL CARE

All of this results in extensive use of medical resources by the elderly. While older people made up for 12.5 percent of the population in 1990, they consumed about one-third of all health care spending (Kingson and Berkowitz 1993). Visiting a doctor for help with a health problem increases with age. According to a 1993 U.S. Senate report, about 85 percent of the elderly living outside a nursing home go to the doctor at least once a year. Older persons are more likely to visit doctors frequently than are younger persons. Persons 65 and older go to the doctor nearly twice as often (nine times to five times) as younger people. About 60 percent of doctor visits by the elderly are to doctors' offices. The rest are made to hospital emergency rooms, to outpatient departments, and by home and telephone consultations (U.S. Senate Special Committee on Aging 1993).

Older persons are likely to have hospital stays twice as often as the rest of the population and stay about 50 percent longer. Between 1965 and 1986, short hospital stays by older persons increased more than 57 percent. Just under one-third of hospitalizations were for people aged 65 and older (U.S. Senate Special Committee on Aging 1993).

PAYING FOR HEALTH CARE: MEDICARE

The good news about covering the costs of acute, short-term hospital stays and physician services is the availability of Medicare, the federal health insurance program for persons 65 years and older. The bad news about Medicare is what it does not cover.

Before Medicare was passed in 1965 and went into effect in 1966, the risk of becoming impoverished by hospital and doctor bills was about the same that older people and their families face today from placement in a nursing home as part of long-term care. Medicare, as part of President Lyndon Johnson's Great Society, went a long way to protect the finances of the elderly and their families. It also provided access to acute care as well as some other health-care services (Kingson and Berkowitz 1993). Currently, fewer than 1 percent of America's older persons are without any health coverage for acute care. Medicare provides health care coverage to nearly all the nation's elderly. In addition, about three-fourths (74.2 percent) of all Americans aged 65 to 84 had supplemental private insurance ("medigap" insurance) in 1989 (U.S. Bureau of the Census 1993). Medigap insurance is purchased to help pay for health-care costs not covered by Medicare, such as deductibles, copayments, and prescription drugs.

Who Gets Medicare?

Medicare is an intergenerational program. To qualify for Medicare health coverage, a person must be 65 years and older; have received Social Security Disability Insurance benefits for 24 months or longer; or be of any age with end-stage renal disease (kidney failure).

What Does Medicare Cover?

Medicare consists of two parts, Part A and Part B.

Medicare Part A   Part A of Medicare is hospital insurance financed by a tax on employers (including self-employed persons) and employees. In 1994, Medicare Part A included the following:

- *Hospitalization*. After the patient pays a deductible of $696, Medicare pays the balance of all allowable charges during the first 60 days of a hospital stay per benefit period. A benefit period begins on the first day a person receives care in a hospital as an inpatient and ends after discharge from the hospital or skilled nursing facility for 60 consecutive days. There is a $174 copayment daily for the next 30 days and a $349 copayment daily for the next 60 days, which are called the lifetime reserve days. These 60 reserve days may be used only once. They are not renewable.

- *Skilled Nursing Care*. A person is entitled to 100 days of skilled nursing care per benefit period. There is a $87 daily copayment for days 21 through 100.
- *No custodial nursing home care*.
- *Home Health Care*. A patient is entitled to unlimited part-time skilled care in one's own home. Medicare pays all approved charges.
- *Hospice Care*. A patient is entitled to 210 days, and when necessary, an indefinite extension; Medicare pays all but limited costs.

There is no cost to receive Part A benefits if a person is qualified.

Medicare Part B   Part B of Medicare is a voluntary program for Part A recipients who chose to pay a monthly premium (fee) to cover physicians' services and medical services. It covers:

- *Medical Services*. Physician's service, inpatient and outpatient visits, supplies, ambulance services, lab tests, and X-rays. Screening pap smears are covered once every three years and screening-mammograms once every two years. The patient pays a $100 annual deductible and a 20-percent copayment on all Part B services. A patient does not have to pay for any excess charge over and above the approved amount if the provider (physician, lab, etc.) accepts assignment in the claim form. If the provider does not accept assignment, the patient is responsible for the deductible, the 20 percent copayment, and any excess charges.
- *Limiting Charge*. Usually, a physician who does not accept assignment may not charge more than 115 percent of the Medicare-approved amount for services.
- *No prescription drug coverage*.

For 1994, the monthly premium for Medicare Part B was $41.10 per person, which is deducted from monthly Social Security benefit checks (Medicare for 1994).

Medicare does not cover:

- Prescription drugs (except during a hospital stay)
- Vitamins
- Dentures
- Routine dental care
- First-aid kits
- Hearing aids and fittings
- Routine hearing aids and vision tests
- Eyeglasses (except after cataract surgery)
- Elective cosmetic surgery
- Personal custodial care
- Homemaker service
- Routine foot care
- Preventive health care (except for pap smears and mammography screening)
- Long-term nursing services
- Private duty nurses
- Health care outside the United States (with limited exceptions) (U.S. Senate Special Committee on Aging 1991).

It is important to note that the Medicare program is geared toward acute or short-term care, not long-term or custodial care. The crisis of long-term care in the United States is explored in the next chapter.

Second Opinions

Before major surgery or medical procedure, many people want a second opinion. They do not want to take the risks or bear the pain and costs of surgery unless they are reasonably comfortable that the procedure recommended is the best way to deal with their medical problem.

Many older people are hesitant to get a second opinion. They feel embarrassed to raise the issue, not wanting to offend their physicians. They should not feel this way. Second opinions can actually improve the quality of medical care for patients.

A patient should find out the certainty of his or her condition as well as any alternative treatments. If a person's doctor resists a second opinion, he or she should get one anyway. Most competent, secure doctors welcome second opinions or consultations.

Medicare pays for a second opinion just as it pays for any physician services—80 percent of the allowable charge. If the opinion of patient's physician and second-opinion doctor disagree, it would be a good idea to get a third opinion. Medicare will pay for a third opinion in the same way it paid for the first and second (U.S. Senate Special Committee on Aging 1991).

There are some steps that an older person can take to get a qualified second opinion:

- Call Medicare's Second Opinion toll-free hotline: 1-800-638-6833; in Maryland: 1-800-492-6603.
- Contact local or state medical societies.
- Ask friends or co-workers for references to specialists they recommend.
- Contact the nearest medical school and ask for a consultation with a specialist (U.S. Senate Special Committee on Aging 1991).

When seeking a second opinion, it is important to avoid duplicate tests. A patient can ask the first physician to send copies of medical records, X-rays, and lab tests to the second opinion doctor.

Helping to Pay for Medicare

For the very-low-income elderly, Medicare may be out of reach even though Medicare Part A has no monthly premium for persons who are eligible for the program. Some older persons simply cannot afford the deductible and copayments in the Medicare program. The Qualified Medicare Beneficiary (QMB) program is designed to help them.

In the QMB program, state governments pay the Medicare premiums, copayments, and deductibles for older persons who cannot afford these charges (U.S. Special Committee on Aging 1991). Persons receiving Supplemental Security Income (SSI) are usually eligible for the QMB program.

Inconsistent Denials for Medicare Claims

As important as Medicare is to older people in the United States as a form of universal health-care coverage, Congressional hearings in 1994 pointed out the troubling inconsistent denials of payments for medical procedures under Medicare across the nation.

To get a better understanding of how the Medicare program actually works, it is important to know that it is administered by the Health Care Financing Administration (HCFA) within the Department of Health and Human Services, which sets up the regulations and policies for the program.

To operate Medicare Part B (physician services, outpatient hospital services, some home health services, diagnostic tests and medical equipment), HCFA contracts with thirty-four private insurance carriers to process and issue benefit payments. During fiscal year 1993, these carriers processed about 576 million Part B claims from about 780,000 physicians and 136,000 suppliers (Chelminsky 1994).

According to an opening statement by Congressman Ron Wyden, chairman of the Committee on Small Business of the U.S. House of Representatives which investigated this problem, high-school graduates without medical training, working for these private insurance carriers, process a new Medicare claim every 72 seconds, 8 hours a day (U.S. House of Representatives Committee on Small Business 1994).

In fiscal year 1993, these processors denied 112 million Part B claims in whole or in part. These denials represented 19 percent of all claims, totaling $17 billion or 18 percent of all billed charges. Some of these claims were correctly denied; they include duplicate claims, ineligible claimants, missing information, and other obvious characteristics that would disqualify them. Other denials deal with medically necessary procedures for patients for which the thirty-four private carriers are given broad latitude. They have been given the primary responsibility for defining the criteria that are used to determine the medical necessity of claims (Chelminsky 1994). It is at this point that there are great discrepancies in claims denials across the nation due to the independent and arbitrary judgments by each of the thirty-four private insurance carriers who administer the Medicare program.

Indeed, a survey in 1993 of the seventy-one most used and costly medical services across six insurance carriers administering the Medicare program was conducted by the U.S. General Accounting Office (GAO). They found a wide range of what was approved for payment among each of the regions. For example, an older woman whose doctor prescribed a mammogram to detect breast cancer was 180 times more likely to have her Medicare claim denied if she lived in southern California than if she resided in northern California. If a physician ordered a chest X-ray to rule out lung cancer, the Medicare claim for this X-ray was 500 times more likely to be denied in Illinois than in South Carolina (U.S. House of Representatives Committee on Small Business 1994).

Reversing Denials of Medicare Claims

Older people across the nation and their families are often bewildered and depressed by the denial of Medicare claims for health services they and their doctors think are absolutely necessary. What can they do? In testimony before the U.S. House of Representatives, the Hotline Director of the Medicare Beneficiaries Defense Fund said there is hope. The Medicare Beneficiaries Defense Fund (MBDF) is a not-for-profit organization that works to provide equal access to quality health care for seniors and people with disabilities on Medicare. MBDF contends that Medicare carriers are denying coverage to Medicare patients in an "arbitrary and irrational manner" (U.S. House of Representatives Committee on Small Business 1994).

Testimony by the Hotline Director indicated that some two-thirds of all claims that are appealed result in the claim being paid, but only 2 percent of all claims that are denied are appealed for an initial review. Claims that are appealed two and three times resulting in second- and third-level reviews also result in about a 60 percent chance of reversal leading to additional benefits.

The lesson is clear: If Medicare claims are denied, it may be necessary to appeal as many as three times if a Medicare participant believes that his or her claim is proper. The chances of winning at one of these levels is excellent.

Medicare and Lifestyle

In recent years there has been considerable discussion over the spiraling costs of the Medicare program—how much more it is costing each year; when the Medicare Trust Fund will run out of money without changes in funding; how costs can be curtailed—leading to debates over the equity of age-based programs and to intergenerational tensions.

On April 11, 1994, the trustees of the Medicare Hospital Insurance Trust Fund warned that the Medicare program would run out of money, given its current spending pattern, in 7 years (Merrill, Fox, and Chang 1994). The expenditures of the Medicare program, which pays for a vast majority of the hospital costs for the elderly and the disabled, continue to grow much faster than the revenues paid into the fund.

Trying to cope with this crisis usually involves proposals to raise taxes to boost revenues or to cut benefits. Little effort has been focused on how to keep older people healthier and thereby avoid many hospitalizations. A major study of the impact of substance abuse on the Medicare program by the Center on Addiction and Substance Abuse at Columbia University in 1994 found that in 1994 alone, substance abuse and addiction added $20 billion to inpatient Medicare hospital costs (Merrill et al. 1994). From 1994 through 2001, substance abuse is projected to cost Medicare almost $170 billion. From 1994 through 2014, a 20-year period. Medicare is projected to pay out more than $1 trillion for hospital care directly related to substance abuse. It is clear that if substance abuse were not a cost factor, there would be no financial crisis for the Medicare Hospital Trust Fund.

Smoking and Medicare

With nearly one out of four (23 percent) dollars paid by Medicare for inpatient hospital care related to substance abuse, it is easy to see that reducing or eliminating substance abuse would provide major savings to the Medicare program. Substance abuse primarily focuses on the use and abuse of alcohol, drugs, and tobacco. The Columbia University study found that more than sixty health conditions were related to substance abuse covering just about every major disease category. For those on Medicare, more than half of hospital admissions were for cardiovascular diseases, 15 percent were for respiratory diseases, 12 percent were for neoplasms (tumors), and 7 percent for burns and accidents in 1991 (Merrill et al. 1994).

More than 80 percent of all the Medicare costs for hospital stays that were the result of substance abuse (alcohol, drugs, and tobacco) was for treating medical conditions directly related to smoking by current and former smokers. These medical conditions ranged from lung cancer to chronic pulmonary obstruction disease to coronary artery disease. It was found that the Medicare population was at a much higher risk for getting diseases that were the result of smoking because people 65 and older who smoked tended to have smoked for longer periods of time than younger persons and were heavier smokers. Almost three out of five (58 percent) current smokers who were on Medicare, and about one-third of former smokers (32.7 percent) who were on Medicare averaged more than ten cigarettes per day for 35 years (Merrill et al. 1994).

By the end of 2001, when the Medicare trust fund has been projected to run out of money, $128 billion of Medicare inpatient hospital costs will be the direct result of cigarette smoking. More than 36 percent of persons who are in the Medicare program are former smokers. Nearly 20 percent of the Medicare recipients were smoking in 1994 (Merrill et al. 1994). Addressing the prevalence of smoking among the elderly, Joseph Califano, Jr., former Secretary of Health, Education, and Welfare, stated in testimony before Congress that the cigarette companies in the early 1960s knew that nicotine was addictive and that smoking caused cancer and heart disease but withheld their knowledge in order to keep selling cigarettes (U.S. House of Representatives Subcommittee on Health and the Environment 1994). Califano pointed out that if the American people had known about the deadly effects of cigarette smoking thirty years ago, hundreds of thousands of premature deaths and billions of dollars in health care costs related to diseases brought about by smoking could have been avoided.

What about the present and the future? What if Medicare recipients stopped smoking? Smoking is the single largest drain on the Medicare program. Smoking-related illnesses resulting in hospital stays are projected to cost the Medicare program $800 billion from 1994 to 2014 (U.S. House of Representatives Subcommittee on Health and the Environment 1994). Abuse of alcohol, drugs, and tobacco will cost the Medicare program more than one trillion dollars over the same period.

Obviously, not everyone who smokes is going to quit. They are addicted to nicotine. What would happen if a certain percentage of smokers quit their habit? It is estimated that between 1965 and 1993, Medicare spent $128 billion on hospital inpatient care as a result of the use of tobacco by Medicare beneficiaries (U.S. House of Representatives Subcommittee on Health and the Environment 1994). If only 10 percent fewer people had smoked during those years, the Medicare program would have saved some $13 billion.

Projecting to the future, if only 10 percent of Americans who smoke quit smoking, the savings would be $80 billion for Medicare hospital costs between 1994 and 2014. If 20 percent of the smokers quit, the savings would double—$160 billion (U.S. House of Representatives Subcommittee on Health and the Environment 1994).

Although there has been increased impetus to point out the dangers to health from tobacco use, especially from U.S. Surgeon Generals' reports and some Congressional subcommittees, the Center on Addiction and Substance Abuse at Columbia University has argued that the United States has not yet made a major commitment to address the problem of substance abuse (Merrill et al. 1994). Their research pointed out that the United States in 1994 was the only industrialized nation among the group surveyed that had a tobacco tax that amounted to less than 50 percent of the cost of a pack of cigarettes. U.S. taxes for a package of cigarettes only averaged about 30 percent. In addition, of nineteen countries rated for control of all forms of advertising of tobacco products, the United States ranked eighteenth (MacKenzie, Bartecchi, and Schrier 1994). As the Columbia University study on this issue concluded:

> The future solvency of the Medicare Trust Fund is inextricably intertwined with what we do *today* to reduce substance abuse in all its forms—among our citizens. Preventing diseases that result from substance abuse and prolonging a healthy life for the elderly can be a much more potent weapon against rising Medicare expenditures than the multitude of other, more frequently discussed cost-containment measures or benefit reductions. If there were no substance abuse, the Trust Fund's solvency would not be in doubt for almost twice the period than the Trustees are now projecting (Merrill et al. 1994: 10–11).

As this study pointed out, ignoring the impact of substance abuse, and not putting major emphases on prevention and treatment of such abuse, impacts more than the financial future of the Medicare program. It impacts all health care issues as the nation continues to wrestle with health-care reform and universal access (Merrill et al. 1994).

"MEDIGAP" INSURANCE

Because Medicare has gaps in coverage as well as copayments, many Medicare-eligible people purchase *medigap insurance*. This is insurance that covers some or all of the gaps and copayments of Medicare, depending on the coverage of the policy. Until July 30, 1992, the medigap insurance market was very confusing, with hundreds of policies available. Older people and their families were routinely misled and confused by

the wide array of insurance products in this category. It was not uncommon for the elderly to purchase overlapping and duplicating policies. In the process, countless older adults wasted their money on policies they did not need or which were not useful.

Legislation to standardize medigap policies went into effect in 1992, setting up ten standard supplemental plans, each covering specific items not covered by Medicare, as shown in Table 17-1.

Each of the ten standardized policies must cover specific expenses that are not covered by Medicare. The *A* policy is the lowest cost. The *J* policy is the most expensive. Each letter policy must cover the same items regardless of the company. With this system, consumers can compare the costs of the policies with the same coverage (Rowland 1992).

Included in the legislation that established the ten standard policies is the provision that a policy a person chooses is guaranteed renewable for life (Rowland 1992). However, if a person wants to change policies, he or she can be denied coverage because of a health condition. (See Table 17-1.)

PAYING FOR PRESCRIPTION DRUGS

One of the biggest gaps in the Medicare program is the coverage of prescription drugs. Various studies released in 1992 indicated that millions of older persons in the United States were not getting the prescription drugs they needed to maintain their lives. These studies were from the American Association of Retired Persons, Families USA, and the U.S. Senate Special Committee on Aging (1993).

These reports all pointed out that many older Americans are not able to buy the prescription drugs they need because of the lack of public and private insurance coverage for drugs and the continuing increases in the prices of drugs. Prescription drug prices increased almost three times the rate of the general inflation rate between 1980 and 1990 (U.S. Senate Special Committee on Aging 1993).

TABLE 17-1

STANDARD MEDICARE SUPPLEMENT PLANS

10 Standard Medicare Supplement Benefit Plans

Core Benefits	Plan A	Plan B	Plan C	Plan D	Plan E	Plan F	Plan G	Plan H	Plan I	Plan J
Part A Hospital (Days 61–90)	X	X	X	X	X	X	X	X	X	X
Lifetime Reserve (Days 91–150)	X	X	X	X	X	X	X	X	X	X
365 Life Hosp. Days—100%	X	X	X	X	X	X	X	X	X	X
Parts A and B Blood	X	X	X	X	X	X	X	X	X	X
Part B Coinsurance—20%	X	X	X	X	X	X	X	X	X	X
Additional benefits	**A**	**B**	**C**	**D**	**E**	**F**	**G**	**H**	**I**	**J**
Skilled Nursing Facility Coinsurance (Days 21–100)			X	X	X	X	X	X	X	X
Part A Deductible		X	X	X	X	X	X	X	X	X
Part B Deductible			X			X				X
Part B Excess Charges						100%	80%		100%	100%
Foreign Travel Emergency			X	X	X	X	X	X	X	X
At-Home Recovery				X			X		X	X
Prescription Drugs								1	1	2
Preventive Medical Care					X					X

Core Benefits pay the patient's share of Medicare's approved amount for physician services (20%) after $100 annual deductible, the patient's cost of a long hospital stay ($163/day for days 60–90, $326/day for days 91–150, all approved costs not paid by Medicare after day 150 to a total of 365 days lifetime), and charges for the first 3 pints of blood not covered by Medicare.

Two prescription drug benefits are offered: 1. a "basic" benefit with $250 annual deductible, 50% coinsurance and a $1,250 maximum annual benefit (Plans H and I above), and **2.** an "extended" benefit (Plan J above) containing a $250 annual deductible, 50% coinsurance and a $3,000 maximum annual benefit.

Each of the 10 plans has a letter designation ranging from *A* through *J*. Insurance companies are not permitted to change these designations or to substitute other names or titles. They may, however add names or titles to these letter designations. While companies are not required to offer all of the plans approved for sale by the individual states, they all must make Plan A available if they sell any of the other nine in a state.

Source: National Association of Insurance Commissioners and the Health Care Financing Administration. 1992. 1992 Guide to Health Insurance for People with Medicare. Washington, D.C.: U.S. Department of Health and Human Services, p. 14.

Every year, some 75 percent of all elderly persons need prescription drugs. The costs of the drugs not covered by Medicare can easily run into the hundreds or thousands of dollars per year. One in five older persons needs at least $500 a year in prescription drugs. For three out of four older persons, drug costs make up their highest out-of-pocket expenses (U.S. Senate Special Committee on Aging 1993). Looking at the medigap insurance plans that have been standardized since 1992, a plan that includes prescription drugs is one of the most expensive, and out of the reach of many older persons.

One of the most important reasons that prescription drugs are so expensive for older persons is that they are taken on a long-term basis for chronic health conditions. This is in contrast to many younger persons who need prescription medicines for an acute, short-term condition such as an infection. It is not uncommon for older persons to have multiple chronic conditions that require multiple prescriptions, for example, hypertension, arthritis, glaucoma, diabetes, and heart disease. In fact, every drug included in the list of the twenty most used drugs by older persons in the Families USA study of prescription drugs and older people, is for chronic, long-term health conditions (U.S. Senate Special Committee on Aging 1993).

Because of ever-increasing prices, the fact that prescription medicines are not covered by Medicare and many other plans, and that so many older persons require long-term drugs, over five million older persons say that they have to choose between buying enough food and paying for their prescription drugs. With the average cost of medicines for older persons at $879 in 1992, it is easy to understand why choosing between eating properly and buying all the prescriptions needed is an impossible choice for so many older people (National Medical Expenditures Survey data in U.S. Senate Special Committee on Aging 1993). Of course, the hardest hit in buying prescription drugs are older people in the lowest income categories, as many do not qualify for Medicaid, the medical assistance program for impoverished people of all ages. Lower-income people can easily spend about 20 percent of their income for medicines.

Many private insurance plans do not include prescription drug coverage because of the rapidly rising costs of drugs. One major exception is employment-based health plans for current and retired workers who have drug coverage as part of their benefits package. These have various levels of copayments. Of the medigap policies that can be purchased by older people to supplement Medicare, only three of the standardized plans include drug coverage. However, even these may require deductibles and copayments that still result in substantial out-of-pocket expenses. President Clinton's initial universal health proposal included adding prescription drug coverage. In this proposal, Americans of all ages, including Medicare recipients, would pay the first $250 (deductible) for medicines each year. Then they would pay 20 percent of the cost of prescriptions. Specifically for Medicare beneficiaries, after they spent $1,000 in deductibles and copayments in a year, the health plan would cover all drug costs for the rest of the year (Hey 1993).

Some states, realizing the burden of prescription drugs on the lives of many older people, have enacted their own prescription-drug assistance programs. Michigan is one state where older residents who meet income guidelines can get assistance in the form of rebates. It is called the Michigan Emergency Pharmaceutical Program (*Aging in Michigan* 1991).

MANAGING PRESCRIPTION DRUGS

As important as affording prescription drugs is to older people, the management of drugs (prescribing, giving, and taking medicines) is equally vital to their well-being. In 1990, people aged 60 and older made up some 17 percent of the population of the United States. This 17 percent received 39 percent of all prescription drugs in the nation (Lamy 1991). As we have already noted, it is common for elderly people to take several drugs on a long-term basis.

Dr. Peter Lamy, director of the Center for the Study of Pharmacy and Therapeutics of the University of Maryland School of Medicine, pointed out that the use of multiple drugs by the elderly is the most important reason for adverse reactions and interactions (Lamy 1991). He indicated that these adverse reactions occur nine million times each year. This is due to elderly patients going to different doctors and not telling each doctor about other medications they are taking. Dr. Lamy also contended that a majority of health-care providers are not trained in geriatrics and do not have an understanding of the complexities of the aging process, how it affects body metabolism, and how substances are excreted from the body. Dr. Lamy cited research that pointed out that the vast majority of illnesses caused by adverse drug actions and interactions come from prescribing the wrong drug (if a drug is needed at all) or the wrong dose of the drug in elderly patients.

Another cause of adverse drug interactions is the mix of prescription and nonprescription drugs. About 40 percent of all the drugs that are administered in nursing homes are nonprescription drugs. For the elderly living in the community, the mix of prescription and nonprescription drugs is about even. Dr. Lamy (1991) contended that physicians often do not either take into account or provide for patients taking the two classes of drugs at the same time.

A crucial factor in the management of prescription drugs is the use of alcohol. Excessive or long-term use of alcohol in combination with many medicines can have serious negative effects. About one-half of all drugs used to treat chronic health conditions interact with alcohol. These interactions can negatively affect almost every organ system of the body (Lamy 1991). It is usually not easy to persuade a patient using prescription drugs and alcohol to stop. It is, however, one of the most important things a caregiver can do.

While he was head of the Department of Health and Human Services, Secretary Louis Sullivan stated that the primary drug-safety issue for the 1990s is related to polymedicine (many medicines) for older people with chronic health conditions (Lamy 1991). To effectively address this issue calls for a preventive approach which includes education for consumers as well as their caregivers.

Long-Term Prescription Drug Use

Using prescription drugs on a long-term basis may result in the depletion of certain vital nutrients. Drugs can change a patient's intake of food because some foods taste differently when certain medicines are used. This may lead to undernourishment. Even in the marginally undernourished elderly, the effects of drugs may change. This can result in overmedication if the body weight of the patient is not taken into account when drugs are prescribed (Lamy 1991). It is important that the patient taking medicines and the caregiver be on the lookout for symptoms of malnutrition. This is vitally important because some experts have contended that up to 50 percent of home-care patients may be marginally undernourished (Lamy 1991). Undernourishment is directly related to diseases and infections.

Although there is general agreement that drugs are the most cost-effective way to manage chronic diseases, the research has found that drugs head the list of disease simulators (Committee on Safety of Medicines 1985).

In order to prevent adverse outcomes of prescription drug use, the patient and the caregiver of an elderly person should ask the following questions:

- Is drug or non-drug therapy best?
- If a drug is used, what is the right dose?
- What good results can be expected?
- What are the side effects?
- Can the patient tolerate the side effects?
- Will the drug interfere with other drugs being taken, exercise, or diet?
- Is the drug affordable?
- Who will monitor the effects of the drug?
- When will the use of the drug be assessed?
- When and under what conditions can the drug be stopped? (Lamy 1991).

All of this takes effort, education, follow-up, and time by the patient, the physician, the pharmacist, and the family or institutional caregiver. The University of Maryland, for example, has established a range of educational programs for medication management for elderly persons themselves, caregivers, health-care providers, and pharmacists (Lamy 1991).

DOCTORS AND OLDER PEOPLE

Dr. Peter Lamy pointed out that not many physicians are trained in geriatrics. In testimony before the U.S. Congress in 1992, Dr. Robert Butler, professor and chair of the geriatrics department of the Mount Sinai School of Medicine, pointed out that there is a major shortage of geriatricians in practice as well as professors of geriatrics in medical schools to train new doctors in this field (U.S. House of Representatives Select Committee on Aging 1992a).

In 1992, there were only 4,084 primary-care physicians in the United States certified in geriatrics. This was more than 15,000 short of the number needed for the older population at that time. By the year 2030, if the current rate of growth of the older population continues, 36,000 geriatricians will be needed (U.S. House of Representatives Select Committee on Aging 1992a). It will be difficult to train the needed number. In 1992, there were about 500 people with the combination of medical, academic, and scientific training to fulfill these roles in medical schools. Of the 126 medical schools in the United States, only thirteen required courses or clinical experience in geriatrics or aging. Not only is there a current major shortage of geriatric physicians, but with a significant shortage of medical school faculty equipped to teach geriatric medicine, the shortage is likely to become worse.

Why Is Geriatric Medicine Important?

If the United States already has a lot of doctors, particularly specialists (only 30 percent of the nation's physicians are primary-care doctors), why are geriatricians important to a nation whose people are growing older? To answer this question, it is first important to know what geriatrics and geriatric medicine are. By Dr. Robert Butler's definition,

> Geriatrics, as a medical discipline, applies the findings from aging research to intervene in the chronic disabilities of aging. Proper geriatric care helps older patients maintain the highest possible degree of function and independence and avoid unnecessary costly institutionalization. . . . As older people tend to suffer from multiple conditions, a geriatrician can assist the patient by assessing and distinguishing disease from the normal physiological changes associated with aging. For the patient, this results in a more accurate diagnosis of illness and a greater degree of self esteem. A key tenet of geriatrics is a realization that aging is not a disease. As a result, the geriatrician urges the family members and society at large not to dismiss the health complaints of older people because of age (U.S. House of Representatives Select Committee on Aging 1992a: 21).

Dr. Butler went on to point out that acute problems often occur on top of one or more chronic diseases in older people. As a result, diseases often appear differently in the elderly. As an example, he pointed out that appendicitis may not give the typical symptoms and signs in an older person.

The geriatric physician is able to treat an older person holistically—as a whole person looking at and distinguishing all of their chronic conditions, their medications, their surroundings, their support systems, their mental health, and their immediate needs. From these considerations an appropriate care plan for each patient can be developed. A care plan can also prevent further decline that could lead to emergency care or placement in an institution.

Geriatrics, according to Dr. Butler, is truly a primary-care specialty. It includes hospital care, office care, day care, nursing-home care, and house-call medicine. He went on to point out that unless a medical student in the 1990s goes into pediatrics, over half of his or her patients will be over the age of 65 once the new doctor starts practicing medicine.

As important as geriatric medicine and geriatric physicians are, it is also important for doctors in primary care and the subspecialties have some training in geriatrics.

> The unprecedented increase in the number and proportion of older people in our population makes a compelling case for integrating geriatrics within all primary care and specialty medicine (with the possible exception of obstetrics and pediatrics). . . . Geriatrics is on the cutting edge. It is the medicine of the future, and it is the new medicine emerging now (Butler 1986: 16).

Choosing a Doctor for Older People

How should an elderly person choose a doctor? Many older people have a doctor they like, a doctor with whom they feel comfortable. But many more reach their later years losing the physician they knew and trusted, for a number of reasons. Like them, their physician may have grown older and retired. Or, as many older people do, they may have moved to be nearer an adult child. Or their doctor may have joined a large group practice or health maintenance organization (HMO) where a patient might have to see any doctor on call. The older patient may develop a condition that requires expertise beyond the scope of his or her personal physician. Many older people and their adult family caregivers face the job of choosing a new physician. What should one look for in a physician for the elderly?

First and foremost is competence in dealing with the condition of the elderly patient. In some instances this may mean a specialist in a particular field. It may mean a physician trained in geriatric medicine. Because geriatricians are trained to look at the whole person, they are able to distinguish diseases from the normal physiological aging processes; they are able to treat acute diseases in combination with underlying chronic conditions; and they are aware of the implications of multiple prescription drugs.

Geriatric medicine minimizes consultation and referrals to multiple doctors (U.S. House of Representatives Select Committee on Aging 1992a). This does not mean that all consultations or referrals are excluded. Some are absolutely needed, such as biopsy examination and consultation. Dr. Burton, clinical Director of Geriatric Medicine at Johns Hopkins University, has contended that frail old people cannot be sent to multiple doctors in various locations.

Dr. Robert Butler contended that the primary-care geriatrician can be like a traffic cop, one who can bring together what is happening to the older patient and not unnecessarily refer older people to increasing numbers of consultations and specialists. Dr. Butler recalled a patient he saw in New York City who was in very good health at age 81. Someone routinely referred him to a gastroenterologist (a specialist in the diseases of the stomach and intestines) for a colonoscopy (examination of the large intestine using a long lighted instrument). Unfortunately, the man's colon was pierced, and he almost died. Dr. Butler went on to indicate that by overreferral to consultants, by referring to too many specialists, older patients may get into trouble (U.S. House of Representatives Select Committee on Aging 1992a).

What can a person use as a guide in choosing a doctor for elderly patients, especially if a geriatrician is not available? The following are some basic questions that can be raised:

- Does the doctor understand the aging process?
- Does he or she attribute most health problems of older people to "just getting old?"
- Has the doctor had any geriatric training in medical school?
- Does the doctor understand the importance of good nutrition for older people?
- Is the doctor willing to have second opinions for serious conditions without appearing threatened?
- Does the doctor understand and practice holistic health care, where the health of the total person is considered rather than only a specific complaint or problem?
- Is the physician willing to work with other doctors on a specific-need basis as necessary?
- Does the physician appear to have experience in dealing with older people?
- Does the physician have an adequate understanding of the community-based support networks that are usually available to assist older people in their special needs of daily living?
- Is the doctor someone the older patient and the caregiver can work with to provide care and assistance? (Riekse and Holstege 1992: 41).

A caring doctor for an elderly patient will take the time for a thorough exam and will clearly point out what the problems are. An appropriate physician will listen carefully to the patient without appearing to be in a hurry. Explaining slowly and carefully the courses of treatment, including drugs, their expected outcomes, and their possible side effects, is important.

If an older patient goes to more than one physician, it is important that each doctor know about the others and the prescription drugs that have been ordered. As much as possible, it is beneficial to choose a doctor with whom the older patient feels relatively comfortable. How a physician relates to a patient is a personal matter and takes some evaluation.

There will be times when a specialist is needed. How can these be selected? Often, referrals are made from the primary-care physician. County medical societies, local hospitals, health agencies, and consumer organizations are also information sources (U.S. Senate Special Committee on Aging 1991).

Beginning in 1991, all telephone directories include a listing in the Yellow Pages of board certified specialists (U.S. Senate Special Committee on Aging 1991). This list is divided by specialty.

In addition, there is a toll-free number (1-800-776-2378) that can be called to check whether a physician is certified to practice in the specialty under which his or her name is listed. This information and telephone line are under the direction of the American Board of Medical Specialists. Qualified specialists can also be checked through a state licensing board for each specialty (U.S. Senate Special Committee on Aging 1991).

NUTRITION AND OLDER PEOPLE

No discussion of medical care and older people can exclude the importance of proper nutrition. Good nutrition is important to everyone, but it is particularly important to older people. It directly relates to their health and health care. According to Dr. Susan Calvert Finn, head of the American Dietetic Association, in hearings before the U.S. House of Representatives in 1992, older persons are at a major risk of malnutrition due to a number of factors.

- Decreased body organ function affects the absorption, movement, metabolism, and elimination of nutrients.
- Decreased physical mobility and dexterity lessen a person's ability to access, prepare, and eat food.

- Poor dental conditions—50 percent of Americans age 65 and older have lost their teeth and many others have teeth in poor condition or have poorly fitting dentures. This severely limits food choices and food intake.
- Multiple prescription drug use—many drugs interfere with digestion, absorption, and elimination of nutrients, which leads to nutrient deficiencies.
- Social isolation and loneliness can result in loss of appetite and unwillingness to prepare adequate meals leading to malnutrition.
- Poverty or near-poverty conditions force millions of elderly persons to choose between heating and eating, housing expenses and enough food, and prescription drugs and proper nutrition.
- Diminished senses (sight, smell, and taste) affect nutritional intake and nutritional health (U.S. House of Representatives Select Committee on Aging 1992b: 51–52).

There is a greater likelihood of chronic health conditions among the elderly. It is common for people as they grow older to have multiple chronic conditions. Osteoporosis, atherosclerosis, diabetes, hypertension, and cancer are some of the conditions older people experience. Nutrition is linked to the prevention and treatment of many of these chronic conditions (U.S. House of Representatives Select Committee on Aging 1992b).

According to Dr. Finn, studies have indicated that up to 50 percent of all older people living independently in communities have specific nutritional deficiencies (U.S. House of Representatives Select Committee on Aging 1992b). Too often, people confuse the signs of malnutrition with the signs of aging. For example, an older person who is dehydrated and malnourished can appear confused and disoriented. This could be viewed as senility instead of the nutritional problem it is. The result of unrecognized or untreated malnutrition, according to Dr. Finn, is often considerable disability, longer hospital stays, reduced quality of life, and in some instances, increased health care cost and premature death (U.S. House of Representatives Select Committee on Aging 1992b).

Older persons with long-term malnutrition often die from infections, the most common of which are pneumonia and urinary sepsis (a toxic condition resulting from the spread of bacteria from the source of infection). Malnourished persons admitted to hospitals have more pressure ulcers than those who are not malnourished. Studies have shown that malnourished older patients require 5.6 more days in the average hospital stay, and the hospital costs of malnourished elderly patients are four times higher than those of older people who are not malnourished (U.S. House of Representatives Select Committee on Aging 1992b).

On the positive side, properly nourished patients have decreased disability, decreased death rates, wounds that heal faster, fewer infections, fewer secondary medical complications, and shorter hospital stays. Older people suffering from diabetes who get proper nutrition services control their disease better and have fewer hospital admissions (U.S. House of Representatives Select Committee on Aging 1992b).

Adequate nutrition services for the elderly include screening, assessment, and counseling as well as adequate nutrition intake. All of these are important because many older people have only a limited understanding of proper nutrition, proper dietary supplements, the interaction of drugs and food, and the good sources of food to meet their nutrition requirements (U.S. House of Representatives Select Committee on Aging 1992b).

Older people have access to nutritional services (screening, assessment, counseling, and therapy) through parts A and B of the Medicare program, state Medicaid home and community-based services waiver program, and the food programs of the Administration on Aging, which also provide meals five or more days a week in group or home settings. Dr. Finn, in the same Congressional hearings where these services were outlined by the director of the Bureau of

Policy Development, Health Care Financing Administration, pointed out that these nutrition services were inadequate. She went on to relate how the University of Michigan Hospital Nutrition Counseling Center estimates that every day three or four older persons refuse nutrition services because they cannot afford the cost. The hospital accepts Medicare payments, but the local carrier will not pay for nutrition services. As a result, the very services that would help them maintain their health, independence, and quality of life are not available. These screenings, assessment, and counseling services are not separately billable through Medicare.

Another problem with nutrition and the elderly is that there are no definite guidelines concerning the actual nutritional needs of older people (York 1992). According to the U.S. General Accounting Office, traditional nutritional research has been primarily focused on the needs of younger adults. It was assumed that what applied to them carried over to the elderly. However, as researchers learn more about nutrition as well as the aging process, it is becoming more evident that the nutritional needs of older persons are different from those of younger people. In addition, the conditions and needs of persons within the elderly population (persons aged 65 and older) are quite different. Similarly, the nutritional needs of a 65-year-old are quite different from those of an 85-year-old (York 1992). For example, the Food and Nutrition Board has established nutritional guidelines known as RDAs (recommended dietary allowances). They are defined as "the levels of intake of essential nutrients that, on the basis of scientific knowledge, are judged by the Food Nutrition Board to be adequate to meet the known nutrient needs of practically all healthy persons" (U.S. House of Representatives Select Committee on Aging 1992b: 33–34). But these RDAs do not take into account old-aged persons; the highest age category of RDA is for persons 51 years old. They are based on the needs of healthy adults and do not take into account the large percentage of older people who have chronic and acute health conditions. In addition, the RDAs do not take into account how prescription drugs interact with food to affect nutrition.

WHEN ENOUGH IS TOO MUCH

Truly we live in an age of medical miracles which have not only dramatically lengthened life but have also greatly improved the quality of life. Access to these medical benefits for older people through physician services, prescription drugs, hospitalization, and long-term care is the focus of many benefit programs. It is also the subject of many public policy debates.

However, in an age of unending expectations from the medical community for overcoming any number of major health conditions, the question still needs to be asked, When is medical treatment enough or appropriate in some circumstances and too much in others?

The following brief essay in *Newsweek* by a young medical specialist conveys the problems and frustrations of our current medical system in facing this question.

We Have Lost Our Humanity

Today is Saturday, and we are almost finished with office hours. I usually feel virtuous after working on Saturday. I am a doctor. Although I prefer to think of myself as a soldier fighting sickness, willing to sacrifice a precious weekend day for a noble cause, I admit that marketplace reality is largely responsible. Most working folks prefer to see their doctor on the weekend.

As I get ready to go home, my nurse hands me a note: "See Mrs. Jones in room 311 Today." Although I have already been to the hospital, it is my weekend on call, so checking on Mrs. Jones is my duty.

I call the hospital, and a nurse fills me in: "Eighty-eight-year-old lady with Alzheimer's transferred to the hospital from the nursing home with a fever and probable blood infection." She pauses. The situation didn't sound serious enough for a gastroenterologist like me to have

been called. "She's got a distended stomach; the internist had to put down a tube to relieve the pressure," the nursed added, sensing my puzzlement. "That must be it."

I inform her that I will be in to see the patient as soon as I finish in the office. At the hospital an hour later I look at the patient's X-rays before seeing her. She has a distended stomach and the tube is properly positioned. When I reach the floor the nurse greets me.

"She's not doing very well. I don't think she's going to make it." The nurse seems less concerned than I would expect. She notices my perplexed expression. "You see, Doctor, when I spoke to you I forgot to mention that she's a DNR [Do Not Resuscitate]. Came that way from the nursing home." So that was it: probably the patient's family, with the advice of the doctor at the nursing home, had made that decision rather than subject her to extensive, expensive and ultimately fruitless measures. But our health-care system won't allow this. And I've allowed myself to be made a pawn in the game.

I have seen this happen time and time again: a human being reaches the end of his or her life, but the family, or the nursing home, doesn't want the person to die there. *Too much trouble; there might be an investigation. So they ship the poor soul—often comatose and "pretzeled," as medical staff sometimes say, in the fetal position—to the hospital. The hospital calls in a specialist (like me) to protect itself from any possible malpractice charges. The specialist in turn orders all sorts of expensive tests, procedures, maybe even surgery. All of which gets billed to Medicaid, i.e., the taxpayers. It's a horror for the patient, a horror for the family and it's costing us all a fortune, money that could be better spent on lives that can be saved.*

"We've got to cover our asses, or they'll sue us or worse. The family wants everything done." We repeat this mantra of self-serving paranoia as we put our patients through paces that frequently serve only our own interests. I understand that if not for patients such as these many

hospitals would be mostly empty. I hear it every day but usually ignore the absurdity. I have become inured to a health-care system gone crazy because I have to function within it. I realize that if DNR meant "Do Not Reimburse" instead of "Do Not Resuscitate" far fewer of the terminally and hopelessly ill would receive pointless treatment.

If I were to suggest in this particular case that nothing be done to try to save this unfortunate woman, her doctor would probably call someone else, never call me again and consider me a troublemaker. My specialty in particular has a reputation, largely earned, for maximizing the dollar value of every patient while internists and family doctors, who work the longest hours, receive far less compensation than their specialist and surgical colleagues. Who was I to tell him that further tests were a waste of money? But if not me, then who?

'Already dead': *The nurse and I pass a half dozen rooms. The faces have no names and blur in my mind as we breeze by. Have I come to see them as human loaves of bread in the health-care supermarket? The anonymity of life in a nation of mass convenience seems even more appalling in these very human terms. I cannot look away. I slow down and examine the faces. Some are asleep; all have slipped closer to the end. Each is attached to at least one piece of technology, modern medicine's bulwark against death, replacing prayer, kindness and compassion. In the name of what? Money?*

Some of them will die alone, hands unheld, faces unstroked, sanitized. Why do we accept this expensive, inhuman set of circumstances? In coming so far it seems we have left some very important things behind.

The nurse reaches the patient's room before me. I have stopped walking. The nurse walks slowly from the room. "She's already dead, Doctor. Sorry." I also am sorry. Faxes, car phones, beepers, scanners, specialists skilled in the latest technology are wonderful. They save time and lives. And we can bill the government for them

because they are easier to quantify than judgment, compassion and kindness.

As I drive home I imagine I am standing on a podium before the entire nation. My speech contains the answers to all the problems that face health care in America. In my Utopia doctors will make enough money but not too much, striving always for what is best for their patients while keeping a vigilant eye on waste. The public will not only take on greater responsibility for their own health but will also come to understand the complexity and limitations of medical technology. The audience roars its approval for this sweeping vision.

I pull the car to the side of the road, next to a small park. It is a beautiful day, and for the moment, I've finished being a doctor. There's a bench near an old maple tree. As I step out of the car a warm breeze strokes my cheek and a tear makes its way across 40 years of hopes and dreams. I sit on the bench to enjoy the moment.

Source: Sam Brody, From *Newsweek,* September 7, 1992, p. 8. © 1992 Newsweek Inc. All rights reserved. Reprinted by permission.

Postmature Death

Until this century, untimely death most always referred to people dying young or relatively young—"dying before their time" (Phipps 1989). Obviously, this still occurs today. A child contracts a fatal disease and dies; a college student collapses on the ballfield and dies; a young mother has cancer that ends her life before her oldest child enters middle school.

Phipps indicated that deaths these days are more likely to be *postmature,* the death of old people whose human functioning had deteriorated irreversibly. He pointed out that thousands of people lie in American hospitals in comatose condition, being kept alive by extraordinary means:

> Their worn-out bodies may be ventilated artificially when no real hope of human life remains. Other comatose patients may be in essentially the same condition, except that the involuntary portion

of their brains are functioning enough to facilitate natural breathing (Phipps 1989: 144).

Why are postmature deaths so common today? Professor Phipps offers some reasons. First, resuscitation techniques have become more advanced and are more widely used. Although these procedures are vital in many, many instances, they can make it nearly impossible for some elderly persons to die at the proper time. Second, some physicians experience feelings of guilt over patient neglect or fear malpractice lawsuits if they do not try every way possible to continue some form of life. Third, private and public health-care funding tempts hospitals to continue to treat hopeless patients because of thousands of dollars of income from treating these patients.

Religious Implications

Theological considerations also play a role in postmature death. Some people believe that limiting heroic and extraordinary means to prolong life is "playing God," which is wrong because one then makes decisions which might shorten the maximum number of days of a person's life. As Phipps pointed out, "by this same logic, however, widely approved measures for extending life also can be viewed as 'playing God.' Scientific medicine and hygiene greatly have prolonged life beyond the average span of earlier centuries, and who would claim that such developments are wrong" (Phipps 1989: 145).

Limiting Medical Treatment

How, then, can a person deal rationally with these tough medical decisions—decisions that relate to postmature death? Phipps (1989) rejected outright mercy killings and suicide. He pointed out that there are generally approved ways to say medical intervention in a particular case is too much. Mentally competent persons have a right to refuse medication and medical intervention. This was decided in 1976 in a law suit in Florida by a 71-year-old man who was suffering from in-

curable amyotrophic lateral sclerosis (Lou Gehrig's disease) who wanted to be removed from a respirator.

Pope John Paul II addressed the issue of medical technology in 1980. He stated:

> When inevitable death is imminent in spite of the means used, it is permitted in conscience to take the decision to refuse forms of treatment that would only secure a precarious and burdensome prolongation of life. Such refusal is not the equivalent of suicide; on the contrary, it should be considered as an acceptance of the human condition . . . (Phipps 1991: 146).

To ensure the level of medical treatment people want, even if they become incompetent or too weak to make their wishes known, advance directives in the form of a "living will" or "medical durable power of attorney" can be drawn up ahead of a medical emergency. These are recognized by most states in various forms.

Both Gallup and Harris polls have indicated that some 80 percent of Americans favor withholding life support systems from terminally ill patients if that is what they want (Phipps 1991). In spite of popular support for withholding extraordinary medical supports from terminally ill patients, a 1993 study found that doctors and nurses often violate their personal beliefs and ignore patients' requests to withhold life support in such cases. In a survey of 1,400 doctors and nurses, nearly half of the attending physicians and nurses and some 70 percent of the resident physicians indicated that they overtreated terminally ill patients, even when there was no chance for recovery. In commentary accompanying this survey, Nancy Wereloff Dubler, a lawyer and bioethicist, indicated that the last days of many patients may not be as comfortable and pain free as good medicine could make them. Indeed, 81 percent of those surveyed pointed out that "the most common form of narcotic abuse in caring for dying patients is undertreatment of pain" (Brody 1993: 2B).

Making sure the patient is comfortable and as free of pain as is medically possible can be the best medical treatment. In the words of the ancient Israelite writer:

> There is a right time for everything:
> A time to be born, a time to die;
> A time to plant
> A time to harvest . . .
> A time to cry;
> A time to laugh;
> A time to grieve;
> A time to dance . . .

Ecclesiastes 3: 1, 2, 4. Scripture verses are taken from *The Living Bible* © 1971. Used by permission of Tyndale House Publishers, Inc. Wheaton, IL 60189. All rights reserved.

SUMMARY

Health care has been one of the most important issues facing our nation. It certainly has become one of the most pressing issues for older people. As people grow older, particularly into the oldest years, their need for medical care generally increases. Even though people are living longer, longevity does not necessarily translate into extended years without chronic health conditions.

There are two types of health conditions people face in life—chronic and acute. Chronic health conditions are those that are expected to be long-term or ongoing for the rest of a person's life. Acute conditions are relatively short-term and can be mild or very serious.

Chronic health conditions are major threats to the well-being of older persons. More than four out of five older people have at least one chronic health condition, and multiple chronic conditions are common among the elderly. Most older people are hospitalized as a result of an acute episode of a chronic health condition. Most visits to the doctor by older people are for chronic conditions.

All of this results in extensive use of medical resources by the elderly. While older people made up 12.5 percent of the population in 1990, they consumed about one-third of all health-care spending. The number of visits to the doctor generally increase with age, and older people are likely to have hospital stays twice as often as the rest of the population.

Medicare is the federal program that covers much of the acute medical costs of the elderly. To qualify for Medicare health coverage a person must be either (1) 65 years and older; (2) receiving Social Security benefits for 24 months or more; or (3) a person of any age who has end-stage kidney disease. Although the focus of Medicare is on the elderly, it is a multigenerational program.

Medicare coverage under Part A focuses on hospitalization for acute conditions, certain types of skilled nursing care, home health care, and hospice care. There is no long-term custodial coverage for long-term care as many people believe. There are no costs (premiums) for Medicare Part A if a person meets one of the three qualifications.

Medicare Part B covers part of physicians' services. How much a person pays depends on whether his or her physician is a participating doctor who accepts Medicare assignments or the rate nonparticipating physicians charge above the amount allowed by Medicare. In 1994, the charges were limited to 115 percent of approved Medicare fees.

The trustees of the Medicare Trust Fund in April 1994 projected that the fund would run out of money in seven years, in 2001. During that same seven years, $128 billion of Medicare inpatient hospital costs will be the result of the use of tobacco. More than 36 percent of Medicare beneficiaries in 1994 were former smokers, with nearly 20 percent current smokers in that year. One out of five hospital admissions paid for by the Medicare program has been the result of the abuse of alcohol, drugs, and tobacco. This accounts for 23 percent of all Medicare dollars for hospital stays. Eighty percent of the dollars Medicare spends on inpatient hospital stays as a result of substance abuse is directly attributed to the use of tobacco.

Between 1994 and 2014, substance abuse of alcohol, drugs, and tobacco is projected to cost the Medicare program one trillion dollars, with

$800 billion attributed to the use of tobacco alone. If just 10 percent of Americans who smoked quit in this 20-year period, there would be a savings of $80 billion to the Medicare program. A 20-percent decrease in smokers would result in reduction of $160 billion to the Medicare system. As a 1994 report by the Center on Addiction and Substance Abuse of Columbia University pointed out, the future health of the Medicare Trust Fund is tied directly to what the nation does today to reduce substance abuse, particularly cigarette smoking.

Medicare does not cover the cost of prescription drugs, which are so important to many older people due to chronic health conditions. To cover prescription drugs as well as other gaps in the Medicare program, many older people buy medigap insurance. Beginning in 1992, by law these policies have to conform to ten standard policy formats so consumers can know what they are buying and what they are paying for at each level of coverage.

Prescription drugs are vital to the treatment and management of both acute and long-term health conditions. Nevertheless, over five million older people each year say that they have to choose between eating adequately and their needed prescription drugs. Prices for medicines increased almost three times faster than the general inflation rate between 1980 and 1990. Because so many prescription drugs are taken on a long-term basis, the costs of these medicines greatly threaten the financial security of older people.

As important as being able to buy prescription drugs is managing them appropriately. Drug potencies and interactions can threaten the health of older people. Much needs to be learned about managing prescription drugs for the elderly. Using alcohol while using prescription drugs also can produce serious negative results.

An important component of the medical care of the elderly is choosing and working with a physician. Geriatricians are specially trained to practice medicine for older people. They can better distinguish diseases from the normal processes of aging. They have a better understanding of the use of prescription drugs in older bodies. Unfortunately, there is a real shortage of geriatricians that will extend into the twenty-first century.

Nutrition is a vital component of the overall health of older people. Proper nutrition can do much to preserve good health and to promote recovery from various diseases. Older people are at particular risk of suffering from malnutrition. This is due to a variety of reasons including decreased body organ function, decreased physical mobility, poor teeth or dentures, multiple prescription drug use, social isolation, poverty or near-poverty, and diminished senses (sight, smell, and taste).

Too often the signs of malnutrition among the elderly are confused with the signs of aging. Malnourishment in older people can lead to infections and other adverse health conditions as well as to more frequent and longer hospital stays. On the positive side, adequate nutrition for the elderly contributes to decreased disabilities, fewer infections, fewer secondary medical complications, and shorter hospital stays.

Despite all the marvelous advances in the quantity (longevity) and quality of life through the modern-day miracles of the basic sciences as applied to the practice of medicine and public health, end-of-life situations inevitably occur for everyone. Until the twentieth century, death was often premature, primarily resulting from infectious diseases and unsanitary conditions which ended the lives of many in infancy, childhood, young adulthood, or middle age. With ongoing scientific advances, longevity has increased considerably. Along with these advances is the development of a growing expectation that medical science can overcome almost any condition, or at least keep people alive.

We have reached a situation in which deaths are increasingly likely to be postmature—people kept alive artificially whose human functioning has deteriorated irreversibly. Many old people are hooked to respirators and other devices to maintain life even though without these extraordinary means they would have died a "natural" death. Issues surrounding these situations are legal, moral, theological, financial, and cultural in nature. Increasingly, people are recognizing that in situations where there is no hope of real revival, enough medical application in some situations is too much in others. There comes a time to call it quits in spite of the availability of advanced medical technology.

REFERENCES

Aging America: Trends and Projections. 1991. Prepared by the U.S. Senate Special Committee on Aging, American Association of Retired Persons, Federal Council on the Aging, and the U.S. Administration on Aging. Department of Health and Human Services Publication No. (FCOA 91-28001).

Aging in Michigan. 1991. Help with Prescription Drug Costs Now Available, 18(1): 11. Lansing, MI: Michigan Office of Services to the Aging.

Brody, J.E. 1993. Doctors, Nurses Admit They Ignore Wishes of Dying Patients. *New York Times.* In *Detroit Free Press,* (January 26): 2B.

Butler, R.N. 1986. Primary Care Geriatrics: Its Time Is Now. *Geriatrics,* 41(9): 16.

Chelimsky, E. 1994. *Medicare Part B: Inconsistent Denial Rates for Medical Necessity Across Six Carriers.* Washington, DC: U.S. General Accounting Office.

Committee on Safety of Medicines. 1985. CSM Update. *British Journal of Medicine,* (291): 46.

Hey, R.P. 1993. Clinton Unveils Health Plan. *NRTA Bulletin,* 34(9): 1, 12.

Kingson, E.R., and Berkowitz, E.D. 1993. *Social Security and Medicare: A Policy Primer.* Westport, CT: Auburn House.

Lamy, P.P. 1991. *The Geriatric Triangle.* The Beverly Lecture on Gerontology and Geriatrics Education. Presented at the 17th Annual Meeting of the Association for Gerontology in Higher Education. Pittsburgh, PA.

The Living Bible. 1971. Ecclesiastes 3: 1, 2, 4. Wheaton, IL: Tyndale House Publishers.

MacKenzie, T.D., Bartecchi, C.E., and Schrier, R.W. 1994. The Human Costs of Tobacco Use. *New England Journal of Medicine,* 330: 978.

Medicare for 1994. 1994. *Older Adult Health Quarterly.* Detroit, MI: Blue Cross and Blue Shield of Michigan.

Merrill, J., Fox, K., and Chang, H-H. 1994. *The Cost of Substance Abuse to America's Health Care System: Report 2: Medicare Hospital Costs.* New York: Center on Addiction and Substance Abuse, Columbia University.

National Hospital Discharge Survey, 1991. 1993. CASA Substance Abuse Epidemiologic Database.

Phipps, W.E. 1989. Health Technology vs. Death: Should We Prolong the Inevitable? *U.S.A. Today Magazine.* In Cox, H. (ed.), 1991. *Annual Editions: Aging,* 7th Ed. Sluice Dock, Guilford, CT: Dushkin Publishing Group, pp. 144–146.

Riekse, R.J., and Holstege, H. 1992. *The Christian Guide to Parent Care.* Wheaton, IL: Tyndale House Publishers.

Rowland, M. 1992. Making Sense of Medigap. *New York Times.* In *Detroit Free Press,* (July 21): 3B.

U.S. Bureau of the Census. 1993. Current Population Reports. Special Studies (P23-178 RV). *Sixty-Five Plus in America.* Washington, DC: U.S. Government Printing Office.

U.S. House of Representatives Committee on Small Business. 1994. *Public Dollars, Private Prerogatives: Lessons From Medicare for National Health Reform.* Washington, DC: U.S. House of Representatives.

U.S. House of Representatives Select Committee on Aging. 1992a. *Geriatricians and the Senior Boom: Precarious Present, Uncertain Future.* Washington, D.C.: U.S. Government Printing Office.

U.S. House of Representatives Select Committee on Aging. 1992b. *Adequate Nutrition for the Elderly.* Washington, D.C.: U.S. Government Printing Office.

U.S. House of Representatives Subcommittee on Health and the Environment of the Committee on Energy and Commerce. 1994. Statement of Joseph A. Califano, Jr., (May 17). Washington, DC: U.S. House of Representatives. 1994.

U.S. Senate Special Committee on Aging. 1991. *An Ounce of Prevention: Health Care Guide for Older Americans.* Washington, DC: U.S. Government Printing Office.

U.S. Senate Special Committee on Aging. 1993. *Developments in Aging: 1992.* Washington, DC: U.S. Government Printing Office.

York, R.L. 1992. Elderly Americans: Nutrition Information Is Limited and Guidelines Are Lacking. In U.S. House of Representatives Select Committee on Aging. Washington, DC: U.S. General Accounting Office.

CHAPTER 18

Long-Term Care

Diane: Forced To Be a Caregiver?

Peter and Diane have a close-knit family. Peter's mother, who lives two miles away, has been widowed for ten years and managed to take care of her own home. Everything was fine until she fell and broke her hip.

Peter's mother was hospitalized for a time, but being immobile and on medication made her chronic conditions worse. Her general health failed rather quickly, and Peter and Diane felt they should do something to help her until she was able to regain her strength. Peter's sister, Jane, lives on the other side of the state and spends most of her time caring for her injured husband. So where should Peter's mother go to recuperate? She can't go to Jane's, so are Diane and Peter expected to take her in?

Diane isn't ready to become a full-time caregiver. She wants to help, but she does not want to give up her job to stay home and care for Peter's mom. Peter and Diane need to find another solution, but they don't know where to look or whom to ask (Riekse and Holstege 1992: 158–159).

Bud and Gladys: The Quick Detour From Easy Street

Bud Hammack was a hard-working, honest American. For 30 years, he rammed sand into molds at the foundry, paid into Social Security, and put a nickel in the pension for every hour he worked. On weekends, he'd fix the house.

As for so many do-it-yourselfers, his home was his masterpiece. He was always digging through scraps of carpet and rusty doorknobs to add a flourish here and there. Tear out the walls, build walls. Stoke the fire in the wood stove. Save a little for the future.

By the time Bud was an old man, he and Gladys were pretty well set. "They thought, 'Gee, we're in wonderful shape. Our house is virtually paid off. We've got money in the bank. We owe nobody,' " said Mike Hammack, their youngest son. They figured they'd be able to leave their little green-shingled bungalow, worth about $50,000, to their three sons—Ron, Floyd, and Mike. Bud

thought this decision would be up to him and Gladys.

"Dad wanted to leave something to us," says Ron Hammack. "That was his big thing because he never got anything himself. I'd tell him, 'Why Dad, don't worry about it?' 'No,' he'd say, 'I want to'."

The first heart attack knocked Bud down in the aisle of the grocery store when he was 59. He picked himself up and walked home. Over the following years, subsequent heart attacks and surgeries weakened him, making it nearly impossible for him to care for his beloved Gladys, whose mind was fading just as surely as Bud's body was failing him. Finally when Gladys was diagnosed with Alzheimer's and needed 24-hour care, she moved to a nursing home and Bud moved in with his son Mike. Before he died, on Father's Day, 1992, Bud said he was ready to go.

The three sons figured they would inherit their father's masterpiece free and clear. Sadly, their mother would never be able to live in the house again. Not long after Bud's death, Ron Hammack received a letter from an attorney named Doug Fellows saying the state of Oregon was going to seize part of their parents' estate to reimburse Medicaid, the government program that had been paying for their mother's care in the nursing home.

The letter, triggered when the brothers tried to cash an $18,000 certificate of deposit in their father's name, came as a shock to the Hammacks. "This wasn't supposed to happen," Ron said. "I didn't understand it."

The Hammack brothers had done everything they could to protect their parents' assets from the exorbitant costs of their mother's nursing-home care. Following their attorney's advice, they had taken the house and savings out of their mother's name. But the state had found a flaw in the brothers' careful plans. They now faced losing the house that represented 40 years of work in the foundry and a lifetime of devotion.

"I just think it's cruel, it's terrible," said Floyd Hammack, a 56-year-old cab dispatcher." "I

think it's a crying shame my father and mother can work all their lives and then have this happen. I think they paid enough" (Ann Japenga 1993: 75–76. Condensed from Health, © *1993).*

WHAT IS LONG-TERM CARE?

Long-term care is a phrase that has become widely used in contemporary America. It "describes health care and other services that help people with disabilities and chronic illness. This includes people with diabetes, Alzheimer's disease, and others too frail to do many things for themselves" (*The Michigan Long-Term Care Reader* 1992: 3). The Special Committee on Aging of the United States Senate described long-term care as follows:

> . . . a wide array of services offered in a variety of settings ranging from institutional settings such as nursing homes to noninstitutional settings such as adult day care centers and a person's own home. Community-based long-term care typically involves a variety of noninstitutional health and social services such as home health care, homemaker, chore and personal services, occupational, physical and speech therapy, adult day care, respite care, friendly visiting, and nutrition and health education" (U.S. Senate Special Committee on Aging 1993: 198).

Another definition of long-term care is:

> . . . care given for a chronic illness or disabling condition over a continuous and long period of time. This care can include medical, social, housing, transportation, or other supportive services. These services can be provided by unpaid family members or friends (informal caregivers) or by specially trained and/or licensed professionals (formal caregivers). The care can be provided in the home, in special community-based programs, or in institutional settings (Rosen and Wilbur 1992: 2).

USERS OF LONG-TERM CARE

Persons needing long-term care include the elderly and nonelderly disabled, the developmen-

tally disabled (mostly the mentally retarded), and the mentally ill. However, older people are the primary users of long-term care services due to their high incidence of chronic illnesses (U.S. Senate Special Committee on Aging 1993). It is important to note that chronic conditions are often difficult to treat medically. Very often, treatment involves maintaining the status quo of the patient. When chronic conditions result in a person's inability to perform normal activities of daily living (ADLs: bathing, dressing, eating, getting in and out of bed, using the toilet), functional or activity limitations are the result. There is a second set of measures of independent living that are not as basic as ADLs. These are called *instrumental activities of daily living* (IADLs), which include shopping, cooking, cleaning, and taking medicines.

Studies have found a strong relationship between increasing age and the need for help with ADLs. Only 2 percent of persons under the age of 65 needed this kind of assistance compared with 9 percent of persons aged 65 to 69, and 45 percent of persons aged 85 and older (Harpine, McNeil, and Lamas 1990).

For each age category, women were more likely to need assistance than men. For persons aged 75 and older who were not living in institutions, 30 percent of the women needed assistance compared with 17 percent of the men. Elderly African Americans and Latinos were somewhat more likely to need daily assistance than whites.

The older people who needed assistance were more likely to live in households with lower incomes than the older persons who did not need assistance (U.S. Bureau of the Census 1984).

A 1990 analysis of data collected in the late 1980s concerning the number of people in the nation who were not in institutions but needed personal assistance with everyday activities indicated that 4.4 million elderly persons needed assistance with one or more activities of daily living (Harpine, McNeil, and Lamas 1990). Of that number, three in five (61.6 percent) were 75 years of age or older. When a broader definition of functionally dependent elderly is used, one that includes at least one ADL and seven IADLs, some 6.7 million noninstitutionalized elderly persons were counted (Hing and Bloom 1990). Add to the number of functionally dependent older people not living in institutions (nursing facilities) the 1.6 million elderly people residing in nursing homes in 1990, and the total swells to over 8 million people (U.S. Bureau of the Census 1990). Projecting into the future, a 1991 study in the *New England Journal of Medicine* reported that although on any given day only about 5 percent of the elderly population is in a nursing home, of those persons who turned 65 in 1990, 43 percent will spend some time in a nursing home before they die (Kemper and Murtaugh 1991). Projections indicate that the nursing home population will increase to 5.3 million elderly persons by the year 2030 (Pepper Commission 1990). Not only will there be more persons overall in nursing homes, but they will be older and have more severe limitations. In the years 2016 through 2020, 51 percent of nursing home residents will be 85 years of age or older, compared to 42 percent in 1986 through 1990 (Rivlin and Siener 1988).

It is important to realize that for every person aged 65 and older who lives in a nursing home, there are nearly twice as many who are not in nursing homes who need some form of long-term care. This long-term care in the community (outside of nursing homes) is provided mostly by informal, family caregivers (U.S. Senate Special Committee on Aging 1993).

LONG-TERM CARE OPTIONS

Long-term care can be provided in a variety of settings, from one's own home or the home of a relative or friend to a nursing home. In this section we will briefly outline various types of long-term care settings. More detailed descriptions of these resources and the implications of each, with the exception of home-based care, are contained in chapter 12.

In-Home Care

Long-term care in one's own home is mostly provided by family members, primarily women (wives, daughters, daughters-in-law). In home settings, care is provided weekly, daily, or around-the-clock, depending on the condition and need of each disabled older person.

An array of services are available in many communities to assist the disabled older person as well as the caregiver in carrying out their tasks. No government program provides for 24-hour, in-home care. Paying for specific in-home services can be tricky. Some are available at little or no cost depending on the service, how it is accessed, or if the recipient qualifies through programs of the Older Americans Act, Medicare, Medicaid, and state social service departments (*The Michigan Long-Term Care Reader* 1992). Usually local Area Agencies on Aging can assist in finding services that meet the needs of specific disabled older persons. These services include:

- *Case care management* is a program designed to assess the needs of an older person who needs assistance arranging for needed services.
- *Home health services*
  —Home nursing care includes services provided by a licensed nurse, including blood pressure readings, changing dressings, and administering medications
  —Personal care services include bathing, dressing, and meal preparation.
- *Homemaker/home chore services* help maintain the home, including laundry, shopping, and light housekeeping.
- *Home delivered meals* provide one or more meals a day, five to seven days per week delivered to an older person's home; also called "meals-on-wheels."
- *Home repair and maintenance* covers minor home repairs and improvements such as building wheelchair ramps, clearing drains, installing smoke detectors, and fixing roof leaks, faucets, toilets, and furnaces.

- *Friendly-Visitor Program* provides people who visit the home to check on the disabled person.
- *Telephone Reassurance Program* schedules regular calls to the home to check on the disabled person (*Michigan Long-Term Care Reader* 1992).

Additional Services Outside the Home

Some additional community-based services are offered to dependent older persons and their caregivers. Further discussion of some of these formal community services are found in chapter 16.

- *Adult daycare* is for persons who are able to get to the centers and who need daytime supervision, some medical services, and social activities.
- *Respite care* provides qualified substitute care to relieve the primary caregiver temporarily.
- *Congregate meals* are hot meals served at convenient locations in the community.
- *Transportation services* include rides to health-care appointments as well as other community destinations (*Michigan Long-Term Care Reader* 1992).

Assisted-Living Facilities

These facilities are described in detail in chapter 13.

Senior-Citizen Housing   A variety of facilities are available in this category. They may be called homes for the aged, continuing-care retirement communities, or senior villages, retirement homes. They may be privately funded and operated or subsidized by some governmental unit, or a combination of these. They may be large, high-rise buildings or single, detached units in a compound setting. The range of services provided depends on the type and purpose of the facility.

Board-and-care Homes/Adult Foster Care Homes   These facilities provide room and board for the aged, including special diets and supervision, and some personal care to adults who are frail but in generally good health.

Nursing Facilities/Homes   These service-based facilities are for persons who need more nursing and personal care than can be provided in their own homes, board-and-care homes, or homes for the aged. Both skilled and basic (intermediate or custodial care) levels of care are provided.

LONG-TERM CAREGIVING: A FAMILY AFFAIR

In the United States, long-term caregiving is for the most part a family affair. One study indicated that more than 27 million unpaid days of informal care—by wives, daughters, daughters-in-law, sons, and friends—are provided each week (U.S. Senate Special Committee on Aging 1993). For men living in the community who needed long-term care, 84 percent of their caregivers were relatives who provided 90 percent of days of care. For women in the community who needed long-term care, 79 percent of their caregivers were relatives who provided 84 percent of days of care. In the mix of caregivers who were relatives, more wives than husbands were caregivers, underscoring the realities that women outlive men by about seven years and that women tend to marry older men (*Aging America: Trends and Projections* 1991).

The commitment and amount of work these family caregivers were extensive. Some 64 percent of the caregivers indicated that they had given care for at least a year. Eighty percent had provided care seven days a week. They averaged some four hours of care a day. Of the more than one million caregivers who had jobs, about one-fifth (21 percent) had reduced their hours at work to have enough time to provide care. In addition, some 9 percent of the 2.2 million caregivers had quit their jobs to accommodate their caregiving (Stone, Cafferata, and Sangle 1987).

Family and Medical Leave Act of 1993

With increasing numbers of caregivers trying to deal with competing interests of jobs and relatives who need care, some relief has been provided by the Federal Family and Medical Leave Act that took effect on August 5, 1993. It provides for up to 12 weeks of unpaid leave each year to care for children, parents, or close relatives. The law guarantees the employee's job or an equivalent job when he or she returns to work, without loss of seniority or benefits (Rosica 1993). Although this law does not provide for the kind of relief long-term family caregivers need, it does give them an opportunity to provide full-time help in a crisis situation with family members for up to 12 weeks without losing their jobs or benefits. In that period they are given the opportunity to survey opportunities in the community for long-term assistance, or make whatever arrangements are necessary to continue care for their relatives, if needed.

Some companies provide additional weeks of leave along with assistance with elder care. Some of these programs make it unnecessary for workers to leave their jobs to help their aged relatives. For example, AT & T, as part of a collective bargaining agreement, provides unpaid leave along with a consultation and referral service for their employees who need assistance in finding care for their elderly relatives. Amoco has a program in which employees can get counseling to deal with the stresses of caregiving. This program also assists employees in finding services in the community for aged relatives. Concerning the new family leave law, Roberta Spalter-Roth, a sociologist at American University and an authority on work and the family stated, "The new law says all workers, regardless of their age or gender, have a responsibility not only to earn a living, but also to care for family members" (Rosica 1993: 5).

Caregiver Burnout

One of the reasons disabled older persons are eventually placed in nursing homes is the wearing down or collapse of their caregivers. It is not difficult to understand why these family caregivers burn out in their caregiving roles. Research since the 1960s has indicated that the primary caregivers of the dependent elderly are usually middle-aged daughters who mostly are married. Many of these women have entered the labor force. Increasingly they have found it difficult to juggle a number of roles—wife, mother, daughter, caregiver, and worker. Unfortunately, too many find trying to carry out all these roles at the same time leads to stress and physical exhaustion. As Abraham Monk, a professor of gerontology and social work pointed out, "There is virtually no end to the caregiving demands assumed by relatives. The burden is relentless and indefinite" (Monk 1988: 177). He went on to point out that caregivers are on call all the time. They sacrifice their own leisure interest and social life along with time spent with their immediate families. Many end up neglecting their own health, which results in their not being able to continue as caregivers.

In the fact of the dire consequences of caregiving for relatives who need long-term care, studies have clearly indicated that families do not flinch from providing care for dependent family members. Most families accept chronic conditions and impairment as a normal part of life and make adjustments accordingly (Kuypers and Bengston 1983; Noelker and Poulshock 1982).

Prospective Payment System and Family Care

In the mid-1980s, Congress instituted a new system to pay for hospital stays under Medicare. It is called the Prospective Payment System (PPS). Under this system hospitals are paid a predetermined rate based on a physician's diagnosis rather than what it actually costs to keep a Medicare patient, depending on their length of stay. Under the PPS, Medicare patients are classified into one of 487 diagnosis related groups (DRGs) based on the patient's diagnosis (U.S. Senate Special Committee on Aging 1993). The specific DRG determines the length of the patient's hospital stay. Hospitals are only paid for the precise number of days for each DRG. Research has indicated that under this system many patients are discharged "sicker and quicker" (Rosenback and Cromwell 1985). Tragically, many patients and their families are not aware that the hospital discharges in the prospective payment system can be appealed, nor do they know how to appeal. Patients are to be informed of their rights upon admission to a hospital. It is important to communicate with the patient's physician regarding all matters of the hospital stay, including discharge. If the patient is to be discharged and the patient or family disagree, a Notice of Non-Coverage should be requested. The hospital cannot charge the patient for care unless such a notice is received and the patient remained in the hospital after the specified date to be discharged (*Michigan Long-Term Care Reader* 1992). The next step is to immediately contact the State Peer Review Organization which is usually a private body funded by Medicare. Telephone numbers and addresses of these organization can be obtained from Long-Term Care Ombudsman Services throughout the United States or Area Agencies on Aging which are listed in most telephone books.

With many Medicare patients being discharged from hospitals "sicker and quicker," increased burdens are placed on family caregivers. In the mid-1980s, not long after the implementation of the DRGs and the prospective payment system, a U.S. General Accounting Office (1985) report indicated that home health agencies were increasing their frequency of visits per case, getting more requests for multiple visits per week, and finding more need for specialized services such as intravenous therapy and catheters. With many patients not qualifying for Medicare-supported home health services, or not finding these services, or not being able to afford them on a private-pay basis, the responsibility falls back on the family caregivers or what has been termed the "no-care zone." There are really no forms of assistance to families in the form of tax exemptions or direct compensation to help them pay for this family caregiving, unlike Sweden and Norway where cash payments have been made to relatives to provide care at home (Monk 1991).

Public Policy, Politics, and Family Caregiving

Gerontologists have pointed out that public policy in the United States regarding long-term care is based upon the willingness of family members to continue indefinitely as primary caregivers (Monk 1991). As has been indicated, families in America take enormous responsibilities in caring for elderly relatives. Does this willingness or sense of responsibility ever decline? Back in the 1970s, long before stories appeared about "granny dumping" or intergenerational competition over resources, a study in New York found that families' ability and willingness to continue to provide caregiving services at home dropped by 50 percent after the second hospitalization of an older relative (Eggert, Granger, Morris, and Pendleton 1977). As Abraham Monk pointed out, the average family is not insensitive or indifferent. Its role in caregiving of an elderly relative simply cannot be taken for granted indefinitely.

Most of our public policy regarding long-term care rests on family responsibility with little assistance to the family in carrying out these complex and demanding responsibilities. Overall, today's caregivers provide care that is much more physically and psychologically demanding than that of 1950. Projecting into the future, including the near future, with the ongoing advance of medical technology, the Census Bureau sees the duration of chronic illness and the need to help these chronically ill older people increase even more.

The heavy dependence on American families for long-term care is no accident of history. In their scholarly analysis of long-term care, Carroll Estes, Jane Swan, and associates (1993) traced the reversal of public policy in the early 1980s that promoted cuts in domestic programs, reduced federal responsibility, and increased family responsibility. Health planning and federal economic policy in the beginning of President Reagan's administration took a radical shift. The economic policies of the early Reagan era were based on the viewpoint that the nation's problems were caused by too much government and too much regulation. These policies were embodied in Reagan's "new federalism" which aimed to reverse the gains made in health and social welfare policy during the 1960s (Estes, Gerard, Zones, and Swan 1984). "New federalism" was to decrease the federal role in health and welfare by shifting responsibility to the state and local levels of government, or away from government entirely. Federal support for social services for the elderly and the disadvantaged took off in 1965 and peaked in 1978 (Estes, Swan, and associates 1993). There was some decline between 1978 and 1981, which set the stage for the larger cuts that wee to come in the first years of the Reagan administration. In the first two years of the Reagan presidency social services were cut by more than 20 percent (Estes 1991).

The Results of the DRGs and Social Service Cuts

As indicated previously, between 1983 and 1985 the Prospective Payment System (PPS), which instituted the Diagnostic Related Group (DRG) method of paying for Medicare, resulted in older patients being released from hospitals "sicker and quicker." Combined with the social service cuts of the 1980s, it is easy to understand that there were major changes in the way services are organized and delivered as part of community-based delivery systems. Estes and Swan (1993) pointed out that the data suggest that the community-based service system has been overloaded with patients who have major health needs. They have filtered down from the hospitals to all levels of the community-care system, including home health agencies, nursing homes, hospices, and adult-care centers. What has resulted is a widening gap between services that are available for the long-term care needs of older adults and the services that are needed by dependent older persons. This care gap has been termed the "no-care zone" by Estes and Swan. Elders caught in this "no-care zone" are forced to rely more and more on the caregiving efforts of families.

Why So Many Female Caregivers?

In looking at the enormous roles families in America play in long-term care as the result of public policy, we have already noted that most of this care (75 percent) is provided by women. Why is this? How did this come about? Elaine Brody (1990) pointed out that in virtually every culture the nurturing role is given to women. She indicated how the sexes learn different roles early in life. Girls are taught to be nurturers, nurses, homemakers, and kinkeepers in the family. Boys are encouraged to be "breadwinners." A daughter's identification with her mother is made stronger when she becomes a mother herself.

Brody went on to show that a female's role as caregiver is so deeply ingrained that most likely it never occurs to her that males (brothers) could become primary caregivers as well. When a son is the provider of parent care, "it is the wife, the daughter-in-law, who carries the responsibilities" (Brody 1990: 81). Brody described the typical family viewpoint in America of women's caregiving roles in the following story:

> An elderly women, following a stroke, moved into her daughter's home. The daughter had four siblings, two sisters, and two brothers. Describing how it happened that she became the main caregiver, the daughter said 'One of my sisters lives in Alaska, and the other is divorced and has to work.' When the interviewer asked 'What about your brothers?' The daughter replied in surprise, 'My brothers? Why would I give my mother to a daughter-in-law when she has daughters?' (Brody 1990: 81).

Brody cited another woman on caregiving: "Caregiving has been my whole life. As women, we're suited for that because we have that nurturing instinct. Even secretarial work is like that." She quoted a woman who is in an advanced position in contemporary society but retains traditional views on caregiving: "My two brothers and I are all busy lawyers. But when my mother got sick—she lives in another state—my brothers just assumed that I would be the one to fly out to her. And you know something? I did it" (Brody 1990: 8, 82).

Daughters-in-law readily accept caregiving roles when the parent-in-law does not have a daughter. When asked how they became caregivers to their in-laws, two women said: "My husband is an only child, so there was no one else. My husband was always the one in the family who took responsibility" (Brody 1990: 82).

Even the new, liberated, "career" woman experiences strains and stresses when it comes to juggling the priorities of her work and parent-care responsibilities. This inner tension occurs even for women who have high-paying jobs, which they keep, and who can afford a range of paid in-home services for the parent who needs care. For many, continuing to work is a great relief from parent care. Work itself can become a respite from the ongoing demands of caring for an elderly parent. As one woman stated:

> Sometimes my work had really helped me to cope. Other times, it's just been another thing on my mind. But sometimes it has helped me to forget things. You become all absorbed with what you're doing at work and forget the personal things in your life (Brody 1990: 224).

For many women the sense of duty, the tug of family responsibilities, the playing out of old roles for women in society are overwhelming. There is a strong pull between their feelings of obligation to care for their dependent parents and the new views of women's roles in contemporary American society. Many continue to work, but others reduce hours at work or leave their jobs. "It is apparent that for such women, the old values about parent care being *their* responsibility had not been driven out by 'new' values concerning women's roles" (Brody 1990: 225). Two studies documented the percentage of women who had left work to care for dependent parents. They are the 1982 Long-Term Care Survey conducted by the U.S. Department of Health and Human Services and the Philadelphia Geriatric Center (PGC) study of daughters who were assisting parents (Brody 1990; Brody, Klebam, Johnson, Hoffman, and Schoonover 1987). In the 1982 Long-Term Care Survey, 11.6 percent of all daughters who were involved in caregiving had

left their jobs to care for elderly parents, and 23 percent had reduced the hours they worked. In the same study, 35 percent of the daughters who worked had rearranged their work hours, and 25 percent had taken time off without pay (Brody, 1990). In the Philadelphia study, 28 percent of the nonworking women had left their work outside the home to take care of their disabled mothers, and 26 percent of the working women were considering quitting or already had reduced their work schedules to take care of their mothers (Brody et al. 1987).

DO AMERICA'S LONG-TERM CARE POLICIES EXPLOIT WOMEN?

With the heavy dependence upon family care (and most of that coming from women) as the result of the public policies that leave so many disabled older people in the "no-care zone," the issue of the exploitation of women has been raised. Numerous recent studies have examined the exploitation of women in regard to their greatly disproportional amount of unpaid family caregiving they undertake in American society (Finch 1989; Okin 1989; Leat and Gray 1987; Baldock and Ungerson 1991; Simonen 1990).

Women's free labor in family caregiving is seen by some conservatives as a means to reduce the cost of care that is financed publicly. It has also been interpreted as a way to restore the patriarchal family and women's traditional role in it (Lloyd 1991). Estes and Swan (1993) pointed out that in the patriarchal family, the basic role of women is caregiving and their status in the family is one of dependency. They went on to argue that because so much of women's work is not visible in terms of pay and benefits, American social policy continues to reflect the idea of women as dependents living in a stereotypical nuclear family. In this approach, women primarily fill domestic and reproductive roles with participation in the work force a secondary consideration. The enormous amount of work women perform as caregivers and the sacrifices they make are often unrecognized because work within the family is seen as free labor, if it is recognized as "labor" at all.

Calling for more family responsibility in long-term care is really a call for increasing women's unpaid work and the hardships that have already been observed that result from caregiving (Binney and Estes 1988). With 80 percent of long-term care already coming from women and other informal caregivers, the call for more family responsibilities in caregiving needs to be looked at in terms of economic, political, and ideological consequences (Estes 1991).

Present public policies regarding long-term care and women's roles as unpaid caregivers clearly show that society has not accepted the reality of the massive numbers and percentages of women who are in the labor force. "The domestic sphere, the world of work, (and) the welfare state are all organized as if women were continuing a traditional role" (Sassoon 1987: 160).

WOULD MORE GOVERNMENT SUPPORT OF LONG-TERM CARE MEAN FAMILY ABANDONMENT?

A major argument against increased government support for long-term care is that it would lead to family members, again primarily women, being less willing to care for their elderly relatives. Estes and Swan (1993) have referred to this as the "myth of family abandonment," because national polling data indicate that Americans remain committed to family care of their dependent elders while at the same time supporting increasing programs to help them in that care. They support assistance programs even if higher taxes are needed to support them (R.L. Associates 1987). In a 1988 Louis Harris and Associates poll, 87 percent of the people polled indicated support for a federal long-term home care program for disabled and chronically ill older adults.

Currently, the vast majority of the severely disabled older people receiving long-term care in a community setting (outside an institution) rely only on family or other unpaid care providers. Some two-thirds of all older people who need assistance on ADLs get no paid assistance at all, and only 3 percent use paid care alone (Pepper Commission 1990; U.S. Senate Special Committee on Aging 1991). Studies have indicated that family caregivers use relatively few community services. Only 10 to 20 percent of family caregivers use paid helpers. Dependent older people receive an average of five times as many hours per week in help from their informal caregivers as they do from paid service providers. Families generally use formal (paid) services only when their older family member's needs are too much for them to cope with (Osterkamp 1988).

In spite of all the evidence which clearly shows the willingness of families (primarily women) to care for disabled older family members, and the tremendous amount of effort spent in family caregiving, the myth of family abandonment has contributed to the hesitancy on the part of policy makers to address the real need of public support for the long-term care needs of older persons as well as the long-term care needs of persons of any age. They fear that increased public aid in long-term care will reduce family commitments in this area (U.S. House of Representatives Select Committee on Aging 1988).

PAYING FOR LONG-TERM CARE

In view of the increasing demands upon family caregivers, senior citizen interest groups, some politicians, and many public policy experts have called for relief for family caregivers in the form of financial support to assist in providing long-term care. This would help in making available affordable and accessible community-based services to assist families with both in-home care of aged relatives as well as placement in nursing facilities.

Paying for long-term care is one of the greatest financial threats to most Americans. The costs are enormous. As the U.S. Senate Special Committee on Aging pointed out in 1993, the costs of long-term care can impoverish all but the most affluent persons. Long-term care, as it exists in the United States in the mid-1990s, is one of the greatest threats to the financial security of older Americans and their families.

Paying for Home Care

Although home care of dependent elderly persons is generally considered less expensive than placing a person in a nursing home because so many of the services are provided by unpaid family caregivers, the costs can add up quickly. In 1990, skilled nursing visits averaged about $79 per visit. Three of these visits per week for one year would add up to $12,324. Add to this the possible need for therapists and rehabilitation specialists at $80 to $100 per visit, and the costs mount quickly (Rosen and Wilbur 1992). Some of these in-home services are covered by Medicare if the patient and his/her needs meet certain requirements. Of the total $6.9 billion spent on home care in 1990 in the United States, $800 million, or 12 percent, was spent by older persons and their families. However, these out-of-pocket expenses documented by the government did not include other home care expenses such as prescription drugs or other community-based services that many dependent older people need.

Paying for Nursing Home Care

Nursing home costs are a major financial threat to older people and their families. In 1992, the average cost of spending a year in a nursing home was about $36,000, but this varies by region of the country. The price can run as high as $50,000 to $60,000 per year. Very few older people and their families can afford this. One study has estimated that about 30 percent of older persons will become impoverished by a 3-month stay in a nursing home (Rosen and Wilbur 1992). A U.S. House Select Committee on Aging report (1987) showed that 70 percent of single older Americans spend down to poverty levels within 13 weeks after admission to a nursing home.

A 1992 report by the Department of Health and Human Services indicated that between 20 and 25 percent of persons who were placed in a nursing facility as private-pay patients became dependent on Medicaid, the program for impoverished persons, for medical and long-term care before they were discharged (U.S. Senate Special Committee on Aging 1993).

Medicaid and Long-Term Care

Outside of the Medicaid program, there are very few public resources available to pay for nursing-home costs. To become eligible for Medicaid for long-term care costs, an older person is required to "spend down" his or her assets to meet Medicaid guidelines. These guidelines require a person to spend their own assets on the nursing home costs until "countable" assets are reduced to about $2,000 (Rosen and Wilbur 1992). This amount varies somewhat from state to state, but the point is, it is not very much to keep after a lifetime of work and saving for most older people.

When qualifying for Medicaid assistance for nursing home costs, older persons may retain some assets that are exempt in determining eligibility. These include:

- Term life insurance which has no cash surrender value
- Life insurance with a face value of less than $1,500
- Personal property (clothing, jewelry, etc.)
- A car
- Household effects
- A prepaid funeral
- A burial account (not to exceed $1,500 in most states)
- A home, regardless of value, used as a primary residence
- Cash ($1,500 to $4,000 depending on the state) (Gordon, and Daniel 1990)

Medicaid Estate Planning

Because some types of assets are exempt from calculating a person's eligibility for Medicaid support in a nursing home, a technique called "Medicaid estate planning" has developed. The goal of this planning is to divest older persons of countable assets so they can qualify for Medicaid assistance with nursing home costs. The beneficiaries of this type of planning are not the persons placed in a nursing home. They are usually the children or other relatives or friends who benefit from transferring assets. When the principal assets are transferred legally and in the proper time (at least 36 months before placement in a nursing home), the government ends up paying the costs of the nursing home through Medicaid. Many people believe this practice is improper, if not highly unethical. The Medicaid program was designed to pay for health care for the poor in America. People are not really poor if they transfer assets to qualify for Medicaid. Other persons reason that because the U.S. government has no policy or programs to help finance long-term care as it does for other health emergencies for older people through Medicare, Medicaid estate planning fills a major support need of older people. They see it as no different than using all the legal loopholes of the Internal Revenue Code.

One of the real difficulties older persons can experience if they transfer assets to qualify for Medicaid assistance to pay for nursing home costs is access to a bed in a nursing home. Because Medicaid pays for nursing home stays at a much lower rate than other forms of payments, patients may have a hard time getting into a nursing home, particularly one of their choice (Miller, Swan, and Harrington 1992).

There is little real information as to how widespread the practice of Medicaid estate planning is. Some observers think that this practice will grow unless people feel they have alternatives to becoming impoverished if they need to be placed in a nursing home (Rosen and Wilbur 1992). Alternatives to our present dilemma for financing nursing home costs include some government program to help people which does not require them to become impoverished first, as is the case with Medicaid, or affordable private long-term care (LTC) insurance. In a 1988 Louis Harris and Associates poll, 87 percent of those polled favored a federal long-term care program for chronically ill and disabled older persons. This is easy to understand given the fact that the most vulnerable persons in the present system of financing long-term care are not only the poor but the middle class as well (Estes, Swan, and associates 1993).

WHO PAYS FOR NURSING HOME COSTS?

Even though large numbers of older people quickly exhaust their assets after spending some time in a nursing home, and even though some families transfer assets through Medicaid estate planning to qualify for Medicaid, out-of-pocket payments by patients and their families account for nearly one-half of the costs of nursing homes. In 1990, 45 percent of nursing home costs came from out-of-pocket-payments from patients and their families; Medicaid also covered 45 percent; private insurance paid for only 1.1 percent. Medicare covered some 4.5 percent of nursing home costs (Levit et al. 1991).

In the years ahead, if the financing of nursing home stays is unchanged, both out-of-pocket expenditures by patients and their families and Medicaid expenditures are expected to increase dramatically as indicated by Figure 18-1.

LONG-TERM CARE INSURANCE

Some people, particularly those in the insurance industry, believe that the way to address the question of financing long-term care is through long-term care insurance. Some 130 companies offer coverage for long-term care (*Consumers Reports* 1991). Between 1987 and 1993, some 2.4 million policies for long-term care were sold in the United States. In 1992, the premiums on these policies totaled one billion dollars, up from almost nothing ten years earlier. This type of insurance has become the fastest-growing type of health insurance sold in recent years (Kerr 1993).

According to the Health Insurance Association of America, private LTC policies cover a wide range of services, from community-based

**Projected Nursing Home Expenditures for People Age 65+,
by Source of Payment: 1990–2020**

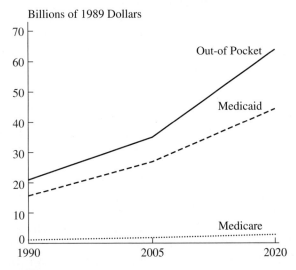

FIGURE 18-1

Sources of nursing home payments. *Source:* U.S. Senate Special Committee on Aging, the American Association of Retired Persons, the Federal Council on Aging. 1991. *Aging America: Trends and projections.* Washington, DC: U.S. Department of Health and Human Services, Chart 5-16, p. 173

care (in-home care) to nursing home placements. The Health Insurance Association of America contends that most of the policies sold today cover various community-based options, including home health, adult daycare, and respite care services. This association points out that the decision to purchase LTC insurance depends on a person's financial resources, if and how he or she wishes to preserve financial resources, concern about the quality of care, and estate planning (Rosen and Wilbur 1992).

Virginia Wilson (1992) argued that persons with assets worth between $100,000 and $1 million (not counting their homes) who want to preserve inheritances for their children or other relatives are candidates for LTC insurance. Millionaires do not have to worry about LTC insurance. They can afford to pay for nursing home costs out-of-pocket.

In looking at long-term care insurance, certain features are important:

- A basic policy should cover the difference between one's daily income and the daily cost of a nursing home. If, for example, one's income is $30 a day and a nursing home costs $100 a day, it is wise to insure for the $70 difference.
- Inflation protection should add 5 percent of one's original benefit each year.
- Waiver of premium should continue coverage with no additional cost while a person is collecting benefits.
- Coverage of any level of care, from custodial to skilled should be included.
- There should be no requirement that a beneficiary be hospitalized before becoming eligible for benefits.

- Mental disorders including Alzheimer's disease should be covered.
- A reasonable waiting period before collecting benefits (such as 100 days) can lower the premium costs.
- The policy should be guaranteed renewable, so the company cannot cancel the policy.

Estimates from the health insurance industry indicate that less than 5 percent of the elderly and 1 percent of the total population have purchased LTC insurance. There are many reasons for this. Not many people plan ahead for a time when they might be in need of long-term care. In addition, the costs of LTC insurance are prohibitive for many people; they simply cannot afford it. When people are younger, the time at which this type of insurance is relatively inexpensive, there are many competing demands for income. When a person reaches his or her mid-sixties, the costs for this type of insurance soar. According to the United Seniors Consumer Group of Washington, D.C., a well-designed policy for a 68-year-old cost $3,400 in 1993 (Kerr 1993). According to a study by the Families USA Foundation, policies that covered two years in a nursing home were unaffordable to 81 percent of Americans aged 55 to 79.

A 1991 study by *Consumer Reports* pointed out some of the major pitfalls of LTC insurance. These include the following:

- Tricky ways which policies are written
- The possibility for large rate increases
- Questions as to whether claims will be paid
- Confusing language in the policies

The *Consumer Reports* study pointed out that not everyone who applies for a policy can get one. Some companies reject as many as 40 percent of their applicants. A company may wait to examine the insurability of an applicant until a claim is filed. This is called post-claims underwriting.

Another potential problem in buying LTC insurance is the question of whether the company this type of insurance is purchased from will be around when the intended beneficiary needs it.

The *Consumer Reports* study found that one-quarter of the companies they rated in 1988 were no longer selling LTC insurance in 1991. "For a variety of disturbing reasons, consumers have little assurance that the company they buy from today will pay their nursing-home bill 15 or 20 years from now" (Consumer Reports 1991: 432).

The Future of Long-Term Care Insurance

With the devastating costs of long-term care hanging over the heads of average Americans, there is little doubt that LTC insurance policies will continue to be sold in increasing amounts. This will be true especially if the government (state or federal) does not adopt long-term care financing programs. To protect consumers, state insurance regulators have been charged with the job of regulating the insurance industry in their states, including LTC insurance. However, the 1991 *Consumer Reports* study clearly indicated that regulation of this type of insurance coverage is mixed. The National Association of Insurance Commissioners (NAIC), the group that develops model laws for all the states to adopt, has attempted to fix the problems with LTC insurance. However, just as one problem is addressed, another one pops up. Clearly state regulation of these types of policies is important and will become more important, as the sales of these policies increase.

With some states developing partnerships with private insurers to make private long-term care policies available to more people, there will be a greater need to put more emphasis on rating policies as to their real long-term value. Already New York and Connecticut have developed these types of partnerships (Kerr 1993). Others are contemplating such joint ventures with private insurance companies.

WHAT ABOUT GOVERNMENT LTC INSURANCE?

Many senior citizen advocates and public policy analysts have strongly advocated a governmental program to help pay for long-term care, much like Social Security and Medicare. In fact, advocates for this approach to long-term care have contended that long-term care coverage is the last major unfinished public business in providing for the major needs of older adults in the United States. With the passage of Social Security in 1935, the enactment of Medicare in 1965, many have contended that a publicly supported long-term care program is needed by 1995, or soon thereafter.

With the realization that long-term care costs, especially for nursing home placements, is the last major threat to economic security for all but the very rich, long-term care financing is a major item for most American families. More than 100 different long-term care bills were introduced in the U.S. Congress by the end of 1992 (Beck, Hager, Springer, and Barrett 1992). However, with price tags ranging from $40 billion to $50 billion, and considering the political pressure to reduce the annual deficits as well as the national debt, the politicians are hesitant to bring such a program to reality (Wiener and Illston 1993).

President Clinton's plan for universal health coverage did not include provisions to pay for placements in nursing homes (Kellogg 1993). Clinton's original universal health plan did include provisions for home-based care from housecleaning services to in-home nurse visits and meals. Even these services were not guaranteed: Services were to depend on the amount of financial resources the government made available. Clinton's long-term care plan, at least initially, was not an "entitlement" program (Patterson 1993). At its minimum, the plan would have provided for an assessment of a disabled person's needs. Only those unable to perform three ADLs (such as cooking, cleaning, dressing, and bathing) without assistance would have been eligible for in-home services. This plan was estimated to cost $15 billion a year, still a hefty price for a government trying to reduce the annual deficit and the national debt.

The Clinton plan was at least a beginning, a beginning for the federal government to provide long-term care beyond the confines of the Medicaid program, which requires a person to become impoverished before getting any help with long-term care costs, and a beginning to really emphasize in-home care for disabled persons. It is important to note that Clinton's long-term care plan was not limited to older people. It was to cover disabled persons of all ages, thereby reducing intergeneration conflict.

STATE PLANS FOR LONG-TERM CARE

Given the reluctance of the federal government to get involved in broad-based long-term care financing beyond the Medicaid program, some states out of necessity have taken the lead in developing long-term care programs. The reason for this is that the Medicaid program that supports so many older persons in nursing homes when they run out of money is a joint federal-state program. Many states are seeing their budgets under severe strain because of their obligations to Medicaid.

Florida, the home of many retirees, spent some $1.2 billion in 1993 for nursing home expenses (Kever 1993). These costs were expected to triple over the next seven years if long-term financing stayed the same.

As an initiative to offer long-term services to more people, and to slow the escalating costs, in 1994 Florida's Department of Elder Affairs proposed to:

- Increase state funding for home or community-based services such as Meals on Wheels and home nursing aides.
- Create a long-term care authority which would be an umbrella organization of fifty-four agencies and special-interest groups. This authority would coordinate services and advise the governor, the legislature, and state agencies.
- Position Florida to take advantage of any federal money that might become available for long-term care as a result of national health reforms.

Florida can well be a model for other states, given the high percentage of older people it has in various regions of the state. Charlotte County, Florida, has the nation's highest percentage of residents aged 65 and older, followed by Sarasota County. The average Floridian placed in a nursing home spends down to Medicaid eligibility after only 56 days. Through this new initiative, Florida hopes to "beef up programs that could help people remain at home," thereby reducing the costs of long-term care (Kever 1993: 64).

The issue of long-term care will not go away. It will only become more intense as the population grows older, particularly in the early part of the twenty-first century when the baby boomers reach their later years.

SUMMARY

Long-term care has become a widely-used term in contemporary America to describe the health care and other services that assist people with disabilities and chronic illness. The settings for these services range from nursing homes, to adult daycare centers, to one's own home.

The users of long-term care include disabled persons of any age, but the focus is on the elderly. The measures of disability are the ability to perform normal activities of daily living (ADLs) such as bathing, dressing, eating, getting in and out of bed, and using the toilet. A second measure used to assess disability are instrumental activities of daily living (IADLs) such as shopping, cooking, cleaning, taking medicines, handling personal finances, traveling, and using the telephone. There is a strong relationship between ADLs and IADLs and increasing age.

Although on any given day only about 5 percent of the nation's elderly population is in a nursing home, of those persons who turned 65 in 1990, 43 percent will spend some time in a nursing home before they die. With the rapidly growing elderly population in the United States, the number of residents of nursing homes is expected to increase dramatically by the year 2030.

Long-term care options include in-home services such as case care management, home health services, homemaker/home chore services, home-delivered meals, home repair/home maintenance, friendly visitor programs, and telephone reassurance programs. Community-based services include adult daycare, respite care, congregate meals, and transportation. Assisted-living facilities can take the form of senior citizen housing, board-and-care homes/adult foster care homes, and nursing facilities.

Long-term caregivers are usually female family members—wives, daughters, and daughters-in-law. Caregiving has become increasingly burdensome for American women with so many older people living longer with multiple chronic health conditions, and with so many women occupied in work outside the home. Studies have clearly shown the adverse effects caregiving of elderly relatives have had on American women, with high percentages forced to sacrifice health, personal life, and jobs. Public policies of the 1980s and the early 1990s added to the burden of family caregiving—the burdens of American women. Some public policy analysts have pointed out that American public policies concerning the burden of caring for elderly Americans represent the exploitation of American women.

One argument against more government support for long-term care is that families would abandon their responsibilities to their elder members. There is no real evidence to support this notion. In fact, the evidence is clear that American families continue to care deeply about helping their older family members. They need help as they assist their older relatives.

Paying for long-term care is one of the largest financial threats to the average American family. The costs of residing in a nursing home can impoverish all but the wealthiest. The only major governmental program that helps pay for long-term costs is the Medicaid program, but to qualify for this program, one must "spend down" his or her assets to a defined poverty level (about $2,000). This results in many older people becoming impoverished for the first time in their lives, or legal transferring of assets to others (usually children) to meet poverty standards.

Long-term care insurance is promoted by some as a way to plan for long-term care costs. Studies have shown the pitfalls of many of the policies that have been sold as well as the fact that a large percentage of Americans cannot afford to buy long-term care insurance.

The issues of the government's responsibility to develop a program to help people pay for long-term care has been raised often. Many senior citizen advocates believe that long-term care protection is the last major missing piece in public support to meet the basic needs of older people, along with Social Security and Medicare. However, with the political push to reduce annual federal deficits and the national debt, which is putting increased pressure on all existing government entitlement programs, there is not much political consensus to enact another major program which is projected to cost between $40 billion and $50 billion per year.

In the face of inaction by the federal government, some states are beginning to experiment with developing long-term care programs. This is due to the increasing number of people who need long-term care, and the fact that Medicaid is a federal-state partnership program which is severely straining the budgets of many states.

The issue of long-term care will not go away. It will only become more important as the population continues to grow older, particularly in the early part of the twenty-first century when the baby boomers move into their older years.

REFERENCES

Baldock, J., and Ungerson, C. 1991. What d' ya want if you don' want money? A Feminist Critique of "Paid Volunteering." In M. McLem, D. Groves (eds.), *Women's Issues in Social Policy*. London: Routledge & Kegan Paul, pp. 136–158.

Beck, M., Hager, M., Springer, K., and Barrett, T. 1992. Planning to Be Poor. *Newsweek*, (November 30) 120(22): 66–67.

Binney, E.A., and C.L. Estes. 1988. The Retreat of the State and Its Transfer of Responsibility: The Intergenerational War. *International Journal of Health Services*, 18: 83–96.

Brody, E.M. 1990. *Women in the Middle: Their Parent-Care Years*. New York: Springer.

Brody, E.M., Klebam, M.H., Johnson, P.T., Hoffman, C., and Schoonover, C.B. 1987. Work Status and Parent Care: A Comparison of Four Groups of Women. *Gerontologist*, 27: 201–208.

Consumer Reports. 1991. An Empty Promise to the Elderly. 5(6): 425–442.

Eggert, G.M., Granger, C.V., Morris, R., and Pendleton, S.F. 1977. Caring for the Patient With Long-Term Disability. *Geriatrics*, 32(10): 102–118.

Estes, C.L., Gerard, L.E., Zones, J.S., and Swan, J.H. 1984. *Political Economy, Health, and Aging*. Boston: Little, Brown.

Estes, C.L. 1991. The Reagan Legacy: Privatization, the Welfare State, and Aging in the 1990s. In J. Myles and J. Quadagno (eds.), *States Labor Markets, and the Future of Old Age Policy*. Philadelphia: Temple University Press, pp. 59–83.

Estes, C.L., Swan, J.H., and Associates. 1993. *The Long-Term Care Crisis: Elders Trapped in the No-Care Zone*. Newbury Park, CA: Sage Publications.

Finch, J. 1989. *Family Obligations and Social Change*. London: Polity Press and Basil Black Well.

Gordon, H., and Daniel J. 1990. *How to Protect Your Life Savings From Catastrophic Illness and Nursing Homes*. Boston, MA: Financial Planning Institute.

Harpine, C., McNeil, J., and Lamas, E. 1990. *The Need for Personal Assistance With Everyday Activities: Recipients and Caregivers*. U.S. Bureau of the Census. Current Population Reports, (Series P-70, No. 19). Washington, DC: U.S. Government Printing Office.

Hing, E., and Bloom, B. 1990. National Center for Health Statistics. *Long-Term Care for the Functionally Dependent Elderly*. Vital and Health Statistics, (Series 13, No. 104, DHHS Pub. No. (PHS) 90-1765). Hyattsville, MD: Public Health Service.

Japenga, A. 1993. The Hammacks: Three brothers must choose whether to shelter their parents' life savings or watch their mother's nursing home costs wipe out their inheritance. *Health: For Our Parents*, 7(6): 75–86.

Kellogg, S. 1993. Clinton Health Plan Quiet on Nursing Home, Adult Foster Care. *Grand Rapids Press* (November 8): B3.

Kemper, P., and Murtaugh, C.M. 1991. Lifetime Use of Nursing Home Care. *New England Journal of Medicine*, 324(9): 595.

Kerr, P. 1993. Elderly Care: The Insurers' Role. *New York Times* (March 16): C1, C6.

Kever, J. 1993. Florida Rethinks Long-Term Care Plans. *Sarasota Herald-Tribune* (December 24): 1A, 6A.

Kuypers, J.A., and Bengtson, V.L. 1983. In T. Brubaker ed. Toward Competence in the Older Family. *Family Relationships in Later Life*. Beverly Hills, CA: Sage, pp. 211–223.

Leat, D., and Gray, P. 1987. *Paying for Care: A Study of Policy and Practice in Paid Care Schemes*. London: Policies Studies Institutes.

Levit, K.R., Lazenby, H.C., Cowan, C.A., and Letsch, S. 1990. National Health Expenditures. In *Health Care Financing Review*. Fall, 1991, 13(1): 40.

Lloyd, P.C. 1991. The Empowerment of Elderly People. *Journal of Aging Studies*, 5: 125–135.

Louis Harris and Associates. 1988. *Majorities Favor Passage of Long-Term Health Care Legislation*. New York: Louis Harris and Associates.

Miller, L., Swan, J.H., and Harrington, C. 1992. *The Annual Per Capita Demand and Supply of Medicaid-Financed Nursing Home Bed Days in the States*. Unpublished manuscript: University of California, San Francisco, Institute for Health Aging.

Monk, A. 1988. Aging, Generational Continuity, and Filial Support. *The World and I*. In *Annual Editions: Aging*, 7th ed. 1991. Sluice Dock, Guilford, CT: Dushkin Publishing Group.

Noelker, L.S., and Poulshock, S.W. 1982. The Effect on Families of Caring for Impaired Elderly in Residence. *Final Report to the Administration on Aging*. Cleveland, OH: Benjamin Ross Institute.

Okin, S.M. 1989. *Justice, Gender and the Family*. New York: Basic Books.

Osterkamp, L. 1988. Family Caregivers: America's Primary Long-Term Care Resource. In *Annual Editions: Aging*, (7th Ed.). Cox, H., (ed.) Guilford, CT: Duskin Publishing Group, pp. 180–183.

Patterson, M-M. 1993. A Boost for the Very Disabled. *NRTA Bulletin*, 34(10): 12.

Pepper Commission (U.S. Bipartisan Commission on Comprehensive Health Care). 1990. *A Call for Action: Executive Summary*. Washington, D.C.: U.S. Government Printing Office.

R.L. Associates. 1987. *The American Public Views Long-Term Care*. Washington, D.C.: AARP and Villers Foundation.

Riekse, R.J., and Holstege, H. 1992. *The Christian Guide to Parent Care*. Wheaton, IL: Tyndale House Publishers.

Rivlin, A.M., and Siener, J.M. 1990. *Caring for the Disabled Elderly: Who Will Pay?* Washington, D.C.: Brookings Institution, 1988; Pepper Commission.

Rosen, A.L., and Wilbur, V.S. 1992. *Long-Term Care: Needs, Costs and Financing*. Washington, D.C.: Health Insurance Association of America.

Rosenback, M.L., and Cromwell, J. 1985. Physicians' Perceptions About the Short-Run Impact of Medicare's Prospective Payment System: Final Report. *Health Economic Research*.

Rosica, J.L. 1993. New Leave Law: Load of Relief. *NRTA Bulletin*, 34(8): 4–5.

Sassoon, A.S. (ed.). 1987. *Women and the State: The Shifting Boundaries of Public and Private*. London: Hutchinson.

Simonen, L. 1990. *Contradictions of the Welfare State: Women and Caring*. Tampere, Finland: University of Tampere.

Stone, R., Cafferata, G., and Sangle, J. 1987. Caregivers of the Frail Elderly: A National Profile. *The Gerontologist* (October). 27: 616–626.

The Michigan Long-Term Care Reader. 1992. Detroit, MI: Citizens for Better Care Press.

U.S. Bureau of the Census. 1982. *Survey of Income and Program Participation, Health-Wealth File*. Wares 3 and 4 (tabulations produced by Arnold Goldstein, Population Division).

U.S. Bureau of the Census Press Release. 1990. *Nursing Home Population Increases in Every State*, (June 28).

U.S. Bureau of the Census. 1992. *Sixty-Five Plus in America*. Current Population Reports Special Studies (P23-178RV). Washington, DC: U.S. Government Printing Office.

U.S. General Accounting Office. 1985. Information Requirements for Evaluating the Impacts of Medicare Prospective Payment on Post-Hospital Long-Term Care Services: Preliminary Report. Report to Senator John Heinz (GAD/PEMD 85-8, February 21): 1–9.

U.S. House of Representatives Select Committee on Aging. 1988. *Exploding the Myths: Caregiving in*

America. Washington, DC: U.S. Government Printing Office.

U.S. Senate Special Committee on Aging. 1991a. *Developments in Aging: 1990*, 1. Washington, DC: U.S. Government Printing Office.

U.S. Senate Special Committee on Aging. 1991b. *Aging America: Trends and Projections, 1991 Edition*. American Association of Retired Persons, Federal Council on the Aging, and U.S. Administration on Aging. Washington, DC: Department of Health and Human Services (FGOA 91-28001).

U.S. Senate Special Committee on Aging. 1993. *Developments in Aging: 1992*, 1. Washington, DC: U.S. Government Printing Office.

Wiener, J.M., and Illston, L.H. 1993. Health Reform Should Address Long-Term Care. *NRTA Bulletin*, 34(3): 18.

Wilson, V. 1992. Policies for Old-Age Care. *Newsweek* (April 20) 119(10): 61.

OLDER PEOPLE AT RISK

CHAPTER 19

Older
Women

Is This Discrimination—Or What?

Joyce Hathaway, 64, is a college professor with two-thirds the average salary of male colleagues. Laura Macy, 57, a marketing researcher for a large corporation, makes half as much as she would have if she hadn't quit work for 12 years to raise a family. "By the time women reach 50 they are considered over the hill," says Macy (not her real name). "Companies don't believe it's worth making career investments in older women. And if you don't promote women, of course, there's going to be a huge earnings gap."

The future indeed looked bleak for Marie Carper, 56, of Duluth, MN, who had five children and no work experience when her husband died in 1972. She enrolled in college, earning all but six credits toward a bachelor's degree in women's studies. But today, working as a $10-an-hour counselor to displaced homemakers, she wonders whether her college education, which left her $9,000 in debt, was worth it.

"I feel like I'm up a creek without a paddle because I don't have retirement benefits and I live from payday to payday," Carper says.

"First of all," she says, "there is discrimination in the job market. And women without experience have an extra strike against them. There just isn't any opportunity for them. What are you going to do if you have never touched a computer and are looking for an office job? Women my age are supposed to be caretakers of the world and not get paid for it," she laments.

Tell that to Eleanor Beadle, a retired 68-year-old Minneapolis real estate agent. Two years ago when she moved 50 miles away to live with her family in Cannon Falls, MN, she sought work as an apartment manager.

"I had the experience and a good résumé, but they didn't want to hire somebody my age" she says. "One gal I interviewed with told me they were very 'youth oriented'."

Now she sells state-licensed gambling cards in a bar that features nude dancers on the second floor. She works until one in the morning for $5 an hour. "It's tough," she says. "I'm on my feet a lot, and it's noisy. But it was the only thing I could get" (Lewis 1991: 12).

Is It Jennie's Job?

Jennie always thought of herself as a loving daughter. Until recently, most of Jennie's worries and joys centered on the normal routines of life. Her job in the local bookstore was a big help in paying college tuition for her sons, and she enjoyed meeting people. Jim, her husband, was even beginning to talk about retirement. On the whole, life was very good.

But Jennie's mother began to change. At first her mom seemed merely forgetful, but then she became confused and did some really strange things. Jennie's dad didn't know what to do, so he called on Jennie for help.

Medical tests determined that Jennie's mom suffered from Alzheimer's disease. She would not get better, and she needed monitoring every day, all day. Jennie's father wasn't up to the job. He had recently suffered a heart attack, and Jennie was careful to shield him from stressful responsibilities.

Jennie and Jim held a family conference with her dad. If Jennie could drop in and fix the meals and help her mom dress, they might get by. But that night, after their discussion, Jennie couldn't sleep. A thousand questions bothered her.

- *Would she be expected to quit her job to care for her mom?*
- *If her dad's pension wouldn't cover the medical expenses, would she and Jim be expected to use their savings to pay the bills?*
- *How could she take care of her own family and her parents?*

(Riekse and Holstege 1992: xii. All rights reserved).

Women Ending Up Poor—True Stories

The following stories of older women facing poverty in old age were told by Rep. Tom Tauke of the U.S. House of Representatives Select Committee on Aging in a hearing held October 3, 1990:

I would like to take this opportunity to share with you a couple of the stories we heard from women in Iowa, particularly farm wives who face unique experiences as a result of the nature of family farm and family-owned businesses. Many women in farming and family-owned businesses are not paid like other employees and, thus, receive no Social Security credits for their contributions to the family business. Nearly half of all farm wives receive a spouse-only benefit—even if they work off of the farm. In addition, farm couples with wives receiving spouse-only benefits have the lowest income of all Social Security beneficiaries.

During the subcommittee field hearing, we heard the story of Pauline Wipperman, a farm wife. She worked part-time off of the farm after her children were raised. For more than ten years, she has been unable to hold a part-time job because she has been caring for her frail, elderly parents and in-laws.

After years of working on the farm, and back and ankle problems, her husband decided to retire last year. Pauline receives less than $100 in benefits because of all of her zero years.

Another woman told the subcommittee her story. She is 79 years old and the widow of a World War II veteran. She and her husband ran a family business—he ran a gas station, and she worked in the attached diner. Since this was a small family business, she didn't receive regular wages and thus paid no Social Security.

Prior to the marriage, and during World War II, she held jobs outside of the home. When her husband's health began to fail, they sold the gas station and she found a part-time job as a maid in a local motel. All of her "zero years" left her with $300 in Social Security based on her husband's record (which disqualifies her for a VA widow's benefit).

We also heard the story of a 61-year-old farm wife whose 67-year-old disabled husband receives $250 in Social Security each month. They rent their farm for $170 per month. This level of monthly income makes them ineligible for the state's medically needy program.

She works outside of the home now in order to supplement their income, and now, at age 61, has paid into Social Security for only 9½ years. If she

claims benefits at age 62, she will receive $80 per month.

We also heard the story of a 78-year-old woman who has never been married. She lived with her parents and cared for them until they died. She never worked outside of the home. She cannot receive Social Security or Medicare, as a result. Her monthly income is $150, which she receives from her sister.

These stories are certainly not unique, but very common. As women become aware of the inequities in Social Security, I believe that Social Security equity for women will become a top priority issue.

(U.S. House of Representatives Select Committee on Aging, 1990, pp. 9–11).

OLDER WOMEN

In this unit we examine older people most at risk in terms of economics, health, and social factors. We will be looking at those who are the most vulnerable in society, vulnerable to abuses of various types, vulnerable to confidence scams, vulnerable to all the things that can impoverish their lives.

The first category of at-risk older people we will look at comprises women. One may question why older women as a category would be so vulnerable in American society. They are, after all, the winners of the longevity race of life.

One could make an argument that women are better off than men because they have greater life expectancies—they live longer than men. In fact at every age, male mortality rates exceed female mortality rates. Today, older women (age 65 and older) outnumber older men three to two; in 1930, both sexes were about equal. As age advances, the number of women relative to the number of men increases. From ages 65 to 69, women outnumber men 5 to 4. For persons 85 years and older, the ratio is 5 to 2. This female advantage in longevity has been increasing for decades. There are some projections that show a slowing of this trend in the twenty-first century because men are expected to increase their numbers compared to women through increased longevity. Even if these projections hold true, there would still be 5 million more elderly women than men by the year 2050 (U.S. Bureau of the Census 1992).

The reason why the advantage of greater life expectancy for women does not translate into their being at an advantage relative to life situations is pointed out by the Census Bureau study *Sixty-Five Plus in America*:

> The death of a husband often marks the point of economic reversals for the surviving wife. The differences of age at marriage between men and women are related to the high proportion of women living alone, the earlier institutionalization of women than men, sharply reduced income and a disproportionately high level of poverty among women, and a need for special support from family members and society (U.S. Bureau of the Census 1992: 2–10).

Not all women ever marry, and not all women become poor following the death of a spouse. But many do outlive spouses, many do become poor or near poor as the result of widowhood, and many outlive their economic and social resources. In this chapter we will examine the factors that put older women at risk. Because women so outnumber men at the upper reaches of the age categories, it is vital to note that the health, social, and economic problems of the oldest categories of the population are, and are likely to remain, basically the problems of women (Taeuber and Allen 1993).

TRADITIONAL ROLES OF WOMEN

It is impossible to understand the vulnerability of older women in American society without examining the social roles women have traditionally held as well as the roles they aspire to hold today. Traditionally, women's roles have focused on being wives, homemakers, mothers, community volunteers, and caregivers of the sick and elderly in family settings. For these roles, so important to any society, women have received no pay and no credits toward any retirement system.

Ruth Jacobs (1993), writing about the need to expand the social roles for older women, put the historical social roles for women in stronger terms. She stated that older women's roles in the United States have been limited by patriarchy, propriety, and patterning. *Patriarchy* refers to the systematic subordination of women where the man in society is always privileged. By *propriety*, Jacobs refers to the standard of what is socially acceptable in behavior and speech which translates to older women being nurturing, asexual, self-sacrificing, restrained, passive, and modest. *Patterning* means that women internalize and conform to stereotypes concerning the proper actions and abilities of older women. As a result, said Jacobs, "women who are no longer young are often allocated an inferior, even despised status due to patriarchy, are constrained by powerful norms to be confined to narrow roles defined by propriety, and are socialized by patterning to keep their proper backstage places" (Jacobs 1993: 192). Jacobs went on to say that these attitudes and constricts placed on women result in their being denied economic security, health care, and expression of their talents. As a result, they suffer economic and social dependency, costly for both them and society.

THE ROLE OF WORKERS OUTSIDE THE HOME

Women are entering and reentering the work force. This is one of the major stories of recent times. It has even reached into the categories of older women. By 1990, three-fourths (74.4 percent) of women in their thirties were in the labor force. This is double the percentage of some three decades earlier, 38.2 percent in 1957 (Herz 1987). Despite the fact that women today who are 50 years of age and older grew up in an era when they were not encouraged as married women to work outside the home, women in their fifties are working at increased numbers. In 1950, only 27 percent of women aged 55 to 64 were working outside the home compared to 45 percent in 1990. The real growth of older women working outside the home has occurred in the 55 to 59 age group. In 1967, 48 percent held paid jobs compared to 55 percent in 1990 (Bureau of Labor Statistics 1991; Herz 1991; Tuma and Sandefur 1987).

Even though more women in their fifties are working outside the home than before, most work in occupations traditionally held by women (Bureau of Labor Statistics 1986; Taeuber and Valdisera 1986). Two in three working women aged 55 and older had jobs in retail sales or administrative support including clerical and services. These types of jobs are often part-time and are less likely to have pension coverage (Herz 1987). Other studies have indicated that older women are more likely to be at the greatest disadvantage in the labor market as they tend to have less work experience and less education (Rones and Herz 1989). It is also important to note that older women workers tend to be more concentrated in declining industries such as manufacturing and textiles, making them more vulnerable to layoffs and job losses.

THE GAP IN WOMEN'S EARNINGS

Across the age span, women are paid about 72 cents for every dollar men earn. As women grow older, the earnings gap widens, resulting in women 50 years of age and older receiving only 64 percent of the wages men are paid. The occupations of today's older women reflect choices made some decades ago when opportunities for women were limited.

Reasons for Lower Incomes

The earnings gap is the result of four main factors, according to analysts:

1. Education. In the past women did not prepare for high-paying jobs.

2. Work experience. Women have less job tenure due to time out for caregiving tasks.
3. Occupational choice and occupational segregation. Women are concentrated in low-paying occupations.
4. Sex discrimination. In spite of the 1964 law banning sex discrimination in employment, it persists in such forms as the "glass ceiling" that prevents women advancing to the top jobs in business and industry (Lewis 1991).

Incomes Lower for Most Jobs

The Bureau of Labor Statistics did a study of occupations in 1990 for the American Association of Retired Persons that compared the earnings for men and women over 50 years of age who work full-time. A study of this type had never been done before. It found:

- Women office clerks aged 50 and older earned 91 percent of what men clerks were paid, and 80 percent of the clerks over the age of 50 were women.
- Women cashiers aged 50 and older earned 80 percent of male cashiers' wages. Women outnumbered males four to one in this category.
- Women janitors and cleaners aged 50 and older were paid 83 percent of what men earned. More than four-fifths of janitors older than 50 years of age were women, indicating poor job prospects for older women, particularly minorities.
- Women managers aged 50 and older in various occupations earned just half of what men were paid. Women held less than a third of these desirable jobs.
- Women college professors aged 50 and older earned $666 a week compared to $918 a week for men (Lewis 1991).

According to Robert Lewis (1991), organized labor has been a major factor in narrowing the earnings gap between men and women. Women in unions earn 83 percent of men's wages compared to 72 percent for women in general. Women unionized teachers over the age of 50 earn 94 percent of what men earn in elementary schools. Secondary women teachers in the same age group earn 90 percent of men's income.

Lewis indicated that researchers do not agree on how much of the earnings gap is caused by discrimination. Some believe that interruptions in work histories are more important than actual discrimination. Whatever the causes, the lower incomes paid to older women weaken their prospects for financial security in retirement. Lower incomes contribute to higher poverty rates for single women over the age of 65 compared to married couples or single men.

Lower Pension Coverage for Women

The pension coverage rate of men was significantly higher than the coverage rate for women. This is also true for pension vesting rates, the ability to receive payments from a pension plan after reaching retirement age. Part of the reason why women are at a disadvantage in pensions is the difference in the earnings between men and women (U.S. Bureau of the Census 1991). Women earn less in the workplace than men, largely because nearly 60 percent continue to work in traditionally female occupations (Rayman, Allshouse, and Allen 1993). It is projected that without changes in pension structures, older women in the future will continue to be at a disadvantage in pension benefits (Older Women's League 1990). The combined Social Security and pension income that men received was 45 percent higher than what women received in 1986 (Short and Nelson 1991). As a result, more and more older women will have to continue to earn money from jobs as long as they are able (Rayman, Allshanse, and Allen 1993). (See Figure 19-1.)

Working Outside the Home a Norm

Even though great numbers of women work outside the home, a majority are at a disadvantage in the types of jobs they hold, the type of industries in which they work, the inferior pay they receive, and the lower retirement benefits for which they may qualify. Projections for the rest of the 1990s and into the beginning of the twenty-first century indicate that most of the growth of the labor force in the United States will result from increased participation by minorities and middle-aged and older women. Women aged 55 to 64 are expected to increase their participation in the labor force to 54 percent by the year 2005, up 9 percentage points from 1990 (Fullerton 1992). For those women between the ages of 25 and 54, some 82

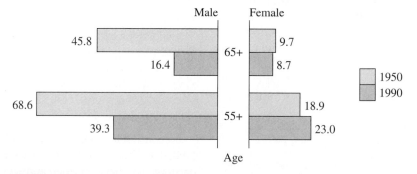

FIGURE 19-1

Percentage of people working by age and sex. (*Source:* U.S. Bureau of the Census. Current Population Reports, Special Studies, P23-178RV, *Sixty-five plus in America.* U.S. Government Printing Office, Washington, D.C., 1993, Figure 4-1, p. 4-1.)

percent are expected to be in the work force by the year 2005. Some experts contend that working in paid employment outside the home will be the norm of a woman's life at least throughout much of her adult life. Baby boomers are expected to spend some three-quarters of their adult lives in the labor force. Gail Sheehy (1993) has contended that American women are beginning to look at menopause as a marking point to their "second adulthood." She says if the age of 45 is the old age of youth, 50 is the youth of a woman's "second adulthood." In the "first adulthood," women will be combining paid employment outside the home with childcare and homemaking. Sheehy contended that in the second adulthood, women cannot afford to retire before their mid-sixties. However, in this phase of life, women are not, and will not be in the future, free of caregiving responsibilities and homemaking. The caregiving role shifts, to a great extent, to parent care often along with some responsibilities left from child care which generally continue into the young adult years of a middle-aged woman's children.

CAREGIVING ROLES OF WOMEN

As women have added to their roles in society in recent years, particularly as workers in the labor force outside the home, they have not walked away from all the other roles they have traditionally held. In fact, as the oldest-old segment of the population becomes the fastest growing sector of the American society, American women are taking on added responsibilities unprecedented in history. Never before have we had so many people live to such old ages. As we have seen in previous chapters, it is the oldest old who are likely to require the most assistance. According to a 1992 Bureau of the Census report, "Longer life expectancy has not necessarily translated into better health for the oldest old. The characteristics of the oldest old differ greatly from those of the younger old" (U.S. Bureau of the Census 1992: 2–5). Not only are great numbers of these persons in need of a range of supportive services to maintain daily

living, but this same report indicated that more and more people in their fifties and sixties who have aging relatives find themselves feeling the concerns, frustrations, perplexities, and expenses of caring for these family members.

Between 80 and 90 percent of all assistance to the oldest old in America comes from family members. Providing assistance and support for dependent older people in America has mostly fallen upon adult children, especially daughters and daughters-in-law who are generally in their middle years. The number of persons aged 85 and older per 100 persons aged 50 to 64 years have been defined as "the parent support ratio." The parent support ratio has tripled from 1950 to 1990 and is expected to triple again by the middle of the next century (U.S. Bureau of the Census 1992).

A recent Bureau of the Census report (1992)—and many other studies—clearly indicated that the pressing daily needs of the oldest old encompass economic, physical, and psychological supports. These pressures and demands are likely to come at the very time when the adult children of the frail oldest old are thinking about or have reached the age of retirement. Some of the 50-to-64-year-old group have health limitations of their own.

In 1950, relatively few people had to worry about caring for the frail elderly. This has changed dramatically. "There is no historical precedent for the experience of most middle-aged and younger persons having living parents." (U.S. Bureau of the Census 1992: 2–14). Another study indicated that one in three 50-year-old women had living mothers in 1940. By 1980, that proportion had doubled to two in three (Menken 1985). This proportion will continue to grow as the number of older Americans continues to increase.

As we have seen, families, especially daughters and daughters-in-law, provide most of the personal care elderly people need such as transportation and shopping (U.S. Bureau of the Census 1992). Further, families provide some 80 percent of medically related services to older people

(Brody 1990). Up to seven million Americans are unpaid caregivers to the elderly. About three out of four of these are women. In her testimony before the House Select Committee on Aging, Louise Glasse (1990), head of the Older Women's League, pointed out that 89 percent of all women over the age of 18 will be caregivers either of children, parents, or both.

Women of the Sandwich Generation

The sandwich generation is made up of those middle-aged persons who feel squeezed by the competing demands of caring for aging parents while still having responsibilities for their own children. The competing demands of providing some supports for children, youngsters to young adults, and to aging parents do not take into account the demands of the care provider's own life, which increasingly means work outside the home. In 1990, two-thirds of all mothers were in the work force, about double the rate for 1955 (Footlick 1990). The real strains in the sandwich generation fall, and will continue to fall on women—daughters and daughters-in-law. They are likely to have full-time jobs and are more likely than in years past to be divorced. Such a woman probably has children who continue to need some type of assistance—financial or emotional—even if they are young adults. She also may have to provide support to husband for health problems he may experience as he grows older. To make matters worse, she may have only one or two siblings to share the burden of caring for her aging parents; they may live at some distance from the parents, or they may expect her to be the primary caregiver (Rieske and Holstege 1992).

The future of the baby boomers as they increasingly take on the responsibilities of the sandwich generation is not any brighter. A Census Bureau statistician, Arnold Goldstein, stated:

> By 2010, Baby Boomers will be torn in two directions. Not only will they be looking after their own children, but they'll be looking after their parents, too. And some of them won't even have sent their children through college yet. Grandparents may be moving in with the rest of the family; parents may have to stay home from work at times to look after them or turn down a job in another city. For some it could be a real strain (Beck 1990: 63).

Characteristics of Female Caregivers

Who are these primary caregivers to the elderly in our society? We already saw that they are primarily daughters and daughters-in-law. But who are these women? What do they take on as caregivers? Studies have found the average age of caregivers of the elderly is 52. Thirty-six percent are aged 65 and older (U.S. House of Representatives Select Committee on Aging 1988). A majority of these caregivers to the elderly provide care for one to four years, with one-fifth of them providing care for five years or more (Stone, Cafferata, and Sangl 1987). These caregivers have no holidays, with 80 percent of them providing care seven days a week. Most are the primary provider of services to their elderly relatives. Most of the responsibilities fall on the daughter or daughter-in-law who lives closest to the dependent elderly person. There is no evidence of primary responsibility by birth order when siblings are present, nor is the "most loved" adult child selected to be the caregiver (Osterkamp 1988). Another study found that primary caregivers spent an average of 12 hours a week taking care of the needs of their elderly dependent family member, 26 hours a week caring for their homes, and hold full-time jobs outside the home. Some caregivers in this same study indicated that the combined hours they spend caring for elderly parents, taking care of their own homes and families, and working outside the home added up to three full-time jobs (Gibeau 1989).

It should be noted that the job of caregiving does not fall on just a few women in American society. The average woman in the United States will spend more years helping elderly frail parents than in raising their own children—18 years in parent care compared to 17 years raising children (U.S. House of Representatives Select Committee 1988). This is due to declining birth rates and increased longevity. For the first time in history, the average American has more living parents than children, a revolutionary change in family status (Beck 1990).

Effects of Caregiving on Women

There are many consequences women face as a result of their caregiving roles, particularly their roles as caregivers for elderly relatives. Most of them are negative. Before we note those effects that put women at a disadvantage in our society, we should recognize that caregiving can result in feelings of self-worth, usefulness, and provide personal satisfaction (Foster and Brizins 1993). Most women feel caring for elderly parents is their duty. They do it out of devotion and love, but often feel conflicting emotions including frustration, anguish, anger, and guilt. All of these emotions get mixed together for family caregivers. "Guilt is such a primary emotion among caregivers," said Lynn Osterkamp, founder and editor of the Parent Care newsletter at the University of Kansas Gerontology Center. "Most people, no matter how much they do, never feel it is enough" (Durso 1988: J7). Psychologist Marilyn Bonjean said, "And there is not one caregiver who doesn't feel it . . . Our emotions are not rational on this issue. It is human to resent our parents for getting older and frail" (Peterson 1989: 4D). Caregiving can be detrimental to a person's physical and emotional health. It can be a tremendous burden as caregivers have less time for themselves, less privacy, diminished or nonexistent social lives, and conflicts over their other roles such as spouse, caring for their own children, homemaking, and all the other things adult women wish, or feel compelled to do (Foster and Brizins 1993). Citing several studies over many years, Elaine Brody cited the following negative results of caregiving:

- Depression
- Frustration
- Guilt
- Sleeplessness
- Demoralization
- Feelings of helplessness
- Irritability
- Lowered morale
- Emotional exhaustion (Brody 1990: 41)

Beyond these feelings and emotions, beyond the threat to physical and emotional health, and beyond the loss of privacy and control over one's life, there are negative effects that jeopardize the financial security of the caregiver's life—both while she is engaged in providing help to aging parents, and for the rest of her life.

Caregiving as a Threat to Work and Financial Security

For many women, caregiving, especially for elderly parents, is a major threat to paid jobs outside the home. A number of studies have documented the numbers and percentages of caregiving women who have rearranged or cut their hours of work to care for elderly parents, quit their jobs, or considered quitting their jobs. The 1982 National Long-Term Care Survey (U.S. House Select Committee on Aging 1988) found that 35 percent of caregiving women rearranged their work schedules to care for elderly parents; 23 percent took time off with no pay. Another study found that 12 percent of women caregivers of elderly parents quit their jobs (Stone, Cafferata, and Sangl 1987). Other studies reported that up to 20 percent quit jobs to care for frail elderly relatives. Blue-collar workers were the most likely to take time off without pay to handle caregiving responsibilities, as they had the least flexibility in their jobs (Osterkamp 1988).

On the whole, caregivers are in the middle-income brackets, but female caregivers are much more likely to be at an economic disadvantage. One of the reasons for this economic disadvantage is diminished or lost opportunities to work in paid employment. With more than half (55.8 percent) of female caregivers of the elderly working outside the home, cutting work hours or quitting jobs is an immediate as well as long-term threat to the economic stability of women (U.S. House of Representatives Select Committee on Aging 1990). When women reduce the number of hours worked—or even more drastic, quit their jobs—to care for dependent elderly relatives, they obviously reduce or eliminate income from jobs. This has long-term consequences as well. According to testimony before Congress in 1990, women, in their caregiving roles, spend 11 years out of the work force caring for children and elderly parents. Men spend an average of 1.3 years in such roles. This has grave consequences in determining Social Security benefits as well as retention of jobs, advancement in professions, and pension benefits. Computing Social Security benefits for a worker takes into account average earnings over a specified number of years. Beginning in 1991, Social Security averaged a worker's earnings in each of 35 years in determining benefits. If a worker has fewer than 35 years of earnings that were covered by Social Security, $0 will be averaged for each year with no earnings (U.S. House of Representatives Select Committee on Aging 1990). The worker's benefits will be reduced by the zero years. With an average of 11 zero years, women are at distinct disadvantage when they reach retirement age. Their benefits will be much less than men who had earned income in all 35 years that Social Security counts. This factor, combined with average lower incomes for years worked, result in lower Social Security benefits for women who worked in paid employment. Proposals have been made to Congress to provide women with Social Security credits for some of their years of caregiving, a role so vital to families and the nation.

As representative Thomas Downey stated in Congressional hearings concerning women, caregiving, and poverty: "Caregiving is a job, an important job, and it should be treated as one" (U.S. House of Representatives Select Committee on Aging, 1990: 20). (See Figures 19-2 and 19-3.)

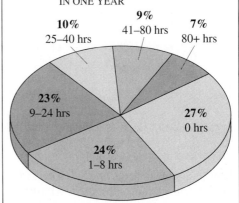

Time Off to Help Out

In a survey of 7,000 federal workers, nearly half said they cared for dependent adults. Of those, three quarters had missed some work.

Hours of Work Missed
IN ONE YEAR

- 10% 25–40 hrs
- 9% 41–80 hrs
- 7% 80+ hrs
- 23% 9–24 hrs
- 27% 0 hrs
- 24% 1–8 hrs

FIGURE 19-2
Women are the big losers in missed work to help older relatives. (*Source: Newsweek*, July 16, 1990, p. 51.)

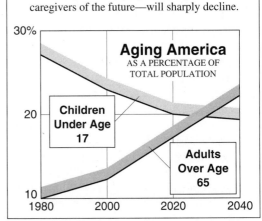

Who Will Care for US?

By the early 21st century, the percentage of Americans who are elderly will double, while the percentage of young people—caregivers of the future—will sharply decline.

Aging America
AS A PERCENTAGE OF TOTAL POPULATION

Children Under Age 17

Adults Over Age 65

30%

20

10

1980   2000   2020   2040

FIGURE 19-3
Caregiving needs and caregivers in the future. (*Source: Newsweek*, July 16, 1990, p. 53. Sotoodeh–*Newsweek*.)

POVERTY AND OLDER WOMEN

In Chapter 8 we saw that older women are among the most economically vulnerable of all older people in American society. We looked at poverty rates for older women and saw that although women made up 58 percent of the elderly population in 1990, they accounted for 74 percent of all poor people aged 65 and older. Of the 2.3 million older persons who lived alone in 1990, nearly two million were elderly women and half of these received means-tested assistance, which meant they met poverty guidelines (U.S. Bureau of the Census 1992). About one million older women who lived alone in 1990 were "near poor." The women were predominately white (89 percent) and mostly lived in metropolitan areas (76 percent) (Littman 1990).

In 1990, only 37 percent of all women age 62 and older received Social Security benefits based solely on their own work records. The average benefit was 76 percent of what male workers received. This translated into an average benefit for women of $518.60 per month compared to $679.20 for men (Social Security Administration 1991). The 1993 Women's Initiative study makes the dire assessment that despite the changes for women in the workplace, most women still get higher retirement income from being wives than from being workers. This depressing view of the poor economic status of women who work is echoed by testimony before the Select Committee on Aging of the U.S. House of Representatives in 1992 by the head of the Older Women's League who stated that although mid-life and older women make up an increasing part of the American work force, these gains in employment do not necessarily mean equal opportunity in the workplace today or in the future. The reason for the unequal sharing of income and retirement benefits is that six out of ten women work in lower-paying occupations. "Most of today's women can expect to do the same low-paying work as their mothers and can expect suffering in poverty in retirement," said Joan Kuriansky, Executive Director of the Older Women's League

(U.S. House of Representatives Select Committee 1992: 150).

A 1992 U.S. General Accounting Office report indicated that elderly women were nearly twice as likely as elderly men to be poor or near poor in 1990. This report went on to point out that the condition that primarily accounts for much more poverty among older women is marital status. Rates for poverty among married women and men were similar in all the age categories of older people in 1990. However, being unmarried—widowed, divorced, separated, or never married—more than doubled the poverty rate for men, and quadrupled it for women. Widows are twice as likely as older married couples to become poor, as the result of declines in income from Social Security, pensions, and assets when a husband dies. For an elderly widow, the death of her spouse is the primary cause of poverty (U.S. GAO 1992; Zick and Smith 1991).

MARITAL STATUS OF OLDER WOMEN

With marital status being a key factor in poverty among the elderly, women are at a great disadvantage. A 1992 Census Bureau report showed that elderly men were nearly twice as likely as elderly women to be married in 1990, 74 percent of men compared to 40 percent of women. Older women were more than three times as likely to be widowed as men, 14 percent of men compared to 49 percent of women in 1990. It is interesting to note that the median age of widowhood for women was 55 in 1985, the latest year these data were available. In 1990, there were 29 unmarried older men for every 100 unmarred women. Never-having-been-married rates were about the same for elderly men and women, 4.2 percent for men compared to 4.9 percent for women (Saluter 1991). As women get older, their chances of being married decreases dramatically. According to the Census Bureau, by the time a person reached ages 85 and older, nearly half (48.7 percent) of white men were still married compared to only 10.3 percent of white women in 1990 (U.S. Bureau of the Census 1992).

WIDOWHOOD IN THE LATER YEARS

As widowhood is the beginning of poverty for many women, women are at a great disadvantage here as well. Widowhood is a common marital status for older American women. In 1990, half of all older women in the United States were widows. As women get older, the likelihood of their being widows increases significantly. One in three (36.1 percent) women between the ages of 65 and 74 were widows in 1990. Three in five (62 percent) women aged 75 to 84 were widows in 1990. In the same year, four out of five women aged 85 and older were widows. Men are much less likely to be widowers. In the age category 65 to 74, only 9.2 percent of men were widowers in 1990. For those men aged 75 to 84, 19.5 percent were widowers that same year. For men 85 and older, well under half (43.4 percent) were widowers compared to about 80 percent of women the same age (U.S. Bureau of the Census 1992).

Widowhood presents especially serious economic problems for older women. This is because so many older women rely on their husbands' work records for their retirement benefits. A retired couple, relying on the husband's work history alone for Social Security benefits, gets 50 percent additional income for the retired wife based on the husband's income. When one spouse dies—typically the husband, as women have longer life spans than men—the benefits are reduced to the level of a single person. A retired couple, for exampie, getting $8,000 in Social Security benefits in 1990 would have lived just above the poverty line with no additional income. The death of one spouse would have reduced the benefits to about $5,360, putting the remaining spouse in poverty (United States General Accounting Office 1992). Because women typically outlive men, most American women will live out their lives as widows. In 1992, over half of all women age 65 and older were widows. About 100,000 women become widows each year (U.S. House of Representatives Select Committee 1992).

As a result, most elderly men are married, while most elderly women are not. Elderly women were more than three times as likely as men to be widowed in 1990. The median age of widowhood for women was 55 in 1985 (U.S. Bureau of the Census, 1992).

A Commonwealth Fund Commission study on elderly people living alone, (U.S. House of Representatives Select Committee 1992) noted some pertinent facts about impoverished widows.

- About half of widows were not poor before the death of their husbands.
- A husband's death can cause his widow's poverty in several ways:
  —Medical and funeral expenses consume resources.
  —Pension income is frequently lost.
- Husbands of poor widows had poorer health and retired earlier. They also earned less when they worked. All of these facts suggest lower income relative to needs during the family's working years, resulting in less savings, and finally resulting in the very low asset income of the elderly who live alone.

Women living alone, widowed, divorced, or never married, will continue to suffer high rates of poverty through the year 2020. In less than 40 years, when today's 25-year-olds retire, fewer women will retire married. As a result, fewer women will have access to their husband's retirement income (U.S. House of Representatives Select Committee 1992).

DIVORCE AND REMARRIAGE IN OLD AGE

As much as widowhood is a major economic threat to older women, divorce is becoming a prime cause of poverty among elderly women. For many older women, divorce dashes their dreams of a happy and financially secure retirement. For more than 100 years, divorce rates in America have risen steadily (Goode 1982). Almost half of all marriages in the United States end in divorce. Current divorce rates are twice those immediately following World War II and three time the rates of the 1920s and 1930s

(Marshall 1991). Although the percentage of divorced persons among the elderly remains relatively low compared to the general population, significant increases have occurred in recent years, and major increases are expected in the near future. In 1960, less than 2 percent of elderly persons were divorced. By 1990, this had increased to 5 percent, more than double the rate. By 2020, it is expected that 14 percent of old persons will be divorced (U.S. Bureau of the Census 1992).

The rates for divorced older men and women who had not remarried were about the same and were quite low (about 5 percent) in 1990 (Saluter 1991). However, for women over 45 years of age, the probability of remarriage is very small. In 1985, only 29 of 10,000 divorced women aged 45 to 64 had remarried, and only five of 10,000

women 65 and older had remarried (Uhlenberg, Cooney, and Boyd 1990). The proportion of divorced women who do not remarry is expected to increase greatly in the future according to a 1993 study by the Policy Center on Aging of Brandeis University (Crown, Mutschler, Schulz, and Loew 1993). Census Bureau data support this projection indicating that by the year 2020, when the baby boomers are elderly, 8 percent of elderly men and 14 percent of elderly women are expected to be divorced (U.S. Bureau of the Census 1992). With only 4 percent of those elderly divorced women receiving alimony payments, the poverty rate for them is as high or higher than for widowed or never-married women. The poverty rate for separated women is even higher than for divorced women (Crown et al. 1993). (See Figure 19-4.)

**Percentage of Persons 65 Years and Over Who
Are Married With Spouse Present, by Age, Sex, Race,
and Hispanic Origin: March 1990**
(Noninstitutional population)

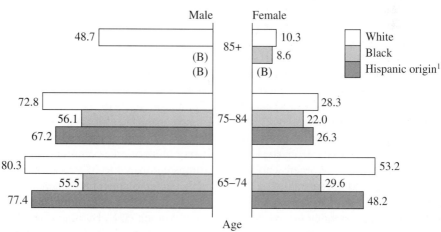

B Base is less than 75,000.
[1]Hispanic origin may be of any race.

FIGURE 19-4

Many more older men have spouses than do older women. (*Source:* U.S. Bureau of the Census. Current Population Reports, Special Studies, P23-178RV, *Sixty-five plus in America.* Washington, D.C.: U.S. Government Printing 1993, Figure 6-1, p. 6-3.)

LIVING ALONE

Older women are much more likely than older men to live alone. This is primarily the result of longer lives for women and their tendency to marry men some years older. In 1990, 9.2 million elderly persons (aged 65 and older) lived alone. Nearly eight in ten (78.8 percent) were women. Among noninstitutionalized persons age 85 and older, white women were about twice as likely as white men (58 percent compared to 30 percent) to live alone in 1990 (U.S. Bureau of the Census 1992). There was an increase from 1980 to 1990 in the percentage of the oldest old (aged 85 and older) living alone, from 39 percent to 47 percent. In the span of the same years, the percentage of the oldest old living with spouses stayed about the same. However, the oldest old living with relatives dropped from 36 percent in 1980 to 25 percent in 1990 (Saluter 1991).

In analyzing the numbers of older women who spend their later years in life widowed and living alone, the 1992 Census Bureau report indicated that if a young woman wants to avoid being alone in her golden years, it would make sense to marry a man at least seven years younger than she. But this did not happen in the past, and it is not happening now. Women still tend to marry men several years older than they are. As a result, the Census Bureau has predicted that by the year 2000, women will head over half (53.2 percent) of all the households run by persons 75 years of age and older (U.S. Bureau of the Census 1986).

On the positive side, older women are better able than older men to cope with the physical and social aspects of living alone. Women who live alone usually have social contacts and diets similar to persons who are married. Older men have less nutritious diets because many do not know how to cook (Riley 1983). Some experts in aging feel that the current generation of older women who live alone are in fact pacesetters for the future. They have coped with the shortage of men in their lives. They have developed new interests and social networks that can prevent or at least help them cope with loneliness (U.S. Bureau of the Census 1992). Research has indicated that the quality and number of companions and close friends in which a person can confide have a lot to do with feelings of well-being (Chappell and Badger 1989). Women are better at developing and maintaining companions, close friends, and social networks. As a result, they survive better living alone, keeping in perspective their economic disadvantages.

One of the biggest disadvantages of living alone is not having someone to rely on for short-term or long-term periods of ill health. This is where older women are at a great disadvantage to older men. As we have seen, of all persons aged 65 and older living alone in 1990, eight out of ten were women. So when they need help with the basic activities of daily living, men are much more likely to have someone (usually spouses) on whom to rely. This obviously becomes more important as people continue to grow older and are more likely to need assistance at various times if not on a long-term basis.

CHRONIC ILLNESS/FUNCTIONAL LIMITATIONS

Not having someone around to help them becomes critical for older women as they grow older. This is due to the fact that as age increases, so does the probability of having chronic illness. Women 60 years of age and older tend to have more chronic health conditions than men. For women 80 years of age and older, 70 percent had two or more of nine common chronic health conditions compared to 53 percent of the men in the same age category (Guralnik et al. 1989). Arthritis and hypertension are especially high among older women (U.S. Bureau of the Census 1992; Havlik et al. 1987).

Women are also more likely to have difficulty with performing personal care tasks and home management tasks, or *functional limitations*. These include bathing, dressing, getting out of bed, continence, and feeding oneself. Elderly women are more likely than elderly men to have difficulty with these tasks. A study by Hing and Bloom (1990) found that one-third (34 percent) of older women were dependent for these functions compared to about one-fifth (22 percent) of older men. Among functionally dependent men 65 years of age and older, 61 percent lived with a spouse compared to 24 percent of functionally dependent women in the same age category. By age 85, 36 percent of these males lived with a spouse compared to only 4 percent of functionally dependent females. Functionally dependent women aged 65 to 84 were most likely to live alone (38 percent). Women aged 85 and older who were functionally dependent were forced to seek help from those other than spouses, with 30 percent living with someone other than a spouse and 38 percent in a nursing home.

NURSING HOME USE BY OLDER WOMEN

Dependency for the activities of daily living leads many more women into nursing facilities than men. With more functional limitations than men, more chronic health conditions than men, many more older women living alone in the older age categories than men, and longer lives, it is not difficult to understand why nursing homes are heavily populated by the oldest-old women (U.S. Bureau of the Census 1992). One study estimated that the lifetime risk of being placed in a nursing home for those persons reaching age 65 in 1990 was 43 percent. Over half (52 percent) of older women compared to one-third (33 percent) of older men would be placed in a nursing home before they die. This increases with age, with some 70 percent of women who lived to be 90 years of age and older having lived in a nursing home between 1982 and 1984 (Kemper and Murtaugh 1991). In 1990, the residents were predominately women, 1.3 million out of 1.8 million total. Two-thirds of the women in nursing homes were 80 years of age or older. A great majority of nursing-home residents were widows in 1990 (61.1 percent) (U.S. Bureau of the Census, Decennial Census 1990).

WOMEN'S HEALTH ISSUES

Although health, fitness, health care, and disease prevention are top priorities for Americans, little is known about diseases that are unique to women. For many years, women were not often included in clinical trials for new medicines and procedures. Most major studies focused on middle-aged men (U.S. Senate Special Committee on Aging 1993).

To correct the problem of excluding women from major health studies, the National Institutes of Health (NIH) has developed the Women's Health Institute, the largest community-based clinical trial ever conducted. It involves up to 140,000 postmenopausal women over a 14-year period. It will study diet, dietary supplements, exercise, hormone therapy, and stopping smoking as a prevention for cardiovascular disease, cancer, and osteoporosis.

Consequences of Poor Health

Although, on average, women live longer than men, they have greater overall rates of physical illness, disability days, physician visits, and prescription and nonprescription drug use than do men. Women are sick more often in the short run and have more chronic health conditions in the long run (Lamphere-Thorpe and Blendon 1993). Some three-fourths of the severely disabled older people live in the community. Two-thirds (67 percent) of these are women (U.S. Bipartisan Commission on Comprehensive Health Care 1990).

Being able to afford living in nursing homes and other forms of long-term care is a major problem for all older people but especially for older women (Rowland 1989). Even though most women aged 65 and older have health insurance through Medicare, most spend substantial amounts of their incomes on health care expenses, more than men spend. Unmarried women aged 65 and older spend an average of over 16 percent of their incomes on medical expenses compared to less than 9 percent for married couples in the same age category. While Medicaid paid for 49 percent of the health-care costs of older unmarried men, it paid for only 33 percent of the health-care costs of unmarried older women (Older Women's League 1989).

Need for Preventive Health Measures

Marianne Fahs (1993) has contended that the development of preventive health measures for older women can save money and add years of healthy life. She pointed out that preventive measures are cost-effective, and they are necessary to offset high rates of disability among older women as well as ever-increasing health care costs. Nonetheless, in the United States only 3.4 percent of the total health care budget is spent on prevention, and almost all of this is spent on the prevention of acute diseases experienced by younger people.

Needed Areas of Research

Three areas of research that can have a major impact on the lives of older women are breast cancer, ovarian cancer, and osteoporosis.

Breast cancer is the second leading cause of death. Some 46,000 women died from breast cancer per year in the early 1990s. One woman in nine acquires breast cancer in her lifetime. The survival rate for treated women with localized breast cancer is 90 percent. For those with breast cancer that has spread, the survival rate is 60 percent. Early detection and treatment are vital (U.S. Senate Special Committee on Aging 1993).

Ovarian cancer is the fourth leading cause of death in women. One woman in 70 will acquire this type of cancer in her lifetime; one in 100 will die from it. But 80 percent of the diagnosed cases of ovarian cancer are in women over the age of 50. The likelihood of tumors that are removed from the ovaries being malignant increases with the age of the patient. Again, early detection is essential (U.S. Senate Special Committee on Aging 1993).

Osteoporosis, the bone disease that results in the loss of bone density, is found in older peo-

ple, particularly older women. Some 24 million people in the United States, of which 80 percent to 90 percent are women, are affected by osteoporosis (U.S. Senate Special Committee on Aging 1993). Osteoporosis is a leading cause of hip fractures, which can be devastating. Following hip fractures, expected years of survival are reduced by 5 percent to 20 percent (Cummings et al. 1985). These fractures can result in disability or death. Fifteen percent of white women, compared to 5 percent of men, will suffer hip fractures during their lives (Fahs 1993). Hip fractures run up costs of $7 billion to $10 billion each year (U.S. Senate Special Committee on Aging 1993).

These health conditions contribute to the disadvantages older women experience in American society, adding to the factors that put them at risk in their later years of life.

PREPARING FOR A LIFE ALONE

With women outliving men and continuing to marry men some years older, what can they do to prepare for widowhood? Some gerontologists have suggested that it would be helpful for them to enrich their present lives. They should cultivate and keep old friends, develop new friends, and maintain their interests and hobbies in life. They should understand the household finances, investments, and credit. In addition, they should become active in organizations they find interesting.

Involvement in outside activities can give meaning and purpose to life. Helping disadvantaged children learn to read, for instance, gives a person purpose and perspective and builds self-esteem. Helping disabled patients in a local hospital often does more for the volunteer than it does for the patient. This type of community service can give older people a sense of well-being, purpose, and importance.

For many of today's older women, the loss of a spouse means the loss of transportation. Many older women never learned to drive, or they gave it up and let their husbands take over. Learning to drive in today's traffic could be helpful for present and future independence.

Both spouses should know how to run the household. The wife should know which mechanic is trustworthy. She should know how to light the pilot light on the furnace if it goes out on a cold morning in January. The husband should know how to cook simple meals and do laundry. The more both spouses know about household maintenance and repair, the less likely they are to be ripped off by a con artist.

Planning for widowhood is not a pleasant prospect, but doing things that promote independence and self-reliance not only helps to prepare for being alone, but also enhances the quality of a person's life while one still has his or her mate (Riekse and Holstege 1992).

SUMMARY

In American society, older women are at risk in a number of ways. Looking at their longer life expectancies, one would at first think they are better off than men. However, this is not really true if all the other factors that affect their lives are considered.

The roles women have traditionally held in America, although essential to families and the larger society, have put them at a great disadvantage socially and economically. Their roles as wives, homemakers, mothers, community volunteers, and caregivers of the sick and the frail in families have provided them with no money compensation or credits toward retirement benefits. In recent years women in large percentages have taken on additional roles as more and more have become workers in the labor force outside the home. In doing so, they have not decreased their traditional responsibilities.

The traditional responsibilities of women have expanded greatly with the increased longevity of older parents. The average American woman now spends more years in parent care than in child care. These responsibilities have caused many women to cut their hours in paid employment or to totally quit their jobs outside the home. The years out of paid employment reduce their opportunities for retirement benefits in private and public pension plans. With lower incomes from employment, fewer opportunities for high-paying jobs, and years out of the labor force for caregiving, women often spend their later years with much less income than men. This is particularly true for women living alone—widowed, divorced, separated, or never married.

The caregiving role of older women for elderly relatives can have many negative consequences. Various forms of stress leading to diminished emotional and physical health are common.

Older women experience more chronic illness and functional limitations in caring for themselves and their homes than do men. In spite of being at a great disadvantage economically, women are better at coping with living alone, especially in developing and keeping friends and social contacts, and being able to cook for themselves. Because so many women end their lives without a mate, and because so many experience chronic health conditions as well as limitations with being able to carry out the daily activities of life, many more women than men end up being placed in nursing facilities.

Overall, older women are an at-risk population with many more disadvantages than older men have. Because of this, it is reasonable to conclude that the real problems of the oldest old in contemporary America are essentially the problems of women.

REFERENCES

Beck, M. 1990. The Geezer Boom. *Special Edition Newsweek: The 21st Century Family, CXIV*(27): 63.

Brody, E.M. 1990. *Women in the Middle: Their Parent-Care Years*. New York: Springer.

Chappell, N.L., and Badger, M. 1989. Social Isolation and Well-Being. *Journal of Gerontology*, 44(5): 169–176.

Crown, W.H., Mutschler, P.H., Schulz, J.H., and Loew, R. 1993. *The Economic Status of Divorced Older Women*. Waltham, MA: Policy Center on Aging, Heller School, Brandeis University.

Cummings, S.R., Kelsey, J.L., Nevitt, M.C., and O'Dowd, K.J. 1985. Epidemiology of Osteoporosis and Osteoporotic Fractures. *Epidemiological Review*, 7: 178–208.

Durso, L. 1988. Preparing to Care for Aging Parents. *Philadelphia Inquirer*, (August 28): J7.

Fahs, M.C. 1993. Preventative Medical Care: Targeting Elderly Women in an Aging Society. In Allen, J. and Pifer, A., *Women on the Front Lines: Meeting the Challenge of an Aging America*. Washington, DC: Urban Institute Press.

Footlick, J.K. 1990. *Newsweek Special Edition: The 21st Century Family*, CXIV(27): 14–20.

Foster, S.E., and Brizins, J.A. 1993. Caring Too Much? American Women and the Nation's Caregiving Crisis. In Allen, J. and Pifer, A., *Women on the Front Lines: Meeting the Challenge of an Aging America*. Washington, DC: Urban Institute Press.

Fullerton, Jr., H.N. 1992. Labor Force Projections: The Baby Boom Moves On. In *Outlook: 1990–2005, BLS Bulletin*, 2402. Washington, DC: U.S. Government Printing Office.

Gibeau, J.L. 1989. Adult Day Health Services as an Employee Benefit. Washington, DC: National Association of Area Agencies on Aging.

Glasse, L. 1990. Statement of Lou Glasse, President of the Older Women's League Before the Subcommittee on Retirement Income and Employment of the House Select Committee on Aging. In *Women, Caregiving, and Poverty: Options to Improve Social Security*, Hearing. Washington, DC: U.S. Government Printing Office: 1990.

Goode, W. 1982. *The Family*. Englewood Cliffs, NJ: Prentice-Hall.

Guralnik, J.M., LaCroix, A.Z., Everett, D.F., and Kovar, M.G. 1989. National Center for Health Statistics. *Aging in the Eighties: The Prevalence of Comorbidity and Its Association With Disability*. Advance Data, Number 170. Washington, DC: U.S. Government Printing Office.

Havlik, R.J., Liu, B.M., Kovar, M.G., et al. 1987. National Center for Health Statistics. *Health Statistics on Older Persons, United States: 1986*. Vital and Health Statistics (Series 3, No. 25), Public Health Service. Washington, DC: U.S. Government Printing Office.

Herz, D.E. 1988. Bureau of Labor Statistics. *Employment Characteristics of Older Women*.

Hing, E., and Bloom, B. 1990. National Center for Health Statistics, *Long-Term Care for the Functionally Dependent Elderly*. Vital and Health Statistics (Series 13, No. 104), DHHS Pub., No. (PHS) 90-1765. Hyattsville, MD: Public Health Service.

Jacobs, R.H. 1993. Expanding Social Roles for Older Women. In Allen, J. and Pifer, A., *Women on the Front Lines*. Washington, DC: Urban Institute Press.

Kemper, P., and Murtaugh, C. 1991. Lifetime Use of Nursing Home Care. *New England Journal of Medicine*, 324(9).

Lamphere-Thorpe, J. and Blendon, R.J. 1993. Years Gained and Opportunities Lost: Women and Health Care in an Aging America. In Allen, J. and Pifer, A., (eds)., *Women on the Front Lines: Meeting the Challenge of an Aging America*. Washington, DC: Urban Institute Press.

Lewis, R. 1991. Equity Eludes Women: Earnings Gap Is Greatest After Age 50. *NRTA Bulletin*, 32(10): 1, 10–13.

Littman, M. 1991. U.S. Bureau of the Census, *Poverty in the United States: 1990*. Current Population Reports, (Series P-60, No. 175). Washington, DC: U.S. Government Printing Office.

Marchall, R. 1991. *The State of Families*. Milwaukee, WI: Family Service America.

Menken, J. 1985. Age and Fertility: How Long Can You Wait? Presidential Address delivered at the annual meeting of the Population Association of America, Boston, MA.

Older Women's League. 1989. The Picture of Health for Midlife and Older Women in America. In Lois Grau (ed.) *Women in Their Later Years: Health, Social, and Cultural Perspectives*. Binghamton, NY: Harrington Park Press.

Older Women's League. 1990. *Heading for Hardship: Retirement Income for American Women in the Next Century*. Washington, DC: OWL.

Osterkamp, L. 1988. Family Caregivers: America's Primary Long-Term Care Resource. *Aging*, 358: 2–5.

Peterson, K.S. 1989. Easing the Emotional Transition. *USA Today* (April 18): 4D.

Rayman, P., Allshouse, K., and Allen, J. 1993. Resiliency Amidst Inequity: Older Women Workers in an Aging United States. In Allen, J. and Pifer, A. (eds.), *Women on the Front Lines*. Washington, DC: Urban Institute Press.

Riekse, R., and Holstege, H. 1992. *The Christian Guide to Parent Care*. Wheaton, IL, Tyndale House Publishers.

Riley, M.W. 1983. Aging and Society: Notes on the Developments of New Understandings. Lecture at the University of Michigan (December 12): 13, Ann Arbor, MI.

Rones, P.L., and Herz, D.E. 1989. Bureau of Labor Statistics. *Labor Market Problems of Older Workers*. Report to the Secretary of Labor. Washington, DC: U.S. Government Printing Office.

Rowland, D. 1989. Measuring the Elderly's Need for Home Care. *Health Affairs*, 8(4): 39–51.

Saluter, A.F. 1991. U.S. Bureau of the Census. *Marital Status and Living Arrangements: March 1990*. Current Population Reports. (Series P-20, No. 450). Washington, DC: U.S. Government Printing Office.

Sheehy, G. 1993. Preference. In Allen, J. and Pifer, A., *Women on the Front Lines: Meeting the Challenges of an Aging America*. Washington, DC: Urban Institute Press.

Short, K., and Nelson, C. 1991. Pensions: Worker Coverage and Retirement Benefits, 1987. Current Population Reports, (Series P-70, No. 25). U.S. Bureau of the Census. Washington, DC: U.S. Government Printing Office.

Social Security Administration. 1991. *Social Security Bulletin, Annual Statistical Supplement*. Washington, DC: U.S. Department of Health and Human Services.

Stone, R., Cafferata, G.L., and Sangl, J. 1987. Caregivers of the Frail Elderly: A National Profile. *Gerontologist*, 27: 616–26.

Taeuber, C.M., and Allen, J. 1993. Women in Our Aging Society: The Demographic Outlook. In Allen, J. and Pifer, A. (eds.), *Women on the Front Line: Meeting the Challenge of an Aging America*. 1993. Washington, DC: Urban Institute Press.

Taeuber, C.M., and Valdisera, V. 1986. Women in the American Economy. Current Population Reports, (Series P-23, No. 146). U.S. Bureau of the Census. Washington, DC: U.S. Government Printing Office.

Tuma, N.B., and Sandefur, G.D. 1987. Trends in Labor Force: Activity of the Aged in the United States, 1940–1980. (unpublished paper).

Uhlenberg, P., Cooney, T., and Boyd, R. 1990. Divorce for Women After Midlife. *Journal of Gerontology*, 45(1): S5.

U.S. Bipartisan Commission on Comprehensive Health Care (Pepper Commission). 1990. *A Call to Action: Final Report*. Washington DC: U.S. Government Printing Office.

U.S. Bureau of the Census. 1980, 1990. Censuses of Population, 1980, from Persons in Institutions and Other Group Quarters, (PC80-2-4D).

U.S. Bureau of the Census. 1987. Current Population Reports. (Series P-70, No. 25). Pensions: Worker Coverage and Retirement Benefits, 1987. Washington, DC: U.S. Government Printing Office.

U.S. Bureau of the Census. 1992. Current Population Reports. (Special Studies, P23-178). *Sixty-Five Plus in America*. Washington, DC: U.S. Government Printing Office.

U.S. Bureau of the Census, Decennial Census. 1990. Census of Population, prepared by the Center Analysis System.

U.S. Bureau of the Census. 1986 unpublished work tables prepared by Bob Grymes in conjunction with *Projections of the Number of Households and Families: 1986 to 2000*. (Series B middle series projections) (Current Population Reports, Series P-25, No. 986). Washington, DC: U.S. Government Printing Office.

U.S. Department of Labor, Bureau of Labor Statistics. 1991. *Employment and Earnings*. 1950 Data from the Bureau of Labor Statistics, (unpublished annual averages from the 1950 Current Population Surveys).

U.S. Department of Labor, Bureau of Labor Statistics. 1986. (Unpublished tabulations from the 1986 Current Population Survey).

U.S. General Accounting Office. 1992. *Elderly Americans: Health, Housing, and Nutrition Gaps Between the Poor and Nonpoor*. Washington, DC.

U.S. House of Representatives Select Committee on Aging. 1988. *Exploding the Myths: Caregiving in America*. Washington, DC: U.S. Government Printing Office.

U.S. House of Representatives Select Committee on Aging. 1990. *Women, Caregiving, and Poverty: Options to Improve Social Security*. Washington, DC: U.S. Government Printing Office.

U.S. House of Representatives Select Committee on Aging. 1992. *Old, Poor and Forgotten: Elderly Americans Living in Poverty*. Washington, DC: U.S. Government Printing Office.

U.S. Senate Special Committee on Aging. 1993. *Developments in Aging: 1992, Vol. 1*. Washington, DC: U.S. Government Printing Office.

Zick, C.D., and Smith, K.R. 1991. Patterns of Economic Change Surrounding the Death of a Spouse. *Journal of Gerontology*, 46(6): S310–20.

CHAPTER 20

Older
Minorities

Jessee: Old, Alone, and Poor

Jessie is a 79-year-old widow. Born in the Mississippi Delta, she was the youngest of ten children. Her father was a sharecropper as were four of her brothers. Being African American 79 years ago in rural Mississippi did not offer her many opportunities for education. As a result, her employment history was limited to domestic work for which she earned no credits towards Social Security.

Her brothers and sisters are now all dead. Jessie's husband has been dead for 20 years. She lives in a house her parents built in 1910. Although she owns the house free and clear, it is hard to keep up with the repairs that are needed. She had been living on $345 a month from her husband's Social Security and was unaware of the Supplemental Security Income (SSI) program. Through her church, an SSI outreach worker made her aware of SSI, which now supplements her income. Getting SSI and Medicaid was a big help because the two programs combined give her more money to live on, and the Medicaid program pays for the medications she needs to control her high blood pressure. However, she does not want to apply for food stamps. There is only so much government assistance she will accept. Having been raised in a rural area, she feels that a person should be able to provide one's own food. Besides, she says that a 79-year-old woman doesn't need to eat too much to get by.

Maria: Helped by Two Major Programs

Maria, a 77-year-old widow, lives in Los Angeles. Although she is a legal immigrant from Mexico and has lived in the United States for 25 years, her use of English is limited.

After her husband died, Maria tried to support herself by babysitting and cleaning other people's houses. She married again after several years, but that marriage did not work out because the second husband did not want to take in Maria's mentally retarded daughter.

At age 70, she suffered a stroke. She could no longer earn even the meager amount of money she was getting from her two domestic jobs. Because she and both of her husbands worked at jobs that did not qualify them for Social Security benefits, Maria was desperate for income to live on and money to pay her medical care. Fortunately, the neighborhood she lived in had a Latino community organization with a Spanish-speaking outreach worker who told Maria about the SSI program and Medicaid. This has enabled Maria to survive in her own place. She doesn't know what she would have done without the outreach worker and the two support programs.

"We're Having Our Say . . ." Centenarian Sisters Recount Their Remarkable Lives—and Share Their Hard-Earned Wisdom

With the perspective that living more than 100 years can bring, Elizabeth and Sarah Delany, two women of color who broke new ground in the fields of health and education, have a loving admonition for America:

"Wake up! Stop dwelling so much on differences in race. Instead, focus more on caring, helping others and maintaining your dignity, independence and personal accountability. There's too much attention paid to color," says Elizabeth Delany, at age 102, two years her sister's junior. "Racism has ruined America. The Founding Fathers didn't intend for it to be like it is right now; they intended for everybody who wanted to make a contribution to be able to make it."

Daughters of a freed slave who became the first elected black Episcopal bishop in the United States, the two sisters have earned the right to speak their minds, and not just because of their longevity.

Elizabeth Delany, known affectionately to her former patients as "Dr. Bessie," battled through both racial and sexual bias to earn a degree in oral surgery at the Columbia University School of Dentistry. In 1923 she became the second Negro woman to be licensed as a dentist in New York state. Her sister, Sarah, whose gentle disposition won her the family nickname "Sweet Sadie," achieved her goal too, as a master's level educator. She became the first Negro high school teacher of domestic science in New York City.

Now the two sisters have reached another milestone. This time they have surprised even themselves by becoming best-selling authors, telling the story of their lives and recounting their remarkable struggle to succeed in a sometimes hostile society.

> Christine Lyons and William Barnhill
> *Source: NRTA Bulletin*, March 1994,
> Vol. 35, No. 3, p. 20

UNEVEN GAINS OF OLDER PEOPLE

Since the enactment of the Social Security Act of 1935, an array of programs and services has improved the health and economic status of the average older person in the United States (Krause and Wray 1992). However, as Bass and his associates have pointed out, "the transition to a social policy that supports a vital and productive old age is still occurring in an alarming uneven fashion" (Bass, Kutza, and Torres-Gil 1990: iv). What this means is that minority older persons continue to be among the poorest and most chronically ill in American society, and consequently, the most in need of social-support and health services (Jackson and Perry 1989; Commonwealth Fund Commission 1989; National Center for Health Statistics 1990).

POOR HEALTH AND THE EFFECTS OF DISCRIMINATION

Many of the minority groups in the United States experience health problems at a greater rate than white Americans. This has resulted in disabilities that have limited work for many members of minority groups. Poorer health and disabilities have played "large parts in their disadvantaged labor force and retirement experiences" (Gibson and Burns 1992: 54). In addition, many elderly persons have experienced a lifetime of discrimination with its range of effects including "lack of perceived control, discouragement . . . that im-

pede the development of motivating aspirations and expectations of a successful life (Jackson, Chatters, and Taylor, 1993: 315). As Jackson and his associates have pointed out concerning African Americans, for example,

> Previous and contemporary cohorts of Blacks have been and are at considerable risks. Blacks have in the past spent and are most likely in the future to spend the majority of their childhood in low-income, single-parent, female-headed households and to be exposed to inadequate educational opportunities. Their job prospects early in life have been poor and will be perhaps even poorer in future cohorts (Jackson, Chatters, and Taylor 1993: 315).

Lifelong discrimination and segregation accompanied by limited access to quality health care, good education, and effective job-training programs have resulted in the disadvantaged conditions of the major minority groups that are described in this chapter. As Fernando Torres-Gil pointed out,

> It is widely agreed that a poor young person is likely to become a poor old person. A functionally illiterate child or teenager lacking basic health care will invariably be highly dependent on public benefits and assistance through old age (Torres-Gil 1992: 169).

DOUBLE AND TRIPLE JEOPARDY OF OLD, MINORITY, AND FEMALE

With older minority persons some of the nation's most vulnerable citizens, a Special Committee on Aging of the United States (1992) pointed out the double jeopardy older minority persons face in American society—the physical changes and social consequences associated with growing older coupled with the cumulative results of lifetimes of discrimination. When being female is added to the consideration of the life circumstances, the situation is even bleaker. As a result, older minority females are among the poorest and most disadvantaged people in the nation.

RAPID GROWTH OF MINORITY AGED

One of the top ten major trends of the elderly population in the United States in the years ahead, as identified by the Bureau of the Census, will be greater racial and ethnic diversity. In 1990, one in ten elderly persons was a member of a minority group. This is expected to increase to about two in ten by the middle of the twenty-first century. With the rapid growth of the Hispanic American population, elderly Latinos are expected to make up a significant proportion of all minority older persons. Where about one in five elderly African Americans and Latinos was 80 years of age and older in 1990, by 2050 one out of three is expected to be 80 years and older (U.S. Bureau of the Census 1992).

This is an important consideration because studies have shown that in several states the white majority will soon become one of several minority groups. Torres-Gil (1992) has pointed out that early in the twenty-first century Asian and Pacific Islanders, Latinos, African Americans, and Native Americans will make up the new majority. By 2056, the white population in the United States is expected to become a minority group (*Time* 1990).

The fastest growing sector of the elderly population (persons aged 65 and older) is among the non-white population, especially Latinos and Asian Americans. Stanford and Yee (1992) have pointed out that gerontology in the United States will not be so focused on an essentially white, relatively homogeneous population. These authors also pointed out that by including a diverse older population in future studies, characteristics such as race would no longer be solely defined as "deviance" or differences from "white standards." This does not mean that comparisons of health, longevity, access to services, and other such measures are not useful as they are utilized in this book. What it does mean, according to Stanford and Yee, is that new approaches to such things as measuring services and service use would benefit from models of study for hetero-geneity within and between various population groups to be studied.

CONDITIONS OF ELDERLY AMERICAN MINORITIES

There are obviously differences in the experiences and conditions of various minority groups, but, as a U.S. Senate report pointed out, there are also similarities in the experiences of each. Each group "has faced discrimination, emotional let down, and economic set backs" (U.S. Senate Special Committee on Aging 1992: 401). This chapter will look at some of the important conditions faced by the most predominant minority groups. There are four federally recognized groups of minority elderly in the United States. They are African Americans, Latino Americans, Asian Americans/Pacific Islanders, and Native Americans including Eskimo and Aleut Americans.

African Americans

According to a report by Samuel Simmons (1992), the President of the National Caucus and Center on Black Aged, Inc., before the House Select Committee on Aging, aged African Americans are among the poorest of the poor in the United States by any objective measure. This report indicated that a large proportion of African Americans have been poor throughout their lives, from conception to death. Growing older makes this problem worse. There are a number of ways to evaluate the condition of elderly African Americans.

Demographics   In 1990 there were nearly 2.5 million African Americans aged 65 and older in the United States. Elderly African Americans made up 8 percent of all persons aged 65 and older. Three out of every five elderly African Americans were women in 1990 (U.S. Bureau of the Census 1991a).

The older African-American population is projected to increase by 25.8 percent from 1990 to 2000, and by 126.1 percent from 1990 to 2020.

This rate of increase for older African Americans is expected to be more than twice that for older whites (58.1 percent) between 1990 and 2020 (U.S. Bureau of the Census 1989).

Income   Inadequate income in retirement is the number-one problem for older African Americans. It is the major cause for almost every problem elderly African Americans face—poor health, inadequate diet, dilapidated housing, and other bad living conditions (Simmons 1992).

The median annual income for aged African-American males was only 50 percent of that of aged white males in 1990. This percentage had decreased from the preceding year. Older African-American females had a median income that was 66 percent of elderly white females. In 1990, elderly African-American males were nearly four times as likely as white elderly males to have incomes below $5,000; elderly African-American females were nearly twice as likely as older white females to have incomes below $5,000 in 1990 (U.S. Bureau of the Census 1991b).

One out of every four (25.3 percent) older African-American males, and four out of every nine (44.3%) elderly African-American females had incomes below $5,000 in 1990. A large majority of all elderly African Americans in 1990 had incomes below $10,000: 64.6 percent of females and 84 percent of males (Bureau of the Census 1991b).

More than half (51.7 percent) of the total income of elderly African Americans in 1990 came from Social Security. Earnings accounted for 17.3 percent of income, followed by pension income at 16.4 percent. Elderly African Americans received more than eight times as much of their incomes from Supplemental Security Income as did elderly whites, indicating their dependence on a poverty income program. One out of six African Americans received SSI, compared to one out of 26 older whites. Elderly whites are two and one-half times as likely to get income from interest earnings as are older African Americans. In 1990, elderly whites were nearly ten times as likely to get income from dividends as were older African Americans, 19.4 percent compared to 2 percent (U.S. Bureau of the Census 1991b).

Poverty   One out of every three (33.8 percent) elderly African Americans was in poverty in 1990. When the near poor (125 percent of the poverty line) and the economically vulnerable (200 percent of the poverty line) were added to those below the poverty line, 64.2 percent of elderly African Americans fell into the combined categories. For elderly African Americans living alone, the percentages were even worse; those living alone or with nonrelatives were among the poorest in the nation. In 1940, 89.3 percent of elderly African-American females in this category were either poor, near poor, or economically vulnerable, and 60.1 percent were below the poverty line and considered poor. Among elderly African-American males, 72.6 percent were either poor, near poor, and economically vulnerable (U.S. Bureau of the Census 1991c).

Older African Americans were more than three times as likely to be poor than elderly whites in 1990, 33.8 percent compared to 10.1 percent. They were nearly twice as likely to have incomes below twice the poverty line (poor, near poor, and economically vulnerable) as older whites (U.S. Bureau of the Census 1991c). The poverty rate for elderly African Americans is 64 percent greater than for children under the age of 18 (33.8 percent compared to 20.6 percent). Between 1986 and 1990, the poverty rate for older African Americans actually increased to about the level it was in 1974. As Samuel Simmons, the head of the National Caucus and Center on Black Aged, Inc., said, "The harsh reality is that older Blacks are on an economic treadmill. They are swirling in an economic rapids that threatens to drown them" (Simmons 1992: 112).

Health   In 1990, two out of five (40.1 percent) African Americans aged 65 and older felt that their health was poor or just fair. Only 31.6 considered their health to be very good or excellent.

Translating this to days confined to bed due to health conditions, elderly African Americans averaged 22.5 days in bed compared to 12.8 days for older whites, a difference of some 76 percent (U.S. Department of Health and Human Services 1991).

Elderly African Americans experience a higher rate of functional limitations—difficulties because of a health or physical problem with the daily activities of living involved with taking care of oneself. Among people aged 65 and older, 74 to 84 percent of African-American women had one or more limitation compared to 58 to 62 percent of white women of the same aged category in a major study. African-American men experiencing one or more limitation ranged from 62 to 76 percent compared with 50 to 54 percent of white men. About half (49 percent) of African-American women had limitations that were severe compared to 31.7 percent of white women and 21.2 percent of white men (McNeil and Lamas 1986). Studies have found that older African Americans who were dependent on others for daily living were more likely to live with someone other than their spouse than were whites in similar dependent conditions (30 percent compared to 18 percent). Elderly whites were more likely than older African Americans to live in nursing homes, 17 percent compared to 10 percent (Hing and Bloom 1990).

Life Expectancy In 1989, life expectancy at birth for African-American males was 64.8 years compared to 72.7 years for white males; 73.5 years for African-American females compared to 79.2 years for white females. At age 65, African-American males could expect to live 13.6 more years compared to 15.2 years for white males; African-American females, 12 years compared to 19 years for white females. With advancing age, the differences between African-American and white life expectancy narrows (U.S. Department of Health and Human Services 1992).

Employment The unemployment rate for African Americans (5.2 percent) aged 65 and older was 68 percent higher than for whites (3.1 percent) in 1991. These rates do not reflect the real size of the unemployment problem among older workers because they do not include "discouraged workers" (persons who wish to work but do not think they can because of such factors as age) and labor force "dropouts" (persons who have given up their search for employment). More older white males were employed than older African-American males, but more older African-American females were in the labor force than were older white females in 1991 (U.S. Department of Labor Statistics 1992).

The median weekly income for elderly African-American males was $270.69 compared to $493.72 for white males in 1991. For females aged 65 and older, African Americans earned $258.19 compared to $323.05 for whites (U.S. Department of Labor Statistics 1991a).

Education Elderly African Americans are among the most educationally disadvantaged in the United States. Males had a median level of education of 8.3 years compared to 12.3 years for older white males. Elderly African-American females had a median level of education of 9.3 years compared to 12.3 years for older white females (U.S. Bureau of the Census 1991a).

Tragically, one out of every four (28 percent) elderly African Americans is functionally illiterate (less than five years of schooling); one out of every seven (13.5 percent) older female African Americans is functionally illiterate. Nearly one-half (45.9 percent) of all elderly African-Americans males and one out of three (34.2 percent) older African-American females have less than an eighth-grade education (U.S. Bureau of the Census 1991a). Older African Americans are four to seven times more likely to be functionally illiterate than elderly whites (Simmons 1992).

Not only do elderly African Americans have much less formal schooling than their white counterparts, the quality of their schooling was markedly inferior because of segregated school systems in many areas of the United States when elderly African Americans went to school. Older whites are more than twice as likely to have graduated from high school as elderly African Americans (Simmons 1992). Clearly, educational deficiencies have been a great disadvantage to older African Americans and continue to place them at risk in American society.

Living Arrangements   With widowhood being a common condition among elderly African-American women, only 37 percent of all African Americans aged 65 and older live with a spouse. About 31 percent of all African Americans live along, 28 percent live with a relative other than a spouse, and 4 percent live with nonrelatives. These percentages are quite different from elderly whites, some 56 percent of whom live with a spouse; only 11 percent live with a relative other than a spouse, and 2 percent live with a nonrelative (Bureau of the Census 1992b).

Older African Americans were more likely than elderly whites to live in households with three or more people. While only 9 percent of elderly whites in 1990 maintained households of three or more people, some 20 percent of older African Americans maintained such multiple-person households. This is partly due to younger elderly grandparents having their adult children and grandchildren live in their homes. But with increasing age, the rate of having three or more persons in an elderly African American's household decreases (U.S. Bureau of the Census 1992b).

Housing   In 1991, five out of every eight (62.6 percent) African-American heads of household aged 65 and older were homeowners, a rate below that for whites of the same age category as well as for all older persons (78.4 percent for whites, 76.8 percent for all races) (Bureau of the Census 1992b). Elderly African Americans (5.5 percent) are more likely to live in housing with serious problems than are whites (3.1 percent) (Naifeh, forthcoming).

Latino Americans

Americans of Hispanic origin are known as Latinos or Hispanic Americans. They are the fastest-growing minority population in the United States. The reasons for this, according to a 1992(a) U.S. Senate report, include changes in immigration laws, lower median age, and higher fertility rates. Persons of Hispanic origin are expected to become the nation's most populous minority after the year 2000. The U.S. Senate report also showed that the Latino population is becoming more diverse. The majority of Latino Americans are from Mexico, Puerto Rico, and Cuba.

Demographics   Between 1980 and 1988, the Latino population increased nearly five times as fast as the non-Hispanic population (Sotomayor 1992). Between 1980 and 1990 the number of elderly Latinos increased from 700,000 to 1.1 million (U.S. Bureau of the Census 1983, 1990c). (See Figure 20-1.)

The elderly Latino population is expected to double by 2010, and to increase seven times by 2050 based on middle (moderate) series projections of the U.S. Bureau of the Census (1988, 1990c). Projections indicate that older persons of Hispanic origin would increase from less than 4 percent of the total elderly population to nearly 12 percent by 2050. The proportion of all older persons in the United States who are of Hispanic origin could exceed the proportion who are African American by the middle of the next century, Figures 20-2, 20-3, 20-4.

The number of Latinos aged 65 and older tripled in the last two decades. Older Latinos make up the fastest-growing group within the Latino population (Sotomayor, 1992).

Income   Elderly Americans of Hispanic origin are at a disadvantage compared to most groups of older people in the United States, especially to older white people. Income from nearly all sources was lower for elderly Latinos than it was for all races. One of the exceptions was the

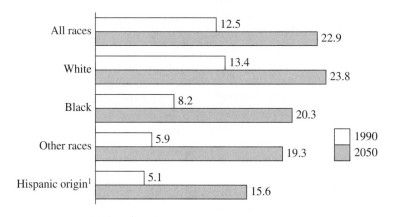

**Percentage of Population 65 Years
and Over, by Race and Hispanic
Origin: 1990 and 2050**

¹Hispanic origin may be of any race.

FIGURE 20-1
Racial makeup of elderly persons in the United States in 1990 and 2050. Growth
of the elderly minority population: 1990–2050 (*Source:* U.S. Bureau of the Census. Current Population Reports, Special Studies, P23-178, *Sixty-five plus in
America.* U.S. Government Printing Office, Washington, DC, 1992, p. 2-15.)

amount received from Supplemental Social Security (SSI), a poverty income program. Even in this income category, Latino Americans are at a distinct disadvantage. Where 56 percent of the elderly poor got SSI benefits in 1990, only 39 percent of eligible Latinos benefitted.

In most categories of income for elderly people in the United States, Latino Americans are at a disadvantage compared to whites, but fare better than African Americans. For example, earnings from work provided the highest mean income for older people in 1990. Older Latinos had a mean income from earnings of $10,331 compared to $9,400 for elderly African Americans and $14,498 for elderly whites. Income from Social Security averaged $6,236 for elderly whites in 1990, $5,159 for older Latino Americans, and $5,081 for older African Americans. From pensions, elderly whites received a mean income of $7,901 and Latinos got $6,825, very similar to el-

derly African Americans' $6,593 (DeNavas and Welniak 1991). While 34 percent of elderly whites received retirement pensions, only 19 percent of Hispanics did (U.S. Bureau of the Census 1992c).

Income from property (including dividends, interest, rents, estates, and royalties) was particularly sparse for Latino Americans as it was for African Americans in 1990. While elderly whites received $5,411 in property income, Latino Americans received $1,853 and African Americans got $1,561 (DeNavas and Welniak 1991).

Elderly Latinos' income has also been influenced by lower-level occupations and wages along with uneven work patterns over a lifetime (Gibson and Burns 1992).

Poverty   Low incomes result in being in or near poverty. With relatively low incomes from most possible sources, it is no surprise that so many el-

**Persons 65 Years and Over,
by Age, Race, and Hispanic
Origin: 1990 and 2050**
(In millions)

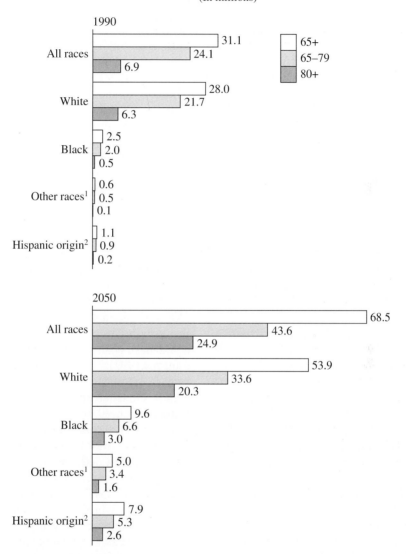

[1]Includes Asians and Pacific Islanders, American Indians, Eskimos, and Aleuts.
[2]Hispanic origin may be of any race.

FIGURE 20-2

Racial makeup of elderly persons in the United States in 1990 and 2050. (*Source:* U.S. Bureau of the Census. Current Population Reports, Special Studies, P23-178. *Sixty-five plus in America.* U.S. Government Printing Office, Washington, DC, 1992, p. 2-12.)

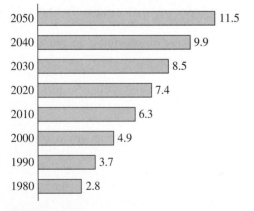

**Hispanic-Origin
Population 65 Years
and Over: 1980 to 2050**
(In millions)

Year	Value
2050	7.9
2040	6.7
2030	5.6
2020	3.9
2010	2.5
2000	1.7
1990	1.1
1980	0.7

FIGURE 20-3

Number of Hispanic-origin persons in the United States in 1980 to 2050. (*Source:* U.S. Bureau of the Census. Current Population Reports, Special Studies, P230178, *Sixty-five plus in America*, U.S. Government Printing Office, Washington, DC, 1992, p. 2-14.)

**Percent Hispanic Origin
of the Total Population 65
Years and Over: 1980 to 2050**

Year	Value
2050	11.5
2040	9.9
2030	8.5
2020	7.4
2010	6.3
2000	4.9
1990	3.7
1980	2.8

FIGURE 20-4

Percentage of elderly persons of Hispanic origin in the United States from 1980 to 2050. (*Source:* U.S. Bureau of the Census. Current Population Reports, Special Studies, P23-178, *Sixty-five plus in America*. U.S. Government Printing Office, Washington, DC, 1992, Figure 2-17, p. 2-14.)

derly Latinos find themselves poor, marginally poor, or economically vulnerable. Of all Latinos aged 65 and older, 22.5 percent were classified as poor in 1990. When the marginally poor (under 125 percent of the poverty line) were added to those defined as poor, 33.5 percent of all elderly Latinos are in this category. When the economically vulnerable (under 200 percent of the poverty line) are counted, 56.6 percent were included (Littman 1991). (See Figure 20-5.)

As age increases, especially past the age of 75, poverty increases for elderly Latinos. Among this age group, 26.2 percent were classified as poor, and an additional 12.4 percent were marginally poor. Similar to other elderly groups, older Hispanic women were more economically disadvantaged than older men of Hispanic origin (Littman 1991).

According to experts and Latino advocates, poverty among elderly Latino Americans is due to a number of factors including lack of access to education, having dropped out of school, limited or lack of marketable skills resulting in underemployment and unemployment, and discrimination resulting in limited access to opportunities that could make positive differences in their lives (Sotomayor 1992).

Health Characteristics   Elderly Latino Americans experienced lower death rates from heart disease and cancer than either older African Americans or older white persons. Whereas the death rate from heart disease was 5 percent higher for African Americans, the death rate for similarly aged Latinos was 35 to 45 percent below that experienced by white older persons in 1988. Similarly, the cancer death rate for elderly African Americans was 17 percent higher than that experienced by older whites, but for elderly Latinos was 40 percent lower than for elderly whites (National Center for Health Statistics 1991).

Elderly Latinos experienced a higher rate of needing assistance with the activities of daily living (ADLs) than did white persons of the same age category (aged 65 and older). In 1986, 19.2 percent of Latino elderly needed help with ADLs

**Percent Poor Elderly in 1990, by Age, Sex,
Race, and Hispanic Origin: March 1991**

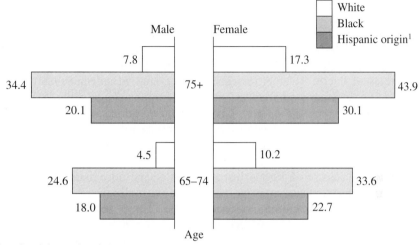

¹Hispanic origin may be of any race.

FIGURE 20-5

Percentage of poor elderly persons in the United States by age, sex, race, and Hispanic origin. (*Source:* U.S. Bureau of the Census. Current Population Reports, Special Studies, P23-178, *Sixty-five plus in America.* U.S. Government Printing Office, Washington, DC, 1992, Figure 4-12, p. 4-14.)

compared to 15.4 percent of older white people (U.S. Bureau of the Census 1990a).

Puerto Rican, Cuban, and Mexican Americans have been found to have poorer health and more work disability than white Americans. Of these groups, Puerto Rican Americans, along with African Americans, have been found to be the least healthy. At the midlife ages (45–64), all three major categories of Latino Americans (Puerto Rican, Cuban, and Mexican) spent more days confined to bed because of disability in 1978–1980. Gibson and Burns (1992) pointed out that poor health and more disability during the working years resulted in disadvantages in work and in retirement. In fact, Puerto Rican Americans and African Americans have been at the bottom of minorities ranked for health, work, and retirement.

Medicare, the national health insurance for older people, is available to nearly all elderly Americans. In addition, some three-fourths (74.2

percent) of all older persons aged 65 to 84 had private supplemental health insurance in 1989. About two-thirds (64.8 percent) of the oldest old (aged 85 and older) had private supplemental health insurance. However, only 29.8 percent of elderly Cuban Americans, 35.7 percent of elderly Mexican Americans, and 20.4 percent of elderly Puerto Rican Americans had private supplemental health insurance (National Center for Health Statistics 1990). Those without this type of coverage are more likely to have functional limitations and severe limitations that negatively impact their lives (McNeil and Lamas 1986). All of these health factors contribute to put Latino Americans at risk among America's elderly population.

Employment Even though minority workers are becoming a greater force in the American workplace, they continue to be at a distinct disadvantage to nonminority workers (Borgas and Tienda

1985). Puerto Rican and Mexican Americans, along with African Americans, continue to be the most disadvantaged of all the minority populations (Gibson and Burns 1992). The levels of occupations in which people work has a real impact on their incomes and work histories. At the end of the 1980s and in the early 1990s, 28 percent of whites were in professional and managerial jobs compared to 11 percent of Puerto Rican Americans and 9 percent of Mexican Americans. In this same era, 14 percent of whites were laborers compared to 22 percent of Cuban Americans, 25 percent of Puerto Rican Americans, and 31 percent of Mexican Americans. These minorities have been concentrated in the lower occupational jobs as the result of lower levels of education, discrimination in the workplace, and language and cultural barriers (U.S. Bureau of the Census 1990b; U.S. Bureau of Labor Statistics 1991; Torres-Gil 1986).

The Immigration Reform and Control Act of the 1980s, designed to regulate the employment of undocumented Latinos and discourage immigration, has resulted in segregating undocumented Latinos in the underground economy where they work long hours in unsafe conditions for below-minimum wages without health insurance, paid holidays, workers compensation, or overtime pay. Even documented immigrants and Latinos born in the United States often experience job discrimination and lack of job advancement just because they are Latinos. There is a fear on the part of some employers that they might be undocumented workers (Hayes-Bautista 1992).

Geographic Distribution In 1990, Latino Americans were about seven times more likely to live in metropolitan areas than not; of all Latino Americans, 1,029,247 lived in metropolitan areas compared to 132,036 in nonmetropolitan areas. Three of four older Latinos lived in the South and West. Nine cities had 10,000 or more elderly persons of Hispanic origin people including (in rank order) New York, Los Angeles, Miami, San Antonio, El Paso, Hialeah (Florida), Chicago, Houston, and San Diego (U.S. Bureau of the Census

1990c). California's Latino population is increasing rapidly. In 1970, Latinos were 10.9 percent of the population (Employment Development Department 1986). By 1990, the percentage of Latinos in California had grown to 25.7 percent (U.S. Bureau of the Census 1991b). By the time the last of the baby boom generation retires, California's Latino population is expected to be about 60 percent (Hayes-Bautista 1992).

Education Educational achievement has become an indicator of the economic and health condition of older people. Some research has demonstrated that older people who are better educated are more likely to be better off economically as well as healthier (Kitagawa and Hauser 1973). Lower levels of education are a significant factor in minority workers being concentrated in lower-status and lower-income jobs (Torres-Gil 1986). Lower-level jobs with lower-level incomes and benefits (or with no benefits) lead to older minority workers either being forced to continue to work in their later years or experiencing greatly disadvantaged incomes in retirement.

Older Latinos are substantially disadvantaged in their levels of formal education. Nearly two-thirds (63.9 percent) of all Americans of Hispanic origin aged 65 and older had only an eighth-grade education or less compared to 57.3 percent of African Americans the same age and 29.2 percent of older people in the same age category of all races in 1989. Not many elderly Latino Americans have completed high school. Just 17.4 percent of Latinos aged 65 and older had completed high school in 1989 compared to 33.2 percent of the elderly of all races. The high school completion rate was about half that of older persons of all races. College completion rates for elderly Latinos (5.9 percent) were also about half the college completion rates for all persons aged 65 and older, 11.1 percent (Kominski 1991).

When the older segments (aged 75 and older) of the elderly population are compared for formal education, Latino Americans are even more disadvantaged. Seven out of ten Latinos (69.5 percent) and African Americans (68.9 percent) aged 75 and older had just an eighth grade education or less in 1989 compared to 38.8 percent of people of all races aged 75 and older (Kominski 1991). When the future older people of various races and ethnic groups are considered, it becomes evident that minorities will continue to be at distinct disadvantages. This is particularly true for future older Latino Americans. In 1989 about one-fourth (23.8 percent) of whites aged 45 to 49 had four or more years of college compared to 14.8 percent of African Americans in that age bracket and only 9.9 percent of Latinos (U.S. Bureau of the Census 1992c).

Marital Status and Living Arrangements As has been previously observed, there is an increasing probability that women will become widowed and live alone as they grow older. This is gener-

ally true for elderly Latino-American women. In 1990, 48.2 percent of elderly Latino women aged 65 to 74 were married with a spouse present compared to 77.4 percent of Latino men of the same ages; 26.3 percent of Latino women aged 75 to 84 were married with a spouse present compared to 67.2 percent of Latino men of the same ages. Insufficient data were available for Latinos aged 85 and older (Saluter 1991). Similarly, the percentages of older Latinos in 1990 showed higher rates of widowhood for Latina women compared to older Latino men as the following figure shows.

It not at all surprising that in 1990 there are about twice as many Latina women aged 65 to 74 living alone as Latino men of the same age category (22.3 percent for women, 12.4 percent for men). For those Latinos aged 75 to 84, 34.4 percent of the women lived alone compared to 22.8 percent of the men (Saluter 1991). (See Figure 20-6.)

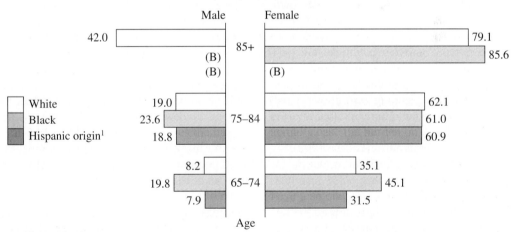

**Percentage of Persons 65 Years and Over
Who Are Widowed, by Age, Sex, Race,
and Hispanic Origin: March 1990**
(Noninstitutional population)

B Base is less than 75,000.
[1]Hispanic origin may be of any race.

FIGURE 20-6
Percentage of elderly persons in the United States who are widowed by age, sex, race, and Hispanic origin. Widowed persons aged 65 and older in 1990. (*Source:* U.S. Bureau of the Census. Current Population Reports, Special Studies, P24-178 RV, *Sixty-five plus in America.* U.S. Government Printing Office, Washington, DC, 1993, Figure 6-2, p. 6-5.)

Housing   The American Housing Survey of 1989 found that 61.4 percent of elderly Latino Americans were homeowners compared to 63.4 percent of elderly African Americans and 77.7 percent of older white persons (Naifeh, in press).

The Commonwealth Fund Commission on Elderly People Living Alone of 1989, a significant study of the major factors that place older people at risk, found that a lower percentage of older Latino Americans (68 percent) lived in houses compared to the total population of elderly people (77 percent). Among older Latinos, 29 percent lived in apartments compared to 16 percent of the total elderly population. The reasons why more elderly Latinos lived in apartments included the fact that large numbers of Cuban Americans and Puerto Rican Americans lived in urban areas that do not have much single-family housing (Lacayo 1992). This is significant not only in the type of housing many Latinos occupy, but also because elderly homeowners spend less of their income on housing than do elderly renters (Naifeh, in press).

Some studies have found that older Latinos have difficulty keeping up the homes they own, and as a result, many live in substandard housing units. They also have had difficulties paying property taxes, making mortgage payments, and paying insurance and utility bills. In addition, as do most minorities, many Latinos have had to deal with "red-lining" by lending institutions which makes it difficult to borrow for houses in areas (typically in a metropolitan area) that are red-lined off limits for lending purposes (Lacayo 1992).

Renting can also be a difficult situation for many elderly Latino Americans. A 1991 study of market rents in areas heavily populated by elderly persons of Hispanic origin showed the following for one bedroom apartments: Los Angeles, $618–$833; San Francisco, $758–$1,063; Chicago, $710–$851; Miami, $532–$711 (U.S. Department of Housing and Urban Development 1991).

One-fourth (25.6 percent) of all households maintained by Latino Americans aged 65 and older had three or more persons compared to less than one in ten (9 percent) of households maintained by elderly whites (Rawlings 1990).

Asian Americans/Pacific Islanders

The following is an analysis of those elderly minority groups (Asian Americans/Pacific Islanders and American Indians) that not only suffer from the results of discrimination and all the other aspects of being minorities in the United States, but are at a disadvantage because of the lack of detailed information concerning their conditions. The basic reason for the sparse information is their relatively small numbers compared to whites, African Americans, and Latinos. Numerous experts on minority elderly persons have recognized and lamented this situation. Stanford and Yee (1992), writing about the diversity of the elderly population in the United States, pointed out that when national studies of older people include minorities, the focus is typically on African Americans or Latino Americans. Krause and Wray (1992) stated that there is a serious lack of research on older adults in minority cultures other than African Americans and Latinos.

Some information concerning elderly Asian Americans and Pacific Islanders is provided by the Census Bureau and reports by the Congress. Out of a total population of over 31 million persons aged 65 and older in 1990, less than one-half million (449,959) were classified as Asian Americans/Pacific Islanders. For the oldest old category, those aged 85 and older, 28,641 were Asian Americans/Pacific Islanders compared to a total population this age of over 3 million (U.S. Bureau of the Census 1990c).

Demographics   In looking at the total population of Asians/Pacific Islanders (of all ages) just 6 percent were elderly (65 and older) compared to nearly 13 percent elderly of the white population (U.S. Bureau of the Census 1992c). (See Figure 20-7.)

The Asian/Pacific Islander population in the United States consists of more than twenty dif-

**Persons 65 Years and Over,
by Specific Race and Hispanic
Origin: 1980 and 1990**
(In millions)

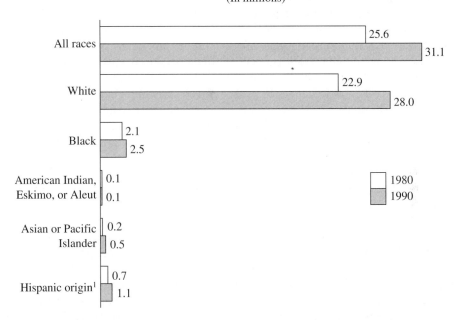

¹Hispanic origin may be of any race.
Note: The data for 1980 does not distribute persons of unspecified races among the specified
races as has been done in the 1990 data. Thus, those elderly who are marked "other race" on
the 1980 Census questionnaire are not included here. In data for 1990 from CPH-L-74
series used here, persons who marked "other race" were assigned the race reported by a
nearby person with an identical response to the Hispanic origin question.

FIGURE 20-7
Racial characteristics of the elderly population of the United States. Racial and Hispanic origin
of the elderly population 1980 and 1990. (*Source:* U.S. Bureau of the Census. Current Population Reports, Special Studies, P23-178RV, *Sixty-five plus in America*. U.S. Government Printing
Office, Washington, D.C., 1993, Figure 2-10, p. 2-10.)

ferent ethnic groups. A 1992 U.S. Senate Special
Committee on Aging report raised the question
of grouping so many different ethnic categories
together. According to this report, more than 50
percent of the Asian/Pacific Islander Americans
live in the Western States. Some 90 percent live
in urban areas. In 1990, the oldest-old Asian/Pa-
cific Islanders were concentrated in four major
cities: Honolulu with 3,922; Los Angeles with
2,374; San Francisco with 2,163; and New York

City with 2,112. Only fourteen other cities had as
many as 100 oldest old Asians/Pacific Islanders.
The three primary groups of Asians/Pacific Islanders are Chinese Americans, Japanese Americans, and Philipino Americans. Each group has
unique characteristics. All three groups have
large numbers of older males living in urban
areas (U.S. Bureau of the Census 1990c).

The Chinese were the first Asians to come to
the United States in significant numbers. The

need for low-cost labor to build the transcontinental railroad and to work the mines of the West motivated the immigration of Chinese males in the mid-1800s. However, the Chinese Exclusion Act of 1882 restricted the number of Chinese immigrants to 105 per year. Not until after World War II were Chinese women in any numbers allowed to come to the United States (U.S. Bureau of the Census 1990c).

The Japanese came to the United States in the early 1900s, but the Oriental Exclusion Act of 1924 stopped all immigration from Japan. During World War II, Japanese Americans on the west coast were relocated to detention camps in isolated areas away from the coast because of fears they would collaborate with the enemy (U.S. Bureau of the Census 1990c).

Many Philipinos came to the United States following the Philipino-American War in the early 1900s. Many Philipino males came as U.S. subjects. In 1934, the Tydings-McDuffie Act limited the number of Philipinos to 50 per year. These were usually single males. Since 1965 there has been a significant change in the number of Philipino immigrants, with many women and children joining family members (U.S. Bureau of the Census 1990c).

Although the Asian/Pacific Islander population is small, their numbers increased dramatically between 1980 and 1990. This is true for all ages, including those aged 65 and older (Vobedga 1991). In fact, the number of Asian/Pacific Islander Americans aged 65 and older more than doubled from 1980 to 1990.

Poverty   The poverty rates for female Asian/Pacific Islander Americans aged 65 and older were the lowest of all of the identified groups— whites, African Americans, Latino Americans, Native Americans (including Eskimo and Aleut Americans) and other Asian/Pacific Islanders. Among these groups, Asian/Pacific Islander older women had a poverty rate of 14.5 percent compared to 15.4 percent for white older women, 28.1 percent for older Latino-American women,

34.2 percent for elderly Native Americans, Eskimos, and Aleuts, and 39.4 percent for older African-American women in 1979, the latest available data of this type (U.S. Bureau of the Census 1980).

Among men aged 65 and older, Asian/Pacific Islander Americans ranked second from the bottom in poverty status to all identified groups by the Census Bureau. The poverty rate for Asian/ Pacific Islander elderly men was 12.3 percent compared to 9 percent for white men of that age, 29.1 percent of older African American men, and 22.4 percent of older Latinos (U.S. Bureau of the Census, 1980).

Marital Status   Rates of widowhood among Asians/Pacific Islanders (API) were similar to other persons aged 75 and older in 1980, the latest year such data were available (Men: API, 22 percent; Latinos, 27 percent; Native Americans, 32 percent; African Americans, 33 percent. Women: API, 73 percent; Native Americans, 72 percent; Latinas, 68 percent; African Americans, 68 percent). The percentages of Asians/Pacific Islanders living alone were similar to those Latino Americans of the same age in 1980, somewhat lower than the rates for African Americans and Native Americans (Men: API, 16 percent; African Americans, 24 percent; Native Americans, 24 percent; Latinos, 17 percent. Women: API, 37 percent; African Americans, 40 percent; Native Americans, 42 percent; Latinas, 31 percent) (U.S. Bureau of the Census 1992c).

Health Conditions   Death rates from heart disease, the major cause of death in the United States at mature ages, were lowest for Asian/Pacific Islander Americans. In fact, they were about 60 percent lower than the death rates white persons experienced in 1988. Adding to that positive news, their death rates from cancer were the lowest for all identified racial and ethnic groups. In 1988 the death rate from cancer for elderly Asians/Pacific Islanders was 549 per 100,000, about half the white rate of 1,062 per 100,000

(National Center for Health Statistics 1991). These are very favorable health conditions for elderly Asian/Pacific Islander Americans. According to a study by the U.S. Public Health Service, eliminating deaths from heart disease would add some 5.1 years to life expectancy at age 65, and 3.5 years at age 85. The impact of eliminating cancer deaths would be significantly less: 1.8 years at age 65 and 0.4 years at age 85 and older (National Center for Health Statistics 1985).

In addition to Medicare, private health insurance was held by almost half (46.9 percent) of elderly Asian/Pacific Islander Americans compared to three-quarters (74.9 percent) of whites, 35.5 percent African Americans, and 20.4 percent of Puerto Rican Americans (National Center for Health Statistics, 1991).

Native Americans

The smallest major elderly minority group is the Native American population, which the Bureau of the Census identifies as American Indians, Eskimos, and Aleuts for statistical purposes. In 1990 there were 116,153 American Indian, Eskimo, and Aleut Americans aged 65 and older. Of that number, only 9,190 were aged 85 and older (U.S. Bureau of the Census, 1990c). Only 6 percent of the Native American population was aged 65 and older in 1990. Compare this to 13 percent of the white population, and 8 percent of the African-American population.

Unlike other minority groups, this sector of the population showed no real increase in numbers between 1980 and 1990, staying at just over 100,000 in the 10-year period (U.S. Bureau of the Census 1990c).

A U.S. Senate Special Committee on Aging (1992: 399) report referred to Native Americans as "the smallest population numerically, the purest culturally, and yet, probably one of the most misunderstood and impoverished communities socio-economically." According to the National Indian Council on Aging, Inc. (1981), there are more than 500 Native American tribes with their own cultures, histories, and languages.

However, only 314 of these are federally recognized. The histories of Native Americans have included "broken treaties, oppression, economic hardship, nonelective movement to reservation land bases, detribilization, removal of large numbers of Native American children from their parents and tribes, and gradual disintegration of traditional family ties and lifestyles" (U.S. Senate Special Committee on Aging 1992: 399–400).

Major differences in values cause the misunderstanding between the general American culture and American Indian culture. Competition versus sharing, focus on individuality versus family and community, and dominating nature versus harmony with nature are examples of different values of the two cultures that lead to basic differences (U.S. Senate Special Committee on Aging 1992). Its older people have experienced lifetimes of discrimination as well as alienation from the larger culture which historically has had different values (National Indian Council on Aging 1981).

Geographical Distribution Older Native Americans were the only minority group more likely to live in nonmetropolitan areas. Three-fourths of them lived in the western and southern states in 1990. Forty percent lived in just three states: Oklahoma, California, and Arizona. The oldest old were also concentrated in western and southern states. The large cities of the United States had very few of the oldest old Native Americans in 1990. New York City had 148, Tulsa had 111, Oklahoma City had 86, and Los Angeles had 84; but most had fewer than 10. Among all Native Americans aged 65 and older, New York City had the most (1,771) followed by Tulsa (1,344), Oklahoma City (1,277) and Los Angeles (958) in 1990 (U.S. Bureau of the Census 1990d).

Health Characteristics In terms of health, death rates from heart disease among elderly Native Americans were 35 to 45 percent lower than those for older whites (National Center for

Health Statistics 1990). This is significant since heart disease is the leading cause of death among elderly people.

Studies reported in the early 1980s indicated that elderly Native Americans were eight times more likely to die from tuberculosis, a figure now reduced (Barrow and Smith 1982). Native Americans were also more likely to die from gastritis, cirrhosis of the liver, influenza, and pneumonia. This population also had high rates of diabetes and arthritis. Fifty-five percent of Native Americans who lived in areas served by the Indian Health Service were covered only by that service. Only 28 percent had additional private coverage and only 11 percent had Medicaid coverage (National Center for Health Statistics 1990).

Their different living situations have resulted in life expectancies shorter than all other racial groups in the United States (National Indian Council on Aging 1981). With a shorter life expectancy, it is pointed out by some experts that the average Native American hardly lives long enough to benefit from most of the nation's entitlement programs (Bane 1992).

As might be expected with such a disadvantaged group as Native Americans, their poverty rates were similar to those experienced by African Americans in 1980 (U.S. Bureau of the Census 1980). Widowhood rates for elderly Native American Indians, Eskimos, and Aleuts were similar to those of other racial/ethnic older persons in 1980. The percentage of elderly Native Americans living alone was about the same as for elderly African Americans, and somewhat higher than those of American Asians/Pacific Islanders and Latino Americans (Taeuber and Smith 1987).

STRENGTHS OF FAMILY TIES AND RESOURCES

Research on social support systems has shown that older people from ethnic minority groups tend to have stronger kinship ties—family ties— than do older whites (Antonucci 1985; Markides and Mindel 1987). Lockery (1992) has pointed out that the informal support network (family, friends, and neighbor), particularly the family, has been the center of life for racial and ethnic minority persons. In later life, this social support system becomes the primary source of caregiving for older minority persons.

Although minority older persons rely heavily on their families for social interaction and support, there are some differences between the major minority groups.

African Americans

African Americans, according to research, are very involved in support between the generations, and are more likely to treat their older members with respect than do others of the general population (Mutran 1985). Without regard to their socioeconomic status, African-American children and grandchildren stand ready to help their older family members. At the same time, older African Americans are more likely to take their grandchildren, nieces, and nephews into their homes (Mitchell and Register 1984).

African-American older people have been found to receive more help from their informal network than white older people receive, including assistance with transportation, banking, homemaker services, and administrative/legal services (Mindel, Wright, and Starrett 1986).

Native Americans

Although there are some tribal differences, Native American cultures have traditionally placed a high value on the extended family (Lockery 1992). Older Native Americans have traditionally been respected for their wisdom, experience, and knowledge of tribal history and customs. The older persons on reservations tend to rely on the extended family for caregiving. Those who live off the reservation are often forced to turn to the formal support networks for assistance (National Indian Council on Aging 1981; Shoemaker 1990).

On the other end of caregiving, older Native Americans are more involved with childcare than whites or Latinos (Harris, Begay, and Page

1989). Helping daughters and grandchildren has been found to ensure the care of Navajo grandmothers in their later years (Shoemaker 1990).

Asians/Pacific Islanders

Even though there is significant diversity within and between Asian American/Pacific Islanders, many of these cultures are influenced by Confucian thought which emphasizes filial piety, with its focus on the moral obligation of children to respect and care for older family members (Koh and Bell 1987).

Restrictive immigration laws and immigration patterns were responsible for weakening the traditional family support system for many Asian American/Pacific Islanders (Lockery 1992).

Large numbers of Asian/Pacific Islander males who came to the United States for jobs grew old as bachelors without traditional family support systems. This was particularly true of Chinese American males who, according to some experts, grew old living in "Chinatowns" of large cities without traditional family supports in their later years. This forced many to become part of the first Asian groups to seek caregiving assistance in their old age from outside the traditional Chinese family support system (Lockery 1992).

Unlike the three primary Asian elderly groups identified by the U.S. Senate 1992 report already cited (Chinese, Japanese, and Philipino), newer waves of elderly Asians follow different patterns of immigration. Elderly Korean immigrants followed their children to the United States (Kiefer et al. 1985). Many were not able to live in the homes of their children, and they too were forced to seek help from outside support organizations (Koh and Bell 1987).

Many Japanese came to the United States in family units (Weeks 1984). Because of this, many were able to maintain family caregiving support systems which by tradition enable them to accept help from their children (Sokolovsky 1990).

The Asian/Pacific Islander population continues to grow rapidly. By March 1994, it was esti-

mated to be 8.8 million, which was an increase from 7.3 million in 1990. This population group has grown about 4.5 percent a year with 86 percent of the growth coming from immigration. By the year 2000, it is projected that there will be 12.1 million Asians/Pacific Islanders in the United States which will be about 4 percent of the total population (U.S. Bureau of the Census, 1995).

Latino Americans

In spite of the many groups (Mexican Americans, Puerto Ricans, Cubans, Central and South Americans, and others) that make up Americans of Hispanic origin, "the Spanish influence on Hispanic subcultures contributes to similar although not identical familial characteristics" (Lockery 1992: 117). Strong family bonds and frequent interaction are traditional with Latino families. A deep sense of obligation to the family often takes precedence over the needs or wishes of individual family members (Lockery 1992). Older Latinos by tradition are held in high esteem and expect their families to help them in their old age (Cuellar 1990).

There are, however, some differences among the groups of Hispanic origin. When they needed help, older Cuban Americans have been found to seek only the assistance of their children, not that of other family members (Escovar and Kurtines 1983). Puerto Ricans, unlike other Latinos, have been found to rely on themselves or friends more than family members when they needed help (Lacayo 1980).

Among Mexican Americans, considerable mutual assistance between the generations was found (Markides and Kraus 1986). Carmela Lacayo (1992) writing about living arrangements among minority elderly persons, pointed out conflicting studies of strong commitments to extended-family ties of older Mexican Americans. She noted some studies that indicated strong extended-family ties. Other studies found these ties decreasing. Demographic trends show that because the average Latino family's income declined (based on poverty rates) from 1978 to 1987, the Latino family became less able to provide for the financial needs of its older members. Some public policies also discourage poor older persons from living in extended-family arrangements. For example, SSI benefits are reduced by one-third when a recipient lives in someone else's household for a full month and gets support. All of these marital-status and living-arrangement factors contribute to putting elderly Latinos at risk.

CHANGING CAREGIVING PATTERNS

The caregiving patterns cited above for various minority groups tend to apply more to first-generation families (Weeks and Cuellar 1983). Subsequent generations often find it helpful to become more like the dominant culture. As a result, although it is important for service provides in the aging networks to be aware of and support family caregiving traditions, they should not perpetuate the myth that minority persons are totally self-sufficient in taking care of their older family members. Policies and practices need to be developed to include more minority persons in the formal caregiving systems (Lockery 1992). Currently, too many eligible minority older persons are not using the assistance programs that could help meet their basic needs and improve the quality of their lives (Kassner 1992). A number of significant barriers have been cited that hinder the participation of minority groups in key assistance programs. They include the following:

- *Fear of the government.* Many elderly poor Latinos and Asians fear giving too much information about themselves to governmental agencies as a result of their experiences with harsh governments back in their countries of origin.
- *Language barriers.* Information application forms and outreach efforts have primarily focused on English-speaking groups, with limited bilingual materials and caseworkers.

- *Verification problems.* It is often difficult for cultural and racial minorities, especially those born in other countries, to verify birth records and other documents needed for many assistance programs.
- *Living arrangements.* As has been pointed out, many cultural and ethnic minority older persons are more likely to live with and be cared for by family members. As a result, they are more likely to be penalized by household eligibility criteria when someone else is officially the head of the household in which they live, preventing them from being eligible for some programs such as Supplemental Security Income (Kassner 1992).

Effectively addressing these and other barriers is essential to assuring greater participation of minority elders in the vital assistance programs that can mean the difference between a minimum and sub-minimum standard of living.

Because Latinos and other minorities continue to work at disadvantaged jobs—disadvantaged for income, continuity, and benefits—it is contended that there is likely to be a growing gap between the "have-not" elderly and the "haves" in the future (Torres-Gil 1992). The job disadvantages of younger minorities that directly affect their income and benefits in their later years carry over to older minority workers. For example, although female whites, African Americans, and Latino Americans 55 years of age and older were nearly equally likely to be in the labor force in 1967, African-American and Latino-American women were more likely to be in low-paying jobs. About half (49.3 percent) of African-American women and about one-third (31.1 percent) of Latino-American women aged 55 to 64 worked in service occupations compared to about one in six (15.9 percent) white women (Herz 1988).

There is little information concerning the unemployment and other labor market problems of older racial and ethnic groups. The reason is because these populations are too small to measure effectively in surveys (U.S. Bureau of the Census 1992c). The National Commission for Employment Policy in 1985 indicated that older Latino Americans were three times as likely as older whites to have labor market problems (Rones and Herz 1989). A 1989 report by the Secretary of Labor stated:

> There is no question that older Blacks and other minorities are far more likely than whites to experience labor market problems. Limited available data suggest that older minority workers, like those of all ages, have higher rates of unemployment and discouragement and lower earnings than do older whites. These lifetime differences in employment and earnings generally mean fewer resources at retirement age. As a result, some older workers must maintain attachment to the job market long after those with greater financial resources might have retired (Rones and Herz 1989: 4).

As has been indicated, those Americans of Hispanic origin aged 65 and older who remain in or re-enter the labor force, earn considerably less income on the average than do elderly whites (DeNavas and Welniak 1991).

Future Prospects

If all of the conditions that describe the status of many elderly minority persons seem rather bad and bleak, the same or worse will be in store for younger and middle-aged minorities if they continue to have restricted access to quality health care, education, and job training programs (Gibson and Burns 1992). It has been argued that current public policies that have been designed for a population made up mostly of white, English-speaking older people whose needs have been quite similar are becoming more and more obsolete (Krause and Wray 1992). For minority older persons who are retired, job retraining should be available for those who want or find it necessary to return to work. The skills of many older minority persons have not kept pace with the skills needed for the changing American workplace (Gibson and Burns 1992).

AN EMPHASIS ON DIVERSITY

According to experts, the aging population will become more diverse by race, gender, income, ethnicity, immigration, and language. The more diverse characteristics of the younger population, with the rapid expansion of minority groups, will be reflected in the older population in the near future. Minority populations continue to swell with growing numbers of non-Europeans including African Americans, Latinos, Pacific Islanders, and Native Americans along with immigrants from Eastern Europe and the Middle East.

Stanford and Torres-Gil (1992) contended that the United States has been moving away from the "melting pot" concept where persons and cultures come closer together and become more alike as they "boil" in the "melting pot" over time. These experts have argued that American society should move toward a concept of diversity that includes the coexistence of different cultures and different ethnic identities. In this approach, Stanford and Torres-Gil have promoted the idea of acculturation as opposed to assimilation. Acculturation means that the goal is to enable persons of all types of backgrounds to function successfully by eliminating barriers such as racism and nativism (favoring native-born people over immigrants) and by promoting economic and social opportunities. Assimilation means giving up the strengths of group identities. They went on to say, however, that diversity should be looked at as an enabling concept and not as an end itself. As the twenty-first century approaches, diversity is the hallmark of the aging population of the United States (Cutler 1992).

SUMMARY

Minority elderly persons are some of the nation's most vulnerable citizens. Older minority persons in American society face a double jeopardy—the physical and social changes and social consequences connected with growing older coupled with the cumulative results of lifetimes of discrimination. When being female is added to these life circumstances, the picture is even bleaker. As a result, older minority females are among the most disadvantaged people in the nation.

Although each racial and ethnic group in the United States has different experiences, there are similarities. Each group has faced discrimination, emotional let-down, and economic setbacks.

Older African Americans are among the poorest of the poor in the nation. A large portion of African Americans have been poor throughout most of their lives. Growing older makes this condition worse and puts them at a disadvantage in income, health, life expectancy, employment, education, living arrangements, and housing conditions.

Americans of Hispanic origin, known as Latinos, are the fastest growing minority in the nation. This is due to changes in the immigration laws, lower median age, and higher fertility rates. The Latino population is expected to double by 2010, and to increase sevenfold by 2050. Older Latinos make up the fastest growing group within the Latino population.

Many older Americans of Hispanic origin find themselves poor, marginally poor, or economically vulnerable. Poverty among elderly Latinos is caused by lack of access to education, school drop-outs, limited marketable skills resulting in underemployment, and discrimination.

Asian Americans/Pacific Islanders not only suffer from the results of discrimination and other aspects of being minorities in the United States, but are at a disadvantage because of the lack of detailed information concerning their conditions. The reason for this sparse data is their relatively small numbers compared to other groups. Just 6 percent of the total population of Asians/Pacific Islanders were elderly (aged 65 and older) compared to nearly 13 percent of the white population.

The Asian/Pacific Islander population in the United States consists of more than twenty different ethnic groups. More than 50 percent of this population sector lives in the western states, with some 90 percent in urban areas. The poverty rates for elderly female Asian/Pacific Islander Americans were the lowest of all the identified female groups—whites, African Americans, Latino Americans, and Native Americans (including Eskimo and Aleut Americans). Among men aged 65 and older, Asian/Pacific Islander Americans ranked second from the bottom in poverty status to the other identified groups.

The smallest major minority group among the elderly is the Native American population, which includes Eskimos and Aleuts. A U.S. Senate report referred to the Native American population as probably one of the most misunderstood and impoverished socio-economically. There has been a history of broken treaties, oppression, economic hardship, and forced movements to reservations which has left older Native Americans in a disadvantaged condition. Their poverty rates are similar to older African Americans.

In the 1990 Census, only one in ten elderly persons was other than white. This is expected to increase to two in ten by the middle of the twenty-first century. The fastest growth will come in the Latino elderly population. As the nation moves into the twenty-first century, the older population will become more diverse by race, gender, income, ethnicity, and immigration. Some public policy experts have promoted the concept of acculturation as opposed to assimilation.

Acculturation means that the goal is to enable persons of all types of backgrounds to function successfully by eliminating barriers such as racism and nativism and by promoting economic and social opportunities. Assimilation means blending into one thereby giving up the strengths of group identities. As we move into the twenty-first century, diversity will be the hallmark of the aging population.

REFERENCES

Antonucci, T.C. 1985. Personal Characteristics, Social Support, and Social Behavior. In Binstock, R.H. and Shanas, E. (eds.). *Handbook of Aging and the Social Sciences*. New York: Van Nostrand Reinhold.

Bane, S.D. 1992. Rural Minority Populations. In E.P. Stanford, and F.M. Torres-Gil (eds.), *Diversity: New Approaches to Ethnic Minority Aging*. Amityville, NY: Baywood Publishing.

Barrow, G.M., and Smith, P.A. 1982. Aging, the Individual and Society. In *The Minority Aged*, 2d Ed. St. Paul, MN: West Publishing.

Bass, S.A., Kutza, E.A., and Torres-Gil, F.M. 1990. *Diversity in Aging*. Glenview, IL: Scott, Foresman.

Beyond the Melting Pot. 1990. *Time* (April 9): 28–35.

Borgas, G., and Tienda, M. (eds.). 1985. *Hispanics in the U.S. Economy*. Orlando, FL: Academic Press.

Commonwealth Fund Commission on Elderly People Living Alone. 1989. *Poverty and Poor Health Among Elderly Hispanic Americans*. Baltimore, MD: Commonwealth Fund.

Cuellar, J.B. 1990. *Aging and Health: Hispanic American Elders*. Stanford, CA: Stanford Geriatric Education Center.

Cutler, N.E. 1992. Targeting and Means Testing, Aging and Need. In E.P. Stanford and F.M. Torres-Gil (eds.), *Diversity: New Approaches to Ethnic Minority Aging*. Amityville, NY: Baywood Publishing Company.

DeNavas, C., and Welniak, E. July 1991. *Money Income of Households, Families, and Persons in the United States: 1990* (Current Population Reports, Series P-60, No. 174). Washington, DC: U.S. Government Printing Office.

Employment Development Department. 1986. *Socioeconomic Trends in California, 1940–1980*. Sacramento: State of California Health and Welfare Agency.

Escovar, L.A., and Kurtines, W.M. 1983. Psychological Predictors of Service Utilization Among Cuban-American Elders. *Journal of Community Psychology*, 11: 355–62.

Gibson, R.C., and Burns, C.J. 1992. The Health, Labor Force, and Retirement Experiences of Aging Minorities. In E.P. Stanford and F.M. Torres-Gil, (eds.), *Diversity: New Approaches to Ethnic Minority Aging*. Amityville, NY: Baywood Publishing.

Harris, M.B., Begay, C., and Page, P. 1989. Activities, Family Relationships and Feelings About Aging in a Multicultural Elderly Sample. *International Journal of Aging and Human Development*, 29: 103–17.

Hayes-Bautista, D.E. 1992. Young Latinos, Older Anglos, and Public Policy. In E.P. Stanford and F.M. Torres-Gil (eds.), *Diversity: New Approaches to Ethnic Minority Aging*. Amityville, NY: Baywood Publishing.

Herz, D.E. 1988. *Employment Characteristics of Older Women, 1987* (Current Population Survey, Monthly Review, unpublished). Washington, DC: Bureau of Labor Statistics.

Hing, E., and Bloom, B. 1990. *Long-Term Care for the Functionally Dependent Elderly* (DHHS Publication No. 90-1765). Hyattsville, MD: Public Health Service.

Jackson, J.J., and Perry C. 1989. Physical Health Conditions of Middle-Aged and Aged Blacks. In K.S. Markides (ed.). *Aging and Health: Perspectives on Gender, Race, Ethnicity, and Class*. New Park, CA: Sage Publications.

Jackson, J.S., Chatters, L.M., and Taylor, R.J. 1993. Status and Functioning of Future Cohorts of African-American Elderly: Conclusions and Speculations. In Jackson, J.S., Chatters, L.M. and Taylor, R.J. (eds.), *Aging in Black America*. Newbury Park, CA: Sage Publications.

Kassner, E. 1992. *Falling Through the Safety Net: Missed Opportunities for America's Elderly Poor*. Washington, D.C.: AARP.

Kiefer, C.W., Kim, S., Choi, K., Kim, L., Kim, B., Shon, S., and Kim, T. 1985. Adjustment Problems of Korean-American Elderly. *The Gerontologist*, 25: 477–82.

Kitagawa, E.M., and Hauser, P.M. 1973. *Differential Mortality in the United States: A Study in Socioeconomic Epidemiology*. Cambridge, MA: Harvard University Press.

Koh, J.T., and Bell, W.G. 1987. Korean Elders in the United States: Intergenerational Relations and Living Arrangements. *The Gerontologist*, 27: 66–71.

Kominski, R. 1991. *Educational Attainment in the United States: March 1989 and 1988*. Current Population Reports, Series P-20, No. 451. Washington, DC: U.S. Government Printing Office.

Krause, N., and Wray, L. 1992. Psychosocial Correlates of Health and Illness Among Minority Elders. In E.P. Stanford and F.M. Torres-Gil (eds.), *Diver-*

sity: New Approaches to Ethnic Minority Aging. Amityville, NY: Baywood Publishing Company.

Lacayo, C.G. 1980. *A National Study to Assess the Service Needs of the Hispanic Elderly, Final Report.* Los Angeles, CA: Associacion Nacional Pro Personas Mayores.

Lacayo, C.G. 1992. Current Trends in Living Arrangements and Social Environment Among Ethnic Minority Elderly. In E.P. Stanford and F.M. Torres-Gil (eds.), *Diversity: New Approaches to Ethnic Minority Aging.* Amityville, NY: Baywood Publishing.

Littman, M. 1991. *Poverty in the United States: 1990.* Current Population Reports, Series P-20, No. 175. Washington, DC: U.S. Government Printing Office.

Lockery, S.A. 1992. Caregiving Among Racial and Ethnic Minority Elders: Family and Social Supports. In E.P. Stanford and F.M. Torres-Gil (eds.), *Diversity: New Approaches to Ethnic Minority Aging.* Amityville, NY: Baywood Publishing.

Lyons, C., and Barnhill, W. 1994. We're Having Our Say. *NRTA Bulletin,* 35(3): 20.

McNeil, J.M., and Lamas, E.J. 1986. *Disability, Functional Limitation, and Health Insurance Coverage: 1984/85.* Current Population Reports, Series P-70, No. 8. Washington, DC: U.S. Government Printing Office.

Markides, K.S., and Kraus, N. 1986. Older Mexican Americans: Family Relationships and Well-Being. *Generations,* 10(4): 31–34.

Markides, K.S., and Mindel, C.H. 1987. *Aging and Ethnicity.* Newbury Park, CA: Sage Publications.

Mindel, C.H., Wright, R., and Starrett, R.A. 1986. Informal and Formal Health and Social Support Systems of Black and Elderly: A Comparative Cost Approach. *Gerontologist,* 26: 279–285.

Mitchell, J., and Register, J.C. 1984. An Exploration of Family Interaction With the Elderly by Race, Socioeconomic Status, and Residence. *Gerontologist,* 24: 48–54.

Mutran, E. 1985. Intergenerational Family Support Among Blacks and Whites: Response to Culture or to Socioeconomic Differences. *Journal of Gerontology,* 40: 382–89.

Naifeh, F.M. *Housing of the Elderly.* Current Housing Reports, Series H-121, forthcoming). Washington, DC: U.S. Government Printing Office.

National Center for Health Statistics. 1985. *U.S. Decennial Life Tables for 1979–81.* Vol. 1, No. 1, DHHS Publication No. (PHS) 85-1150-1). Wash-

ington, DC: Public Health Service, U.S. Government Printing Office.

National Center for Health Statistics. 1990. *Health United States, 1989.* Hyattsville, MD: Public Health Service.

National Center for Health Statistics. 1991. *Health United States, 1990.* Hyattsville, MD: Public Health Service.

National Indian Council on Aging. 1981. *American Indian Elderly: A National Profile by the National Council on Aging.* Albuquerque, NM.

Rawlings, S. 1990. *Households and Family Characteristics: March 1990 and 1989.* Current Population Reports, Series P-20, No. 447. Washington, DC: U.S. Government Printing Office.

Rones, P.L., and Herz, D.E. 1989. *Labor Market Problems of Older Workers.* Report of the Secretary of Labor. Washington, DC: U.S. Government Printing Office.

Saluter, A.F. 1991. *Marital Status and Living Arrangements: March 1990.* Current Population Reports, Series P-20, No. 450. Washington, DC: U.S. Government Printing Office.

Shomaker, D. 1990. Health Care, Cultural Expectations and Frail Elderly Navajo Grandmothers. *Journal of Cross-Cultural Gerontology,* 5: 21–34.

Simmons, S.J. 1992. Testimony in *Old, Poor, and Forgotten: Elderly Americans Living in Poverty.* U.S. House of Representatives Select Committee on Aging. Washington, DC: U.S. Government Printing Office.

Sokolovsky, J. 1990. Bringing Culture Back Home: Aging, Ethnicity, and Family Support. In J. Sokolovsky (ed.), *The Culture Context of Aging: Worldwide Perspectives.* New York: Bergin and Garvey.

Sotomayor, M. 1992. *Old, Poor, and Forgotten: Elderly Americans Living in Poverty.* Testimony before the U.S. House of Representatives Select Committee on Aging. Washington, DC: U.S. Government Printing Office.

Stanford, E.P., and Torres-Gil, F.M. 1992. *Diversity: New Approaches to Ethnic Minority Aging.* Amityville, NY: Baywood Publishing.

Stanford, E.P., and Yee, D.L. 1992. Gerontology and Relevance of Diversity. In E.P. Stanford and F.M. Torres-Gil (eds.), *Diversity: New Approaches to Ethnic Minority Aging.* Amityville, NY: Baywood Publishing.

Taeuber, C.M., and Smith, D. 1987. *Minority Elderly: An Overview of Characteristics and 1990 Census Plans* (unpublished paper, available from Age and Sex Statistics Branch, Population Division). Washington, DC: U.S. Government Printing Office.

Torres-Gil, F.M. (Ed.). 1986. *Hispanics in an Aging Society*. New York: Carnegie Corporation.

Torres-Gil, F.M. 1992. *The New Aging: Politics and Change in America*. New York: Auburn House.

U.S. Bureau of the Census. 1980. *Census of Population and Housing, Special Tabulations for National Institute on Aging*. Summary Tape File 5A. Produced by Age and Sex Statistics Branch, Population Division.

U.S. Bureau of the Census. 1983. *1980 Census of the Population: General Social and Economic Characteristics*. (PC80-1-C1). Washington, DC: U.S. Government Printing Office.

U.S. Bureau of the Census. 1988. *Projections of the Hispanic Population: 1983 to 2080*. Current Population Reports, Series P-25, No. 995. Washington, DC: U.S. Government Printing Office.

U.S. Bureau of the Census. 1989. *Projections of the Population of the United States, by Age, Sex, and Race: 1988 to 2080*. Current Population Reports, Series P-25, No. 1018. Washington, DC: U.S. Government Printing Office.

U.S. Bureau of the Census. 1990a. *The Need for Personal Assistance With Everyday Activities: Recipients and Caregivers*. Current Population Reports, Series P-70, No. 19. Washington, DC: U.S. Government Printing Office.

U.S. Bureau of the Census. 1990b. *The Hispanic Population in the United States, March 1989*. Current Population Reports, Series P-20, No. 444. Washington, DC: U.S. Department of Commerce.

U.S. Bureau of the Census. 1990c. *1990 Census of Population and Housing: Modified and Actual Age, Sex, Race and Hispanic Origin Data*. Series CPH-L-74. Washington, DC: U.S. Government Printing Office.

U.S. Bureau of the Census. 1990. *1990 Census of Population and Housing*. Summary Tape File 1A. Washington, DC: U.S. Government Printing Office.

U.S. Bureau of the Census. 1991a. *Age, Sex, Race, and Hispanic Origin Information From the 1990 Census*. 1990 CPH-L-74. Washington, DC: U.S. Government Printing Office.

U.S. Bureau of the Census. 1991b. *Money Incomes of Households, Families, and Persons in the United States: 1990*. Current Population Reports: Consumer Income, Series P-60, No. 174. Washington, DC: U.S. Department of Commerce, Economics, and Statistics Administration.

U.S. Bureau of the Census. 1991c. *Poverty in the United States: 1990*. Current Population Reports: Consumer Income, Series P-60, No. 175. Washington, DC: U.S. Department of Commerce, Economics, and Statistics Administration.

U.S. Bureau of the Census. 1992a. *Household and Family Characteristics: March 1991*. Current Population Reports, Series P-20, No. 458. Washington, DC: U.S. Department of Commerce, Economics, and Statistics Administration.

U.S. Bureau of the Census. 1992b. *Marital Status and Living Arrangements: March 1990*. Current Population Reports, Series P-20, No. 450. Washington, DC: U.S. Department of Commerce, Economics, and Statistics Administration.

U.S. Bureau of the Census. 1992c. *Sixty-Five Plus in America*. Current Population Reports, Special Studies, P23-178. Washington, DC: U.S. Government Printing Office.

U.S. Bureau of the Census. 1995. *Population Profile of the United States*. Current Population Reports, Series P23-189. Washington, DC: U.S. Government Printing Office.

U.S. Department of Health and Human Services. 1991. *Current Estimates from the National Health Interview Survey, 1990*. Washington, DC: U.S. Government Printing Office.

U.S. Department of Health and Human Services. 1992. *Advance Report of Final Mortality Statistics, 1989*. Monthly Vital Statistics Report, Vol. 40, No. 8, Supplement 2. Washington, DC: U.S. Government Printing Office.

U.S. Department of Housing and Urban Development. 1991. *Section 8 Housing Assistance Payments Program: Fair Market Rents for New Construction and Substantial Rehabilitation for All Market Areas*. Federal Register 56(70): 18887–943. Washington, DC: U.S. Government Printing Office.

U.S. Department of Labor Statistics. 1991a. *Current Population Survey, 1991 Annual Averages*. (unpublished data). Washington, DC: U.S. Government Printing Office.

U.S. Department of Labor Statistics. 1991. *Employment and Earnings* (March) 38(3). Washington, DC: U.S. Department of Labor.

U.S. Department of Labor Statistics. 1992. *Employment and Earnings* (January). Washington, DC: U.S. Government Printing Office.

U.S. Senate Special Committee on Aging. 1992. *Developments in Aging: 1991* (Volume 1). Washington, DC: U.S. Government Printing Office.

Vobedga, B. 1991. Asian, Hispanic Numbers in the U.S. Soared in 1980s, Census Reveals. *Washington Post* (March 11): 5.

Weeks, J. 1984. *Aging: Concepts and Social Issues.* Belmont, CA: Wadsworth.

Weeks, J., and Cuellar, J. 1983. The Role of Family Members in the Helping Networks of Older People. *The Gerontologist*, 21: 388–94.

CHAPTER 21

Elder Abuse— Crimes/Scams/Cons

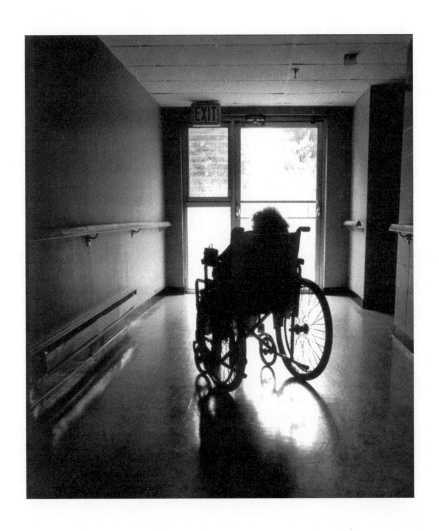

Older Victims of Abuse or Fraud

Mr. W. had promised his wife that he would never put her into a nursing home. Even though she has severe Alzheimer's Disease, he still tries to take care of her at home. He is 82 and she is 81. He has arthritis and has difficulty bending. He frequently shouts at his wife. Over and over he says, "Rose, don't do that. Rose don't do that." He also slaps her hands. He told a visitor that he stopped trying to prevent her from eating the dog's food. Rose spends much of her time crawling on the floor. Mr. Winter said that what helps him get through the day is a fifth of gin.

Mr. P. is 62 years old, unemployed, an alcoholic and lives with his 82-year-old mother. She is mentally alert but not able to get around without a walker. She depends totally on her son for groceries and for any transportation. Mr. Polski charges her $20 for any place he takes her. In addition, he demands that she give him "loans" of several hundred dollars. If she refuses, he becomes verbally and physically abusive. She usually gives him money, knowing he will use it for alcohol. She feels there is no alternative because she has no other children and is isolated from other people.

Ms. W. is 72. Her mother is 92. Ms. Waterfeldt is suffering from congestive heart failure and is trying to take care of her aged mother. She is also suffering from depression, and over the last four months she has really neglected her mother's basic needs. On top of this, Ms. Waterfeldt is suffering from guilt feelings because she has screamed at her mother, calling her a whiner. In the last week she slapped her mother several times for her incontinence. She is thinking about suicide.

Ms. S. has an income of over $300,000 dollars a year by being involved in telemarketing scams. For years she has been calling older people and is good at winning their confidence. She tells them she is interested in their financial future. She tells them about high-paying securities that she is selling, warns them that they will be sold out within the next 24 hours, and hopes that they will not lose an opportunity to buy these "gold-plated" financial instruments. Ms. Sunderland then asks for their savings account number and recommends that they not purchase anything less than five thousand dollars worth of these securities. Her voice sounds caring, soothing, confident, and trustworthy. Her financial instruments are virtually worthless and most of her clients lose most of their money.

Mrs. B. received a call from a person offering a comprehensive physical exam, including state-of-the-art diagnostic testing, at "very little cost." The caller on the phone was so friendly and sounded so knowledgeable, it was a pleasure to talk to him. Mrs. Brown was not feeling ill at all, but after the friendly person called a number of times, she figured, given her age, why not give it a try. The two-hour exam ended up costing Mrs. Brown $7,500.

ELDER ABUSE: A NATIONAL ISSUE

Elder abuse, according to many experts, is one of the most underrecognized, and as a result, one of the most underreported social problems in the United States (Tatara 1994). When the problem began to be recognized the following statement was published in *Public Welfare*:

> Elder abuse is a shocking revelation to most Americans, and the average citizen may find it hard to believe that the problem exists. Studies suggest, however, that elder abuse is a widespread phenomenon, affecting hundreds of thousands of vulnerable people across all classes of society. Because it is still largely hidden, elder abuse is difficult for the professional community to address effectively (Public Welfare 1988: 5).

Elder abuse as a national issue first surfaced in 1978 when Representative Claude Pepper, a tireless advocate for the needs and rights of the elderly, held Congressional hearings to expose the problem. The hearings were followed by a joint hearing by the U.S. Senate and U.S. House of Representatives in 1980. This led to a report recommending that the federal government help the states deal with elder abuse by establishing a Prevention, Identification, and Treatment of Elder Abuse Act (Wolf 1988).

There was essentially no federal action until 1987 when Representative Pepper tried a new strategy. He was able to add amendments to the 1987 reauthorization of the Older Americans Act (OAA) which defined elder abuse and authorized $5 million worth of program grants for elder abuse services and education. Although $5 million was authorized in 1987, Congress waited until 1990 to appropriate $2.98 million for fiscal year 1991 for these services. In the 1992 amendments to the Older Americans Act, $15 million was authorized to fund elder abuse programs; however only $4.399 million was actually appropriated for fiscal year 1993 (Gelfand 1993; Tatara 1994).

Defining Elder Abuse

The Older Americans Act defines elder abuse, neglect, and exploitation. Protection against these misdeeds is listed as part of the overall goals of the Declaration of Objectives for Older Americans of the OAA as amended in 1972. State laws define elder abuse, but the definitions vary from one state to another. The National Center on Elder Abuse has organized the definition of elder abuse into the following three basic categories:

- Domestic elder abuse
- Institutional elder abuse
- Self-neglect or self-abuse (Tatara 1994)

Domestic Elder Abuse   Domestic elder abuse generally refers to many forms of mistreatment of an older person by someone who has a special relationship (a spouse, a child, a friend, a caregiver, a sibling) in the older person's home or in the home of the person caring for the elder:

- Physical abuse: The deliberate use of physical force that results in bodily injury, pain, or impairment.
- Sexual abuse: The nonconsensual sexual contact of any kind.

- Emotional or psychological abuse: The willful infliction of mental or emotional anguish by threat, humiliation, intimidation, or other verbal or nonverbal abusive conduct.
- Neglect: The willful or nonwillful failure by the caregiver to fulfill his or her caretaking obligation or duty.
- Financial or material exploitation: The unauthorized use of funds, property, or any resources of an older person.
- All other types: All other categories of elder maltreatment that do not belong to the above-mentioned five categories (Tatara 1993).

Institutional Abuse   Institutional abuse generally refers to the abuse that occur in facilities designated for older people such as foster homes, group homes, nursing homes, and board-and-care facilities. Persons inflicting institutional elder abuse usually are those who have a legal or contractual obligation to provide care and protection to the victims. They may include paid caregivers, staff, and professionals (Tatara 1994).

Self-neglect or Self-abuse   Self-neglect or self-abuse refers to neglectful or abusive behavior by an older person that is threatening to his or her own safety or health. This type of activity generally results from the physical or mental impairment of the older person. According to data available in 1994, not all forms of elder abuse are crimes in every state of the nation (Tatara 1994). Most instances of physical, sexual, and financial/material abuses are classified as crimes in all states. Certain emotional abuse and neglect cases are considered criminal offenses depending on the perpetrator's conduct and the consequences on the victims. On the other hand, self-neglect is not considered a crime in all states. Some elder abuse laws in some of the states do not even address self-neglect.

Intentional and Unintentional Abuse   Some analysts break elder abuse and neglect into two major categories, intentional and unintentional.

Intentional is defined as "a conscious or deliberate attempt to inflict harm or injury, such as verbal abuse or battering" ("Elder Abuse Is On The Rise" 1993). Intentional elder abuse is simply willfully and intentionally abusing the rights of an older person. It is an active decision to carry out an abusive act. In a hearing of the U.S. Senate Special Committee on Aging, the following case was described by a home health aide from Alabama, a story that could come from any location in the nation.

> I have a patient there that lives in a home with the granddaughter. The granddaughter has three children. One time there, the granddaughter was taking the grandmother's money and spending it and buying clothes for herself and for her children, so the grandmother decided that she would hide the money. So the daughter would leave the room and leave one little boy there to spy on the grandmother. They would watch what she'd do with the money, and if he could find it, they would still use it for themselves (U.S. Senate Special Committee on Aging 1991a: 6).

Another case from the same hearing, presented by an adult protective services worker, also illustrates willful, intentional elder abuse.

> Another case involved the exploitation of an elderly man who resided in a health care facility. The son, who had power of attorney and access to the victim's substantial income and resources, was not using the money to pay his father's bills. We received a report that the victim was being evicted for nonpayment of bills to the nursing home. Several months passed and various informal agreements were made and broken by the son. Only after we filed a petition for the appointment of a conservator did the son agree to a consent agreement that involved another relative handling his father's financial matters (U.S. Senate Special Committee on Aging 1991a: 13).

Unintentional abuse or neglect, some contend, is the result of:

- Ignorance
- Caregiver lacking desire to provide care

- Self-neglect among the elderly (Elderly Abuse on the Rise 1993)

Supporting these reasons for elder abuse, it is pointed out that the role of caregiver is stressful for anyone. When added pressures such as economic stresses, lack of community support, and increasing care needs enter the life of the caregiver, heightened tensions and increased frustration may lead to abusive behavior (Elder Abuse is on the Rise 1993).

The following case illustrates the real-life factors that can lead to elder abuse. This story comes from testimony before the Special Committee on Aging of the U.S. Senate.

> Mrs. O is an 83-year-old female. She has chronic health problems and has been maintained in her home setting over the past few years with the services of Coffee County Home Health and our community-based Waiver Services. Over the last several months, her physical condition has deteriorated to the point that she can no longer get out of bed on her own, and what this means is that our services alone are not sufficient to keep her in the home setting.
>
> But we could not impress on the daughter the need that her mother required 24-hour care, so what happened in this case is that Mrs. O lay unattended from Friday p.m. when our homemaker left until Monday a.m. This means that she went without food and water and also that she was forced to lay in her own body excrement. The Department of Human Resources was notified by our community-based Waiver Services case manager, and with a doctor's help, we were able to force the family to take some action. A granddaughter took Mrs. O into her home. She kept Mrs. O for one week, but she returned her to her own home. Legally, DHR or the Health Department could do nothing because this lady is mentally competent, and she did not want to leave her home.
>
> What finally happened was that she became so ill that we were able to force the daughter to take her to the hospital, and from the hospital we did place her in a nursing home. Sadly, this was a 9-month period which the lady was in this condition (U.S. Senate Special Committee on Aging 1991a: 20).

How Widespread Is Elder Abuse?

According to the National Aging Resource Center on Elder Abuse, "the true national incidence or prevalence of domestic elder abuse is not known" (Tatara 1993: 2). There are two basic reasons for this. First, reporting and research in the field is incomplete, mostly because the adult protective information systems in many states are incomplete. Surveys are based on these reporting systems.

Second, because elder abuse is far less likely to be reported than child abuse, the true scope of elder abuse is difficult to determine. A 1990 survey by the Subcommittee on Health and Long-Term Care of the U.S. House of Representatives found that where one out of three cases of child abuse was reported, only one out of eight cases of elder abuse was reported (U.S. House of Representatives Select Committee on Aging 1990).

The number of cases of elder abuse that were actually reported has increased dramatically. In fiscal year (FY) 1986, there were 117,000 reports; 128,000 reports for FY 1987; 140,000 reports for FY 1988; 211,000 reports for FY 1990; and 227,000 for FY 1991, the latest year this information was available (Tatara, 1993). There was a 94-percent increase in the number of domestic elder abuse cases reported from fiscal year 1986 to fiscal year 1991. As with many reports of these types, it is not possible to determine whether there is a real increase in the incidence of elder abuse, or whether more people are reporting these types of situations (Tatara 1993).

Data Based on Local Studies   Attempting to determine the total number of elder abuse cases, reported and unreported, has been the subject of several surveys over the last fifteen to twenty years. Most of these studies were based on small samples of the population, reviews of agency records, or interviews with staff who work with elderly persons (Tatara 1993). In 1979, Lan and Kosbery reported that 9.6 percent of the elderly clients served by an agency in Cleveland, Ohio,

had been abused. In 1981, Steinmetz reached the conclusion that 2.5 million older people were the victims of abuse. Gioglio and Blakemore (1983) estimated that only 1 percent of the elderly population were victims of elder abuse based on their random survey. However, Pillemer and Finkelhor (1988) estimated that the incidence of elder abuse was 3.2 percent of the elderly population. This translated into between 701,000 to 1,093,560 abused older people. It should be noted that the Pillemer and Finkelhor study was based on a random sample survey of over 2,000 elderly persons in the Boston, Massachusetts metropolitan area, from which they projected national estimates.

The Subcommittee on Health and Long-Term Care of the U.S. House of Representatives in 1990 estimated that more than 1.5 million older persons may be victims of elder abuse (U.S. House of Representatives Select Committee on Aging 1990). This represented about 5 percent of the elderly population, or about one out of every twenty elderly persons.

Data Based on National Surveys   Basing its projections on data compiled from a nationwide survey of elder abuse reports, the National Aging Resource Center on Elder Abuse (NARCEA) estimated that nearly 1.57 million older people were abused in 1991 (Tatara 1993). This estimate was arrived at by determining the substantiated number of elder abuse cases nationwide (112,415) and multiplying that number by 14, the number arrived at by Pillemer and Finkelhor (1988) based on their estimate that only one out of fourteen cases of elder abuse is reported.

WHO ARE THE VICTIMS?

Over one-fourth (28.1 percent) of all reported cases of elder abuse in 1991 were for self-neglect or self-abuse. Of the confirmed cases, the majority (51.4 percent) of elder abuse cases were instances of self-neglect or self-abuse (Tatara 1994). It should be noted that while most states offer some protective services for elderly persons who neglect themselves, the states are careful to consider a person's right to refuse these services. This may result in a guardianship being established through court action, where a person appointed by the court can act on the self-abused's/neglected's behalf. Sometimes self-neglect results in placing the person in an institution, again through court action. These procedures usually are used only as last resorts for people in situations that are threatening to their health and safety.

Of the victims of abuse, neglect, or exploitation by the actions of others, the rate of abuse for 1991 based on nationwide data is shown in Table 21-1.

Characteristics of the Victims   As to the characteristics of the victims, based on data compiled from their random survey of elderly persons in the Boston, Massachusetts area, Pillemer and Finkelhor (1988) found that the rates of abuse and neglect were similar for minority and white elderly persons. There were no significant differences based on religion, economic, or educational backgrounds.

In this same study, there were some groups of older persons who had different rates of abuse. The elderly living alone had much lower rates of abuse than those living with other people. Those elderly persons who were widowed, divorced, or never married were less likely to be abused. Those in poor health were three to four times more likely to be abused.

Based on data compiled from nationwide reports of elder abuse, the National Aging Resource

TABLE 21-1

Physical abuse	19.1%
Sexual abuse	0.6%
Emotional abuse	13.8%
Neglect	45.2%
Financial exploitation	17.1%
All other types	4.0%
Unknown	0.2%

Source: Tatara 1994: 6.

TABLE 21-2

ELDER ABUSE VICTIMS

	Percentage	
Sex of victims	FY90	FY91
Male	31.3%	32.0%
Female	68.6%	67.8%
Unknown/missing data	0.2%	0.2%
Totals:	100.0%*	100.0%

*Due to rounding errors, the totals are not exactly 100.0%
Source: Tatara 1993: 24

Center on Elder Abuse, which in 1993 became the National Center on Elder Abuse (NCEA), outlined the characteristics of the victims of elder abuse and of self-neglect, as shown in Table 21-2 (Tatara, 1993).

As Table 21-2 indicates, a little more than two-thirds of the elder abuse victims were females in 1990 and 1991. About one-third of the victims were males.

As this chart shows, people aged 85 and older (the oldest old) accounted for a little more than one-fifth of the victims of elder abuse and made up the age group with the most victims in 1991. When the 80-to-84-year-olds are added to the oldest-old group, combined they accounted for more than two-fifths of all elder abuse victims.

TABLE 21-3

ELDER ABUSE BY AGE

	Percentage	
Age of victims	FY90	FY91
60–64	7.8%	7.6%
65–69	11.2%	10.5%
70–74	15.0%	15.5%
75–79	17.4%	17.1%
80–84	19.2%	19.4%
85 and up	22.2%	23.1%
Missing data	7.2%	6.8%
Totals:	100.0%*	100.0%

Source: Tatara 1993: 25

This same study showed that persons in the younger age groups (aged 60 to 64 and aged 65 to 69) are less likely to be victims of elder abuse. Persons aged 69 and younger accounted for only about one-half as many elder abuse victims who are aged 80 and older. The median age of elder abuse victims based on nationwide data was 78.8 years of age in 1991 (Tatara 1993).

As Table 21-4 indicates, almost two-thirds of the self-neglecting elderly people were women in 1990 and 1991, based on nationwide reports (Tatara 1993). About one-third were males in each year. This pattern is similar to the pattern for elder abuse victims.

Table 21-5, also based on national data for the fiscal years 1990 and 1991, shows that the age of an elderly person relates to his or her being more likely to be a victim of self-neglect (Tatara 1993). Those who are older among the elderly are more likely to be self-neglecting than younger elderly persons. Older people aged 80 and older made up nearly two-fifths of all self-neglecting elderly persons in 1990 and 1991. Persons aged 69 and younger accounted for only about one-fifth of self-neglecting older persons.

The median age of self-neglecting older people in 1991 was 77.8 years. This was a little bit younger than elder abuse victims.

Who Are the Abusers?

Who is mostly responsible for elder abuse? Different studies resulted in different answers to this question. The Pillemer and Finkelhor study (1988) of older people in the Boston area found that the majority of elder abuse was committed by spouses (58 percent) compared to adult children (24 percent). The national data of the National Aging Resource Center on Elder Abuse which was based on elder abuse reports from seventeen states in 1990 and eighteen states in 1991 showed a clear predominance of male abusers (51.8 percent) in 1991 over female abusers (42.5 percent) (Tatara 1993). Because the reporting for this particular finding came from about one-third of the states, the NARCEA study did not claim certainty as to whether the same rates on the sex of the abusers holds true nationally. Table 21-6.

TABLE 21-5

SELF-NEGLECT BY AGE

	Percentage	
Age of self-neglecting elders	**FY90**	**FY91**
60–64	9.9%	9.4%
65–69	13.0%	11.8%
70–74	14.8%	15.3%
75–79	18.3%	16.7%
80–84	18.5%	18.8%
85 and up	18.0%	20.3%
Missing data	7.6%	7.6%
Totals:	100.0%*	100.0%

*Due to rounding errors, the totals are not exactly 100.0%
Source: Tatara 1993: 28.

TABLE 21-4

SELF-NEGLECTING ELDERS

	Percentage	
Sex of self-neglecting elders	**FY90**	**FY91**
Male	32.4%	35.2%
Female	62.5%	62.1%
Unknown/missing data	3.2%	2.8%
Totals:	100.0%*	100.0%

*Due to rounding errors, the total is not exactly 100.0%
Source: Tatara 1993: 27.

TABLE 21-6

PERPETRATORS OF ELDER ABUSE BY SEX

	Percentage	
Sex of perpetrators	**FY90**	**FY91**
Male	52.3%	51.8%
Female	41.8%	42.5%
Unknown/missing data	5.8%	5.8%
Totals:	99.9%*	100.1%

*Due to rounding errors, the total is not exactly 100.0%
Source: Tatara 1993: 21.

Concerning the types of abusers and their frequency, the National Aging Resource Center on Elder Abuse report (Tatara 1993) based on national reporting data is clearly different from the Pillemer and Finkelhor random sample study (1988). Where spouses represented by far the most frequent abusers in the random sample study of older people in Boston, the NARCEA study gave a clear edge to adult children. In fact, in the NARCEA study, adult children were the most frequent abusers of older people, accounting for nearly one-third of the reported cases (32.5 percent in 1991). In this study spouses were the second most frequent abusers, but their rate of causing elder abuse was only about one-half that of adult children. As Table 21-7 below indicates, "other relatives" ranked third as abusers of the elderly, closely behind spouses. The "all other categories," item, although higher in percentage of frequency of elder abuse than "spouse" or "other relatives," was not compared to the other categories because it included a number of categories of persons such as unrelated caregivers, former spouses, housemates and former housemates, and lovers or mistresses (Tatara 1993).

TABLE 21-7

**PERPETRATORS OF ELDER ABUSE
BY RELATIONSHIP**

	Percentage	
Types of abusers	FY90	FY91
Adult children	31.9%	32.5%
All other categories	16.7%	18.2%
Spouse	15.4%	14.4%
Other relatives	13.0%	12.5%
Friend/neighbor	7.3%	7.5%
Service provider	6.6%	6.3%
Grandchildren	4.0%	4.2%
Sibling	2.6%	2.5%
Unknown/missing data	2.5%	2.0%
Totals:	100.0%*	100.0%

*Due to rounding errors, the total is not exactly 100.0%.
Source: Tatara 1993: 22.

Causes of Domestic Elder Abuse

A number of theories have been developed as to why elder abuse occurs. Why does a person become an abuser of an elderly individual? What are the circumstances that tend to lead to the abuse of an elder?

The National Center on Elder Abuse pointed out that elder abuse, similar to any type of domestic violence, is very complex and many factors are involved in its causes (Tatara 1994). Psychological, social, and economic factors that affect interpersonal and family relationships often combine with the physical and mental conditions of older persons and their potential abusers to result in domestic elder abuse according to this approach to analyzing the problem. When new stresses are added to already stressful situations that exist between elderly persons and the people around them, elder abuse may result. There is a mix of the existing situation between elderly persons and the people around them, their physical and mental conditions, and added stresses that enter their lives. The added stresses may be psychological, social, or economic, or a combination of these.

The National Center on Elder Abuse has formulated four major theories to explain the causes of elder abuse based on observations from professionals who work with elder abuse victims, their families, and their abusers (Tatara 1994). In looking at these categories, it is important to note that they often combine to produce instances of abuse.

Stress of the Caregiver   As has been pointed out previously, caregiving for older people is a stressful role. This role is made more difficult when the older person being cared for is mentally or physically impaired, the caregiver has severe limitations because of his or her own problems or lack of knowledge of how to be a caregiver, and support from other family members is lacking. This theory stresses that a combination of internal factors in the caregiver (lack of coping skills, emotional problems) combined with external factors (mental or physical impairment of the older person being cared for, the financial burden of caregiving, lack of family or community supports) can result in elder abuse (Tatara 1994). This theory has had wide support in the professional community.

Increased Dependency of Older Persons The vast majority of dependent older people are cared for at home by family members. It has been found by researchers that older people in poor health are more likely to be victims of abuse than those in good health. This theory of elder abuse holds that abuse often occurs when the stress level of the caregiver is increased as a result of the worsening of the physical or mental condition of the older person. The increased stress level causes the caregiver to react in an abusive way in given situations (Tatara 1994).

Cycle of Violence Some families are simply more prone to violence than others. Reacting to given situations in a violent way is a learned behavior that is passed from one generation to another. For these families, violence remains a normal behavior pattern throughout their lives—from child abuse through elder abuse. Clinical workers who have worked in both child abuse and elder abuse have observed these ongoing patterns of violence (Tatara 1994).

Personal Problems of the Abusers It has been found that persons who abuse older people (most often adult children) usually have more personal problems than nonabusers. The adult children who abuse their parents often have mental and emotional problems, financial problems, or substance-abuse problems. As a result of these problems, these adult children are often dependent on their parents for support—the parents they end up abusing. This theory contends that the abuse of these parents by these dependent adult children is a response to their feelings of inadequacy (Tatara 1994).

In looking at these and other possible theories to explain the causes of elder abuse, it is important to consider that no single theory can give a complete explanation. More research is needed to explore the causes of elder abuse as the aging revolution continues into the twenty-first century.

Retirement and Elder Abuse

There is evidence from research of a relationship between stress resulting from major life events and family violence (Straus and Gelles 1990). Retirement is a major life event that has the potential to result in some stresses. The question has been raised, does retirement play a role in elder abuse? With spouses the second leading type of offenders in domestic elder abuse, and with retirement an accepted part of American life, this is an important question.

In the popular media, retirement is often seen as a stressful situation with much potential for marital conflict (Bachman and Pillemer 1992). This is particularly true when the husband retires. "What will I do with him all day?" wives ask in popular books and articles (Bachman and Pillemer 1991: 76). Stress, according to the popular notion, is supposed to result from having the husband around so much of the time (Herbert 1987). After a lifetime of going off to work, the wife has to put up with not only having her spouse around much of each day, but having him interfere in her daily routine and ways of doing things around the house if the wife focused her work in the home. Even if the wife worked outside the home, once both spouses retire they probably will be spending considerably more time together. Does this lead to stressful situations that could result in elder abuse by a spouse?

The evidence is that retirement does not have a negative impact on health status, psychological well-being, or how people interact within marriage. This is true for women as well as men. In addition, retirement has not been found to negatively affect marital satisfaction (Vinick and Eckerdt 1988). Adjustment problems after retirement, if any, have been found to be minor and of short duration. Some research has revealed no negative effects of retirement on marital satisfaction. Other research has found a positive effect of retirement on marital relations (Bachman and Pillemer 1991).

With marital satisfaction not being negatively affected by retirement, additional research has found that retirement has little or no effect on spousal violence, which in the case of retirees would be a form of elder abuse (Bachman and Pillemer 1991). This is due to an important component in male-female relationships as they progress into the later years of life. The imbalance of power between husbands and wives has been found to contribute to spousal violence—spouse abuse. The greater power held by husbands in the marital relationship makes violence possible (Coleman and Straus 1990). Research has shown that the power imbalance held by men in the younger years is likely to be equalized by the aging of the spouses (Bachman and Pillemer 1991). As a result, in their retirement years, women tend to be less vulnerable to abuse.

Bachman's and Pillemer's research (1991), using a nationally representative sample of persons aged 55 and older, demonstrated that in regard to marital conflict and physical violence, there were no significant differences between retired spouses and spouses who were not retired. Both groups scored similarly on measures of depression, stress, and marital conflict. There were no significant differences in regard to physical violence between the retired and nonretired spouses. There is no reason to expect increased marital conflict or spousal abuse as a result of retirement. This, according to Bachman and Pillemer, does not mean that stressful life events and major changes in one's life have no impact on elder abuse. It simply means that for many people, retirement is not a particularly stressful situation.

Who Reports Elder Abuse Cases?

All of the states plus the District of Columbia, Guam, and the Virgin Islands have some legislation that deals with domestic or institutional elder abuse. This includes reporting procedures to identify elder abuse cases. In 1994, forty-two states plus Washington, D.C., Guam, and the Virgin Islands had provisions which made it mandatory for certain professionals to report elder abuse cases. Typically these included staff of law enforcement agencies, adult protective services staff, medical doctors and health care professionals, and staff of residential facilities for older people. In some states, the public is required to report elder abuse cases.

Reporting elder abuse is obviously very important. It is the principal way cases can be identified and investigated. It is also important in informing the public as to the importance of the problem. An efficient reporting system documents the need for public and private support to provide appropriate protective services or treatments to the victims of elderly abuse and their families.

As Table 21-8 shows, service providers (homemakers/chore services, home health care, personal care, and other in-home services) most often report cases of domestic elder abuse (Tatara 1993). Doctors and other health-care professionals are the next most frequent reporters of these cases. The category "all other types" was not counted in these rankings as it includes many types of elder abuse reporters. It does indicate that there is a wide variety of persons who report cases of elder abuse. Not too many cases are reported by law enforcement staff. Friends and neighbors make up less than 10 percent of elder abuse reporters.

Elder Abuse and Medical Practice

Elder abuse has only recently attracted the attention of the medical profession. According to a practitioner and researcher in emergency medicine, Dr. Jeffery Jones (1994), this is surprising for two reasons: (1) Elder abuse is a major health problem which affects hundreds of thousands of vulnerable older people across the nation in all socioeconomic classes; and (2) physicians played a prominent role in defining and publicizing the

TABLE 21-8

WHO REPORTS ELDER ABUSE?

	Percentage of reports made	
Reporter category	FY90	FY91
Family member/relative	14.9%	15.0%
Friend/neighbor	8.8%	8.2%
Service provider	28.1%	26.7%
Physician/health care professional	17.0%	18.0%
Law enforcement	4.3%	4.3%
Clergy	0.1%	0.1%
Bank/business	0.2%	0.2%
Elder victim	5.6%	4.6%
All other types	18.7%	21.0%
Unknown/missing data	2.2%	2.0%
Totals:	*99.9%	100.0%

*Due to rounding errors, the totals are not exactly 100.0%
Source: Tatara 1993: 15

problem of child abuse and had a significant role in shaping public policy concerning that issue.

Jones (1994) pointed out that emergency health care providers who are on the front lines in dealing with elder abuse face a number of critical issues.

Confusing Definitions   Lack of standardized definitions of elder abuse, according to Jones (1994), has made it impossible to compare research findings. This has also resulted in difficulties in tabulating national data on elder abuse and in transferring model programs between states. Jones pointed out that at least thirty-three different types of elder abuse have been identified in various studies. It is important for physicians to be familiar with the elder abuse laws in their states and know how they apply to their practices.

Research Gap   Compared to the number of scientific studies on child abuse, the number of scientific investigations into elder abuse has been minimal (Jones 1994). Jones pointed out that emergency physicians can play a very valuable role in promoting and being involved in research on risk factors, procedures for detecting instances of elder abuse, identifying and meeting the needs of older people, how to best treat them, and strategies for prevention.

Procedures for Reporting/Follow-up   A 1992 report of practicing emergency physicians found that 27 percent of those who responded to a survey had formal protocols (procedures) for reporting and follow-up for cases of elder abuse compared to 75 percent who had protocols for child abuse (McNamara, Rousseau, and Sanders 1992). Jones (1994) contended that every clinical setting should have guidelines regarding what information is necessary to assess and report elder abuse cases. The American Medical Association has urged all physicians to routinely ask their elderly patients if anyone in their home has threatened, scolded, or hurt them; if they are often alone; and if they are afraid of anyone who lives in their home (Aravanis et al. 1992).

More emphasis needs to be placed on having physicians use the procedures for referring suspected cases of elder abuse (Jones 1994). Most of the states have mandatory reporting laws.

Lack of Financial Support   There is a shortage of money to adequately support adult protective services (Jones 1994). To make matters worse, competition between child protective services and adult protective services has increased, with the adult services losing out in many states (Tatara 1990). While the states were spending an average of $22 per child for child protective services, they spent an average $2.90 per elderly person for adult protective services (AMA Council on Scientific Affairs 1987).

As a result, many states also suffer from a lack of community services such as adult foster care, group homes, counseling, chore services, medical services, home health, diagnostic and assessment services, respite care, and legal services (Jones 1994). The lack of these community resources can have an impact on the incidence of elder abuse.

Jones (1994) urged that emergency health care providers become involved in planning programs for elderly patients who have physical and social needs. In addition, he urged health care providers to become familiar with available community resources that can assist vulnerable elderly persons.

Lack of Coordinated Services In the various states, elder abuse cases are assigned to fifteen different types of agencies. These include adult protective services, sheriff's departments, police, state attorney general's offices, and prosecuting attorneys. Often these agencies are not coordinated in their efforts, which results in poor services for the victims. Jones (1994) suggested that physician-related services, such as the social-work staff in the emergency department of a hospital, can assist in referring the victims of elder abuse to appropriate resources, as well as monitoring the follow-up status of patients.

The Key Role of Doctors in Elder Abuse
Doctors play a key role in identifying, treating, and reporting cases of domestic elder abuse. It is the doctor who often has the best opportunity to detect cases of elder abuse. It is the doctor or other health-care worker to whom the victim is brought to be treated for physical abuse or physical neglect. It is the doctor who is often able to win the confidence of the victim so the abusive situation can surface.

Many victims are very fearful to report their situations to anyone. "They fear losing their homes. They fear it means they're going on welfare. They fear somebody's going to put them in a nursing home. They fear it means they've lost their independence and their ability to take care of themselves" said Elizabeth Clemmer, senior coordinator with AARP's Public Policy Institute, pointing out why so many older people are afraid to report elder abuse or accept elder abuse services (McLeod 1993: 15). This is where doctors can be important. They can gain the confidence of the patient and help him or her look at elder abuse services in a different light, according to Clemmer (McLeod 1993).

To help doctors better detect and treat elder abuse victims, the American Medical Association in 1992 developed guidelines for doctors. Doctors have been urged to ask probing questions of their patients to try to find out if they are afraid of anyone they are living with, if any one abuses them in any way, or if they are neglected. These are important questions because it is often very hard to determine from examining patients if they have suffered from abuse.

Dr. James O'Brien, a professor of family practice at Michigan State University's College of Human Medicine, has pointed out that the clues doctors would normally use to detect a case of elder abuse are hard to separate from the normal experiences of older persons (Freedman 1992). That is because older people bruise more easily, fall more frequently, and break bones more often than younger people. It is the author's experience that an older person can appear to be "beat up" because of large bruises, but in reality the person merely bumped a leg, an arm, or other part of the body on a table or chair without even realizing it. Because of these realities, O'Brien said:

> It is important for doctors to think beyond the immediate medical problems for their older patients and consider the environment in which the older

adult is living. If the suspicion of abuse is there, doctors can suggest assistance in the home, day care, counseling, or a respite for the caregiver (Freedman 1992: B5).

"This is where doctors can be so useful," according to Elizabeth Clemmer, senior coordinator with AARP's Public Policy Institute. She advises older people who go to their doctor and are asked some probing questions about their personal lives:

> Don't be offended if your doctor asks these questions. If they don't apply to you, great. But keep in mind that this is a way of screening for people who may not even raise the issues themselves but who really could benefit from these services (McLeod 1993: 15).

Institutional Abuse and Neglect

Up to this point, we have focused on domestic elder abuse. It is important to describe briefly another setting of elder abuse—institutional settings such as nursing facilities/homes or mental hospitals.

The rate of elder abuse is unclear for many institutional settings except community-based nursing facilities. Research has indicated that 36 percent of community nursing home staff have seen physical abuse by other staff such as using excessive restraints (Pillemer and Moore 1989). In addition to physical abuse, 81 percent of nursing home staff reported that they have seen psychological abuse such as yelling at patients.

The American Medical Association has reported that at least half of all nursing facility residents suffer from some form of dementia-mental illness or impairment (Aravanis et al. 1992). Other sources have placed those in nursing facilities with mental illness or dementia as high as 80 percent. These types of patients are particularly vulnerable to elder abuse and are unlikely to report instances of it. Only 5 percent receive psychiatric care (U.S. Senate Special Committee on Aging 1991a).

In addition to those staff reporting what they saw others do, 10 percent admitted to physically abusing patients themselves, and 40 percent admitted they psychologically abused patients (U.S. Senate Special Committee on Aging, 1991a).

Causes of Elder Abuse in Nursing Facilities

The reason for elder abuse in nursing facilities has been traced to four major underlying problems: (1) the lack of understanding of the cause of patient behavior; (2) dissatisfaction among the staff; (3) increased staff/patient conflict; and (4) increased burn-out among the staff. What these conditions result in is clear:

> A population of elder patients that is at highest risk for abuse, as predicted by their multiple psychiatric and medical problems, is cared for predominantly by young, marginally educated individuals. They in turn are supervised by professional staff with limited experience in psychiatric diseases (U.S. Senate Special Committee on Aging 1991a: 64).

Prevention of Elder Abuse in Institutions

There is a consensus that education is the most important factor in decreasing elder abuse in the institutional setting (U.S. Senate Special Committee on Aging 1991a). Doctors and nurses need to be educated about mental illnesses and dementias in the elderly and how they affect the behavior of their patients. They, in turn, need to educate the nurse-assistant staff (aides) about the potential behaviors of their patients and how to deal with them on a one-to-one basis. In addition, more psychiatric services for patients need to be made available.

Assistance in Institutional Settings   Where can a patient or the relatives and friends of a patient in an institutional setting go for help if anyone of them experiences or suspects elder abuse? The Long-Term Care Ombudsman programs, which are found around the nation, are excellent sources of help. These programs are funded through the Older Americans Act. Part of the responsibility of these programs is to receive, investigate, and resolve complaints made by residents of long-term care facilities or by others acting for them. Some of the complaints deal with the mistreatment of older people in these facilities.

Services Available for Elder Abuse Victims and Their Families

To effectively deal with the serious issue of elder abuse, it is essential to be aware of the fact that elder abuse is a multidimensional problem that needs to be addressed in many ways using a variety of services. Ideally, according to the National Center on Elder Abuse, the four following types of approaches or services should be developed in communities across the nation to cope with elder abuse (Tatara 1994).

Elder Abuse Treatment　Given the fact that almost 20 percent of elder abuse victims have been physically or sexually abused, medical treatment is vital. In addition to these cases, victims of neglect are likely to need medical attention. Hospitals, especially emergency departments, need programs to identify, diagnose, treat, and follow up cases of elder abuse. Dr. Jeffrey Jones (1994) has outlined specific goals and tasks for physicians/health care workers in the hospital setting.

Protective Services　Most states designate adult protective services (APS) as the lead agency in domestic elder abuse cases (Tatara 1994). Some other public agencies are used in some instances. The APS agency usually is responsible for the following:

1. Operating a system to receive reports and referrals of suspected elder abuse cases
2. Investigating these cases
3. Substantiating or refuting the reports based on the evidence
4. Providing emergency services to the victims and their families
5. Administering assessments, tests, or evaluations, as needed

6. Preparing legal procedures as needed
7. Referring cases to appropriate service programs
8. Removing elder abuse victims or abusers from the home as necessary
9. Providing advocacy services
10. Training agency staff, professionals, and volunteers
11. Educating the public
12. Collecting appropriate statistics

Prevention Services　The most common form of prevention of elder abuse is the education of professionals who deal with older people and the general public concerning elder abuse. These educational programs should focus on making professionals and the public aware of the problem and provide them with "abuse/neglect indicators and warning signs" (Tatara 1994: 21). Education in this area could also include providing training for professional and informal caregivers in how to care for the elderly. These kinds of training programs have been shown to help prevent the potential abuse and neglect of older persons.

When Area Agencies on Aging across the nation were asked what activity was most successful in reducing elder abuse, the most frequently cited response was public education (Blakely and Dolon 1991). Along with public education, of the issue of increasing public awareness of elder abuse is vitally important.

Support Services　Support services for elder abuse victims and their families vary from one state to another and from one community to another, but they are usually available in some form in most places. They should be expanding, as more recognition is given to the problem of elder abuse. These services generally include guardianship programs, legal advocacy, financial planning for the elderly, self-help groups, respite care, foster care and group homes, and transportation (Tatara 1994).

Possible Signs of Physical Abuse and Neglect

Physical abuse

1. Unexplained bruises and welts:
   a. on face, lips, mouth, torso, back, buttocks, thighs.
   b. human bite marks in various stages of healing (it is advisable to note site of bruising).
   c. clustered, e.g. forming regular patterns.
   d. reflection of shape of article used to inflict abuse, (e.g. electric cord, belt buckle)
   e. different surface areas noted.
   f. regular appearance after absence, weekend, or vacation.
2. Unexplained burns:
   a. cigar or cigarette burns, especially on soles, palms, back, or buttocks.
   b. immersion burns (sock-like, glove-like, doughnut-shaped, on buttocks or genitalia).
   c. patterned like electric burner, iron, etc.
   d. rope burns on arms, legs, neck, or torso.
3. Unexplained fractures:
   a. to skull, nose, ear (cauliflower ear), facial structure.
   b. in various stages of healing.
   c. multiple or spiral fractures.
4. Unexplained lacerations or abrasions:
   a. to mouth, lips, gums, eyes, ears.
   b. to external genitalia.
5. Unexplained hair loss:
   a. hemorrhaging beneath scalp.
   b. possible hair pulling, self or other.
   c. possible evidence of underlying severe head injury (subdural hematoma).
6. Evidence of past injuries:
   a. Deformities—skull, nose and ears, cauliflower ear, hands (twisting reflex).
   b. Contractures resulting from restraint and delay in seeking treatment.
   c. Dislocation, pain, tenderness, and swelling (N.B.: dislocation may be due to incorrect lifting).

Physical neglect

1. Consistent hunger, poor hygiene, inappropriate dress including soiled clothing, unexplained weight loss, dehydration.
2. Consistent lack of supervision, especially in dangerous activities or long periods.
3. Constant fatigue or listlessness, unexplained or increasing confusion.
4. Unattended physical problems or medical needs, including urine burns or pressure sores.
5. Lost or nonfunctioning aids, e.g. glasses, dentures, hearing aids, walking aids and wheelchairs.
6. Over/under-medication.
7. Abandonment, immobility, hypothermia indicating possible isolation.

Sexual abuse

1. Difficulty in walking or sitting.
2. Torn, stained, or bloody underclothing.
3. Pain or itching in genital area.
4. Bruises or bleeding in external genitalia, vaginal, or anal areas.
5. Unexpected and unreported reluctance to cooperate with toileting and physical examination of genitalia.

Emotional mistreatment

1. Habit disorder (sucking, biting, rocking, etc.).
2. Conduct disorders (anti-social, destructive, self and others).
3. Neurotic traits (sleep disorders, speech disorders, inhibition of play).
4. Psychoneurotic reaction (hysteria, obsession, compulsion, phobias, hypochondria).

Note: It is necessary to assess whether symptoms and signs disappear in hospital or residential care over a period of time (Decalmer and Glendenning 1993: 39–41).

OTHER CRIMES AGAINST OLDER PEOPLE

As important as elder abuse is in contemporary American society, older people are victimized by other forms of crime—the types that have become a focus of national attention in recent years. These include strong-arm robbery, purse snatching, burglary, theft of checks, fraud, vandalism, murder, rape, and aggravated assault.

It is important to note that older people tend to have more fear of crime than younger persons, and yet generally there is less violent crime committed against them than against people who are younger (La Grange and Ferraro 1987). This is particularly true for murder, rape, and aggravated assault (U.S. Senate Special Committee on Aging 1991b).

This does not mean that there are not many older people living in high-crime areas where it is dangerous for them to leave their homes. The fear and reality of "street crimes" have resulted in many older people, particularly those who live in urban settings, becoming virtual prisoners in their own homes. As Matthew Sutherland of the American Association of Retired Persons (AARP) Criminal Justice Services Program said in testimony before Congress,

> A trend causing widespread concern is the increase in "street crimes" associated with crime-prone young males, particularly those youths involved with illicit drugs. Such street crimes are the ones having the greatest impact on urban life; they restrict movement, lessen the quality of life, reduce property values, erode the tax base, and cause extensive and debilitating changes in lifestyles (U.S. Senate Special Committee on Aging 1991b: 19).

An example of this violent type of crime was presented at this same Congressional hearing.

> On June 10, 1991, at approximately 6:30 A.M., I receive a phone call from my 82-year-old aunt indicating that she wanted me to go her home as soon as possible. Because of her apparent urgency and the fact that she never wants to bother anyone, I rushed over immediately. She lives only three blocks from my home. When I arrived, I discovered that someone had broken into her home, attacked her, bound and gagged her, struck her in the head, thereby knocking out her front teeth and rendering her unconscious. She had extensive bruises to her hands, feet, to her neck and face.
>
> She did not want to call the police nor go to the hospital. However, I convinced her that we had to contact the police as well as seek medical attention for her own good.
>
> Prior to the attack of June 10, 1991, my 82-year-old aunt was a very strong, proud, independent, and self-sufficient woman. She was born, raised, and lived all her life in her home. She was never married and has no children. She no longer feels safe, comfortable, or happy in her own home.
>
> During the attack, she apparently suffered a minor stroke which has slightly impaired her speech and her sense of balance. This has totally destroyed her quality of life. Anyone, no matter what age, would be traumatized by such an experience, but to an older adult, this is an almost unrecoverable catastrophic experience (U.S. Senate Special Committee on Aging 1991b: 3–4).

Sutherland pointed out that once an older person experiences this or similar types of crime, the fear that remains can become worse than the crime itself, lasting long after the injuries to the victim heal or the economic losses are overcome (U.S. Senate Special Committee on Aging 1991b).

As people grow older, they become more vulnerable to certain types of crimes. Many older persons are more fragile as a result of a variety of conditions such as reduced muscle ability, osteoporosis, reduced vision or hearing, slower reaction times, and psychological changes. As people become more frail with advancing age, their fear of crime is likely to increase. This potential for increased fear of crime has been demonstrated by a nationwide survey of persons aged 55 and older conducted by the AARP (1990). In their outlook at the time of the survey, 58 percent indicated that they felt "very secure" in their homes from crime, with 38 percent "somewhat secure." Projecting into the future, 29 percent said they were "very concerned" about their security and safety, and 38 percent indicated that they were "somewhat concerned." So while over 90 percent were either "very secure" or "somewhat secure" in their present situation concerning crime, looking ahead to older age resulted in two-thirds (67 percent) of those responding to the survey saying that they were "very concerned" or "somewhat concerned" about crime.

Many older people, because of their particular vulnerability, are more fearful of crime than some rates of crime against them would indicate. Nevertheless, it is difficult to generalize about the victimization of older people for some types of crime, especially crimes of violence. While older people are victimized less than younger persons in some of the most violent crime categories (murder, rape, and aggravated assault), a qualifier needs to be added: "It depends." It depends on where the older person lives, on lifestyle to some extent, on her or his economic condition, and on a number of other factors (U.S. Special Committee on Aging 1991b).

What is certain is that once an older person is a victim of crime, it is far more likely that this person will greatly change her or his lifestyle as well as develop and keep a high level of fear of crime which older friends and relatives are likely to develop as well (U.S. Special Committee on Aging 1991a).

FRAUDS, SCAMS, AND CONS—RIPOFFS OF OLDER PEOPLE

A series of crimes that older people are not immune from, and indeed are the prime targets for, are frauds, scams, and confidence schemes—all classified as consumer fraud. While older people make up about 12 percent of the population, over 30 percent of consumer fraud is directed at them (U.S. Senate Special Committee on Aging 1993).

In some areas of consumer fraud, older people are nearly the only target. A survey of 331 police departments found that 99 percent of home improvement swindles are committed against the elderly. These victims were mostly between the ages of 65 to 79, and primarily women living alone (U.S. Senate Special Committee on Aging 1993).

Why Older People Are Targets of Consumer Fraud

There are a variety of reasons why older people are so often the victims of consumer fraud.

- Older Americans are easier for the con artist to reach.
- Older consumers are more easily contacted by telephone.
- Retired people tend to spend much time at home, making them available to the swindler.
- Older people who suffer from health problems or who have restricted mobility tend to spend most of their time at home.
- Older people tend to be more trusting of salespeople.
- Older consumers tend to be less informed of their consumer rights.
- Many older persons welcome someone to talk with and are likely to let the con artists into their homes (U.S. Senate Special Committee on Aging 1993).

These factors do not mean older people are less intelligent. Older people experienced earlier business times when trust was based on knowing the seller. In addition, older consumers often are inclined to rely on the expertise of salespersons who seem trustworthy and knowledgeable. This is particularly true for complex products about which an older person has little or no knowledge. Some are pressured by high-handed tactics of salespersons who get into their homes and will not leave until the older person agrees to "sign on the dotted line." They literally become hostages in their own home. These predators of the elderly look for the most vulnerable older persons and then try to wear them down, play on their fears and needs, and increase their sense of helplessness. They end up robbing them of their money, dignity, and self-confidence (U.S. Senate Special Committee on Aging 1993).

Types of Scams, Cons, and Fraud Pulled on the Elderly

Some of the types of crimes that follow are old schemes pulled on elderly people, such as the pigeon drop scam and the bank examiner con. They have been around for many years and are still reported regularly. Many of the current scams focus on the vulnerability and needs of older people and use modern technology.

The Pigeon Drop Scam   This involves at least two people acting as if they do not know each other. One of them "finds" a large amount of money. They then ask an older person who is sitting, for example, at a bus stop, if he or she could help them keep the money until they can divide it up after work. They ask the victim to put up an amount of cash to show his or her trust and good faith. They then put all of the money into one pot so the victim can deposit it in his or her bank account until they can get together later. Usually a sign of good faith requires the victim to take several thousand dollars out of his or her account. They help the older person obtain the cash withdrawal from his or her bank account, look it over, and then give the victim the cash withdrawal and the "found" money. When the victim attempts to deposit the money in a bank there is no money at all in the envelope in which the "found" and the withdrawn monies were supposedly mixed together. There is only shredded paper because the crooks switched the envelopes, and have disappeared. Swindlers frequently target older persons who have not only a significant bank balance, but who also are beginning to lose mental competence or show a certain amount of greed and larceny on their part.

The Bank Examiner Con   In the bank examiner ploy, the swindlers will call potential victims and represent themselves as either bank officials or a members of the police department. They then ask their victims about the amount of money in their bank accounts and explain that they would appreciate their cooperation in catching a bank embezzler. They ask the targeted older persons to take out a sum of money, say $2,000 dollars. Then they come to the home of the victims to take and hold the $2,000, for which they will give a receipt. They thank their target for being so cooperative and tell them that after they examine the bank records and the records of the specific teller, they will return the money. Of course, they are never seen again.

Home Improvement/Repairs Schemes   In the home improvement/repair con, the perpetrators attempt to get an older person to prepay for an improvement or repair which they offer at greatly reduced prices. After receiving the money they disappear and never do the agreed-upon job. A variation of this is to actually complete the repair with very inferior materials, and then threaten their victim if they complain; or they may pressure the older person to accept a new, more expensive contract for additional work, which they never complete. Siding, roofing, and sidewalk or driveway repairs frequently tend to be a part of this type of swindle.

At times these repair scams are tied in with predatory lenders, where an older targeted person signs up for a balloon payment, meaning that after a certain amount of time, she or he has to repay the entire loan. Often these swindlers try to get the older person to take out an equity loan on the house. If the payment is not made on time, whoever holds the loan can foreclose on the house, and the older person will lose his or her home. In Atlanta alone, more than 2,500 homeowners had law suits against banks, claiming either home repair fraud or extremely high finance charges (Kane 1992). One older resident in Atlanta had a broker knock on his door and sign him up on a debt consolidation loan using his house as collateral. The $53,000 loan paid off his mortgage and his repair debts, but it had a 21-percent interest rate with finance charges of $581 per month. This person had an income of $80 a week, and the bank threatened foreclosure on the loan and eviction of the resident.

In a case in Wisconsin, a home improvement contractor convinced a 73-year-old woman and her blind husband to sign loan documents they did not understand and forged others. This left the couple with monthly loan payments of $796 on an income of less than $10,000 a year. This same contractor took over $97,000 from another older woman for work that had a value of $20,000. The value of the house was only $26,000 (U.S. Senate Special Committee on Aging 1993).

Telemarketing Scams   Telemarketing scams involve using the telephone to contact people in their homes with intent to defraud them. Telephone scams frequently target older people. A 1991 report by a U.S. House of Representatives Committee estimated that fraud by telephone costs consumers between $3 billion and $15 billion annually.

In one version of these scams, older persons are asked to call an "800" or "900" number. They will then be offered prizes or low-priced trips, or an easily obtained loan. The "guaranteed" prize is one of numerous telephone-marketing scams. Often the caller will request a credit card number, which is then used by the caller to make purchases charged to an older person. These callers often work from "boiler rooms," in which groups of persons will be calling constantly, trying to make "connections" with older people. They usually tell the person that he must accept the offer immediately because it is only good for 24 hours. Some fraudulent telemarketing outfits contract with legitimate nonprofit organizations to raise funds but keep most of the funds for themselves to cover the "expenses" of calling. One version of this type of scam is to offer needed items such as trash bags, light bulbs, ironing board covers, or birthday/holiday cards. These items usually are quite inferior and are very high priced. The telemarketing schemers then keep most of the profits (Reyes 1993).

Other telephone scams involve "cheap" trips, or "free trips," or vacation housing at reduced prices, if the person acts immediately, which usually means giving a credit card number. The swindlers will usually be willing to settle for a checking account number. Once the telemarketers have the checking account numbers, they put them on "demand drafts," which function much like checks but do not require signatures. Often the victims are unaware that the bank has

paid the drafts until they receive their monthly statement. As one older victim said,

> They called and told me I'd won an all-expense paid trip to Hawaii. All I had to do was purchase a round-trip ticket to Los Angeles. I gave them my checking account number and they took out $800 the next day. Two weeks passed and I hadn't heard from them. Turns out the company didn't exist (Reyes 1992: 72).

Gottschalk, after investigating telemarketing fraud, wrote:

> Telemarketing scamsters abound, operating out of "boiler rooms" in Southern California, Texas, Las Vegas, and southern Florida. These smooth-talking "yaks"—as they are known in the telemarketing trade—just love to talk to polite senior citizens who won't hang up on them (Gottschalk 1994: 16).

Con artists have found that it takes no more time to swindle $100,000 out of an older person than it does to swindle a younger person out of $3,000. Although persons 65 and over comprise about 12 percent of the population, they control over 30 percent of the wealth.

Gottschalk found that these kinds of frauds have included investments in silver, gold, and foreign currencies, second mortgages and mortgage-backed securities, promissory notes, and real estate. He believed that low interest rates in the early 1990s made retired persons very susceptible to con artists because they were seeking higher rates of return on their money. Some of the current telemarketing scams include oil leases, gasoline futures, vending machines, and wireless cable licenses. Gottschalk stated that the biggest mistake an older person can make is to send money on the basis of a telephone call. He warned that the caller will be friendly, smooth, solicitous, and will, as other investigators have found, pressure the older person to send money immediately because of a time limit on "the deal."

According to the North American Securities Administrators Association, telemarketing fraud amounts to over $10 billion in investor losses each year (Bekey 1991). John Perkins, president of NASAA, stated that telephones are now the vehicle of choice for committing fraud: In illustrating this, Bekey stated,

> Authorities don't know a scam is taking place until they're notified by scorched investors—but many victims don't realize they've been had until months later and many are too embarrassed to come forward when they do grasp what's happened. Further, they may not even have a correct name or phone number for the company they dealt with. Some artists frequently initiate calls and do business under several names (Bekey 1991: 1).

Telephone scam artists tend to work from a prepared script using the same words over and over so that they get very good at it. They work hard at sounding sincere. They know people will initially be suspicious so they have to overcome suspicion. Some will ask that a person give them just 1 percent of his or her trust and time, so that they can earn the other 99 percent. They have heard all the objections before and are prepared to give answers.

Mail Fraud   The mail service is frequently used to defraud older persons as well as persons of any age who are able to respond to mail-order advertisements.

Some real-life deals in mail-order advertisements include:

A "universal coat hanger" advertised for $3.99. What did consumers get stuck with? A sturdy 10-cent nail.

A "solar clothes dryer" for only $39.99. Trouble is, it looked just like the clothesline and clothespin we used in the old days.

An ad for a "15-piece wicker set" including a table, settee, two chairs and a rocker guaranteed that the set would be exactly like the picture; that is just what you got—a copy of the picture.

One ad showed an actual photo of the product (a complete tool set and box for $40), so you couldn't be fooled, right? The ad was carefully worded to mention only the box—which was all you got (Bekey 1991: 33).

Medical Quacks/Frauds

Medical quackery is largely targeted at older people. It is estimated that more than $40 billion a year is swindled out of the American people, most of it from the elderly, according to Congressional sources (Barnhill 1991). Others have put the amount swindled from fraud and abuse in the health-care field between $50 billion and $80 billion each year (Witkin, Friedman, and Guttman 1992).

There is almost no limit to the fraudulent products and procedures offered to older people to reverse the aging process and treat or cure almost anything from athlete's foot to cancer (Barnhill 1991). In testimony before the Congress in 1992, the U.S. Assistant Chief Postal Inspector stated that medical and investment scams are targeted to address the particular needs of older persons (U.S. Senate Special Committee on Aging 1993).

To pitch their quack remedies, the con artists use modern-day marketing techniques including ads in national magazines, supermarket tabloids, direct-mail flyers, television promotions that look like talk shows ("infomercials"), door-to-door salespeople, and telemarketing. Two-thirds of the money that comes from medical quackery are generated by "nutritional" remedies (Barnhill 1991).

It is no surprise that anti-aging products flood the market promising new vitality and enhanced sexual vigor. "You Can Now Enjoy An X-Rated Sex Life Up To Age 100 And Beyond," one ad claimed. "Give a 50-year-old man the energy and performance he had when he was 20," another ad promised (Barnhill 1991: 2).

There is metabolic therapy, in which the attempt is made to detoxify the body of impurities and to boost the immune system. The movie star Steve McQueen, dying of cancer, went to Mexico to receive coffee enemas to stimulate his liver, and thereby eliminate toxins from his body. He gave a personal testimonial to the benefits of this treatment. He died shortly after his testimonial (Wolfman 1990).

People with arthritis are especially vulnerable to medical quackery because most forms of arthritis go through exacerbations and remissions, meaning that there are periods in which the disease flares up, and then temporarily subsides. Knowing that, it is easy to claim that virtually any treatment will be effective because sooner or later the person will go into a natural remission, at which time the claim can be made that the treatment works. When the symptoms come back with a natural exacerbation of the disease, it can be claimed that the person should either increase the treatment, or just wait, and the treatment will become effective. That is why persons who wear cooper bracelets for arthritis will claim that it is effective. One might just as well wear an onion around one's neck, because sooner or later it will be "effective" (Wolfman 1990).

Food and Drug Administration (FDA) officials stated: "There are so many phony arthritis cures we can't keep track of all the names." The list of "cures" includes alfalfa and algae pills, cow dung baths, and "Extract of Green-Lopped New Zealand Musel." Dr. Floyd Pennington of the Arthritis Foundation stated, "As the population ages, we're going to see a tremendous growth in the number of people with arthritis problems. It's a great market for fraud" (Wolfman 1990: 44).

Some of the medical frauds sold to the elderly not only hurt their pocketbooks, but can be very harmful physically. One investigator stated,

> Laboratory analysis of various quack remedies reveal they can contain anything from human waste to deadly poisons, from herbal substances to potent chemicals known to have powerful—and sometimes devastating—effects on the body.
>
> Thousands of elderly people each year suffer needless injury or death because of quack medical products, and millions suffer financial losses they cannot afford (Barnhill 1991: 2).

Congressman Ron Wyden, a member of the Energy and Commerce Subcommittee on Health, pointed out that the products and methods of health quacks may change, but they all offer essentially the same product:

> Hope. To the sick, they promise new health. To the dying, they promise life. To the elderly, they promise youth. But what they provide is disappointment, disillusionment, and despair (Barnhill 1991: 2).

Not only are medical scams costly to the victims in terms of lost money and potential harm to the body, but relying on fraudulent products and treatments delays seeking diagnosis and treatment from reputable medical providers; and delays can be deadly in many instances.

Investment Fraud

With many older people trying to live on savings they accumulated over years of work, the elderly are natural targets of fraudulent investment schemes. These schemes may include phony art works, gold, wines, gemstones, leveraged precious metals, rare coins, oil and gas leases, cellular telephone licenses, and wireless cable licenses (U.S. Senate Special Committee on Aging 1993). They may include investments that are legal but simply not appropriate for older persons because their risks are so high. As an example,

> To Earl Bonsey of Dover-Foxcroft, Maine, it sounded almost too good to be true. As it turned out, it was. The 69-year-old retired carpenter thought he was investing $15,000 in a safe, high-yield mutual fund. Instead, he got a high-risk junk bond fund and lost a third of his money (Lewis 1993: 1).

With bank certificates of deposit paying relatively low interest rates in the early 1990s, older people across the nation were looking for higher returns from their investments so they could have a higher level of income. As a result, they were ready potential victims of investment fraud, with countless numbers having been bilked out of millions of dollars each year and many having lost their life savings, according to Kent Brunette of the American Association of Retired Persons (Lewis 1993).

Older people are especially vulnerable to investment fraud because they generally have more assets than younger people, live on fixed incomes, and often suffer from loneliness. Widows often are more vulnerable because many have had limited experience in managing financial assets (Vilbig 1993). Sophisticated, computer-generated lists provide the con artists with ways to identify newly retired employees, those receiving lump-sum pension payments, newly widowed older women, or older persons who sell their homes.

The real-life story was related about a man who retired from the University of Northern Colorado and moved to San Diego, California. He bought a house and arranged for a major securities company to invest $90,000 in safe, short-term securities that he planned to use to pay off his mortgage. Instead of a safe haven for his money, the broker sold him high-risk securities such as oil and gas limited partnerships that lost much of their value and were not marketable shortly after he bought them (Lewis 1993).

Living Trust Scams

An emerging scam largely targeted at older people is the high-pressure sale of living trusts. A living trust is a legal device to transfer real or personal property into something called a trust. The trust is managed by a trustee who may be the same person who set up the trust. It is an estate planning device that avoids probate. With this device a person's property does not have to be processed through a Probate Court, which takes time and costs money.

This scheme takes advantage of the fact that between 30 percent and 50 percent of all the adults in the United States at any given time have not made adequate financial arrangements relating to their death (U.S. Senate Special Committee on Aging 1993). As a result, slick-talking salespersons approach older Americans telling them how they can save purchasers of living trusts thousands of dollars in taxes and probate costs by "signing on the dotted line" and giving them what amounts to enormously inflated prices for what is often a very inferior service. They generally charge far beyond what local attorneys would charge for something that may be inappropriate for an older individual's circumstances. The product (the living trust) that the con artists sells is often defective, as demonstrated in the following example:

> A Connecticut couple paid $6,900 for a living trust and membership in one of these organizations. The attorney who prepared the trust was from Arizona, not Connecticut. This couple had great difficulty reaching the attorney. When they finally received the document, it was riddled with mistakes that even a non-lawyer could identify. Their fear was that it contained other mistakes that were not immediately apparent (U.S. Senate Special Committee on Aging 1993: 99).

In an AARP-sponsored survey of attorneys in different parts of the nation, fees ranged from $150 to $1,000 for drafting a trust valued at $80,000 and $350 to $1,850 for a $200,000 estate, well under the amounts charged by the living-trust con artists.

Phony Prizes   Either by telephone or by mail, these fraudulent schemes are used to notify potential victims that they have won a valuable prize such as a vacation, car, cash, or jewelry. Using various misrepresentations, these con artists lead the victim into buying items at prices that far exceed the value of the products or the value of the prizes (U.S. Senate Special Committee on Aging 1993).

Through these schemes, it is easy for people to spend hundreds and even thousands of dollars on nearly worthless items. In many instances, the consumers never get the prizes that were promised.

Misuse of Guardianships   Another major area of fraud against the elderly is the misuse of guardianships. E. McRae Mathie writing in the *FBI Law Enforcement Bulletin* said,

> One area in which law enforcement has seen an increasing number of complaints is financial exploitation of the elderly through the mismanagement of their income and assets. These incidents usually occur when individuals are given legal guardianship or power of attorney over the victim's finances (Mathis 1994: 1).

Guardianships are granted by a court order to manage the affairs of individuals who are judged incompetent to manage their own financial and personal business. Once a guardianship is granted by the court, it is not easy to reverse.

Mathis pointed out that most states do not demand much accountability of guardians. Many courts are simply too busy to become very involved in examining in any great detail the activities of the guardians. Proving financial exploitation is difficult because it usually requires the examination of savings accounts, items of deposit, retrieving canceled checks, and following the flow of the victim's and the victimizer's funds.

Added to these difficulties is the probability that if a guardianship was granted, the victim is not able to provide testimony because of physical or psychological conditions. In other situations, the victimized person may be dead, and the guardian's exploitation of his or her estate may never become known. Mathis gave an illustration of a guardian who misspent an older person's funds:

> . . . she purchased a Corvette, a boat, a home computer, a tanning bed, furniture, a refrigerator, a dishwasher, and gold jewelry, in addition to paying her own utility bills. Even though the victim was deceased at the time of the trial, friends and acquaintances described her as "tight," a "miser" and a person who "kept close to her money," wore old clothes, and drove a 12-year-old automobile. They also testified that the defendant had not allowed the victim to see the financial records from the joint accounts (Mathis 1994: 3).

These are some of the old as well as the newer frauds that are targeted at older people. The types and variations of scams and cons committed on older persons is endless. They continue to evolve, and marketing techniques continue to develop based on new technologies and strategies. What does not change is the fact that older people are exploited by greedy, ruthless con artists—exploitation that can result in financial ruin and health loss up to death.

Preventing Crime Against the Elderly

In order to combat crime against the elderly, some communities have formed something called Triad/SALT organizations. Triads are organized when the local police and sheriff's departments agree to work cooperatively with senior citizens to prevent victimization of the elderly (Cantrell 1994). The Triad concept began in 1987, when members of the American Association of Retired Persons (AARP), the International Association of Chiefs of Police (IACP), and the National Sheriffs' Association (NSA) met to consider methods of reducing crime against the elderly. Most Triads also include representatives from other organizations and agencies such as the Area Agencies on Aging, senior center representatives, adult protection services, and other organizations promoting the reduction of crime among the elderly.

The SALT (Seniors and Lawmen Together) is the organization that the Triad usually creates when law enforcement personnel ask older persons, as well as people who work with them, to serve on an advisory council. The SALT organization typically conducts a survey to determine the needs and concerns of older people in their region regarding criminal activity.

In describing the operation of the program, Cantrell wrote,

> . . . volunteers may staff reception desks in law enforcement agencies, present programs to senior organizations, conduct informal house security surveys, and become leaders in new or rejuvenated neighborhood watch groups. They may also provide information and support to crime victims, call citizens concerning civil warrants, or assist law en-

forcement agencies in maintaining records or property rooms at substations or in other areas (Cantrell 1994: 2).

In some areas the Triad creates telephone programs in which older persons are called daily. In other areas they have created senior shopping programs where grocery stores provide vans to transport older persons in regularly scheduled shopping trips. Triads also teach older persons safe ways to carry money and other valuables, as well as carjacking prevention.

Mel Weith, writing to law enforcement officials in the *FBI Law Enforcement Bulletin* stated:

> Very few, if any, police inservice programs deal with crimes involving elders, including abuse, neglect, theft, and con games . . .
>
> In short, proper training regarding basic gerontology and the problems that face our elders on a daily basis is greatly needed. If it is not provided, we are failing to address the issues that concern a large segment of our "at risk" population . . . through education of law enforcement personnel, we have the potential to eliminate this fear and guarantee that the elder population does more than just survive (Weith 1994: 24).

SUMMARY

Elder abuse is one of the most underrecognized, and as a result, one of the most underreported social problems in the United States. It first surfaced as a national issue in 1978 with Congressional hearings conducted by the late Representative Claude Pepper, a tireless advocate for the elderly. It was not until 1987 that the federal government took any action to define or prevent this type of abuse. It did so by adding amendments to the reauthorization of the Older Americans Act. There are three broad categories of elder abuse: (1) domestic elder abuse; (2) institutional elder abuse; and (3) self-neglect/abuse. Domestic elder abuse refers to many forms of mistreatment of an older person by someone who has a special relationship in the older person's home or in the home of the person caring

for the elder. These abuses include physical abuse, sexual abuse, emotional or psychological abuse, neglect, and financial exploitation. Institutional abuse refers to the forms of abuse listed above that occur in facilities designed for older persons, such as foster homes and nursing facilities. Self-neglect/abuse refers to neglectful or abusive behavior by an older person on himself/herself.

There was a 94 percent increase in the number of elder abuse cases reported from 1986 to 1991. It is estimated that only one out of fourteen elder abuse cases is reported. The majority of elder abuse cases that were reported and confirmed were for self-neglect/abuse.

Based on the latest available national data, about two-thirds of the victims of elder abuse are women. The median age of victims was 78.8 years. A majority of the abusers were men, with adult children leading the categories of types of abusers.

A number of theories concerning the causes of elder abuse have been put forward. For unintentional abuse, the causes include:

- Ignorance
- Caregiver lacks desire to provide care
- Caregiver lacks ability to provide care
- Self-neglect

Underlying some of these causes is caregiver burnout and stresses on the caregiver. In addition, some families are more prone to violence than others. There is no indication that retirement contributes to elder abuse.

The medical community plays a vital role in identifying, treating, and preventing elder abuse. This is particularly true of emergency department personnel in hospitals. All health-care workers have a vital role in the problem of elder abuse. To this end, the American Medical Association has developed guidelines to assist physicians in their vital role.

There are a variety of services available in many communities to assist in the overall problem of elder abuse. Not the least of these is the

Long-Term Care Ombudsman Programs which receive, investigate, and act on reports of suspected elder abuse in long-term-care facilities such as nursing homes.

Crime is a big issue with older people. Even though some types of violent crime—murder, rape, and aggravated assault—are less frequently committed against the elderly, older people have more fear of crime than younger persons. Nevertheless, "street crime" is a reality for older people. The fear of these types of crimes causes many to become virtual prisoners in their own homes. Older people, because of physical changes due to the aging process or chronic health conditions, have a tendency to feel particularly vulnerable to crime.

Frauds, scams, and cons are particularly targeted at older people. Even though the elderly make up about 12 percent of the population, they account for over 30 percent of the consumer fraud victims. Some types of fraud, such as home improvement scams, are almost totally targeted at older people.

Older people are targets of consumer fraud because they are easy targets. They are home most of the time and therefore can be reached by the con artists. Many are more trusting of friendly salespeople. Others, because of boredom and loneliness, welcome salespeople into their homes, which can be a big mistake because it can be very hard to get rid of them.

Types of consumer fraud targeted at the elderly include the pigeon drop, the bank examiner con, home improvement schemes, telemarketing scams, medical quackery, investment fraud, living trust scams, phony prizes, misuse of guardianships, and a variety of others.

In order to prevent crimes and confidence scams against the elderly, the International Association of Chiefs of Police, the National Sheriffs Association, and the American Association of Retired Persons have joined together to promote the development of Triads/SALTs in communities across the nation. The Triads are the three groups working together to form Seniors and Lawmen Together (SALT) to mobilize community resources to fight crime.

REFERENCES

American Association of Retired Persons. 1990. *Understanding Senior Housing for the 1990s*. Washington DC: AARP.

American Medical Association Council on Scientific Affairs. 1987. Elder Abuse and Neglect. *JAMA*, 257: 966–971.

Aravanis, S.C., Adelman, R.D., Breckman, R., et al. 1992. *Diagnostic Treatment Guidelines on Elder Abuse and Neglect*. Chicago, IL: AMA.

Bachman, R., and Pillemer, K.A. 1991. Retirement: Does It Affect Marital Conflict and Violence? *Journal of Elder Abuse and Neglect*, 3(2): 75–88.

Barnhill, W. 1991. Pulling the Plug on Quacks. *NRTA Bulletin*, 32(7): 2, 7.

Bekey, M. 1991. Dial S-W-I-N-D-L-E-. *Modern Maturity* (April/May): 31–41.

Blakely, B.E., and Dolon, R. 1991. Area Agencies on Aging and the Prevention of Elder Abuse: The Results of a National Study. *Journal of Elder Abuse and Neglect*, 3(2): 21–40.

Cantrell, B. 1994. Triad: Reducing Criminal Victimization of the Elderly. *FBI Law Enforcement Bulletin*, (February): 19–23.

Coleman, D., and Straus, M.A. 1990. Marital Power, Conflict, and Violence in a Nationally Representative Sample of American Families. In M.A. Straus and R.J. Gelles, (eds.). *Physical Violence in American Families*. New Brunswick, NJ: Transaction Books.

Decalmer, P, and Glendenning, F.. 1993. Clinical Presentation. In Decalmer, P. and Glendening, F. (eds.). *The Mistreatment of Elderly People*. Newbury Park, CA: Sage Publications.

Elder Abuse Is On the Rise. 1993. *Older Adult Health Quarterly* (Spring): 7. Detroit, MI: Blue Cross and Blue Shield of Michigan.

Freedman, M. 1992. Elder Abuse Not Seen as a Problem. *The Grand Rapids Press*. (March 22): B5.

Gelfand, D.E. 1993. *The Aging Network: Programs and Services*. New York: Springer.

Gioglio, G.R., and Blakemore, P. 1983. *Elder Abuse in New Jersey: The Knowledge and Experience of Abuse Among Older New Jerseyans*. Trenton, NJ: New Jersey Department of Human Resources.

Gottschalk, J. 1994. Telemarketing Scams. *Modern Maturity* (April/May): 13–16.

Herbert, E. 1987. *Marriage and Retirement: Advice to Couples in Popular Literature*, (November). Presented at National Council on Family Relations. Atlanta, GA.

Jones, J.S. 1994. Elder Abuse and Neglect: Responding to a National Problem. *Annals of Emergency Medicine*, 23 (April): 845–848.

Kane, M. 1992. Poor or Elderly Homeowners Lose Their Homes to Predatory Lenders. *The Grand Rapids Press* (May 10): A-9.

LaGrange, R.L., and Ferraro, K.F. 1987. The Elderly's Fear of Crime: A Critical Examination of the Research. *Research on Aging*, 372–391.

Lan, E., and Kosberg, J.I. 1979. Abuse of the Elderly by Informal Care Providers. *Aging* (September/October): 11–15.

Lewis, R. 1993. Stock Schemes a New Peril. *NRTA Bulletin*, 34(7): 1, 6, 7.

McLeod, D. 1993. How Are Things at Home? *NRTA Bulletin*, 34(1): 2, 15.

McNamara, R.M., Rousseau, E., and Sanders, A. 1992. Geriatric Emergency Medicine: A Survey of Practicing Emergency Physicians. *Annals of Emergency Medicine*, 21: 796–801.

Mathis, E.M. 1994. Policing the Guardians: Combating Guardianship and Power of Attorney Fraud. *FBI Law Enforcement Bulletin*, (February) *Vol. No.*, 1–4.

Pillemer, K., and Finkelhor, D. 1988. The Prevalence of Elder Abuse: A Random Sample Survey. *The Gerontologist*, 28(1): 51–57.

Pillemer, K., and Moore, D.W. 1989. Abuse of Patients in Nursing Homes: Findings From a Survey of Staff. *The Gerontologist*, 29: 314–320.

Public Welfare. 1988. The Vexing Problem of Elder Abuse. (Spring): 5–6.

Reyes, K.W. 1992. You've just won . . . *Modern Maturity* (June/July): 10.

Reyes, K.W. 1992. Scambusters. *Modern Maturity* (December/January): 72.

Steinmetz, S.K. 1981. Elder Abuse. *Aging* (January/February): 6–10.

Straus, M.A., and Gelles, R.J. 1990. *Physical Violence in American Families*. New Brunswick, NJ: Transaction Publishers.

Tatara, T. 1990. *Elder Abuse in the United States: An Issue Paper*. Washington, D.C.: National Aging Resource Center on Elder Abuse.

Tatara, T. 1993. *Summaries of the Statistical Data on Elder Abuse in Domestic Settings for FY90 and FY91*: A Final Report. Washington, D.C.: National Aging Resource Center on Elder Abuse.

Tatara, T. 1994. *Elder Abuse: Questions and Answers*. Washington, D.C.: National Center on Elder Abuse.

U.S. Department of Health and Human Services. 1980. USDHEW Publication OHDS 79-3021. 47–80 Washington, DC: USDHEW.

U.S. House of Representatives Select Committee on Aging. 1990. Sub-Committee on Health and Long-Term Care. *Elder Abuse: A Decade of Shame and Inaction*. Washington, DC: U.S. Government Printing Office.

U.S. Senate Special Committee on Aging. 1991a. *Elder Abuse and Neglect: Prevention and Intervention*. Washington, DC: U.S. Government Printing Office.

U.S. Senate Special Committee on Aging. 1991b. *Crimes Committed Against the Elderly*. Washington, DC: U.S. Government Printing Office.

U.S. Senate Special Committee on Aging. 1993. *Consumer Fraud and the Elderly: Easy Prey?* Washington, DC: U.S. Government Printing Office.

Vilbig, P. 1993. Dodging Financial Deceit. *Maturity News Service*. In *Detroit Free Press* (June 15): 3C.

Vinick, B., and Eckerdt, D.J. 1988. *The transition to Retirement: Accounts of Husbands and Wives*. Annual meeting of the Gerontological Society of America, San Francisco, CA.

Witkin, G., Friedman, D., and Guttman, M. 1992. Health Care and Fraud. *U.S. News and World Report* (February 24): 34–43.

Weith, M.E. 1994. Elder Abuse: A National Tragedy. *FBI Law Enforcement Bulletin* (February): 24–25.

Wolf, R.S. 1988. The Evolution of Policy: A 10-Year Retrospective. *Public Welfare*. (Spring) 46(2).

Wolfman, I. 1990. Special Report: Health Fraud 1990. *New Choices* (February 24): 43–45.

PART SEVEN

PUBLIC POLICY AND POLITICS

Chapter 22   **PUBLIC POLICY AND THE POLITICS OF AGING**

Public Policy
and the Politics of Aging

Running Out of Money?

John and Mae thought they had earned a pretty good living in their business. John was a painter, and Mae worked in an office. After they were married in 1928, Mae continued to work in the office until her first child was born. She never went back to work, and in the next six years the family added two more children. It was rough raising a family during the Great Depression, but John managed to keep going by painting homes and commercial properties.

During World War II, painting jobs were easy to get. With the end of the war and the building boom that followed, John expanded his business and hired other painters to work for him. The children were growing up, and Mae was eager to do some work outside the home, so she and John decided to open a paint store.

It was a smart move. Millions of returning servicemen and women were eager to settle down and establish their own homes and families. Because John and Mae were hard workers, knew their business, and had timed their expansion well, their business prospered. They did not get rich, but they sent all three children to college and generously supported their church. They had nice clothes, a good car, and took a vacation every year.

Life was good beyond their dreams. Although becoming wealthy had never been their highest goal, a sense of financial security was nice. In 1963, John and Mae began to think about retirement. Their children were grown, and John felt it was time to slow down and get out from under the pressure of the business. He and Mae wanted to enjoy life while they were still young enough to travel and do the things they had been too busy to do while running their own business.

John and Mae sold their paint store and invested the proceeds for retirement income. They thought they had enough money to last them the rest of their lives. In addition to their Social Security income, they were sure their investments would allow them to live the comfortable, modest life they had enjoyed.

But they didn't plan to live as long as they did. John and Mae had no way of knowing how much inflation would affect the economy. They never dreamed the cost of living would rise so dramatically in thirty years.

Even though John and Mae do not need a nursing home yet, they are facing lean times as they continue to grow older in an economy with ever higher prices. Any illness they face may require large sums of money in spite of Medicare. How will they raise that money with their fixed income and continual cuts in the Medicare program?

"Economic Spat Rocks the Ages"

WASHINGTON—Hear the sound of youthful voices raised in anger? To some, it's the righteous clamor of millions of teen-agers and twenty somethings denouncing society's inequitable protection of the elderly at the expense of the young.

To others, it's the irritating self-indulgent whine of a spoiled and lazy generation raised in luxury and expecting the same as adults.

Whether you hear the former or the latter, the hubbub signals the newest inter-generational war.

Unlike previous generational disputes, this one isn't borne of differences over politics and culture. Today's division is about jobs and economic security.

Acting on their anger, young people are joining national advocacy groups—Lead . . . or Leave and another called Third Millennium—to attack such sacred cows as Social Security and Medicare. And they are urging the federal government to refocus its support for youth-oriented programs ranging from education to job creation.

"The entire system is slanted to benefit senior citizens," said Rob Nelson co-founder of Lead . . . or Leave. "That would be OK if young people weren't suffering at the same time."

The economic disparities between the elderly and the young are evident in U.S. Census data. National statistics show that:

- *15.9 percent of 18- to 24-year-olds are in poverty, compared with 12.2 percent of people 65 years or older;*
- *99.1 percent of people over the age of 65 were covered by health insurance in 1990, compared with only 73.9 percent of people between the ages of 18 and 24; and*
- *the median net worth for people under the age of 35 was $6,078 in 1988, compared with $61,491 for senior citizens. About 40 percent of seniors' net worth is home equity.*

Nelson believes such inequities are sparking a firestorm of youthful discontent. But John Rother, AARP's chief lobbyist in Washington, believes disenchantment isn't unique to the younger generation. It mirrors the entire society's "skepticism about the long-term future," he says.

For Benjamin Bolger of Ann Arbor, it's much more than a feeling of skepticism. He says he is frustrated by the federal government's biases toward the elderly and wants to overhaul the system.

A 17-year-old junior at the University of Michigan, Bolger is hoping more of his peers will hear that message this fall, as Lead . . . or Leave kicks off seminars on 10 university campuses around the country. An Ann Arbor teach-in is scheduled for Oct. 7 on U-M's campus.

At the top of Bolger's list of concerns is Social Security. Like many young people, he fears the federal pension system will be bankrupt when he retires. Official estimates show a surplus into the next century, although the massive baby boomer generation is expected to deplete the fund within the next 25 years.

"A lot of young people are legitimately concerned about the future of Social Security," Bolger said. "We're paying in now, but there's no guarantee it will be there for us. What will we do then?"

To slow the drain on Social Security, Bolger endorses Lead . . . or Leave's proposal to prevent affluent seniors from collecting benefits. He also backs income testing for Medicare, the federal

government's health insurance program for the elderly.

But talk of trimming Social Security payments and limiting access to Medicare has angered seniors.

"We're not greedy geezers," said 72-year-old Phyllis Wilde, of Portage. "We've worked all our lives for what we've got. Social Security is just one piece of that."

Dick Wilde, Phyllis' 76-year-old husband, said Social Security also eases the burden on family members.

"Sure, I'm having direct transfers of money from younger people to Phyllis and me," said Dick Wilde, who is active on senior issues. "When that happens, my children don't have to take care of me. Other children don't have to take care of their parents. It's a cycle that works to everyone's advantage."

As the battles continue, finding a common ground between the two generations may be difficult, especially as the heat of the rhetoric rises.

Senior groups have called this group of young people baby bummers, for their fatalistic attitude, while young people have labeled their elders as nothing more than "greedy geezers."

"This is a hard time for young people," said Sidney Callahan, a New York psychologist and author who specializes in inter-generational issues. "There is no American dream for this generation. They feel like everybody before them took it all. Now, they're left with nothing."

Sarah Kellogg
Grand Rapids Press Bureau
(*The Grand Rapids Press*,
September 26, 1993, p. A3)
Reprinted with permission of Booth Newspapers

WHAT ARE PUBLIC POLICY ISSUES?

Much of what is discussed and reviewed in some of the previous chapters directly relates to the development of public policy issues and the political process in America. For many people in contemporary America, students not excluded, this seems to be either a dull subject or something that is not too relevant to their lives. In reality, nothing could be further from fact. The development of public policy and the political process in American life are simply ways of defining social decision making. Who make decisions in a free society? How are they made?

Public policy decisions are ongoing. They deal with important questions all of us face on a daily basis. If Aunt Francis has to go to a nursing home, who will pay the $35,000 bill she will ring up in a year? Why do I have to pay so much FICA tax each week when I have real doubts that there will be any money in the Social Security trust fund when I retire in 35 years? Why is it important to have entitlements specifically for older people when so many kids in our country are so poor? How did the "greedy geezers" get so greedy anyway? These are but a few of the questions and public policy issues people of all ages raise which ultimately get translated into political issues and become part of the political process.

HOW DO PUBLIC POLICY ISSUES DEVELOP?

In a democracy, the development of public policy and the political process are the means by which we address the pressing issues that many of us face in our daily lives. One might argue that it really is not necessary to do very much, if anything, in a political way to address many of the problems and issues most people face in their lives. But in reality, this approach in itself is a way of dealing with issues. In fact, this has been a common approach throughout American history to many policy issues—a hands-off approach. Let each individual take care of himself/herself or rely on family or immediate social institutions, such as one's church, to do so.

When specific problems and issues begin to grow larger, either because more and more people experience them or the problems themselves become more complex and involved, it has been the American experience that they then become

the subject of public policy debates and find their way into the political process.

The health-care delivery debate is a ready example. Although health-care delivery for all Americans was promoted by President Harry Truman in the late 1940s and early 1950s, not until the presidential campaign of 1992 did it become a primary public policy issue and end up as a centerpiece of Bill Clinton's political campaign. How did it happen? With the economic difficulties the nation experienced in the late 1980s and early 1990s, because of structural economic changes—downsizing of companies, mergers, long-term layoffs, more part-time employment with no benefits—increasing numbers of people found themselves with no health care coverage at a time when medical care became more and more complex and more and more expensive. Following the 1992 election, the issue became *how* to achieve universal health coverage, not *whether* the United States have health coverage for all its citizens. Thus, health coverage became a public policy issue that ultimately entered the political arena.

AGING AND PUBLIC POLICY

Dealing with public policy issues that end up in the political process can be looked at similarly. In his book, *The New Aging: Politics and Change in America*, Fernando Torres-Gil, head of the Administration on Aging in the Clinton administration and former professor of gerontology at the University of California at Los Angeles (UCLA), pointed out that the history of aging in America can be divided into three basic periods as it relates to public policy. The first period, "Young Aging," covers the history of America until 1930. The second period extended from 1930 to 1990 and is referred to as "Modern Aging." The third period, "New Aging," began in 1990.

The first period, "Young Aging," extended from the beginning of the nation to the Great Depression era. In this long span of time, the needs of older people were seen as the responsibility of the family and the local community. The family was, of course, the key element. For those poor elderly persons whose families could not or would not provide for them, many local communities established "poor farms" or some such institutions in which they could take refuge. However, it is important to note that there were not that many older people in the general population. With the average life expectancy of some 47 years in 1900, and with older people comprising only 4 percent of the population, caring for older people was not an enormous issue during most of our early history. Coupled with the agrarian, rural nature of our society at that time, with a large percentage of the people rooted to the land or small towns, providing for the needs of elderly people was relatively manageable.

With the coming of the Great Depression in late 1929, America took a more active role in dealing with its major social issues and problems. Many businesses and industries collapsed, resulting in large numbers of unemployed people across America. Economic survival became a key concern for most Americans and many problems of daily life became public policy issues, resolved through the political process. The political process resulted in the coming of the New Deal of President Franklin Roosevelt. The federal government played a whole new role in developing policies, structures, and institutions to deal with the pressing daily needs of people.

In this period of Modern Aging, the pressing needs of the elderly, as well as the pressing needs of many persons of other age categories, became public policy issues which found their way into the political process (Torres-Gil 1992).

This dramatic shift in approach to public policy did not occur in a vacuum, nor did it come about without tremendous forces and pressures. The Great Depression was a devastating time for millions of Americans. It threatened the economic survival of the middle class. Across America people lost their jobs, their homes, and their savings. Older people especially were hard hit (Torres-Gil 1992). Great numbers lost their homes as well as

what retirement savings and incomes they had, and because their families were hit so hard by the collapse of so much of the economy, they could not turn to them for help. People, young and old, lost faith in themselves, their economic prospects, and their government. Out of despair and great economic need, they turned to a new approach to solving their basic needs, a new approach in dealing with social issues.

The economic demands of the Great Depression were not the only forces that brought about a shift in public policy approaches in addressing the needs of older people in the Modern Aging period. Andrew Achenbaum (1983) noted four major shifts that resulted in the coming of the "Modern Aging" approach. These are: (1) demographic trends (increases in life expectancy as well as the numbers and percentage of older people in society); (2) changing images of old age (older people increasingly looked at as a social problem); (3) group action among older persons (interest group activities and political action); and (4) new directions in social welfare (activist policies and programs as a result of the Great Depression).

This analysis of how America got into the Modern Aging activist period follows our earlier illustration of how many particular problems people face in their daily lives become public policy issues and enter the political arena for possible solution in a democratic society. The numbers of older people began to increase in the twentieth century with more and more people living longer. In addition, the problems of this age group became more complex during the Great Depression; families were not able to meet the support needs of a growing elderly population due to their own pressing economic needs and the fact that increasing numbers of families were dependent on an industrial economy which was primarily urban based and in a state of collapse.

The Rise of Senior Citizen Activism

Added to the basic components needed to elevate issues and problems to the status of public policy issues was the development of citizen activism for and by older people—the beginnings of senior power. The foundation for this citizen activism was developed in the 1920s, prior to the beginning of the Great Depression in October 1929. Three organizations emerged which promoted the adoption of old-age pensions. They were the American Association for Old Age Security, The American Association for Labor Legislation, and the Fraternal Order of Eagles (Day 1990). Although all their efforts failed, they were the trailblazers for other movements that would follow.

One of the major efforts to develop public policy to improve the economic lives of older people was the Townsend Movement of the 1930s. This movement was headed by Dr. Francis E. Townsend who was motivated by the plight of so many older persons who became destitute as the result of the Great Depression. Dr. Townsend was a 60-year-old physician who had lost his job as assistant medical officer in Long Beach, California during the Depression. He originally outlined his pension idea in a letter to the *Long Beach Press-Telegram* on September 20, 1933, at the depth of the Depression. His idea grew into a nationwide movement of two million people who organized 7,000 clubs. Although the movement never achieved its objective, it stirred public debate and elevated the economic security of older people into the public policy arena. It is credited with paving the way for proposals which became part of the Social Security Act of 1935 (Schulz 1992).

A New Approach to Active Government

With the Townsend Movement of 1933 and the enactment of the Social Security Act in 1935 as a part of President Franklin Roosevelt's New Deal, a whole new approach to dealing with the basic needs of older persons in America was launched. In commenting on his 53 years of working in jobs relating to aging, including his early years in the Roosevelt administration at the beginning of the New Deal, Clark Tibbits, one of the pioneers in the field of aging, stated:

I agreed with the late professor Fred W. Cottrell's appraisal that enactment of this Social Security legislation represented the most radical extension of government into the private lives of citizens ever taken by the American government (Clark Tibbits, in Schulz 1992: XIV).

With this new approach to the role of the federal government in providing for the needs of citizens, especially older citizens, senior citizen interest groups and the Aging Enterprise emerged (Torres-Gil 1992). Over this 60-year period a whole range of programs, agencies, and benefits emerged to assist older people in many aspects of their daily needs. A variety of providers of services to the elderly emerged. For many of these services and benefits, age was the only criterion for eligibility. These are called age-segregated programs, or entitlements. A person receives benefits when he or she reaches a certain age, usually 60, for most of the programs of the Older Americans Act. Torres-Gil has pointed out that it is this series of programs and benefits for older people that comprise the system upon which the elderly of the nation and their families depend for support. Some social policy experts, such as Harry Moody (1990), have contended that these age-segregated programs are based on a view of the elderly that is outdated—a view that portrays older people as a vulnerable or needy group with nothing much to contribute.

IS THE AGING ENTERPRISE ENDING?

With the very large annual federal deficits, the multi-trillion federal debt which is only added to by the annual deficits, escalating health-care costs reflected in Medicare and Medicaid expenditures because of the rising needs of an ever-increasing older population (particularly those 85 and older who use most of the medical services of the older age categories), and the suspicion of younger workers that they are supporting benefits for older persons that they themselves may never receive, there is intense pressure to reevaluate the programs and benefits of the aging enterprise which have developed since the 1930s. Fernando Torres-Gil contended that the Modern Aging period has ended. He asked,

> Can we afford to maintain age-segregated entitlements for the elderly when up to a quarter of the population will be 55 or over by 2010? Can we continue to spend up to 26 percent of the federal budget on benefits and services to an older population (Torres-Gil 1992: 2).

Former Colorado Governor Richard Lamm caused a public debate when he agreed that too much is done for the elderly at the expense of younger persons. Organizations such as Americans for Generational Equity and the American Association of Boomers have contended that programs and benefits for the elderly should be reduced so that more could be spent on groups that are needier.

INTERGENERATIONAL CONFLICTS

The view of the elderly as needy and dependent began to shift in the 1980s (Torres-Gil 1992). "Greedy geezers" became a phrase that portrayed people as well-off, healthy, enjoying high retirement pensions (including Social Security), and living in luxury and leisure, much at the expense of poorer younger people in America (Fairlie 1988). With rising budget deficits and difficult economic conditions for millions of job seekers, including recent college graduates, many viewed the benefit programs for older persons as luxuries the nation could no longer afford (Torres-Gil 1992).

In the fall of 1993, ten seminars around the nation were launched by a group called Lead . . . or Leave, urging the federal government to refocus its support from programs and benefits for older people to youth-oriented programs ranging from education to job creation. Lead . . . or Leave has contended: "The entire system is slanted to benefit senior citizens. That would be OK," says Rob Nelson, co-founder, "if younger people weren't suffering at the same time" (Kellogg 1993a: A8).

Lead . . . or Leave has noted that the federal government spent $354 billion in assistance to older people compared to $65 billion for programs for children, teen-agers, and young adults (Kellogg 1993a). However, advocates of senior citizen groups have pointed out that when state and federal spending is combined, spending for the two groups—old and young—is about equal, taking into account state spending for education and social programs targeted at younger persons.

Some of Lead . . . or Leave's spokespeople have argued that there are inequities in expenditures in federal spending that are sparking a firestorm of discontent among the young. Many of them believe that the federal pension system, Social Security, will be bankrupt when they retire even though official projections show huge surpluses into the twenty-first century. They believe the baby boomers will drain the system before they get a chance to collect any benefits. As a result, many of the leaders of such organizations as Lead . . . or Leave have promoted preventing affluent older people from collecting Social Security benefits. They also have supported means (income) testing for Medicare.

Spokespersons for the elderly have contended that most older people are not "greedy geezers." They have pointed out that older people have worked all their lives for the benefits they receive, including Social Security income. They also have shown that benefits such as Social Security, Medicare, and other age-related benefits actually ease the burden on younger members of the families of older people who traditionally assume the burdens of caring for aging parents in American society. Some advocates of the elderly have also claimed that many of the complainers of the younger generation are unwilling to work hard for their successes, although members of the older age groups were. Some have contended that the younger complainers are spoiled. "They lived the good life with their parents, and they just expected that to continue," said Jim Wolverton, a senior advocate from Bay City, Michigan (Kellogg 1993a: A8).

Some senior advocates have also pointed out that older people have few opportunities to improve their lots in life. Young people can basically go out and get a job. It may not be the best job, or even a job for which they were trained. Many older people, especially the oldest old, those with physical limitations, and those particularly discriminated against because of gender or minority status, have few if any opportunities for meaningful employment to improve their economic status. Their incomes are basically fixed for the rest of their lives, usually based upon earning and economic conditions of an earlier, pre-inflation period.

Is Intergenerational Conflict Inevitable?

Is the wave of the future the "Baby Bummers" versus the "Greedy Geezers?" Is intergenerational warfare central to public policy debates of the future regarding programs and benefits for any category of citizens? Organizations such as Generations United try to work to promote policies that will benefit the young and the old (Kellogg 1993a). Generations United includes such influential and diverse groups as the American Association for Retired Persons and the Children's Defense Fund, two groups with successful records of advocating for their respective constituencies—the old and the young. Many public policy experts believe the United States is at a crossroads in providing for the needs of older people in the twenty-first century. In 1992, Arthur Flemming, a pioneer in civil rights and programs for the elderly, stated, "The field of aging is at an important crossroads. The choices our nation makes will determine whether our society is going to contribute constructively to the well-being, not only of older persons, but of all age groups" (Torres-Gil 1992: ix). In 1992, Fernando Torres-Gil, wrote: "The United States is in the throes of fundamentally transforming its manner of treating elderly people. Recognizing that programs, benefits, and services developed in the past will inadequately serve the elderly of the next century, we are shifting our attitudes and

viewing older people differently then ever before" (Torres-Gil 1991: xi). He went on to state that the 1990s will be a time of change, a time to make public policy decisions that respond realistically to an older and more diverse population than the United States has had.

This view relates to the question raised by the *Economist*:

> With a few blips, such as the depression of the 1930s, the notion (of the American Dream) has come true for every generation in the past 200 years . . . Now, as communism crumbles, America's ability to deliver the dream also is in doubt . . . (*Economist* 1991: 78–79)

Dealing with this issue, Robert Binstock, a noted professor and author in the field of aging, wrote:

> From the New Deal to the present, public policies have substantially improved the well-being of older Americans. But as the twentieth century comes to a close, policies on aging are approaching an important set of crossroads. There are still many urgent needs within the elderly population. Yet our political system may not respond to these needs (Binstock 1992: 1).

Binstock pointed out that by 1992 about 30 percent of the federal budget, nearly $450 billion, was spent on benefits to older people, an increase from the percentage (26 percent) Fernando Torres-Gil cited in his 1992 book. The elderly have emerged as a scapegoat, portrayed by many younger people, as well as some journalists, academics, policy analysts, and politicians as prosperous, hedonistic, politically powerful, and selfish. As such, they are seen as being responsible for the injustices experienced by younger people who have inadequate nutrition, health care, education, and poor family environments. Can ways be found to reconcile the competing claims and needs of each generation? Binstock and other policy analysts have pointed out that "the future of American policies toward older people is uncertain" (Binstock 1992: 7). He went on to indicate that the idea of intergenerational equity is clearly prominent among political leaders as well as leaders in the public and private sectors. The keynote speaker at the 1992 Democratic convention, which nominated Bill Clinton for president, called for cutting mandatory entitlement programs (Social Security and Medicare) to implement generational equity. With the coming avalanche of retiring baby boomers in the early part of the twenty-first century, how can benefits and programs for older people in America be preserved without generational warfare? Is it inevitable? Is the dismantling of the "Aging Enterprise" inevitable?

Approaches to Avoid Generational Conflict

Policy analysts have taken different approaches to the fundamental issues that have placed the United States at the crossroads of deciding whether and how programs and benefits for older people can be maintained and in some cases expanded. There are politicians who have simply called for the dismantling of the Aging Enterprise that was built up over the last 60 years. They feel that government is too big and should not be involved in the affairs of so many of its citizens. America should essentially retreat to the public policy position that predominated prior to the Great Depression, with older family members being the responsibility of their families, or local institutions such as churches.

This approach ignores the realities of an urban and complex economic society where individuals and families are not always in control of their own economic, or even their personal, lives. Jobs are lost or merged; people get sick, divorced, separated, or widowed; times get tough for millions of well-intentioned hard-working people as well as for those who are not so well-intentioned or hard-working. The Great Depression brought the United States face to face with the realities of life in the modern era, with the resulting Modern Aging approach of the aging enterprise that developed from 1930 to 1990.

Ross Perot, the unsuccessful presidential candidate of 1992 who fostered the independent movement United We Stand America, which was supported by millions of Americans, took another approach. Cutting the deficit and the federal debt has been the major theme of this movement. Among the ways this could be done would be for wealthier Social Security recipients to voluntarily give up their benefits. If they did not, Perot indicated that he might undertake a policy that would force them to do so (Binstock 1993a).

Program-by-Program Cuts Some congressional leaders have proposed other approaches to deal with the spiraling governmental expenditures they attribute to ever-growing entitlements, many of which have been developed for older persons. One such congressional approach is program-by-program cuts. This would involve going through mandatory spending programs one by one, trying to find ways to cut benefits, limit eligibility, or require recipients to pay more in the way of premiums, fees, or other payments. In this approach federal, civil, or military retirees might have their cost-of-living adjustments cut. More well-to-do Medicare recipients might be required to pay higher premiums for their coverage. The *Congressional Quarterly* pointed out that revising programs one by one might be the fairest method to cut spending on benefit programs, but it is a difficult process for politicians to follow (Hager 1993). They do not want to take benefits away from any group of voters.

Entitlement Caps Another approach to curtailing federal spending for older people is to cap, or put a ceiling on, entitlements. If Congress is unable to make program-by-program cuts, across-the-board spending cuts on entitlements could be devised. A group in the U.S. Senate led by Senator John Danforth, (R-MD) and Senator David Boren (D-OK), singled out entitlements, and the Americans who receive them, as the targets for reducing the federal deficit. The primary entitlements affecting older people in this approach include Social Security, Medicare, Medicaid, and veterans' health benefits. Horace

Deets, Executive Director of the American Association of Retired Persons, contended that this approach is off target. Entitlement caps, he argued, "would hit the poor, the middle-class, the young, the disabled, and the elderly with both barrels—by lowering income and increasing health-care costs. Hardest hit will be low- and middle-income Americans" (Deets 1993: 3).

Emma Francis, 80, a widow who lives on $747 a month from Social Security, said she did not really understand the term "entitlement cap" that she kept hearing in the news according to a 1993 article in *The Detroit News*. "I think it means that if everything keeps going up the way it is, I won't be able to afford to live," said Francis, a retired bookkeeper (Claiborne 1993: 2A). To Francis and millions of others in her situation, entitlement caps would mean more out-of-pocket expenses for medical care and sharp cuts in other benefits for the poor and the elderly. These added costs, they point out, would strain already tight budgets.

Means Testing   Another approach to curtailing federal expenditures for a growing elderly population is to means-test benefits for the recipients. In this approach benefits would be scaled back or denied to anyone of more than modest income and resources. Benefits would be targeted at the truly needy (Hager 1993).

Influential media sources, have contended that "it makes little sense to give Social Security benefits to many elderly households with sizeable earning and assets" (*Business Week* 1989: 20). The same *Business Week* article went on to say that the United States will be forced to replace Social Security systems in their present form with systems that benefits only the needy elderly.

According to Congressional Budget Office (CBO) statistics, about 80 percent of entitlement benefits go to recipients without regard to their incomes. There is real debate over whether too many people get federal program benefits they really do not need. CBO figures show that more than two-thirds of the households that receive Social Security and Medicare benefits have incomes of less than $30,000 a year, and less than 2 percent of these benefits go to households with incomes of more than $100,000 (Hey 1992).

Fernando Torres-Gil has argued that means-testing Social Security would result in the loss of its support as a system. "It cannot be means-tested without losing the political support of those who pay into it through payroll taxes" (Torres-Gil 1992: 112). He went on to contend that in means-testing, "the more affluent and educated will depend on personal savings, asset accumulation, and private pensions. They will lose interest in preserving the basic structure of the Social Security system." He argued that this approach will only put future poor elderly persons in a more precarious situation.

IS THERE HOPE FOR PRESERVING BENEFITS?

If dismantling major benefit programs for the elderly is not the way to treat older people and not politically feasible anyway, or if cutting programs across the board, capping them, means-testing them, or freezing them is unfair to needy older people and counterproductive to their stability, are there any approaches to the benefit/entitlement dilemma that take into account the real needs of the growing number of older people as well as the pressing needs of persons in younger age groups in a nation with a growing national debt? Some approaches to these tough issues have been offered by responsible policy makers for review and debate.

Horace Deets, Executive Director of the American Association of Retired Persons (AARP), has contended that "the most effective way to reduce the federal deficit is to control health-care costs throughout society, with a guarantee of affordable, high quality coverage—including long-term care—for everyone" (Deets 1993: 3). He pointed out that the primary factor behind the entitlement growth has been federal health spending, which, he argued is symptomatic of a system-wide crisis in health care.

The only way to reduce health-care costs is through comprehensive, system-wide controls on all health-care costs. If we're really serious about cutting the federal deficit—and AARP believes President Clinton and the Congress are serious—we can't afford to be side-tracked by legislation that portrays entitlements and beneficiaries as villains. To cure America's economic ills, including deficits, we need health care reform and we need it soon" (Deets 1993: 3).

This approach is similar to President Clinton's approach to reining in health care costs while at the same time providing universal access for all Americans to a comprehensive package of health-care benefits. Under President Clinton's original health-care plan, through managed competition and other cost-containment mechanisms, the spiraling growth of the cost of health care as a percentage of the national gross domestic product would be brought in check, benefiting the cost of doing business in America, the cost to the consumers of health care, and the ongoing federal deficits which directly impact the ability of the government to fund benefit/entitlement programs for older people (Fein 1992; Hey 1993a; NRTA and Hey 1993b).

A Sweeping Approach—The New Aging

Fernando Torres-Gil (1992) has taken a sweeping approach to dealing with the issues raised by growing numbers of older people, pressures to limit their benefits, ongoing federal deficits, and competition among age groups for benefits and entitlements. He has contended that "the 1990s, much like the 1930s, will provide an opportunity to respond to the immediate social needs and prepare for the inevitable social and demographic changes by revamping not only the current age-based system of benefits and services, but all social welfare policies" (Torres-Gil 1992: 6). He went on to point out that the 1990s will require changes in the legacy of the New Deal while at the same time keeping its values, which include (1) an activist role for government, (2) concern for the needs of all, (3) understanding the social

relationships and interdependencies of those with much and those who have little, and (4) a willingness to give up today in order to have benefits in the future. Torres-Gil has argued that the nation needs to redevelop the social contract between individuals, society, and government. In this redesign, the individual would have more responsibility for taking charge of personal and economic well-being with government having the responsibility for needs in education, health, and public safety. Such a redefined social contract between individuals, society, and the government would also involve a new view of the life-cycle process taking into account increased longevity and a more diverse population. The redefined social contract would also involve redefining who is eligible for benefits and services and how they are financed.

How do the principles of New Aging translate into specific approaches to benefits and entitlements for the rest of the 1990s and the coming realities of the twenty-first century?

Torres-Gil contended that in order to avoid the kind of intergenerational warfare that has already been outlined, currently and in the future, it is essential to move away from age-defined expansion of benefits toward intergenerational and age-integrated solutions. The goal of "the New Aging is to gradually integrate benefits of the young, middle-aged, and old in the 1990s" (Torres-Gil 1992: 113). An example of this is President Clinton's original proposal in his health reform legislation of 1993 to phase in long-term care for disabled persons of any age. It is not difficult to see the impact of Torres-Gil, the Assistant Secretary for Aging in the Department of Health and Human Services (HHS), in this important component of President Clinton's health proposal. "Avoiding single-generation financing and moving toward intergenerational programs will prevent many of the tensions and conflicts otherwise possible in the economics of the New Aging" (Torres-Gil 1992: 113–114).

Torres-Gil outlined some specific approaches to the growing elderly population/intergenerational conflict/increasing federal deficit/entitlements dilemma. They include:

1. Raise taxes to improve the nation's educational system. A poor young person is more likely to become a poor old person; a functionally illiterate child will lack the skills to provide for herself/himself through life, including the later years which will further burden the public benefit system (Torres-Gil 1992).

2. Develop a social-insurance form of health and long-term care. Both are essential to the vitality and productivity of the nation's citizens as well as reining in health care costs as a percentage of gross domestic product. The for-profit and private sectors have shown that they are not capable of providing for the long-term care for the poorest and the most needy (Torres-Gil 1992).

3. Invest in the social needs of the young. In his book, *Dollars and Dreams*, Frank Levy (1987) detailed the negative consequences for the nation as the result of one-fifth of its children being raised in poverty. He pointed out that developing benefit programs to help people at the low end of the economic ladder will improve productivity; rising productivity is directly linked to rising living standards which in turn can help fund benefits for the elderly.

4. Reduce the federal deficit during the 1990s so a greater portion of tax revenues can be used for benefit programs for the old and the young in the future (Torres-Gil 1992).

5. Prepare younger people to plan for their future retirement economic security. This planning process should include teaching younger people the realities of the demographic revolution that is occurring in America and how increased longevity will affect their lives. Planning for retirement also involves promoting saving for the later years. In this regard, incentives such as tax credits and Individual Retirement Accounts (IRAs) should be instituted to promote saving for retirement income (Torres-Gil 1992).

6. Gradually raise the age of retirement with full benefits. As we pointed out in an earlier chapter, using the age 65 for retirement is a carryover from Otto von Bismarck in Germany in the nineteenth century. Increasingly, people are living longer and are healthier. As a result, 65 years of age today is not what it was over 50 years ago. It has been calculated that in determining equivalent retirement ages based on increases in life expectancy, if 65 years was the retirement norm in 1940, 70 years would be the equivalent in 1995, and 73 years by 2040 (Chen 1987). This does not mean that all workers can make it to 70 or 73. Torres-Gil (1992) argued that expanded benefits in the Disability Insurance and Worker's Compensation programs need to go along with increased retirement ages to provide for workers in physically demanding and/or dangerous occupations. He also advocated retaining an early retirement option at age 62 with reduced benefits with premiums for those who work beyond age 70.

7. Promote additional work opportunities for older persons. In this approach, older people are encouraged and helped to remain or become productive members of society as long as possible instead of just dependent old people. Harry Moody advocated a "politics of productivity" instead of a "failure model of old age (which costs) the elderly in an outdated stereotype of a vulnerable or needy group to justify entitlement programs" (Moody 1990: 136).

It is contended that early retirement policies will no longer be workable as businesses face worker shortages in the future. Torres-Gil (1992) has argued that flexible working conditions will be needed to facilitate the use of older workers. Moody (1990) pointed out that greatly expanding the use of older workers would diminish the need to increase the retirement age.

8. Eliminate the earnings limits for Social Security. Taking away the penalty persons under age 65 now pay for earning over $7,680 and those between ages 65 and 69 pay for earning over $10,560 in 1993 would open the door for many more older persons to stay in or reenter the work force. The penalty older workers pay for exceeding these limits is the reduction in their Social Security benefits of $1 for every $2 earned over the limits for persons under the age of 65, and $1 for every $3 earned over the limit for those aged 65 to 69.

9. Promote and facilitate late-life reeducation. Life-long education and training/retraining programs for the changing workplace will be essential to keep older people employed or to enable them to return to the changing world of work with new technologies. Skilled jobs require training and retraining.

10. Develop policies to protect pensions. Torres-Gil (1992) pointed out that pensions may be the most vulnerable component of retirement income. The failure of many pension plans in the 1980s and the current underfunding of many plans make oversight a key component of stability of future retirement income. With no cost-of-living increases in so many private pensions, many retirees run short of money. Torres-Gil has called for a presidential commission to investigate and respond to the problems many pension programs face currently and in the near future.

11. Return the financing of Social Security to a pay-as-you-go system. In 1990 and 1991 Senator Moynihan (D-NY) suggested this approach, contending that it would reduce Social Security taxes on current workers and lessen their rising doubts about the whole program. It is argued that Social Security taxes are regressive and represent a dishonest method of helping to pay for the deficit run up by other governmental operations (U.S. Senate Special Committee on Aging 1993). Pay-as-you-go financing of Social Security would reduce tensions between the generations.

12. Take Social Security "off budget." Removing the revenue of the Social Security taxes from the federal budget deficit estimates will make the system less political while helping to preserve the future stability of the program.

13. Tax Social Security benefits. Torres-Gill advocates fully taxing the Social Security benefits of all recipients. Increasing the taxes on upper-income Social Security beneficiaries was part of the Clinton tax plan of 1993. The 1983 Social Security reforms placed a tax on 50 percent of the Social Security benefits of upper-income recipients. The Clinton tax bills of 1993 levied taxes on 85 percent of these benefits for individuals with combined incomes over $32,000 and couples with combined incomes above $40,000 (Hey 1993b).

14. Reverse the trend toward early retirement. This has been a driving force among American workers. In order to promote productivity among older people, keep them earning money longer to support their increased longevity, and to increase the pool of employees available to counteract the decreasing number of younger workers, the trend toward early retirement needs to be reversed.

Torres-Gil, in summarizing the need for the types of changes outlined above in policies and programs, stated:

> The 1990s might be our last chance to make the difficult political decisions required in reforming the policies of the Modern Aging. In just twenty years, the baby boomers will reach retirement. We must be ready with social policies that respond to increased life expectancies, new definitions of old age, and immeasurable diversity. We must welcome and nurture changing attitudes about government, the individual, and the family (Torres-Gil 1992: 71).

Not All Bleak for Dependency Ratio

In addressing the issue of whether the Aging Enterprise, as we know the array of benefits and programs for the elderly, can be maintained economically and politically in the years ahead. Robert Binstock (1992) has made some interesting observations. He indicated that the major worry revolves around the increasing dependency ratio—the number of retired dependent people compared to the number of younger people still working who pay taxes to finance old age benefits and entitlements.

Binstock pointed out that for the immediate future, during the time the baby boomers are still working, the dependency ratio will remain quite stable. Beginning in 2010, when the Baby Boomers begin to retire, the percentage of the population that is working is projected to decline gradually from about 60 percent until it reaches 54 percent in 2035, after which it will remain stable. Even though the huge surpluses in the OASI trust fund may be depleted by Congress for other purposes, the future is not all bleak. Binstock projected that there will likely be declines in the child dependency ratio which will offset increases in the elderly dependency ratio.

Importance of Productivity

In addition, Binstock (1992) has contended that the productive capacity of a nation's economy is the result of many factors including capital, natural resources, balance of trade, and technology along with the number of workers.

Looked at from this perspective, and understanding that benefits for older people, particularly Social Security benefits, do not always have to be financed by payroll taxes on workers, "the economic consequences of population aging do not appear dim" (Binstock 1992: 9). Binstock argued that the future benefits for the elderly in America will not depend on the proportion of workers to retirees, but on the ability of the American economy to generate enough resources that can be transferred to the old and on the political will to make such transfers.

NEED FOR NEW APPROACH

In order to maintain programs and benefits for growing numbers of older people in the long-term

future, Binstock has indicated the need for "a major reconceptualization of governmental responsibilities for older persons and perhaps, for human welfare, generally" (Binstock 1992: 11). This is particularly important when the present entitlement and benefit programs do not adequately deal with the unmet needs of older people. A different approach to determining who among the old will receive benefits will need to emerge.

Needs or Entitlements?

Despite all the current benefits of the Aging Enterprise, Binstock has pointed out that about one-third of all older people face difficult economic situations in their lives, especially older women and minorities. When two-thirds of single older people and one-third of older married people fall into poverty after being in a nursing home just thirteen weeks, there is real unfinished business in meeting the needs of older people in contemporary America (U.S. House Select Committee on Aging 1987). President Clinton's original health plan, although proposing some in-home, long-term-care benefits, had no provisions to help Americans pay for nursing-home care or adult foster care (Kellogg 1993). Gerontologists such as Robert Binstock (1992) have indicated that these types of needs cannot be met through the incremental additions to the Aging Enterprise that characterized the development of the array of programs and benefits the elderly have experienced.

Many years ago gerontologist Bernice Neugarten (1979) suggested altering the eligibility criteria for the entitlements and benefits programs by focusing more on need than age. She contended that the characteristics of older people were changing. Age was no longer a predictor of lifestyle or need. Other policy analysts, who have taken into account the real success of the Social Security program, have contended that such a need-based approach would destroy the social-insurance principle which generated widespread political support as well as income to support the major old age benefit programs (Binstock 1992).

A proposal by two other gerontologists, Neil Howe and Phillip Longman, to develop the "Next

New Deal" incorporated need-based policies while trying to keep broad-based political support. In this proposal all benefits, including mortgage-interest deductions, farm subsidies, Social Security, and tax exclusions for Part B Medicare premiums, would be based on a recipient's economic need. Benefits would be adjusted on a graduated scale providing at least a minimum benefit for everyone, even the rich, in order to keep some portion of the social contract concept of traditional social insurance programs (Binstock 1992).

Robert Binstock has pointed out that whatever policies are adapted to meet the growing needs of an aging population, "it is likely that they will centrally involve complex mechanisms for balancing age and need as eligibility criteria for public benefits. Such mechanisms will be critical in determining whether still urgent needs within the older population are to be met" (Binstock 1992: 13).

IMPORTANCE OF ECONOMIC GROWTH

James Schulz, the author of many books on the subject of economics and older people, has contended that the nation's ability to provide for the needs of people in various age groups is complex. He pointed out that at any time, past, present, or future, the most important factors that determine the economic well-being of people of all ages are those that influence growth: labor force participation, savings, investments in human and business capital, technological change, initiatives in entrepreneurship, managerial skills, and government's support of infrastructure (Schultz 1992). Even moderate rates of real economic growth would enable the United States to increase real support for nonworkers (young, old, or disabled persons) without much increase (if any) in the taxes on workers in the future (Schutz, Borowski, and Crown 1991).

MAKING HARD CHOICES

In addition to economic growth as a central answer to providing for needs, Schulz (1992) recommended (1) raising the Social Security

"normal" age of eligibility; (2) increasingly penalizing the early retirement policies of private pensions, even through government action; (3) promoting the employment of older workers; (4) providing for the training of older persons for the changing world of work; and (5) preparing for the retirement years by making hard economic choices and tradeoffs such as sacrificing consumption in the earlier years of life in order to enjoy a higher standard of living in the retirement years. Schulz summed up this last approach by stating: "Whether we like it or not, the 'economics of aging' begins for most of us quite early in life" (Schulz 1992: 273).

THE POLITICS OF AGING

All of these issues are directly tied to the political process. Who will make these decisions? How are they made in the context of various competing interests? What is the role of the elderly in the political process? How are older people themselves likely to vote when it comes to issues such as health care, pensions, or Social Security? How are older people organized to promote their political agenda?

These questions will be addressed by looking at the basic elements of the political process as they apply to the needs of older people.

Voting: A Powerful Tool of the Elderly

Certainly, older people represent a significant voting force. Overall voter participation has declined in presidential elections in the United States since the mid-1960s. This is true for all age groups except the elderly. Since 1964, when the presidential election turnout for all age groups was 69.3 percent, the percentage of people voting has fallen to 57.4 percent. However, the percentage of elderly voting in presidential elections has remained high, with more than three in five elders voting in presidential elections since 1964. Among the elderly population as a whole, persons aged 65 to 74 have

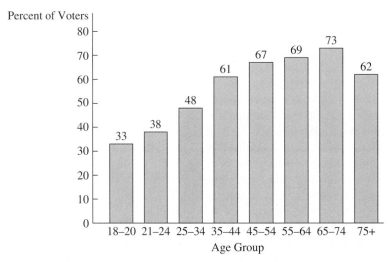

**Percent Who Reported Voting,
by Age Group: 1988**

FIGURE 22-1

Percentage of persons who voted by age groups. (*Source:* U.S. Special Committee on Aging, the American Association of Retired Persons, the Federal Council on Aging, and the U.S. Administration on Aging. 1991. *Aging America: Trends and projections.* Washington, DC, U.S. Department of Health and Human Services, Chart 6-6, p. 202.)

been the most likely to vote (73 percent) (U.S. Bureau of the Census 1992). (See Figure 22-1.)

Voting participation declines for those aged 75 and older. But even with declining voter participation of those aged 75 and older, this group was more likely to vote than persons younger than age 35 (U.S. Senate Special Committee on Aging 1991).

A higher percentage of men have voted over the years. Among the racial and ethnic groups, aged 65 to 74, whites and African Americans have been more likely to vote than Latinos (Jennings 1989). A primary reason for this is that some 17 percent of the Latino population were not U.S. citizens and as a result, not eligible to vote (U.S. Bureau of the Census 1992). Among all elderly groups, white men have been the most likely to vote (71.9 percent) with Latino women the least likely (29.1 percent) (Jennings, 1989).

Do Older People Vote Conservatively?

Contrary to some stereotypes, older people do not necessarily vote conservatively. They tend to be more conservative on such issues as women's rights, abortion, gay and lesbian rights, and issues of "law and order." However, older people are less conservative on such issues as pensions, health care and employment, and a high standard of living where they favor government actions (Hudson and Strate 1985). This reflects their historical legacy from the New Deal approach which resulted in Social Security, Medicare, the Older Americans Act with its various programs, as well as other benefits developed through governmental action (Torres-Gil 1992).

More persons have identified with the Democratic Party in all age categories, as Table 22-1 indicates (U.S. Bureau of the Census 1991b).

TABLE 22-1					

POLITICAL PARTY IDENTIFICATION OF THE ADULT POPULATION BY AGE, 1988

Age	Total	Democrat[a]	Republican[b]	Independent	Apolitical
Under 30 years old	100	44	42	14	2
30–35 years	100	45	41	13	1
46–61 years	100	52	41	7	1
61–77 years	100	50	41	7	2
78+ years	100	48	42	9	3

[a]Includes those who identify as weak Democrat, strong Democrat, and independent Democrat.
[b]Includes those who identify as weak Republican, strong Republican, and independent Republican.
Source: U.S. Bureau of the Census 1991, Table 452.

Similar to persons in all the age categories, this does not mean that older people always vote for the candidate of one of the parties. They tend to follow the national trends in major elections. In the 1992 presidential election, Democratic candidate Bill Clinton was swept into office, winning 370 electoral votes compared to the Republican George Bush's 168 and none for third party candidate Ross Perot. In the popular vote, Clinton won just 43 percent of the vote compared to 38 percent for Bush and 19 percent for Ross Perot. However, among people age 60 and older who voted, 50 percent voted for Clinton, 38 percent for Bush, and 12 percent for Perot. Voters in no other age group gave Clinton more than 44 percent of their vote (Carlson 1992b). No other group supported Clinton so strongly as did voters age 60 and older. The 1992 election was the first presidential election since 1972 in which older people voted substantially differently from voters in other age groups. In 1972, older voters supported Democratic candidates from 6 to 8 percentage points higher than voters in other age groups (Binstock 1993b).

Older People and Third Parties

The support given by older voters to Ross Perot, the independent, third-party candidate, was significantly lower than provided by other voters. Even though older voters tend to switch voting behavior between Democratic and Republican candidates in about the same patterns as other voters, research has indicated that they tend to stick with the traditional political parties (Wallace and Williamson 1992). This was demonstrated in the 1980 presidential election when independent candidate John Anderson got voter support among younger groups between 8 percent and 11 percent; but among older age voting groups only 4 percent to 5 percent supported him.

Basic Issues and Voting by Older People

Another explanation for Ross Perot's relatively low voter support from people 60 years of age and older was his position that wealthier Social Security beneficiaries should voluntarily give up their benefits, and if they failed to do so, he might undertake action to make them do so. Barbara Jordan's keynote speech at the Democratic convention called for sacrifices in federal benefit programs to achieve "generational equity." In analyzing these positions, including Bush's pledge to "not touch Social Security," Robert Binstock contended that "on balance, issues targeted at or especially affecting elderly persons seem to have played little role in the 1992 elections" (Binstock 1993: 3). Clinton's campaign focus on controlling rising health-care costs while providing universal access to health care, including beginning steps to provide for long-term care, was an important issue with many older people. At the American Association of Retired Persons biennial convention during the presidential campaign of 1992,

AARP Executive Director Horace B. Deets took issue with the critics who blame spending on programs for the elderly for the nation's economic troubles. He argued that increased spending on the elderly is due to (1) the dramatic growth in the size of the older population, (2) inflation, and (3) rising medical costs (Carlson 1992a). Acting in his capacity as chair of the Leadership Council of Aging Organizations, a coalition of more than thirty aging groups (representing consumers, educators, volunteers and others), Deets wrote the new President, indicating that fast action on long-term care is needed because "(many) family caregivers are forced to leave jobs and lose family income as a consequence of their caregiving efforts" (Carlson 1993b: 1).

New Deal Legacy

Given their legacy from the New Deal approach to major concerns such as the necessity to provide assistance to pay for long-term care, it seems reasonable that a case could be made that support of older voters for Bill Clinton in the 1992 presidential election was related to his concern for issues that affected older people. This leads to an examination of the political power of older people in contemporary America.

SENIOR POWER

In this chapter we have already traced the beginnings of interest and pressure groups on behalf of older people beginning in the 1920s, with three organizations advocating the adoption of pensions (Torres-Gill 1992). These efforts laid the basis for government responsibility for old-age economic security (Day 1990).

The 1940s saw a decline in senior-citizen activism. These were the years of World War II and the immediate postwar era that launched the baby boom as well as a prosperous economy. Senior citizen activism flourished again in the 1950s and 1960s, with the establishment of the National Council on Aging in 1950, the American Association of Retired Persons in 1958, and the National Council of Senior Citizens in 1961, along with many other groups representing and promoting older people and their needs (Torres-Gil 1992).

An array of organizations currently exists to promote the varied interests of older people. They can be divided into three categories:

1. *Membership of older people and their advocates*: American Association of Retired Persons (AARP) and its division, the National Retired Teachers Association (NRTA); Asociacion Nacional Pro Persons Mayores (ANPPM), promoting the interests of older Latinos; Catholic Golden Age (CGA); Families USA Foundation (FUSAF); Gray Panthers Project Fund (GPPF); National Association of Retired Federal Employees (NARFE); National Alliance of Senior Citizens (NASC); National Caucus and Center on Black Aged, Inc. (NCBA); National Citizens' Coalition for Nursing Home Reform (NCCNHR); National Council on the Aging (NCOA); National Council of Senior Citizens (NCSC); National Displaced Homemakers Network (NDHNN); National Hispanic Council on Aging (NHCoA); National Indian Council on Aging, Inc. (NICOA); National Pacific/Asian Resource Center on Aging (NP/ARCA); Older Women's League (OWL); Save Our Security Coalition (SOS).

2. *Professional organizations promoting the interests of older people*: Association for Gerontology in Higher Education (AGHE); American Geriatrics Society (AGS); American Society on Aging (ASA); Gerontological Society of America (GSA); National Senior Citizens Law Center (NSCLC).

3. *Provider groups*: American Association of Homes for the Aging (AAHA); American Health Care Association (AHCA), representing licensed nursing homes and long-term facilities; National Association of Area Agencies on Aging (NAAAA or N4A); and the National Association of State Units on Aging (NASUA); (*Acronyms in Aging* 1990 AARP).

AARP: A Major Interest Group

Of all of the groups promoting the interests of older people, the American Association of Retired Persons (AARP) is a giant. It has over 33 million members aged 50 and older. In 1990, it had 1,100 employees in its Washington, D.C. headquarters which it leases for about $16 million a year; spent some $10 million on consultants and $2 million in lawyer's fees; and generated revenues of about $300 million a year from its nine business enterprises including group health insurance (Lindeman 1992). The AARP magazine, *Modern Maturity*, is the most widely circulated membership magazine in the world (Jacobs 1990). The AARP has been and continues to be very active in promoting and lobbying for a wide range of issues affecting older persons in the United States—particularly access to health care for persons of all age categories, long-term care, employment and income opportunities for older workers, pension protection, and entitlement benefits including Social Security and Medicare. In addition, it facilitates a national network of volunteers to assist in educational and community service programs and offers a range of services to its members.

TAKING A BROADER VIEW

In the face of criticisms that powerful organizations such as the AARP which promote the interests of older persons are only looking out for the welfare of the elderly thereby diverting resources from other needy groups such as children, AARP leaders have spoken out. "To think, as some people do, that programs like Social Security and Medicare are the cause of the growing rate of poverty among children is wrong," stated Lovola Burgess, AARP president. "The issue isn't old versus young. It's the 'haves' versus the 'have nots' in our society. There are old and young people alike who are in need—who are 'drowning' " (Carlson 1992a: 1).

The AARP leadership has stressed the need to support intergenerational issues and programs to dispel the notion that all older people are "greedy geezers." This has meant older people taking a broad view of their responsibilities in contemporary America, including being sensitive to and supporting the needs of children and of families. It has called for support of children in education, income security, and health care. A specific example of the AARP's approach to health-care reform has been "Health Care America," the association's draft proposal to "reach the goal of affordable, high-quality health care for everyone, regardless of age, income or employment status" (Carlson 1992a: 5). Intergenerational action has been cited by many policy analysts as a key to meeting the real needs of people of all ages while at the same time reducing generational conflict over spending on various benefit programs (Carlson 1992a; Torres-Gil 1992; Binstock 1992). This is a complex issue that will require careful balancing of interests, needs, and some successful benefit programs for the elderly that have been quite widely supported by the American people.

It is important to remember that through its various provisions, the Social Security Act is more than a retirement income and protection program for the elderly. It provides disability income for workers at any age, survivors insurance for the family members of deceased workers, Supplemental Security Income for the blind and disabled, Medicare for some disabled persons under the age of 65, medical assistance (Medicaid) for certain low-income individuals and families, and block grants to states for social services including child care and protective and emergency services for children as well as adults (Acronyms in Aging 1990). It is also important to note that specifically designed benefit programs to assist elderly people in America take some of the burdens of supporting older people off children and grandchildren. This has resulted in increased freedom and social mobility for the younger generations (Torres-Gil 1992).

UNFINISHED BUSINESS

In spite of the real gains that have been realized in improving the lives of America's elderly since the inception of the Social Security Act of 1935, and taking into account the rising opposition of those in our society who would decrease the benefits going to older persons, there are still real needs among older people that call for attention.

Continuing Areas of Poverty

In the area of poverty, although the overall defined rate of poverty for older Americans has dropped from 35 percent in 1959 to 12.2 percent in 1990, when the near poor (125 percent of poverty) are included, the percentage rises to 19 (U.S. Bureau of the Census 1991).

Some policy analysts have argued that even this combined figure (poor and near poor elderly) is low. One study, for example, pointed out that different consumption patterns are used to define poverty for the elderly population. If the measures used for the rest of the population were applied to the elderly, they would increase the elderly poverty rate by 165 percent (Rugges 1990).

There are significant numbers of individuals within the elderly population who are experiencing high levels of poverty. Elderly women, minorities, and persons over the age of 75 were more likely to be poor than the overall elderly population in 1990. Elderly women were twice as likely to be poor or near poor than were elderly men. Persons in the older age categories (age 75 and older) were also twice as likely to be poor or near poor than persons between 65 and 74 (General Accounting Office 1992).

Addressing the Causes of Poverty Among the Elderly

The reasons for high levels of poverty among older women, older minority persons, and persons in the older age categories, were explored in previous chapters. The public policy issues associated with these reasons call for discussion and action if they are to be addressed adequately in a society that is growing older. Marital status, low or nonexistent earnings over their lifetimes, and poor pension protection have been cited by a 1992 General Accounting Office report as leading causes of high rates of poverty among women. Added to these are the vital caregiving roles women fill in society for which they receive no income and no pension credits. Legislation to give women Social Security credits for caregiving has been introduced in the U.S. House of Representatives, but this legislation has stalled (U.S. House of Representatives Select Committee on Aging 1992).

It is not hard to determine why there is so much poverty among elderly women with women (1) continuing to outlive men, while continuing to marry older men resulting in added years of widowhood; (2) continuing to work at jobs that pay less than men overall; (3) working at jobs with little or no pensions; and (4) continuing to provide most of the caregiving for the young and the old in families for which they receive no income or pension credits. It is important to note that this does not just describe today's elderly.

ECONOMIC VULNERABILITY OF BABY BOOM WOMEN

Testimony by the Older Women's League (OWL) before the U.S. House of Representatives included the following projection for today's young women:

> In less than 40 years, when today's 25-year-olds retire, fewer women will be retiring married, and therefore fewer will have access to a husband's retirement income. Seven out of ten baby-boom women will outlive their husband and can expect to be widows for at least 15 years. In the year 2030, only one in three women over age 65 will be married, compared to 40 percent today. More than one out of every five older women will be divorced, a 40 percent increase over today (U.S. House of Representatives Select Committee on Aging 1992: 156).

To address these potentially bleak realities, the Older Women's League, along with other interest groups on behalf of the elderly, have proposed significant changes in the Social Security Act, public and private pension provisions, Supplemental Security Income, Medicare and Medicaid, public housing provisions, and the Older Americans Act (OAA). These issues concerning pressing needs can only be addressed by public policy debates and political action.

RISING HEALTH-CARE COSTS

A common perception is that the health-care costs of older people are pretty much covered by Medicare, the health insurance program for people aged 65 and older. However, a February 1992 report by Families USA showed that older people in 1991 spent more than twice as much in inflation-adjusted dollars on health-care than they did before Medicare was established (U.S. House of Representatives Select Committee on Aging 1992). It is not surprising that some of the most powerful organizations promoting the interests of older people have supported health-care reform, including strategies to contain the growth of health-care costs.

THE CRISIS OF PAYING FOR LONG-TERM CARE

Paying for long-term care has become a crisis issue for most Americans. Not only do they dread going to a nursing home or placing a loved one in such a facility, but most people do not have sufficient funds to pay for any length of stay in a nursing home. In order to qualify for Medicaid to pay for nursing-home expenses, a person is forced to "spend down" to poverty level. Although there are no national data concerning spending down to poverty and the length of stay in a care facility, some studies have painted a bleak picture for many older people. The majority of older people who need long-term institutional care end up poor and dependent on the government to pay their nursing home bills (Estes, Swan, and Associates 1993). About two-thirds of older persons who go into nursing homes spend down their resources and become dependent on Medicaid (U.S. House of Representatives Select Committee on Aging 1987).

Long-term care for the elderly, and for persons of any age who need it, is high on the list of unfinished business in the public policy arena. What strategies can be devised to pay for it if so many people end up needing it? Many people end up needing it. Although only about 5 percent of people 65 and older reside in nursing homes at any one time, of those persons who turned 65 in 1990, 43 percent will enter a nursing facility before they die (Kemper and Murtaugh 1991). The number of elderly persons living in nursing facilities will go from 1.5 million in 1990 to 5.3 million by 2030 (U.S. Bipartisan Commission on Comprehensive Health Care 1990).

Proposals for Financing Long-Term Care

A variety of proposals have been made to deal with financing long-term care ranging from relying mostly on private resources (including private long-term care insurance) to a new federal entitlement program based on social-insurance principles. Given the realities of the federal deficits, the national debt, and the pressures for fiscal restraint, the outcome will probably be a mixture of funding mechanisms, even though President Clinton's initial long-term-care plan as part of health reform called for gradually phasing in home-based care (including copayments which varied by income). A key element of Clinton's proposal was that it provided services regardless of age or income. Under this plan, benefits would have been limited by the amount of money available from the government. Only an assessment of a person's eligibility for the program would be provided as an entitlement (Patterson 1993). Nevertheless, limited as this proposal was, it attempted to move away from the present system which relies on spending down to poverty to qualify for Medicaid, a welfare program described by many as a disgraceful way to treat older people or disabled people of any age.

OTHER PENDING POLICY ISSUES

The National Legislative Council of the AARP identified a range of issues that affect older people as well as others in the nation that they considered noteworthy for legislative action in 1993 (AARP 1993). They include the following:

- Reduce the federal deficit, including reducing health-care cost increases.
- Increase revenues on the federal and state levels by increasing some tax rates and by broadening some tax bases.
- Protect Social Security funding to ensure current and future benefits.
- Protect and expand pension coverage, including improving the portability of pension contributions.
- Enforce with vigor statutes against age discrimination in employment.
- Afford access to health care for all and control health-care costs through a comprehensive restructuring of reimbursement without increasing the burden of already high out-of-pocket costs.
- Offer high-quality long-term care to all chronically ill people with disabilities regardless of income and age through a coordinated system of home- and community-based services in a variety of settings which attempt to maintain the autonomy of the persons who need services.
- Invest in the needs of children, including immunizations against childhood diseases, access to health care for pregnant women and children, and better and more equitable funding of schools.
- Enhance the quality of life for future generations through preserving the environment.
- Improve the food stamp program, extend Medicaid to all the poor, increase asset limits for Supplemental Security Income (SSI), and develop a more effective outreach program for SSI.
- Address the homeless issue, including the older homeless, and extend housing and energy assistance programs.

- Strengthen consumer protection in financial services, communications, and insurance.
- Improve food safety.
- Improve transportation services for the frail elderly, people with disabilities, and rural residents.
- Improve protection against elder abuse and criminal victimization and fairly enforce personal and legal rights.
- Adopt comprehensive campaign reform, improve voter-education efforts, and simplify voter procedures.

INTERGENERATIONAL APPROACH

It is evident from this AARP public policy agenda that this major interest group on behalf of older people is taking an intergenerational approach to addressing human needs in the United States. This approach, while dealing with the unmet needs of older people, is designed to lessen intergenerational conflict that has been developing in an era of rapidly increasing numbers of older people and increasing competition for public resources. As stated in *Aging Public Policy: Bonding the Generations*:

> Our society is desperately in need of social and political leadership that strengthens the bonds between generations, that minimizes differences between groups, and that gives testimony to the idea that we are all responsible for the others in society (Koff and Park 1993: 276).

Developing public policies and political agendas that result in programs to address the real needs of persons of all ages in American society seems to be gaining some momentum as we move toward the twenty-first century.

SUMMARY

This chapter addresses the range of public policy issues that affect the well-being of older people and the political realities of developing solutions to these needs and concerns.

To make public policy issues and the politics of aging meaningful to the everyday lives of Americans of any age, it is important to keep in mind that we are dealing not just with abstract ideas and concepts, but with real questions: Who will pay for Aunt Francis when she is forced to move to a nursing home? Why do I pay so much in FICA taxes? Will Social Security be there for me when I retire?

To gain a better understanding of public policy issues, Fernando Torres-Gil (1992) has outlined an overview of the development of how older people's issues were treated throughout the history of the United States. In the Young Aging period, from the beginning of the nation to 1930, a "hands-off" approach was taken; older people, not too numerous in the early years of the nation, were the responsibility of families and the local community. In the Modern Aging period, from 1930 to 1990, the federal government played an activist role beginning with the passage of the Social Security Act of 1935 stretching through the various provisions of the Older Americans Act. The Great Depression of the 1930s, along with the rise of senior citizen activism, played major roles in this period.

Torres-Gil has argued that America has been in a "New Aging" period since 1990. With massive federal deficits, increased longevity, dramatically increasing numbers of older people, competition for governmental benefits, and rising intergenerational conflict, he contended that a new approach to governmental and personal responses to the needs of elderly persons should be developed. In this new era, many public policy experts have contended that the United States in the 1990s is at a crossroads in the development of public policies to address the real ongoing needs of the elderly and other age groups, particularly children.

Various public policy experts in the field of aging have provided a range of approaches that could be developed to adequately address the real needs of persons of all ages in American society and thereby diminish the rising intergenerational conflicts that are embodied in such groups as Lead . . . or Leave. These approaches range from a continuation of strictly age-based entitlements, a combination of age-based benefits and need-based benefits on a sliding income/asset scale, a cap on entitlements, to strictly need-based benefits. They include specific proposals to raise taxes, develop social insurance programs for health and long-term care, invest more in the needs of the young, raise the age of retirement, eliminate Social Security earnings limits, promote older worker training/retraining and hiring, protect pensions, reverse the trend toward early retirement, put Social Security back on a pay-as-you-go basis, and reduce the federal deficit.

Robert Binstock and James Schulz have pointed out that benefits for the elderly will always be tied to the economic vitality and productivity of the nation. If these rise, even modestly, there is less resentment toward the entitlements the elderly receive. Still, the emphasis clearly seems to be the promotion and adoption of an intergenerational approach to needs and benefits. In this regard, the multigenerational approach of a program such as Social Security needs to be emphasized. Not only does it provide an income base for older people which of itself relieves younger generations from the financial burdens of supporting parents, grandparents, and great-grandparents, but it affords protection to the disabled worker and her or his dependents as well as the survivors of deceased workers.

By looking at the public policy agendas of some of the nation's most powerful interest groups promoting the causes of older people, recognizing the rising intergenerational tensions in an era of high federal deficits and tight federal and state budgets, an intergenerational approach to the politics of aging seems to be emerging. With 76 million baby boomers ready to retire relatively early in the twenty-first century and adding to the dramatically increased numbers of older people already among us, creative public policy solutions that will meet the real needs of people of all ages while keeping the faith and confidence of the American people in programs that have worked to date will need to emerge.

REFERENCES

Achenbaum, A. 1983. *Shades of Gray: Old Age, American Values, and Federal Policies Since 1920.* Boston: Little, Brown.

Acronyms in Aging. 1990. National Gerontology Resource Center. Washington, DC: AARP.

American Association of Retired Persons. 1993. Toward a Just and Caring Society. *AARP Public Policy Agenda.* Summary. Washington, DC: AARP.

Binstock, R.H. 1992. *Policies on Aging at the Crossroads.* Unpublished address for the Holland Home, Grand Rapids, MI.

Binstock, R.H. 1993. The Votes of Older Persons in the 1992 Presidential Elections. *University Center on Aging and Health Newsletter, 12*(1). Cleveland, OH: Case Western Reserve University.

Carlson, E. 1992a. Bush, Clinton Hit High Note: AARP's New Chief Defends Elderly, Asks Aid for Kids. *NRTA Bulletin, 33*(7). Washington, DC: AARP.

Carlson, E. 1992b. Clinton's Win Lifts Age Issue. *NRTA Bulletin*, 33(11).

Carlson, E. 1993. Clinton Told Care "a must". *NTRA Bulletin*, 34(2): 1, 4–5.

Chen, Y.-P. 1987. Making Assets Out of Tomorrow's Elderly. *Gerontologist, 27*(4): 410–16.

Clairborne, W. 1993. *Washington Post.* Entitlement Cap: Less Money for Elderly When They Need It Most? *The Detroit News.* (May 31): 2A.

Day, C. 1990. *What Older Americans Think: Interest Groups and Aging Policy.* Princeton, NJ: Princeton University Press.

Deets, H.B. 1993. Attack on Entitlements Mock Shared Sacrifice. *NRTA Bulletin, 34*(7).

Economist. 1991. Grey Peril—American Pensions. (May 11).

Estes, C.L., Swan, J.H., and Associates. 1993. *The Long-Term Care Crisis: Elders Trapped in the No-Care Zone.* Newbury Park, CA: Sage Publications.

Fairlie, H. 1988. Talkin' bout My Generation. *The New Republic* (March 28): 19–22.

Fein, R. 1992. Prescription for Change. *Modern Maturity.* (August/September)

Hager, G. 1993. Entitlements: The Untouchable May Become Unavoidable. *Congressional Quarterly*, 2. (January 2)

Hey, R.P. 1992. Entitlements Under Fire, But No Big Changes Wow. *NRTA Bulletin, 33*(11).

Hey, R.P. 1993a. Coming: Price Controls? *NRTA Bulletin, 34*(4).

Hey, R.P. 1993b. Clinton Unveils Health Plan. *NRTA Bulletin, 34*(9).

Hudson, R.B., and Strate, J. 1985. Aging and Political Systems. In R. Binstock and E. Shanas (eds.), *Handbook of Aging and the Social Sciences.* 2d ed. New York: Van Nostrand.

Jacobs, G. 1990. Aging and Politics. In R.H. Binstock and L. George (eds.), *Handbook of Aging and the Social Sciences*, 3d Ed. New York: Academic Press.

Jennings, J. 1989. U.S. Bureau of the Census. *Voting and Registration in the Election of November 1988*, Current Population Reports, Series P-20, No. 440. Washington, DC: U.S. Government Printing Office.

Kemper, P., and Murtaugh, C.M. 1991. Lifetime Use of Nursing Home Care. *New England Journal of Medicine, 324*(9): 595.

Kellogg, S. 1993a. Generational Gulf: Economic Spat Rocks the Ages. *Grand Rapids Press* (September, 26): A8.

Kellogg, S. 1993b. Clinton Health Plan Quiet on Nursing Home, Adult Foster Coverage. *Grand Rapids Press* (November 8): B3.

Koff, T.H., and Park, R.W., Hendricks, J. (ed.). 1993. *Aging Public Policy: Bonding the Generations.* Amityville, NY: Baywood Publishing.

Levy, F. 1987. *Dollars and Deams: The Changing American Income Distribution.* New York: Russell Sage Foundation.

Lindeman, B. 1992. AARP—Too Much Greed? *Detroit Free Press* (July 7): 3C.

Moody, H. 1990. The Politics of Entitlement and the Politics of Productivity. In *Diversity in Aging*, S. Bass, E. Kutza, and F. Torres-Gil (eds.). Glenview, IL: Scott, Foresman.

Neugarten, B. 1979. Policy for the 1980s: Agers Need Entitlement? In National Journal Issues Book, *Aging: Agenda for the Eighties.* Washington, DC: Government Research Corporation.

Paterson, M-M. 1993. A Boost for the Very Disabled. *NRTA Bulletin, 34*(10).

Ruggles, P. 1990. *Drawing the Line: Alternative Poverty Measures and Their Implications for Public Policy.* Washington, DC: Urban Institute Press.

Schutz, J.H., Borowski, A., and Crown, W.H. 1991. *Economics of Population Aging: The "Graying" of Australia, Japan, and the United States.* New York: Auburn House.

Schutz, J.H. 1992. *The Economics of Aging*, 5th Ed. New York: Auburn House.

Smart, W.E. 1986. Caught Between the Generations: Middle-Aged and Caring for Young and Old. *The Washington Post*. (December 5).

Social Security Should Benefit Only the Elderly Poor. 1989. *Business Week*, (January 16).

Torres-Gil, F.M. 1992. *The New Aging: Politics and Change in America*. New York. Auburn House.

U.S. Bipartisan Commission on Comprehensive Health Care (Pepper Commission). 1990. *A Call for Action*. Washington, DC: U.S. Government Printing Office.

U.S. Bureau of the Census. 1991a. *Poverty in the United States: 1990*. Current Population Reports, Series P-60, No. 175. Washington, DC: U.S. Government Printing Office.

U.S. Bureau of the Census. 1991b. *Statistical Abstract of the United States, 1991*. Washington, DC: U.S. Government Printing Office.

U.S. Bureau of the Census. 1992. Current Population Reports, Special Studies, P23-178 RV, *Sixty-Five Plus in America*. Washington, DC: U.S. Government Printing Office.

U.S. General Accounting Office. 1992. *Elderly Americans: Health, Housing, and Nutrition Gaps Between the Poor and Nonpoor*. Washington, DC.

U.S. House of Representatives Select Committee on Aging. 1987. *Long Term Care and Personal Impoverishment: Seven in Ten Elderly Living Alone at Risk*. Washington, DC: U.S. Government Printing Office.

U.S. House of Representatives Select Committee on Aging. 1992. *Old, Poor, and Forgotten: Elderly Americans Living in Poverty*. Washington, DC: U.S. Government Printing Office.

U.S. Senate Special Committee on Aging. 1991. *Aging America: Trends and Projections*, Washington, DC: U.S. Department of Health and Human Services.

U.S. Senate Special Committee on Aging. 1993. *Developments in Aging: 1992:1*. Washington, DC: U.S. Government Printing Office.

Wallace, S.P., and Williamson, J.B. 1992. *The Senior Movement: References and Resources*. New York: G.K. Hall & Company.

Glossary

accessory apartment   An independent apartment within a single-family home that provides secure living arrangements for an older person close to the family while still maintaining the privacy and independence of his or her own living space.

Action   An independent government agency set up to administer all domestic volunteer programs under a single authorizing law.

active euthanasia   To purposely and deliberately take action to end an individual's life.

active life expectancy   The expected years of physical, emotional, and intellectual vigor of functional well-being, or how long a person can be independent in their ADLs.

activities of daily living (ADLs)   Functions such as bathing, dressing, getting out of bed, going to the bathroom, and feeding oneself.

acute condition   A condition which can be either mild or serious that is expected to be of a limited duration, such as simple bruises, broken bones, or heart attacks.

Administration on Aging (AoA)   The federal level of the Aging Network which administers most of the programs that come under the Older Americans Act; the primary federal agency to advocate for older persons, overseeing a network of state units on aging.

adult daycare   A community-based group program designed to meet the needs of functionally impaired adults through an individual plan of care; a structured, comprehensive program that provides a variety of health, social, and related support services in a protective setting during any part of a day but fewer than 24 hours a day.

aged   The second of the three subcategories of the elderly population defined by the U.S. Bureau of the Census. This category consists of people between the ages of 75 and 84 years.

age discrimination   Prejudiced treatment on the basis of age.

Age Discrimination in Employment Act (ADEA)   A congressional act designed "to promote employment of older persons based on their ability rather than age; to prohibit arbitrary age discrimination in employment; and to help employers and workers find ways of meeting problems arising from the impact of age on employment." The act covers persons aged 40 to 70.

age in place   A phrase used to indicate how people continue to get older in the places they have been living regardless of the condition of the living unit, the changing nature of the neighborhood, or the special needs of many older people.

age-integrated housing   Older persons living among people of all ages, young, middle-aged and older.

ageism   Prejudice against the elderly.

age-segregated housing Older persons living among persons about their own age.

Aging Network A nationwide system of federal, state, and local agencies that focus all or part of their activities on meeting the needs of older people.

agnosia A condition, resulting from a stroke, in which a person cannot recognize everyday objects such as a key, pencil, or comb.

AIDS (acquired immunodeficiency syndrome) A disease characterized by a deficiency in the immune system.

Alzheimer's disease A progressive, degenerative, irreversible brain disease first diagnosed by a German physician, Dr. Alois Alzheimer.

Americans with Disabilities Act (ADA) An act involving approximately 43 million Americans, which requires a range of public and private individuals and organizations to make "reasonable accommodations" to a variety of diverse needs.

angina pectoris Significant pain in the chest brought about by a reduction in oxygen to the heart muscle.

anxiety An aspect of the "flight-or-fight" syndrome with physical symptoms such as sweating, diarrhea, palpitations, headaches, dizziness, and for some, hyperventilation. Anxiety can also lead to problems with memory, concentration, and shortened attention span.

apraxia A condition, resulting from a stroke, in which a person has an inability to control motor tasks such as writing or feeding themselves.

Area Agencies on Aging (AAAs) Geographic service areas on the state level that are established by the state units on aging. These agencies can be a unit of county, city, or town government, or a private, nonprofit agency. AAAs develop their own 3-year plans to serve the older people of their areas.

arteriosclerosis A general term describing the hardening of or loss of elasticity of the arteries.

arthritis A degenerative disease of bone joints.

atherosclerosis A condition when the inner walls of the arteries become thickened by fat deposits.

autoimmunity theory of aging One popular physiological theory of aging that says two important changes occur with increasing age. First, the body begins to lose the ability to distinguish between foreign and nonforeign particles, and therefore antibodies and cells begin to attack normal, healthy cells. Second, the body begins to produce more mutations in its DNA structure as a cell divides, which the body responds to as foreign matter.

baby boomers A term used to describe the largest group of persons ever born in one period of American history, those born between 1946 and 1964.

baby boomlet A term used for the children of the baby boomers.

baby bust A term used for the generation that followed the baby boomers.

baby echo A term used for the children of the baby boomers.

bereavement The condition a person is in upon having lost a significant other to death.

beta-amyloid plaques Waxy protein substances deposited in nerve cells, found in patients with Alzheimer's disease.

biogerontology The scientific study of the aging processes.

bipolar depression A type of depression in which a biochemical imbalance brings about emotional mood swings. A person with bipolar depression may change from mania to depression.

board-and-care homes Homes which provide supervision, supportive services, and assistance for persons who cannot live alone because of physical or mental impairments, but who do not require institutional care.

caregiver burnout The wearing down or collapse of caregivers.

case care management A program designed to assess the needs of older persons who require assistance and to help in arranging for needed services.

case management A community-based service, usually in conjunction with a community-based agency, in which the responsibility for assisting the needs of older people and finding and/or negotiating for services to meet the identified needs is undertaken by a qualified person or team.

cataracts A condition in which the lens of the eye becomes cloudy which causes the person to suffer from blurred or misty vision.

categorical programs Programs are designed to benefit all people who fall into specifically defined groups.

cellular theories of aging Theories that postulate that aging occurs because processes within the cell malfunction. Several popular cellular theories are mutation, error catastrophe, cellular theory, genetic switching, and free-radical theory.

cellular theory of aging A theory stating that cells have a finite number of replications; after cells have replicated as many times as possible, the cells die.

chronic condition A condition that is expected to be long-term or permanent, such as heart disease, high blood pressure, hearing loss, vision impairment, diabetes, and arthritis.

circuit-breaker program A property tax relief program which provides tax cuts or refunds to older homeowners when property taxes go above a certain percentage of their household income.

club-sandwich generation A term which refers to older persons who have the responsibility of caring for their own parents, their children, and their grandchildren.

common-law states States that do not have specific laws dividing up property at the time of divorce.

community property states States that have specific laws which categorize the property of married couples as jointly held property, and hence at divorce evenly divide it between the divorcing couple.

condominiums Housing units that are individually owned but are usually part of a multifamily housing setting on a common grounds area that typically has support facilities and may have recreational facilities.

congregate living Housing units that have a common dining room in which meals are served on a regular basis along with access to social and recreational services. This type of care is designed to provide services in a residential setting for persons who need some form of assistance with daily living but do not require continuing medical or nursing care.

congregate meals A program designed to provide both meals and opportunities to socialize for older persons.

continuing-care retirement communities (CCRCs) A living arrangement in which incoming residents enter into a contractual agreement to pay an entrance fee and monthly fees that will provide for their care for the rest of their lives regardless of the status of their mobility and health.

continuum-of-care An environment where levels of supportive care are provided as needed.

coronary thrombosis A heart attack caused by a lack of blood and oxygen going to the heart because of a blockage of an artery.

cross-sectional research Research in which two or more groups are tested at the same time.

crystallized intelligence Learned patterns of culture and linguistic ability acquired from experience and education.

cultural norms Behavior that is accepted as normal.

defined-benefit pension plan A plan in which the employer saves and invests for the workers and guarantees a certain level of benefits in retirement.

defined-contribution pension A plan in which employees set aside part of their wages in tax-sheltered accounts for their retirement. In this type of pension, employers may contribute to these plans but are not required to do so.

Department of Housing and Urban Development (HUD) The federal department that pays money for housing to persons who show financial need to make up the difference between 30 percent of a person's income and what is considered fair-market rent.

dependency ratio The number of retired dependent people compared to the number of working younger people who pay taxes to finance old-age benefits and entitlements.

diagnostically related groups (DRGs) Medicare patients are classified into one of 487 diagnostically related groupings which determine the payments hospitals receive for Medicare patients.

discretionary income Money that is available to purchase items people want.

domestic elder abuse Many forms of mistreatment of an older person by someone who has a special relationship in the older person's home or in the home of the person caring for the elder.

durable power of attorney An individual designated to make treatment decisions for a person who no longer has the mental capacity to do so.

economically vulnerable Persons who have incomes not exceeding twice the poverty rate.

elder abuse A concept defined by the Older Americans Act and organized into three basic categories: (1) domestic elder abuse, (2) institutional elder abuse, and (3) Self-neglect or self-abuse.

eldercare locater A service which taps into an extensive network of organizations that are familiar with state and local community resources for older persons. Information is provided about resources such as adult daycare centers, legal assistance, home health services, and transportation resources.

elder cottage housing opportunity (ECHO) Small, free-standing, removable housing units placed on the side or back yard of a single-family home to provide private, independent housing for elderly parents close to the home of an adult child.

elderly   A term used for persons 65 years of age and older.

electroconvulsive therapy (ECT)   A treatment for depression in which a very slight electrical impulse is sent through the frontal part of the brain.

emerging old   Persons who are not old yet but are getting close to being old.

emotional or psychological abuse   The willful infliction of mental or emotional anguish by threat, humiliation, intimidation, or other verbally or non-verbally abusive conduct.

Employee Retirement Income Security Act (ERISA)   A law designed to expand the supervision and regulation of private pension plans by the federal government and to create tax-exempt individual retirement accounts for persons not covered by a qualified pension plan.

encoding   The storage and retrieval of learned material.

endogenous depression   A type of depression brought about by a biochemical imbalance.

entitlement caps   An approach to curtailing federal spending by putting a ceiling on entitlements.

error catastrophe   A cellular theory proposed by Dr. Leslie Orgel in 1963. The theory claims that aging is caused by damaging RNA, enzymes, and certain proteins.

estrogen therapy   A supplement to a woman's estrogen level that is taken after menopause.

expressive aphasia   A condition caused by a stroke, in which a person cannot form words.

extended family   A family form relied upon in the traditional agricultural society. It consists of mother, father, sons, and their wives and children.

Family and Medical Leave Act of 1993   A federal law which provides employees up to 12 weeks of unpaid leave each year to care for children, parents, or close relatives. Persons are covered if they work for firms that employ 50 or more people.

family councils   Councils established by the provisions of OBRA of 1987 which provide a means for the loved ones of residents of nursing facilities to band together to have input into the operation and to address any issues and concerns that may arise.

family reciprocity   The idea that adult children think they owe total care to their parents because their parents took care of them when they were young and dependent.

fantasy therapy   A therapeutic emphasis in which staff members relate to the reality being constructed by a person with a irreversible brain disease.

Federal Housing Administration (FHA)   A federal agency that provides for a loan program which aids persons in purchasing homes at reasonable prices and low interest rates.

FICA taxes   Contributions that both employees and employers make to the Social Security Trust Fund. Self-employed persons must fund the total statutory required amount.

financial abuse   The unauthorized use of funds, property, or any resources of an older person.

fluid intelligence   Analytical or instant reasoning ability.

Food Stamp program   The federal program set up to alleviate malnutrition and hunger among low-income persons by increasing their food purchasing power through issuing coupons to purchase food in accordance with guidelines established by the U.S. Department of Agriculture (USDA).

Foster Grandparent program   A program that provides part-time volunteer opportunities for low-income persons 60 years of age and older to help them provide supportive services to children with physical, mental, emotional, or social disabilities.

401K plans   Defined-contribution pensions in which employees set aside part of their wages in tax-sheltered accounts for their retirement. In this type of pension, employers may contribute but are not required to do so.

frail elderly   Persons 65 years and older with significant physical and mental health problems.

free-radical theory of aging   A cellular theory which claims that oxygen radicals or superoxides are able to destroy cells. The theory states that the constant pounding by free radicals eventually wears down the system over a period of time, and that it requires antioxidants to be constantly working against the effects of free radicals.

Friendly-Visitor program   A program that provides visits to the home to check on a disabled person.

functional dependency   A term which indicates a need for assistance with one or more ADLs.

functional limitations   A term which indicates difficulty with performing personal care tasks and home management tasks.

generation gap   The tension which some children experience with their parents because each are members of different generations with distinctly different experiences.

generational equity   Equitable distribution of resources, especially governmental resources, between and among the generations.

generations united   An organization that attempts to promote policies that benefit both young and old. It includes persons from such diverse groups as the American Association of Retired Persons and the Childrens Defense Fund.

generic program   A program designed to be of assistance to people of any age.

genetic switching theory of aging   A cellular theory which proposes that certain genes can be switched on and off. Because genes that encode DNA become inactive, DNA is no longer produced and the cells "age".

geriatricians   Doctors who focus on the health needs of older people.

geriatrics   The medical field specializing in treatment of the medical conditions of older persons.

gerontological phobia   A fear and distaste of aging.

gerontology   The study of aging.

gerontophilia period   A term which refers to the period of American history between the years 1600 and 1800 when old age was generally honored and older persons were respected.

gerontophobia period   A term which refers to the period of American history beginning around 1800 in which older persons were increasingly mocked and disrespected, and the aging process was feared.

glaucoma   A condition in the eye in which a buildup of pressure causes damage to the optic nerve resulting in a loss of peripheral vision. Untreated, the condition results in tunnel vision and loss of sight.

greedy geezers   A phrase which portrays older persons as well-off, healthy, enjoying high retirement pensions (including Social Security), and living in luxury and leisure, much at the expense of poorer younger people in America.

grief   Emotional response to the loss of a significant other.

guardianships   Granted to persons called guardians by a court order to manage the affairs of individuals who are judged incompetent to manage their own financial and personal business.

health maintenance organization (HMO)   A large group medical practice where a person might see any doctor on call.

heterogeneous   Possessing differences.

heterosexual   Sexual desire for persons of the opposite sex.

home-delivered meals   A program which provides one or more meals a day, five to seven days per week, delivered to an older person's home; also called *meals-on-wheels*.

home equity conversion mortgage   A mortgage which turns the equity value in an older person's house into a source of monthly income without the need to sell or move out of the home.

home health services   Services made up of two types of programs: (1) home nursing care, and (2) personal care services.

homemaker/home chore services   Services provided to maintain the home, including laundry, shopping, and light housekeeping.

homestead exemptions   A property tax relief program which provides fixed percentage reductions in the assessed valuation of an older person's primary residence.

homosexual   Sexual desire for persons of the same sex.

hormonal theory of aging   One popular physiological theory of aging which explains that aging occurs because the endocrine system begins to "shut down," and certain hormones are depleted.

hot flashes, flushes   A feeling of heat usually spreading over the upper body which is experienced by most women going through menopause.

hypothermia   A reduction in body temperature with a danger that the body temperature may get so low that the person is endangered.

incontinence   The involuntary leaking out of urine.

information superhighway   Technology which utilizes computers to transmit information on current issues and problems.

inhibited sexual desire   A term used to describe persons with no known physiological dysfunctions but with little or no sexual motivation.

in-home services   Services which enable older people to remain in their own homes in community settings. These services can be grouped into three basic categories based on the level of service needed: (1) intensive or skilled services which are ordered by a physician and supervised by a nurse; (2) personal care or intermediate services for older persons who are medically stable but need help with some activities of daily living; (3) homemaker services.

insomnia   A condition in which a person has difficulty sleeping.

institutional elder abuse   Physical, sexual, emotional, or financial abuse or neglect that occurs in facilities designed for older people.

instrumental activities of daily living (IADLs)   Activities such as shopping, cooking, cleaning, taking medicines, handling personal finances, traveling, and using the telephone.

intentional abuse   Willfully and intentionally abusing the rights of another person.

intergenerational approaches/age-integrated approaches   A movement away from age-defined benefits and toward a gradual integration of the benefits of the young, middle-aged, and old.

interiority   A loss of interest in the outside world and a preoccupation with oneself that often occurs as one ages.

Job Training Partnership Act (JTPA)   An act established by the federal government to be a nationwide system of job training programs administered jointly by local governments and private-sector planning agencies.

legal hotlines   Legal assistance for the elderly in which legal advice is given to callers over the telephone by attorneys.

Legal Services Corporation (LSC)   A legal assistance resource for persons with an income no higher than 125 percent of the poverty line.

lesbians   Homosexual women.

life-care contracts   A form of housing insurance that can be grouped into three categories: (1) extensive, (2) modified, and (3) fee-for-service. Each of the three categories include shelter, residential services, and amenities, but they differ in the amount of long-term nursing care provided.

life expectancy   The average number of years a person in a particular society is expected to live. It can be measured from birth or from any given year.

life span   The number of years human beings can live under optimal conditions.

living environment   The type and condition of a person's dwelling unit and the general characteristics of the neighborhood.

living trust   A legal device to transfer real or personal property into a trust managed by a trustee; essentially an estate planning device that avoids probate court.

living will   A written document which allows persons to indicate their wishes about the type of medical care they wish to have or not to have under specified conditions.

longevity-inflation squeeze   The concept that peoples' savings and investments do not keep up with the underlying inflation.

longitudinal studies   The test of the same group of people over a period of time (weeks, months, years, or decades).

long-term care   Care given over a continuous and long period of time, which can be offered in a variety of settings, either institutional or community-based.

Long-Term Care Ombudsman Program   A program set up as an amendment to the Older Americans Act to: (1) investigate and resolve complaints made by or on behalf of residents of long term care facilities; (2) monitor the development and operation of federal, state, and local laws, regulations, and policies for long-term facilities; (3) provide information about the problems of residents of long-term care facilities to appropriate public agencies; (4) provide training to staff and volunteers to participate in the ombudsman program; and (5) serve the residents of board-and-care homes.

macula   The most sensitive area of the eye; located in the center of the retina in the back of the eye and packed with light receptors which enable one to see fine detail.

macular degeneration   A condition in the eye resulting in vision in which words increasingly become blurred, straight lines seem to have a kink in them, and colors tend to become dimmer. Central vision is eventually lost.

masturbation   Achieving sexual release through self-stimulation.

matrix family   An adult-centered family unit spanning generations that is bound together by friendships and circumstances as well as by blood relationships.

meals-on-wheels   A program in which home-delivered meals are provided to home-bound older people to enable them to have nutritional meals on a regular basis.

means-testing   A method of determining benefits based on a person's financial status.

Medicaid   A federally funded, means-tested, medical program for the indigent.

Medicaid estate planning   A type of planning used to divest older persons of countable assets so they can qualify for Medicaid assistance with nursing home costs.

Medicare   A federally funded health insurance program for persons 65 and older.

medigap insurance   A privately funded supplemental health insurance policy for the elderly that aids in covering medical costs not covered by Medicare.

menopause   The process, usually around age 50, in which ovulation and the menstrual cycle cease.

microbiological theory of aging   A theory which states that the aging process is controlled by maintaining an internal balance within the body. Contained in this theory is the *homeostatic imbalance theory* which explains that various organs within the body attempt to maintain an internal balance between the heart, lungs, kidney, and liver.

micturition   The signal a person receives when he/she has to urinate.

mixed aphasia   A condition resulting from a stroke in which a person has difficulty speaking and understanding words.

mobile/manufactured homes   Moveable homes usually found in mobile home parks which provide the independence and privacy of a home at an affordable cost.

multi-infarct dementia   Minor strokes that damage the brain by reducing blood flow to the brain.

multipurpose senior centers   A community focal point where older persons come together as individuals or in groups for services and activities which enhance their dignity, support their independence, and encourage their involvement in and with the community.

mutation theory of aging   A cellular theory which claims that the process of aging is directly related to the production of mutated DNA of vital organs.

mutual masturbation   Bringing pleasure to each partner through touching, caressing, massaging, hugging, fondling; bringing each partner to orgasm by manipulation.

myocardial infarction   A heart attack.

NCOA   National Council on the Aging.

NCSC   National Council of Senior Citizens.

near-death experience   Persons who believe that they experience themselves dying, leaving their bodies, and then coming back to life.

near poor   Persons income at 125 percent of the poverty line.

neglect   Failure by the caregiver to fulfill his/her caretaking obligation or duty.

neurofibrillary tangles   Twisted filaments of nerve cell endings found in patients with Alzheimer's disease.

new federalism   A term referring to a decrease in the federal role in health and welfare by shifting the responsibility to the state and local levels of government.

no-care zone   A term used for the widening gap between services that are available for the long-term care needs of older adults and the services that are needed by dependent older persons.

nocturia   The need to get up in the night to urinate.

non-proprietary facilities   Not-for-profit operations.

notice of non-coverage   A notice that is requested if a patient in a Prospective Payment System is to be discharged and the patient or family disagree. A hospital cannot charge a patient for care unless such a notice is received and the patient remained in the hospital after the specified date to be discharged.

nuclear family   A family centered around children, usually a two-generation family.

nursing homes/nursing facilities   Service-based facilities for persons who need more nursing and personal care than can be provided in their own homes, board-and-care homes, or homes for the aged.

Older Americans Act of 1965 (OAA)   An act which grew out of the deliberations of the 1961 White House Conference on Aging. OAA laid the foundation for the wide array of community services to meet the social and human needs of older people.

older workers   A term used for workers over 50 years of age who are experiencing the processes, realities, and consequences of aging.

oldest old   The third of the three subcategories of the elderly population defined by the U.S. Bureau of the Census. This category consists of people aged 85 years and older.

Omnibus Budget Reconciliation Act of 1987 (OBRA)   An act designed to address the conditions that were documented by investigations and studies by the U.S. Senate Special Committee on Aging (1986), the U.S. Government Accounting Office (1987), and the Institute of Medicine, which found that thousands of frail elderly people were in nursing homes that did not provide care that met their most basic health and safety needs. This act addressed many issues, from the definition of nursing facilities to the details of staffing and operating a nursing facility.

open-ended questions   Questions that enable the respondent to their feelings and thoughts at length.

osteoarthritis   A common form of arthritis, sometimes referred to as degenerative joint disease. It results in the breakdown of joint tissue producing pain and stiffness in the joints.

osteoporosis   The loss of mass in the bones causing them to become brittle.

ostomy   An operation to make an artificial opening to empty the large or small bowel or the bladder.

overflow incontinence   A condition where the bladder becomes too full and urine leaks out.

over-housed   A term used for older persons who do not want to give up ownership of their homes, and as a result have too much house for their present needs.

OWL   Older Women's League.

parent-support ratio   The number of oldest old people (85 years and older) likely to need support and assistance for every 100 persons aged 50 to 64 years, who are the likely family-member caregivers.

passive euthanasia   Deliberately not taking any action to prolong the life of someone who is dying or is existing in a vegetative state.

Patient Self-Determination Act   A federal law, passed on December 1, 1991, which requires hospices, nursing homes, hospitals, and other home-health care agencies to provide patients with information about the right to determine whether they want "extraordinary" or other means used to keep them alive if they become comatose or hopelessly ill.

patriarchy   The systematic subordination of women in society where the man is always privileged.

Pension Benefit Guaranty Corporation (PBGC)   An agency established under ERISA as part of the Department of Labor. It is designed to guarantee payment of pension checks to retired workers and future payments to vested workers when a pension plan is terminated or runs out of money.

pension portability   The ability to shift monies for retirement when an employee changes jobs.

physical abuse   The deliberate use of physical force that results in bodily injury, pain, or impairment.

physiological theories of aging   Theories which propose that aging occurs because there is a breakdown in the functioning of a particular organ system or physiological control mechanism. Two popular theories are the *autoimmunity* and the *hormonal theories*.

planned-unit development (PUD)   Developments of apartment buildings, mobile home parks, public housing complexes, or condominiums involving a defined tract of land.

poor farms   Living situations in which indigent older persons dwelled together on government-owned farms. They received shelter, food, and basic support, and were expected to work, to the extent possible, on the farm.

post-claims underwriting   Policy whereby an insurance company waits to examine the insurability of an applicant until a claim is filed.

post-industrial society   A society marked by a shift away from the ongoing expansion in manufacturing and industry. Some believe that such a society may bring reduced working hours, the 4-day work week, and a diminished emphasis on the Protestant work ethic.

postmature death   A person whose condition has deteriorated irreversibly and who is kept alive by extraordinary means.

poverty line   The official economic line established by the federal government under which persons are considered poor.

presbyopia   A condition in which the aging eye losses accommodation, meaning it becomes more difficult for the eye to adjust to different distances, to darkness, and to glare. It is caused by the hardening of the lens.

productive capacity   The result of a nation's capital, natural resources, balance of trade, technology, and number and quality of workers.

proprietary facilities   For-profit operations.

prospective payment system (PPS)   A system in which hospitals are paid a predetermined rate based on a physician's diagnosis rather than what it actually costs to keep a Medicare patient in the hospital.

pseudodementia   A reversible condition in which the symptoms are similar to an organic, irreversible brain disease such as Alzheimer's disease.

public housing   Subsidized housing for low-income individuals and families.

qualified Medicare benefit (QMB)   A government program in which the state government, for income qualified older persons, pays the Medicare premiums, copayments and deductibles.

random sample   A sample in which all persons in the desired population have an equal probability of being chosen.

ratio of two elderly generations   The number of persons 85 years and older for every 100 persons 65 to 69 years of age. This ratio is used to gain a better understanding of the aging of the aged.

reactive depression   A type of depression that is brought about by certain events in the life of the depressed person.

reality therapy   A therapy technique in which staff members emphasize the time of day, the day of the week, and other aspects of reality to enable the patient to recover cognitive functioning.

receptive aphasia   A condition resulting from a stroke in which a person has difficulty understanding spoken words.

refractory period   The length of time after ejaculation before a male is able to have another erection.

religiosity   A concept that includes both a moral belief system, involving such things as prayer and meditation, and certain behaviors that may allow the individual to associate with others who share their belief system.

religious   A word used to describe individual or group relations with a supernatural power, whether called God, or spirit, or vital force.

replication studies   Further research on the same topic.

rescue fantasy   An idea held by some adult children in which they believe that they should rescue their aging parents from illness or other problems.

resident councils   Councils established by the provisions of OBRA of 1987 that provide both a means for the ongoing input of the residents of nursing facilities as well as a means to disseminate information to the residents.

respite care   Qualified, temporary substitute care to relieve a caregiver.

retinopathy   Damage to the eye caused by diabetes in which blood vessels in the retina leak, close, or produce new growth. This leads to fluid buildup, bleeding, and/or scarring that can impair or destroy vision.

Retired Senior Volunteer Program (RSVP)   A program that offers a variety of volunteer opportunities to persons 60 years of age and older.

retirement   The termination of and formal withdrawal from a regular job under the provisions of a statutory pension system, a demographic category, an economic condition, a social status, a developmental phase in the human life span, the transition to old age, and a lifestyle dominated by leisure pursuits or, at least, by economically nonproductive activity.

reverse mortgage   A mortgage which turns the equity value in an older person's house into a source of monthly income without the need to sell or move out of the home.

rheumatoid arthritis   An autoimmune condition causing swelling, stiffness, tenderness, and pain in the joints. The disease is systemic, resulting in symptoms such as fatigue, fever, and weight loss.

role reversal   The concept that persons who were independent and the caregivers of others are now dependent and have to be cared for by the very people they raised.

sandwich generation   Those persons in the middle age category who are caught with competing responsibilities for dependent parents and dependent children.

scapegoat   Someone who is blamed for the problems of others, such as when the elderly are seen as being responsible for the injustices experienced by younger people.

seasonal affective disorder (SAD)   A condition in which persons begin to feel chronically depressed as winter approaches and the days grow shorter.

self-abuse   Neglectful or abusive behavior by an older person himself/herself that is threatening to that person's safety or health. This generally results from the physical or mental impairment of the older person.

self-selected sample   A sample in which persons are asked to volunteer to take part in the study.

senile dementia   Loss of brain function caused by disease related to the aging process.

senior companion program   A program designed to provide volunteer opportunities for low income persons 60 years of age and older to help provide supportive services to "vulnerable, frail older persons," such as those who are homebound, in institutions, or enrolled in community health programs.

senior power   Organizations and interest groups which exist to promote the varied interests of senior citizens.

Seniors and Lawmen Together (SALT)   An advisory council made up of law enforcement personnel, older persons, and people who work with older persons to determine the needs and concerns of older people in their region regarding criminal activity.

sex ratio   The number of men in a given age category for every 100 women in the same age group. This number decreases with age.

sexual abuse   Nonconsensual sexual contact of any kind.

sexual apathy   A refusal of sexual activity or a significant reduction in the amount and type of sexual contact.

sexual dysfunction   Loss of sexual desire.

sexual partner   Someone with whom a person is sexually intimate.

sexual response   A complex process affected by peoples' physiological and psychological condition as well as their relationship with their sexual partner.

shared housing   A living arrangement in which two or more unrelated people live in and share the same home.

simple hysterectomy   Surgery to remove the uterus and cervix.

single-room occupancy (SRO)   Single rooms that people of any age occupy in inner-city hotels and rooming houses, usually with a shared or common bath and no kitchen unit.

sleep apnea   A condition in which a person, during sleep, struggles to breathe and is short of breath. The condition involves snorting and snoring during sleep, and there is a cessation of breathing for several seconds.

Social Security Act of 1935   An act designed to provide economic stability for older Americans. Title II of the Act was designed to replace a portion of a person's income when he or she retired or died.

spiritual   A word that reflects one's search for the meaning and purpose in life and an attempt to put meaning into the many events of daily living.

spirituality   A reflection of past and present experiences and relationships in order to understand one's purpose in life.

state units on aging (SUAs)   Agencies which receive federal funds to implement state plans on aging which are approved by the AoA. These units can be independent units of state government or part of existing state agencies.

stress incontinence   Incontinence brought about by a laugh, a cough, a sneeze, or lifting.

structural economic changes   Economic changes including such things as downsizing of companies, mergers, long-term layoffs, and more part-time employment with no benefits.

subacute facilities   Facilities that provide a level of care just below acute care hospitals.

supplementary security income (SSI)   A federal program that guarantees a specific amount of monthly income for persons aged 65 years and older, and the disabled, if they qualify under income guidelines.

support groups   Small group structures for mutual aid and the accomplishment of specific purposes.

symbols   Objects, ideas, or events which represent something else and are used to give meaning and direction to life.

systemic   Not limited to one area, but rather encompassing several areas or symptoms.

telemarketing scans   The use of the telephone to contact people in their homes with intent to defraud them.

testosterone   A male hormone thought to be related to sexual drive.

total hysterectomy   Surgery to remove the uterus, cervix, ovaries, and fallopian tubes.

Townsend movement   Social movement started in the 1930s by Dr. Francis E. Townsend, who recommended that older Americans receive $200 a month, which they had to spend within 30 days to keep the economy growing.

transfer trauma   A term used to describe the difficult change of being placed in a nursing facility or other congregate living facility.

triad   An agreement between local police and sheriff's departments to work cooperatively with senior citizens to prevent victimization of the elderly.

unintentional abuse   Abuse which occurs as a result of ignorance, lack of desire to provide care, or self-neglect among the elderly.

urge incontinence   The sudden urge to go to the bathroom without time to get there.

vaginal elasticity   The elasticity and expansive qualities of the vagina. With age, the vagina has reduced elasticity and expansive qualities.

vested workers   Workers who have been employed long enough to collect under a pension plan.

vesting   The right to receive benefits from a pension plan.

Volunteers in Service to America (VISTA)   A program developed as a "domestic Peace Corps" for volunteers to work full-time in projects intended to reduce poverty. Volunteers work primarily with the handicapped, the homeless, the jobless, the hungry, and the illiterate or functionally illiterate.

widow's hump   A condition caused by osteoporosis that results in a curvature of the spine which makes a person look round-shouldered.

Widowed Persons' Service (WPS)   An organization founded by the American Association of Retired Persons to meet the emotional and practical needs of newly widowed persons.

widower's syndrome   A condition in which a man who has not had sexual contact for some time may have difficulty having an erection.

work ethic   A term used to describe the commitment to quality, company loyalty, coolness in crisis, and practical knowledge; often displayed by older workers.

young old   The first of the three subcategories of the elderly population defined by the U.S. Bureau of the Census. This category consists of people between the ages of 65 and 74 years.

Resource List

ACTION

Volunteers in Service to America
1100 Vermont Avenue NW
Washington, DC 20525
(202) 606-4855/(800) 424-8867

ACTION is an agency of the federal government that sponsors a number of volunteer programs conducted by older adults, including the Foster Grandparent Program, Retired Senior Volunteer Program, and the Senior Companion Program.

Administration on Aging

330 Independence Avenue SW
Washington, DC 20201
(202) 619-0641

The AoA, an agency of the Department of Health and Human Services, develops federal government programs and coordinates community services for older people.

Alzheimer's Association

Suite 1000
919 North Michigan Avenue
Chicago, IL 60611
(312) 335-8700/(800) 272-3900

The Alzheimer's Association is a voluntary organization that sponsors public education programs and offers supportive services to patients and families who are coping with Alzheimer's disease.

Alzheimer's Disease Education and Referral Center

P.O. Box 8250
Silver Spring, MD 20907-8250
(301) 495-3311/(800) 438-4380

The Alzheimer's Disease Education and Referral (ADEAR) Center, a service of the National Institute on Aging, distributes information about Alzheimer's disease to health professionals, patients and their families, and the general public.

American Association of Homes for the Aging

Suite 500
901 E Street NW
Washington, DC 20004-2037
(202) 783-2242

The American Association of Homes for the Aging (AAHA) is the national association of not-for-profit organizations dedicated to providing quality housing, health, community, and related services to older people. AAHA's mission is to represent and promote the common interests of its members through leadership, advocacy, education, and other services in order to enhance members' ability to serve their constituencies.

American Association of Retired Persons

601 E Street NW
Washington, DC 20049
(202) 434-2277

511

The American Association of Retired Persons (AARP) is a nonprofit organization dedicated to helping older Americans achieve lives of independence, dignity, and purpose.

American Cancer Society

1599 Clifton Road NE
Atlanta, GA 30329
(404) 320-3333/(800) 227-2345

The American Cancer Society (ACS) is a national, voluntary health organization dedicated to eliminating cancer as a major health problem by preventing cancer, saving lives from cancer, and diminishing suffering from this disease, through research, education, and service.

American Council of the Blind

Suite 720
1155 15th Street NW
Washington, DC 20005
(202) 467-5081/(800) 424-8666

American Diabetes Association

1660 Duke Street
Alexandria, VA 22314
(703) 549-1500/(800) 232-3472

The American Diabetes Association (ADA) is a voluntary organization that supports research to find a cure for diabetes and seeks to improve the well-being of people with diabetes and their families.

American Foundation for the Blind

15 West 16th Street
New York, NY 10011
(212) 620-2000/(800) 232-5463

The American Foundation for the Blind (AFB) is a national, nonprofit organization that advocates, develops, and provides programs and services to help people who are blind and those with visual impairments achieve independence in all sectors of society.

American Geriatrics Society

Suite 300
770 Lexington Avenue
New York, NY 10021
(212) 308-1414

The American Geriatrics Society (AGS) is dedicated to improving the health and well-being of all older persons. It is a not-for-profit organization of physicians and other health-care professionals committed to providing quality health care for older persons. As the primary organization representing geriatrics, the Society provides leadership for professionals, policymakers, and the public. To ensure the delivery of quality health care to older persons, the Society develops, implements, and advocates for programs in patient care, research, professional education, public policy, and public information.

American Heart Association

7272 Greenville Avenue
Dallas, TX 75231
(214) 373-6300

The American Heart Association is a voluntary health organization that funds research and sponsors public education programs to reduce disability and death from cardiovascular diseases and stroke.

American Lung Association

1740 Broadway
New York, NY 10019-4374
(212) 315-8700

The American Lung Association is a voluntary health organization that conducts public and professional education programs on preventing, detecting, and treating lung diseases and on living with disabled breathing.

American Medical Association

515 North State Street
Chicago, IL 60610
(312) 464-5000

The American Medical Association (AMA) is a professional organization that represents the interests of physicians and patients.

American Parkinson's Disease Association

Suite 401
60 Bay Street
Staten Island, NY 10301
(718) 981-8001/(800) 223-2732

The American Parkinson's Disease Association is a voluntary organization that funds research to find a cure for Parkinson's disease, educates the public about this illness, and offers assistance to patients and their families.

American Podiatric Medical Association

9312 Old Georgetown Road
Bethesda, MD 20814
(301) 571-9200/(800) 366-8227

The American Podiatric Medical Association (APMA) is a professional society of doctors who specialize in diagnosing and treating foot injury and disease. Podiatrists also make devices to correct foot problems, provide care for nails, prescribe certain medications, and perform foot surgery.

American Sleep Disorders Association
Suite 300 1610 14th Street NW
Rochester, MN 55901

The American Sleep Disorders Association is an organization of health professionals and facilities with a special interest in sleep disorders medicine. Sleep disorders include persistent insomnia (sleeplessness), narcolepsy (recurrent, uncontrollable episodes of sleep), sleep apnea syndrome (breathing stops many times during the night), and sleep pattern disturbances (disruption of sleep time).

American Society on Aging
Suite 512
833 Market Street
San Francisco, CA 94103
(415) 882-2910

The American Society on Aging is a nonprofit, membership organization that informs the public and health professionals about issues that affect the quality of life for older persons and promotes innovative approaches to meeting the needs of these people.

American Speech-Language-Hearing Association
10801 Rockville Pike
Rockville, MD 20852
(301) 897-5700/(800) 638-8255 (outside Maryland)

The American Speech-Language-Hearing Association is a professional society that supports the study of communication and funds research to improve the treatment of communication disorders.

Arthritis Foundation
1314 Spring Street NW
Atlanta, GA 30309
(404) 872-7100/(800) 283-7800

The Arthritis Foundation is a nonprofit, voluntary organization that supports research to find a cure for and ways to prevent all forms of arthritis and distributes information to the public about arthritis and rheumatic diseases.

Association for Adult Development and Aging
5999 Stevenson Avenue
Alexandria, VA 22304
(703) 823-9800

The Association for Adult Development and Aging provides leadership and information to gerontological

counselors and others on matters related to the development and needs of adults across the life span.

Association for Gerontology in Higher Education
Suite 410
1001 Connecticut Avenue NW
Washington, DC 20036-5504
(202) 429-9277

The Association for Gerontology in Higher Education (AGHE) is a professional organization that includes colleges, universities, and other educational institutions that offer training in the field of gerontology (the study of the biological, clinical, economic, and psychosocial aspects of aging).

Better Hearing Institute
P.O. Box 1840
Washington, DC 20013
(703) 642-0580/(800) 327-9355

The Better Hearing Institute is a nonprofit, educational organization established to provide the general public with information on hearing loss and to encourage the use of available resources and assistance.

Better Vision Institute
Suite 904
1800 North Kent Street
Rosslyn, VA 22209
(703) 243-1528

The Better Vision Institute (BVI) is an organization dedicated to serving as a credible source of news and information on the health aspects of vision care.

B'nai B'rith International
1640 Rhode Island Avenue NW
Washington, DC 20036
(202) 857-6600

B'nai B'rith International is a voluntary service organization that helps people of all faiths.

Catholic Golden Age
430 Penn Avenue
Scranton, PA 18503
(717) 342-3294/(800) 233-4697

Catholic Golden Age sponsors charitable work and offers religious worship opportunities for older people.

Center for Social Gerontology
Suite 204
117 North First Street

Ann Arbor, MI 48104
(313) 665-1126

The Center for Social Gerontology advances the well-being of older people in the United States through research, education, technical assistance, and training.

Children of Aging Parents

Suite 302-A
1609 Woodbourne Road
Levittown, PA 19057
(215) 945-6900

Children of Aging Parents (CAPS) is a nonprofit organization that provides information and emotional support to caregivers of older persons. CAPS serves as a national clearinghouse for information on resources and issues dealing with older people.

Concerned Relatives of Nursing Home Patients

3130 Mayfield Road
Cleveland Heights, OH 44118
(216) 321-0403

Concerned Relatives of Nursing Home Patients is a consumer group made up of persons who have had, currently have, or soon will have a family member or a friend in a nursing home. The goals of this group are to maintain quality care and improve services for all nursing home residents.

Consumer Product Safety Commission

Office of Information and Public Affairs
5401 Westbard Avenue
Bethesda, MD 20207
(301) 504-0580/(800) 638-2772

The Consumer Product Safety Commission (CPSC), an agency of the federal government, develops safety standards to protect the public against injury from consumer products, helps consumers evaluate product safety, and promotes research into the causes and prevention of product-related injury.

Courage Stroke Network

Courage Center
3915 Golden Valley Road
Golden Valley, MN 55422
(612) 588-0811/(800) 553-6321

The Courage Stroke Network links stroke survivors, their family members, and the professionals who serve them by providing a forum for sharing knowledge and experiences related to living with a stroke.

Department of Labor

Consumer Affairs
Room S1032
200 Constitution Avenue NW
Washington, DC 20210
(202) 219-6060

The Department of Labor is the Federal Government agency that guarantees workers' rights to safe working conditions, a minimum hourly wage and overtime pay, freedom from employment discrimination, unemployment insurance, and workers' compensation. The Department also protects workers' pension rights, provides job training programs, helps workers find jobs, and keeps track of changes in employment. Special efforts are made to help older workers, women, minorities, and people with disabilities.

Department of Veterans Affairs

Office of Public Affairs
810 Vermont Avenue NW
Washington, DC 20420
(202) 233-5187

The Department of Veterans Affairs (VA) is the federal agency that provides benefits to veterans of military service and their dependents.

Elderhostel

75 Federal Street
Boston, MA 02110-1941
(617) 426-7788

Elderhostel is a nonprofit organization that sponsors educational programs for persons 60 years of age and older.

Epilepsy Foundation of America

4351 Garden City Drive
Landover, MD 20785
(301) 459-3700/(800) 332-1000
(800) 332-4050 (National Epilepsy Library [for professionals])

The Epilepsy Foundation of America is a national, voluntary health organization dedicated to the prevention and cure of seizure disorders, alleviation of their effects, and promotion of optimal quality of life for people who have these disorders. To accomplish this mission, the Foundation supports research, education, advocacy, and service.

Equal Employment Opportunity Commission

1801 L Street NW
Washington, DC 20507
(202) 663-4900/(800) 669-3362

The Equal Employment Opportunity Commission (EEOC) is the federal agency responsible for eliminating discrimination based on race, color, religion, sex, national origin, age, or disability in hiring, promoting, firing, and all other conditions of employment.

Federal Council on the Aging
Room 4280 HHS-N
330 Independence Avenue SW
Washington, DC 20201
(202) 619-2451

The Federal Council on Aging, an advisory group authorized by the Older Americans Act of 1965, is selected by the President and the Congress. The fifteen members represent a cross-section of rural and urban older Americans, national organizations with an interest in aging, business, labor, and the general public.

Food and Nutrition Information Center
Room 304
U.S. Department of Agriculture
National Agricultural Library Building
Beltsville, MD 20705-2351
(301) 504-5719

The Food and Nutrition Information Center provides information to professionals and the general public on human nutrition, food service management, and food technology.

Foundation for Glaucoma Research
Suite 830
490 Post Street
San Francisco, CA 94102-9950
(415) 986-3162

The Foundation for Glaucoma Research is dedicated to improving the well-being of people with glaucoma through education and research.

Foundation for Hospice and Home Care
519 C Street NE
Washington, DC 20002
(202) 547-6586

The Foundation for Hospice and Home Care promotes hospice and home care, establishes responsible standards of care, develops programs that ensure the proper preparation of caregivers, educates the public, and conducts research on aging, health, and social policies.

Gerontological Society of America
Suite 350
1275 K Street NW
Washington, DC 20005-4006
(202) 842-1275

The Gerontological Society of America (GSA) is a professional organization that promotes the scientific study of aging in the biological and social sciences.

Gray Panthers
Suite 602
1424 16th Street NW
Washington, DC 20036
(202) 387-3111

Gray Panthers is an advocacy and education group that works to eliminate ageism, discrimination against older people on the basis of chronologic age. It is currently engaged in a national health system campaign that will ensure health protection for all Americans.

Green Thumb, Inc.
Suite 600
2000 North 14th Street
Arlington, VA 22201
(703) 522-7272

Green Thumb works to improve the social and economic condition of older Americans by promoting employment and training opportunities and by providing essential community services, particularly in rural areas. The ultimate goal is to promote job placement outside the program.

Health Care Financing Administration
6325 Security Boulevard
Baltimore, MD 21207
(410) 966-3000/(800) 638-6833

The Health Care Financing Administration (HCFA) coordinates the federal government's participation in Medicare (a health insurance program for people 65 years of age and older and certain disabled persons) and Medicaid (a health insurance program for people who need financial aid for medical expenses). HCFA also sponsors health care quality assurance programs such as the Medigap Hotline.

Help for Incontinent People
P.O. Box 544
Union, SC 29379
(803) 579-7900/(800) 252-3337

Help for Incontinent People (HIP) is a patient advocacy group that works to educate the public and health professionals about the prevalence, diagnosis, and treatment of urinary incontinence.

Huntington's Disease Society of America
6th Floor
140 West 22nd Street
New York, NY 10011-2420
(800) 345-4372

The Huntington's Disease Society is a voluntary organization that serves patients with Huntington's disease, a hereditary, degenerative neurological disease.

Hysterectomy Educational Resources and Services Foundation
422 Bryn Mawr Avenue
Bala Cynwyd, PA 19004
(215) 667-7757

The Hysterectomy Educational Resources and Services Foundation (HERS) is a nonprofit organization that provides information to the general public about hysterectomy (surgical removal of the uterus) and oophorectomy (removal of the ovaries).

International Hearing Society
20361 Middlebelt Road
Livonia, MI 48152
(313) 478-2610/(800) 521-5247

The National Hearing Aid Society is a professional organization designed to promote the welfare of the hearing impaired by providing quality care, support, and informational resources.

International Tremor Foundation
360 West Superior Street
Chicago, IL 60610
(312) 664-2344

The International Tremor Foundation is an international, nonprofit membership organization established to provide patient services and education and support research in tremor disorders.

Japanese American Citizens League
1765 Sutter Street
San Francisco, CA 94115
(415) 921-5225

The Japanese American Citizens League (JACL) is a nonprofit, educational organization that works to ensure equal opportunities for Americans of Japanese ancestry.

Legal Services for the Elderly
17th Floor
130 West 42nd Street
New York, NY 10036
(212) 391-0120

Legal Services for the Elderly is an advisory center for lawyers who specialize in the legal problems of older persons.

Make Today Count
P.O. Box 6063
Kansas City, KS 66106-0063
(913) 362-2866

Make Today Count is a nonprofit, self-help organization that provides emotional support to patients with life-threatening illnesses and their families.

Medic Alert Foundation
P.O. Box 1009
Turlock, CA 95381-1009
(209) 668-3333/(800) 344-3226

The Medic Alert Foundation is a worldwide nonprofit organization dedicated to providing personal medical information to protect and save lives.

National Action Forum for Midlife and Older Women
c/o Dr. Jane Porcino
P.O. Box 816
Stony Brook, NY 11790-0609

The National Action Forum for Midlife and Older Women (NAFOW) serves as a clearinghouse of information dealing with issues of special concern to middle-aged and older women.

National Aging Resource Center on Elder Abuse
c/o American Public Welfare Association
Suite 500
810 First Street NE
Washington, DC 20002-4205
(202) 682-2470

The National Aging Resource Center on Elder Abuse (NARCEA) is a joint project operated by the American Public Welfare Association, the National Association of State Units on Aging, and the University of Delaware. The purpose of NARCEA is to develop and provide information, data, and expertise to states, communities, professionals, and the public to help them effectively combat the problems of elder abuse.

National AIDS Hotline
P.O. Box 13827
Research Triangle Park, NC 27709
(919) 361-8430/(800) 342-2437/(800) 344-7432
   (Spanish)

The National AIDS Hotline, a service of the Centers for Disease Control, is the primary HIV/AIDS information, education, and referral service for the United States.

National AIDS Clearinghouse
P.O. Box 6003
Rockville, MD 20849-6003
(800) 458-5231

The National AIDS Clearinghouse is the Centers for Disease Control's primary reference, referral, and publication distribution service for HIV and AIDS information. The Clearinghouse acquires, organizes, reviews, updates, and distributes this information. Services are aimed primarily at professionals, including public health professionals, educators, social service workers, attorneys, employers, and human resources managers.

National Alliance of Senior Citizens
Suite 401
1700 18th Street NW
Washington, DC 20009
(202) 986-0117

The National Alliance of Senior Citizens is a consumer group that advocates policies and programs to enhance the lives of older people.

National Arthritis and Musculoskeletal and Skin Diseases Information Clearinghouse
P.O. Box AMS
9000 Rockville Pike
Bethesda, MD 20892
(301) 495-4484

The Clearinghouse, a service of the National Institute of Arthritis and Musculoskeletal and Skin Diseases (part of the National Institutes of Health), helps health professionals and the public locate up-to-date information about arthritis, musculoskeletal disorders, and skin diseases.

National Association of Area Agencies on Aging
Suite 100
1112 16th Street NW
Washington, DC 20036
(202) 296-8130

The National Association of Area Agencies on Aging (NAAAA) represents the interests of Area Agencies on Aging across the country.

National Association of Community Health Centers
Suite 122
1330 New Hampshire Avenue NW

Washington, DC 20036
(202) 659-8008

The National Association of Community Health Centers is a professional organization that represents community-based, primary health programs that provide services to medically underserved people.

National Association of the Deaf
814 Thayer Avenue
Silver Spring, MD 20910
(301) 587-1788

The National Association of the Deaf (NAD) is a nonprofit organization that advocates on behalf of people who are deaf or hard of hearing and distributes information to the public about hearing loss and related subjects.

**National Association for Hispanic Elderly/
Asociacion Nacionial Pro Personas Mayores**
Suite 800
3325 Wilshire Boulevard
Los Angeles, CA 90010-1724
(213) 487-1922

The National Association for Hispanic Elderly works to ensure that older Hispanic citizens are included in all social service programs for older Americans.

National Association for Home Care
519 C Street NE
Washington, DC 20002
(202) 547-7424

The National Association for Home Care (NAHC) is a professional organization that represents a variety of agencies that provide home care services, including home health agencies, hospice programs and homemaker/home health aid agencies.

National Association of Meal Programs
206 E Street NE
Washington, DC 20002
(202) 547-6157

The National Association of Meal Programs is a group of professionals and volunteers who provide congregate and home-delivered meals to people who are frail, disabled, or home-bound.

National Association of Professional Geriatric Care Managers
1604 North County Club
Tucson, AZ 85711
(602) 881-8008

Publishes a directory of private care managers for families involved in the home care of an elderly relative who lives at a distance.

National Association for Practical Nurse Education and Services
Suite 310
1400 Spring Street
Silver Spring, MD 20910
(301) 588-2491

The National Association for Practical Nurse Education and Services is a professional organization of licensed practical nurses (LPNs). LPNs are found most often in hospitals and long-term care facilities, where they provide much of the direct patient care.

National Association of State Units on Aging
Suite 304
2033 K Street NW
Washington, DC 20006
(202) 785-0707

The National Association of State Units on Aging (NASUA) is a public interest group that provides information, technical assistance, and professional development support to SUAs. This organization is funded by the Administration on Aging of the Department of Health and Human Services and by membership dues.

National Cancer Institute
Office of Cancer Communications
Building 31, Room 10A16
9000 Rockville Pike
Bethesda, MD 20892
(301) 496-5583/(800) 422-6237

The National Cancer Institute (NCI), part of the National Institutes of Health (NIH), is the Federal Government's principal agency for funding cancer research and for distributing information about cancer to health professionals and the public. One of NCI's top priorities is cancer in older Americans. Among its activities is a national education initiative targeting people age 65 years and older and the health professionals who treat them.

National Caucus and Center on Black Aged, Inc.
Suite 500
1424 K Street NW
Washington, DC 20005
(202) 637-8400

The National Caucus and Center on Black Aged is a nonprofit organization that works to improve the quality of life for older African Americans.

National Center for Health Statistics
6525 Belcrest Road
Hyattsville, MD 20782
(301) 436-8500

The National Center for Health Statistics (NCHS), part of the Centers for Disease Control of the Public Health Service, collects, analyzes, and distributes data on health in the United States.

National Clearinghouse for Primary Care Information
Suite 600
8201 Greensboro Drive
McLean, VA 22102
(703) 821-8955

The National Clearinghouse for Primary Care Information collects and distributes information to help administrators and health professionals plan, develop, and deliver health-care services to urban and rural areas where there are shortages of medical personnel and services. Community health clinics and migrant health centers are examples of ambulatory care centers.

National Commission on Working Women, Wider Opportunities for Women
Lower Level
1325 G Street NW
Washington, DC 20005
(202) 638-3143

The National Commission on Working Women advocates on behalf of women in nonprofessional occupations such as retail sales, service industries, clerical work, and factory jobs.

National Council on Alcoholism and Drug Dependence
Eighth Floor
12 West 21st Street
New York, NY 10010
(212) 206-6770/(800) 622-2255

The National Council on Alcoholism and Drug Dependence, a private, nonprofit organization, works to educate the public about the disease of alcoholism.

National Council of Senior Citizens
1331 F Street NW
Washington, DC 20004
(202) 347-8800

The National Council of Senior Citizens is an advocacy organization of senior activists in affiliated local clubs and area and state councils. Together, NCSC members work for state and federal legislation to benefit older people and advocate senior citizens' interests in communities across the United States.

National Diabetes Information Clearinghouse
Box NDIC
9000 Rockville Pike
Bethesda, MD 20892
(301) 468-2162

The Clearinghouse, a service of the National Institute of Diabetes and Digestive and Kidney Diseases of the National Institutes of Health, offers information about diabetes to health professionals, patients, and the general public.

National Digestive Diseases Information Clearinghouse
Box NDDIC
9000 Rockville Pike
Bethesda, MD 20892
(301) 468-6344

The Clearinghouse, a service of the National Institute of Diabetes and Digestive and Kidney Diseases of the National Institutes of Health, offers information about digestive diseases to health professionals, the general public, and patients and their families.

National Displaced Homemakers' Network
Suite 300
1625 K Street NW
Washington, DC 20006
(202) 467-6346

The National Displaced Homemakers' Network is dedicated to empowering displaced homemakers and assisting them to achieve economic self-sufficiency. Displaced homemakers are women who have lost their principal means of financial support through widowhood, divorce, separation, a husband's long-term unemployment or disability, or the discontinuation of public assistance.

National Hispanic Council on Aging
2713 Ontario Road NW
Washington, DC 20009
(202) 265-1288

The National Hispanic Council on Aging is a private, nonprofit organization that works to promote the well-being of older Hispanics.

National Hospice Organization
Suite 901
1901 North Moore Street

Arlington, VA 22209
(703) 243-5900/(800) 658-8898

The National Hospice Organization (NHO) promotes quality care for terminally ill patients and provides information about hospice services available in the United States. Hospices provide medical care for dying patients, as well as counseling and supportive services for the patient and family members.

National Indian Council on Aging
City Centre, Suite 510W
6400 Uptown Boulevard NE
Albuquerque, NM 87110
(505) 888-3302

The National Indian Council on Aging, a nonprofit organization funded by the Administration on Aging, works to ensure that older Indians and Alaskan Native Americans have equal access to quality, comprehensive health care, legal assistance, and social services.

National Information Center on Deafness
Gallaudet University
800 Florida Avenue NE
Washington, DC 20002
(202) 651-5051

The National Information Center on Deafness collects and distributes information on deafness to the general public and health professionals.

National Institute on Aging
Public Information Office
9000 Rockville Pike
Building 31, Room 5C27
Bethesda, MD 20892
(301) 496-1752/(800) 222-2225

The National Institute on Aging (NIA), part of the National Institutes of Health, is the federal government's principal agency for conducting and supporting biomedical, social, and behavioral research related to aging processes and the diseases and special problems of older people.

National Institute on Drug Abuse
5600 Fishers Lane
Rockville, MD 20857
(301) 443-6245/(800) 729-6686

The National Institute on Drug Abuse (NIDA), part of the Public Health Service, is the federal government's principal agency for research on narcotic addiction and drug abuse.

National Interfaith Coalition on Aging
c/o National Council on the Aging
Suite 200
409 Third Street SW
Washington, DC 20024
(202) 479-1200

The National Interfaith Coalition on Aging, a program of the National Council on the Aging (NCOA), includes representatives of the Roman Catholic, Jewish, Protestant, and Orthodox faiths and people concerned with religion and aging. The Coalition supports individuals and religious groups that serve older people.

National Kidney Foundation
30 East 33rd Street
New York, NY 10016
(212) 889-2210/(800) 622-9010

The National Kidney Foundation is a nonprofit organization that promotes the prevention, treatment, and cure of kidney diseases.

National League for Nursing
350 Hudson Street
New York, NY 10014
(212) 989-9393/(800) 669-1656

The National League for Nursing works to improve the standards of nursing education, nursing service, and health care delivery in the United States.

National Library of Medicine
8600 Rockville Pike
Bethesda, MD 20894
(301) 496-6095/(800) 272-4787

The National Library of Medicine (NLM), part of the National Institutes of Health, is the world's largest medical research library, containing more than 4.5 million journals, technical reports, books, photographs, and audiovisual materials covering more than forty biomedical areas and related subjects.

National Mental Health Association
1021 Prince Street
Alexandria, VA 22314-2971
(703) 684-7722/(800) 969-6642

The National Mental Health Association established the National Mental Health Information Center to meet the needs of the general public, consumers of mental health services and their families, and other concerned individuals and groups.

National Multiple Sclerosis Society
Sixth Floor
733 Third Avenue
New York, NY 10017
(212) 986-3240/(800) 227-3166/(800) 624-8236
    (publication orders)

The National Multiple Sclerosis society is a nonprofit organization dedicated to the prevention, treatment, and cure of multiple sclerosis (MS) and to improving the quality of life for people with MS and their families.

National Organization for Victim Assistance
1757 Park Road NW
Washington, DC 20010
(202) 232-6682

The National Organization for Victim Assistance (NOVA) is a private, nonprofit group of criminal justice professionals, former crime victims, professionals who help witnesses of crimes and crime victims, and others committed to the recognition of victim rights.

National Osteoporosis Foundation
1150 17th Street NW
Washington, DC 20036-4603
(202) 223-2226

The National Osteoporosis Foundation is a voluntary health agency dedicated to reducing the widespread incidence of osteoporosis, a condition seen most often in older women. Osteoporosis causes bone density to decrease, which produces weaknesses throughout the skeleton and leads to an increased risk of fractures.

National Pacific/Asian Resource Center on Aging
Melbourne Tower, Suite 914
1511 Third Avenue
Seattle, WA 98101
(206) 624-1221

The National Pacific/Asian Resource Center on Aging is a private organization that works to improve the delivery of health care and social services to older members of the Pacific/Asian community across the country.

National Rehabilitation Information Center
Suite 935
8455 Colesville Road
Silver Spring, MD 20910-3319
(301) 588-9284/(800) 227-0216

The National Rehabilitation Information Center (NARIC), funded by the National Institute on Disability and Rehabilitation Research (NIDRR) of the U.S. Department of Education, provides information to the public, professionals, and others involved in the rehabilitation of people with physical or mental disabilities.

National Self-Help Clearinghouse

Room 620
25 West 43rd Street
New York, NY 10036
(212) 642-2944

The National Self-Help Clearinghouse collects and distributes information about self-care and self-help groups throughout the country and provides technical assistance and advice to these groups.

National Senior Citizens Law Center

Suite 700
1815 H Street NW
Washington, DC 20006
(202) 887-5280

The National Senior Citizens Law Center (NSCLC) is a public interest law firm that specializes in the legal problems of older people.

National Society to Prevent Blindness

500 East Remington Road
Schaumburg, IL 60173
(708) 843-2020/(800) 331-2020

The National Society to Prevent Blindness works to preserve sight and prevent blindness by sponsoring community services, offering public and professional education programs, and funding research.

National Technical Information Service

5285 Port Royal Road
Springfield, VA 22161
(703) 487-4650/(800) 553-6847 (rush orders only)

The National Technical Information Service (NTIS), an agency of the Federal Government, is the central source for the public sale of U.S. Government-sponsored research, development, and engineering reports and documents, as well as analyses prepared by local government agencies or special technology groups.

National Urban League

500 East 62nd Street
New York, NY 10021
(212) 310-9000

The National Urban League is a nonprofit, community service organization dedicated to assisting African Americans to achieve social and economic equality. The League implements its mission through advocacy, research, program services, and bridge building.

National Women's Health Network

Lower Level
1325 G Street NW
Washington, DC 20005
(202) 347-1140

The National Women's Health Network works to ensure that women have access to quality, affordable health care and serves as a clearinghouse of information on women's health issues.

Older Women's League

Suite 700
666 11th Street NW
Washington, DC 20001
(202) 783-6686/(800) 825-3695

The Older Women's League (OWL) seeks to educate the public about the problems and issues of concern to middle-aged and older women.

Organization of Chinese Americans

Room 707
1001 Connecticut Avenue NW
Washington, DC 20036
(202) 223-5500

The Organization of Chinese Americans (OCA) works to ensure equal opportunities for Americans of Chinese ancestry.

President's Council on Physical Fitness and Sports

Suite 250
701 Pennsylvania Avenue NW
Washington, DC 20004
(202) 272-3421

The President's Council on Physical Fitness and Sports (PCPFS) encourages Americans to raise their fitness levels.

SeniorNet

399 Arguello Boulevard
San Francisco, CA 94118
(415) 750-5030

SeniorNet is a national nonprofit educational organization founded to teach computer skills to older adults and to provide a means for older adults to access information and to form friendships within an online network community.

Social Security Administration

Office of Public Inquiries
6401 Security Boulevard
Baltimore, MD 21235
(410) 965-1234/(800) 772-1213

The Social Security Administration is the Federal Government agency responsible for the Social Security retirement, survivors, and disability insurance program, as well as the Supplemental Security Income program.

United Parkinson Foundation
360 West Superior Street
Chicago, IL 60610
(312) 664-2344

The United Parkinson Foundation is a nonprofit organization that provides supportive services to patients with Parkinson's disease and their families and funds research to find a cure for this progressive neurological condition.

Visiting Nurse Associations of America
Suite 900
3801 East Florida
Denver, CO 80210
(303) 753-0218/(800) 426-2547

Visiting Nurse Associations are community-based and supported nonprofit home health care providers, governed by voluntary boards of directors. The mission of the Visiting Nurse Associations is to provide quality care to all people, regardless of their ability to pay.

Index

Page numbers set *Italic* indicate figures.
Page numbers followed by *t* indicate tables.